HISTORY
OF
BLACK AMERICANS

From the Compromise
of 1850
to the End
of the Civil War

Philip S. Foner

Contributions in American History, Number 103

GREENWOOD PRESS
Westport, Connecticut • London, England

Library of Congress Cataloging in Publication Data

Foner, Philip Sheldon, 1910–
  History of Black Americans.

  (Contributions in American history, ISSN 0084-
9219; no. 40)
  Bibliography: v. 1, p.
  Includes index.
  CONTENTS: v. 1. From Africa to the emergence of
the cotton kingdom—   —v. 3. From the Compromise of
1850 to the end of the Civil War.
  1. Afro-Americans—History. I. Title. II. Series.
E185.F5915   973'.0496073   74-5987
ISBN 0-8371-7529-1 (v. 1)
      0-8371-7967-X (v. 3)

Library of Congress Catalog Card Number: 74-5987
ISBN: 0-8371-7529-1 (v. 1)
      0-8371-7966-1 (v. 2)
      0-8371-7967-X (v. 3)
ISSN: 0084-9219

First published in 1983

Greenwood Press
A division of Congressional Information Service, Inc.
88 Post Road West
Westport, Connecticut 06881

Printed in the United States of America

10 9 8 7 6 5 4 3 2 1

Contents

Preface

This is the third volume in the projected multivolume *History of Black Americans*. The second volume (*From the Emergence of the Cotton Kingdom to the Eve of the Compromise of 1850*) concluded on the eve of the Compromise of 1850. This volume begins with the enactment of the Compromise, including one of the most vicious pieces of legislation in U.S. history—the Fugitive Slave Act of 1850—and concludes with the victory of the Union in the Civil War and the abolition of slavery. The volume stresses four themes: (1) black resistance to the Fugitive Slave Act; (2) black emigration during the 1850s; (3) black participation in the political struggles over slavery during the same decade; and (4) the role of blacks in the Civil War.

Although a number of these subjects have been dealt with in detail in general and specialized American historical works, the black dimensions, except for specialized doctoral and master's dissertations and articles in scholarly journals, have been neglected. This volume seeks to fill this important gap in our historiography. The role of blacks in the Civil War has been the subject of a number of important studies, but no general history of black Americans has, in my judgment, heretofore done justice to this vital subject.

Although they are personally offensive, I have retained words that are scurrilous so as to keep the record intact.

I wish to express my gratitude to Professor Jon Wakelyn of Catholic University of America for taking the necessary time from his schedule and reading the entire manuscript and offering valuable suggestions.

I have received the kind cooperation of many libraries and historical societies in the preparation of this volume. I wish to take this opportunity to thank the staffs of the Historical Society of Pennsylvania, Library Company of Philadelphia, Library of Congress, National Archives, Free Library of Philadelphia, Cincinnati Historical Society, Boston Public Library, Rare Book Room, New-

York Historical Society, Cleveland Public Library, Lancaster County Historical Society, New York Public Library, Manuscripts Division, Schomburg Division of the New York Public Library, and the staffs of the following university and college libraries: Stanford University, University of Missouri, Tulane University, Dillard University, Southern Illinois University, Northwestern University, Vanderbilt University, Louisiana State University, Howard University, University of Cincinnati, Lehigh University, Washington University (St. Louis), Syracuse University, University of Virginia, University of Chicago, Atlanta University, Duke University, University of Ottawa, Swarthmore College, University of California, Berkeley, Miami University (Ohio), Harvard University, University of Rochester, Columbia University, University of Buffalo, Lincoln University (Pennsylvania), Temple University, and University of Pennsylvania.

Philip S. Foner
December 1982

Professor Emeritus of History
Lincoln University, Pennsylvania
Visiting Professor of Economics
Haverford College

1

The Compromise and the Fugitive Slave Act of 1850: Background of the Compromise

As the year 1850 opened, John C. Calhoun wrote from Washington: "The Southern members [of Congress] are more determined and bold than ever I saw them. Many avow themselves to be disunionists, and a still greater number admit that there is little hope for a remedy short of it." The *Charleston Mercury* spelled out precisely what Calhoun meant in an editorial stating that the "only remedy" to protect the planters "from Northern oppression [and] from the Wilmot Proviso," with its intention of keeping slavery out of all the former Mexican territories, was *"the secession of the slaveholding states in a body from the union and their formation into a separate republic."*

Until the 1840s, the political balance between North and South in Congress was maintained by the admission of equal numbers of slave and free states. But the rapid growth of the population of the North and the West, induced by the arrival of millions of immigrants from strife-torn Europe, made it clear that the number of free states would soon exceed that of the slave states. This would mean that the power the slaveowners exercised in the federal government to protect the interests of slavery would be reduced and ultimately would disappear. In addition to maintaining its political control, slavery had to expand to meet the problem of a falling rate of profit as the soil devoted to slave cultivation became worn out. In 1844 the *Jacksonville* (Alabama) *Reporter* put it bluntly: "The balance of power is already against us. Under the circumstances the addition of Texas with its slaves is the only means of saving the South."

Texas was annexed in 1845, but in 1846 and 1848, Iowa and Wisconsin entered the Union as free states. By 1848 the slave states were well outnumbered in the House of Representatives, and while the South and North had an equal number of senators, the future looked bleak for the South. It appeared certain that the slave interest would soon become a permanent minority in Congress—unless all of the territories acquired in the war with Mexico were allowed to enter as slave states.

The Wilmot Proviso (providing that slavery should never exist in any part of the territory that might be acquired from Mexico as a result of the war then in progress) had been defeated, but the principle of keeping slavery out of the territories was being boldly asserted in Congress by Northern members in the closing months of 1849. The answer given by southerners was that either all of the territories obtained from Mexico must become slave states or the South would secede from the Union.

The initial reaction in the North was voiced by the *Cleveland Plain Dealer:* "Rather than see slavery extended one inch beyond its present limits we would see this Union rent asunder." How typical this feeling was is illustrated by the fact that the conservative New York merchant, Philip Hone, noting the Southern threat of a dissolution of the Union, wrote in his diary: "Well, be it so; if faction is to prevail and the South can get along without us, the sooner the issue the better. New York, Pennsylvania, and Massachusetts are able to take care of themselves."

But as it became clear that the disunionists in the South were not bluffing, anger was replaced by alarm. Mississippi's call for a Southern convention in Nashville to discuss action in the event that the Wilmot Proviso was adopted by Congress brought a quick response from six Southern states who appointed delegates, and some even appropriated money for "necessary measures for protecting the State . . . in [the event of] the passage of the Wilmot Proviso."

Now the businessmen and other conservatives of the North became thoroughly frightened as they saw the destruction of the Union becoming a reality and the prospects of future prosperity endangered. "A dissolution of the Union, which until now it was treason to think of, much more to utter," Philip Hone wrote in alarm, "is the subject of daily harrangues of Congress." At this point, all eyes turned to Henry Clay, who once again was called upon to use his parliamentary skills to bring about a peaceful solution, as he had done thirty years before in the Missouri Compromise.

On January 29, 1850, Henry Clay introduced his Compromise resolutions in Congress. They provided for the admission of California as a free state and for settlement of the boundary between Mexico and Texas. The rest of the Mexican acquisitions—New Mexico, Nevada, Arizona, and Utah—were to be organized into territories without any mention of slavery. The determination of their status—free or slave—was to be left to the people of these territories, under the principle of popular sovereignty. The slave trade would be abolished in the District of Columbia, but slavery there would not be touched unless Maryland consented.

In Clay's proposals southerners were asked to surrender a parity of free and slave states, which the admission of California as a free state meant, in return for equal access for slaveowners to the rest of the Mexican cession and a new fugitive slave law. In turn antislavery forces were to be pacified with abolition of the slave trade in the District of Columbia. However, Clay made it clear that ending the slave trade in the District was not to set any precedent. Congress had no power to "prohibit or obstruct" the interstate slave trade.

Although the rejection of an amendment by Senator William H. Seward of New York to abolish all slavery in the nation's capital (with the approval of the residents) aroused indignation in the North, the most explosive part of Clay's package was a revised and strengthened Fugitive Slave Act.

BACKGROUND FOR THE NEW FUGITIVE SLAVE LAW

Attempts in Congress to achieve a more stringent fugitive slave law were made in 1796, 1801, 1817, and 1822, but all in vain. Meanwhile various Northern states passed laws to define and limit the state's role in enforcing the 1793 federal statute. The Pennsylvania legislature passed such laws in 1820 and 1826. Although these laws regulated the procedure by which claimants might recover their property, they also stipulated somewhat more adequate protection for alleged fugitives. They provided, for instance, that their cases would be heard by judges rather than by aldermen or justices of the peace and that certain standards of evidence would be maintained. They also levied severe penalties against the illegal seizure (kidnapping) of free blacks.

More persistent and overt opposition to the 1793 law emerged with the new antislavery movement after 1831. The formation of vigilance committees in cities to which runaways most frequently came and the action of local blacks in rescuing fugitives and preventing kidnapping impeded efforts of slaveowners to recapture their alleged fugitives. An official list of the "causes" of the 1834 antiblack riots in Philadelphia noted

the conduct of certain portions of the colored people, when any of their members are arrested as fugitives from justice. It has too often happened, that . . . the colored people have not relied on the wisdom and justice of the judiciary . . . or on the active and untiring exertions of benevolent citizens . . . but they have . . . forcibly attempted the rescue of prisoners.

In 1842 the Supreme Court of the United States moved to define more precisely the states' responsibility in fugitive slave cases. Edward Prigg, a Maryland resident, had seized his fugitive slave and her children and removed them from Pennsylvania in clear violation of the legal processes required by the state's 1826 law. After a state court had tried and convicted Prigg, he appealed to the Supreme Court. The decision, written by Justice Joseph Story, definitely affirmed Congress' right to legislate on the subject of fugitive slaves. Second, it denied to the states the power of legislating on the subject of slavery since that subject came within exclusive national jurisdiction. Third, it left up to the state governments the choice between extending or denying to their officials the duty of helping to execute the federal act. In short, while *Prigg* v. *Pennsylvania* invalidated the 1826 Pennsylvania personal liberty law, holding that it contravened the federal Fugitive Slave Act of 1793, it also ruled that there was no constitutional requirement that state authorities must in any way assist in returning fugitive slaves, although state magistrates might, if they chose, "exercise that authority, unless prohibited by state legislation."

In spite of the *Prigg* decision, personal liberty laws similar to those of Pennsylvania spread throughout the Northeast. Massachusetts, responding specifically to the arrest of the fugitive George Latimer in Boston, prohibited the use of state jails in returning fugitives, as well as any participation by state officials in enforcing the fugitive slave law. Subsequently Pennsylvania, Rhode Island, and Vermont also forbade state officials to assist in any way in enforcing the law.

In the 1844 case of *United States* v. *Weld,* the Supreme Court held that "a patrol authority by the master to his agent, is sufficient to authorize a seizure of a fugitive from labor." But interference with both masters and agents by Vigilance Committees and others associated with the Underground Railroad made it difficult for them to return alleged fugitives to slavery. As Joseph L. Nogee points out in his study of the situation of fugitive slaves between 1842 and 1850:

Between 1842 and 1850 fugitive slavery in the northeastern states was characterized by two conditions: (1) number of fugitives increased greatly and (2) Southern slaveowners made almost no use of the federal machinery to recover their runaways. It was becoming increasingly difficult to secure the recapture and return of the increasing number of fugitives.

When slaveowners or their agents tried to recapture blacks they claimed to be their runaway slaves, they met with resistance in Northern communities. When whites refused to assist them in frustrating the slave catchers, blacks acted alone. The following report appeared in the *Carlisle* (Pennsylvania) *Herald* of June 3, 1847:

Our town was thrown into great commotion and excitement yesterday afternoon, by an attempt on the part of a large portion of our colored population to rescue several slaves who had been arrested as fugitives. The slaves (one man, a woman and little girl) were . . . taken before Judge Hepburn . . . which resulted in their being fully identified as the property of Col. Hollingsworth and Mr. Kennedy, of Hagerstown, Md. They were therefore remanded to their owners.

During the hearing a large crowd of infuriated negro men and women gathered in and about the Court House, who evidenced by their violent conduct a disposition to rescue the fugitives by force. An attempt was made first in the court room, but quickly frustrated by the constables.

A second attempt was made as the slaves were brought down from the court room to the carriage which resulted in a serious riot.—The attack was commenced at the door of the carriage, where, before the slaves got into the vehicle, a general rush was made on the slave owners and constables by the negro men and women, and a frightful melee ensued in the street in which for some minutes paving stones were hurled in showers, and clubs and canes used with terrible energy. The result was that the woman and girl escaped, while the man was secured and taken back to Maryland. We regret to say that Mr. Kennedy, one of the owners, was very severely hurt, having been felled to the earth under a succession of blows from stones and clubs which completely disabled him.

. . . Much excitement prevails in our community in relation to the unfortunate affair, and the Sheriff and Constables have arrested a score or more of negroes, who were identified as leaders in the riot, who are now confined to jail to await their trial.—Our citizens generally made no interference. The evidence that the slaves were fugitives was clear, and the mass of our citizens therefore regarded them as rightful property of their owners.

The Carlisle paper subsequently announced the death of slaveowner James H. Kennedy from injuries received in the "riot." Eleven black men were sentenced on a misdemeanor charge to three years in the Eastern Penitentiary and were released on a technicality in June 1848 after serving about a year in prison.

The same year events took place in Marshall, Michigan, that further increased the demand for a more effective fugitive slave act. In August 1843, upon learning that their master was planning to break up their family, the slaves Adam and Jane Crosswhite and their four children fled from Kentucky across Ohio in a skiff and landed in Madison, Indiana. Fearing capture, the family separated, with each parent keeping two children. They were reunited in Marshall, Michigan, a town inhabited by men and women with strong antislavery sentiments, among whom were about sixty free blacks. Served by the Michigan Central Railroad, Marshall was also a leading station on the Underground Railroad. The Crosswhites settled in a small cottage, obtained work as handyman and domestic servant, and sent their children to the local school. Soon they had another child.

On January 26, 1847, Francis Troutman, grandson of one of Crosswhite's previous owners and a nephew of Frank Giltner, Crosswhite's last master, arrived in Marshall. He was accompanied by three others, one of them Giltner's son. After learning of Crosswhite's whereabouts, Troutman and his fellow Kentuckians entered the fugitive's house and told the family he had come as an agent of Frank Giltner to arrest them as fugitive slaves. He said he would take the six who had escaped before a justice for a hearing but made no claim respecting the youngest child, who, having been born in Michigan, was free.

Crosswhite then set out with deputy sheriff Harvey Dickson to procure counsel. While he was away, a group of local people, black and white, came to the house. The blacks threatened Troutman with a knife and club, declaring that they would not allow the family to be taken back to slavery. Although Troutman was able to prevent injury to himself by drawing his gun, the size of the crowd increased, and together, blacks and whites passed two resolutions. One declared that "these Kentuckians shall not take the Crosswhite family by virtue of moral, physical, or legal force." The other went: "*Resolved* that these Kentuckians leave town in two hours or they shall be tarred and feathered and rode on a rail, and, in addition, they shall be prosecuted for kidnapping or housebreaking."

Troutman asked for the names of those responsible for preventing him from taking the Crosswhites and, probably to his surprise, received them. One of the blacks when giving his name also requested that he take it down in capital letters "and bear it back to the land of slavery, as an evidence of the example we intend to make of you." In the end, the Crosswhite family was taken by team and covered wagon to Jackson, Michigan, where they boarded a train to Detroit and then crossed into Canada.

When Francis Troutman returned to Kentucky empty handed, indignation meetings were held in the state, and resolutions were adopted requesting the state legislature "to instruct their Senators and Representatives in Congress to take the matter into consideration and insist upon the passage of a law by Congress, making the offense of engaging in such a mob punishable by imprisonment, [and] in addition to furnish all assistance as may be in their power to enable . . . Giltner to obtain redress."

Eventually the Kentucky slaveowner did obtain some redress, even though the Crosswhites were never returned to slavery. A first trial of the black and white men charged with having interfered with the return of the Crosswhites ended in a hung jury. But in a second trial, they were found guilty and ordered to pay $1,926 damages for loss of the slaves and court costs. Since most of the defendants, particularly the blacks, were men of small means, Zachariah Chandler, a wealthly Detroit antislavery Whig, put up the money. But the slaveowner and his witnesses had had to spend several months in the prosecution of the men of Marshall.

THE FUGITIVE SLAVE BILL OF 1850

On December 20, 1847, acting on instructions from the state legislature, Kentucky Senator Joseph Underwood urged Congress to enact laws that would facilitate the recovery by citizens of slaveholding states of slaves who had escaped to the North. The issue was referred to the Senate Judiciary Committee, where it died.

The mounting tension over the question of slavery in the territories acquired from Mexico gave slaveowners' representatives in Congress the opportunity to link the demand for a more effective fugitive slave law with other issues being considered as part of the Compromise of 1850. On January 14, 1850, Senator Andrew P. Butler of South Carolina said: "The act of 1793 recognized the unquestionable right of the owner to apprehend his own slave—and recognized as an unquestionable duty, that the State should cooperate through their State officers and courts, to give them aid in the enforcement of this right." But what had happened? Every effort of the masters to exercise their legal and constitutional right had been and was being frustrated, and even their lives were being put into jeopardy. If nothing were done to change this situation, Butler warned, secession sentiment in the South would be difficult to suppress. Supporting

Butler's warning, Senator John Mason of Virginia introduced a new fugitive slave bill, the terms of which he had worked out with the South Carolina senator. The need for the measure, Mason told the Senate, was clear: "You may as well go down into the sea, and endeavor to recover from his native element a fish which had escaped from you as to expect to recover a fugitive."

On January 29, 1850, Henry Clay included Mason's new fugitive slave bill within the package of resolutions that made up the Compromise of 1850. He proposed that "more effectual provision ought to be made by law . . . for the restitution . . . of persons bound to service . . . in any State, who may escape into any other State." In arguing for his proposal, Clay dwelt on the impediments encountered by slaveowners in reclaiming runaway slaves. He asserted that his own state of Kentucky was second only to Virginia in the number of slaves lost, and "I know too well that it is only at the utmost hazard of life itself, that a Kentuckian can . . . take back the . . . slave . . . . in every case . . . where an appeal has been made to the courts . . . they have asserted the rights of the owners and the juries have returned . . . verdicts in favor of the owners." But this was cold comfort to owners or their agents, threatened with lynching and tar and feathers and required to spend months and money in trial procedures.

The fugitive slave provision of the proposed Compromise of 1850 was entitled "An Act to amend, and supplementary to the Act entitled, 'An Act respecting the Fugitive from justice, and Persons escaping from the services of their Masters.' " It supplemented the Fugitive Slave Law of 1793 with the aim of rendering its execution more effective. It provided for the appointment of special federal commissioners to facilitate the reclaiming of runaways. These commissioners could appoint marshals to arrest fugitives, and these marshals could, in turn, "call to their aid" any bystanders at the scene of an arrest, who were "commanded" to "assist in the prompt and efficient execution of this law." A federal marshal or deputy refusing to execute the certificate issued by the commissioner authorizing the arrest of a fugitive slave would be fined up to one thousand dollars. Law officers were liable for the value of any slave escaping their custody. Fugitives could not testify in their own behalf and were denied trial by jury. An affidavit claiming title was deemed sufficient evidence of ownership. The measure went on: "Any person obstructing the arrest of a fugitive or attempting his or her rescue, or aiding him or her to escape, or harboring and concealing a fugitive, knowing him to be such, shall be subject to a fine of not exceeding one thousand dollars, and be imprisoned not exceeding six months, and shall also forfeit and pay the sum of one thousand dollars for each fugitive so lost." The law provided for a ten dollar fee for commissioners if the fugitive was returned, but if the black was released, the fee was five dollars.

The slaveowner was authorized to use all "reasonable force" necessary to take a fugitive back to the place of his or her escape. If a slaveowner feared "that such fugitive will be rescued by force," it was the duty of the officer involved to employ any number of persons necessary "to overcome such force" and deliver the fugitive back to the fugitive's claimant.

NATURE OF THE FUGITIVE SLAVE BILL

Unlike the fugitive slave law of 1793, the proposed bill of 1850 placed the hearing of cases within strict federal jurisdiction. Therefore state courts and magistrates would not be allowed to hear cases. The bill provided for what is known as a commission system, under which all commissioners were appointed by the circuit courts to hear fugitive slave cases. Yet even though these positions were appointive, the commissioners were to be invested with concurrent jurisdiction on a level with judges of the circuit and district courts of the United States and to decide upon the cases that came before them.

The procedure for apprehending an alleged fugitive under the proposed bill was simple. The claimant had only to go before the court of the state from which the fugitive had fled to prove his claim. After he gave testimony, either orally or by written affidavit, as proof that the person in question was a fugitive slave, the court of the slave state made a record of the claim, including a general description of the runaway. The court then prepared an official transcript, which was presented to its clerk, who was authorized to issue certificates. The certificate, when issued to the claimant, was "held and taken to be full and conclusive evidence of the fact of the escape, and that the service or labor of the person escaping is due to the party in such record mentioned."

With this evidence in hand, the claimant could proceed to the free state to reclaim his property. There he had to go before the commissioner empowered to issue warrants for the arrest of fugitives. The warrants were issued to a U.S. marshal, who was ordered to seize and arrest the fugitive in question. In certain cases, fugitives could be seized without warrants. After seizure and arrest, the fugitive was brought before a commissioner who would examine him. The hearing was to be conducted with dispatch, and if the affidavit and other evidence presented by the claimant were accepted as sufficient proof, the commissioner would issue a certificate establishing the right of ownership. And, said the bill: "In no trial or hearing under this act shall the testimony of such alleged fugitive be admitted in evidence."

Clearly the claimant held the upper hand. The court of his home state could be expected to be friendly to him and inclined to accept his oral testimony or written affidavit at face value. The court certificate he brought with him to the North was therefore difficult to challenge. No set rules or procedures were laid down for determining the identity of the fugitive. A slave could have escaped in his youth, and the owner might decide to pursue him. After years had elapsed, during which the fugitive's personal appearance, along with any other marked peculiarities, might have undergone considerable change, the claimant may have caught a glimpse of the alleged fugitive and concluded that, because of certain mannerisms, he was the slave that had run away years before. On the strength of such an encounter, he could decide to have the person arrested as a fugitive, and the machinery would be set in motion to return the person to slavery—even though he might not be the actual fugitive and even if he had a family and a well-established place in the Northern community. Judge Robert Kane of the U.S. Circuit Court put his finger on one of the many inequities in the proposed bill when he observed: ''The best physicians concur in the doctrine that after twenty years, the difference of identity is so great, where there is no mark, no peculiar bodily conformation, no marked physiognomy, that courts of justice are advised to regard with very great caution evidence of personal identity in such cases.''

Central to the problem of the system of proofs and identity was the role of the commissioner during the hearing. What he did or failed to do could spell freedom or slavery for the accused. Even though the commissioners were to be appointed by the judges of the U.S. Circuit Courts and to exercise concurrent jurisdiction with them, their position was not salaried; instead they received fees for performing their duties: ten dollars if they delivered a fugitive to a slaveowner and five dollars if they freed the black claimed. The fees paid to the commissioners thus established a built-in system of bribery designed to ensure that they rendered a decision favorable to the claimant. This evil was compounded by the fact that at the hearing itself, the commissioner served as judge, juror, and prosecutor. The alleged fugitive was completely at his mercy. To be sure, the hearing before the commissioners was only preliminary. The commissioners had only to establish the right of claim; after the alleged fugitive was returned to the slave state, theoretically he could then sue for trial. In other words, the decision of the commissioner was not final but was subject to review in the claimant's state court. But what if, as actually did happen, free Negroes claimed as fugitives were sold into slavery immediately on reaching the South? What chance did they have of proving their real status? In practice, it turned out that the hearing before the commissioners was in fact final, because U.S. Attorney General John Jay Crittenden, in a sweeping legal opinion, maintained that under the Fugitive Slave Act of 1850

Congress has constituted a tribunal with *exclusive* jurisdiction to determine summarily and without *appeal,* who are fugitives from service or labor under the second section of the fourth article of the constitution, and to whom such service or labor is due. The judgment of every tribunal of *exclusive* jurisdiction where the appeal lies is of necessity, conclusive upon every other tribunal. And therefore, the judgment of the tribunal created by this act.

Thus federal commissioners, not judicial officers, determined the status of fugitives. A judicial process was thus converted into an administrative one.

REACTION TO THE FUGITIVE SLAVE BILL

It became clear that under the provisions of the proposed fugitive slave bill, the fugitive would be effectively stripped of practically all legal protection and that in an effort to mollify the South by opening territories to the extension of slavery, free blacks, whether fugitives or born in freedom, would be confronted with the real danger of being legally kidnapped and enslaved. This realization produced the most heated debates in the history of Congress. William H. Seward of New York argued in the Senate for the admission of California but against the extension of slavery and the enactment of the new fugitive slave law. Seward urged that slavery be excluded from the territories and that fugitive slaves be treated as human beings; he went on to say to those who claimed that the measures in the proposed Compromise of 1850 were all constitutional: "But there is a higher law than the Constitution, which regulates our authority over the domain, and devotes it to the same noble purposes." Clay angrily replied that this theory was one of the "wild, reckless and abominable doctrines, which strike at the foundation of all property and threaten to crush in ruins the fabric of civilized society." Horace Mann of Massachusetts, the noted educational reformer and a leading "Conscience" (antislavery) Whig and John Quincy Adams' successor in the House of Representatives, insisted that "the man who can read this [fugitive slave] bill without having his blood boil in his vein, has a power of refrigeration that should cool the tropics." Mann was enraged by the failure of the bill to provide a trial by jury for an alleged fugitive slave. The Constitution, he asserted angrily, did not establish classes of criminals in American society, some of whom were entitled to a trial by jury and others not. He was also appalled by the extent of the judicial power placed in the hands of commissioners who were not judges and insisted that this was contrary to Article III of the Constitution. Further, he maintained, the bill lacked protection of the common law. That any of the evidence could be taken against an alleged fugitive without his knowledge and that there could be no real appeal from the decision of a commissioner and no resort to habeas corpus, Mann added, made this bill utterly reprehensible. He concluded: "I say that a law so worthy of abhorrence, so truculent, so fiendish, is not to be found upon the statute book of any other civilized nation on the globe."

But Daniel Webster, the former antislavery senator from Mann's state of Massachusetts, stood up in the Senate, and, in his notorious speech of March 7, 1850, announced his support of the entire Compromise of 1850 package, including the fugitive slave bill "now before the Senate . . . which I propose to support, with all its provisions, to the fullest extent." He continued:

One complaint of the South has, in my opinion, just foundation; and that is, that there has been found at the North, among individuals and among legislators, a disinclination to perform, fully, their Constitutional duties in regard to the return of persons bound to service, who have escaped into the free States. In that respect, it is my judgment that the South is right, and the North is wrong. . . . Here is a ground of complaint against the North well founded, which ought to be removed, which it is now in the power of different departments of the Government to remove; which calls for the enactment of proper laws authorizing the judicature of this Government, in the several States, to do all that is necessary for the recapture of fugitive slaves, and for the restoration of them to those who claim them.

In the printed version of his March 7 speech, Webster complained that Northern free Negro sailors were unjustifiably imprisoned in Southern ports, but he had omitted this in the oral delivery. He also added to the printed version his support for the denial of jury trial for alleged fugitive slaves, saying:

Nothing is more false than that such jury trial is demanded, in cases of this kind, by the Constitution, either in its letter or its spirit. The Constitution declares that in all *criminal* prosecutions, there shall be a trial by jury; the reclaiming of a fugitive slave is not a criminal prosecution. The Constitution also declares that in suits of common law, the trial by jury shall be preserved; the reclaiming of a fugitive slave is not a suit at common law; and there is no other clause or sentence in the Constitution having the least bearing on the subject.

Ralph Waldo Emerson voiced a common reaction in Massachusetts to the oral and printed version of Webster's March 7 speech when he commented bitterly that the word *honor* in the mouth of Daniel Webster was like the word *love* in the mouth of a whore.

Samuel Ringgold Ward, the New York minister and former fugitive slave whose oratorical ability caused him to be referred to (before March 7, 1850) as the "black Daniel Webster," was the main speaker at the anti-Webster rally of the "colored citizens of Boston and Vicinity." Accusing Webster of having sold out to the slaveowners, Ward cried out: "This is the question. Whether a man has a right to himself and his children, his hopes, and his happiness, for this world and the world to come." Already slave hunters were "infesting Boston and other cities and towns in the North, as an immediate result of Mr. Webster's speech." He had only one word of advice to members of Boston's black community in the event the new fugitive slave bill became law: "Resolve to live in Boston; live *freemen* in Boston, and die *freemen* in Boston."

One of the speakers at the meeting was Calvin Fairbank, just released from a Kentucky prison, and the audience was moved to tears when he was introduced by Lewis Hayden as the man who had gone to prison for having rescued Hayden, his wife, and his child from slavery. Fairbank related his harrowing experiences in prison and "pledged himself ready and willing, at every hazard, to join issue for the slave against his master."

Resolutions proposed by a committee headed by William C. Nell were read and adopted. They began:

Whereas, however deeply other classes may be interested in the question of slavery, and injured by its existence and extension, it is still the colored race upon whom the burden of its yoke, and the galling prejudice that springs from it, bear with the most deadly weight; and

Whereas, if the cruel provisions of the Bill for the recovery of fugitive slaves, now before the U.S. Senate, should pass into law, it is *our households* and *our children* which will be outraged by its atrocious violations of all legal provisions for the security of citizens, and even of the Constitution of the United States.

After excoriating "the recent speech of Hon. Daniel Webster," the resolutions noted "the ominous fact" that "Mr. Webster's recreancy to Freedom" had brought the senator the congratulations of Calhoun and other Southern senators for the service "rendered" the slaveowners. The resolutions asked Webster to raise the question to himself: "What treason to liberty have I been guilty of, that such men should applaud my effort?" The final resolution read:

Resolved, That whereas the crisis has arrived when the liberties of every colored men are at stake; it is their duty, as members of the human family, to enter into a solemn pledge, that come what will, their motto will be, Liberty or Death.

THE COMPROMISE OF 1850 BECOMES LAW

Throughout the spring and summer of 1850, the rancorous debates continued in Congress. In spite of Clay's parliamentary skill, it seemed doubtful that the Compromise would be adopted. Then in June, when only nine Southern states sent representatives to the Nashville Convention and these delegates voted not to recommend secession but to await the passage of the Compromise of 1850, it became clear that the Southern Unionists had gained the upper hand over the secessionists. On July 9, while the struggle over the Compromise was reaching a climax in Congress, President Zachary Taylor died. His successor, Millard Fillmore, worked hard to secure passage. Early in September 1850, all of the bills in the Compromise of 1850 package passed both houses of Congress and were signed into law.

On September 9, 1850, Philip Hone wrote joyfully in his diary: "These horrible slavery questions which have suspended the public business for more than eight months are settled." But Walt Whitman's poem, "The House of Friends," condemned the Northern politicians, supposedly friends of freedom, who had compromised with the defenders of slavery. He called them contemptuously:

> Doughfaces, Crawlers, Lice of Humanity—
> Terrific screamers of Freedom
> Who roar and bawl, and get hot i' the face . . .
> Much-worms creeping flat to the ground
> A dollar dearer to them than Christ's blessing.

Once the Compromise of 1850 had become law and the danger to the Union had subsided, it became even clearer that on almost every point, human rights were sacrificed in the new Fugitive Slave Act to protect property rights. Still, while many Northern journals agreed that the law was "injudicious," "unstatesmanlike," "unjust," and "oppressive" and that "some of the provisions are directly opposed to what are considered in the North as sacred and personal rights," they counseled obedience while political leaders worked for either changes in the measure or its outright repeal. But in January 1851, forty-five members of Congress, headed by Henry Clay, issued a manifesto declaring that sectional controversy over slavery could be avoided only by strictly adhering to every part of the Compromise. In obedience to this warning, Congress turned down proposals to grant fugitive slaves a jury trial, to exempt conscientious objectors from noncooperation penalties relating to fugitive slave recapture, and all other petitions asking for modification or repeal of the Fugitive Slave Act.

But the slaveowners' representatives and their Northern allies (the "Doughfaces, Crawlers, Lice of Humanity" of Walt Whitman's poem) could not prevent the people of the North, black and white, from modifying and even repealing the infamous Fugitive Slave Act of 1850 through direct action.

2

Black Reaction to the Fugitive Slave Law of 1850: Terror in the Black Community

The passage of the Fugitive Slave Act of 1850—the "Bill," as it was often referred to—sent a shudder through every black in the North. Unlike the Fugitive Slave Act of 1793, which was not stringently enforced, all indications were that this latest action of the federal government to appease the slaveowners would receive both prompt and vigorous enforcement. As the law went into effect, an attempt was made to kidnap Henry "Box" Brown in broad daylight in Providence. Scarcely a month after the new law was passed, Adam Gibson was seized on the streets of Philadelphia because he resembled a black who had escaped from William S. Knight of Cecil County, Maryland. Gibson was dragged before Commissioner Edward D. Ingram and, despite his insistence that he was free and could produce papers to prove it, was ordered remanded to his claimant in Maryland. Fortunately for Gibson, upon his arrival in Cecil County, his alleged owner admitted that Gibson was not his slave, and the Philadelphia black was reunited with his family. But others were not so fortunate. A report in the press read:

Elizabeth Williams, negro woman in West Chester, Pa. was taken before a United States Marshal, charged with being a fugitive slave, and while the citizens were yet generally in bed, without witnesses, without counsel—without the presence of a solitary friend,—after a trial occupying fifteen minutes, was delivered to her claimant, placed in a closed wagon, and driven rapidly from the state.

It was thus clear very early that nothing could prevent a slaveowner or his agent from coming up to any Negro on the streets of any Northern city and accusing him or her of being a sought runaway. It also became clear that certificates were being issued by state courts in the South to claimants without the slightest evidence. "These transcripts which come up from the South," abolitionist Gerrit Smith noted, "are of no more legal value than so many pieces of blank paper. . . . The proceedings before the State judge might be ever so full of perjury, and no prosecution for perjury could be sustained."

Since kidnapping was a highly profitable enterprise during the 1850s when prices for slaves were mounting, no black could be guaranteed immunity from the law's operation. A letter from a southerner found in possession of a well-known counterfeiter requested him to "go among the niggers, find their marks and scars, send good descriptions of them and I'll find owners."

After a rumor spread that slave catchers were in New York City, the *New York Tribune* reported that "a negro named William Gordon became so much excited by fright, that it threw him in a state of paralysis by which he died this morning."

The terror that struck every Northern black community was best explained by the Massachusetts Anti-Slavery Society:

It is not the actual number of slaves that may be recaptured under the law; it is the perpetual sense of danger which haunts the fugitive and his friends that constitute the main wickedness of this new abomination. The sword of Damocles may never fall; but as long as it is suspended by a single hand, it creates a suspense worse than death in the hearts of those over whose heads it hangs.

FLIGHT TO CANADA

Many fugitives reacted to the new law by fleeing to the safety of Canada. The Boston African Methodist Episcopal Church lost eighty-five members, the African Methodist Episcopal Zion Church lost ten members from its small congregation, and the Twelfth Baptist Church lost more than one-third of its members. The *Pennsylvania Freeman* later estimated that within twenty-four hours of the passage of the new law, 40 percent of Boston's 8,900 blacks had fled to Canada. While the exact number is impossible to determine, the fact is that work on one black church that was in the process of construction at the time of the act's passage, the bulk of whose parishioners were to be fugitives, was halted as soon as the law was passed.

Nor was Boston exceptional in this respect. Of the 114 members of the Colored Baptist Church of Rochester, 102 left for Canada immediately after the law went into effect. The Baptist Colored Church in Buffalo lost 130 members through flight to Canada. The black population of Columbia, Pennsylvania, decreased by more than one-half, from 943 to 437. A black settlement at Sandy Lake, in northern Pennsylvania, broke up altogether. The *Pennsylvania Freeman,* after reporting that in Allegheny County, Pennsylvania, more than 150 blacks were heading for Canada, added: "Mothers and daughters, fathers and sons, brothers and sisters, were clinging to one another in despair at the thought of separation, which they seem to feel would be for life." Shortly after the passage of the law the principal hotels in Pittsburgh announced that they were without servants since all had left for Canada with their families. In Ohio, the

Cleveland True Democrat reported that blacks were "leaving by the droves due to the panic spread by the Fugitive Slave Law."

Some blacks who had left for Europe before passage of the law did not return until years later. Reverend William C. Pennington, pastor of the Shiloh Church in Cleveland, had left for Europe two years earlier to raise funds to help pay off the debts of his former church in Hartford. Even though he had escaped from Maryland twenty years before, Pennington delayed his return because he feared that it would mean instant seizure and permanent separation from his family.

Reverend Theodore Parker, the abolitionist Congregational preacher, after revealing the fact that a number of the 400 to 600 fugitives in Boston belonged to his church, went on to urge the "fugitive and colored inhabitants of Boston and the neighborhood to remain with us, for we have not the smallest fears that any one of them will be taken from us and carried off to bondage, and we trust that such as have fled in fear will soon return to their business and homes." Parker assured the blacks that he would act with any serious men to resist the law in any manner not involving the use of deadly weapons.

But other ministers refused to join Parker in providing this assurance. Reverend Miles M. Rogers, an orthodox minister of Boston, declared in a sermon: "When the slave asks me to stand between him and his master, what does he ask? He asks me to murder a nation's life; and I will not do it because I have conscience—because there is a God." He further claimed that it was the duty of all citizens to obey the provisions of the law, and "if ordered to take human life, in the name of God take it." Reverend John C. Lord of Buffalo hailed the departure of fugitives for Canada and praised the law for ridding the community of men and women who were just "bad." "They are a trouble to us," he complained. "They corrupt our population, overload our prisons and one of the benefits of this law is that they are so rapidly disappearing from the midst of us."

Blacks were faced with the question of what to do about the law if they did not emigrate. Even though a considerable number of their white abolitionist friends were at first prepared to refuse to obey the new measure, they would not go any further. Horace Mann, for example, who bitterly opposed the law, placed his reliance on repeal rather than nullification. "The only true and enduring remedy is repeal," he assured blacks. "Those who would forcibly resist the law lose half their motive and impulse for repeal." He would help the fugitive escape, he declared, but he would not resort to armed resistance.

GARRISONIAN ADVICE

William Lloyd Garrison was even more opposed to a frontal assault on a law that he characterized as "an edict so coldblooded, so inhuman and so atrocious, that Satan himself would blush to claim paternity to it." His response, however, was to assure blacks that, in the long run, the righteousness and morality of their cause would bring them victory without their having to flee to Canada or abandon the principles of nonviolence and nonresistance. Garrison had arrived late at the anti-Webster meeting of Boston's blacks held before passage of the law, and he delivered only a brief address. Although he was pleased by the fact "that the colored citizens had rightly appreciated the trying circumstances in which the March 7th speech of Webster and the present aspect of Congress had placed them," he cautioned them that even though vigilance was useful, it must be nonviolent and nonresistant. A report of the meeting indicated that he gave blacks his personal assurance that a fugitive slave "could not be recaptured in Massachusetts. He relied much for the safety of the colored population in a cultivation of their self-respect, and its influence upon the surrounding community."

Garrison's assurance had some merit. In no other Northern city had blacks found a safer haven than in Boston. It was Boston that had led the way in the petition movement that produced the first personal liberty law after the *Prigg* decision in 1843, which had practically nullified that decision in the state of Massachusetts by forbidding judges or other law enforcement officers to implement the constitutional requirement for the return of fugitive slaves.

But Boston blacks could not leave it at that. They were convinced that the federal government was intent upon enforcing the new law and they could not rely upon the goodwill of the community to maintain their freedom. Even a number of Garrison's white associates recognized the inadequacy of his approach in meeting the threat posed by the Fugitive Slave Act. The board of managers of the Garrisonian Massachusetts Anti-Slavery Society advised Negroes to fight the new law with all the strength at their command and, at the very least, to nullify it by word and deed:

As citizens, it is your prerogative to question the constitutionality of any enactment of Congress and, in case you are convinced of its illegality, to contest it . . . till a final decision is made by the rightful judicatory. As moral and religious men, you cannot obey an immoral and irreligious statute. . . . This law is to be denounced, resisted, disobeyed. . . . Its enforcement on Massachusetts soil must be rendered impossible.

Disagreeing with his colleague's call for nonresistance, Wendell Phillips insisted that

the path to the jury box lies through defiance of the law. If he concealed a slave, he was liable to a fine of $1,000, but a Massachusetts jury must try him. . . . The remedy, therefore, lies in defiance; and a jury is at last reached in a defiance of the law. . . . We must trample the law under our feet. . . . There is not treason in that. The law expects disobedience . . . and God forbid that it should be disappointed.

ADVICE OF BLACK LEADERS

Among some blacks, the Garrisonian influence was still strong. A Negro sent a letter to the *Liberator* condemning the Fugitive Slave Act yet cautioning against physical violence. "We believe," he wrote, "that more can be accomplished by the all-controlling power of *public sentiment* than by guns, bowie knives, or pistols. Why should it not be so?" A black Baptist pastor in Buffalo told his congregation that while he found examples in the gospels that justified running away, there were no examples approving of violence as a method of resistance.

But even among Garrisonian blacks, the Fugitive Slave Act produced a new militancy. Starting in 1850 with the passage of the law, blacks still under Garrison's influence systematically departed from his principles. William C. Nell, one of the leading black Garrisonians, urged fugitives to stay in the United States and resist. He also advised blacks to act if they were in danger of being seized by slave catchers "as they would to rid themselves of any wild beast." Asked by friends to express his position on the new law, Reverend Jermain W. Loguen of Syracuse, a moral suasionist Garrisonian, gave the following answer:

I want you to set me down as a *Liberator* man, I am with you in heart. I may not be in *hands* and *head*—for my hands will fight a slaveholder—which I suppose the *Liberator* and some of its good friends would not do. . . . I am a fugitive slave, and you know, that we have strange notions about many things.

Martin R. Delany declared that his house was his castle and that if any man should "approach that house in search of a slave . . . if he crosses the threshold of my door, and I do not lay him a lifeless corpse at my feet, I hope the grave may refuse my body a resting place."

Samuel Ringgold Ward, the brilliant black orator and editor of the *Impartial Citizen* (published in Boston), advised blacks not to be overly dependent on their white friends for advice on how to deal with the crisis:

I think, that in our unprotected state, we are driven to the most desperate circumstances. We must act according to our desperation. Let no man consent to be a slave. Let no man be taken from the north alive. . . . What little we do enjoy is too precious to be yielded up without a struggle. Let us die for it, if need be.

Later Ward expanded upon this theme. He charged that the fugitive slave law had stripped blacks of all protection and that they were therefore justified in falling back upon the inalienable right of self-defense. He asked his people "whether we will submit to being enslaved by the hyenas which this law creates and encourages or whether we will protect ourselves, even if, in so doing we have to peril our lives." He concluded with a warning:

Let the men who would execute this bill beware. Let them know that in the business of catching slaves, of kidnapping freemen, [there] is an open warfare upon the rights and liberties of the black man in the North. Let them know that to enlist in that warfare is present, certain, inevitable death and damnation.

Immediately after the law was passed, Ward made a vow: "I pledge you there is one whose name is Sam Ward, who will never be taken alive." He was forced to leave for Canada, but he kept his vow.

The Reverend Jermain W. Loguen of Syracuse was particularly vulnerable to capture. He was a frequent speaker in pulpits, was often quoted in the press, and was pointed to as a fugitive slave who, by dint of hard work and thrift, had accumulated a considerable amount of property and had contributed much of his wealth to the antislavery cause. He had married a free black woman, and they had two children.

Shortly after the passage of the law, Loguen was advised by his friends and urged by his wife to leave for Canada. He refused. When, on October 4, 1850, the people of Syracuse filled the city hall to hear a discussion of the recently passed law, Loguen told them that it was their duty to stand up against it and "crush it by force or be crushed by it." He then pledged that "whatever may be your decision, my argument is taken. I have declared it everywhere. It is known in and out of the State. I don't respect this law—I don't fear it—I won't obey it. It outlaws me, and I outlaw it and the men who attempt to force it on me. . . . I will not live a slave, and if force is employed to reenslave me, I will make preparations to meet the crisis as becomes a man." Loguen then called upon the whites to stand by the blacks in "resistance to this measure." and he assured them that in so doing "you will be the saviors of your country." He pleaded that Syracuse be made an "open city" for fugitive slaves. Loguen's plea moved his listeners, and after he finished, the Reverend R. R. Raymond, a white minister of a local Baptist church, arose to declare:

How can we do to others as we would that they should do to us, if we do not resist this law? Citizens of Syracuse, shall a live man ever be taken out of our city, by force of this law? Let us tell the Southerners, then, that it will not be safe for them to come or send agents here to take away a fugitive slave. I will take the hunted man to my own house and he shall not be torn away, and be left alive.

By a vote of 395 to 96, the meeting decided in favor of Loguen's proposal that Syracuse be made an open city for fugitives.

In nearby Rochester, New York, Frederick Douglass was urged by friends to leave, even though his freedom had been purchased. It was felt that because of his position as a leader of blacks, he was in danger of being seized by slave catchers. Douglass conceded the danger but refused to leave his work as publisher and lecturer for the cause of the slaves and free blacks. A year later, Douglass wrote in his paper that he had made the correct decision:

We have lost some of our strong men—Ward has been driven into exile; Lougen has been hunted from our shores; Brown and Crummell, men who were our prize and hope, we have heard signified their unwillingness to return again to their National field of labor in this country. Bibb has chosen Canada as his field of labor—and the eloquent Remond is comparatively silent—all because of the hideous operations of this hideous law.

The passage of the Fugitive Slave Act marked another turning point in the life of Frederick Douglass. As Leslie Goldstein points out, it was at this point that "Douglass totally abandoned what was left of his opposition to violence." He openly counseled resistance and the "shooting down," if necessary, of any "creature" who would rob the life and liberty of a human being. Speaking at a large meeting of abolitionists and their sympathizers at Faneuil Hall in Boston on October 14, 1850, he described the terror that the law had struck in the hearts of thousands of escaped slaves in the North and declared that it was the universal feeling of his black brothers and sisters "to die rather than be returned to slavery." He warned the slave catchers that should "this law be put into operation . . . the streets of Boston would be running with blood." To his people, Douglass issued the following advice:

Every colored man should sleep with his revolver under his head, loaded and ready for use. Fugitives should, on their arrival in any Northern city, be immediately provided with arms, and taught at once that it is no harm to shoot any man who would rob them of this liberty. . . . Every slave-hunter who meets a bloody death in this infernal business, is an argument in favor of the manhood of our race. Resistance is, therefore, wise as well as just.

The only way to make the Fugitive Slave Law a dead letter is to make a half a dozen or more dead kidnappers. . . . The man who takes the office of a bloodhound should be treated as a bloodhound.

Douglass justified his position by boldly asserting that there never was nor ever could be "more sacred rights to defend than were menaced by slave hunters. . . . Life and liberty are the most sacred of all rights. If these may be invaded with impunity, all others may be, for they comprehend all others. . . . The man who rushes out of the orbit of his own rights, to strike down the rights of another does, by that act, divest himself of the right to live: If he be shot down, his punishment is just."

To make his point, Douglass made effective use of bitter sarcasm. Under the Fugitive Slave Act, he said,

the colored man's rights are less than those of a jackass. No man can take away a jackass without submitting the matter to twelve men in any part of this country. A black man may be carried away without reference to a jury. It is only necessary to claim him, and that some villain should swear to his identity. There is more protection there for a horse, for a donkey, or anything, rather than a colored man—who is, therefore, justified in the eye of God, in maintaining his right with his arm.

Since the slaves were not protected in their rights by the government, Douglass argued, they were thrown back upon the original law of nature. By the natural, God-given law of self-preservation, slaves were bound to defend themselves against those who would deprive them of their liberty and thereby of the capacity to preserve their own lives. Men who were acting to try to enslave their fellow men had put themselves "on a footing with the wild beasts of the forest which live and prey upon each other." To act to enslave a fellow man was to declare war against him and to endow him with the right of war—the liberty to kill his aggressor.

But there was still another reason for this type of resistance. When blacks passively allowed themselves to be dragged off into slavery, they had "well-nigh established that they were conscious of their own fitness for slavery." The quiet submission by blacks to the violation of their rights had only served to create contempt for them in the public mind. By fighting against his enslavers, the black man could gain not only self-respect but a measure of public dignity. The manhood of black people now had "to be defended, for mankind generally does not respect a person who will not stand up to tyranny and fight for his rights." Thus, violent resistance to enslavement was not only just but also strategically correct.

BLACK PROTEST MEETINGS

Faced with the prospect of seeing so many who had been living as free men and women thrown back into slavery, blacks organized to meet the danger. In most communities, their first act was to distribute handbills urging all Negroes to be "careful in their walks through the highways and by-ways of the city by day; and doubly so if out at night, as to where they go, how they go, and who they go with." They were warned to be "guarded on each side and watchful as *Argus* with his hundred eyes, and as executive as *Briereus* with as many hands . . . [and] if seized by any one to make the arie resound, with the signal word that all within hearing may know and witness the deed over which angels weep and demons exult for joy."

This done, blacks at various meetings and conventions set out to evaluate the situation facing them and to outline a program of resistance. Boston blacks, with so many fugitives in their midst, were the first to meet. Late in September 1850, they gathered at Reverend Samuel Snowden's church on West Centre Street to discuss the grave situation. Lewis Hayden, William C. Nell, and John Hilton were among those present, together with the recently escaped William Craft. The meeting adopted resolutions affirming their determination to stand firm and fight for their freedom:

as we prefer *liberty* to *life,* we mutually pledge to defend ourselves and each other in resisting this God-defying and inhuman law, at any and every sacrifice . . . they who would be free, themselves must strike the blow. . . . We are now Resolved, to organize a League of Freedom, composed of all those who are ready to resist the law . . . [and] rescue and protect the slave, at every hazard.

The meeting advised all blacks "against . . . leaving the soil of their birth, consecrated by their tears, toils and perils, but yet to be rendered, truly 'The land of the free and the home of the brave.' "

In his speech, William C. Nell cautioned blacks to be watchful on the streets of Boston, lest they become prey to kidnappers. Blacks, however, were advised not to wait passively for the slave catchers but instead to arm themselves and shoot anyone who would try to enslave them. Nell also condemned anyone who would "deliver up a fugitive slave to a southern highwayman under the infamous and unconstitutional law" and urged the entire community to take action against such a villainous individual.

At a follow-up meeting held on October 4 at the Belknap Street Church, the League of Freedom was launched, composed of Lewis Hayden, president, John T. Hilton, William Craft, and Henry Watson, vice-presidents, and William C. Nell and Isaac H. Snowden, secretaries. The audience was made up almost entirely of blacks, "including Fugitives and their Friends," and a goodly proportion of "men of overalls—men of the wharf—those who do the heavy work in the hour of difficulty." Evidently the militant tone struck at the first meeting alarmed the Garrisonians, which probably explains the mild, religious tone of the resolutions. The only recommendation for action was the promise of convening "a New England convention of the friends of Liberty to operate against the Fugitive Law and to devise ways and means of consolidating their resources here on the soil."

After the resolutions had been accepted and John T. Hilton had denounced Daniel Webster for his perfidy in defending the Fugitive Slave Act, Joshua B. Smith arose and criticized the passive tone of the proceedings. *"If Liberty is not worth fighting for,"* he cried, "it is not worth having." He advised "every fugitive to arm himself with a revolver—if he could not buy one . . . to sell his coat for that purpose." As for himself, "he should not be taken ALIVE, but upon the slave catcher's head be the consequence."

Robert Johnson followed and called upon the women who visited the hotels and boardinghouses in the course of their work to "be on the constant lookout for the Southern slave catchers or the Northern accessory, and if they valued their liberty [to] be prepared for any emergency." The audience responded enthusiastically, "some remembering that the spirit exhibited by the women years since, in a slave rescue from the Supreme Court, was yet alive and ready for action." The reference was to what is known as the abolition riot, when, in the summer of 1836, Eliza Small and Polly Ann Bates, fugitives from Baltimore, were captured in Boston by slave hunters and brought before a judge to be returned to their master. At a signal, a group of black women rushed into the courtroom and whisked the runaways out of the building to a waiting carriage and out of the city. Johnson concluded with the advice to be cautious and not seek out the slave hunter, "but when he rushes upon our buckler—*kill him.*"

This type of talk brought Garrison to the platform, and he argued that "the fugitives in this city and elsewhere would be more indebted to the moral power of public sentiment than by any display of physical resistance." He was grateful that the resolutions invoked "the religious sentiment in behalf of the poor fugitive," and he announced that he had framed an address to the clergy of Massachusetts, which he submitted to the chair. The address was read and incorporated into the minutes. Entitled "Address of the Fugitive Slaves to the Clergy of Massachusetts," it implored the ministers "to 'lift up your voices like a trumpet' against the Fugitive Slave Bill, recently adopted by Congress."

After Garrison had resumed his seat, Father Henson, the famous fugitive slave and Underground Railroad conductor, addressed the audience and said bluntly that while he agreed "with Mr. Garrison and others in a reliance upon moral power, . . . in a crisis for *Liberty or Death,* the speaker would not be quietly led like a lamb to the slaughter." Any people who "condemned resistance on the part of the colored people" were "denouncing the examples of WASHINGTON and JEFFERSON and all Martyrs of Liberty."

"Liberty or Death" was the motto adopted by the meeting of blacks in Springfield, Massachusetts, and they went on to announce that they would defy the new law and continue to

welcome to our doors everyone who feels and claims for himself the position of a man, and has broken from the Southern house of bondage, and that we feel ourselves justified in using every means which the God of love has placed in our power to sustain our liberty.

Springfield blacks were urged to form themselves into a "Vigilance Association, to look out for the panting fugitive, and also for the oppressor when he shall make his approach."

The best organized and best attended meeting was held in New York City on the evening of October 1, when thirteen hundred blacks jammed the Zion Chapel Church in response to a handbill circulated in the black community calling them to the meeting

for your Liberty, [since] your Fire-side is in danger of being invaded! Devote this night upon the question of YOUR FUTURE in the CRISIS.

Shall we resist Oppression? Shall we defend our Liberties? Shall we be FREEMEN OR SLAVES?

The handbill was signed by the Committee of 13, among whom were William P. Powell, James McCune Smith, and Samuel E. Cornish.

Several days before the meeting, Powell, the black secretary of the Manhattan Anti-Slavery Society and the proprietor of the Colored Seamen's Home, visited Mayor C. S. Woodhull accompanied by black seamen from the home, to find out whether the civil authorities would protect free colored persons from being carried off into slavery. It is possible that the news that black seamen were part of the delegation frightened the mayor, for he was not in his office when they arrived. Powell left a letter asking the mayor

what protection we, the free colored people, may expect under the operation of the Fugitive Slave Law. The peculiar position we occupy in this State—depending upon the magistery of the People of New York to defend her citizens against the operation of an unjust law, requires that we solicit in the name of our families that information from you which the nature of the case demands. Please answer and address William P. Powell, Colored Seamen's Home, 330 Pearl Street.

When the mayor's answer came after several days, he assured Powell in person that in case of the arrest of a fugitive, he had ordered policemen or any other officers of the city to refrain "from assisting the slaveholder in returning the slaves under the late act of Congress." However, he could not tell free colored people what course they ought to pursue in the event of seizure. "I assured his Honor," Powell reported to the mass meeting at the Zion Chapel Church, "that in the event of my friend Robert Hamilton (who was present) being arrested under the Fugitive act with the intent to reduce him to Slavery, that we would not allow him to be taken out of the city—to which the Mayor made no reply."

In addition to presiding at the packed meeting, Powell delivered a militant speech denouncing the fugitive slave law and asking the audience of black New Yorkers a series of questions:

Shall the iniquitous Fugitive Slave bill, which subjects every free colored man, woman and child, to be seized upon, handcuffed, and plunged into perpetual Slavery, be resisted or acquiesced in? Shall the blood-thirsty slaveholder be permitted by this unrighteous law to come into our domiciles, or workshops, or the places where we labor, and carry off our wives and children, our fathers and mothers, and ourselves, without a struggle—without resisting, even if need be, unto death? Or, shall we sit down and tamely submit our necks to the halter, whether it be backwards or forwards, will be followed by consequences too vast, too momentous to be considered by any one present; upon your decision this night hangs suspended the fate of millions. . . . When the mother country imposed on the infant colonies the three-and-a-half percent tax, and the Stamp Act, the first blood that was shed in resistance of the odious act was shed by Attucks, a colored man, and he was the first to receive the fire of the British soldiery, and throughout the revolutionary and late war, colored men stood side by side with white men, and achieved a most glorious victory in the name of liberty. We have met this night to decide, not whether to pay the government a three-and-half percent tax or an impost duty, but whether we will suffer ourselves and our families to be made slaves. . . . You are told to submit peacefully to the laws; will you do so? You are told to kiss the manacles that bind you; will you do so?

The response was instant and unanimous: loud cries of "No! No! No! No!" reverberated through the church. Powell concluded by paraphrasing a Garrisonian dictum but discarded Garrison's advice to blacks on how to meet the crisis. He declared the law to be a "covenant with Death and an agreement with hell and must be trampled underfoot, resisted and disobeyed at all hazards and by all means, non-violent and violent."

One of the resolutions adopted struck the same note, declaring that if "any attempt to execute its [the law's] provisions on any one of us either by invading our homes or arresting us on the street, we will treat such a one as assaulting our persons with intent to kill, and, God being our helper, will use such means as will repel the aggressor and defend our lives and liberties.'' Another resolution called upon Chairman Powell to set up a secret committee that would receive the names of fugitives who wanted help and to assist them in escaping. Powell was also called upon to appoint a committee to advise fugitives to remain in the city and not to flee to Canada and, at the same time, to devise methods to rescue any if any attempt was made to capture them. This plan of action was unanimously approved.

John S. Jacobs, a fugitive from South Carolina, warned his brothers to be constantly vigilant and, in an obvious slap at Garrison, criticized those white abolitionists who offered their assurances that the slaveholders "cannot take us back to the South." "Under the present law they can," he said flatly. He then told blacks that if they had to be taken, "let them take only your dead bodies." Jacobs concluded: "I would, my friends, advise you to show a front to our tyrants and arm yourselves; aye, and I would advise the women to have their knives too."

At this point, a man in the gallery stood up and remarked that although the meeting was hearing fine speeches, his black brothers and sisters were fleeing from the city. He called upon the chairman to appoint a committee to advise fugitives to remain and if any attempt be made to capture them, to protect them by all possible means. The plan of action was approved by the meeting.

Jeremiah Powers, a member of the Committee of Thirteen, arose from the audience and insisted that it was not enough merely to listen to speeches and adopt resolutions. He expressed the fear that resistance would begin and end right there—with words. The only argument that could be used effectively against the fugitive slave law, he insisted, was the "bowie knife and the revolver." Amid loud applause for these remarks, the meeting of black New Yorkers adjourned.

Philadelphia blacks, although still under Garrisonian influence on most issues, also responded militantly to the Fugitive Slave Act. Indeed most of the city's black leaders abandoned their Garrisonian view for this emergency and publicly announced that violent physical resistance was the only language slaveholders understood. Meeting in the Belknap Church, black Philadelphians approved this view and resolved that "God willed us free: Men willed us slaves. We will as God wills [it to] be done." They then declared their determination "to resist oppression by any means necessary—and we pledge ourselves at all hazards, to resist unto death any attempt upon our liberties."

Such language enraged the *Philadelphia Evening Bulletin,* which editorially condemned "that class of agitators who advise the colored population to make forcible resistance to the law of the land." Even some white abolitionists were made uneasy. The Garrisonian Pennsylvania State Anti-Slavery Society vigorously attacked the Fugitive Slave Law but expressed opposition to any violent resistance by blacks. "Many of you," the society observed, "are fearing that the iron hand of oppression may be laid on you . . . and under this feeling you have resolved upon armed resistance, and have determined to surrender your lives, rather than your liberties. This is natural." However, the society went on to insist, resort to violence would conflict with the precepts of Christianity. It therefore called upon blacks "not to oppose this iniquitous law by open violence, but rather trust to the operation of a humane and enlightened sentiment to do it away."

How little impression the society made is indicated by the fact that when they learned on October 16 that an alleged fugitive had been picked up on the streets of Philadelphia and would be brought before a commissioner and returned to the South, leading blacks met and called upon all members "of the colored race to arm themselves against the law, and shoot down the officers of the law if they should attempt to drag the unfortunate man back to slavery." Upon the publication of this notice, Judge Robert C. Grier, who was acting as commissioner, announced that he would "maintain the law" even if he had "to order every man who put himself in armed position to prevent its execution to be shot down." He further warned that "the first officer killed would be the signal for the extermination of the black race." But when the alleged fugitive was released because the certificate carried by the slave catchers bore no signature or seal, the press commented that the black threat of action may have influenced the decision.

At a meeting in Cleveland's Second Baptist Church on October 7, 1850, blacks resolved to "oppose this nefarious and abominable law" by every means and advised "all colored people to go continually prepared that they may be ready at any moment to offer defense in behalf of their liberty." The meeting appointed five men to act as a vigilance committee. In November, Muskingun County blacks in Zanesville, Ohio, announced that they would assist any person arrested as a fugitive by any means necessary.

By December 1850, most of the black opposition voiced at meetings had tapered off, but on January 9, 1851, the Anti-Fugitive Law Convention assembled in Syracuse, New York. Frederick Douglass was elected president and introduced the following resolution: "Resolved, That it is the duty of 'good citizens' to resist the execution of the Fugitive Slave Law, even to the taking of life." When a substitute resolution was offered asserting that "it is our duty to peril life, liberty and property, in behalf of the fugitive slave, to as great extent as we would peril them in behalf of ourselves," Douglass spoke in favor of the original resolution, emphasizing that it was his firm belief that "the law of God . . . required the death of the kidnappers." He declared that he thought it "benevolent to kill the slave-holding and slave-catching tyrants. The fall of such must cause triumph among the angels. The negroes of this country must show that they are worthy of liberty, by fighting for it." After further discussion, the original resolution was adopted, and the delegates also resolved to resist the fugitive slave law "actively as well as passively, and by all means, as shall, in our esteem, promise the most effectual resistance."

A more conservative position was adopted by the State Convention of the Colored Citizens of Ohio, meeting a week later in Columbus. John Mercer

Langston presented a clear picture of why the fugitive slave law (which he described as "a hideous deformity in the garb of law" and an "abomination of all abominations") was unconstitutional:

It is unconstitutional for the following considerations:—It strips man of his manhood and liberty upon an ex parte trial; sets aside the constitutional guarantee of the writ of *Habeas Corpus,* which, under the Constitution, can never be suspended, except in cases of rebellion or invasion; declares that the decision of the commissioner, the lowest judicial officer known to the law, upon the matter of personal liberty—the gravest subject that can be submitted to any tribunal, shall be final and conclusive; holds out a bribe in the shape of double fees, for a decree contrary to liberty and in favor of Human Slavery; forbids any enquiry into the facts of the case by confining it to the question of personal identity. Thus the law strikes down all the shields of liberty, by aiming to make a local crime a national sin.

But there was no mention of any proposal for resistance in this, the only speech at the convention on the law. The resolution adopted by the delegates condemned the fugitive law as "more unjust than any law ever passed" and the men in Congress who voted for it "more cruel and Heaven-daring than any law makers that ever legislated." But it refrained from advocating resistance of any form, urging only "the necessity of its immediate and unconditional repeal."

The New York State Convention of Colored People held in Albany from July 22 through 24, 1851, was as vigorous as the Ohio convention in denouncing the fugitive slave law. Unlike the latter, however, it took a stand on resistance, calling upon the people to follow the divine command: "*Hide the outcast; betray not him that wandereth; be thou a cover to them from the face of the spoiler.*" No man, whatever his color, could obey this "ODIOUS AND CRUEL LAW . . . without palpable and flagrant disobedience to God." The convention advised blacks "to refuse to surrender rather than to be taken into slavery." It summed up its position in three brief resolutions:

Resolved: That the fugitive slave law is the law of tyrants.
Resolved: That disobedience to tyrants is obedience to God.
Resolved: That we will obey God.

ARMING FOR SELF-DEFENSE

While the blacks were meeting and denouncing the fugitive slave law in speeches and resolutions, the Ohio *Anti-Slavery Bugle* urged them not to forget that words alone would accomplish little. Blacks could flee to Canada, it went on, but there was another course of action for those who refused to leave: they should arm themselves at once, and "if the slave-catcher comes, receive him with powder and balls, with dirk or Bowie Knife, or whatever weapons be most convenient." And in the language used by David Walker in his 1829 *Appeal,* it urged: "Do not hesitate. Slay the miscreants."

Soon after the passage of the fugitive slave law, blacks did begin to arm themselves. In a dispatch from western Massachusetts, in late September 1850, a reporter wrote that "colored people are determined to resist to a man—and woman too—any attempt to take a fellow being back to bondage and have already armed themselves. Should the slaveholder come hither for that purpose, he will find the colored people are prepared to give him a warm reception." In Springfield, Massachusetts, blacks began to arm themselves after receiving word that slave catchers were in town. "The colored people are arming," a report from the city read, "and the town hall is thronged by excited people who are determined that not a slave shall come from Springfield—Law or no Law." At a meeting in Pittsburgh in late September, blacks pledged never to allow the law to go into operation in the city. A short time later, Parker Pillsbury, the noted white abolitionist, wrote to Oliver Johnson, editor of the *Anti-Slavery Bugle,* that blacks were prepared to resist the law to the last man or woman in Pittsburgh, and that "revolvers, bowie knives, and other deadly weapons found a ready sale." The headline in the *Oberlin* (Ohio) *Evangelist* of November 6, 1850, read: "Colored Brethren to Resist an Attempted Arrest by Force of Arms."

Thus, although the fugitive slave law had spread considerable panic and alarm in black communities all over the North, causing many to flee to Canada, the majority refused to leave. Nearly all vowed at meetings to resist even with their lives, and some, as the *Rochester Advertiser* pointed out, were "pricing and buying firearms . . . with the avowed intent of using them against the ministers of the law."

On January 15, 1851, in Springfield, Massachusetts, John Brown organized a black self-defense group called the U.S. League of the Gileadites. (Brown took the group's name from the biblical command, "Whosoever is fearful or afraid, let him return and depart early from Mount Gilead.") The agreement and rules of the league, written by Brown, were signed by forty-four predominantly black men and women of Springfield. The black Gileadites pledged the armed, organized rescue of any arrested fugitive and cautioned blacks: "Hold on to your weapons, and never be persuaded to leave them, part with them or have them far away from you. *Stand by one another, and by your friends, while a drop of blood remains; and be hanged, if you must, but tell no tales out of school. Make no confession.*"

While blacks were reacting militantly to the fugitive slave law in meetings, by arming themselves and by forming self-defense groups, many whites did not take this seriously, claiming that all these actions had been taken "in the heat and passion of the hour," and that when tempers cooled, blacks could be expected to return to passivity while the law was fully enforced.

Throughout the 1850s, however, the militancy of the black community expressed by leaders and at meetings and conventions was translated into action. Before turning to this dramatic story, we should note that the machinery of black resistance to slave catchers and kidnappers had been in existence long before the passage of the Fugitive Slave Act of 1850. Blacks had resisted kidnapping and slave catching since the Fugitive Slave Law of 1793. The Underground Railroad and the Vigilance committees also predated the 1850 law, although it is true that black resistance reached its highest point in the decade following its passage.

Physical resistance by blacks also had its pre-1850 antecedents. In 1833 blacks in Detroit overpowered officials who sought to return two fugitive slaves to their southern owners. This "insurrection" of the blacks frightened white Detroit, and troops were summoned amid fears that black arsonists were planning to set fire to the city and then cross the river to Canada.

Even before that, in 1820, John Read, a fugitive from Maryland who had settled in Kennett township near West Chester, Pennsylvania, shot and killed his former master and clubbed his overseer so severely that the latter died eight days later of his wounds, received when the two attempted to capture Read. Read turned himself over to the authorities, was indicted and tried for murder, and, in the first trial, was found "not guilty of killing his former master, on the ground that he had acted in self-defense." In a second trial, however, he was found guilty of manslaughter and sentenced to nine years in prison.

The area in which Read had established his home after his flight from slavery was populated by many fugitive slaves. In the same region, a group of white toughs organized the Gap Gang, named after the town of Gap, Pennsylvania, where most of them lived. The Gap Gang made a substantial profit from seizing black residents in the southeastern corner of Pennsylvania, especially in the area around Gap and Christiana, and either transporting them across the Maryland border for sale or delivering them to their owners for a price. In many cases, the Gap Gang did not bother to determine whether the Negro seized was a fugitive slave or a free-born or manumitted black. The method of seizure they usually practiced was to knock the Negro senseless and speed with him or her toward the border before any opposition could form.

The Gap Gang operated freely until 1841. William Parker, a fugitive slave from a plantation in Anne Arundel County, Maryland, who settled in Lancaster, Pennsylvania, decided to organize black resistance. In late 1840, Parker became the leader of his people in fighting the Gap Gang kidnappers who had held the blacks in a constant state of terror. As he later recalled:

a number of us had formed an organization for mutual protection against slaveholders and kidnappers, and had resolved to prevent any of our brethren being taken back into slavery, at the risk of our own lives. . . . Whether the kidnappers were clothed with legal authority or not, I did not care to inquire, as I never had faith in or respect for the Fugitive Slave Law.

Together with five to seven other black men, Parker set up the "organization for mutual protection." Soon after its formation, the black self-defense organization went into action against the slave catchers, and within a few months it had slowed down the number of kidnappings by mobilizing many of the former fugitive slaves in the area into an armed body of men and women ready to respond at a prearranged signal to rescue a victim of the Gap Gang. When the Fugitive Slave Act of 1850 was passed, the black self-defense organization in southeastern Pennsylvania was fully prepared to intensify its activities.

Blacks were not alone in the determination to resist the fugitive slave law. Ralph Waldo Emerson said: "I will not obey it, by God!" Senator Salmon P. Chase of Ohio declared: "Disobedience to the enactment is obedience to God." Joshua R. Giddings, Ohio's abolitionist congressman, went so far as to urge armed resistance to slave catchers and federal marshals. Giddings repeatedly declared that the northern portion of his state would not "arrest nor return fugitive slaves." He asked: "Do you think they would take him, in the presence of our people, and drag him back to a land of sighs and tears?"

The same applied to other parts of the North. At times, whole communities threw their protective shield over the alleged fugitive. Gordon Casey points out in his study of the operation of the Fugitive Slave Act of 1850:

If any owner pursued his runaway slave promptly, and caught him before he had gained a settled residence in any Northern community, he generally had little or no difficulty in carrying him back. There was however, in the minds of the free people of the free states, an unwritten statute of limitations which barred the claim of a dilatory owner, and a slave who had settled and proved himself a useful and law-abiding resident of such a community could not, as a rule, be retaken, without considerable opposition.

To this I must add, however, that there were not a few in the Northern white communities who were swayed more by the influence of a law-and-order mentality and a fear of severing the Union than by the claims of humanity. In the main and in the end, it was black resistance to the fugitive slave law of 1850 that most often rendered this statute null and void.

3

Black Resistance to the Fugitive Slave Act of 1850: Early Phase

So incensed were blacks over the operation of the Fugitive Slave Act of 1850 that even when a fugitive was freed for lack of evidence, they vented their anger at the authorities charged with carrying out the law. On October 18, 1850, a number of blacks gathered at the office of the mayor of Philadelphia to learn the outcome of a fugitive slave case. After the hearing, the alleged fugitive was discharged from custody. Upon learning of this, the crowd, instead of dispersing, went after both the marshal and the commissioner. When they were held back by the police, they turned on the officers. A violent battle followed in which a police officer was severely beaten and one of his fingers nearly bitten off. Two blacks—James Berry and John Freeman—were arrested as instigators and held in $1,000 bail to answer the charges of assaulting the police and inciting to riot.

The number of cases dismissed were few and far between, however. In most instances, blacks had to act, either alone or in cooperation with whites, to prevent the enslavement or achieve the return of a Negro carried into slavery.

PURCHASE OF JAMES HAMLET

The first case under the Fugitive Slave Act of 1850 involved the latter operation. On September 26, 1850, James Hamlet, a Negro residing in New York City, was claimed as the slave of Mary Brown of Baltimore. Hamlet, who was about thirty years of age, had been living in the city for three years and had a wife and family. Thomas J. Clare, the claimant's agent, brought the case before commissioner John Gardiner, clerk of the Circuit Court of New York, who, after a cursory examination of the affidavit presented by the claimant, issued a warrant for Hamlet's arrest. Hamlet was at work as a porter in the firm of Tilton & Maloney when he was seized by the U.S. marshal. He was taken to city hall, where the commissioner, without assigning an attorney or rendering any other kind of assistance, accepted the ex parte testimony of Clare and Gustavus Brown, the son of the alleged claimant. Quite by accident, a man of antislavery sympathies heard about these proceedings and obtained an attorney for Hamlet. At the hearing, Hamlet told the commissioner that his mother was a free Negro and that he was therefore entitled to his freedom. Commissioner Gardiner, however, after pointing out that the Fugitive Slave Act prohibited the testimony of an alleged fugitive, refused to receive the statement into evidence and ordered Hamlet returned to slavery.

Hamlet was not even allowed to say farewell to his wife and children. Upon arriving in Baltimore, he was put in prison until he could be sold farther south, where, in the words of fellow blacks in Maryland, he would "wear out his life quickly in severe and unrequited labor on cotton or sugar plantations." New York City's black community was enraged by Hamlet's capture and return to slavery, leaving behind a wife and two children, and even the commercial interests of the city were moved by the inhumanity of the case.

The reaction of blacks was swift, united, and firm. Upon learning that Hamlet's owner was willing to accept a price for his freedom, fifteen hundred blacks gathered at a church and subscribed $500 to ransom him from slavery. One black contributed $100. When an additional $300 was contributed by New York merchants and white antislavery adherents, Hamlet's freedom was purchased for $900.

At noon on October 5, 1850, New York's blacks met for the first time in a public park. Five thousand people (including whites) gathered to welcome James Hamlet home. William P. Powell opened the meeting by thanking the audience for their presence "to honor a man, the first victim arrested under an unconstitutional act, and brought to trial without due process of law." He read the resolutions thanking those who had "so generously contributed to the emancipation of James Hamlet," hailing the restoration of his freedom and predicting that his return would mark "the time of our complete enfranchisement." Powell's speech, however, was much less sanguine over the significance of Hamlet's release, since he had been redeemed "not by the irresistible genius of universal emancipation, but by the irresistible genius of the almighty dollar." Nevertheless, in a voice filled with deep emotion, he proclaimed that "in the name of Almighty God and his holy angels, beneath an October sun, and in the name of humanity all over the earth, I welcome you, James Hamlet, back to your wife, your children and your home once made desolate by an awful abduction of your person but now to be made happy by your speedy return, not as a slave, but as a *Freeman*." At this point Powell shook Hamlet's hand accompanied by an outburst of cheers, mingled with sobs and tears. After the meeting, Hamlet was escorted home "amid great cheering, shouting, and rejoicing."

RETURN OF HENRY LONG TO SLAVERY

While Powell's comment on the limited nature of the victory did not lessen its value for James Hamlet, it did foreshadow the difficulty of preventing slave hunters from carrying out their operations in New York City, which was so dependent on the Southern trade. Late in October 1850, merchants engaged in the Southern trade joined with other conservative businessmen and professionals in organizing the Union Safety Committee, with the aim of defending and helping to enforce the Compromise of 1850, including the Fugitive Slave Act. Two months later, when Henry Long was seized by federal authorities as a fugitive slave, the committee had an opportunity to prove that the city could be depended upon to uphold the legal and constitutional rights of the slaveowners. Long's case was moving along quickly and appeared to be about over when the Manhattan Anti-Slavery Society, headed by William P. Powell, came to his aid and hired an attorney to defend him. At this point, the Union Safety Committee entered the scene. It publicly deplored the fact that the case was dragging along in the court, thereby adding considerable expense to the Southern claimant, and it announced that it considered the case crucial in keeping intact Southern approval of the Compromise. The committee further declared:

The failure of the law to accomplish its object in a case so plain and palpable in the City of New York, too, where so strong a Union sentiment has been manifested, would have been regarded as equivalent to an acknowledgment that the law could not be enforced.

The Union Safety Committee raised $500 to aid in restoring Long to his owner and succeeded in having the court rule that the fugitive should be delivered back to slavery. The committee made an effort to purchase Long's freedom, but his owner refused on the ground that once the slaves of the South knew that they would have their freedom purchased if they fled to New York, the new law would be of little value.

Two hundred New York City policemen led Henry Long, heavily chained, through the streets to the ferry that was to take him to the ship that would carry him back to slavery. When Frederick Douglass learned that, despite their pledges not to submit to the law, not one New York City Negro had interfered to save Long, he was furious. He began a speech in Rochester's Corinthian Hall on January 12, 1851:

I rise to give my seventh lecture on American slavery under feelings of very deep seriousness. The return of Henry Long to all the horrors of a life of endless slavery, has shrouded my spirit in gloom. . . .

It is stated that there was not a sign of "disturbance" when the unfortunate man was taken to the ferry from which he departed to the South. . . . If this be so, it is a shame and a scandal which the colored people of New York should seize the first opportunity to wash out. It is humiliating in the extreme, that, in a city with a colored population of more than twenty thousand, such a high-handed and daring atrocity could be perpetrated without any intervention on the part of any among them.

Nothing short of physical resistance, Douglass warned, would keep blacks in the North "safe from the horrible enormities which must result from the execution of the fugitive slave law; and I had rather have heard that colored men had been beaten down by the two hundred policemen employed on the occasion, than that there should have been no manifestation of physical resistance to the re-enslavement of poor Long.''

By way of contrast, Douglass pointed to what had happened in Boston when slave hunters attempted to do what they had succeeded in accomplishing in New York City.

DEFENSE OF WILLIAM AND ELLEN CRAFT

The first case in which the entire machinery of the fugitive slave law was sabotaged and an attempt to reenslave fugitives was defeated occurred in Boston. It involved William Craft and his wife, Ellen, the famous couple who had escaped from slavery in Macon, Georgia, in 1848, using an ingenious plan under which Ellen, light enough to pass for white, posed as a white gentleman, while the darker William played the role of a servant accompanying his ill master to the North for medical care. Thus disguised, they made their way to freedom. After spending a year in Boston addressing abolitionist meetings, the Crafts toured Scotland and England for six months, accompanied by William Wells Brown, where they related their story at public meetings. They returned to Boston in the fall of 1850 and participated in meetings of the black community to protest the fugitive slave law. William Craft became vice-president of the League of Freedom, which was established to resist the new law.

The Crafts were among the first targets of the slave hunters under the new law. Their owner, Dr. Robert Collins, had been following with mounting anger their activities in the antislavery movement as reported in the abolitionist press, and when they returned to Boston, he dispatched two agents to bring them back to slavery.

On October 26, 1850, the agents arrived in Boston and obtained warrants for the arrest of William and Ellen Craft. William, forewarned, vowed that he would never be taken and armed himself with two guns and a knife. For safety's sake, however, the couple was separated, hidden in the homes of various members of the Vigilance Committee, and moved frequently to avoid capture. At one point, Ellen was hidden at the Brookline home of Ellis Gray Loring, and William in Lewis Hayden's Boston home on Beacon Hill. George Thompson, the British abolitionist, described the visit he and Garrison made to Hayden's home:

on entering the house after the doors were unbarred—there with windows barricaded and doors double locked and barred—sat around a table covered with loaded weapons Lewis Hayden, his young son and a band of brave colored men armed to the teeth and ready for the impending death struggle.

Two kegs of gunpowder were placed on the front porch. When the two slave hunters tracked William Craft to Hayden's home and arrived there with a warrant, a U.S. marshal, and an armed posse, the entire group was confronted on the front porch by Lewis Hayden with a torch in his hand. As the slave hunters and their allies watched with mingled horror and amazement, he lit the torch and threatened to blow up his house, himself, and anyone attempting to enter, rather than surrender the fugitive. The invaders hastily retreated.

Throughout the slave hunters' stay in Boston, the streets around their hotel became a meeting place for a large crowd of angry blacks who repeatedly warned the southerners to leave. Finally, after being told that they were risking their lives if they stayed any longer in the city, the slave hunters left without their quarry.

Upon learning of the frustrated attempt to retrieve the Crafts, President Millard Fillmore informed the Georgia claimant that if another attempt were made, he would employ "all the means which the Constitution and Congress have placed at his disposal, to enforce the law." The publication of the president's letter resulted in preparations to send William and Ellen Craft out of the country. On November 11, 1850, they sailed for England on the *Cambria,* but not before they were legally married by Reverend Theodore Parker at a joyous wedding at Lewis Hayden's home, now converted into a festive salon.

RESCUE OF SHADRACH

The Crafts arrived in England safely and joined William Wells Brown who, having escaped North from Mississippi in 1834, had decided to leave the United States after the new fugitive slave law was passed. Meanwhile, the slave catchers had returned to Boston. This time they were seeking Frederick Wilkins, a waiter at Taft's Cornhill Coffee House. Wilkins had escaped from Norfolk, Virginia, in May 1850 and after arriving in Boston had taken the name Shadrach. John Debree, his master, learned of his whereabouts, made out an affidavit in the Virginia courts, and in February 1851 sent John Capehart to bring his runaway back to slavery. Commissioner George Ticknor Curtis issued a warrant for Shadrach's arrest and sent the U.S. marshal and a deputy marshal to apprehend the fugitive.

With cruel irony, Shadrach was served with the warrant while he was waiting on his arresting officers. Deputy Marshal Patrick Riley later bragged of how "we got a nigger." His captors rushed Shadrach, still in his waiter's apron, to the federal courthouse, ignoring the black man's vows that he would never allow himself to be returned to slavery alive. Within moments after the arrest, word had spread and a crowd assembled around the courthouse. A number of lawyers from the Vigilance Committee, including Robert Morris, a black, volunteered to act as counsel for the fugitive. Richard Henry Dana, author of the classic *Two Years before the Mast,* was chosen along with Morris as one of the two assistant counsels. Dana tried to have Chief Justice Lemuel Shaw issue a writ of habeas corpus freeing Shadrach, but the judge refused, basing his decision on the absence of any such provision in the fugitive slave law.

In order to prepare the defense, Shadrach's counsel asked for a delay in the proceedings until February 18. Commissioner Curtis granted the request. Shadrach was put under the custody of the deputy marshal and remained guarded in the courtroom since fugitives were not allowed to be kept in the state jails. When he had first been brought into the courtroom, an angry crowd of some two hundred blacks was waiting outside, with Lewis Hayden acting as leader. Just after the order was given to clear the courtroom and after everybody but Robert Morris had left, the black lawyer suddenly opened the courtroom doors and a group of fifty blacks, led by Lewis Hayden, burst into the room. The invaders seized Shadrach before the marshals could prevent his rescue, and he was rushed to a waiting carriage and brought to the city's black section. So sudden was the rescue that no pursuit was attempted. That evening Hayden drove Shadrach to Concord, Massachusetts, where Francis Edwin Bigelow, a white blacksmith, was waiting to transport him safely to Canada.

Once again, President Fillmore was informed that Boston's blacks and their white friends had defeated the fugitive slave law. He responded instantly and furiously: "Nothing could be more unexpected than that such a gross violation of law, such a high-handed contempt of the authority of the United States should be perpetrated by a band of lawless confederates at noonday in the city of Boston and in the very temple of justice." He issued a proclamation ordering that "prosecutions be commenced against all persons who have made themselves aiders or abettors in this . . . violation of the law." Daniel Webster agreed with the president's proclamation and condemned the rescue as treason.

Eight men were arrested for aiding in the Shadrach rescue, all held in the high bail of $3,000 each. Four of the eight were blacks—Robert Morris, Lewis Hayden, John A. Coburn, and James Scott. The four whites were Elizur Wright, Jr., editor of the *Boston Commonwealth,* who happened to be in the courtroom a few minutes before the daring rescue, Dana, and two of his white assistants.

Morris and Hayden were defended by two white lawyers, and bail for Morris was furnished by Josiah Quincy, the former mayor of Boston. The trials were long, but no one was ever convicted, prompting the infuriated *Savannah Republican* to denounce Boston as the center of treason, a "black speck on the map—disgraced by the lowest, the meanest, the BLACKEST kind of NULLIFICA-TION." But Reverend Theodore Parker called the rescue "the noblest deed done in Boston since the destruction of the tea." Probably because no violence had been involved in the rescue, Garrison forgot his advice to blacks to rely primarily on moral suasion in combating the fugitive slave law and declared jubilantly:

Thank God Shadrach is free, and not only free, but safe under the banner of England. On the Canadian soil he is now standing erect, redeemed and disenthralled, bidding defiance to President Fillmore and all his Cabinet, though backed by the Army and Navy of the United States.

It is likely that the fact that the rescue had entailed no violence was responsible for the black-white unity that marked its achievement. The integrated Vigilance

Committee, many of whose white members were still moral suasionists, contributed funds to pay former slave George Latimer to keep Shadrach's owner under surveillance and to cover the cost of the carriage used in the rescue. White lawyers joined black attorney Robert Morris in the defense, and a white blacksmith helped Shadrach escape to Canada. By coincidence, he was also a member of the jury that later refused to convict Hayden.

But it was the black Bostonians who initiated and mainly effected the rescue. Henry Clay declared angrily on the floor of the Senate:

By whom was this mob impelled onward? By our own race? No, sir, but by negroes; by African descendants, by people who possess as I contend, no part in our political system; and the question which arises is whether we shall have law, and whether the majority of the government shall be maintained or not; whether we shall have a government of white men or black men in the cities of this country?

Clay urged the passage of an even more stringent fugitive slave law. Small wonder, then, that when Frederick Douglass learned of Henry Clay's death in late June 1852, he wrote:

Henry Clay has gone up to his Maker a holder of slaves, a man-stealer, having done more than any other man in this country to make slavery perpetual. . . . His career may be traced by the blasted soil of Virginia; by the whipping posts of Kentucky; by the slave-hunts of New England; and by the domineering pride of men, whose property is human flesh; whose motive to industry is the lash; whose protection is in the ignorance of their victims; and who are driven, by their iniquitous position, to plot, war, and repine upon their neighbors. From a life and death like his, we may all reverently say, "Good Lord! deliver us."

FAILURE OF THE SIMS RESCUE

On April 1, 1851, the Massachusetts legislature, sitting in Boston, began debating a personal liberty bill calling for a jury trial for anyone claimed as a runaway slave. Two days later, another episode involving a fugitive slave occurred in Boston. Thomas Sims was arrested on a warrant issued by Commissioner George T. Curtis on the claim of James Potter of Chatham, Georgia. Two police officers were deputized by U.S. Marshal Danvers as federal officers and set out to find Sims. They sighted him on a street corner and arrested him. Informed that the charge was theft and knowing himself to be innocent, the twenty-three-year-old Sims accompanied the police officers peacefully, but when he learned that he had actually been arrested as a fugitive slave, he put up a fight, wounding one of the arresting officers with a knife. Sims was finally subdued with the aid of some nearby hotel workers and brought directly to the guard room of the courthouse where he was accused of being James Parker's escaped slave.

This time the federal authorities, aided by Boston officials, took no chances. The courthouse was surrounded by heavy chains and ringed by a company of police guards, accompanied by dogs, and several platoons of soldiers, later referred to as the "Sims brigade." Only those who had official business were allowed to enter. Judges had to kneel under the chains in order to enter the building. These precautions prevented Boston's blacks, aided by their white allies, from rescuing Sims.

At the hearing before Chief Justice Shaw, Sims was defended by Charles G. Loring and Robert Rantoul, members of the Vigilance Committee, who tried to bring the case before the state supreme court through a writ of habeas corpus. Shaw rejected the request, and a similar application before the U.S. District Court also ended in failure. Shaw also rejected Frederick Douglass' written plea asking for Sims' release. The chief justice had just one answer to everyone making such a request: Sims had to be returned to his master. Another effort along legal lines challenged the constitutionality of the fugitive slave law, but this was overruled by Commissioner Curtis.

Throughout these nine days of legal maneuverings, Sims remained imprisoned in a room three stories above the ground. Crowds of blacks gathered outside the area encircled by chains and were joined by a number of whites. The city was tense with excitement. The black community was furious over the role played by Boston's police in the capture of Sims and the protection afforded the officials who were to send him back to slavery. Signs appeared in the city denouncing the police as slave catchers and kidnappers. Blacks were further angered by the fact that Negroes were regularly stopped in the street and searched. Anyone found with a weapon or anything that resembled a weapon was arrested.

After every legal effort had failed, it became clear that unless he was rescued, Sims would be extradited to Georgia. Lewis Hayden, Thomas Wentworth Higginson, and several others agreed on a plan. The room in which Sims was imprisoned had no bars. During a visit to the prisoner, Leonard Grimes, a black clergyman, told him that if he jumped out of the window of his third floor cell, he would land on mattresses, which would be placed on the ground a few minutes earlier, and a carriage would be waiting to whisk him away to freedom.

Sims eagerly agreed, and all preparations were made. At the appointed hour, the rescuers waited with the mattresses spread out, expecting Sims to come hurtling down. But Sims could not jump. It was never learned whether the plan was betrayed or the news of it leaked out, but workmen had placed bars on the cell window, preventing the escape. Sims, heavily chained, was brought before Commissioner Curtis, who announced that before he signed the certificate for the return to Georgia, he would take the unprecedented step of determining if Sims was the actual fugitive indicated in the warrant from the Southern court. Several witnesses from Georgia identified Sims as Thomas Potter's slave. As they started to leave, a Negro tried to hit one of the witnesses with a club, but he was immediately seized and locked up.

Commissioner Curtis then signed the certificate and ordered Sims remanded to slavery. On April 11, 1851, Thomas Sims was taken from his cell, surrounded by three hundred policemen and a detachment of federal troops, and led to the Long Wharf to board the brig *Acorn* for his journey to Savannah and slavery. Although it was five in the morning, the streets were lined with onlookers, many of whom cried out "Shame! Shame!" and "Where is Liberty?"

At least one hundred members of Boston's Vigilance Committee, black and white, were at the pier as Sims, his cheeks bathed in tears, was brought aboard the vessel. As he came on deck, a voice cried out, "Sims preach liberty to the slaves!" Finally the ship set sail taking Sims back to Georgia. It had cost the federal government $10,000 and the city of Boston $4,000 to return Sims to slavery.

Theodore Parker was so enraged by Boston's surrender of Sims that he called on his state to take its "historic mantle, wrought all over with storied memories of two hundred years, adorned with deeds in liberty's defense, and rough with broidered radiance from the hands of sainted men, [and to] walk backwards, and cover up and hide the public shame of Boston, drunk with gain, and lewdly lying in the street." In a poignant editorial, Frederick Douglass wrote: "Let heaven weep and let hell be merry. Daniel Webster has at last obtained from Boston, the cradle of liberty, a living sacrifice to appease the slave God of the American Union." But the Boston press, apart from the *Liberator*, had no regrets. On the contrary, the papers rejoiced that the city, only recently denounced in the South as the "black speck on the map," was once again a citadel of law and order. The *Boston Courier* exulted: "The country will learn with infinite gratification, that all fears of a forcible resistance to the law in this city are at an end." Now, perhaps, it continued, the "colored population of this city, who, when left to themselves are peaceable and orderly, the most harmless and quiet of those who dwell among us," will realize how they had been "most cruelly deceived and misguided by the fanatical abolitionists who have endeavored to incite them to deeds of violence."

Nothing could have been further from the truth. In the Sims case, black members of the Vigilance Committee had called for open resistance, but the majority of white abolitionists would not agree, and so many blacks had left for Canada that the blacks could no longer carry open resistance into effect by themselves. Thomas Wentworth Higginson described the situation:

It is impossible to conceive of a set of men, personally admirable, yet less fitted on the whole than this [Vigilance] committee to undertake any positive action in the direction of forcible resistance to authorities. In the first place, half of them were non-resistants, as was their great leader Garrison, who stood composedly by his desk preparing his next week's editorial and almost exasperating the more hotheaded among us by the placid way in which he looked beyond the rescue of an individual to the purifying of a nation. On the other hand, the "Political Abolitionists," or Free-Soilers, while personally full of indignation, were extremely anxious not to be placed for one moment outside the pale of good citizenship. The only persons to be relied upon for action were a few whose temperament prevailed over the restrictions of non-resistance and politics on the one side and of politics on the other; but of course their discussion was constantly damped by the attitude of the rest.

"All this would not, however, apply to the Negroes," Higginson emphasized, and he added that when he told this to the Vigilance Committee members, Lewis Hayden assured him that Boston blacks were ready for any action necessary to rescue Sims. Yet after the meeting, the black leader informed him that so many Negroes had fled to Canada from Boston that it was difficult to mobilize effective black resistance.

A year after he was returned to slavery in Georgia, Sims was sold to a slaveholder in Vicksburg, Mississippi. He was located in 1860 and Lydia Maria Child learned that he could be purchased for $1,800. She was finally able to raise the money, but the outbreak of the Civil War prevented the sale's consummation. When Grant's men were besieging Vicksburg in 1863, one of the many slaves who escaped to the Union army was Thomas Sims, who was given a pass by General Grant that allowed him to return to Boston. He arrived just in time to witness the presentation of the colors to the great Negro regiment, the Fifty-fourth Massachusetts.

The recapture of Sims brought with it a new danger for Boston's blacks since it had demonstrated how fully involved the city officials were in aiding in the enforcement of the new fugitive slave law. On April 24, 1851, Boston's buildings were plastered with handbills reading:

CAUTION!!!
COLORED PEOPLE OF BOSTON, ONE & ALL,
You are hereby respectively CAUTIONED and advised,
    to avoid conversing with the
Watchmen and Police Officers of Boston
For since the recent ORDER OF THE MAYOR & ALDERMEN,
    they are empowered to act as KIDNAPPERS and
                SLAVE CATCHERS,
And they have already been actually employed in Kid-
    napping, Catching, and Keeping Slaves.
Therefore, if you value your LIBERTY, and the *Welfare*
of the Fugitives among you, shun them in every possible
manner, as so many HOUNDS on the track of the most
unfortunate of your race. . . .

THE JERRY RESCUE

One of the most famous of the rescues of this period involved a second successful attempt after the first had failed. This exciting episode occurred in

Syracuse, New York, in late September and early October 1851 and became known as the "Jerry rescue."

Eight days after President Fillmore signed the fugitive slave bill, the citizens of Syracuse met in the city hall and, after listening to Reverend Jermain W. Loguen, the black minister (himself a fugitive slave), adopted thirteen resolutions calling on the people of the state to oppose all attempts to enforce the new law. The most significant resolution was the one that read: "Resolved, that we recommend the appointment of a Vigilance Committee of thirteen citizens whose duty it shall be to see that no person is deprived of his liberty without 'due process of law.' And all good citizens are earnestly requested to aid and sustain them in all needed efforts for the security of every person claiming the protection of our laws." The Vigilance Committee, composed of black and white Syracusans, was headed by Reverend Samuel J. May as chairman and Reverend Loguen as vice-chairman. A plan was adopted under which anyone learning of a black man or woman in danger was to ring the bell at a meeting house ten times, at which the committee members were to meet and decide on what action to take to prevent the black's enslavement. The Vigilance Committee announced to "Southern oppressors" that "the people of Syracuse and its vicinity" were prepared to resist "the encroachments of despotism."

While May, an adherent of nonviolence, continued to counsel his Unitarian parishioners in Syracuse to be prudent and discreet in opposing the evil law, he nonetheless called upon them to defy it, totally and firmly. "We must," he wrote in a public letter, "trample this infamous law under foot, be the consequences what they may." And to the Syracuse Anti-Slavery Convention, held in March 1851, he declared: "We *must* come into collision with the American Government. I say *must,* for the Fugitive Slave Bill shall never be enforced throughout the land." A month later, he advised his congregation: "It is not for you to choose, whether or not to obey such a law as this. You are as much under obligation not to obey it, as you are not to lie, steal, or commit murder."

The entire Vigilance Committee of black and white residents of Syracuse was imbued with this spirit of resistance. The first opportunity it had to prove this in deeds involved a fugitive living in Syracuse named William McHenry, popularly known as Jerry, who was employed as a cooper. McHenry had escaped from John McReynolds of Marion County, Missouri. McReynolds discovered that he was living in Syracuse and sent James Lear as his agent to bring him back. On Lear's request, Commissioner Joseph F. Sabine issued a warrant for McHenry's arrest and sent a deputy U.S. marshal, Henry V. Allen, with a police officer to seize the fugitive. McHenry was arrested at his place of work, handcuffed, and told that he was charged with theft. On that pretext, he was brought before Commissioner Sabine in the courthouse, where he learned that he had really been arrested under the fugitive slave law.

All this took place at the time when the Liberty party convention was in session in Syracuse's Congregational church. When news of the arrest was brought to the meeting, the convention adjourned and the Liberty party men went in a body to the courthouse. Gerrit Smith, leader of the Liberty party, arrived early and took his seat near Leonard Gibbs, who had been appointed by the Vigilance Committee as the prisoner's counsel. The alarm bells were rung, and soon all the committee members, black and white, assembled in the courthouse. Church bells were also tolled, and a large crowd of blacks and whites gathered outside.

The preliminary examination began about one o'clock in the afternoon; thereafter the court adjourned for a half-hour in order that a larger room might be found for those seeking to get inside. Just as the adjournment was announced, a band of blacks and whites suddenly closed in on McHenry, still heavily manacled, and rushed him through the door, which was immediately slammed shut by a powerful black man. The men threw McHenry down the stairs, and he rolled head over heels to the sidewalk below. Scampering to his feet, he took off in flight. The crowd outside the courthouse opened to let him through but closed on Deputy Marshal Allen and his officers. However, they succeeded in forcing their way through and caught up with McHenry, put him in a dray, and, with officers sitting on him to keep him down, transported him back to the courthouse. McHenry was put in a back room with his legs shackled and a guard of marshals and policemen to watch over him, day and night. McHenry was in such a rage that the Reverend Samuel J. May was summoned to quiet him down. During their conversation, May alerted him to the fact that a second attempt would be made to rescue him and disclosed some of the details.

That afternoon, a second rescue attempt was organized. Meeting at the home of Dr. Hiram Hoyt, a local physician, Smith, May, Loguen, and A. A. Wheaton worked out the strategy. The group's attitude, Smith later revealed, was that even an acquittal by the commissioner would be "as nothing to a bold and forceful rescue. A forcible rescue will demonstrate the strength of public opinion against the legality of slavery and this Fugitive Slave Law in particular. It will honor Syracuse and be a powerful example everywhere."

In the second rescue attempt, a group of blacks and whites broke into the courtroom, smothered the guards with their bodies, and rushed McHenry out to a buggy furnished by the Vigilance Committee. The driver, a committee member, rode through the city pretending that he was not being pursued. In this manner, he reached the center of Syracuse, where he was joined by two other men. McHenry was taken to the home of Caleb Davis, a former proslavery Democrat who had turned against the institution after the passage of the Fugitive Slave Act. McHenry remained with Davis for four days and then was taken to Mexico, New York, where he stayed several days and from which he was taken to a place near Oswego. After another week, he arrived in Kingston (Ontario), Canada, where he lived a free man until his death two years later.

Many papers were quick to point out that the daring rescue had occurred in the very city where only shortly before Daniel Webster had told the citizens of Syracuse: "Depend upon it, the law will be executed in all of the great cities— here in Syracuse, in the midst of the next Anti-Slavery Convention."

Twenty-six men were indicted by a grand jury, and bail was posted at $2,000 each. Among the whites indicted were May and Smith, and among the twelve blacks were Loguen and Enoch Reed. All but three of the blacks escaped to Canada and never stood trial. Loguen, one of those who fled, called upon Governor Hunt of New York to guarantee him the protection of a safe return so that he could stand trial for the "crime of loving liberty." With one exception, none of the trials of those who remained behind got under way before January 1853 because of several postponements. All of the defendants were acquitted.

Enoch Reed's trial was separated from the others and brought up first. In addition to the charge against all the defendants of resisting the marshal, interfering with the law, and disturbing the peace, the black laborer had been indicted for homicide because of the death of an Irish worker resulting from his blow. An attempt had been made to procure an indictment for murder, but the grand jury refused to go along since the evidence showed that Reed had fought back in self-defense. Even then the jury found him guilty only of resisting the marshal. Reed was released on bail while the verdict was appealed. He died soon after the trial ended. As Frederick Douglass noted: "Death has severed the bail bond—set the prisoner free from his accusers, and removed the whole proceedings to the great tribunal of the universe." These were the closing words of Douglass' tribute to Reed, which went in part:

Enoch Reed, one of the *Jerry Rescuers,* was a young colored man of about thirty, or thirty-five years of age. He was one of the foremost to rush to the side of his outraged brother—thrust the kidnappers from around him—knock off his chain—force a passage with him through the immense crowd—wave his hat on high—and send the shouts of victory to the glad heavens. He was a brave man; and though his education and associations did not give him a place on the high platform of morals, refinement and intelligence, with many of his colored brothers, he was always respected for his kind impulses, stalwart physical powers, and unflinching courage in the time of danger. He was ever ready to raise a hand to help a friend or to smite a foe. On an occasion like the kidnapping of Jerry, he could neither be quiet or out of sight.

Samuel J. May had hoped to be among the group of rescuers hailed before the court, but he was not indicted. "I have seen," he wrote to Garrison after the rescue, "that it was necessary to bring the people into direct conflict with the Government—that the Government be made to understand that it has transcended its limits—and must recede." May informed New York's Senator William H. Seward that both he and Gerrit Smith (who had been indicted) had given notice "that if tried, we should acknowledge our participation in the rescue, and rely upon justifying ourselves to the jury for resisting the execution of a Law so extremely wicked." May went on to express to Seward his regret over the fact that despite his acknowledged role in the rescue, the government had not filed any charges against him.

For his part, Frederick Douglass always regretted that his own absence from the area because of lecture commitments had prevented him from participating in the Jerry rescue (or perhaps more properly, the McHenry rescue). But he did play an important role in the black resistance in Christiana, Pennsylvania. In the entire history of black resistance to the Fugitive Slave Act of 1850, "the battle for liberty at Christiana" (as Douglass called it) was a seminal event and one of the major harbingers of the Civil War.

4

Black Resistance to the Fugitive Slave Act of 1850: "Freedom's Battle" at Christiana, Pennsylvania

The October 1911 issue of the *Crisis,* official organ of the National Association for the Advancement of Colored People, featured an article entitled "The First Bloodshed of the Civil War," marking the sixtieth anniversary of the battle for freedom at Christiana, Pennsylvania, popularly called the "Christiana Riot." The article opened: "The Christiana riot has not been widely celebrated, like the Boston massacre, although it bears to the Civil War exactly the same relation that the affair in New England did to the Revolution."

BACKGROUND

In the early morning of September 11, 1851, one week short of the first anniversary of President Fillmore's signing of the bill amending and supplementing the Fugitive Slave Act of 1793, a group of armed men silently approached a two-story stone house located two miles from the village of Christiana, Pennsylvania. One of the eight, a guide, pointed to it and departed. The others walked on. Suddenly a man appeared at the entrance to a lane that led to the stone house. He was a Negro. Several members of the approaching party cried, "Catch him!" and broke into a run. The Negro bolted back toward the house. His shouts of "Kidnappers!" "Kidnappers!" awakened the sleeping men and women in the house and residents of the valley.

This was the beginning of the black resistance at Christiana. It took place soon after the arrival from Maryland of Edward Gorsuch, along with a group of his relatives and friends and a party of law officers. They had come to the home of William Parker to capture Gorsuch's fugitive slaves. Almost two years after his four slaves had escaped, Gorsuch received a letter from a Pennsylvanian informing him that he had the "required information" as to the whereabouts of two of the men. Confident that he would reclaim his slaves under the new fugitive slave law, Gorsuch decided to leave his prosperous farm in Baltimore County, Maryland, and travel by rail to Philadelphia on September 8, 1851. With him were his son, Dickinson, his nephew, Dr. Thomas Pearce, his cousin, Joshua M. Gorsuch, and two neighbors, Nathan Nelson and Nicholas Hutchings.

The Gorsuch farm, located approximately twenty miles north of Baltimore, used slave labor in raising grains and garden produce for the Baltimore market. Gorsuch, fifty-seven years old at the time, was an important member of the Methodist Episcopal church in his community.

In Philadelphia, Gorsuch went to see Commissioner Edward D. Ingraham, and on September 9, 1850, he obtained four fugitive slave warrants. Commissioner Ingraham directed Henry H. Kline to head the posse as deputy marshal. Two other officers agreed to join. The entire group set out for Gap, Pennsylvania, from where they were to continue to Christiana and the home of William Parker where, according to Gorsuch's informant, his slaves were staying.

The village of Christiana, Pennsylvania, located in Lancaster County, eighteen miles east of the city of Lancaster, was originally the site of Noble's Foundry and was named Christiana in 1846, when the construction of the Pennsylvania Railroad required the erection of water works with a foundry and small machine shops and a boardinghouse for the workers. Even when it was without a real name, the area around Christiana was a haven for fugitive slaves. The lines of the Underground Railroad located there extended from Columbia to Phoenixville. A large percentage of the population were blacks, and it was no secret that many had been slaves. The blacks were led by William Parker, an extraordinary figure, at whose stone house the black resistance occurred.

William Parker was born a slave in Anne Arundel County, Maryland. His mother died while he was still young, so he was sent to live in the quarters, a low building housing slaves of both sexes. One building was for single people and children whose parents had been sold or had died. At an early age, he learned to take care of himself, for the smallest children were forced continuously to fight for food. Put to work in the fields, Parker resolved to run away when he watched his friends being sold. At seventeen, he did escape. His master had picked up a stick to whip him for refusing to go to work in the rain. Parker seized the stick, whipped his master, and left. His brother joined him on the journey northward. Near York, Pennsylvania, they were stopped by three white men. A battle followed, and the whites fled. When they reached Columbia, Parker recognized the voice of his master speaking to someone, and he and his brother ran and hid in the bushes. They finally arrived in Lancaster County and were hired by farmers.

Establishing himself in the area of Christiana, Parker married Eliza Ann Elizabeth Howard and became a lay preacher. He also became the leader of the black community in resisting the Gap Gang kidnappers, who were keeping the blacks in a state of constant terror. In an account he wrote with the aid of other blacks and published in the *Atlantic Monthly* in 1866, Parker related how he and his friends organized the black self-defense organization to prevent the Gap Gang from kidnapping Negroes and selling them as slaves. On one occasion, they freed a black girl taken from Moses Whitson's farm and administered a beating to the Gap Gang members, resulting in the death of two of the kidnappers.

In the year before the Christiana riot, the herculean strength and remarkable courage of William Parker had galvanized the blacks of southeastern Pennsylvania into active defense of their freedom. "Certain names of colored men and women stand out prominently in the strange annals of the Underground Railway," M. D. Maclean wrote in the *Crisis* article on the resistance at Christiana. "William Still, chairman of the Philadelphia Vigilance Committee, and Harriet Tubman the 'Moses of her people,' and others are better known than Parker, because they shared more largely in the organization and devoted their entire time to the work of helping their brothers and sisters from slavery, but nobody could have been braver or more loyal than was William Parker in his less conspicuous way."

After the passage of the Fugitive Slave Act of 1850, tension mounted in Lancaster County. On October 11, 1850, a meeting of white citizens in Bart resolved that they would "harbor, clothe, feed and aid the escape of fugitive slaves in opposition to the law." At about the same time, armed blacks paraded through the streets of Lancaster vowing their determination to find and kill all slave catchers.

Nevertheless violent seizures of black residents continued to take place throughout the county. On the evening of January 16, 1851, a group of men headed by William Baer and Perry Marsh, leaders of the Gap Gang, forcibly entered the house of William Chamberlin on the road from Christiana to Gap and horribly beat an alleged fugitive. James Miller McKim, editor of the *Pennsylvania Freeman,* informed Garrison that the black man was gagged and "dragged like a plain beast from the house to a wagon about a hundred yards distant" and from there "conveyed across the line—which was about 20 miles south of the scene and that was the last—as I know—that has ever been heard of him." An elderly black man sitting in the kitchen sounded the alarm after the Gap Gang had left, and a band of blacks, armed with double-barreled guns and led by William Parker, was soon on the scene. But the kidnappers and their victim were already across the state border into Maryland. The Gap Gang reportedly received two hundred dollars for the capture, despite the fact that the black man was so badly maimed from his beating that he was almost incapable of work.

So bold had kidnapping attempts become that the *Pennsylvania Freeman* declared that "every week brings some fresh instance of outrage upon the homes of industry and peace. Must we fear the ravages forever? Must we sit inactively and see our neighbors torn from home and happiness to feed the insatiable avarice of Southern slave-barterers?" Blacks were unwilling to wait for their white friends to do something about slave catching so they resolved to move by themselves. Shortly after the brutal beating of the alleged fugitive by the Gap Gang, a Lancaster paper reported that "for several weeks, there has been an organization among the blacks to prevent the arrest of fugitive slaves. Armed gangs have patrolled the neighborhood during the night and guarded particular persons that were supposed to be in danger from slave hunters.'' When Samuel Worthington of Maryland, who had come into the Christiana area in pursuit of his slave Jacob Berry, arrived at the house where Berry was supposed to be living, he was greeted at gunpoint. Upon hearing horns and bells sounding to summon support for the fugitive, Worthington made a hasty departure without his slave.

The next occasion on which horns were blown was to summon support for the fugitives sought by Edward Gorsuch and his posse.

"FREEDOM'S BATTLE"

When Gorsuch and Marshal Kline left Philadelphia, they did not know that their activities in the city had been watched by the Vigilance Committee of the Underground Railroad or that they had been overheard mentioning some fugitives in the vicinity of Christiana. Samuel Williams, a trusted black agent, was immediately dispatched with instructions "to put all persons supposed to be in danger on their guard." Williams rode to Christiana on the morning of September 10 in the same coach as several members of the Gorsuch party.

When Parker learned of the impending assault on his house, he was not unduly alarmed, probably because he was confident that the self-defense league the blacks had organized could handle the situation. However, he told his landlady, Quaker Sarah Pownal, that the slave hunters were on the way. She advised him not to resist by violence. Parker replied that if the law protected blacks as it did whites, he, too, would be nonviolent and would appeal to the law for protection. Whites, he said, "have a country and may obey the law. But we have no country." So the blacks, who could have fled northward to Canada before the arrival of Gorsuch and his party, remained to confront them at Parker's house.

At about four o'clock on the morning of Thursday, September 11, the posse, led by a guide, started from Gap to Christiana. When they came near Parker's home, the guide pointed to it and left. Just then, Joshua Kite, one of Gorsuch's fugitives, left Parker's home and started for work. He met the posse, and, racing back to the house, burst open the door and ran upstairs to where the others were sleeping, crying, "Kidnappers! Kidnappers! William, Kidnappers!" Parker told the blacks "not to be afraid, nor to give up to any slaveholder, but [to] fight until death."

In an effort to impress the blacks with his authority, Marshal Kline read his warrants aloud a number of times and pretended to send Hutchings for one hundred men to enforce them. At about this time, someone fired a shot at Gorsuch from a window on the second floor. His aim was high, and the bullet ploughed into the earth. Kline fired back through a window but with no effect.

Upon entering the house, Gorsuch called upon Nelson and Joshua, two of the fugitives, to come down and give themselves up. Gorsuch and Kline then decided to go upstairs where the slaveowner recognized Nelson and told him to come down, pointing out that resistance was futile. Gorsuch continued upstairs, but someone threw down a fish jig (a pitchfork-like instrument with blunt prongs). Then an axe was thrown down, but it hit no one. Parker appeared in person to warn Gorsuch and Kline that if either took another step, his neck would be broken. Before Gorsuch and Kline could proceed, a group of blacks descended upon them, forcing them downstairs and outside. At this time, Gorsuch's nephew, Thomas Pearce, who had remained outside the house, was struck above the right eye by a piece of wood thrown from one of the windows.

A stalemate had been reached. Neither Kline nor any member of the Gorsuch party dared to climb the stairs again. Gorsuch again attempted to persuade his slave, Nelson Ford, to give up by saying: "Come down, Nelson, I know your voice, I know you. If you come down and go home with me without trouble I will look over the past." One of the blacks replied: "If you take one of us, you must take him over our dead bodies."

Following this exchange, the white men were startled by the sound of a dinner horn blown by Parker's wife from a second floor window. Assuming that this was a signal, the men surrounding the house opened fire on her, but she ducked below the sill and continued blowing.

It soon became evident from the prompt response it produced that the sounding of the horn was some sort of signal used by the blacks in case of an emergency. A group of blacks, armed with guns, swords, corn cutters, and scythes, came running across the fields and out of the woods in response to the horn.

News of the trouble at Parker's house also had been spread by other means. Isaiah Clarkson, an old black man who passed by shortly after the Gorsuch party arrived, hurried on to Elijah Lewis' store in Coopersville and told Lewis that Parker's place was "surrounded by kidnappers, who had broken into the house and were about to take fugitives away." Lewis, a white Quaker, went at once toward Parker's house and, passing the mill of Castner Hanway, another Quaker, told him what he knew. Hanway, who was ill at the time, saddled his horse and rode the mile to Parker's house. Both Lewis and Hanway believed that the Gap Gang had attacked Parker's house to kidnap him and his wife.

When Hanway arrived, the besieged blacks and those who had gathered outside in response to the horn made "a great rejoicing and a great noise." Nicholas Hutchings later testified that "they appeared to be in great spirits—all of them hallowing and shouting and singing."

Nothing indicates that Hanway was in any way involved with the blacks in their plan for a concerted defense against the slave hunters. He had never been in sympathy with the Underground Railroad or participated in meetings called to defy the Fugitive Slave Law. In fact he had resided in the Christiana area only since the spring of 1851. He would have preferred that the fugitives flee rather than fight.

As for the jubilation and singing, it was probably caused by the fact that Samuel Thompson, one of Gorsuch's fugitives, had just reminded the slave owner that he was a "class leader" in his church. At this, Parker recalled, Gorsuch "hung his head but said nothing." The blacks then taunted Gorsuch by singing a popular spiritual:

> Leader, what do you say
> About the judgment day?
> I will die on the field of battle,
> Die on the field of battle,
> With glory in my soul.

When Gorsuch saw Castner Hanway, he asked Marshal Kline to speak with him. Under the new Fugitive Slave Act, Hanway, as a bystander, could legally be commanded by a U.S. marshal to assist in the arrest of fugitive slaves. At first, according to Kline, when he asked Hanway to assist him under the provisions of the fugitive slave law, the latter replied that he would not and that he did not care for that act of Congress or any other act. Later Kline changed the story somewhat, indicating that Hanway had said only that "colored people had a right to defend themselves and that he would not assist."

After realizing that he could not depend on any help from either Hanway or Lewis and observing the increasing number of hostile blacks, Marshal Kline again called for a retreat. Gorsuch, however, was determined to move ahead relentlessly. "I will have my property or go to hell," he told the marshal.

It is a matter of some controversy as to how many blacks were present by this time. Various estimates place the figure as low as a dozen and as high as two hundred. Jonathan Katz, in *Resistance at Christiana*, a meticulous re-creation of the event, puts the number of black participants at "from 15 to 25," but other studies, equally painstaking, place the figure at fifty.

It is difficult to reconstruct precisely what happened after the exchange between Marshal Kline and Edward Gorsuch, but it appears that while the others in the party retreated, Gorsuch remained in front of Parker's house. Those blacks who were grouped outside then moved in on the slaveowner, while those in the house emerged and also advanced toward him. Gorsuch was struck down, and when he tried to rise, he was shot fatally through the chest. His son, Dickinson, in an effort to save his father, rushed back and attempted to fire his revolver. However, it was knocked down from his hand and at the same time, he received a blast of squirrel shot from very close range. The younger Gorsuch fell, coughing blood, and crawled a few yards into the lane, where he collapsed. After a short while, he was taken to the Levi Pownall farmhouse where he recovered.

Freedom's Battle at Christiana was over. The posse and the blacks had scattered. Edward Gorsuch was dead and his son severely wounded. His nephew, Thomas Pearce, had had "a very severe blow over the eye," had a shot in his wrist, another in his shoulder blade, two in his back, plus a scalp wound and a bullet wound through his hat. His cousin, Joshua R. Gorsuch, wrote in his diary that he had been "knocked out of my mind" and was wandering dazedly through the woods with a scalp wound. Marshal Henry H. Kline, Nathan Nelson, and Nicholas Hutchings, having left early, escaped without injury. Two blacks, Henry C. Hopkins and John Long, had received gunshot wounds, which were attended to by a sympathetic doctor.

FLIGHT TO CANADA

"Having driven the slavocrats off in every direction, our party now turned towards their several homes," Parker wrote later. But three of the participants— Parker himself, Alexander Pinckney, and Abraham Johnson—having been warned by sympathizers that officers would soon come to arrest them, decided to leave that night for Canada. They went forth, Parker wrote, "with heavy hearts, outcasts for liberty," provided with disguises and food by friendly Quaker neighbors. The three blacks traveled from station to station on the Underground Railroad, through Pennsylvania into upstate New York, and finally reaching Rochester. There they were led by a black man whom they met to the home of Frederick Douglass. Even though he was aware that the authorities were close on their trail, Douglass took them into his home and gave them shelter. "There are three men now at my house who are in great peril. I am unwell. I need your advice. Please come at once," Douglass wrote in a hastily scribbled note dated "Sept. 1851" to his white Rochester friend, Samuel D. Porter. The note was signed "D. F." in case it was intercepted.

While the men remained in hiding, Julia Griffiths, Douglass' assistant, drove to the boat landing on the Genessee River and made arrangements for their passage to Canada. When the fugitives boarded the boat, Parker gave Douglass "the revolver that fell from the hand of Gorsuch when he died." Years later, Douglass wrote: "I could not look upon them as murderers, to me they were heroic defenders of the just rights of men against men-stealers and murderers."

On September 21, Parker and his two comrades landed in Kingston, Ontario, Canada. "On Monday evening the 23rd," Parker wrote, "we started for Toronto, where we arrived safely the next day. Directly after landing, we heard that Governor Johnston of Pennsylvania had made a demand on the Governor of Canada for me, under the Extradition Treaty."

The Webster-Ashburton Treaty of 1842 provided for the extradition of fugitive criminals but not runaway slaves. The return of fugitive slaves from Canada could be accomplished only by claiming them as "fugitives from justice." But no precedents for such criminal extradition existed, and the British government refused to honor the governor's request. On November 24, 1851, Eliza Ann Elizabeth Parker joined her husband in Canada. "The Christiana Hero is in Canada," read a headline in *The Voice of the Fugitive*, published by Henry Bibb in Sandwich, Canada West. In welcoming Parker, Bibb wrote:

If we had thousands of such colored men scattered over the nominally free States, the Fugitive Slave Bill would soon become a dead letter. This man, in our estimation, deserves the admiration of a Hannibal, a Toussaint L'Ouverture, or a George Washington. A nobler defense was never made in behalf of human liberty on the plains of Lexington, Concord, or Bunker Hill than was put forth by William Parker at Christiana. We bid him, with his family, and all others, from that hypocritical Republic welcome to this our glorious land of adoption, where no slave hunter dare to step his feet in search of a slave.

REACTION

Before midday of September 11, 1851, exaggerated accounts of the resistance at Christiana had reached Philadelphia and were transmitted by telegraph throughout the country. Southern journals were soon picturing the Gorsuchs, father and son, as "writhing in agony," with Negroes "beating them with clubs and stones." Slaveowners in Maryland immediately gathered at indignation meetings. It was clear from their speeches that they saw in a man like William Parker the embodiment of all they hated and feared and that they were terrified of what might happen if the slaves learned about Freedom's Battle in Christiana against slave hunters. They demanded swift action to punish the "ruthless band of negroes, headed and led by brutal abolitionists and fanatics who had butchered Gorsuch."

The Southern press joined in this call. "The body of the murdered man calls not more loudly for vengeance, than do the faith of the Government and the provisions of the law," cried the *Augusta* (Georgia) *Chronicle and Sentinel*. The *Nashville Christian Advocate* warned that the crisis had come:

This affair will test the matter. It will now be demonstrated whether or not the laws of Congress will be maintained, and the rights of Southern citizens be respected, and the cold-blooded murder punished, or the rights of Southern citizens be trampled under foot, and their blood cry in vain for justice.

"Unless the Christiana rioters are hung," said the *North Carolina Chronicle* bluntly, "the Compromise will be a rope of sand and the Free States will obey it only as it may suit their convenience or pleasure." In that case, the Compromise, with the new Fugitive Slave Act, "may as well be torn up."

Governor E. Louis Lowe of Maryland made the same point in a letter to President Fillmore in which he urged immediate action to apprehend and severely punish the blacks involved. "I do not know of a single incident," he concluded, "that tends more to weaken the bonds of union, and arouse dark thoughts in the minds of men, than this late tragedy." '

Fillmore responded by placing a company of forty-five marines at the disposal of the U.S. marshal in Philadelphia, with orders to track down the parties involved at Christiana. In Maryland, however, armed riflemen acted on their own. They prowled the countryside, looking for blacks to seize and punish for Gorsuch's murder. Men and women alike were beaten and arrested. Their fury also descended upon Joseph S. Miller, a white man who had come to Baltimore to seek Rachel Parker, a free black servant who had been kidnapped from his home in West Nottingham Township, Chester County, Pennsylvania, and had been carried into Maryland and slavery. Miller followed the kidnappers into the slave state, but his train was stopped near Baltimore. He was bound and gagged, taken to an isolated wooded section, and lynched. On his lifeless body was pinned the message: "In revenge for the death of Gorsuch at Christiana."

Most Northern papers that commented on the events in Christiana struck three main themes. One was the intensified need to uphold the supremacy of the law. Another was that the murder of Gorsuch was the result of abolitionist agitators. The *Philadelphia North American* blamed it on the influence of "The Frederick Douglasses." The *Public Ledger* of the same city maintained that both white and black abolitionists were men "who excite the ignorant and reckless to treasonable violence, from which they themselves shrink, but who are, not only in morals but in law equally amenable to punishment with the victims of their inflammatory rhetoric." A third theme was that the riot proved there was no room for blacks in the free states. "Such scenes as those in Pennsylvania," declared the pro-Southern *New York Express*, "are demonstrating that the white man and the black man cannot live in the Free States together." The same idea was enunciated at a meeting in Philadelphia's Independence Square on the night of September 17, 1851, where resolutions were adopted demanding "immediate prosecution of the negroes involved in the Christiana riot" and proposing that "negroes who cannot be our social or political equals, must be kept out of the Free States."

The antislavery press defended the blacks of Christiana, although some did so with qualifications. Garrison's *Liberator* refused to "hold the Negroes guilty of the crime of murder. They acted against one law, it is true, but they had another on their side, and that a law august and divine . . . the law of nature. These blacks are fully justified in what they did by the Declaration of Independence and the teachings and example of Washington, Warren, and Kossuth." (The last named was the Hungarian revolutionist who led the unsuccessful attempt to end Russian rule in 1848.) A week later, however, Garrison qualified his endorsement by reminding blacks: "No man, bearing arms enters into the kingdom of Heaven. . . . A truly brave man never yet took up the sword."

Theodore Parker exhibited a similar change of tone. He was "glad some black men have been found at last, who dared to resist violence with powder and ball. . . . I rejoice that a negro has shot a kidnapper. Black men may now hold up their heads before those haughty Caucasians, and say, 'You see we also can fight.' The power to kill is not a monopoly of the slave hunter!" "But," he went on, "I deplore violence; let us do without it while we can, forever if we can. . . . Let us have firmness without fight, as long as possible."

But the Garrisonian *National Anti-Slavery Standard* and the *Pennsylvania Freeman* did not qualify their endorsement of the black resistance at Christiana. That Gorsuch "should have been shot down like a dog," declared the *Standard*, "seems to us the most natural thing in the world, and the only wonder is that such catastrophe has not occurred in every case where a fugitive slave has been arrested." The *Freeman* believed that the "calm and candid thinker cannot fail to see that it [the incident at Christiana] has grown legitimately—necessarily— from the passage and the attempt to enforce the cruel and disgraceful provisions of National law." It continued:

What right has the American nation to expect anything else from its own teachings, and its own actions? Have they not proclaimed, "Liberty or death;" "Resistance to tyrants is duty to their God," as their National creed? Have they not honored and rewarded the daring and exploits of the battleground as true heroism? Rebellion or flight is the slave's only hope of freedom. The government now lets loose its minions upon them, refuses them the shelter of the law, gives its law as an engine of cruelty into the hands of the man-hunters. What wonder that, outlawed as they are, they think it no crime for them to defend their liberties by the same means, for using which the "revolutionary heroes" of our own and other countries are glorified?

Horace Greeley argued in his *New York Tribune* that "the negroes in firing did no more than they knew would be done to them." In addition, a higher law justified them: "They defended an inalienable right to their own persons." "Would it not, in truth," Greeley asked, "have been a worse murder had the negroes been shot down in defending their freedom?" Yet for all this, Greeley insisted that "the blacks fell into a lamentable error. They ought to have fol-lowed the advice of their *friends* and escaped from the country."

Blacks did not equivocate in hailing the Christiana fighters for freedom. Charles Lenox Remond claimed that the Negroes of New England were "en- couraged" that Pennsylvania's blacks had showed their willingness to defend themselves by armed resistance. Robert Purvis insisted that the men at Chris-tiana, in their self-defense actions, had been "true to themselves, to liberty, and to God." From England, William and Ellen Craft wrote joyfully: "We think a few more such cases as the Christiana affair will put a damper on slave-catchers."

On September 25, 1851, five days after William Parker and his two comrades had passed through Frederick Douglass' Rochester home, his paper carried an editorial headed "Freedom's Battle at Christiana." In sarcastic and biting words, Douglass wholeheartedly justified the armed resistance. "Everybody seems astonished," wrote Douglass, "that in this land of gospel, light and liberty . . . there should be found men so firmly attached to liberty and so bitterly averse to slavery as to be willing to peril even life itself to gain one and to avoid the other." Proslavery men, he went on, were especially "in a state of amazement at the strange affair. That hunted men should fight with the biped bloodhounds that had tracked them, even when the animals had a *paper* authoriz-ing them to hunt, is to them inexplicable audacity." What could "have got into these men of sable coating? Didn't they know that slavery, not freedom is their natural condition? Don't they know that their legs, arms, eyes, hands and heads, were the rightful property of the white men who claimed them?" Didn't they know that "in the seventy-fifth year of the freedom and independence of the American people *from the bondage of a foreign yoke,*" a new fugitive slave law had been decreed? And that by signing the law, President Fillmore had commanded that black men should cease to be men? But, said Douglass,

> if the story gets afloat that these negroes of Christiana did really hear the words of the mighty Fillmore commanding them to be brutes instead of men and they did not change as ordered—why, the dangerous doctrine will also get afloat presently that there is a law higher than the law of Fillmore.

The Christiana resistance, Douglass declared, had demonstrated

> that all NEGROES ARE NOT SUCH FOOLS AND DASTARDS AS TO CLING TO *LIFE* WHEN IT IS COUPLED WITH CHAINS AND SLAVERY.
> This lesson, though most dearly bought, is quite worth the price paid. . . . The frequency of arrests and the ease with which they were made quickened the rapacity, and invited these aggressions of slave-catchers. The Christiana conflict was therefore needed to check these aggressions and to bring the hunters of men to the sober second thought. But was it right for the colored men to resist their enslavers? We answer, Yes, or the whole structure of the world's theory of right and wrong is a lie.—

On November 5 and 6, Douglass and Remond defended the action of the blacks at Christiana at a meeting of the Rhode Island Anti-Slavery Society. Remond "exhorted his people to a brave and manly bearing . . . and reminded them that there was one avenue left to them—that they could be traitors to the government that oppressed them, and if they died in heroic defense of their rights, posterity would reverence and cherish their memories while their oppressors would inherit an immortality of infamy." Douglass put forth his case for forcible resistance to the fugitive slave law and ended by saying of slave catchers "that every one of them ought to be killed." But the resolutions on Christiana embodied the Garrisonian principle of "spiritual resistance to the diabolical law" rather than the position advocated by Remond and Douglass.

In Christiana itself, most whites refused to condemn the blacks, but the newspapers in nearby Lancaster were horrified. The *Lancaster Sunday Express* denounced the resistance and called the events at Christiana "Civil War—The First Blow Struck." A group of Pennsylvania citizens sent a memorandum to Governor William Johnson asking him to take appropriate steps to apprehend the persons responsible for the Gorsuch murder. The governor pointed out proudly that he had offered a reward of $1,000 for information leading to the capture of Gorsuch's murders and that the state authorities had already arrested many blacks and a number of whites. He vowed that "as soon as the guilty agents are ascertained they will be punished in the severest penalty by the laws of Pennsylvania."

TREASON

On September 13, 1851, as ordered by President Fillmore, a force of forty-five U.S. Marines and about the same number of citizens in a civil posse arrived in Christiana from Philadelphia. In addition, another strong force was present under the command of district attorney John L. Thompson. But they had no one to arrest. Castner Hanway and Elijah Lewis, upon learning that they were wanted for questioning, turned themselves over to the authorities on September 12. Three of the blacks who had been present at Parker's house, including Parker himself—the chief target of the authorities—had fled to Canada, and the others had gone into hiding far from Christiana. Nevertheless, the three forces scoured the area, and, in their zeal to arrest and prosecute any blacks who could be linked directly or indirectly to the murder of Gorsuch, the federal and Pennsylvania authorities left local residents, especially blacks, with the feeling that they had undergone a "reign of terror." One reporter wrote: "The colored people, though the great body of them had no connection with this affair, are being hunted like partridges upon the mountains by a relentless horde which has poured forth upon them under the pretext of arresting the parties concerned in the battle at Christiana."

When the hunt was ended, over thirty black men and several white men had been arrested. (Among the whites were Hanway and Lewis, who had already voluntarily given themselves up.) Legal hearings began September 23 before Alderman J. Franklin Reigert in the Lancaster County courthouse. Thaddeus Stevens defended the prisoners at the preliminary hearings in Christiana and Lancaster. Stevens was a strong antislavery Whig of the faction derisively called "Wooly Heads" by proslavery elements and was highly respected by antislavery groups in southeastern Pennsylvania for his declarations of "unchangeable hostility to slavery in every form, in every place." But as a lawyer and a duly elected and sworn member of the House of Representatives, Stevens had also declared his "determination to stand by all the compromises of the Constitution and carry them into faithful effect."

The hearings resulted in the indictment by the grand jury of thirty-six black men and five whites for treason against the United States. All but one of the men indicted were sent to Philadelphia's Moyamensing Prison to await trial before the U.S. Circuit Court. These forty-one citizens (the number was later reduced to thirty-eight) remain the largest number of persons ever charged at one time with treason against the United States. They were accused of the highest crime in the land, punishable by hanging.

Only a few of the thirty-six black men charged had been active in the battle, and of the five whites, only Hanway and Lewis had been at the scene. James Jackson had not even been near Christiana at the time of the resistance and had no direct relation to it. "The federal government," Jonathan Katz observes, "apparently included the treason charge against Jackson simply to test the prosecution of an abolitionist whose speeches or writings might be interpreted as inciting resistance to the fugitive law." The indictments against Jackson and two other whites were withdrawn, leaving thirty-six blacks and two whites (Hanway and Lewis) to stand trial for treason.

"This," Douglass wrote when he heard of the indictments, "is to cap the climax of American absurdity, to say nothing of American infamy. Our government has virtually made every colored man in the land an outlaw, one who may be hunted by any villain who may think proper to do so, and if the hunted man, finding himself stript of all legal protection, shall lift his arm in his own defense, why, forsooth, he is arrested, arraigned, and tried for high treason, and if found guilty, he must suffer death!" Continuing in this vein, Douglass wrote brilliantly:

The basis of allegiance is protection. We owe allegiance to the government that protects us, but to the government that destroys us, we owe no allegiance. The only law which the alleged slave has a right to know anything about, is the law of nature. This is his only law. The enactments of this government do not recognize him as a citizen, but as a thing. In the light of the law, a slave can no more commit treason than a horse or an ox can commit treason. A horse kicks out the brains of his master. Do you try the horse for treason? Then why the slave who does the same thing? You answer, because the slave is a man, and he is therefore responsible for his acts. The answer is sound. The slave is a man and ought not to be treated like a horse, but like a man, and his manhood is his justification for shooting down any creature who shall attempt to reduce him to the condition of a brute.

But there is one consolation after all about this arraignment for treason. It admits our manhood. Sir Walter Scott says that treason is the crime of a gentleman. We shall watch this trial in Philadelphia, and shall report the result when it transpires. Meanwhile, we think that fugitives may sleep more soundly than formerly.

Many others were also watching. The black self-defense at Christiana and the subsequent prosecution of thirty-eight persons, thirty-six of them blacks, for treason on account of their defiance of the fugitive slave law had breathed new life into the fugitive aid movement. In Philadelphia, the response to the resistance at Christiana and to the needs of the Christiana "conspirators" was the appointment of a Vigilance Committee "to take charge of the cases growing out of the recent Fugitive Slave Act." This committee secured legal counsel for the defendants in the Christiana cases and urged black churches and beneficial societies to aid them. Five Negro churches and two beneficial societies subscribed over $100 to the cause. In four months, through appeals signed by black leaders John P. Burrn, J. Gould, Bliss, William Forten, and N. W. Dupee, the Vigilance Committee raised $663.41 for the "Christiana patriots." The committee was able to provide clothing and food to "these noble men" to make them comfortable during their confinement.

In New York City, black leaders Dr. James McCune Smith, the Reverend Dr. J. C. Pennington, William P. Powell, Thomas Downing, and Charles W. Ray attended "a small but spirited meeting in the Shiloh Church basement" to "raise money to defend the Christiana Patroits." In Columbus, Ohio, blacks contributed funds in honor of the "victorious heroes of Christiana," and when a meeting of Chicago's black citizens proposed "means to aid the Christiana sufferers on trial in Philadelphia," the "Ladies of the Chicago Mutual Protection Society" contributed ten dollars on the spot. In Detroit, a large meeting of black people appointed a Committee of Vigilance, took a collection, and issued an appeal to all churches "in behalf of the Christiana sufferers." Five days later a second large Detroit meeting reported a good response to its earlier appeal from churches and "friends in all parts of the country." Among these contributors, a group of Detroit black women raised thirty dollars and sent it with a note to the Special Vigilance Committee of Philadelphia "in behalf of our noble-hearted, liberty-loving patriots of Christiana." The note said:

Approving, as we do, of that most noble and manly stand taken by them in the defense of their lives, their liberties, and the peace and happiness of their families, we feel ourselves (females as we are) specially called upon to answer that portion of your appeal which relates to their suffering families.

The reply from the Philadelphia Committee thanked the Detroit women for their money but added that they "by no means like the insinuation 'females as we are' as though you were not a part of the great chain of humanity, and bound by every tie that links us to God our great father, and to our common destiny. In this cause which is really and truly the cause of Christ, there is neither male nor female."

THE TRIAL

The U.S. prosecuting attorney decided to use Castner Hanway's trial as a test case upon which the fate of the other thirty-seven prisoners would be decided. The specific charges against Hanway were that (1) he, with a "large number" of armed persons, "wickedly and traitorously did intend to levy war against the . . . United States . . . [by a] combination to oppose, resist and prevent the execution of the Fugitive Slave Laws of 1793 and 1850''; (2) that Hanway and others did forcibly and "traitorously resist" Henry J. Kline, a U.S. officer, in the process of executing the laws of the United States; (3) that Hanway and others "liberated" from Kline's custody the fugitive slaves of Edward Gorsuch; (4) that Hanway and others did "meet, conspire and consult" to resist forcibly the laws of the United States; and (5) that Hanway, acting on his "traitorous intentions," prepared and distributed various "books, letters, resolutions, addresses, etc.," inciting "fugitives and others" to forcibly resist the laws of the United States.

The case of *United States* v. *Hanway* opened in the second-story room of Independence Hall in Philadelphia on November 24, 1851. The clerk read the indictment and asked: "How say you, Castner Hanway, are you guilty or not guilty?"

Hanway: Not guilty.
Clerk: How will you be tried?
Hanway: By God and my Country.
Clerk: God send you good deliverance.

U.S. attorney John W. Ashmead of Philadelphia opened for the prosecution and stressed that the jury would be judging a crime of an "extraordinary character":

In monarchical governments, it is true, crimes of this description are of frequent occurrence, but in a government like ours they are seldom committed. The tyranny to which the subjects of despotism are exposed, may so burden and oppress them that longer submission becomes intolerable. . . . In governments so constituted, the only hope for a change exists in revolution, and hence the attempt made is to overturn the whole fabric of government. Under such circumstances, treason may become patriotism, and the friends of liberty throughout the world may ardently wish for its success. No such excuse, however, exists with us; for our institutions are based upon the inherent right of the people to change and modify their forms of government. . . . If obnoxious acts of Congress are passed they can be changed or repealed. Hence this defendant, if he has perpetrated the offense charged, . . . has raised his hand without excuse . . . against the freest government on the face of the earth.

After noting that without the fugitive slave clause, the Constitution of the United States "never could have been adopted; . . . and the powerful, prosperous, and glorious Republic of the United States, never could have existed among the nations of the earth," Ashmead declared that the Compromise of 1850 and the new Fugitive Slave Act had saved that Republic when it seemed to be about to be destroyed by sectional conflict. It was this federal law that had been attacked at Christiana. If this law could not be enforced, the prosecuting attorney warned, "then, indeed, is the beginning of the end." Ashmead asked the jury to consider "the influence your verdict may have on the future harmony and permanence of the National Union." They would decide, he concluded, whether the Constitution, and the laws based on it, would be recognized throughout the Union as supreme. He hoped that "this venerated hall from which the Declaration of Independence was first proclaimed to an admiring world, never can be the scene of the violation of Constitution, the noblest product of that Independence."

The presentation of evidence and examination of witnesses began on November 28, and it did not take long for the reporters and spectators to realize that the prosecution's case was untenable. The only man against whom any concrete evidence might have been brought was William Parker, and he was in Canada. In Hanway's case, the evidence did not substantiate the charge. Theodore A. Cuyler, who, with Thaddeus Stevens and John M. Read, made up the counsel for the defense, predicted in his opening speech that the defense would prove the case "to be the most absurd and groundless prosecution ever instituted in this or any other court of justice.'' The Christiana ''outrages,'' said Cuyler, did not amount to treason; there was no conspiracy against the fugitive slave law involved. In fact, Cuyler went on, ''It was because of previous kidnappings that the blacks, exercising but a fair and natural right, armed themselves, and to some extent organized purely for their own protection.''

As for the charge of ''levying war'' against the United States, Cuyler was scathing in his sarcasm:

Sir—Did you hear it? That three harmless non-resisting Quakers and eight-and-thirty wretched, miserable, penniless negroes, armed with corn cutters, clubs, and a few muskets, and headed by a miller, in a felt hat, without a coat, without arms and mounted on a sorrel nag, levied war against the United States.

Even though he stretched the truth in mentioning three Quakers when there were only two, and in placing the white miller at the head of the black resistance, Cuyler made his point eloquently.

Judge Robert C. Grier, an associate justice of the U.S. Supreme Court, who was one of two judges in the trial, criticized the defense for using the term *kidnapper,* in this case calling it a ''cant phrase,'' covering even an authorized ''master seeking to recover his slave.'' Thaddeus Stevens replied that the defense wished to introduce testimony about previous kidnappings

to show, may it please your honors, that if anybody should suspect in that neighborhood that there is a covert term or slang phrase used, and that kidnappers did not mean kidnappers—to show that it did mean those who followed that business for a living.

Following this exchange, Judge Grier allowed the evidence on kidnapping to be received.

In its summation, the prosecution tried to explain the lack of direct evidence linking Hanway with the blacks in a general conspiracy to resist the fugitive slave law. It was not to be expected, it argued, that ''in a case like this that direct proof shall be brought, where the whole region is infected, and where every white man in that immediate neighborhood . . . is leagued with the traitors.'' Maryland's attorney general, Robert J. Brent, who represented his state as part of the prosecution, attempted finally to bolster the case by conjuring up the following frightening specter: ''If this armed resistance at Christiana by a band of one hundred men, be not treason . . . then an army of ten thousand blacks may raise in the free States for armed resistance to this law of Congress, and it would not be treason.''

On December 11, Judge Grier delivered his charge to the jury. The Supreme Court Justice had vowed just after the Fugitive Slave Act had passed that ''as the Lord liveth and as my soul liveth,'' he would rigorously enforce the act ''till the last hour it remains on the books.'' But his charge made it clear that while he still fully supported the Fugitive Slave Act, he did not believe that Hanway's resistance to it rose to the status of treason. It was the abolitionists, according to Judge Grier, who deserved the blame for riots such as the one that occurred at Christiana because their teachings incited the blacks to acts of violence. Concluding his charge, Grier pointed out that grave dangers lay in the doctrine of constructive treason. He added that the persons involved in the Christiana riot had no intentions of making a "genuine and public" resistance to a U.S. law and were interested only in protecting one another from kidnappers. After hearing Grier's charge, the jury took only fifteen minutes of discussion to reach a verdict of "Not Guilty!"

In view of the decision rendered by the jury, Ashmead declared that the prosecution would not proceed any further in its actions against Hanway. Ashmead also stated that he was unwilling to prosecute the other thirty-seven bills of treason and thereby washed the federal government's hands of the affair.

The entire group of thirty-eight blacks and whites were still subject to prosecution in the Lancaster County courts, but the charges were ignored and the prisoners were freed. The judicial aftermath of the Christiana resistance came to a conclusion when a jury in the U.S. District Court in Philadelphia found Samuel Williams not guilty of what William Still described in a letter to the *Voice of the Fugitive* as the "enormous offence of going from this city with the intelligence to Christiana, that kidnappers were about."

AFTERMATH

In the same letter, Still called the outcome of the trials "a sad day for the slaveholders and their allies." History has confirmed the truth of this contemporary evaluation. As Benjamin Quarles has noted, the resistance at Christiana and the failure of the treason trials contributed to a resurgence of the antislavery movement and of organized aid to fugitives and brought widespread support for these efforts. The event convinced the Pennsylvania Anti-Slavery Society of the value of Underground Railroad activity to the antislavery movement. "The riot," one student concludes, "exacerbated public revulsion against slavery more successfully than did lectures and petitions." In *Ordeal of the Union*, Allan Nevins observes that the Christiana resistance "was an important factor in shaping, and in some cases, altering American public opinion." It forced the American people "to reconsider the feasibility of the compromise solution that had seemed a final settlement of the sectional controversy at the time of its enactment."

On June 30, 1911, the Lancaster Historical Society marked the sixtieth anniversary of the resistance at Christiana with a series of papers. One bore the title, "The Christiana Riot: Its Causes and Effects, from a Southern Standpoint." The author, a white southerner, wept for Edward Gorsuch, "a kind and indulgent master," murdered by "ungrateful negroes." He lamented the acquittal in the first treason trial and the dismissal of the others and concluded sadly: "The

Christiana riot was the beginning of the end that led to the firing on Sumter and the beginning of a terrible war.'' What the author did not mention was that that war also brought an end to the right of one man to hold another in property. This issue was dramatized by remarks made in the dialogue between two of the participants in Freedom's Battle at Christiana:

Edward Gorsuch: My property is in this house. I've come for it.
William Parker: Go in the room down there, and see if there is anything belonging to you. There are beds and bureau, chairs, and other things. Then go out to the barn; and there you will find a cow and some hogs. See if any of them are yours.

5

Black Resistance to the Fugitive Slave Act of 1850: The Middle Phase

CONFLICTING ADVICE

Analyzing the effect of the Fugitive Slave Act of 1850 on black communities in the North by the spring of 1852, Dr. James McCune Smith, leader of New York City's black community, concluded that as far as achieving its main object—the return of large numbers of fugitives to slavery—was concerned, the law was "a failure, from the fact that very few have been taken in its meshes." Nevertheless, "the results had been extremely disastrous to the prosperity and happiness of a large class of our colored citizens; for by its operations, not much less than 30,000 of this unfortunate class have been driven from their homes, and from the land of their nativity, to undergo the toils and hardships of sustaining themselves in a foreign land."

One of the thirty thousand who had fled was Reverend Samuel Ringgold Ward, and, from his new home in Canada, he became embroiled in a controversy with blacks who remained in the United States. In the summer of 1851, Reverend Ward was touring the Midwest, speaking at antislavery meetings on the fugitive slave law. Ward and his wife were in Ohio and had almost finished the tour when they "saw in the papers an account of the Gorsuch case in Christiana." Ward read of the arrest of the blacks who had resisted and of their prosecution by a government which, he wrote,

seemed determined to have their blood. Upon reading this, I handed the paper containing the account to my wife; and we concluded that resistance was fruitless, that the country was hopelessly given to the execution of this barbarous [fugitive slave law] enactment, and that it were vain to hope for the reformation of such a country.

On September 29, 1851, Ward wound up his affairs in the United States, and he, his wife, and their children left for Canada. On March 1, 1852, in a letter from Toronto, published in *Frederick Douglass' Paper*, Ward wrote to the millions of brothers and sisters he had left behind, voicing the opinion that in view of the "persevering and increasing hardness of the American heart," further resistance to the fugitive slave law was "fruitless" and that there was nothing to be gained either for the slaves or the "nominally free" from such struggles. "I do believe," he closed, "God will allow this to go on till, like the Israelites, you suffer still more, when you will, as you ought like Israel, cry to him, and he will appear for your deliverance, and the oppression will be overthrown."

Ward's advice brought an enraged response from blacks all over the North. The "spurious doctrine" of "our pretended leader" was condemned in letters to Douglass' paper, and blacks were advised that "the sooner it is that this philosophy is hurled into oblivion, the better for us, and for those who are to come after us." What right, asked one critic, did blacks who had "left for the Canadian hills" have to counsel "black men of the United States" and "tell them for their consolation that 'God will suffer them to be oppressed a little longer'?" Pointing to the resistance at Christiana and the failure of the treason trial as well as to the rescue of Shadrach and the Jerry rescue, Johnson Wooden of Philadelphia argued:

If the colored people are ever delivered from their present condition it must be by their own effort and action, and not by any outward miracle, as in the case of the Israelites. To look beyond this for deliverance, is to look for an effect without a cause.

NEW RESCUES

Ward's advice was rejected in every Northern black community. Fugitive slaves were assisted, and while blacks continued to be returned to slavery, the rescues also continued. Blacks in Sandusky, Ohio, were alerted during the afternoon and evening of October 20, 1852, to the fact that a group of fugitives, made up of two men, two women, an infant, and a number of children, had arrived in the city on the Mad River and Lake Erie train. The fugitives had proceeded directly to the steamship *Arrow*, which was scheduled to leave for Detroit that evening. Just when the ship was ready to depart, the Sandusky city marshal, his assistants, and a slaveowner boarded and forcibly removed the blacks. The young mother, with her baby in arms, broke loose from her captors, ran several steps, threw her baby to the ground, and then returned to the slave catchers. She later refused to acknowledge any relationship to the child. A black spectator picked up and refused to surrender the child.

The marshal and deputies marched their prisoners through an angry crowd to Mayor F. M. Follett's office for a hearing. The crowd, including twenty enraged blacks (one carrying the infant), followed. The slaveowner, marshal, deputies, fugitives, and spectators crowded into the mayor's office. Meanwhile the Sandusky blacks had sent for attorney Rush R. Sloane to represent the fugitives.

When the lawyer appeared, he asked the city marshal if the men, women, and children were in his custody. The marshal answered in the negative. Sloane then asked if the blacks were in the custody of any U.S. officer or commissioner in the room. When no one replied, Sloane demanded that those responsible for the refugees' detention submit warrants authorizing an arrest. The marshal said there were no such documents. Sloane asked for any paper as evidence under which the blacks could be detained, and when none was submitted, he informed both the fugitives and the spectators that there appeared to be nothing that required the detention.

Immediately blacks in the crowd rushed the captives out of the door. At that point a man shouted, "Here are the papers—I own the negroes—I'll hold you [Sloane] responsible for the escape." It was too late. Sandusky's blacks rushed the fugitives to the wharves and arranged with Captain James Nugent to transport them to Canada on his sailboat.

The slaveowner filed suit against the attorney, Sloane. He was tried before the U.S. District Court in October 1854, found guilty of charges of violating the fugitive slave law, and fined $3,000 plus the costs of prosecution, amounting to $333.30 court fees plus $1,000 attorney fees. About $400 of this amount was raised by popular subscription, and Sloane paid the balance.

A widely reported and much commented on self-rescue occurred in Cincinnati in the fall of 1853. Lewis, a Kentucky fugitive slave who had deserted his master several years earlier and had settled in Columbus, was arrested on a writ obtained by his master who had been informed of his location. The deputy marshal who arrested Lewis started to transport him back to Kentucky, but Lewis' black friends in Columbus wired attorney John J. Jollife of Cincinnati for help. The lawyer obtained a writ to arrest Lewis' master for kidnapping, and when the Columbus party arrived in Cincinnati, the sheriff took the slave catcher into custody. If Lewis were free under Ohio law, the master was guilty, but if he were a fugitive, he would be returned to slavery.

The decision was never made public. The case was heard in a long room divided by a table around which the participants sat. On one side, just behind Lewis and the deputy marshal, stood the white spectators, with the blacks on the other side. Commissioner Wright was reading his decision in a low voice. All the spectators had to lean forward to hear his words—all, that is, but Lewis. He stood up and, unnoticed, walked behind the spectators, and "donning a good hat," proceeded down the stairs, "through an alley, across the canal, through the German settlement, and by an indirect route to Avandale, where he knew the sexton of the colored burying ground." Lewis was taken to a black man's house and "placed in an upper room . . . where he remained about a week."

The alleged fugitive had not been missed at the Cincinnati courtroom for about five minutes, enough time to enable Lewis to escape. From Avandale, Lewis was driven to Sandusky and took a boat to Canada. When news reached Cincinnati that the daring fugitive had arrived safely in Canada, the black community, reported the *Cincinnati Daily Commercial,* immediately made plans to "celebrate the event, with songs, parade, dancing, bonfires, [and] cannons.'' For weeks the antislavery press chuckled over Lewis' self-rescue.

Another self-rescue occurred at about the same time in Pennsylvania. On September 3, 1853, Deputy Marshal Wnykoop and four other men (three of them from Virginia) seized William Thomas, a black waiter at the Phoenix House in Wilkes-Barre, knocked him down with a club, and slipped a handcuff on his right wrist. Thomas struggled hard against the five men, succeeded in shaking them off, and, with the handcuffs dangling from his wrist, rushed from the hotel. He plunged into the river close by, shouting, ''I will be drowned rather than be taken alive.'' He was pursued, fired upon repeatedly, and ordered to come out of the water, where he stood immersed to his neck, on threat that his pursuers ''would blow his brains out.'' ''I will die first,'' Thomas replied to every demand. The kidnappers fired again four or five different times. The last shot apparently struck him in the head, for his face was instantly covered with blood. A group of bystanders on the shore then cried out ''Shame!'' and the kidnappers stopped shooting, retired a short distance, and began to consult with each other as to the next step. Meanwhile, Thomas dragged himself out of the water and lay down on the shore, barely able to breathe. One of the Virginians among the pursuers said cynically, ''Dead niggers are not worth taking South,'' and the group prepared to leave.

Thomas, however, recovered and was helped to his feet by a black man, whereupon the kidnappers quickly returned and took steps to capture him. Thomas again ran into the river where, a reporter for the *New York Tribune* at the scene wrote, ''he remained upwards of an hour, nothing but his head above water, covered with blood, and in full view of hundreds who lined the banks.'' The kidnappers were afraid to pursue Thomas into the water since he called out that he would ''die contented, could he carry two or three of them with him under the water.'' Finally the kidnappers departed. Thomas came out of the water, ran off, and was found in a nearby cornfield, unconscious. He was carried to an Underground Railroad station and transported to Canada after his wounds were dressed.

Wnykoop and another deputy marshal were later arrested in Philadelphia on a charge of causing a riot. But Justice Grier of the U.S. Supreme Court—who had also presided at the Christiana treason trial—denounced the constable for arresting the two marshals, saying: ''I will not have the officers of the United States harassed at every step in the performance of their duties by every petty magistrate who chooses to harass them.'' Grier ordered the prisoners discharged, arguing that he could not see ''anything worthy of blame in the conduct of these officers in their unsuccessful endeavors to fulfill a most dangerous and disgusting duty.'' He felt, however, that they had not shown sufficient ''perseverance in the attempt to execute the writ,'' since William Thomas was now a free man in Canada instead of a slave in Virginia.

Ohio was the scene of another rescue, this time in 1854. James Worthington, a resident and property owner in Akron for more than a dozen years, was arrested on a charge of counterfeiting. The public soon learned that he had really been seized as a fugitive. When authorities attempted to remove Worthington to the South, a crowd of blacks and whites rescued him, and he was sent off to Canada. His family soon followed.

But the 1854 Worthington rescue was overshadowed by the tremendous struggle that took place in Boston that year to prevent the return to slavery of Anthony Burns.

RENDITION OF ANTHONY BURNS

The return of Thomas Sims to slavery on April 11, 1851, had both depressed and invigorated the black community and many white abolitionists. No other event was so influential in galvanizing the city and increasing support for the protection of fugitives. The number of black and white members of the Vigilance Committee increased, as did its finances. More blacks than ever attended committee meetings, especially those held in Lewis Hayden's home, which were frequent, since Hayden offered his home any time the committee wished to meet.

Most white abolitionists of Boston, the seat of Garrisonianism, were now ready for forcible resistance to the Fugitive Slave Act. Included among them was William Lloyd Garrison himself. Shortly after the Jerry rescue, Reverend Samuel J. May had written to Garrison explaining his participation in the rescue and adding: ''You will think I go too far in enjoining it upon all men to act against the Fugitive Slave Law.'' That was in December 1851. But at a meeting in April 1852, marking the anniversary of the rendition of Sims, Garrison offered an amendment to a resolution that had called for opposition to the fugitive slave law by peaceful means only. Garrison urged instead opposition by all means necessary—violent as well as peaceful. In arguing in favor of his amendment, he pointed out that if ''the Revolutionary fathers were justified in wading through blood to freedom and independence, then every fugitive slave is justified in arming himself for protection and defence, in taking the life of every marshal, commissioner or other person who attempts to reduce him to bondage.'' Clearly there was no qualification this time.

Not everyone agreed with Garrisons' changed views. Abby Kelly Foster was still committed to nonviolence but pledged herself to action when necessary by ''throwing her body in the way of the kidnappers, and sacrificing her life.'' Horace Mann also refused to abandon nonviolence, asserting that he would still take the Quaker position: ''I will not assist to execute it, though I should suffer it to execute itself on me.''

This split over tactics in resisting the fugitive slave law surfaced in the next crisis. Nevertheless all members of the Boston Vigilance Committee agreed there would be no more renditions of fugitive slaves. In the first test of this resolution, the result was no different from what it had been in the Sims case. In August 1853, Washington McQuery was captured in Boston, and, although his arrest caused great excitement among black and white abolitionists, all efforts to effect his rescue failed, and he was returned to slavery.

After this, enforcement commissioners avoided a confrontation with the abolitionists and looked away while the flow of fugitives into Boston continued. But on May 24, 1854, the quiet was broken.

Anthony Burns, the slave of Charles Suttle, shopkeeper, politician, and militia colonel of Alexandria, Virginia, had learned to read and write during slavery; he had joined a church and become a preacher. His work had been varied—personal servant, sawmill worker (in which trade he mangled his hand), and tavern servant. Sent to Richmond by his master, Burns not only hired his own time but supervised the hiring out of four other slaves belonging to Suttle. As in the case of many other urban slaves who were hired out or who hired themselves out, Burns paid his principal employer a stipulated fee for the privilege.

If any slave should have exemplified the proslavery thesis that bondspeople enjoyed great freedom, it was Anthony Burns. Yet at the first chance he took the opportunity to escape aboard a northbound vessel. As he put it in his narrative:

Until my tenth year, I did not care what became of me; but soon after I began to learn that there is a Christ who came to make us free; I began to hear about the North, and to feel the necessity for freedom of soul and body. I heard of a North where men of my color could live without any man daring to say to them, "You are my property;" and I determined by the blessing to God, one day to find my way there. My inclination grew on me, and I found my way to Boston.

Arriving in Boston in March 1854, Burns was befriended by blacks and given a job cleaning clothes in a clothing store on Brattle Street operated by Coffin Pitts, leader of the black community. Burns foolishly made use of his ability to write to send a letter to his brother, still a slave of Colonel Suttle. The letter, sent by way of Canada, was intercepted by Suttle, who left for Boston to reclaim his slave after obtaining the necessary documents from the Virginia court.

Burns was arrested on May 24 as he left work. The arresting officer was Asa O. Butman, the policeman who had been stabbed by Sims during his capture and who was now a U.S. deputy marshal. He charged Burns with robbing a jewelry store, and the latter, feeling that there had been some mistake, accompanied the marshal peacefully. When he realized that he had been seized as a fugitive and was to be sent back to slavery, the six-foot tall, broad-chested, and solidly built Burns began to resist arrest. A group of whites in a nearby saloon, overhearing the struggle, rushed to aid the marshal. Burns was quickly subdued and taken to the federal courthouse, which served as a jail for fugitives, where Suttle was waiting for his arrival. Burns then made a second mistake by recognizing the Virginian and referring to him as "master," acknowledged his slave status, and explained his presence in Boston by the fact that he had come north by accident after having fallen asleep while working aboard a boat as a stevedore.

As soon as he heard of Burns' arrest, Richard Henry Dana, who had acted as counsel in the Shadrach case, volunteered to serve as Burns' attorney. Burns rejected the offer, partly because he feared that if he lost in court, his angered master might sell him down the river and partly because he was suspicious of a white lawyer. Dana then asked Commissioner Edward G. Loring for a delay on the ground that Burns needed time to decide whether he desired counsel. Commissioner Loring granted the delay and adjourned the proceedings until the morning of May 27. By that time, however, Robert Morris had entered the case as assistant counsel, and Burns agreed to be represented by Dana and Morris. At the same time, Lewis Hayden filed suit against Burns' master "for $10,000 damage and for well knowing the said Burns to be a free citizen of Massachusetts and conspiring to have Burns arrested and imprisoned . . . and carried to Virginia."

On Friday morning, two days after Burns' arrest, handbills printed by the Boston Vigilance Committee were distributed in the city, reading:

A MAN KIDNAPPED

A Public Meeting will be held at Faneuil Hall this evening, May 26, at 7 o'clock, to secure justice for a man claimed as a slave by a Virginia kidnapper and imprisoned in Boston Court House in defiance of the laws of Massachusetts. Shall he be plunged into the hell of Virginia slavery by a Massachusetts judge?

At another meeting held that evening, blacks filled the basement of Tremont Temple to vent their anger over the arrest. After several speeches, an appeal came from the platform "for persons to come forward and give in their names that they might be called upon at any moment to discharge not only a responsibility but a dangerous duty." The "dangerous duty" was the rescue of Anthony Burns. A number of black men stepped forward and signed their names; some who were illiterate made a cross. Charles Lenox Remond was deeply moved as he saw black men, most of them unskilled or semiskilled workers, quickly come forward to aid in rescuing Burns. "My heart," he wrote, "has not been so encouraged for many a day as when I witness a large group of colored men present walk up to that stand, with an unfaltering step, and enroll their names as men who would run the risk of death in the name of freedom."

At nearby Faneuil Hall the Vigilance Committee-sponsored meeting was under way. Resolutions were presented condemning the arrest and urging that the outrage not be submitted to "tamely." Black minister Robert A. Grimes, black lawyer Robert Morris, Reverend Theodore Parker, and Wendell Phillips all demanded in their speeches that Burns be freed, by force if necessary. Phillips, never a pacifist, urged street fighting if necessary to thwart the kidnappers. In this he was echoing the sentiments of his invalid wife, Ann Phillips, who wrote on the eve of the Fanueil Hall meeting: "If this man is allowed to go back, there is no anti-slavery in Mass[achuset]ts—We may as well disband at once if our meeting & papers are all talk & we never are to do any[thing] but talk."

It turned out that there was to be much more than talk that Friday evening, May 26, 1854. The tone of the resolutions adopted at the Faneuil Hall meeting indicated that the audience would not accept an outcome in the Burns' case similar to that of Thomas Sims, who had been sent back to slavery after legal efforts had failed to save him. They read:

Resolved, That the time has come to declare and to demonstrate the fact that no slave-hunter can carry his prey from the Commonwealth of Massachusetts.
Resolved, That in the language of Algernon Sydney, "that which is not law ought not to be obeyed."
Resolved, That, leaving every man to determine for himself the mode of resistance, we are united in the glorious sentiment of our Revolutionary fathers—"Resistance to tyrants is obedience to God."

In his speech that evening, Wendell Phillips was even more fiery than the resolutions. Boston's Mayor Smith, he told the audience, had forbidden the city police to assist federal officials in the Burns case as they had in the Sims case. Hence, whether Burns was returned or not was to be decided by the people. Would Boston, he asked, "adhere to the result of the case of Shadrach or the case of Sims?" In conclusion, Phillips urged: "See to it, every one of you, as you love the honor of Boston, that you watch this case so closely that you can look into that man's eyes. When he comes up for trial get a sight of him—and don't lose sight of him. There is nothing like the mute eloquence of a suffering man to urge to duty; be there, and I will trust the result." The implication was clear: Burns should be rescued from the hands of the law and the slave catchers during the legal proceedings the next day.

Theodore Parker, who followed Phillips, was even more precise. Although he was "a clergyman and a man of peace," he was not unwilling to mark out a course of direct action. "Now," he told the audience, "I am going to propose that when you adjourn, it be to meet at *Court Square, tomorrow morning at nine o'clock.*"

While Parker was still speaking, a man in the audience at Fanueil Hall interrupted with the startling announcement that a "negro mob" was attacking the courthouse. Immediately the meeting adjourned to the courthouse, although not without some confusion. At the courthouse, armed blacks, led by Thomas Wentworth Higginson, the white minister, and Lewis Hayden, armed with two pistols, had laid siege to the west entrance. About two hundred members of the Faneuil Hall audience joined the assault upon the courthouse, the "Bastille of the Slave Power," as Higginson called it. Some of the attackers, headed by a stout Negro, brought up a wooden beam to smash their way through the west door in order to climb up the stairway to Burns. A group of some twelve to fourteen black and white men, including Higginson, then charged up the courthouse steps and started pounding the middle door of the building with the beam. Except for Higginson, they were variously armed. Some carried axes, others butchers' meat cleavers; at least two men carried revolvers. As the heavy blows against the door resounded through Court Square, the crowd, which grew rapidly from several hundred to its peak of some two thousand, encouraged the attackers by hurling brickbats, stones, wooden sticks, and other objects and by firing revolvers at the building, at the same time yelling, "Bring him out," "Rescue him," "Where is he?"

Burns, manacled and placed against the wall between two windows, was on the third floor of the building. His guards crouched in a far corner to escape injury from the bombardment. A box of pistols and cutlasses for ready use at infighting rested on the floor of the cell, which was sealed from the outside by a door barricaded by seven large iron bars extending at one-foot intervals from top to bottom. In addition to Burns' guard, U.S. Marshal Watson Freeman earlier that day had stationed some forty to fifty special deputies throughout the building and had also deposited a sufficient number of cutlasses in his first floor office for just such an emergency.

Although Freeman himself and a number of his special deputies were trying to brace up the splintering door, it took only two to three minutes of battering and chopping efforts for the attackers to splinter a panel and snap a hinge, and the partly shredded door swung ajar briefly. There was just enough time and sufficient space for two or three men to follow one another through the inside entryway before the breach was slammed shut. Higginson and a black rushed through together.

There, in the entry way, the two men found themselves confronted by some six to eight special deputies, who quickly drove them against the wall and began clubbing them about the head with their billies. Outnumbered and unarmed, the two men, vainly warding off blows and counterpunching with bare knuckles, were soon pushed through to the outside steps.

During all this, a shot had been fired, and one of the special deputies suddenly sprang back, exclaiming: "I am stabbed," and fell into the arms of another constable. James Batchelder, a Charlestown drayman, serving as a special deputy on his third fugitive slave case, had received a severe wound in the left groin of the lower abdomen. Carried to the marshal's office, he was laid out on the floor and died within a few minutes.

The invading band now halted their attack, and the appearance of two military companies finally restored order. Indictments for Batchelder's murder were soon issued against Thomas Wentworth Higginson, whom the authorities accused of being the leader of "the mob," Wendell Phillips, Theodore Parker, and Lewis Hayden, who were blamed for instigating the riot. The officers who served Hayden with the writ found him at the office of the Anti-Slavery Society. When they arrived, Hayden was in the back of the office speaking with an escaped slave mother and child. Rather than betray the presence of the fugitives, Hayden stepped to the outer office and allowed himself to be arrested.

Writing to Garrison in late June 1854, Higginson noted that "the attack [on the courthouse] was planned deliberately, cautiously, and (as the *almost* success proved) most judiciously.'' It all began at a meeting of the Vigilance Committee. Martin Stowell, a principal organizer of the Jerry rescue in Syracuse, now living in Worcester, had arrived in Boston with fifty supporters. Stowell convinced Higginson and others on the committee that an attack on the courthouse should be made the night of the scheduled meeting at Fanueil Hall instead of the following morning, as originally planned. Accordingly the Tremont Temple meeting of blacks was organized so that volunteers could be mobilized to attack the courthouse, and a plant was stationed at the Faneuil Hall meeting to interrupt Parker's speech and inform the audience of the black assault on the courthouse. Axe handles had been placed in strategic positions at both the Tremont Temple and Faneuil Hall meetings.

According to Stowell's plan the Faneuil Hall meeting would draw the attention of the police while the initial attack began. Originally it had been planned to begin the attack at the meeting at Fanueil Hall, but when Stowell learned that the authorities were anticipating an attack at that time, he shifted it to an earlier time. When Phillips' speech was interrupted, he and Parker were to issue the call and bring the entire gathering to the courthouse.

The attack failed, according to Higginson, because of the hesitancy of many of those at the Vigilance Committee meeting to join the battle immediately. His first reaction as he saw the reinforcements arrive from Faneuil Hall for the joint assault was that they were the ''froth and scum of the meeting, the fringe of idlers on its edge.'' The more respectable members of the audience had held back and, when they did arrive, were fearful of becoming involved in violent direct action. The attack was also poorly planned. Higginson blamed the ''extraordinary forgetfulness'' of the platform speakers who did not inform Phillips of the change in the timing of the attack, while Parker claimed that he had only half-comprehended the entire operation. But others criticized the plan because it had concentrated the attack on the least vulnerable section of the building.

For years Hayden suspected that he was responsible for Batchelder's death, the single fatality in all of Boston's rescues. Not until thirty-four years later was it learned that the coroner's report of death from a knive wound was incorrect. No autopsy had been performed. Martin Stowell, the mastermind of the raid, had himself shot the special policeman.

The rescue effort having failed, attempts were made to purchase Burns' freedom. A fund for that purpose was rapidly collected in the black community, but two obstacles could not be overcome. Each time a figure was agreed upon, Suttle increased the price until he made it clear that he would not take even $100,000 for his slave. He had not come to Boston, he told the agents for the purchasers, to ''sell niggers.'' But even while Suttle appeared to be negotiating, U.S. district attorney B. H. Hallet indicated he would block any sale. He insisted that Burns must first be returned to the South, after which his freedom might be purchased. Pointing to Batchelder's death spot on the floor of the marshal's office, he angrily told the agents: ''This man's blood must be avenged.'' Hallett doomed the sale. ''He came not simply as the government attorney,'' Jane H. Pease and

William H. Pease point out, ''but as the agent of an administration determined that in this case nothing must abort its efforts to satisfy the slaveholding South by successfully enforcing the law.''

No ''courthouse rioter'' was ever convicted for Batchelder's murder. Federal Justice B. R. Curtis squashed the indictment on the ground that it was incorrectly based on a federal statute of 1790 instead of the fugitive slave law of 1850, and the cases against all the defendants were then dismissed. The general opinion in Boston was that if the cases had gone to the jury, all defendants, black and white, would have been found not guilty and that the government, anticipating a defeat, had decided to let the indictments be quashed.

After the incident, security for Burns was doubled. During his trial, he was guarded by 125 militiamen selected by U.S. Marshal Watson Freemen, chosen, in the words of an antislavery tract, ''from the vilest sinks of scoundrelism, corruption, and crime in the city, to be Duty Marshals for the occasion. These men, with every form of loathsome, impurity and hardened villainy stamped upon their faces, sat constantly around the prisoner, while in the courtroom, the handles of pistols and revolvers visibly protruding from their breast-pockets.'' Even the commercial Boston press agreed that these men were ''hired bullies, pimps, gamblers, and fighting men.''

A company of marines from the Naval Yard guarded the courthouse and its entrances. Also called to keep order was an artillery company from Fort Independence and the entire city militia numbering fifteen hundred to eighteen hundred men. Admission to the courthouse was severely restricted, but crowds of seven thousand to eight thousand people, many traveling from rural areas and outlying towns, thronged Court Square outside. Many had walked from as far away as Worcester, responding to the Vigilance Committee's call to the ''yeomanry of New England to come and view the Mock Trial of Anthony Burns.'' Handbills distributed in surrounding towns, however, urged that those coming to Boston in support of Burns should bring no arms.

During the trial, feeling ran so high in Boston that a further attack on the courthouse was not ruled out, and more troops were hurried to the city. Black laborers were arrested for even threatening to rescue Burns. Wherever Marshal Butman, who had arrested Burns, walked in the city, he was followed by angry blacks insulting him and threatening violence. When he visited Worcester on business, he was stoned by blacks and driven out of the city. Boston's black waiters and caterers also showed their feelings toward the authorities by refusing to serve troops brought to the city to guard Burns. The waiters employed by J. B. Smith, himself a fugitive, made this fact known by placing a sign outside the establishment indicating that the soldiers were not welcome.

At the trial itself, defense counsel at first argued that the fugitive slave law was unconstitutional. When the federal court refused to rule on the law's constitutionality, the defense attempted to present the defendant as a person other than the Anthony Burns who had been a slave of Charles F. Suttle in Virginia. William Jones, a black day laborer, was put on the witness stand, and he testified that he had known and worked with the defendant at the Mattapan Iron Works in South Boston during a period before Burns was supposed to have escaped from slavery in Virginia. Jones' testimony was corroborated by eight other witnesses, including a Boston policeman and a member of the common council. Unfortunately Burns had been overheard addressing Suttle as "master" immediately following his arrest. Therefore the testimony that he was someone else was thrown out, along with Lewis Hayden's suit against Suttle for having caused the arrest of a free black man.

Burns' trial lasted from May 29 to June 3, 1854, when Commissioner Edward Greeley Loring issued his verdict stating that

if extradition is the only purpose of the statute Fugitive Slave Law of 1850, and the determination of the identity is the only purpose of these proceedings . . . it seems to me that the objection of unconstitutionality to the statute, because it does not furnish a jury trial, to the fugitive, is answered. There is no provision in the Constitution requiring the identity of the person to be arrested should be determined by a jury. . . . Whether the statute is a harsh one or not, is not for us to determine.

Loring based his ruling calling for Burns' extradition on Chief Justice Shaw's past decisions in similar cases, and, to prevent further trouble in the city, he ordered that Burns be sent back to Virginia the next day. President Franklin Pierce immediately ordered the marines to cooperate to the fullest in carrying out the order, and had the U.S. naval cutter *Norris* dispatched to take Burns back to slavery.

Immediately, too, Boston's mayor, J. V. Smith, issued a proclamation urging the citizens to clear the streets and not to obstruct or molest any civil or military officer. John Greenleaf Whittier, the abolitionist poet and a nonviolence advocate, issued a plea to "our colored friends to bear and forbear. . . . Oh let them beware of violence." The Vigilance Committee advised:

Let there be no armed resistance; but let the whole people turn out, and line the streets, and look upon the shame and disgrace of Boston, and then go away and take measures to elect men to office who will better guard the honor of the state.

On Saturday, June 2, 1854, while church bells rang, a groaning, hissing, straining, crying mass of Bostonians, estimated at fifty thousand, lined the streets of the city. Shouting "Kidnappers, Kidnappers," they watched a lone, handcuffed black man, his head held high, being led back to slavery. In front of the courthouse was a cannon; soldiers around it were looking nervously at the growing crowd of angry Bostonians. Twenty-two companies of state militia, four platoons of marines, a battalion of U.S. artillerymen, and the city's police force were used to ensure the carrying out of the shameful act. One scholar has estimated that Burns' rendition cost the federal government $100,000.

At least one police officer refused to take part in Burns' return. Captain Hayes resigned at 10 o'clock that morning. His official statement said in part:

Through all the excitement during the arrest and trail of Anthony Burns by the U. S. government, I have not received an order which I could not carry out as an officer of the police until today, when I received an order which would involve me in carrying out the unjust Fugitive Slave Bill. I therefore resign.

As Burns was taken back to slavery, citizens draped their stores and offices in black and hung the American flag upside down. A huge coffin labeled "Liberty" was suspended across State Street. Blacks had remained on the sidewalk in an all-night vigil before the hotel where Burns' master was staying. It took enormous willpower for them not to break through the military and police lines, even after General Edmonds, military commander of the entire operation, announced that he had ordered the troops to fire at the crowd if anyone crossed the lines.

During Burns' march several soldiers mockingly sang, "Carry me back to Old Virginny." Burns, seeing the enormous crowd that had come to watch him go, turned to one of the men accompanying him, and, according to one report, noted with surprise and sadness how "there was lots of folks to see a colored man walk through the streets."

Burns was marched first to Long Wharf, but the proprietor refused admittance to the procession, and the point of embarkation was changed to "T" Wharf, from which Burns was ferried to the cutter *Morris,* for his return to bondage. At 3:20 that afternoon the *Morris,* with Burns aboard, left for Richmond.

REPERCUSSIONS

That night Bronson Alcott, abolitionist educator, noted in his journal:

Witnessed Burns's rendition today sadly, and ashamed of the Union, of New England, of Boston, almost of myself too. I must see to it that my part is done hereafter to give us in Boston a mayor, a governor and a President—if indeed a single suffrage, or many, can mend matter essentially. So I shall vote as I have never done hitherto, for a municipal government and a state. Possibly a country may yet be rescued from slavery. . . . Yet something besides voting must do it effectually.

"Anthony Burns Returned to Slavery," read the heading in *Frederick Douglass' Paper* of June 9, 1854. His caustic editorial began:

Now let all true patriotic Christian Republicans rejoice and be glad! Let a grand Festal day be at once proclaimed from the august seat of government. Let the joyous thunders of ten thousand cannon jar the earth and shake the sky with notes of gratitude, in fitting acknowledgement of this mighty victory! Let the churches be flung open and the pulpit resound with thanksgiving, that our beloved country has been saved, and that Republican Liberty is still secure, and the example of the model republic still shines refulgently, to the confusion of tyrants and oppressors in Europe. After a mighty struggle continued through a great many bitter, dreadful, stormy and anxious days and nights the arms of the Republic have gloriously succeeded in capturing Anthony Burns—the clothes cleaner—in Brattle Street, Boston! Under the Star Spangled Banner, on the deck of our gallant warship *Morris,* the said Burns, whose liberation would have perhaps rent asunder our Model Republic, has been safely conveyed to slavery and chains, in sight of our nation's proud Capitol!

Douglass' editorial, "Is It Right and Wise to Kill a Kidnapper?" written in response to denunciations of the men who had murdered James Batchelder, reflected the sentiments of many blacks. He wrote:

We hold . . . that when James Batchelder, the truckman of Boston, abandoned his useful employment as a common laborer, and took upon himself the revolting business of a kidnapper, and undertook to play the bloodhound on the track of his crimeless brother, Burns, he labelled himself the common enemy of mankind, and his slaughter was as innocent, in the sight of God, as would be the slaughter of a ravenous wolf in the act of throttling an infant. We hold that he had forfeited his right to live, and that his death was necessary, as a warning to others liable to pursue a like course.

At the antislavery picnic in Framingham, Massachusetts, on July 4, 1854, Massachusetts abolitionists cheered when Garrison burned first a copy of the fugitive slave law, then a copy of the court's charge and decision in the Anthony Burns case, and finally a copy of the Constitution of the United States. "So perish all compromises with tyranny! And let the people say Amen," Garrison said to cheers.

The nationally publicized rendition of Anthony Burns, occurring only days after the Senate passed the unpopular Kansas Nebraska bill, which opened new territories to slave expansion, converted many to the antislavery point of view. There was clear evidence in Boston of a more open hostility to slavery and the slave power among the populace. Moreover, like Bronson Alcott, many nonvoting abolitionists decided to use their ballot against officials who had taken part in the return of Burns to slavery. Every Massachusetts official who had participated was defeated at the next election.

Because of Judge Edward Greeley Loring's key role in Burns' extradition, a petition drive was begun by a group of women to have him removed from his post as judge of probate for Suffolk County. This drive snowballed until seventeen thousand signatures had been accumulated. Meanwhile Loring lost his job as lecturer at the Harvard Law School as a result of continuing student complaints against him. Legislative committees were set up to determine Loring's status, and each time the general court voted for his removal. However, time and again, Know-Nothing Governor Henry Gardiner vetoed the legislature's action. Loring's removal was finally approved by Republican Governor Nathaniel Banks in March 1858 after nearly four years of continuing attempts. But the commissioner quickly received a vote of confidence from President James Buchanan, who immediately appointed him chief justice of the Court of Claims in Washington.

The revolution of public opinion in Massachusetts was indicated by the number of signatures to a petition for the immediate repeal of the fugitive slave law. In Boston there were three thousand signatures, including those of members of the mercantile community. "Conservative feeling," Edward Everett noted, is "utterly . . . crushed out," and merchant and textile magnate Amos A. Lawrence wrote that "we went to bed one night, old fashioned, conservative, compromise, Union Whigs and waked up stark mad Abolitionists." They did not, to be sure, remain "stark mad Abolitionists" for long, but long enough to sign petitions to the state legislature calling for a stronger personal liberty law. The legislature overwhelmingly passed such a law in May 1855—over the advice of Chief Justice Lemuel Shaw and over Governor Gardiner's veto.

The law, "An Act to Protect the Rights and Liberties of the People of the Commonwealth of Massachusetts," provided for a jury trial for an alleged fugitive. Although it also stipulated that the accused could not testify at the trial, it provided that he could not be forced to testify against himself. Section 6 provided:

Upon every question of fact involved in the issue, the burden of proof shall be on the claimant and the facts alleged and necessary to be established must be proved by the testimony of at least two credible witnesses.

Section 7 marked a great advance in checking the menace of kidnapping of free blacks. Anyone found guilty of this offense or of assisting in it "shall be punished by a fine of not less than one thousand dollars, and by imprisonment in the State Prison not less than one year nor more than five years." The act also provided that ex parte affidavits were not to be admitted in evidence. For a state officeholder to issue a warrant under the fugitive slave law was tantamount to resignation, for an attorney to assist the claimant was to forfeit his rights to practice in the courts, and for a judge to do either was to subject himself to impeachment or removal from office. It was the duty of the governor to appoint county commissioners to help defend fugitives and secure a fair trial for them.

Garrison hailed the law as one "intended to deny a plain constitutional provision: intended to nullify a law of Congress; intended to bring the authorities of the Commonwealth in conflict with the authorities of the United States: intended to involve the community in Civil War." Although a slave was returned to the South from Hyannis, Massachusetts, in May 1859, Anthony Burns was the last fugitive returned from Boston.

In less than a year after his rendition, Burns returned to Boston a free man. Leonard A. Grimes, Coffin Pitts, and the members of the Twelfth Baptist Church, the most active of the black churches in support of fugitive slaves, collected funds and arranged to purchase Burns' freedom for $1,300. Burns spent two years at Oberlin College and at the Fairmount Theological Seminary in Cincinnati but left before he completed his studies because of lack of funds. He made antislavery speeches and sold copies of his narrative to help raise money to complete his studies. His speeches were illustrated by, in his own words, "a panorama, styled the Grand Moving Mirror-scenes of real life, startling and thrilling incidents, degradation and horrors of American slavery." The presentation was set forth with great skill. "His lecture," reported one observer, "cannot fail to kindle anew in the hearts of all a stronger opposition to that curse of all curses—American Slavery."

When he finished his studies, Burns took a post as pastor of a colored Baptist church in Indianapolis, Indiana; however, because of Indiana's notorious black laws, he eventually settled in Canada, where he died in July 1862, apparently from overwork.

OTHER RESCUES AND A COURT DECISION

A few weeks after the rejection of Anthony Burns' counsel's challenge of the constitutionality of the Fugitive Slave Act, the Supreme Court of Wisconsin sustained a decision against its constitutionality pronounced by one of the justices of that court. The decision stemmed from an action against an alleged fugitive slave, James Glover, claimed by B. S. Garland of St. Louis, Missouri. On March 10, 1854, Glover was arrested by five men who suddenly came into his shanty in Racine, Wisconsin, put a pistol to his head, threw him to the ground, handcuffed him, and took him in a wagon to the Milwaukee jail, a distance of twenty-five miles. "We found him in his cell," wrote a reporter for the *Milwaukee Sentinel* who visited Glover. "He was cut in two places on the head; the front of his shirt and vest were soaking and stiff with his own blood." Upon reading this report, several hundred blacks and whites collected around the jail and courthouse. A Vigilance Committee of twenty-five black and white Milwaukee residents was appointed to watch the jail at night and see that Glover was not taken away secretly. The next afternoon, when U.S. Judge Miller refused to release Glover, a crowd of blacks and whites, armed with axes, attacked the prison door while others brought up planks to force it open. The door was broken down, and the inner door and wall were smashed. Glover was snatched from the prison guards, rushed outside, placed in a wagon, and quickly transported to Canada.

Sherman Booth, editor of the *Milwaukee Free Democrat,* and three others, one of them a black, were arrested for aiding and abetting the rescue. Brought before Judge Smith of the Wisconsin Supreme Court on a writ of habeas corpus, Booth was set at liberty on the ground that the fugitive slave law was unconstitutional. Upon appeal, the Wisconsin Supreme Court, with one dissent, approved Judge Smith's opinion. The court, in its decision, noted:

We are of opinion, that so much of the act of Congress in question, as refers to the Commissioners for decision the questions of fact which are to be established by evidence, before the alleged fugitive can be delivered up to the claimant, is repugnant to the Constitution of the United States, and therefore void, for two reasons: First, because it attempts to confer upon those officers judicial powers; and secondly, because it is a denial of the right of the alleged fugitive to have the questions tried and decided by a Jury, which, we think, is given him by the Constitution of the United States.

In effect, the Wisconsin Supreme Court was stating the arguments raised against the fugitive slave law's constitutionality since the law was passed. The law was attacked because no provision was made for trial by jury to determine the status of the alleged fugitive. The argument was also frequently advanced that the commissioners, who were appointed by U.S. circuit courts and who were empowered under the Fugitive Slave Act of 1850 to issue certificates for the rendition of fugitive slaves, were exercising judicial functions. Thus, it was claimed, they should be appointed by the president with the consent of the Senate and receive a fixed salary rather than the fees set by the fugitive slave law.

It was not until 1859, in the Booth case growing out of the Wisconsin decision, that the Supreme Court upheld the constitutionality of the Fugitive Slave Act of 1850.

Salem, Ohio, was distinguished mainly by the fact that the organ of western Garrisonianism, the *Anti-Slavery Bugle*, was published in the town by Marius Robinson, the leading Garrisonian of the West. On August 28, 1854, the Western Anti-Slavery Society convention was meeting in Salem. At about four o'clock that afternoon, news arrived that a slaveowner and his slave were on a train headed for Salem. The convention adjourned, and the delegates, black and white, went en masse to the depot. Ben Brown and another black, plus two whites, Henry B. Blackwell and Dr. Abram Brooks, were delegated to board the train and rescue the slave.

When the three boarded the train, they found the slave to be a ten-year-old girl sitting with her mistress, a Mrs. Robinson. When Brown asked the ten-year-old who she was and where she was going, Mrs. Robinson angrily retorted that "it was none of his business." Brown ignored the woman and "asked the child if she wished to be free." According to the antislavery press account of the episode, the young slave answered "Yes." In any event, she was taken from her owner by Brown and Blackwell (who apologized to the southerner "for his rudeness") and placed on the shoulders of a black man outside the coach. The abolitionists then held a victory parade down Salem's main street. At a meeting after the celebration, fifty dollars was collected to purchase clothes for the ex-slave. Marius Robinson later informed his readers that "the little chattel of Tennessee . . . is in the hands of kind and conscientious friends, who provide for her interest." Her foster parents renamed her Abby Kelly Salem in honor of the famous female Garrisonian abolitionist and the place where she had been rescued and emancipated.

THE PHILADELPHIA RESCUE

In commenting on the Wisconsin Supreme Court decision declaring the Fugitive Slave Act of 1850 unconstitutional, the *Christian Recorder,* official organ of the African Methodist Episcopal church in Philadelphia, correctly predicted: "The case will no doubt be taken up to the Supreme Court of the United States, for the final adjudication of the important question involved." But, the journal went on, while the case of Sherman Booth of Wisconsin was making its way to the Supreme Court for decision, blacks should not lessen in the slightest their vigilance or resistance to the vicious fugitive slave law.

Philadelphia blacks quickly agreed. At a public meeting in the summer of 1854, they adopted a resolution in which they replied to criticism in the city's press that they were lax in upholding the law of the land. Their rejoinder began:

Those who without crime, are outlawed by any Government, can owe no allegiance to its enactments—that, being condemned and treated as outlaws by Government for no crime but that of claiming to be men rather than beasts and chattels, we hereby declare ourselves absolved from all obligations to obey its slaveholding behests, and fall back upon our natural rights—that we adopt and advise all oppressed to adopt the motto, "Liberty or Death."

They went on to warn slaveowners that they "will not allow any fellow beings to be enslaved if we can prevent it—that resistance to the slave hunters is obedience to God, and we pledge ourselves to resist all such laws by such means as we shall deem right and expedient."

A year later, they had an opportunity to make good on their warning. On July 18, 1855, John H. Wheeler, U.S. minister to Nicaragua, was traveling through Philadelphia en route to New York City, where he was to embark on a voyage to resume his duties in the Central American nation. Accompanying Wheeler were three Virginia slaves whom he had purchased two years earlier—Jane Johnson and her sons, Daniel and Isaiah. After Wheeler had warned Jane to talk to no one, the party proceeded to Bloodgood's Hotel, near the Walnut Street wharf on the Delaware River. During the two-and-a-half hour wait at the hotel, Jane, disregarding her owner's orders, twice informed passing blacks that she was a slave and desired her freedom. She did this while Wheeler was eating dinner. Immediately after completing his meal, Wheeler rejoined his slaves and then boarded the *Washington,* a boat upon which they were scheduled to sail at 5:00 P.M.

But Wheeler did not know that Jane Johnson's plea for assistance had been transmitted to William Still. At 4:30 P.M., Still received a hastily written note informing him of the plight of the Wheeler slaves. Being the secretary of the General Vigilance Committee, Still immediately relayed the message to Passmore Williamson, one of the initial white members of the Philadelphia General Vigilance Committee when it was revived in December 1852. He also served with Still on its four-member Acting Committee. Boarding the *Washington,* Williamson and Still located Jane Johnson. Williamson informed her that she and her children were free according to Pennsylvania law, whereupon Wheeler, Williamson, Still, and a white bystander vigorously argued this question until the final bell for going ashore rang. Williamson then told the slave woman that she must act at once if she desired her freedom. Jane attempted to rise from her seat, only to be pushed down by Wheeler. As she struggled to rise a second time, Williamson interposed and prevented further interference by her master. Jane and her sons were conducted off the ship to a waiting carriage by a group of blacks who had followed Williamson and Still aboard, and were carried away to safety.

Released by Williamson, Wheeler pursued his slaves, but he was physically restrained by two blacks who threatened ''to cut his throat from ear to ear.'' Five blacks had assisted Williamson and Still in the rescue of Jane Johnson and her sons.

The dramatic episode in Philadelphia is listed in ''The Fugitive Slave Law and Its Victims,'' *Anti-Slavery Tract Number 18,* probably because Jane Johnson and her children were rescued from slavery and did become fugitives from their master, but the incident is not related to the fugitive slave law. Since Wheeler's slaves had been brought into Pennsylvania and had not escaped from another state, the law had no bearing in the matter. Pennsylvania's so-called personal liberty law of 1847 had repealed the right of slaveholders to bring their slaves into the state, established in 1780. Thus, a slave brought into Pennsylvania by his or her master could be considered free the moment he or she entered the state. Pennsylvania was not alone in this respect. Other free states usually followed the principle that when a master took a slave into a free state, even without the intention to remain permanently, the slave could refuse to leave. The master could not invoke the fugitive slave law because the slave had not come into the free state as a fugitive. Wheeler, aware of this, contended in court that he based his claim on Virginia law that regarded his slaves as his property. He appealed to Judge John K. Kane of the U.S. District Court in eastern Pennsylvania for a writ of habeas corpus to compel Williamson to bring the slaves to Kane's court. The judge issued the desired writ. When Williamson failed to produce the slaves, he was imprisoned for three months in an iron and stone cell at Moyamensing Prison for contempt of court until public pressure compelled his release.

The ordeal of Passmore Williamson in the cause of freedom is well known. Less known is the trial of the five blacks who had assisted Williamson and Still. (Even *Anti-Slavery Tract Number 18* mentions only ''the celebrated case of Passmore Williamson.'') On July 19, Wheeler brought complaints against them, a warrant was issued, and all were arrested. After being charged with highway robbery, inciting to riot, and assault and battery, they were forced to remain in jail when alderman James B. Freeman set bail at the exorbitant sum of $7,000 a person. Bail was later reduced to $1,000 a person, and the only charges mentioned in their indictment were riot and assault and battery. But a sixth defendant was added—William Still—who was also indicted on charges of assault and battery.

The trial of the six blacks began in the Court of Quarter Sessions in Philadelphia on August 29. Wheeler testified that his slaves had not desired their freedom, that they had been forcibly abducted, and that he had been violently manhandled. Since it appeared that the only available witnesses for the defense were either on trial or in jail, it seemed that Wheeler's testimony would go unchallenged. At this juncture, Jane Johnson, the "abducted" slave, dramatically arose in the courtroom gallery, where she had been seated with members of the Philadelphia Female Anti-Slavery Society. After her rescue, she had been taken to New York and then to Massachusetts, but had been brought back to Philadelphia to help defend those who had assisted her. Here are some excerpts from her dramatic testimony:

I can't tell my exact age; I guess I am about 25; I was born in Washington City; lived there this New Year's, if I should live to see it, two years; I came to Philadelphia about two months ago.

I came with Col. Wheeler; I brought my two children, one aged 10 and the other a year or so younger; we went to Mr. Sully's and got something to eat; we then went to the wharves; then into the hotel.

Col. Wheeler did not let me go to dinner, and sent by the servants some dinner to me, but I did not desire any; after dinner he asked me if I had dinner; I told him that I wanted none; while he was at dinner I saw a colored woman and went to her and told her I was a slave woman traveling with a very curious gentleman, who did not want me to have anything to do or say to colored persons; she said she was sorry for me; I said nothing more; . . . I had made preparations before leaving Washington to get my freedom in New York; I made a suit to disguise myself in—they had never seen me wear it—to escape in when I got to New York; Mr. Wheeler has that suit in his possession in my trunk; I wasn't willing to come without my children; . . . while Col. Wheeler went on board the boat a colored man asked, did I want to go with Col. Wheeler; I told him, "No, I do not."

Jane Johnson's testimony clearly contradicted Wheeler's on nearly all of the major points: she had desired her freedom, it was Wheeler who had restrained her, and she had not been forced off the ship.

Before the jury retired to deliberate the case, the presiding magistrate, William D. Kelley, made the final charge, in which he reminded them: "When Jane was brought here by Col. Wheeler she and her children were as free as he was." The verdict of the jury exonerated all the defendants of the riot charge and declared only two guilty of assault and battery. When these two were sentenced to a week in jail and fined $10 and court costs, Frederick Douglass announced in his paper under the headline, "The Noble and the Brave Acquitted": "Our readers will rejoice to know that the brave colored men of Philadelphia who were charged with riot, and assault and battery upon the Nicaraguan Minister, have all been acquitted of riot, and but two of them convicted of assault." The proceedings against brave black men and the imprisonment of Passmore Williamson, Douglass insisted, like the return of Anthony Burns to slavery, were rapidly adding friends to the slaves' cause. As evidence of the truth of this conclusion, Douglass reprinted the comment of the *Philadelphia Daily Sun* that the conduct of the authorities in the matter of the rescue of Colonel Wheeler's slaves "has made more 'abolitionists' and excited a more rancourous feeling against slavery than all the debates, feuds, and broken compromises of the past."

A PARTIAL RESCUE

A somewhat similar rescue effort involving a young slave woman occurred in Cincinnati at around the same time, but the outcome was not as fortunate as in the case of Jane Johnson. Sixteen-year-old Rosetta Armstead and the infant child of her dead mistress were being transported from Louisville, Kentucky, where Mrs. Henry M. Dennison, her mistress, had died, to Richmond, Virginia, where the husband, an Episcopal clergyman, was preaching. Reverend Dennison had arranged for Dr. Jones Miller to take the slave and child directly to Richmond, but heavy ice forced the river steamer to stop in Cincinnati. Miller planned to proceed to Wheeling, Virginia, by rail, but scheduling problems caused a delay, and he decided to visit his brother, John G. Miller, in Columbus.

While on the train, Rosetta Armstead seized an opportunity to speak with "a colored man . . . [and learned] that she had a right to her freedom inasmuch as she had come into the State by consent of her master or his agent." Upon arriving in Columbus, the black man, who remained unnamed, alerted members of the black community. During that late afternoon, "some colored women managed to get a conversation with the slave girl, who repeated to them her desire to be free." After some difficulty, W. B. Ferguson, a leader of the Columbus black community, procured a writ of habeas corpus in Rosetta Armstead's behalf. Many black men and women attended the court hearing on her case. The judge pronounced her free, and, at the suggestion of her lawyer (who had been hired by the black community), placed her under the guardianship of Louis G. Van Slyke.

Reverend Dennison, Rosetta's owner, immediately set off for Columbus and tried to persuade the former slave to return with him, but she refused. He then informed her in front of witnesses that if she repeated her wish not to return, he would not force her to do so, but when she did that, the Kentucky minister obtained a warrant for her arrest as a fugitive slave. U.S. Marshal Hiram H. Robinson transported Rosetta to Cincinnati and put her in jail to await trial before Commissioner John L. Pendery. Cincinnati blacks organized at once to help her, and Charles H. Langston, the black educator, secured a writ of habeas corpus, claiming that the black woman was illegally imprisoned. Judge Parker then ordered the prisoner set free, but Marshal Robinson rearrested her. When Van Slyke, who had accompanied Rosetta to help protect her rights, complained to the court, the marshal was held in contempt and fined $50.

Fortunately Commissioner Pendery ruled that Reverend Dennison was "bound by the act of his agent Miller; that there was no escape on Rosetta's part; that bringing her to Columbus and there offering her freedom was equivalent to emancipating her." But Reverend Dennison appealed the decision, and it was overturned by Justice John McLean of the U.S. Supreme Court. While police and marshals stood by to prevent a rescue, Rosetta Armstead was remanded to Reverend Dennison and returned to slavery in Virginia.

6

Black Resistance to the Fugitive Slave Act of 1850: The Last Phase

THE TRAGEDY OF MARGARET GARNER

The *New York Times* of January 28, 1856, carried a brief telegraph from its Cincinnati correspondent. The message said: "A stampede of slaves from the border counties of Kentucky took place last night. One slave woman finding escape, cut the throats of her children, and severely wounded others. Six of the fugitives were apprehended, but eight are said to have escaped." The dispatch lifted the curtain on one of the most emotional events that grew out of the enforcement of the Fugitive Slave Act and one of the major fugitive slave cases of the 1850s—one, moreover, that was to arouse the nation as much as the return of Anthony Burns to slavery in 1854.

Late on the night of January 27, 1856, a group of slaves belonging to John Marshall and Archibald K. Gaines of Boone County, Kentucky, crossed the frozen Ohio River in a large horse-drawn sleigh belonging to Marshall. The runaway party consisted of Simon Garner, his wife, Mary, his son, Simon, Jr., the latter's wife, Margaret Garner (who was pregnant), and the couple's four children, together with nine slave friends from other plantations. Nine of the seventeen fugitives soon reached black operators on the Underground Railroad and were led to Canada. The other eight—the Garner family—stayed in the Cincinnati home of their kinsman, Elijah Kite. Kite went to the shop of Levi Coffin, "president" of the Underground, who instructed him as to the quickest way to dispatch his kinsmen to the next station of the Railroad. But by the time Kite reached home, it was too late to carry out the plan.

Upon discovering the slaves' absence a few hours after their flight, Gaines had set off in pursuit. In Cincinnati, he learned that the fugitives were hiding in Kite's home. Gaines procured the necessary warrants from U.S. Commissioner John L. Pendery, formed a posse led by the marshal and made up of a deputy marshal and a large body of assistants, and went to the Kite home the following day. The posse surrounded the house and urged the fugitives to surrender since they were hopelessly outnumbered.

Inside Kite's cabin, the fugitives (the two older parents, Simon and Mary, Simon, Jr., and Margaret and their four children) put up a fight to resist capture. The family was a closely knit one; they had been in Cincinnati several times before with their master, and on one such occasion, Simon, Jr., had abandoned an opportunity to escape because he did not want to go without his parents, wife, and children. Simon, Jr., fired two rounds from a revolver, and this kept the arresting party off for a while, but all of the fugitives knew that the odds were hopelessly against them.

Suddenly Margaret Garner, seeing the futility of resistance, shrieked that she would kill her four children and herself rather than be returned to slavery. She seized a kitchen knife and turned upon her three-year-old daughter, hacking at the child's throat. Again and again, she struck until the little girl was nearly decapitated. Margaret Garner then turned to one of her little boys who pleaded with his mother not to kill him. Margaret, however, turned a deaf ear to his appeal and called out to old Mary Garner: "Mother, help me to kill the children." But the old black woman started to scream and wail and ran under a bed for refuge. Finally Elijah Kite's wife managed to disarm Margaret Garner, who broke down and sobbed that "she would rather kill every one of her children than have them taken back across the river."

Some of the raiding party broke into the cabin but were attacked by the blacks with clubs and pistols. A bullet struck Deputy Marshal John Patterson, tearing off a finger of his right hand, after which the ricocheting bullet struck him in the lip, dislocating several of his teeth. The posse then brought up heavy timber and battered down the front door. Margaret Garner fought wildly but was at last overpowered. Inside the cabin, the raiders found the almost lifeless body of the little girl. Two other children were bleeding profusely, and a fourth, an infant, was badly bruised. A member of the posse took the dying girl into his arms, but the crowd that had gathered would not let her be taken with the other fugitives. A moment later, the child was dead.

The remaining members of the Garner family were brought to the U.S. District Courthouse in Cincinnati. On reaching the marshal's office, the fugitives seated themselves dejectedly around the stove and maintained a moody silence, either answering questions in monosyllables or refusing to answer at all. When Margaret Garner was asked how she had received a scar on the left side of her forehead that ran down to her cheekbone, she replied, "White man struck me." Her only extended response came when she was asked whether madness had provoked her to kill her child. She replied: "No, I was as cool as I now am, and would much rather kill them at once and end their suffering than have them taken back to slavery, and be murdered piecemeal."

The fugitives were taken downstairs to be transported to the Hamilton Street station house, but when they reached the street, they were met by a crowd of blacks and some whites. The posse guarding the Garners was strengthened and the fugitives were led to several coaches, which were to drive them to the station house. But when the crowd cried, "Don't take them!" the coachmen drove off, fearing an assault on their horses and carriages, while one openly declared his sympathy for the fugitives. The posse had to walk their prisoners through the streets of Cincinnati to the Hamilton Street station house.

Prodded by abolitionists, the state of Ohio raised the claim that the Garners had been made free by their previous visits to Cincinnati and that they were actually free persons at the time of their flight from Kentucky on the night of January 27, 1856. The claim gained the immediate support of Governor Salmon P. Chase, who had been elected on a Free Soil–Republican party ticket. On this basis, Judge John Burgoyne of the state probate court issued a writ of habeas corpus in order to try the legality of the detention of the fugitives by the U.S. authorities. But the U.S. marshal refused to obey the state's writ and turn over the prisoners. After a furious tug of war between the two authorities, during which it appeared that crowds of blacks and white sympathizers would seize the slaves by force and rescue them, the Garners were locked in the county jail.

Hearings began on January 30, three days after the escape from Kentucky, with John Joliffe, a prominent Cincinnati antislavery attorney, acting as chief counsel for the Garner family. He obtained a postponement in order to obtain further evidence as to the actual status of the fugitives.

When the hearings resumed, blacks were kept out of the courtroom, but many distinguished white persons attended, and some even visited the Garners in prison. One was Lucy Stone, famous abolitionist and women's rights advocate, who once again achieved national attention when she was accused of seeking permission from a deputy marshal to pass a knife to Margaret Garner with which the slave mother could kill herself if the commissioner ordered her sent back to slavery. Stone's request to defend herself in court was rejected, but she did address a crowd outside the courthouse and drew tears from the audience as she pleaded for sympathetic understanding of Margaret Garner:

The faded faces of the negro children tell too plainly to what degradation female slaves submit. Rather than give her little daughter to that life, she killed it. . . . With my own teeth would I tear open my veins and let the earth drink my blood, rather than to wear the chains of slavery. How then could I blame her for wishing her child to find freedom with God and the angels, where no chains are.

During the hearing, Joliffe asked the commissioner to allow state officers to arrest the Garners at once. It might appear strange, he observed, for an attorney to seek the arrest of his own clients for murder, but all of the Garners, and especially Margaret, had assured him "they would go singing to the gallows rather than be returned to slavery." The right of Ohio to punish for crime, he insisted, must be superior to private claims of slaveowners.

By the time U.S. Commissioner Pendery was ready to hand down his decision, a Hamilton County grand jury had indicted Margaret and Simon Garner,

Jr., for murder, but Pendery ordered all seven blacks returned to their owners. He conceded that in coming to Ohio with the slaves on previous occasions, "the master voluntarily abandoned his legal power over the slave" but then added that "in returning voluntarily, the slave has equally abandoned his claim to freedom."

State officials continued to insist that Margaret and Simon must remain in Ohio for trial under the murder charge, but federal authorities demanded that all the fugitives be remanded. The stalemate was broken when the commissioner's decision was upheld by U.S. District Judge Humphrey H. Leavit, who ordered the prisoners removed from the custody of the U.S. marshal and turned over to the claimant. Within an hour after Judge Leavit had issued his order, the Garners were once again in slavery in Kentucky.

Frustrated in the effort to keep the Garners from being returned to slavery on the murder charge, Governor Salmon P. Chase asked the governor of Kentucky to return "the escaped murderers." The Southern governor, hoping to establish a precedent to ease the return of fugitives from Ohio, agreed. But before Kentucky authorities could gain custody of Margaret and Simon Garner, Jr., they were removed with their children to the Deep South.

The final tragedy in the story came during the trip to the Deep South. The ship carrying the Garners was in a collision, and Margaret Garner fell into the water with her child in her arms. The mother was rescued, but the child was drowned. Margaret Garner rejoiced that still another of her children had found death rather than slavery.

Margaret Garner's infanticide stirred deep emotions. In a letter to the *Liberator,* abolitionist Henry C. Wright wrote that Margaret "sought to destroy her own life and the lives of her children, to escape the doom of what slaveowners dare to call the God-ordained and Christ-sanctioned institution of slavery." But Wright judged her to be wrong in her action because "the absolute sanctity of human life was the only principle that would save the world from slavery, war, anarchy, and murder." Many white abolitionists and nearly all blacks, however, viewed Margaret Garner's desperate attempt to liberate her children as noble. Thousands of copies of the sermon delivered by Reverend H. Burnell of Cleveland, Ohio, who visited Margaret Garner in the Cincinnati prison, were distributed. He revealed that when he had asked the fugitive why she killed her child, she had replied: "It was my own, given me of God, to do the best a mother could in its behalf. *I have done the best I could!* I would have done more and better for the rest! I knew it was better for them to go home to God than back to slavery." When the minister asked why she had not waited and hoped and trusted in God, she answered: "I did wait, and then we dared to do, and fled in fear, but in hope; hope fled—God did not appear to save us—*I did the best I could!*" And to his own question: "Who was this woman?" Reverend Burnell replied:

A noble, womanly, amiable, *affectionate* mother. "But was she not deranged?" Not at all—calm, intelligent, but resolute and determined. "But was she not fiendish, or beside herself with passion?'' No, she was most tender and affectionate, and all her passion was that of a *mother's fondest love*. I reasoned with her, . . . ; tried to awaken a sense of guilt, and lead her to repentance and to Christ. But there was no remorse, no desire of pardon, no reception of Christ or his religion. To her it was a religion of *slavery,* more cruel than death. And where had she lived? Where thus taught? Not down among the rice swamps of Georgia, or on the banks of Red River. No, but within sixteen miles of the Queen City of the West! In a nominally Christian family—whose master was most liberal in support of the Gospel, and whose mistress was a communicant at the Lord's table, and a professed follower of Christ! Here, in this family, where slavery is found in its mildest form, she had been kept in ignorance of God's will and word, and learned to know that the mildest form of American slavery, at this day of Christian civilization and Democratic liberty, was worse than death itself! She had learned by an experience of many years, that it was so bad she had rather take the life of her own dearest child, without the hope of Heaven for herself, than *it* should experience its unutterable agonies, which were to be found even in a Christian family!

The failure of Ohio's antislavery governor to prevent the return of the Garners to slavery further convinced Garrison of the futility of relying on politics. "And this is all," he wrote, "in the last resort, that Free Soil Republican Governor Chase can do, either to protect personal liberty or to vindicate the laws of Ohio in an acknowledged case of homicide committed on her soil! No Union with Slaveholders!"

Actually it was not all. When the second Garner child died by drowning, public feeling in Ohio reached the highest pitch of anger. The state legislature, responding to the public indignation, enacted a law requiring state officers to take persons out of the possession of U.S. authorities upon the issuance of a state writ of habeas corpus. It also denounced the fugitive slave law as unconstitutional and "repugnant to the plainest principles of justice and humanity."

THE ARCHY LEE RESCUE

The first organized activity of San Francisco's black community occurred in March 1851 and involved a fugitive slave. A Missouri slaveowner had brought his slave, named Frank, to work in the mines. After Frank fled to the Sierras, his master tracked him down and had him confined in preparation for his return to Missouri. Legal aid was furnished Frank by San Francisco's black community, which hired attorney S. W. Halliday to defend him. A request was presented to Judge James Morrison to set Frank free, and the judge did precisely that, claiming that California laws demanded it. The national Fugitive Slave Act of 1850 was not involved, the judge argued, reasoning that Frank did not come to California as a fugitive. His flight took place within the boundaries of the state, which was not an offense under California law. During the interrogation, Frank had stated that he had been a slave in Missouri, but Judge Morrison, in an ironic twist, rejected this testimony because the California state legislature the year before had made Negro testimony illegal in civil and criminal cases.

The decision in the Frank case infuriated pro-Southern forces in the California legislature, and in January 1852 Assemblyman Henry A. Crabb, a Southern aristocrat, introduced a fugitive slave bill that gave white men arbitrary powers in returning Negroes whom they claimed as slaves in Southern states. Although Crabb's bill did not define any limits on how long a slaveowner might remain in California, it was passed by the legislature. The California Fugitive Slave Act of 1852 permitted the arrest of any escaped slave found in the state and his return to servitude, provided that he was taken out of California. The law specified, too, that "in no trial or hearing under this Act shall the testimony of such alleged fugitive be admitted as evidence." Thus California had the distinction of being the only state in the Union that doubly barred black testimony.

The constitutionality of the 1852 Fugitive Slave Act was tested in the Perkins case. A Mississippi slaveowner named Perkins claimed, through an agent, that three Negroes working in Placer County, two of them bearing the name Perkins, were his fugitive property. A justice of the peace and then a county judge gave the three blacks to Perkins' agent. But the San Francisco black community again hired attorneys to defend the alleged fugitives, and they managed temporarily to rescue the three from a ship that was about to leave the city. The case was brought directly to the state supreme court. The slaves were unable to testify that Perkins had promised them their freedom when he had brought them into the state in 1849 and had allowed them to work to save money to buy themselves out of slavery. The proslavery court upheld the entire California Fugitive Slave Law, including the section that had made it difficult for free blacks to maintain their freedom in California. The three fugitives were transported back to slavery in Mississippi.

Although the California Fugitive Slave Act lapsed in 1855, southerners continued to operate under the federal law. They developed a clever but cruel device. Masters brought their slaves into California as "indentured servants," exploited them as slaves, collected their wages when they hired them out, and when they were ready to return to the South, declared their "servants" to be in fact fugitive slaves. Under the provisions of the Fugitive Slave Act of 1850, they received federal assistance in returning their "fugitive slaves" to the South.

The issue did not stir much of a dispute until the Archy Lee case in 1858. Archy Lee, a nineteen-year-old slave, had been brought to California as a "manservant" by his Mississippi master, Charles A. Stovall. Stovall claimed that he was traveling through the state for his health and did not plan to reside there permanently. However, he purchased a ranch in the Carson Valley, stocked it with a herd of cattle, hired a schoolroom in Sacramento, and advertised for pupils. He had put Archy Lee out to work and was collecting his wages.

In January 1858, Stovall decided to return to Mississippi and, claiming that Archy Lee was his fugitive slave, took steps to have him brought back with him to the South. When Lee refused, Stovall went before the U.S. commissioner to obtain an order forcing him to return to Mississippi with his claimant. But a group of San Francisco blacks came to Lee's defense and hired legal counsel to defend him. The commissioner ruled that Lee was not a fugitive slave and therefore could not be taken back to the South, but he declined to decide what should be done with Archy and turned the case over to the state court.

San Francisco blacks again raised funds for Lee's defense, but Stovall received help from the state legislature. On January 18, 1858, just a week after the case had become public knowledge, Assemblyman A. G. Stokes introduced a bill providing that when a slave "shall be brought or may have been heretofore brought" into California by an owner only traveling through or briefly sojourning, the owner should have his property restored to him if the slave attempted to escape. The bill, with its ex post facto provision, gave Stovall legal grounds for regaining possession of Archy Lee, but the bill never became law because the state supreme court made it unnecessary by coming to Stovall's assistance.

In February 1858, the Supreme Court of California handed down its decision in the Archy Lee case: "a decision," notes Crawford Killian, "which at once took its place as one of the most astounding judicial farces in American history." Chief Justice Terry and Judge Burnett ruled that Stovall was not visiting or traveling in California and was therefore a resident of a free state who was trying to uphold slavery in that state. But since Stovall was ill, insolvent, and young and this was the first such case in California, they continued, "we are not disposed to rigidly enforce the rule for the first time. But in reference to all future cases it is our purpose to enforce the rules strictly according to their true intent and spirit." In this instance, however, Stovall could take Archy Lee back to slavery.

A later California Supreme Court judge, in commenting on this decision, concluded that it "gave the law to the north and the nigger to the south." He added that Terry and Burnett in effect had declared that the constitution "did not apply to young men traveling for their health; that it did not apply the first time; and that Supreme Court decisions were not to be taken as precedents." Not surprisingly, the court's decision was indignantly denounced by San Francisco's black community as "an outrage." But Stovall now had possession of Archy Lee, and he kept him secretly locked up in the San Joaquin County jail. Blacks, however, discovered his location and hired an attorney who applied for a writ of habeas corpus to gain his release. Stovall evaded service of the writ, hid Archy Lee elsewhere, and arranged to sail with him for Panama on March 4 on the steamer *Orizaba*. But the blacks made plans for a dramatic last-minute rescue.

The *Orizaba* left San Francisco as scheduled on March 4, but Stovall and Archy Lee were not aboard. Thinking he would successfully outwit San Francisco blacks, Stovall had hired a small boat and, as the steamer approached the Golden Gate, this boat, with Stovall and Lee aboard, came alongside the *Orizaba*. Stovall waved farewell to San Francisco and prodded Lee to board the steamer. To his surprise and rage, however, he found policemen on board the steamer with a warrant for his arrest on a charge of kidnapping. San Francisco's blacks had outwitted the outwitter. Furious, Stovall drew a pistol but was quickly disarmed by the police. "The Supreme Court gave me this boy," he shouted, "and I'll be damned if any other Court in this state will take him away."

The police took Stovall and Archy Lee back to the San Francisco docks where they were met by a joyous crowd of blacks. Their elation was somewhat dimmed when someone appeared with the news that the Senate judicial committee in Sacramento had recommended continuance of the prohibition against black testimony. Under the existing law, Stovall might well escape punishment for kidnapping.

On March 5, a mass meeting was held in the Zion Methodist Episcopal Church at Pacific and Stockton to rally the entire community behind Archy Lee's cause. The audience, predominantly black, contributed $150 to his legal costs and set up a committee to raise more. Three days later, in a packed courtroom, Judge Freelon turned down Stovall's application to dismiss the writ of habeas corpus. Stovall's lawyer then consented that Archy Lee be granted his freedom. But before the crowd in the courtroom could cheer, Lee was arrested as a fugitive slave and ordered back to jail. A near-riot broke out, and the U.S. marshal charged with escorting Lee to jail had to call for reinforcements before he could get the young black out of the courtroom. As Lee was dragged, struggling, through the streets of San Francisco to the jail, he was followed by an angry procession of blacks and sympathetic whites. Several black men were arrested for assault and battery before Lee was put behind bars again.

The case of Archy Lee took another bizarre turn. Stovall made a new affidavit in an attempt to make Archy Lee seem to be a fugitive slave. He now claimed that Lee had assaulted someone in Mississippi in January 1857 and had then fled west. According to his account, Stovall, traveling west a little later, had encountered his slave by chance on the North Platte River and traveled to Sacramento with him. Obviously Stovall was relying on the California Civil Practices Act forbidding Negro testimony to keep Lee from disproving this new story. But U.S. Commissioner George Pen Johnston, who heard the case, although politically a Democrat and sympathetic to the slaveowner, could not allow Stovall's latest trickery. He ruled on April 14, 1858, that Archy Lee was not a fugitive slave and granted him his freedom.

That evening, a victorious mass meeting was held in Zion Methodist Episcopal Church. The meeting opened with a hymn, "The Year of Archy Lee," composed for the occasion: The first stanza went:

> Blow ye the trumpet! Blow!
> The gladly solemn sound.
> Let all the nations know
> To earth's remotest bound
> The year of Archy Lee is come.
> Return, ye ransomed Stovall, home.

Another song to celebrate the rescue of Archy Lee was called "Song of Paradise" and subtitled "For the Benefit of Those Named. Therein."

> Sound the glad tidings o'er land and o'er sea—
> Our people have triumphed and Archy is free!
> Sing, for the pride of the tyrant is broken,
> The decision of Burnett and Terry reversed.
> How vain was their boasting! Their plans so soon broken;
> Archy's free and Stovall is brought to the dust.
> Praise to the Judges and praise to the lawyers!
> Freedom was their object and that they obtained.
> Stovall was shown it was time to be moving;
> He left on the steamer to lay deeper plans.
> But there was a Baker, a Crosby, and Tompkins,
> Before Pen Johnston and did plead for the man.

After Archy Lee was presented to the cheering crowd of five hundred, the meeting turned to raising an additional $400 for his legal costs and then to discussing possible destinations for a mass emigration of the black community.

Racist legislators in California, of whom there was always a plentiful number, had been much chagrined by the militancy of San Francisco's black community in the Archy Lee case. They decided that the time had come to teach the blacks that they were not welcome in the state. On March 19, 1858, during the battle to prevent Archy Lee from being taken back to slavery, Bill 339 was introduced in the legislature. It was entitled "An Act to restrict and prevent the immigration to and residence in the State of negroes and mulattoes." Under its provisions, no black would henceforth be allowed to migrate to California; those who did would be deported at their own expense, for the state would be empowered to hire them out to anyone "for such reasonable time as shall be necessary to pay the costs of the conviction and transportation from this state before sending such negro or mulatto therefrom." Blacks already residing in the state would be required to register; failure to do so would be a misdemeanor. Every registered black would have to be licensed to work, and anyone employing an unlicensed black would be heavily fined. Probably the cruelest provision of the bill would have made it a misdemeanor to bring a slave into California with the intent of freeing him. This provision was aimed at blacks who, having bought their freedom and earned enough money, wished to buy the freedom of their own families still in the slave states. However, efforts to penalize a slaveowner who brought a Negro into the state after the effective date of the law were defeated.

The bill was passed overwhelmingly in the assembly and sent to the senate. There, Senator Edrain Merrit, supporting the measure, pointed to the conduct of the San Francisco blacks in the Archy Lee case as evidence that "he [the Negro] becomes insolent and defiant, and, if in sufficient numbers, would become dangerous, as evidenced by recent occurrences in one of our cities."

As the bill worked its way through the legislature, a number of California newspapers voiced opposition to the measure, in part because they felt it would prove to be unenforceable. In urging defeat, the *San Francisco Daily Evening Bulletin* saw some merit in preventing further immigration of Negroes but pleaded for more kindness in treating the resident black population, which, it argued, was "the best of the free negro group in the United States." Mifflin Wistar Gibbs, one of the leaders of the San Francisco black community, rejected this kind of support. In a letter to the *Evening Bulletin,* Gibbs defended free Negroes everywhere in the United States. He began:

I appeal with pride to the history of the free colored people for the last twenty years in every free state in the Union. . . . During all that time, notwithstanding they have been subjected to the most unjust enactments and coerced by rigorous laws, pursued by a prejudice as unrelenting as inhuman, disregarded by the Church, and persecuted by the State—they have made steady progress, upward and onward, in oral and intellectual attainments.

He closed:

Let the bill now before the Legislature take what turn it may, the colored people in this state have no regrets to offer for their deportment. *Their* course has been manly, industrious, law-abiding. To this Legislature and the press that sustains them be all the honor, glory and consequences of prosecuting and abusing an industrious, unoffending and defenceless people.

When the senate included some minor provisions in the bill that required its return to the assembly for approval, the immediate threat to the black community ended, for in the meantime, the assembly had adjourned, and the bill died.

When the anti-immigration bill appeared certain of passage, however, blacks in San Francisco were conducting indignation meetings and talking about mass emigration. At the same time, excitement was mounting in California as a result of the Frazier River gold rush. Owing to the Frazier River fever, British officials in Victoria, British Columbia, found it necessary to expand governmental functions, which in turn required a building program that called for a large number of laborers. The gold rush had also created a severe labor shortage in Victoria. At the Zion Church black mass meeting hailing the victory in the Archy Lee rescue, the members of the audience were informed that they would be welcome in Victoria, where there were both employment and land.

On April 19, another meeting was held to form a "Pioneer Committee" of sixty-five blacks who were to embark for Victoria the next day on the *Commodore.* Only thirty-five of them were able to clear up their affairs in time, but the next day they were seen off by almost the entire black community. One of the thirty-five was Mifflin Wistar Gibbs. Another was Archy Lee. Within a few days after his release, Archy Lee and the rest of the Pioneer Committee stepped off the *Commodore* onto British soil.

THE OBERLIN-WELLINGTON RESCUE

The celebrated Oberlin-Wellington rescue involved John Price, an eighteen-year-old black who had escaped from John Bacon of Macon County, Kentucky, during the winter of 1858. Price had worked around and about Oberlin, Ohio, as a farm hand without any trouble until August Jennings arrived in the village looking for fugitives from his uncle's plantation. While Jennings was unsuccessful in locating his uncle's property, he learned that a slave belonging to his uncle's neighbor was working nearby. He then offered a thirteen-year-old white boy $20 to get Price out of town. When the young lad offered Price excellent wages if he would help dig potatoes at a farm several miles from town, the black fugitive refused, but he agreed to take the boy to another black man who might want the work. About two miles from the village they were intercepted by Jennings, Mitchell, a deputy U.S. marshal, and a deputy sheriff, who arrested John and headed toward Wellington to catch the next train for Cincinnati.

Two youths en route to Oberlin recognized Jennings, Mitchell, and the law officers but could not identify the prisoner. They sped to Oberlin to report what they had witnessed. Oberlin citizens, black and white, rushed toward Wellington to assist the fugitive. By this time the posse had discovered to their dismay that the next scheduled train did not depart until five o'clock that evening. While they waited for the train in a Wellington hotel, a crowd gathered and grew increasingly militant. Some members of the crowd forced the windows, and others raised ladders to the third floor. Several Oberlin students reached the attic door and forced it open. During a verbal confrontation, John Price was sneaked down the stairs and away in Simeon Bushnell's buggy. It was later learned that John spent several days at Professor James Fairchild's home in Oberlin before fleeing to Canada. The victorious rescuers paraded the nine miles back to Oberlin. At a mass meeting in the square, they pledged that no man or woman would ever be returned to slavery from their community.

The enraged federal government reacted immediately. The U.S. District Court at Cleveland issued warrants for the arrests of thirty-seven citizens of the two towns of Oberlin and Wellington. W. B. Evans, J. H. Scott, John A. Copeland, Jr. (later to be associated with John Brown at Harpers Ferry), and Charles H. Langston, brother of John Mercer Langston, were among the eleven blacks summoned to appear before the grand jury. John, who had been absent on business during Price's rescue, questioned the grand jury's objectivity since Lewis D. Boynton, father of the boy who had betrayed John Price, was a member.

On December 7, 1858, all thirty-seven were indicted for "rescuing a fugitive from services" or "abiding, abetting, and assisting to rescue a fugitive from

service and labor." They pleaded not guilty and asked for a speedy trial. However-
er, the cases were postponed, first to March 8, 1859, and then to April 5. During
that time, the defendants, who refused to post bail, were released "upon their
own recognizance of one thousand dollars each."

Some indication of the effect the trial of the Oberlin-Wellington rescuers had
on some Ohioans is indicated by the reaction of Joshua R. Giddings. The political abolitionist announced that he was prepared to challenge the entire system of
American government if the rescuers were not acquitted by the trial court or on
appeal. In that event, Giddings wrote, the people, finding their government
"destructive of the lives, the liberties and the happiness of its citizens, will
ALTER OR ABOLISH IT: *and organize its powers in such forms as to them shall
seem most likely to effect their* SAFETY AND HAPPINESS." His program was
simple: "I would take every possible measure to release those men peacefully,
and when all peaceful measures shall be exhausted, I would strike for freedom so
long as I could raise an arm; and when that should become paralyzed, I would
retire and pray for the liberty of our State and nation until my voice shall be
hushed in the silence of death." To cooperate with black resistance to the
Fugitive Slave Act, Giddings organized, in Ashtabula County, the Sons of Liberty, a Vigilance Committee composed of blacks and whites.

Simeon Bushnell, the white who had driven Price to Oberlin in his buggy, was
the first to be tried. After two weeks of testimony and cross-examination, the
jury found Bushnell guilty, and he was sentenced to sixty days' imprisonment
and fined $600, plus the cost of prosecution, amounting to $2,000. In protest
against the "unjust verdict," Charles H. Langston and twelve other "rescuers"
dismissed their counsel and pledged to make no defense. When the accused
protested that the jury was prejudiced against their cases, the court decided to
impanel a new jury before the next case—that of Charles H. Langston.

A new jury was sworn in on April 19, 1859, and testimony opened in the
Langston case. Witnesses testified that the defendant was not only present but
very active at the scene of the rescue. He was alleged to have denounced
emphatically a suggestion that a writ of habeas corpus be obtained to liberate
Price legally. According to the witnesses, Langston's insistence on a rescue was
instrumental in rescuing the fugitive from the law. On May 10, 1859, the jury
held Langston guilty as charged.

Before pronouncing sentence, Judge H. V. Wilson asked the black rescuer if
he had any comments. Langston's challenge to the court is one of the great
speeches in the antislavery struggle and was widely reprinted in newspapers and
pamphlet form. In it, Langston asked no favors, insisting that "the courts of this
country . . . the laws of this country . . . the government of this country, are so
constituted as to oppress and outrage colored men, men of my complexion." He
could not expect, "judging from the past history of the country, any mercy from
the laws, from the constitution, or from the courts of the country." What, he
asked, was the situation in Oberlin when John Price was seized? Everywhere
blacks were frightened by rumors "that slave-catchers, kidnappers, negro steal-

ers were lying hidden and skulking about, waiting for some opportunity to get their bloody hands on some helpless creature to drag him back—or for the first time, into helpless and life-long bondage.'' Mothers did not dare send their children to school for fear that they would be caught and carried off.

It was in the midst of such fears that news came on September 13, 1858, of "an actual seizure.'' When he thought of John Price, the black who had been seized, Langston did not see a slave, "but a *man,* a *brother,* who had a right to his liberty under the law of God, under the laws of Nature, and under the Declaration of Independence.'' He "identified with that man by color, by race, by manhood . . . [and] by sympathies such as God'' had implanted in all people. It was therefore his "duty to . . . do what I could toward liberating him,'' and he had no apology to offer for the part he had played in ensuring Price's freedom.

Langston insisted that he should be found not guilty. The law under which he had been arraigned—the Fugitive Slave Act of 1850—was "an unjust one, one made to crush the colored man, and one that outrages every feeling of humanity, as well as every rule of right.'' And there was another reason: he had not had a trial before a jury of his peers. The common law of England and the Constitution of the United States guaranteed "to *all persons* a trial before an *impartial* jury. I have had no such trial.'' Members of his jury "shared largely'' in "certain universal and deeply fixed prejudices,'' and he considered them neither "impartial'' nor "a jury of my peers'':

I was tried by a jury who were prejudiced; before a court that was prejudiced; prosecuted by an officer who was prejudiced, and defended, though nobly, by counsel that were prejudiced. And therefore it is, your Honor, that I urge that by all that is good and great in manhood that I should not be subjected to the pains and penalties of this oppressive law when I have not been tried either by a jury of my peers or by a jury that were impartial.

Langston said that he had gone to Wellington from Oberlin "knowing that colored men have no rights in the United States which white men are bound to respect'' (a reference to the words of Supreme Court Chief Justice Roger B. Taney in the *Dred Scott* decision), that there was not "a spot in this wide country where any colored man dare to ask a mercy of a white man.'' Referring to the building where the Declaration of Independence was signed, Langston declared:

Let me stand in that [old Philadelphia] Hall and tell a United States marshal that my father was a revolutionary soldier; that he served under Lafayette and fought through the whole war, and that he fought for *my* freedom as much as his own; and he would sneer at me, and clutch me with his bloody fingers, and say he has a *right* to make me a slave! And when I appeal to Congress, they say he has a right to make me a slave; when I appeal to your Honor, *your Honor* says he has a right to make a slave, and if any man, white or black seeks an investigation of that claim, they make themselves amenable to the pains and penalties of the fugitive Slave Act, for *black men have no rights which white men are bound to respect.* (Great applause.)

Finally, Langston vowed that after he had served his sentence, he would do the same thing again if he should ever see another man seized as a fugitive:

So help me God, I stand here to say that I will do all I can for any man thus seized and held, though the inevitable penalty of six months imprisonment and one thousand dollars fine for each offense hangs over me! We have all a common humanity, and you all would do that; your manhood would require it, and no matter what the laws might be, you would honor yourself for doing it, while your friends and your children to all generations would honor you for doing it, and every good and honest man would say you had done *right*!

The court record reads that after Langston completed his speech, there was "great and prolonged applause in spite of the efforts of the Court and marshal." The court appears to have been impressed, for Judge Wilson handed down the relatively light sentence of imprisonment for twenty days and a fine of one hundred dollars and court costs.

While in jail, Langston and other rescue prisoners issued, with permission of the jailer, *The Rescuer,* which carried the information that it was "edited and printed from a Cuyahoga County jail cell." It was to be issued every other Monday as a means of keeping the prisoners' views before the public. As it turned out, only one issue, the first, appeared. It carried the following item:

PAINFUL DEATH

Died in the cells of the Jail in this city early this morning, Ohio State Rights, aged just Eighty-three years.

The deceased was one of a numerous family, all born July 4, 1776. The father's name was American Independence.

*   *   *   *

On the 8th of December, 1858, at Lorain County, Ohio State Rights received a severe blow, which has been followed by a succession of blows laid on at the U.S. Court-House by the paid agents of Slavery and Federalism.

On the 11th of May the fatal stab was given, and on the 25th the mangled body was taken to the operating-room at the State House before the full board of L.L.D.'s. . . . After much loss of blood from a severed artery, the patient has at length ceased to breathe.

Funeral takes place this afternoon, July 4th, 1859.—The body will be buried in the northwest corner of the Jail yard.—Procession will form upstairs—Friends are invited.

From *The Rescuer,* published in the Cuyahoga Jail by the Political Prisoners.

A kidnapping indictment was secured by Oberlin abolitionists against the marshals and Kentuckians who had captured Price. After some negotiations, the charges against both "kidnappers" and "rescuers" were dismissed. All of the prisoners were freed on July 6, 1859.

After the release of the rescuers, however, the Ohio Supreme Court, by a three-to-two majority, delivered a blow to the joyful black and white Ohioans by upholding the constitutionality of the fugitive slave laws of 1793 and 1850. But the fact remained that John Price had been rescued from slavery and that those participating had escaped severe punishment.

John Mercer Langston wrote an account of the "Oberlin-Wellington Rescue" in the *Anglo-African* magazine of June 1859, including the complete text of his brother's magnificent speech to the court. He described Charles H. Langston as follows: "He is widely known as a devoted and laborious advocate of the claims of the Negro to liberty and its attendant blessings. Discreet and far-seeing, uncompromising and able, he has labored most efficiently in behalf of the slave and the disfranchised American."

THE LAST CRISIS

Charles H. Langston was also involved in the last major crisis over the enforcement of the Fugitive Slave Act. This occurred in January 1861 in Cleveland. Sara Lucy Bagby, a twenty-year-old fugitive from Virginia slavery, found employment as a domestic in the lake city. On January 17, 1861, John Goshorn and his son, William, arrived in Cleveland from Wheeling, Virginia, for the purpose of removing Bagby. The Goshorns led a posse of U.S. deputy marshals to the home of L. A. Benton, her employer. The officers forced entrance and removed the fugitive without interference. Benton informed William E. Ambush, the chairman of the local Fugitive Aid Society, an all-black organization (as distinguished from the biracial Vigilance Committee). News of the kidnapping spread through the black community, and Ambush called "a strong delegation of the Society" into action. Their first problem was to locate the fugitive. At the train depot, they learned that she had not been taken from the city by the eight o'clock train. She was then found in the county jail, where Ambush interviewed her.

Bagby told Ambush that she had crossed the Ohio from Virginia to Beaver, Pennsylvania, in the company of her master's daughter, Isabella, and that she was aided in her escape by a "gentleman" who took her to Pittsburgh. She arrived in Cleveland several days later. Ambush attempted to obtain a writ of habeas corpus from probate judge D. R. Tilden. After C. W. Palmer and A. G. Riddle were engaged by the Fugitive Aid Society to represent Bagby, Judge Tilden granted the writ.

While legal machinery was being set in motion, a potentially explosive situation developed in the streets around the jail. Large crowds of blacks and a few whites gathered. Several members of the crowd "openly announced that they cared nothing for the hearing or the Judge's action after the prisoner was once out of the jail." Newspapers reported that it was assumed that she would be rescued "by a negro force large enough to overpower the sheriff's posse, and spirited away before a recapture could be made." Authorities, sensing the danger, increased the number of police guarding the prisoner. The crowd also increased in both size and determination. Officers took a butcher knife from a black man and searched others for weapons.

When the courthouse doors opened for the hearing, the excited crowd packed the courtroom. The authorities decided to keep the prisoner in jail beyond the reach of potential rescuers. Judge Tilden heard the arguments of both sides, and the hearings continued until January 21, 1861, an hour before the U.S. commissioner was to hear the case. On that day a large police force was on hand at the courthouse, and the Cleveland Gray, a military company, was nearby in case an attempt was made to rescue the prisoner. Judge Tilden ruled that the local jail could not legally be used by federal officers to confine their prisoner. The gesture was academic since in less than an hour Bagby was to appear before the U.S. commissioner as a fugitive slave. At the hearing before Commissioner Bushnell White, the defense was unable to produce evidence in her behalf, and Commissioner White remanded her to the Goshorns, who left immediately with her and a posse of U.S. marshals for Wheeling.

Cleveland's black and white abolitionists were severely criticized by the antislavery press for having allowed the slave catchers to invade the most publicized abolitionist stronghold west of Massachusetts and remove their victim with relative ease. The Clevelanders had made no serious rescue attempt. Stung by the criticism, the local biracial Vigilance Committee conducted an investigation of the conduct of William Ambush to determine whether he should be charged with neglect as a member of the Fugitive Aid Society.

The investigation took place in the old Baptist church before a large black audience. The evidence presented proved that Thomas Norris, the abolitionist who had assisted Bagby's escape to Pittsburgh, had informed Ambush that the Goshorns were pursuing the young fugitive. Ambush had read Norris' letter to two associates and together they had approached Bagby, but she had refused to leave Cleveland for a safer place. Ambush's accusers claimed that as chairman of the society, he should have called an emergency meeting of the group and that his failure to do so had led to the fugitive's arrest. Ambush claimed that according to society bylaws, "when a fugitive refuses to be governed by the Committee, he or she is to be 'given up' and left to care for himself or herself." After a heated argument, the jury returned a verdict of not guilty.

This final crisis under the fugitive slave law continued after Bagby was taken out of Cleveland, for black Ohioans attempted to rescue her when her train passed through Stark County. Charles H. Langston, the organizer of the rescue effort, traveled to Alliance on the morning of January 23, 1861, and conferred with black residents there. Alliance, however, posed a number of problems. Few blacks lived there, but large numbers of antiabolitionists did. Alliance also had a telegraph station, and outside aid could be mustered on short notice. However, at Lima Station, there was no telegraph terminal and few whites could be assembled to resist.

W. J. Whipper, a black from the vicinity of Youngstown, and W. H. Tyler, a white Oberlinite, boarded the train at Hudson. Whipper carried an iron bar under his coat to knock out the coupling pin and sever the prisoner's car from the rest of the train. Tyler's mission was to prevent the marshals from shooting members of the assault party that was supposed to stop the train at Lima Station. The conductor, however, became suspicious, and both men were arrested. Meanwhile armed blacks formed lines on both sides of the tracks at the Lima Station. The conductor had informed his engineer of the expected assault, and as the station came into view, the engineer eased up on the throttle and started to brake the train. Just before reaching the station, he laid on full steam and the train passed by rapidly, with the blacks unable to do anything.

In the last case under the Fugitive Slave Act of 1850 before the outbreak of the Civil War, a black—Sara Lucy Bagby—was returned to slavery. She was freed the following year when Union troops occupied Wheeling. Soon, especially after blacks joined its ranks, the Union army became the greatest of all rescuers of slaves.

Although the fugitive slave law of 1850 was not repealed until June 28, 1864, very few, if any, attempts were made to seize fugitives after the outbreak of the Civil War except for a brief period when the Union Army was under the command of General George B. McClellan. For all practical purposes, the outbreak of the Civil War repealed the measures that Ralph Waldo Emerson aptly labeled "a hell-born enactment."

THE FRUITS OF RESISTANCE

The traditional view among many American historians has been that in the main, the fugitive slave law of 1850 soon became a dead letter and that enforcement was almost impossible. This view was challenged by Stanley W. Campbell in his 1967 Ph.D. dissertation, "The Enforcement of the Fugitive Slave Law, 1850–60," and in the somewhat expanded version published a year later under the title, *The Slave Catchers: Enforcement of the Fugitive Slave Law, 1850–1860*. Campbell documents black resistance to the law, but the works are mainly devoted to establishing his thesis that "in spite of hostility and opposition, the [fugitive slave] law was enforced" and that the personal liberty laws did not obstruct "justice." In his 1976 work, *The Impending Crisis, 1846–1861*, David Potter (who ignores black resistance) came down on Campbell's side and argued that no convincing evidence exists to indicate that a majority of northerners were prepared to violate the Fugitive Slave Law. Hence, "an overwhelming northern defiance must be qualified."

Campbell set up four criteria for measuring the effectiveness of the fugitive slave law. First, he compared the annual decrease with the annual increases in the number of fugitive slaves; second, he compared the number of slaves returned with the number of fugitives escaping from their owners; third, he compared the number of fugitive slaves arrested and remanded to their owners with the number of claims made upon the fugitive slave tribunals; and fourth, he used the number of convictions for harboring, concealing, or rescuing fugitive slaves.

Measured by the first criterion, Campbell concluded the law was a failure. This was so because variations in annual increase and decrease of fugitive slaves remained relatively unchanged in the decade preceding the Civil War. The fugitive slave law thus did not act as a deterrent to the escape of slaves, but then, Campbell argues, the express purpose of the law was not to prevent Negroes from escaping but to facilitate their arrest and return. One would think, however, that if the law was effectively enforced, it would have some bearing on the number of escapes.

Campbell concludes that the only reliable means for measuring the fugitive slave law's effectiveness is by utilizing criteria three and four. He concedes, however, that there is no reliable way for gaining the complete records of the various claims made upon the tribunals but argues that the cases that were reported in the press could provide an "adequate basis for estimating the effectiveness of enforcement procedures." However, since arrests of fugitives were frequently not reported in the press, this approach would not seem to be too convincing. Still, by relying on newspaper accounts and on extant court records, Campbell concludes that the Fugitive Slave Act of 1850 was generally enforced. In the cases that actually came before the fugitive slave tribunals established by law, Campbell contends, approximately 92 percent of the runaway slaves were returned to their owners, while 8 percent were rescued or otherwise escaped from federal custody.

But even if one is to say with Campbell that the law on the whole was enforced, it is still not to say that it was effective. Even Campbell admits that it was highly ineffective. He points out that the record of convictions for those charged with violations of the fugitive slave law from 1850 to 1860 was "not good" and that jurors in the federal courts were "highly reluctant" to convict those charged with violating the law. Campbell also maintains that the reason the fugitive slave law became a "dead letter" in New England was because it was not "economically feasible" to trace, capture, and return fugitives. Costs were "prohibitive" when a southerner must travel to New England, where his runaway was near Canada. Although in cases where the danger of rescue was acute, the commissioner might require the government to pay some of the costs of rendition, such costs excluded the owner's and agents' expenses, legal and witness fees, the posting of bail, and fees incurred in securing the process. In the case of Anthony Burns, Suttle, the claimant, maintained that these costs amounted to $400.

Although Campbell discounts the effect of public opinion as a factor contributing to the difficulties of enforcing the Fugitive Slave Act and places major emphasis on the impracticality of enforcement, the "impracticality" itself resulted from the effect of public opinion, partly through the enactment of personal liberty laws, in hindering enforcement. Campbell acknowledges that while the Fugitive Slave Act was generally effectively enforced during the decade

1850–1860, after 1855, with the Kansas-Nebraska Act and the Burns and Booth cases, all of which were well publicized, there was "a groundswell of public reaction against the inhumanity of the law."

In general, Campbell maintains that enforcement of the fugitive slave law required a "favorable climate of public opinion" but goes on to insist that although the Northern attitude was for the most part ambiguous, the law on the whole was "acquiesced" in by the public.

Yet the evidence is overwhelming that the law's blatant violation of the rights of anyone accused of being a fugitive slave aroused enormous indignation in the North, and not only among antislavery men and women. Many northerners who had little concern for the slaves themselves were affected by the sight of a man or woman who had lived peacefully in the community, raised a family, and participated in the religious, social, and cultural activities of black society, being suddenly torn from all this and deprived of liberty by slave catchers. A letter to the *New York Tribune* described an incident that occurred in Springfield, Massachusetts, "some weeks after the Fugitive Slave Act was passed" but was common throughout the North:

A noted "Mr. C." spoke convincingly on the constitutionality of the Act and its need for support. A friend then asked him, "Suppose that Jim there—pointing to a colored waiter who was cleaning the table—should come rushing up to you, trembling and agitated, and say, 'Oh, Mr.—the sheriff is after me! I am a fugitive and shall be dragged back into slavery if somebody don't assist me. Won't you assist me? Won't you hide me from my pursuers?'

"I want to know (said the friend) whether you would coldly repulse him and give him up."

After a moral struggle, Mr. C. smashed his fist against the table and exclaimed, "No, I'll be d———d if I would!"

The law turned law-abiding citizens into lawbreakers. Failure to join in hunting down Negroes, failure to be an active accomplice in slavery, was pronounced a violation of the law (even treason in the case of Castner Hanway) by the government. In this violation, every man and woman of conscience wholeheartedly joined. Joseph P. Bloss, a prominent citizen of Rochester, New York, remembered that in his boyhood days in the city, his father led him to a woodshed of their home on East Avenue. There he was told to lay his fingers in the deep whip welts on the back of an escaped woman slave who was in hiding there until she could be sent to Canada. Said the elder Bloss: "I am subject to a fine of $1,000 and an imprisonment of six months for giving this woman a crust of bread, a cup of water—for not arresting her, or for in any way aiding her to escape from her master. But I shall disobey this law, and when there is another like this in the land, you disobey it." In Madison County, New York, Judge Joseph Nye, a man sworn to uphold the law, exclaimed vehemently:

I am an officer of the law. I am not sure that I am not one of those officers who are clothed with anomalous and terrible powers by this Bill of abominations. If I am, I will tell my constituency that I will trample that law in the dust, and they must find another man, if there be one who will degrade himself, to do this dirty work.

The scriptural injunction "not to deliver unto his master the servant that has escaped" was a powerful factor in Northern opposition to the law. "In some places," wrote Theodore Parker, "all the people rose up against the Fugitive Slave Bill, the whole town a vigilante committee." Even so, there were still many whites who abhorred the law but felt upon reflection that "it was better for one or a dozen men to suffer than that the moral supremacy of the law should be abolished."

It is becoming increasingly evident that the persevering, unqualified resistance on the part of blacks during this entire period goaded many of the reluctant whites into taking a more forthright position. Because slaves also learned of their kinsmen's resistance, more of them escaped from 1850 to 1860 than had fled during the previous twenty years. Despite the threat of jail terms, black men and women assisted them. So, too, did whites. But blacks most often furnished the initiative and most of the bodies to resist enforcement of the law. They were the most active in rescues.

Not all of the rescues were associated with carefully laid plans by well-organized groups. Rather, they were a blend of personal courage, aid from unknown blacks—many of them unskilled workers—and from organized bodies set up for precisely this purpose and in which blacks represented either the only members or the predominant membership. The most important catalytic agent in every rescue was the participation of the free blacks who came to the aid of their black brother or sister.

When Peter H. Clark, Cincinnati's black educator, was criticized for calling slave catchers "scoundrels," he replied angrily: "Who is afraid to call them scoundrels? Not I. I hated them, and what I hate I would destroy." Blacks everywhere shared his view, and they also agreed when Clark continued with the angry comment that perhaps an even greater scoundrel was a black informer who betrayed fugitives to the slave catchers. Cincinnati blacks showed their feelings on this issue when they learned that James Brodie had led two black fugitives into the hands of Kentucky slave hunters, for which act of treachery he had received three hundred dollars. They seized the "black traitor" and placed him on trial. "[Reverend Henry Highland] Garnet was present at the trial, and it was mainly owing to his intercession that Brodie was not torn limb from limb," William C. Nell wrote after hearing a report of the trial by Garnet. "He escaped with life, after the infliction of three hundred blows with a paddle—one blow for each dollar of blood money he had received for doing the infamous work of these Kentucky hunters of men." Cincinnati blacks still threatened to take Brodie's life. "Brodie delivered himself into the hands of the authorities, who put him in jail to save his life," Nell reported. State warrants were issued for the arrest of several men charged with participating in the trial, but they fled to Canada before they could be arrested.

The effort to protect and rescue fugitives during the decade of the 1850s was the most significant and unifying force in the antebellum black community of the North. It was instrumental in galvanizing the community spirit of the 1830s and 1840s into virtual solidarity of action, which cut across class lines. More and more, blacks came to agree with Frederick Douglass that "every slave hunter who meets a bloody death in his infernal business, is an argument in favor of the manhood of our race." James Oliver Horton and Lois E. Horton point out that "black militancy which had been growing steadily for more than twenty years, came of age during the decade before the Civil War." Nothing was more responsible for this than the black resistance to the Fugitive Slave Act of 1850. In Boston, Horton and Horton note:

The protection of the fugitives was an antislavery activity of the greatest significance. . . . It demonstrated most vividly the extent to which the issue of freedom united the black community in common action. To the extent that whites as individuals or as members of the Vigilance Committee were willing to stand with blacks, even against the law, risking life and limb, a bond of trust was built between peoples. Both victories and failures served to strengthen the resolve of blacks and whites in their fight against the fugitive slave law.

In the 1850s, Gerrit Smith noted growing evidence that blacks were no longer accepting "the insults and outrages heaped upon them," and he pointed, in particular, as "among these signs . . . the manly resistance to the kidnappers at Christiana, and the brave and beautiful bearing of the black men at Syracuse [during the Jerry rescue]." Frederick Douglass, whose own transition from a largely moral suasionist abolitionist to the most advanced advocate of militant abolitionism occurred during these years, pointed to the same significant aspect of black resistance to the Fugitive Slave Act in his great West India emancipation speech August 4, 1857. (It was in this speech that the words often associated with Douglass—"If there is no struggle there is no progress"—were first used.) At the close of the speech, after examining every weapon that had to be used in the black liberation struggle, Douglass reminded his people: "If we ever get free from the oppression and wrongs heaped upon us, we must pay for their removal. We must do this by labor, by suffering, by sacrifice, and if needs be, by our lives and the lives of others." For illustrations, Douglass turned to the history of black resistance to the Fugitive Slave Act of 1850 up to the time he was speaking:

Hence, my friends, every mother who, like Margaret Garner, plunges a knife into the bosom of her infant to save it from the hell of our Christian Slavery, should be held and honored as a benefactress. Every fugitive from slavery who like the noble William Thomas at Wilkesbarre, prefers to perish in a river made red by his own blood, to submission to the hell hounds who were hunting and shooting him, should be esteemed as a glorious martyr, worthy to be held in grateful memory by our people. The fugitive Horace, at Mechanicsburgh, Ohio, the other day, who taught the slave catchers from Kentucky that it was safer to arrest white men than to arrest him, did a most excellent service to our cause. Parker and his noble gang of fifteen at Christiana, who defended themselves from the kidnappers with prayers and pistols, are entitled to the honor of making the first successful resistance to the Fugitive Slave Bill. But for that resistance, and the rescue of Jerry, and Shadrack [sic] the man-hunters would have hunted our hills and valleys here with the same freedom with which they now hunt their own dismal swamps.

Resistance made the fugitive slave law largely inoperative. Through organization and agitation, numerous state governments were forced to enact laws forbidding state officials from assisting in the law's execution. The cases in which the federal government succeeded in returning fugitives to slavery were really pyrrhic victories, for they served mainly to increase antislavery sentiment in the nation. The day of the Jerry rescue was commemorated annually to keep the people constantly aware of its significance. At the first anniversary in 1852, Theodore Parker, in a letter to Samuel J. May, congratulated the rescuers: "Do it continually, till the American Government shall understand that though they made wicked statutes in the name of the 'Union,' the people will violate any such wicked device and bring it to naught."

Campbell concedes that in Massachusetts, Pennsylvania, and Ohio, where the fugitive slave law presented the greatest problems, the abolitionists picked up considerable support, but he contends that on the whole, those states still "favored enforcement of the law over disunion." But the more important point was made by a slaveowner who, after several years of operation of the Fugitive Slave Act of 1850, concluded that the South had gained nothing from the law. He voiced the sentiments of many of his Southern colleagues when he wrote: "The value of the slave lost is eaten up, if capture follow, while hatred to the institution abroad, and opposition to it at home are increased by the hard features and the barbarous enforcement of them."

To this should be added the fact that out of the indignation against the law, the most powerful of all antislavery writings—Harriet Beecher Stowe's *Uncle Tom's Cabin*—was written in 1852.

7

Blacks and *Uncle Tom's Cabin*

THE WRITING OF *UNCLE TOM'S CABIN*

"It was the fugitive slave law that produced *Uncle Tom's Cabin*," wrote literary critic Charles Dudley Warner in 1896. Soon after the law was passed in 1850, Harriet Beecher Stowe received a letter from her sister-in-law in Boston, Mrs. Edward Beecher. "Hattie," she wrote, "if I could use a pen as you can, I would write something that will make this whole nation feel what an accursed thing slavery is." Mrs. Stowe read the letter to her children, and they recalled years later that their mother, then a woman of thirty-nine, who had suffered much poverty, illness, and personal distress, crumpled the letter, rose to her feet, and said quietly: "I *will* write something. I will if I live." She herself recalled for one of her grown children: "I well remember the winter you were a baby, and I was writing *Uncle Tom's Cabin*. My heart was bursting with the anguish excited by the cruelty and injustice our nation was showing to the slave, and praying God to let me do a little and to cause my cry for them to be heard. I remember many a night weeping over you as you lay sleeping beside me, and I thought of the slave mother whose babies were torn from them." One of her seven children died while still an infant. "It was at his dying bed," she wrote, "and at his grave that I learned what a poor slave mother may feel when her child is torn away."

But writing a book was no simple matter for a mother of six children who had to make ends meet on Calvin Stowe's salary as a professor of natural and revealed religion at Bowdoin College in Brunswick, Maine. There was an infant to nurse—"as long as the baby sleeps with me nights I cannot do anything"— and to stretch out the family income, Mrs. Stowe turned out short journalistic sketches.

For eighteen years, Harriet Beecher Stowe had lived in Cincinnati, where her father headed the Lane Theological Seminary. She married Calvin Stowe, raised a large family, and began writing for money. During these years, too, she had seen organized proslavery mobs, "composed in the main of young men of the better class," wreck the printing press of abolitionist James G. Birney's *Philanthropist*. She herself had helped her brother, Henry Ward Beecher, with a loaded revolver at his elbow, edit a journal that Southern postmasters banned from the mails because of its views, as they said, "on a certain subject." She had witnessed the destruction of the Negro ghetto of Cincinnati, the brutal capture of slaves who had escaped, like Eliza Harris in *Uncle Tom's Cabin* across the frozen Ohio. Her home was a haven for fugitives, and she herself helped a young black woman in her employ slip away from a master on her trail.

Mrs. Stowe's first antislavery story, "The Two Altars," written while she was still a young housewife in Cincinnati, is a sentimental portrayal of the domestic life of a sober working-class family—a family that is unusual only in that the husband is "colored" and the wife a "mulatto." The tale concludes with the arrest of the husband as a runaway slave and his removal to Georgia. "Think for one hour," asked Mrs. Stowe, "What if this that happened to this poor mother should happen to you?"

Mrs. Stowe had seen the peculiar institution itself at first hand during her visits to Kentucky across the river. These experiences, which were to form the rich soil of her novel, had deepened her antislavery convictions and caused her to sympathize with the abolitionists (although she did not become a full-fledged one herself). She had been held back not only by the need to care for her family but also by social pressures against a woman's taking an active part in politics, by a rather unworldly husband wrapped up in his theological researches, and by her own pacifist and conciliationist leanings, which were in conflict with the growing militancy of the antislavery movement.

Harriet Beecher Stowe came back North in 1850 to escape the horrors of slavery, but there was no refuge from the national crime. With the passage of the Fugitive Slave Act in the year of her return, the die was cast. At the height of the resistance to the act, inspired by what she described as a vision in church, Harriet Beecher Stowe resolved to write *Uncle Tom's Cabin*. She wrote to Dr. Gamaliel Bailey, editor of the antislavery weekly *National Era*, published in Washington, D.C.:

Up to this year I have always felt that I had no particular call to meddle with this subject, and I dreaded to expose even my own mind to the full force of its exciting power. But I feel now that the time is come when even a woman or a child who can speak a word for freedom and humanity is bound to speak. The Carthaginian women in the last peril of their state cut off their hair for bow-strings to give to the defenders of their country and such peril and shame as now hangs over this country is worse than Roman slavery, and I hope every woman who can write will not be silent.

In the novel she wrote, an early chapter, entitled "An Evening in Uncle Tom's Cabin," introduces Uncle Tom as "the hero of our story." Uncle Tom is a white-haired, pious, loyal slave foreman, a man of African descent:

He was a large, broad-chested, powerfully-made man, of a full glossy black, and a face whose truly African features were characterized by an expression of grave and steady good sense, united with much kindliness and benevolence. There was something about his whole air self-respecting and dignified, yet united with a confiding and humble simplicity.

Although warned that he is about to be sold by his master to whom he had been loyal, Tom feels it is against his Christian principles to run away, and he goes without reproach:

"If I must be sold, or all the people on the place, and everything go to rack, why let me be sold. I s'pose I can b'er it as well as any of 'em," he added, while something like a sob and a sigh shook his rough chest convulsively. "Mas'r always found me on the spot—he always will. I never have broke trust, nor used my pass noways contrary to my word, and I never will. It's better for me alone to go than to break up the place and sell all. Mas'r ain't to blame, Chloe; and he'll take care of you and the poor."

While being shipped down river, Uncle Tom leaps overboard and saves a wealthy man's small daughter, Little Eva, from drowning. The grateful father buys Uncle Tom, and in a New Orleans mansion the old slave and the angelic child read the Bible and sing hymns.

One of the new characters in the novel at this stage is Topsy, who, as everyone knows, "just grow'd." But considering the fact that she was raised by a speculator, who bought her from a slave breeder, the miracle is that she survived to grow at all. At any rate, there is a significant conversation between Little Eva and Topsy in which the truth of Topsy's words would be difficult to refute:

"What does make you so bad, Topsy? Why won't you try and be good? Don't you love *anybody,* Topsy?

"Dun know nothin' 'bout love: I loves candy and sich, that's all," said Topsy. . . .

"But, Topsy, if you'd only try to be good, you might—"

"Couldn't never be nothin' but a nigger, if I was ever so good," said Topsy. "If I could be skinned, and come white, I'd try then."

"But people can love you, if you are black, Topsy. Miss Ophelia would love you if you were good."

Topsy gave the short, blunt laugh that was her common mode of expressing incredulity.

"Don't you think so?" said Eva.

"No, she can't be'er me, 'cause I'm a nigger!—she'd 's soon have a toad touch her. There can't nobody love niggers, and niggers can't do nothin'. I don't care," said Topsy, beginning to whistle.

Little Eva develops tuberculosis. Dying, she extracts her father's promise to free Uncle Tom. But before he can, the grieving father is killed in a brawl. His widow sells all her slaves to the cruel, Yankee-born slave dealer, Simon Legree. The slave dealer turned plantation owner loses no time in telling Tom to discard his religion:

"Well, I'll soon have that out of you. I'll have none o' yer bawling, praying, singing niggers on my place; so remember. Now, mind yourself," he said, with a stamp and a fierce glance of his grey eye directed at Tom, "I'm your church now! You understand—you've got to hear what I say."

Ordered by Legree to flog another slave, Uncle Tom refuses, on Christian grounds, and is flogged himself. Legree then threatens to beat him to death unless he betrays the escape plans of two slave women. Uncle Tom refuses and begs Legree to avoid damning himself through needless cruelty. Legree has the fatal beating administered, as Uncle Tom prays to God to forgive Legree.

Uncle Tom, dying, sees his original good master's son arrive to buy his freedom. The young master berates Legree, knocks him down, and swears, "From this hour, I will do what *one man can* to drive this curse of slavery from our land."

THE MIRACLE OF *UNCLE TOM'S CABIN*

Uncle Tom's Cabin began as a series of sketches in the *National Era* in June 1851. Mrs. Stowe conceived it as a serial of three or four installments, but the subject would not let go, and neither would the readers of the *National Era,* who begged the author to go on and protested vehemently to the editor when the paper missed an installment. Contemporary observers tell of how families read aloud (and wept over) each installment of Mrs. Stowe's saga and of how copies of the magazine were passed from household to household. So on went the serial until nearly a year passed, and there were forty sections, for which the author was paid the sum originally contracted for—$300.

The paper's circulation was tiny, but word of the astonishing serial passed through the country, and a demand for a book arose. Finding a publisher for the book was another matter. The Boston firm of Phillips, Sampson and Company turned it down. It would never sell a thousand copies, they said, and besides, success would be even worse than failure, for success would "ruin our business in the South."

Fortunately a Boston woman, Mrs. John R. Jewitt, had been moved by the serial, and she induced her husband, who owned a small publishing house, specializing in "practical" books, to gamble on a novel. Mr. Jewitt was worried and offered to split the investment with the author and divide the improbable profit evenly, but Harriet's husband held out for a straight 10 percent royalty. Mrs. Stowe was pleased and said: "I hope it will make enough so I may have a silk dress."

The two-volume work, *Uncle Tom's Cabin; or Life among the Lowly,* was published on March 20, 1852. It was not the first antislavery novel to be published, but it was still a rare event for any fiction dealing with slavery to appear. Although many Northern poets were ready to use that form of literature in the antislavery campaign, few novelists were prepared to do so. As Van Wyck Brooks has pointed out, novelists hesitated because of the dangers to their literary careers: "If one published a plea for the slaves, one's fame went out like a candle."

Although Lydia Maria Child's 1832 appeal for *That Class of Americans Called Africans* (see volume 2 for a discussion) was one of the most influential antislavery tracts, her one antebellum novel dealing with slavery, *Philthea,* published in 1836, is set in ancient Greece. The first antislavery novel was published anonymously by Richard Hildreth. In 1836, after two years spent on a Southern plantation for health reasons, Hildreth issued *The Slave; or Memoirs of Archy Moore.* The book purported to be the actual account of an escaped slave, and many accepted it as such. The 1852 edition, however, acknowledged Hildreth as its editor. In the preface to the 1840 edition, Hildreth explained that the book had been rejected by New York publishers before a Boston firm consented to issue it, but without using its name on the title page. The reissuing of the book in 1852 with identification of author and publisher is indicative of the change wrought by *Uncle Tom's Cabin.*

The first edition of Mrs. Stowe's novel was 5,000. No reviews appeared, but they were hardly necessary. The 5,000 copies were gone in two days, and from the first it was impossible to keep up with the demand, despite the four power presses working day and night and 200 bookbinders pressed into service. By the end of the first year, 300,000 copies were sold in this country—the equivalent of 4 million today—and by 1857 over a half-million copies had been sold. In the 1850s, a book that sold more than 50,000 copies in its first year after publication was regarded as a best-seller by the standards of the period. A book that sold more than 20,000 copies was considered highly successful, and a book that sold 5,000 copies or more was profitable to both author and publisher.

No other American book, before or since, has been so widely read and has had such a profound impact abroad. In England nearly 200,000 copies were sold in its first year in editions pirated by twenty different publishers. The book was translated into Bengalese, Danish, Chinese, Persian, Bohemian, Swedish, Japanese, Armenian, German, Finnish, and Russian. In Paris, three newspapers serialized the book simultaneously in three different translations.

The reaction of the British people is vividly depicted by black abolitionist leader William Wells Brown, who in 1853 published his own antislavery novel, *Clotel,* the first novel by an American Negro. Writing to Garrison from London on May 17, 1853, Brown described an overflow meeting of 5,000 at Exeter Hall, which Mrs. Stowe attended on her first trip abroad:

No time could have been more appropriate for such a meeting than the present. *Uncle Tom's Cabin* has come down upon the dark abodes of slavery like a morning's sunlight, unfolding its enormities in a manner which has fastened all eyes upon the "peculiar institution," and awakening sympathy in hearts that never before felt for the slave. . . . At this stage of the meeting when Mrs. Stowe appeared there was a degree of excitement in the room that can better be imagined than described. The waving of hats and hand-kerchiefs, the clapping of hands, the stamping of feet, and the screaming and fainting of ladies, went on as if it had been in the programme, while the thieves were at work helping themselves out of the abundance of the pockets of those who were most crowded. A few arrests by the police soon taught the latter that there was no room for pickpockets. Order was at once restored, and the speaking went on.

REACTION TO *UNCLE TOM'S CABIN*

In the South, Harriet Beecher Stowe became a hated woman, whose book, according to a literary journal, was ''a criminal prostitution of the high functions of the imagination.'' Thus, when a Baltimore constable examining the room in which Samuel Green, a former slave, who was manumitted after working for thirty years for his master, found a copy of *Uncle Tom's Cabin,* Green was tried, convicted by a Maryland court in 1857, and sentenced to the Baltimore penitenti-ary for ten years. He served five years until 1862 when the governor of Maryland released him from jail on condition that he leave the state.

A Mobile bookseller was run out of town for stocking *Uncle Tom's Cabin.* Mrs. Stowe herself received threatening letters, and one day there arrived in the mail a package containing an ear cut off from the head of a Negro. Southern children were taught to chant:

Go, go, go,
Ol' Harriet Beecher Stowe.

The *Alabama Planter* editorialized: ''For her own domestic peace we trust no enemy will ever penetrate into her household to pervert the scenes he may find there with as little logic or kindness as she has used in her *Uncle Tom's Cabin.*'' Very quickly there appeared a raft of proslavery ''anti-Tom'' books such as Robert Criswell's *''Uncle Tom's Cabin'' Contrasted to Buckingham Hall, the Planter's Home, or, A Fair View of Both Sides of the Slavery Question* (1852); Mary Eastman's *Aunt Phillis's Cabin; or Southern Life as It Is* (1852); J. W. Page's *Aunt Robin in Her Cabin in Virginia and Tom Without One in Boston;* J. R. Thornton's *The Cabin and the Parlor* (1853); and Caroline Rush's *North and South, or Slavery and Its Contrasts* (1852).

In *Aunt Phillis's Cabin,* Mrs. Eastman describes Susan, a slave, who like all other slaves, is ''illy calculated to shift for herself.'' Susan has a kind mistress, a good home, and light work, but abolitionists convince the ''simple-minded girl'' that the evils of slavery will one day destroy her. Susan is put to work for a family of ten for $4 a week and is overworked. When Susan escapes the clutches of the abolitionists, her severest punishment is that her former owners refuse to claim her. They do, however, give her $10 to help her out, and eventually all ends happily—for other kind southerners allow her to attach herself to their household.

Mrs. Rush's novel begins in the squalor of New York, where the wife of a drunken husband tries to care for their nine children, but without success. Then the novel shifts to the bounty of a Mississippi plantation, where the slaves are all happy and well fed and totally removed from the cares and worries of free workers in the North.

Black leaders were quick to welcome *Uncle Tom's Cabin* as a weapon for emancipation. Frederick Douglass told the readers of his paper that the novelist had "unfolded the secrets of the slave's lacerated heart" and had done so with "deep insight into human character, melting pathos, keen and quiet wit, powers of argumentation, exalted sense of justice, and enlightened and comprehensive philosophy."

After the first five installments of the story appeared in the *National Era,* Mrs. Stowe had written to Douglass for help in portraying the reality of life on a cotton plantation. "I have before me an able paper written by a Southern planter," she wrote, "in which the details and *modus operandi* are given from his point of view. I am anxious to have something from another standpoint." Douglass assisted Mrs. Stowe in her prodigious research to recreate reality, and he rejoiced in the universal appeal of the "master book of the nineteenth century":

One flash from the heart-supplied intellect of Harriet Beecher Stowe could light a million camp fires in front of the embattled hosts of slavery, which not all the waters of the Mississippi, mingled as they are with blood, could extinguish. The present will be looked to by aftercoming generations as the age of anti-slavery literature—when supply on the gallup could not keep pace with the ever growing demand—when a picture of a Negro on the cover was a help to the sale of a book.

Less than a year after the novel was published, a call to the National Negro Convention to be held in Rochester, New York, cited "the propitious awakening to the fact of our condition at home and abroad, which has followed the publication of *Uncle Tom's Cabin.*" Sojourner Truth made a trip to greet Harriet Beecher Stowe, while Francis E. W. Harper, in her poem "Eliza Harris," evoked one of the most moving passages of the book.

The tradition was to continue with black poet Paul Lawrence Dunbar's sonnet to Mrs. Stowe in 1898:

> She told the story, and the whole world wept
>   At wrongs and cruelties it had not known
> But for this fearless woman's voice alone.
>   She spoke in consciences that long had slept;
> Her message, Freedom's clear reveille, swept
>   From heedless hovel to complacent throne.
>
> Command and prophecy were in the tone

And from its sheath the sword of justice leapt,
Around two peoples swelled a fiery wave,
 But both had come forth transfigured from the flame.
Blest be the hand that dared be strong to save
 And blest be she who in our weakness came—
Prophet and priestess! At one stroke she gave
A race to freedom and herself to fame.

In 1927, the eminent black historian, Dr. Carter G. Woodson, defended the novel against a white magazine writer who ridiculed its portrait of slavery's horrors. "*Uncle Tom's Cabin* met the test of realism," Dr. Woodson declared.

HARRIET BEECHER STOWE AND FREDERICK DOUGLASS

Deeply disturbed by the charges of inaccuracy in her novel, Mrs. Stowe gathered up supporting research material and published it in 1853 under the title *A Key to Uncle Tom's Cabin.* She included large extracts from the *Narrative of the Life of Frederick Douglass, an American Slave, Written by Himself* (1845), and she recommend Douglass' *Narrative* "to anyone who has the curiosity to trace the workings of an intelligent and active mind through all the squalid misery, degradation and oppression of slavery." Mrs. Stowe drew materials from Douglass' self-portrait for her characterization of the heroic mulatto in her novels—George Harris in *Uncle Tom's Cabin* and Harry Gordon in *Dred,* her second antislavery novel, published in 1856. When the *Key* was published, Douglass wrote:

The most unwise thing which, perhaps, was ever done by slaveholders, in order to hide the ugly features of slavery, was the calling in question and denying the truthfulness of *Uncle Tom's Cabin.* They had better have owned the "soft impeachment" therein contained—for the *Key* not only proves the correctness of every essential part of *Uncle Tom's Cabin,* but proves more and worse things against the murderous system than are alleged in that great book.

Douglass praised Mrs. Stowe for using some of the money she obtained in royalties to assist black causes. "There are, at this moment," he wrote on May 16, 1853, "two colored young ladies, at Oberlin College, being educated, at the charge of Harriet Beecher Stowe, and these two ladies were snatched from a fate worse than death. They were intended by American refinement and civilization, for the New Orleans Market, where their youth and beauty would have commanded the highest prices." Stowe also came vigorously to the defense of Douglass in his dispute with Garrison. Thus, she wrote to the editor of the *Liberator:*

I am satisfied that his change of sentiments was not a mere political one but a genuine growth of his own conviction. A vigorous reflective mind like his cast among those holding new sentiments is naturally led to modified views.

At all events, he holds no opinion which he cannot defend, with a variety and richness of thought and expression and an aptness of illustration which shows it to be a growth from the soil of his own mind with a living root and not a twig broken off other mens' thoughts stuck down to subserve a temporary purpose.

His plans for the elevation of his own race, are manly, sensible, comprehensive, he has evidently observed carefully and thought deeply and will I trust act efficiently. . . .

I must indulge the hope you will reason at some future time to alter your opinion and that what you now cast aside as worthless shall yet appear to be a treasure.

There is abundant room in the antislavery field for him to perform a work without crossing the track of impeding the movement of his old friends and perhaps in some future time meeting each other from opposite quarters of a victorious field, you may yet shake hands together.

Mrs. Stowe was earnestly trying to arrange a reconciliation between Garrison and Douglass, both her friends. But her words were wasted on the leader of the American Anti-Slavery Society. However, Mrs. Stowe's prediction did come true in that when the Civil War was over and victory over slavery achieved, Douglass and Garrison did allow bygones to be bygones, even though they never restored the close relationship they once enjoyed.

Mrs. Stowe's reference to Douglass' plans "for the elevation of his own race" included one in which she herself was involved. In March 1853, Douglass visited Mrs. Stowe at her home in Andover, Ohio, to consult with her as to some method that "should contribute successfully, and permanently to the improvement and elevation of the free colored people in the United States." Mrs. Stowe asked Douglass to propose the best plan to achieve that goal. He replied:

What can be done to improve the condition of the free people of color in the United States? The plan which I humbly submit in answer to this inquiry—and in the hope it may find favor with you, and with many friends of humanity who honor, love and co-operate with you—is the establishment in Rochester, N.Y., or in some other part of the United States equally favorable to such an enterprise, of an *industrial college* in which shall be taught several branches of the mechanical arts. This college is to be opened to colored youth.

A fervent believer in education as a major instrument in helping solve the "Negro problem," Mrs. Stowe responded enthusiastically and asked Douglass to spell out his plan more precisely. Douglass drew up a detailed plan for the institution, which was to be known as the American Industrial School. It was to be located within one hundred miles of Erie, Pennsylvania, on a site of at least 200 acres of land, 150 of which would be used as a farm for agricultural instruction. Teachers would be selected and students admitted to the school "without reference to sex or complexion," and special efforts would be made "to aid in providing for the female sex, methods and means of enjoying an independent and honorable livelihood." For every course in literature, there would be a course in handicraft. Each student would occupy half his time while at school working at some handicraft or on the farm, and all handicrafts produced would be sold at a market within easy access of the school.

It was an ambitious program, one that anticipated the curriculum and organization of most of the manual labor schools established after the Civil War, but its fulfillment hinged upon the raising of a fund sufficient to launch the institution. Even though the National Negro Convention held at Rochester in 1853 endorsed the plan, Mrs. Stowe reconsidered her offer to help the project with a substantial contribution and, for reasons not divulged, decided against the plan. In the end, Douglass' ambitious program came to naught.

HARRIET BEECHER STOWE AND SLAVERY

Mrs. Stowe's book was originally to be called *Uncle Tom's Cabin; or, The Man That Was a Thing.* Her subtitle was changed to *Life among the Lowly,* but the original one expressed her real intention to make vivid the individual, personal cruelties of the slave system, especially as it tore families apart, and to expose the monumental insensitivity of those who countenanced it. In the introduction to chapter 44 of *Dred, A Tale of the Great Dismal Swamp,* her antislavery novel that followed *Uncle Tom's Cabin* and that was inspired by Nat Turner's rebellion, she wrote:

We have been accustomed to look on the arguments for and against the system of slavery with the eyes of those who are at ease. . . . We shall never have all the materials for absolute truth on this subject till we take into account . . . the views and reasonings of those who have bowed down to the yoke, and felt the iron enter their souls. . . . We have seen how the masters feel and reason. . . . We must add also, to our estimate, the feelings and reasonings of the slave; and therefore the reader must follow us again to the fastness in the Dismal Swamp.

Her account of the slave's experience has been criticized on the ground that she overemphasized the house slave and ignored the field hand, but she did clearly understand the pecuniary and property aspect of slavery. Very shrewdly, she made one of her characters in *Uncle Tom's Cabin* say concerning the argument that the Bible sanctioned slavery:

Well, suppose that something should bring down the price of cotton once and forever, and make the whole slavery property a drug on the market, don't you think we should soon have another version of the Scripture doctrine? What a flood of light would pour into the church, all at once, and how immediately it would be discovered that everything in the Bible and reason were the other way?

One of the characters in *Dred* makes the point:

> Those among us who have got the power in their hands are determined to keep it, and they are wide awake. They don't let the first step [to emancipation] be taken. . . . They'll die first. Why, just look at it! There is at least twenty-four millions of property held in this way. . . . These men are our masters; they are yours, they are mine; they are masters of everybody in these United States.

In *Uncle Tom's Cabin,* Mr. Selby, the slaveowner, sells Uncle Tom down the river, against every instinct, every principle, and every personal feeling, because he is in debt to Haley, the slave trader. "All's equal with me," says Haley of his trade; "li'ves trade 'em up as down, so I does a good business. All I want is a living, you know, ma'am, that's all any of us wants, I s'pose." After one of Haley's articles of slave merchandise throws herself into the river, "the trader sat discontentedly down, with his little account book, and put down the missing body and soul under the head of *losses.*"

In *Dred,* Mr. Carson, a visitor from New York to the Gordon plantation, asks the lawyer Mr. Jekyl: "What do you call your best investments, down here—land, eh?"

> Mr. Jekyl shook his head.
> "Land deteriorates too fast. Besides, there's all the trouble and risk of overseers, and all that. I've look this thing over pretty well, and I always invest in niggers."
> "Ah!" said Mr. Carson, "you do?"
> "Yes, sir, I invest in niggers; that's what I do; and I hire them out, sir,—hire them out. Why, sir, if a man has a knowledge of human nature, knows where to buy and when to buy, and watches his opportunity, he gets a better percentage on his money that way than any other. Say, now, that you give one thousand dollars, for a man,—and I always buy the best sort, that's economy,—well, and he gets—put it at the lowest figure—ten dollars a month wages, and his living. Well, you see there, that gives you a pretty handsome sum for your money. I have a good talent of buying. I generally prefer mechanics. . . . I own two first-rate carpenters, and last month I bought a perfect jewel of a blacksmith.

Thomas P. Ruggio points out that "Mrs. Stowe's decision to make the novel's [*Uncle Tom's Cabin*] archvillain [Simon Legree] a nightmare version of the Yankee peddler . . . highlighted the capitalist basis of slavery, and implicated the North as well as the South."

"UNCLE TOM"

It is ironical that this book, which played such a dramatic part in the struggle for emancipation, has itself been an instrument for giving wide currency to slanders against the Negro people. The fault is mainly in the cheapening and distortion of the book by its many dramatizers. The first of the countless dramatizations opened in September 1852 for a one hundred-night run in Troy, New York. These productions retained only the most sentimental scenes, joined together by the blackface minstrel-show dances and lyrics. These dramatizations have created the image of a groveling Uncle Tom, a monstrously stereotyped Mammy, a ludicrous Topsy. Although Mrs. Stowe did not write of any dogs, the theater invented the classic chase of Eliza crossing the ice. British companies added a scene in which Simon Legree, with dogs, closed in on a runaway slave, with horrible off-stage noises as the pack mangled their quarry. And whether American or British, there was always the grinning, bowing, praying, forever forgiving Uncle Tom. The tragic elements of the story were stripped, the evils of slavery converted into parodies of an oppressed people, and the dignity and deeply felt moral outrage of the book destroyed.

To be sure, in her portrait of Uncle Tom, Mrs. Stowe became the victim of her evangelical fervor. The man of great heart becomes almost a person without any heart in his capacity for forgiving even a Simon Legree, who is murdering him, and the dignity he assumes is undermined by his infinite ability to suffer indignities. At the same time, it should be noted that Uncle Tom goes to his death rather than betray the escaping Cissy, the victim of Legree's brutal lust.

While Garrison could applaud the pacifistic nonresistance philosophy of Mrs. Stowe's hero, black leader Charles L. Remond declared at a Massachusetts state convention of Negroes in 1858, where he called for militant resistance, that he "did not go so far as Uncle Tom and kiss the hand that smote him." Reverend Josiah Henson, who was the real model for Mrs. Stowe's hero, was present at the convention and remarked, "When I fight, I want to whip somebody." It is known that Henson told Mrs. Stowe his own story before she set out to write *Uncle Tom's Cabin.* But the novel would have been much the better if the fictional hero had really been based on the experiences of the real-life hero. After he escaped from slavery by the Underground Railroad to Canada, Henson quickly became a leader there among the fugitive slaves. He then commenced a succession of daring returns to the South until he ranked as one of the Underground Railroad's most able conductors, having helped 118 slaves escape to freedom.

The novel suffers, too, from its extreme sentimentality, especially in regard to little Eva. The distinctions made between the lighter-skinned and darker-skinned blacks is another serious flaw. The former are always handsome, while only the latter speak in a dialect, with occasioned "comic effects."

But outweighing such flaws of form and content is the powerful indictment of the institution of chattel slavery. The system itself is the villain. Mrs. Stowe's conscious aim was to show its inherent barbarism. The book is rich in scenes that evoke the heartbreak of families split up and the unbearable anguish of mothers whose babies are snatched from them on the auction block. One of the most memorable is the scene on the steamboat *La Belle Riviere,* with its fashionable white folks sunning themselves on the top deck while on the freight deck below, the young Negro mother, Lucy, tormented beyond human endurance, hurls herself into the river to escape "into a state which *never will* give up a fugitive— not even at the demand of the whole glorious Union."

The better-known scene of Eliza Harris crossing the ice with her son, Harry, after she had won some precious time because her pursuers were misdirected by black men is truly heroic. And the author does not hesitate to speak directly to her white women readers:

If it were *your* Harry, mother, or your Willie, that were going to be torn from you by a brutal trader, tomorrow morning—if you had seen the man, and heard that the papers were signed and delivered, and you had only from twelve o'clock till morning to make good your escape,—how fast could you walk?

GEORGE HARRIS

In many parts of the novel, as in the case of George Harris, Mrs. Stowe shows the moral and intellectual superiority of blacks over their white rulers. Harris, the husband of Eliza and brother of Cissie, had seen his mother put up at a sheriff's sale with her seven children. He is sent by his owner to work in a bagging factory, where he invents a machine for the cleaning of hemp. George Harris "talked so fluently, held himself so erect, looked so handsome and manly, that his master began to feel an uneasy consciousness of inferiority. What business had his slave to be marching round the country, inventing machines and holding up his head among gentlemen? He'd soon put a stop to it."

But George Harris refuses to go back to the field. While on a visit to Eliza's residence (they were kept apart by separate masters), he divulges his plan of escape and asks what justice made him a slave and the white, his master: "I'm a better man than he is, I know more about the business than he does, I am a better manager than he is, I can read better than he can, I write a better hand—and I've learned it all myself, and no thanks to him."

Black resistance to the Fugitive Slave Act of 1850 finds its place in *Uncle Tom's Cabin* during the escape of George Harris. Disguised as a Spanish gentleman, Harris marches across Kentucky to Ohio, where he is reunited with Eliza, who had earlier escaped with their son, Harry. In a confrontation with a slave catcher's posse, George Harris shouts from a rock fortress to his would-be captors:

"I know very well that you've got the law on your side and the power. . . . You mean to take my wife to sell in New Orleans, and to put my boy like a calf in the trader's pen, and send Jim's old Mother to the brute that whipped and abused her before, because he couldn't abuse her son. You want to send Jim and me back to be whipped and tortured, and ground under the heels of them that you call masters; and your law *will* bear you out in it—more shame for you and them! But you haven't got us. We don't own your laws; we don't own your country; we stand here as free, under God's sky, as you are; and by the great God that made us, we'll fight for our liberty till we die."

And Harris also declares, "I'm a free man, standing on God's free soil, and my wife and child I claim as mine. . . . We have arms to defend ourselves and we mean to do it." And do it he does. He sends a bullet into the advancing slave catcher, dispersing the posse. Harris, his wife, and his child reach Canada, where he finds employment as a machinist.

Through the character of George Harris, Mrs. Stowe interjected her colonization views. Too ambitious to remain an artisan, Harris enrolls in a French university where he spends four years in study. But in the closing pages of the novel, he departs with his family for Liberia, where a new and promising republic has arisen:

"I want a country, a nation, of my own," he declared. "I think that the African race has peculiarities, yet to be unfolded in the light of civilization and Christianity, which, if not the same with those of the Anglo-Saxon, may prove to be, morally, of even a higher type. . . . As a Christian patriot, as a teacher of Christianity, I go to *my country,* my chosen, my glorious Africa."

Indeed Mrs. Stowe also proposed that eventually all Negroes should be sent to Africa:

Let the Church of the North receive these poor sufferers in the spirit of Christ; receive them to the educating advantages of Christian Republican society and schools, until they have attained to somewhat of a moral and intellectual maturity, and then assist them in their passage to the shores of Africa, where they may put into practice the lessons they have learned in America.

THE COLONIZATION CONTROVERSY

This feature of *Uncle Tom's Cabin* was heatedly discussed by irate black abolitionists. George T. Downing argued that George Harris was the only black character in the novel who "really betrays any other than the subservient, submissive Uncle Tom spirit, which has been the cause of so much disrespect felt for the colored man." Harris' exile to Liberia was thus a tragedy. The year following publication of *Uncle Tom's Cabin,* the American and Foreign Anti-Slavery Society recommended that something should be done to counteract the novel's colonizationist influence. Mrs. Stowe protested that she was not a colonizationist but that Liberia ought not to be ignored, since its presence as an independent nation lent dignity to Negroes everywhere. A delegate who claimed to speak for Mrs. Stowe produced a letter from the harried author reassuring Negroes that if she were to rewrite the novel, Harris would not emigrate to Liberia or counsel Negroes to do so. It should be noted, however, that in *Dred,* she again spoke favorably of colonization but explained that she expressed such sentiments only out of utter despair that either emancipation or any reform of slavery would be achieved in the United States.

Still, in *Dred,* she saw a little more clearly that the end of slavery could not come without great struggle. The father of the black hero of the novel, Dred, was Denmark Vesey, and he had absorbed the doctrine "that all men were born equal and had an *inalienable* right to life, liberty and the pursuit of happiness; and that all governments derive their just power from the consent of the governed." After his father was executed for attempting to achieve this idea, Dred dedicated his life to freeing the slaves, inspired "by memories of self-sacrificing ardor with which a father and his associates had met at the call of freedom." Dred's plan to lead a slave insurrection thus conforms to the political ideals of America. As a white southerner tells Dred's lieutenants:

I admit the right of an oppressed people to change their form of government *if they can.* I admit that your people suffer under greater oppression than ever our fathers suffered. And if I believed that they were capable of obtaining and supporting a government, I should believe in their right to take the same means to gain it.

Living in the swamp on an almost inaccessible island, Dred defies the slaveowners and helps the oppressed find freedom. When Harry, a slave foreman, is faced with the danger that his wife, Lisette, will be forced to sleep with the slaveowner, Dred challenges him to seek freedom and protection for his wife in the forest. The challenge is a brilliant passage:

"Look here, Harry," said Dred, speaking in bitter irony, "did your master strike you? It's sweet to kiss the rod, isn't it? Bend your neck and ask to be struck again! . . . You are a *slave,* and you wear broadcloth and sleep soft. . . . Don't fret about your wife. . . . Take it meekly, my boy! 'Servants, obey your masters.' Take your wife when he's done with her—and bless God that brought you under the light of the Gospel! Go! You are a slave! But, as for me," he said, drawing up his head and throwing back his shoulders with a deep inspiration, "I am a free man! Free by this," holding out his rifle. . . . "I sleep on the ground, in the swamps! You eat the fat of this land. I have what the ravens bring me! But no man whips me!—no man touches my wife!—no man says to me 'Why do ye so?' Go! You are a slave! I am free!"

Eventually Harry flees with Lisette to Dred's colony.

Mrs. Stowe has been accused of racism by James Baldwin, among others, because her elitist characters are "really" whites, that is, half-white in parentage. That Harriet Beecher Stowe shared many of the misconceptions of race common in her lifetime was practically unavoidable. Yet to a remarkable degree, she was able to rise above the sentiments then prevalent. She realized that the reason white Americans did not see slavery as cruel and unjust was that they denied the humanity of the Negro. She expressed this view bluntly in *A Key to Uncle Tom's Cabin*:

It is because the negro is considered an *inferior animal* and not worthy of any better treatment, that the system which relates to him and the treatment which falls to him are considered humane.

Take any class of white men, however uneducated, and place them under the same system of laws and make their civil condition in all respects like that of the negro and would it not be considered the most outrageous cruelty.

In 1854, in an introduction to William C. Nell's *Colored Patriots of the American Revolution,* she admitted that the acceptance of racial stereotypes was all too common among white Americans:

The colored race have been generally considered by their enemies, and sometimes by their friends, as deficient in energy and courage. Their virtues have been supposed to be principally negative ones. This little collection of incidents, made by a colored man, will show how much injustice there may often be in a generally admitted idea.

In the last chapter of *Uncle Tom's Cabin,* Harriet Beecher Stowe makes an impassioned appeal to white Americans, devoting a few lines to sailors, shipowners, and farmers, and then addresses the force she feels must play the vanguard role:

Mothers of America,—you, who have learned, by the cradles of your own children, to live and feel for all mankind,—by the sacred love you bear your child; by your joy in his beautiful, spotless infancy; by the motherly pity and tenderness with which you guide his growing years; by the anxieties of his education; by the prayers you breathe for his soul's eternal good;—I beseech you, pity the mother who has all your affections, and not one legal right to protect, guide, or educate the child of her bosom! By the sick hour of your child; by those dying eyes, which you can never forget; by those last cries, that wrung your heart when you could neither help nor save; by the desolation of the empty cradle, that silent nursery,—I beseech you, pity those mothers who are constantly made childless by the American slave-trade! And say, mothers of America, is this a thing to be defended, sympathized with, passed over in silence?

RECENT ESTIMATES OF *UNCLE TOM'S CABIN*

In 1956, J. C. Furnas, in *Goodbye to Uncle Tom,* attempted to show that Mrs. Stowe's widely read book was in tune with notions of Negro inferiority popular in her day and that an Uncle Tom stereotype was established that has distorted white America's view of the Negro down to the present. In Akron, Ohio, in 1962, a local Negro political and civil leader, Mrs. Bertha B. Moore, brought suit for libel against a black weekly newspaper, the *Cleveland Post,* for printing a "false report" that she had been called an Uncle Tom. Mrs. Moore won her suit—and $32,000 in damages—from an all-white jury.

Yet the late American literary critic, Edmund Wilson, insisted that *Uncle Tom's Cabin* does not deserve the general contempt in which it is currently held. For all its faults, he noted, it had a grandeur of conception and what Wilson called a "certain eruptive force" that overwhelms these deficiencies. And Wilson observed that even militant blacks "have forgotten that Uncle Tom rebels and is beaten to death for rebellion." In *The Negro in American Fiction,* Howard University professor Sterling Brown observed:

It is not like that there were no slave auctions, slave cellars such as the ones where the flies "got to old Prue," public whipping posts, mothers separated from their children, and slaves like Cissy whose beauty was their doom. With allowances for sentimentality and melodramas, essential truth is in *Uncle Tom's Cabin.* To argue against its artistic faults and to consider it incomplete representation are possible. The charge of lying, however, is confusing. Mrs. Stowe showed that slavery was a great wrong, and that Negroes are human. Is it here that critics believe she lies?

In sharply and effectively criticizing J. C. Furnas' *Goodbye to Uncle Tom,* Ernest Kaiser, the black curator of the Schomburg Collection of the New York Public Library, located in Harlem, makes an essential point:

Striking ostensibly an "objective" position between liberals and racists, the book is actually a venomous, repetitious diatribe and hymn of hate against Harriet Beecher Stowe, *Uncle Tom's Cabin* and all liberal arguments on the Negro question. Furnas blames *Uncle Tom's Cabin* for creating and perpetuating most of the current stereotypes of the Negro. But pro-slavery and segregation propaganda before and after the Civil War is the real source of Negro stereotypes; *Uncle Tom's Cabin* was accepted during its time by Negro Abolitionists as a blow against slavery. Furnas is mistaken in thinking that since "Uncle Tom" is a term of opprobrium among Negroes today and the N.A.A.C.P. fights against all black-face minstrelsy and stereotyped revivals of *Uncle Tom's Cabin* as a play, the impact of the novel was negative in its time. Furnas's synopsis of *Uncle Tom's Cabin* shows clearly, although unintentionally, the anti-slavery tenor and drive of the book; its trenchant, unanswerable criticisms of slavery and its curses.

One of the many positive effects of the novel in its time is noted in the following excerpt, which appeared in William Still's "Journal of Station No. 2, U[nder] G[round] R[ail] R[oad]:

Oct. 21, 1854. Arrived Chas. Thompson, age 40 Chestnut Color, active, well informed, etc. Bad treatment had driven Chas. to the necessity of making his escape. Adding to the natural prompting of his heart for liberty, he had recently been much stimulated by the reading of *Uncle Tom's Cabin.*

Of the countless tributes paid to Harriet Beecher Stowe—by writers like Heine, Dickens, Tolstoy, George Sand, Frederika Bremer, and Macaulay and by artists like Van Gogh—she probably would have appreciated most the one by Charles Thompson.

8

Black Emigration, 1850–1861
I: Issues and Personalities

LIBERIA AND ITS MEANING

In the period from the 1820s through most of the 1840s, colonization met with almost universal condemnation in the black communities of the North. As long as these communities equated emigration overseas as part of "a diabolical scheme of the American Colonization Society to rid the country of free Negroes,", there could be no real support for these projects. While several hundred blacks did emigrate to Liberia with the aid of the Colonization Society, to most blacks the only really acceptable place to emigrate to in those decades (because of hatred of the society) was Canada, Haiti, or the British West Indies. In fact, however, even though several national and state black conventions revealed an interest in Canadian settlement during these years, resistance to emigration of any kind was the dominant feeling from 1817 to 1850. When most blacks thought of emigration, there immediately came to mind the following typical statements in the *African Repository,* official organ of the American Colonization Society:

The African in this country belongs by birth to the very lowest station in society, and from that station he can never rise.

Here [in the United States] they must be forever debased; more than this, they must be forever useless, more even than this, they must be forever a nuisance, from which it were a blessing for society to be rid. And yet they only are qualified for colonizing Africa.

Free Blacks are a greater nuisance than even slaves themselves.

Such statements reflected what the American Colonization Society really thought of black people, and even though the *African Repository* toned down the invective contained in such racist editorials, this did not prevent most blacks from continuing to denounce the society. N. D. Artist, who lectured in favor of colonization, wrote to Reverend William McLain, one of the society's chief officials: "It must be well known to you how deep the prejudice of most of our free colored people is against any thing that the Colonization Society has anything to do with or any control over." Frederick Douglass spoke for "most of our free colored people" when he wrote: "The great mass of the free people of color in the United States . . . cannot for their lives, see why a society, which can look with complacency upon the enslavement of three millions of colored men should be so alive to the sufferings of five hundred thousand free people of color."

Even during these years a few black voices spoke out in favor of breaking the opposition of free Negroes to overseas emigration. Writing in the *Colored American* of May 3, 1838, "Augustine" (whom Floyd J. Miller has identified as Lewis Woodson of Ohio and has called the Father of Black Nationalism) contended that the animosity of the black community to emigration was simply a reaction to the effort of the American Colonization Society to exile the free Negroes and that this was not a legitimate reason for such opposition. Referring a few months later to the belief expressed by some blacks that they would face death rather than allow themselves to be removed from America for any cause whatsoever, Woodson wrote: "After much reflection upon this highly important point, I am free to acknowledge that I am not one of that number." Noting that too many blacks were "just beginning to live happily in the West Indies, and in Canada," he declared that "for me to think of dying just now would be absurd." He suggested that he would "rather be a *living freeman,* even in one of these places, than a 'dead nigger' in the United States."

Although Woodson's arguments fell mainly on deaf ears, colonization continued to exert some influence among black Americans. In 1847, the Republic of Liberia was born, and the settlements fostered by the American Colonization Society achieved their independence. To many black Americans, Liberia no longer symbolized a white man's attempt to rid the United States of free Negroes. Rather, it was now another nation in the firmament of black republics to be added to Haiti, one to which blacks in the United States could look with some pride and hope for the future.

Other black Americans, however, still would have nothing to do with Liberia. In their opinion, it represented no more than a scheme to perpetuate slavery by draining off the free Negro population. They pointed, too, to the exploitation of and limited rights extended to the native African population, who vastly outnumbered the black emigrants from the United States. Finally, they insisted that the Liberian economy did not offer a sufficiently strong inducement to potential settlers, and on this last point, even a number of the pro-Liberian blacks agreed.

Nonetheless, these arguments were growing less persuasive as the 1840s drew to a close. "In Liberia, colonization has established an entire nation of colored people," wrote one black American in 1849, "who elect not only their constables, but their own legislature and president and judges." Another saw Liberia as "the Land of Refuge, . . . Equality, wealth, Dignity and Peace"—a veritable "Israel for the sons of Ham."

HENRY HIGHLAND GARNET: CHAMPION OF LIBERIAN EMIGRATION

The most important convert to the cause of the new black republic was the Reverend Henry Highland Garnet. Before 1849, Garnet had repeatedly questioned the desirability, or even the possibility, of emigration, arguing that the races were so inextricably intermixed that it was "too late to separate the black and white people in the New World." Thus, he told members of his congregation in Troy, New York: "We are now colonized. We are planted here and we cannot as a whole be reconciled back to the fatherland." In 1848, he wrote:

It is impossible, like the children of Israel, to make a grand Exodus from the land of bondage. The Pharaohs are on both sides of the blood-red waters! You cannot remove *en masse* to the dominions of the British Queen—nor can you pass through Florida, or overrun Texas and at last find peace in Mexico. The propagators of American slavery are spending their blood and treasure, that they may plant the black flag in the heart of Mexico, and riot in the halls of the Montezumas.

Yet later that same year, Garnet's ideas shifted, and in an article in the *North Star* of January 26, 1849, he made it clear that while he still opposed the American Colonization Society in its philosophy that the Negro could never rise to equality in the United States, he was now ready to accept the long-hated society's help "to the land of my fathers." Frederick Douglass, who never wavered in his firm opposition to the Colonization Society, immediately demanded an explanation from Garnet for this change in attitude. To this Garnet replied:

My opinion of the Colonizationists has undergone no change. But new developments have been made in relation to the descendants of once glorious but now fallen Africa and these have changed my mind.

1. I believe that the Republic will succeed—and that its success will be highly beneficial to Africa.

2. I believe that the new Republic will succeed—and that its success will curtail the slave trade on the coast.

3. I believe that every political and commercial relationship which President Roberts [of Liberia] negotiates with European powers goes far to create respect for our race throughout the civilized world.

4. I believe that every colored man who believes that he can never grow to the stature of a man in this country ought to go there immediately, if he desires. I am in favor of colonization in any part of the United States, Mexico or California or in the West Indies or

Africa, wherever it promises freedom and enfranchisement. In a word, we ought to go anywhere where we can better our condition.

Evidently Garnet had concluded that blacks should rather be free in lands beyond the borders of their country than slaves or quasi-free in the United States. He now looked to Liberia to become a great commercial and political benefit to Africa and expected the new black republic to check the slave trade "by the diffusion of light and knowledge, and by turning the attention of the black traders to some other and honorable business, and by sweeping off the white ones as with the hand of an avenging God."

With this response, a vitriolic debate broke out between Douglass and Garnet on the issue of colonization. Douglass minced no words in denouncing Garnet and separating himself from his position. He made his stand clear in an editorial entitled "Colonization":

We do not mean to go to Liberia. Our minds are made up to live here if we can, or die here if we must; so every attempt to remove us, will be, as it ought to be, labor lost. Here we are, and here we shall remain. While our brethren are in bondage on these shores, it is idle to think of inducing any considerable number of free colored people to quit this for a foreign land.

In a speech at the great anticolonization mass meeting of the Colored Citizens of the City of New York held on April 24, 1849, and called, in part, to criticize Garnet's stand, Douglass summed up his position:

the fundamental and . . . the everlasting objection to colonization is this; that it assumes that the colored people, while they remain in this country, can never stand on an equal footing with the white population of the United States. This objection, I say, is a fundamental one; it lies at the very basis of this enterprise, and, as such, I am opposed to it, have ever been opposed to it, and shall, I presume, ever to continue to oppose it. It takes the ground that the colored people of this country can never be free, can never improve here; and it is spreading throughout the country this hope-destroying, this misanthropic doctrine, chilling the aspirations of the colored people themselves, and leading them to feel that they cannot, indeed, ever be free in this land. In this respect the influence of the Colonization scheme has been most disastrous to us.

FUGITIVE SLAVE ACT OF 1850, BLYDEN AND CRUMMELL

All of this controversy over colonization, moreover, occurred even before the passage of the Fugitive Slave Act of 1850. When Garnet spoke in March 1848 of having changed his mind on colonization because of "new developments" affecting black Americans, it was a mild statement compared to the effect of the passage of the hated law on the attitude of blacks toward emigration. The Fugitive Slave Act of 1850 made every black man, woman, and child feel not only a sense of alienation from the body politic but a sense of insecurity, as every free black became potentially enslavable at the whim of any local magistrate. Under these circumstances, no free black could escape the influence of emigrationists' arguments.

For the free black community in the United States, the 1850s proved to be a decade of growing despair. The Kansas-Nebraska Act of 1854, four years after the Fugitive Slave Act, the *Dred Scott* decision three years later, the expulsion of free black populations from several Southern states, and the serious attempt to reopen the African slave trade all made it increasingly clear that the future of the free blacks was very much in doubt. Although many blacks grudgingly resigned themselves to an inferior status, a persistent number sought to demonstrate that environmental factors, not inherent racial traits, accounted for their degradation and that in a significantly altered environment, blacks could prove their fitness for citizenship. With the growing despair over their future in the United States, once again, as in the late 1820s and 1830s, the decision to leave the United States became a burning issue for blacks.

For some the decision was easy. Thus, the Fugitive Slave Act of 1850 brought to Liberia a young West Indian who had come to the United States from his native St. Thomas to seek entrance into a theological college. This black American was Edward Wilmot Blyden who has recently been described as "easily the greatest of the Pan-African figures of the Nineteenth Century." Not only were his applications for college in the United States turned down because of his race, but he had the traumatic and humiliating experience of witnessing the application of the fugitive slave law against free blacks of New York. Fearing that he himself would be seized as a slave and convinced from his experience and readings that black people would never be treated as the equals of whites in the New World, he became excited by the possibilities of the development of Liberia. Accordingly, Blyden emigrated to Liberia, arriving there in late January 1851. In his first letter to the *New York Colonization Journal,* Blyden wrote:

You can easily imagine the delight with which I gazed upon the land of Tertullian, ancient father in the Christian Church; of Hannibal, and Henry Diaz, renowned general; yes, and the land of my forefathers. . . . The land here is teeming with everything necessary for subsistence of man.

Asserting that Negroes could never be integrated into the American body politic, Blyden favored colonization of black Americans, and his articles in the American press and, later, his speeches in the United States promoting Liberian emigration brought about some emigration of blacks to the African black republic. Although Blyden's formal education never went beyond the high school level, because of his broad reading, his wide travels, and his unceasing application, he became a versatile scholar—a linguist who read and spoke all of the Romance languages, as well as Arabic and Hebrew, and several West African languages; a classicist who read Greek and Latin fluently, a theologian, historian, and sociologist. In Liberia, Blyden was principal of Alexander High School from 1858 to 1861 and again from 1874 to 1877; professor of classics at Liberia College, 1862–1871; secretary of state, 1864–1866; ambassador to Britain, 1877–1878 and again in 1892, and to Britain and France in 1905; president of Liberia College, 1880–1881 and again in 1900; and minister of the interior, 1880–1882. In Sierra Leone he was agent to the interior, 1872–1873, and director of Muslim education, 1901–1906; and in Lagos he was agent for native affairs, 1896.

Joining Blyden in promoting the emigration of black Americans to Liberia was another remarkable Negro, Reverend Alexander Crummell. Although he left from England for Liberia, his encounters with racism in the United States made him a devoted advocate of Liberia as a home for black Americans.

Born in New York City on March 8, 1819, Crummell escaped exposure to the life of slavery. Well educated for the times, he first attended the African Free School on Mulberry Street and then the Canal Street High School for classical studies for Negroes, of which he was one of the first pupils. In 1835 when the abolitionists of New Hampshire opened a new school at Canaan for all races and sexes, Crummell went from New York City with Garnet and another black youth to extend their education. Crummell's description of their journey is heartrending. Garnet was a crippled, weak youth who had to ride on top of a coach most of the way. Inns and hotels refused to serve them, and people sneered at them. Upon their arrival at the academy in Canaan, they were greeted by about forty white students. Their studies, along with those of the other Negroes present, progressed smoothly until the white people of New Hampshire could no longer accept the idea of a "nigger school" in their midst. On July 4, 1835, the white farmers met at Canaan and resolved to remove the academy, which they proceeded to do on August 10. Using ninety oxen, they spent two days in successfully dragging the schoolhouse into a nearby swamp, ending the educational experience in New Hampshire for Crummell and his friends. They were ordered to leave the state within two weeks and returned to New York.

It was just at this time that the Oneida Institute, a manual labor seminary in Whitesboro, New York, opened its doors to blacks. For three years, Crummell studied at Oneida, and in 1839, he became a candidate for holy orders. On the advice of Reverend John Williams, Crummell applied to the General Theological Seminary of the Episcopal church in New York. But prejudice again stood in the way, and he was refused admission. Not easily discouraged, Crummell appealed directly to the board of trustees, but to no avail. In fact, he was called in before Bishop Onderdonk of New York and severely rebuked for his insolence. From then on, Alexander Crummell was a "marked man," for no other black had previously dared to contest discrimination in the entrance procedures at the General Theological Seminary. Later Crummell rather charitably attributed his treatment to the fact that South Carolina had endowed a professor's chair at the seminary for several thousand dollars and that Bishop Onderdonk did not want to offend the slave state by permitting a Negro to enter the seminary.

Again fortunately for Crummell, William Jay and John Jay, the son and grandson of the first chief justice of the Supreme Court, along with Charles King, editor of the *New York American,* came to his aid and helped the black New Yorker go up to Boston where, in 1842, he received deacons' orders from Bishop Griswold of St. Paul's Church. Then, in 1844, after another course of preparation, he was ordained into the Episcopalian ministry.

Crummell's first ministerial experience was in Providence, Rhode Island, and it was a disaster. His sermons were considered too intellectual, too full of "high ethics," and with too little emotional appeal. He soon made his way to Philadelphia where another Bishop Onderdonk (the brother of the New York bishop) refused to receive him into the diocese unless he promised never to apply for a seat in the church convention for himself or his black constituents. Crummell refused and set out on his own. His sermons were no better appreciated in Philadelphia than they had been in Providence.

Depressed and practically penniless, Crummell returned to New York. There he discovered a chapel for which he could work—St. Mathews, the second Episcopal church in New York for black people. The congregation was so poor that it had been worshipping in hired rooms when funds could be raised to pay for them. It needed a building desperately. After several years of such difficult ministerial existence, Crummell, at the suggestion of a fellow minister, decided to go to England to raise money for a building. With the financial support of John Jay, Crummell made his way across the Atlantic to London, where he arrived on January 26, 1847. He preached and lectured throughout the British Isles and was even licensed for six months to a curacy in Ipswich. The bishop in Liverpool was so impressed with Crummell that he invited him to be the minister of St. George's Church at Everton. There, during 1848, Crummell amazed his audience with his dignity, diction, lucidity, and depth of knowledge.

He got results too. The bishops of London and Oxford were among those who helped raise money for his New York church. So impressed were the British that a committee in Bath, England, proposed in 1848 that Crummell should receive a British education and recommended further that his wife and children should come over from the United States to join him and also receive an education. With this aid, Crummell went to Queen's College, Cambridge University, for two years and received his bachelor's degree in classics and theology in 1853.

Despite the different life he led in England from that he had known in the United States, Crummell had no intention of living in the British Isles. His aim was to return to his New York congregation, for as he put it: "My heart from youth, was consecrated to my race and its interests." However, throughout his five years in England, Crummell was constantly battling poor health. Finally, his doctors suggested that instead of returning to New York, he live in a warmer climate. Crummell chose the land of his father, Boston Crummell, who had been taken from Africa as a boy, and he settled in Liberia.

He arrived with his family in Monrovia (Liberia's capital, named after President James Monroe) on July 15, 1853. He had come to Liberia primarily as a missionary with no civil or national interests. Yet he became a citizen soon after arriving. As he put it: "I had not been in the country three days when such was the manliness I saw exhibited, so great was the capacity I saw developed, and so many were the signs of thrift, energy, and national life which showed themselves, that all my governmental indifference at once vanished."

Crummell occupied himself in Liberia as a pastor, missionary, farmer, master of a high school, and a college professor. Like Blyden, he wrote letters and articles in the American press urging blacks to emigrate to Liberia, and he returned to the United States with Blyden to present the argument for Liberian emigration to black audiences.

While Blyden and Crummell extolled Liberia as the logical place for black Americans to settle, welcomed the American Colonization Society's assistance to potential emigrants to the black republic, and served as agents for the society, most emigrationists in the 1850s still rejected their position. In fact, at this time, the major emphasis was placed on emigration rather than colonization. The main difference between the two was that the emigrationists took up a rhetoric of independence from whites. Martin R. Delany, who investigated the possibilities of migration to a number of sites in both the Old and New Worlds, showed open contempt for the American Colonization Society and Liberia.

EMIGRATIONISM AND NATIONALISM

Discussions of black emigrationism during the 1850s place major emphasis on the despair that swept the black communities during that decade. There is no question that this did play an important role. Yet emigrationism of the 1850s was not motivated by despair alone. It was related also to the European nationalist fervor unleashed by the Revolution of 1848 and by the well-publicized visit of Louis Kossuth, the Hungarian patriot, to the United States. This same period also witnessed the battles of peoples throughout Europe for their national independence, and advocates of black emigration saw parallels between the black experience in America and those of oppressed nations in Europe. Emigrationists were very much influenced by the European conceptions of nationalism as advanced by the Italian Mazzini, the Frenchman Guizot, and the German theorists Johann Gottfried von Herder and Friedrich Schleiermacher.

Von Herder rejected the idea that nationality was only a figment of the imagination. He argued that each nation was an organic unity and that each was "part of the divine plan in history." In the development of each nationality, he saw the unfolding of divine will. Schleiermacher, whose thought ran in the same direction, wrote:

Every nation is destined through its peculiar organization and its place in the world to represent a certain side of the divine image . . . for it is God alone who directly assigns to each nationality its definite task on earth and inspires it with a definite spirit in order to glorify himself through each one in a peculiar manner.

Parallel ideas were present in the thinking of black American emigrationists, as the following by Edward Wilmot Blyden makes clear:

As in every form of the inorganic universe we see some noble variation of God's thought and beauty, so in each separate man, in each separate race, something of the absolute is incarnated. The whole of mankind is a vast representation of the Deity. Therefore we cannot extinguish any race either by conflict or amalgamation without serious responsibility.

When Blyden visited the United States in 1861, he was accompanied by Alexander Crummell as an official representative of the Liberian government in order to encourage emigration to Liberia. Crummell and Blyden both emphasized the divine nature of their mission. "Races, like families, are the organisms and the ordinance of God," Crummell said, "and race feeling, like family feeling, is of divine origin."

Black emigrationists voiced conceptions of nationality then prevalent, emphasizing that each race was entitled to the hereditary realm in which God had originally placed it. They adopted the rhetoric of the Christian expansionism and manifest destiny and spoke either of the duty of black Americans to support the work of civilizing the blacks of West Africa and elevating them to self-governing status or of carrying out this mission in the black Caribbean.

The great influx of immigrants to the United States during this same period was another influence in the rise of emigrationist sentiment, for it continually reminded black Americans of their oppressed status in American society. America, the land of their birth, continued to extend the welcoming hand to displaced Europeans, while it actively denied blacks the basic rights articulated in the Declaration of Independence and the Constitution. Martin R. Delany expressed the black reaction most clearly when he wrote in 1852: "We love our country, dearly love her, but she does not love us—she despises us, and bids us gone, driving us from her embrace." If blacks were a colonized group within the United States, Delany argued, they must emigrate to decolonize themselves.

NEW YORK BLACKS REJECT COLONIZATION

The Fugitive Slave Act of 1850 marked the beginning of a new attitude among free blacks toward emigration. Yet it was to take time before the influence of twenty years of anticolonization feeling was overcome. (In Boston it was never overcome.) Shortly after the fugitive slave law was passed, Douglass wrote bitterly:

While the colored people are thus elbowed out of employment, while a ceaseless enmity in the Irish is excited against us, while we are hunted like wild beasts . . . the American Colonization Society, with hypocrisy written on its brow, comes to the front, awakens to new life, and vigorously presses its scheme for our expatriation. . . . Evidently this society looks upon our extremity as its opportunity.

To most blacks a good example of what Douglass referred to occurred in the fall of 1851. Lewis H. Putnam, a New York City Negro, tried to break the old pattern. Together with a group of his friends, he organized the Liberian Agricultural and Emigration Society and sought funds from the black communities of the North. Immediately Putnam came under attack. At a public meeting of black New Yorkers on October 6, 1851, Putnam's organization was called simply a black version of the American Colonization Society, and a report submitted by a committee favoring emigration to Liberia was refused even a hearing. The Reverend Samuel E. Cornish, Robert Hamilton, George T. Downing, and others supported this decision; Putnam and one other black were the only ones opposing it. Before the meeting adjourned, a series of resolutions were adopted. One made clear the fixed determination of blacks to oppose all colonization schemes and declared their "abhorrence" for its designs, whether "promulgated by the American Colonization Society or by renegade colored men, made under the guise of emigration society." Another asked Putnam to "disconnect himself from the negroes of New York . . . seeing that he has found it to his interests to connect himself with the American Colonization Society, our enemy and vilifier." A final resolution called upon blacks in the city to refrain from contributing funds to the "so-called Liberian Emigration Society, as the colored citizens of New York have no connection or sympathy with it."

Lewis Putnam not only persisted but won some support from Governor Washington Hunt. In his annual message to the New York state legislature in January 1852, Hunt called upon that body to make a "liberal appropriation" to aid the American Colonization Society and the Liberian Emigration Society to help in colonizing New York blacks who were desirous of emigrating to Liberia. On the day the governor's message was made public, the Committee of Thirteen, a watchdog body representing the interests of blacks in New York City and Brooklyn, promptly called upon the governor to disavow the scheme. They pointed out that his proposal would be "pernicious to us and the state" and "if suffered to go unrebuked" would lead to further deterioration in the status of blacks in New York. The group then announced plans for a state convention to be held at Albany on January 20, 1852, to deal with this problem.

In the meantime the Committee of Thirteen called a meeting for January 13 at the Abyssinian Baptist Church in Manhattan and issued a circular entitled, "IMPORTANT NOTICE. COLOURED MEN AROUSE! AROUSE! AROUSE!" In the circular the committee declared:

There are traitors among us—coloured men allied with our oppressors—men who, to satisfy their selfish ends, to put money in their purses, are uniting their influence with

those who would drive us from our country. Is this to be? You will not remain indifferent
with this fact before your eyes! No! No!

. . . Come one, come all—maidens and mothers, brothers and sisters, fathers and all—
come, come, and proclaim to the world your resolve not to leave the country.

At the meeting, a number of resolutions were adopted, one of which branded
Governor Hunt's colonization program as "both unchristian and
unconstitutional":

Unchristian because it does not recommend to the wrong-doer instantaneous cessation
from his evil course, and unconstitutional because there is no power given to the Legislature, by the constitution, to make appropriation of public funds for the purpose of removing citizens beyond the bounds of the state.

Jeremiah Powers, a member of the Committee of Thirteen, declared, to great
applause, that in view of Governor Hunt's policies, blacks would refuse to
support the Whig party, of which he was a leader. Powers promised that "in the
future we will vote for no man that will not vote for us and the cause of
humanity. We will vote Gov. Hunt out next time. He was elected by only two
hundred and fifty of a majority and these were the votes of the Colored
population."

Across the state, local meetings also voted their disapproval of Hunt's recommendation. The New York State Convention of Colored Citizens, meeting under
the chairmanship of Reverend James W. C. Pennington in Albany's city hall on
January 20, 1852, adopted a vigorous protest calling Hunt's action "unconstitutional," since the tenth section of article 7 of the state constitution declared that
the "credit of the state shall not in any manner be given or loaned to, or in aid of
any individual association or incorporation," and the American Colonization
Society was definitely an association. Moreover, a contribution to the organization would pledge the good faith of the state "to the cruel and monstrous
doctrines on which that Society is founded—that a man has no right to live in the
land of his birth." The appropriation was also unnecessary since there were in
the entire state not fifty blacks "who desire to emigrate to Africa." If New York
blacks ever decided to emigrate, the protest went on, they would do so with their
own means, and they would go not to Liberia but to

Canada, from whose fertile fields and equal institutions, we might be permitted to witness
the prosperity of that state which, in giving us birth, has entwined in its commonwealth
every fibre of our being; this would take away half the bitterness of exile.

Finally the convention's delegates opposed the appropriation because they
remembered those who were still in bondage, "bone of our bone, and flesh of
our flesh, may evil betide us when the hope of gain, or the fear of oppression,

shall compel or persuade us to forsake them to the rayless gloom of perpetual slavery.''

On January 26, 1852, a special meeting at the Abyssinian Baptist Church in New York City heard a report from the delegation to the Albany convention. At this gathering, George T. Downing gave an extended account of the visit of the black delegates to Governor Hunt at the executive mansion. The governor tried to impress the delegation with the fact that he harbored no hostile attitudes toward the black citizens of the state and viewed colonization only as an attractive alternative for some blacks who wanted to leave. He assured the delegation that he would urge defeat of an appropriation of funds for colonization and that if it passed over his opposition, he would veto it.

Thus, the Hunt plan died, killed by the massive and overwhelming opposition of New York blacks. But the story did not end there. On April 22, 1853, the proslavery *New York Herald* urged a revival of Governor Hunt's proposal. The editorial, ''The African Race in New York,'' opened on a humanitarian note:

All persons having a shade of philanthropy in their composition, must have that feeling excited by witnessing the poverty and degradation in which the African race exist in this city. Systematically shut out from all mechanical pursuits, and expelled from almost all the inferior positions they were once allowed to hold here, they have seen their places filled by Germans and Irish; and now there are not more than half a dozen occupations in which they can engage. Even as waiters in our hotels—one of the last and best strongholds left them—they find that they are constantly losing ground by the abler competition of immigrants from Europe.

The *Herald* did not, however, urge employers to open their shops and factories to black workers or the trade unions to open their ranks to them. Instead it offered the following proposal:

Under the circumstances, would not the wisest and most philanthropic measure be, to promote, by all possible means, the emigration of the colored people of this State to the republic of Liberia? and would it not be prudent and politic in our government to appropriate a certain annual sum for this purpose. . . . The State of New York should not remain passive to the wretched condition of so many of her colored citizens, but do what humanity and sound policy alike suggest—make such an appropriation as would enable all negroes wishing to emigrate to Liberia to do so free of expense. We trust that the Legislature, at its next session, will not be unmindful of the claims of the poor African, condemned to a life of abject poverty and destitution in this State, and longing for means to enable him to become a good citizen of the modern black republic. Let him have them.

MARTIN R. DELANY, EMIGRATIONIST

So few New York blacks were actually ''longing'' to emigrate to Liberia and so many were enraged by the *Herald*'s stance that the legislature ignored the suggestion. However, one black American, while he did not favor the specific area to which blacks should emigrate suggested by the *New York Herald,* agreed with its analysis of the miserable status of black workers in the North and had himself gravitated toward support of emigration. The same year in which Governor Hunt's proposal to assist blacks to emigrate to Africa was defeated marked the appearance of this black American on the emigration scene, and he was soon to become the dominant figure in the emigration movement. He was Martin Robison Delany, a Harvard-trained black physician, dentist, journalist, and novelist. As late as 1851, Delany had expressed opposition to all emigrationism, even emigration to Canada. In 1852, however, his conversion got under way. "I am not in favor of separation of the brotherhood of mankind and would as willingly live among white men as black," he wrote to William Lloyd Garrison in May 1852, "if I had an *equal possession and enjoyment* of privileges; but shall never be reconciled to live among them, subservient to their will—existing by mere *sufferance,* as we, the colored people, do, in this country." "Blind selfishness on the one hand, and deep prejudice on the other," he continued, "will not permit them to understand that we desire the *exercise* and *enjoyment* of these rights, as well as the *name* of their possession. If there were any probability of this, I should be willing to remain in this country, fighting and struggling on, the good fight of faith. But I must admit that I have no hopes in this country—no confidence in the American people—with a *few* excellent exceptions—therefore, I have written as I have done."

Further elaborating his argument in *The Condition and Elevation, Migration, and Destiny of the Colored People,* published at his own expense that same year, he wrote:

The bondsman is disfranchised, and for the most part so are we. He is denied all civil, religious, and social privileges, except such as he gets by mere sufferance, and so are we. They have no part nor lot in the government of the country; neither have we. They are ruled and governed without representation, existing as mere nonentities among the citizens, and excrescences on the body politic—a mere dreg on the community, and so are we. Where then is our political superiority to the enslaved?

Delany argued that in certain periods of a people's history, emigration became a political necessity; that although black Americans loved their country, the society had rejected them; that blacks were too poor and therefore could not compete on an equal basis with white Americans; and that emigration of black Americans would stimulate the reemergence of the race to its former glory.

The appendix to Delany's book contained a now-famous sentence: "We are a nation within a nation; as the Poles in Russia, the Hungarians in Austria; the Welsh, Irish and Scotch in the British dominions." The only remedy for this black nation within a nation was for blacks to leave the United States. "Where shall we go?" Delany asked. In his answer, he rejected Liberia because of its unhealthy climate and its domination by American whites. Canada had a better climate, he reasoned, but was also subject to American influence and would probably soon be annexed by the United States. He concluded that Central America was the logical area to which emigrationists should turn. The climate was excellent; the land was rich; racial discrimination was totally absent; the black population was 20.5 million; there was no possible fear of annexation by the United States, as was the case with Canada, and it was within easy reach for fugitive slaves. Although Delany called for an "expedition to the Eastern Coast of Africa, to make researches for a suitable location on that section of the coast, and for the settlement of colored adventurers from the United States and elsewhere," the focus of his interests remained Central America.

But Delany's book was received so poorly in the black communities that he ordered a halt to its sale. Most blacks had their attention fixed on the forthcoming National Negro Convention scheduled to meet in Rochester in 1853, and after that great gathering, they were excited by the program drawn up by Frederick Douglass and endorsed by the delegates calling for the establishment of national and regional councils by which programs for improved academic education and vocational training would be instituted. Many blacks believed that united action behind the program of the Rochester convention would improve the political and economic position of the Negro and enable blacks to "grapple with the various systems of injustice" more effectively.

THE NATIONAL EMIGRATION CONVENTION OF 1854: THE CALL AND THE CONTROVERSY

The emigrationists were not persuaded by the program of the 1853 convention. On the contrary, convinced of its inadequacy in solving the pressing problems of black Americans, they issued a call shortly after the Rochester gathering for a convention in Cleveland on August 24, 1854, to discuss emigration. The idea of such a convention had been advanced at the 1852 Ohio black state convention in Cincinnati. There, the key issue had been colonization, and the discussion of the reports of the committee on the subject occupied two sessions. Unable to agree, the committee had issued separate majority and minority reports. The former condemned the American Colonization Society as attempting to make slavery more secure by its program of colonization and advanced the idea that a settlement of free blacks somewhere on the American continent rather than in Africa would have a salutory effect on slavery by the example of its development. It also recommended a national meeting to deliberate on emigration and to appoint an agent who would investigate suitable locations where black Americans might settle within the Western Hemisphere. The minority statement emphasized the inexpediency of emigrating anywhere while slavery existed in the United States. It stressed the absence of sufficient means with which black Americans could accomplish such a large enterprise, as well as the fact that no nation had offered to accept them (thereby ignoring Liberia's invitation). Reaffirming America as the land of the black American's birth, the minority report asserted that the duty of black men in the United States was to struggle for citizenship rights where they were and not elsewhere.

After two days of heated discussion on the two reports, the delegates voted. By a majority of thirty-six to nine, they came out against a mass emigration of black Americans even to a destination within the borders of the United States. During the discussion of the reports, however, John Mercer Langston, H. Ford Douglass, and Charles H. Langston, while condemning the American Colonization Society and advocating voluntary emigration to some region on the American continent, had also recommended the calling of a national black convention to consider the subject and to send a delegation to explore the most suitable location for "the establishment of an independent nationality." The emigrationists at the convention then communicated with leaders in other states who shared their convictions. To promote and organize the movement and advance the cause, the emigrationists began to plan for a national convention of those blacks who favored colonization in the Americas.

The call for the Emigration Convention was issued in July 1853 and was signed by eleven blacks from Pittsburgh, nine from Allegheny City, Pennsylvania, four from Philadelphia, and three from New York. It was written by Martin R. Delany, one of the signers from Pittsburgh. The call opened:

Men and Brethren: The time has fully come when we, an oppressed people, should do something effectively, and use those means adequate to the attainment of the great and long desired end—do something to meet the actual demands of the present and prospective necessities of the rising generation of our people in this country. To do this, we must occupy a position of entire *equality,* of *unrestricted* rights, composing in fact an acknowledged necessary part of the *ruling element* of society in which we live. The policy *necessary* to the *preservation* of this *element* must be in *our favor,* if ever we expect the enjoyment, freedom, sovereignty, and equality of rights anywhere. For this purpose, and to this end, then, all colored men in favor of Emigration out of the United States, and *opposed* to the American Colonization scheme of leaving the Western Hemisphere, are requested to meet in *Cleveland, Ohio,* Tuesday, the 24th day of August, 1854, in a great *National Convention,* then and there to consider and decide upon the great and important subject of Emigration from the United States.

The call warned that "no person will be admitted to a seat in the convention, who would introduce the subject of emigration to the Eastern Hemisphere—either to Asia, Africa, or Europe—as our object and determination are to consider our claims to the West Indies, Central and South America, and the Canadas." All persons attending the convention had to bring with them "credentials properly authenticated" or give "verbal assurances" to the Committee on Credentials "of their fidelity to the measures and objects set forth in this call, as the Convention is specifically by and for the friends of Emigration, and none others—and no opposition to them will be entertained."

Assuring all who fought "for the bettering of our condition in this country" that the sponsors were their friends, the call went on to note that the subject of emigration was of "vital importance" but had always "been shunned by all delegated assemblages of our peoples," and that the time had finally come to conduct an "intelligent inquiry" into and the carrying out of plans for emigration to the West Indies and Central and South America,

the majority of which are peopled by our brethren, or those identified with us in race, and what is more *destiny,* on this continent—all stand with open arms and yearning hearts, importuning us in the name of suffering humanity to come—to make common cause, and share one common fate on the continent.

After advising colonizationists "that no favors will be shown to them or their expatriating scheme, as we have no sympathy with the enemies of our race," the call concluded: "We must make an issue, create an event, and establish a position *for ourselves.* It is glorious to think of, but far more glorious to carry out."

Before the Emigration Convention met, the black community witnessed an ideological battle between those favoring emigration and those advocating remaining in the United States. The chief protagonists were James M. Whitfield for the emigrationists and Frederick Douglass for the antiemigrationists. These articles (plus a few by William J. Watkins, another antiemigrationist) were published in a pamphlet entitled *Arguments, Pro and Con, on the Call for a National Emigration Convention to be Held in Cleveland, Ohio, August, 1854, by Frederick Douglass, W. J. Watkins, J. M. Whitfield, with an Introduction by J. Theodore Holly.*

Both Whitfield and Holly emphasized that national Negro conventions were really nothing but "a kind of national organization . . . under the overshadowing influence of their oppressors." Respect and equality for black Americans, they insisted, would come only after they could show "men of their own race occupying a primary position instead of a secondary and inferior one." Emigration was inevitable, and while the first step might be feeble, it was preferable to "crawling again in the dust to the feet of our oppressors." This did not mean that emigration would mean a mass exodus of blacks. Rather, some would emigrate and those who did "should go forth and build up their own institutions, and conduct them in such a manner as to furnish occular proof of their . . . capacity . . . to fulfill ably all the duties of the highest as well as the lowest positions of society."

"We have no sympathy with the call for this convention," Douglass announced in his paper on July 25, 1853. He branded the call "uncalled for, unwise, unfortunate and premature" and said he was convinced that "a majority of our intelligent thinking colored men" would agree with this judgment. To them, as to himself, he went on, the timing indicated an intention to undercut the National Negro Convention, just held in Rochester, which had rejected the idea of settlement outside the United States and had outlined a clear program for black equality. Douglass also condemned the exclusion of all but supporters from the proposed Emigration Convention as "illiberal and cowardly" and charged that its promoters were "afraid to meet the colored people of the United States on the question of emigration." He expressed the hope that in the twelve months before the convention met in Cleveland, no black American would hesitate to purchase various forms of property, including a house and farm, "which looks to permanent residence here," because of "any prospective Canaan which may be spread out in the lofty imaginations of the projectors of this Cleveland Convention." Douglass was convinced that if blacks continued to pressure the white community, they would obtain full civil rights. We are "not aliens," he insisted, but "a component part of the nation." He was convinced, too, that black Americans had no "wish to form a separate nation," and he advised his people to concentrate on achieving equality and not to be distracted by wild plans founded upon "despondency and despair."

Replying to Douglass' criticism of the proposed convention, James M. Whitfield charged that the only good that would come from the Rochester National Negro Convention was that it would

ultimately lead "*intelligent thinking* colored men" to the conclusion which many of us ignorant and thoughtless ones have arrived at intuitively—that is, that colored men can never be fully and fairly respected as the equals of the whites, in this country (or any other) until they are able to show in some part of the world, men of their own race occupying a primary and independent position, instead of a secondary and inferior one, as is now the case everywhere. In short, that they must show a powerful nation in which the black is the *ruling* element capable of maintaining a respectable position among the *great* nations of the earth; and I believe that the reflex influence of such a power with the increased activity that its reaction will excite in the colored people of the country, will be the only thing sufficiently powerful to remove the prejudices which ages of unequal oppression have engendered.

Whitfield then asserted boldly that he and his fellow emigrationists believed that it was "the destiny of the Negro, to develop a higher order of civilization and Christianity than the world has yet seen" and that it was part of "his 'manifest destiny' to possess all the tropical regions of this continent, with the adjacent islands." Since the Negro outnumbered all others in that entire region, the only question to be resolved was, "Shall they exercise the power and influence their numbers entitle them to, and become the ruling political element of the land in which they live? or shall they, as too many of our brethren in this country seem to be willing to do, tamely submit to the usurpation, of white aristocracy, naturally inferior to themselves in physical, moral and mental power, and devote their lives to building up a power whose every energy will be wielded to crush them!" If the Cleveland convention gave a proper response to these questions, as emigrationists hoped it would, its position would be "as much more manly than that assumed by the Rochester Convention, as freedom is superior to slavery, or self-reliance to childish dependence on others."

Whitfield called Douglass' criticism of the convention call because it excluded all but friends of emigration "too ridiculous to deserve serious comment." Would Douglass, he asked, expect Whigs or Democrats to admit their political opponents to their conventions? The friends of emigration were not afraid to meet blacks in a debate on the subject, but they were ready to be accused of cowardice rather than "*prove* themselves fools by admitting the avowed enemies of a measure, as the ones to devise ways and means for promoting its success." They could only hope that those blacks who differed with them would do the emigrationists "the justice to believe that our position in favor of emigration is the result of no rash and hasty speculation, but of full and well matured deliberation." All of the arguments against emigration had already been studied "without at all shaking our confidence in the wisdom and policy of Emigration." Whitfield concluded by repeating the argument that the emigrationists did not anticipate an exodus of the colored people in the United States en masse. Indeed no fact was "better fixed in the world's history" than that "a people who have passed the pastoral state, never can be any possibility be brought to emigrate *en masse.*"

In his concluding remarks, Whitfield had echoed Douglass' famous comment that "individuals emigrate—nations never," and Douglass, in his reply, asked what, then, was the point of calling the Cleveland convention. Was it to achieve individual emigration? But the call was for a national emigration, and "national emigration means emigration of the nation." Thus, the purpose was already condemned beforehand. Yet all this, Douglass declared, was really of no great importance. What was important was the fundamental difference between black emigrationists and antiemigrationists: whether black Americans could ever be equals of the whites in the United States. The emigrationists said never and that "we must, therefore, prepare for our exodus." Douglass disagreed:

We, who are opposed to Emigration, occupy a different position. In waging war with the enemy, and believing in the final triumph of the right, we do not believe that we are the victims of a miserable delusion. A contemplation of the past, and its contrast with the present, inspire us with confidence and hope for the future. We, therefore, intend to work faithfully and fearlessly, and hopefully for our elevation HERE, till victory perches upon our banner.

THE NATIONAL EMIGRATION CONVENTION OF 1854: PROCEEDINGS AND REACTION

Public meetings in Northern black communities—in New Bedford, Boston, Chicago, Elmira, New York, Columbus, Ohio, and other cities—supported Douglass; they urged continuation of the struggle for liberation and equality and condemned the policies enunciated by Whitfield, as well as the unrepresentative nature of the call for the Emigration Convention. But this did not deter 141 elected black men and women from gathering in Cleveland on August 24 to attend the National Emigration Convention. The fact that the call was for a gathering of "Colored Men" and addressed "Men and Brethren" did not prevent the seating of women, and among the women delegates was the convention's second vice-president, Mary E. Bibb, wife of Henry Bibb, of Canada. The delegates came principally from three states: 81 from Allegheny County in western Pennsylvania, 25 from Ohio, and 17 from Michigan. Eleven states were represented, including Louisiana, New York, and Rhode Island. But the fact that most of them came from western Pennsylvania, Delany's own territory, led George Vashon to ask whether it was only a "convention of Pittsburghers" and to quip that it would have been wiser for the delegates to have stayed home and saved transportation costs.

Each delegate was questioned by the five-member Committee on Credentials. Only those who favored emigration and who subscribed to the stated aims were admitted. However, William H. Day, who attended as editor of the *Aliened American,* an Ohio black weekly, was permitted by unanimous vote to remain as a delegate, even though it was known he disagreed with the emigrationists on "minor points."

Despite the care taken to prevent controversy, some conflicts did arise. John Mercer Langston, although not a delegate, had been invited to address the convention, and he attacked its aims and blamed "youthful enthusiasm" for his previous support of emigration. He was answered by H. Ford Douglass (no relation to Frederick Douglass), a delegate from New Orleans, Louisiana, who had escaped from slavery in Virginia, settled in Cleveland some time after his fifteenth birthday, become a barber, educated himself, and emerged as a great orator whose speeches revealed "a remarkable mastery of the Bible, classics, history, drama, literature, and poetry." (H. Ford Douglass is an interesting figure in the emigrationist movement. In his study of emigrationism during the decade before the Civil War, Floyd J. Miller lists nationalist and missionary emigrationists, but Robert L. Harris adds a third category, which he classes "anti-slavery emigrationists," and he cites H. Ford Douglass as an outstanding example of this latter group.) Douglass' reply to Langston at the Cleveland convention is a fine example of antislavery emigrationism. The twenty-three-year-old Douglass rebuked Langston for vacillation and went on to defend emigrationism, observing:

A truth told by a patrician would be no less the truth when told by a plebian. Because Mr. [Frederick] Douglass, Mr. [J. McCune] Smith, or Mr. [J. Mercer] Lansgston tell me that the principles of emigration are destructive to the best interests of the colored people in this country, am I to act the part of a "young robin," and swallow it down without ever looking into the merits of the principle involved? No! Gentlemen, you must show more plausible reason for the faith which is within you.

Douglass then explained that the migration of people in and out of nations was a natural event of world history, and he went on: "Let us then be up and doing.

To stand still is to stagnate and die. . . . Shall we then refuse to follow the light which history teaches, and be doomed, like our 'fathers' to perish in the dark of the wilderness of oppression?'' The answer, he maintained, was ''no.'' The degraded condition of black Americans demanded positive action, which did not permit them to wait indefinitely for the nation to alter its opinion of them. He reminded his audience that those few blacks who became enamored of the country because of their personal advancement forgot the compelling reasons for a ''Colored Nationality.'' He warned them that whites viewed every achievement, contribution, or significant act performed by blacks with contempt, and he insisted that prejudice against blacks mounted almost in direct proportion to their accomplishments.

Blacks, Douglass continued, could never anticipate equality while slavery existed in the United States, and he was not optimistic about its imminent destruction:

You must remember that slavery is not a foreign element in this government, nor is it really antagonistic to the feelings of the American people. On the contrary, it is an element commencing with our medieval existence, receiving the sanction of the early Fathers of the Republic, sustained by their descendants through a period of nearly three centuries, deep and firmly laid in our organization, completely interwoven into the passions and prejudices of the American people. It does not constitute a local or sectional institution . . . but is just as national as the Constitution which gives it an existence.

In Douglass' view, the Constitution was a proslavery document, and black Americans, in effect, sustained bondage by remaining in the nation and submitting to its fundamental document. What is more, he declared, he owed nothing to the country that had inflicted so many wrongs on his people:

I hate this Government without being disloyal, because it has stricken down my manhood, and treated me as a saleable commodity. I can join a foreign enemy and fight against it, without being a traitor, because it treats me as an ALIEN and a STRANGER, and I am free to avow that should such a contingency arise, I should not hesitate to take any advantage in order to procure indemnity for the future.

Douglass rejected the argument that blacks should stay in the United States because it was the land of their birth. Although they had fought the nation's wars and had enriched its soil, black Americans were regarded as inferior to any recently arrived immigrants who had never contributed anything to the nation. Moreover, neither religion nor rhetoric could improve conditions for black Americans. Amalgamation was no solution. It virtually conceded that blacks were inferior, since it required their virtual disappearance as a distinguishable group. Hence, emigration was the only viable alternative for an oppressed people such as black Americans, who were mentally and physically imprisoned by superior numbers. Emigration would provide black Americans with the power essential to control their own political and intellectual future; it would work as a tactical measure to uproot slavery. As for himself, he had made his decision:

When I remember that from Maine to Georgia, from the Atlantic waves to the Pacific shore, I am an alien and an outcast, unprotected by law, proscribed and persecuted by cruel prejudice, I am willing to forget the endearing name of home and country, and as an unwilling exile seek on other shores the freedom which has been denied me in the land of my birth.

While H. Ford Douglass had referred to "Colored Nationality" in his speech, his major emphasis was on emigration as a means of combatting slavery. He made it clear that he refused to conduct himself as an American citizen "while the nation sheltered bondage."

The National Emigration Convention's business committee was chaired by Martin R. Delany, who was primarily responsible for its report, "The Platform: or Declaration of Sentiments of the Cleveland Convention." The document was designed to answer the question, "What is it you black people want?" Black Americans, it declared, had "been looking, hoping and waiting in expectation of realizing the blessings of Civil Liberty," but instead they had "met with disappointment, discouragement and degradation." What they wanted was spelled out in thirty-one resolutions. These affirmed a belief in the "natural equality of the Human Race" and insisted that man was "by nature free" and "cannot be enslaved except by injustice and oppression." Blacks had to possess land to be independent and had to be independent to resist enslavement. Their rights as freemen and to be represented in government, as well as the right to vote, were essential, but these required the removal of restrictive national, state, and local ordinances. Black Americans sought "absolute control of their own political destiny." They demanded "every political right, privilege, and position to which whites are eligible in the United States and we will attain to these or accept nothing." They wanted economic equality, respectable jobs at equal pay, and equal educational opportunities for their children. "No people," the platform stated, "can ever attain to greatness who lost their identity." Therefore, they wanted the relative terms "Negro, African, Black, Colored and Mulatto" to be held in "the same respect and pride as the terms Caucasian, White, Anglo-Saxon and European." In short, black Americans wanted nothing more than those rights, privileges, and respects enjoyed by their white brothers and sisters—and would settle for nothing less. But upon reviewing the discrimination blacks endured in America, the report observed: "The rights of no oppressed people have ever yet been obtained by a voluntary act of justice on the part of the oppressors." Since their rights could not be obtained in the United States, blacks would have to migrate to the West Indies, Central or South America, or Canada.

The delegates, however, regarded Canada warily, for they questioned whether Canada would long remain separated from the United States. On the other hand, many believed that in the West Indies, or in Central or South America, safely separated from their "oppressors," blacks could achieve the equality and other aspirations listed in the platform for themselves and their posterity.

Delany delivered a long report at the convention (later published as the "Political Destiny of the Colored Race on the American Continent"), in which he argued that the central flaw in American life, which made emigration necessary, was not a question of the rich against the poor, or the common people against the higher classes, but a question of white against black—every white person being held superior by legal right to a black or colored person. He denied that blacks were either free men or citizens, contending that his people could not be free unless they constituted a majority of the ruling class:

Were we content to remain as we are, sparsely interspersed among our white fellow-countrymen, we never might be expected to equal them in any honorable or respectable competition for a livelihood. For the reason that, according to the customs and policy of the country, we for ages would be kept in a secondary position, every situation of respectability, honor, profit or trust, either as mechanics, clerks, teachers, jurors, councilmen, or legislators, being filled by white men. Consequently, our energies must become paralyzed or enervated for the want of proper encouragement.

"Where then," he asked, "is our hope of success in this country? Upon what is it based?" Where was the justification for the advice of "our political leaders and acknowledged great men—colored men we mean"—who insisted that "we should be patient, remain where we are; that there is a 'bright prospect and glorious future' before us in this country?" The truth was that American blacks had experienced and would continue to experience an oppression similar to that of Latin American Indians, with whom they could now join in establishing a new nation south of the border.

As he had in the past, Delany associated Africa with the work of the American Colonization Society. He called Liberia a "burlesque on government" and "that miserable hovel of emancipated and superannuated slaves." He forecast that Canada was destined to come into the United States "at no very distant day" and therefore recommended the former as a "temporary asylum" only. Delany strongly favored emigration to Central America, South America, and the West Indies, with Canada as a last resort if it remained independent and if the other places proved to be unfeasible. Later, however, Delany revealed that Africa had not been entirely ignored. In a "secret session," he disclosed, the convention had agreed to hold Africa in reserve.

To implement their program, the emigrationists formed a national board of commissioners, with Delany presiding, with the central office in Pittsburgh and branches in Cincinnati, Detroit, Louisville, New Orleans, Nashville, St. Louis, and Essex County, Canada. The board appointed agents to investigate Haiti, Central America, and even the Niger Valley as possible settlement sites, indicating again that Africa was not completely neglected.

In the official report of their deliberations, the emigrationists claimed that they had "transacted business equal to the duration of a season, and of vastly more importance than any other similar body of colored people ever before assembled in the United States.'' The antiemigrationists ridiculed this pretentious remark, commenting that the two days of proceedings at Cleveland had been reminiscent of the American Colonization Society and that, like that organization, the new one would succeed only in removing the most enterprising free blacks who should stay at home and continue the struggle against slavery. Thus, their only contribution would be to prolong slavery in the United States. The convention's opponents scoffed at the emigrationist argument that slavery would cease when blacks had created a separate nation. As John Goines of Cincinnati put it referring to Haiti: ''What benefit is this to us? Has it abated one jot of prejudice? Has it removed one unholy law?'' He believed that ''a Negro Republic, on the coast of Africa, the Caribee Islands, or South America, will never induce the haughty Saxon to respect us at home, unless it be a power physically as strong as Russia and morally [as strong] as England or France.'' To which Frederick Douglass, who published Goines' letter, said ''Amen,'' and added that the emigration furor was only diverting attention from slavery and indefinitely postponing emancipation.

EMIGRATIONISTS AND ANTIEMIGRATIONISTS

Before the decade of the 1850s was several years old, black American leaders could easily be classed in one of two opposing groups. On one side were the black nationalists, favoring emigration, among whom where Martin R. Delany, Henry Highland Garnet, James M. Whitfield, H. Ford Douglass, James T. Holly, and Alexander Crummell. The other view—the exponents of egalitarianism in American society and opponents of emigration—was represented by Frederick Douglass, William Wells Brown, Charles Lenox Remond, James C. Pennington, William Whipper, James McCune Smith, and George T. Downing. The latter group—the black egalitarians—believed in self-evident truths and unalienable rights, and they conceived of all humanity as brothers and sisters, essentially equal. They preferred not to see themselves as ''darker brothers and sisters,'' denied their rightful place in the family of the American people, but entitled to all the benefits of U.S. citizenship that any white American enjoyed, and more than those exercised by the recently arrived emigrants. They sought to solve racial problems through appeals to the conscience of society at large in addresses, resolutions, editorials, and articles, but they also advocated agitation, both nonviolent and violent (if necessary), to bring the issue of equality to the fore. They considered the race problem one that all Americans must solve and sought to change society to one in which blacks would receive all the rights enjoyed by other Americans. They were confident that they would succeed in this mission. William Wells Brown chose an interesting method of asserting his belief in integrationist possibilities in the United States: ''I have some white neighbors around me in Cambridge; they are not very intellectual; they don't associate with my family; but whenever they shall improve themselves, and bring themselves up by their own intellectual and moral worth, I shall not object to their coming into my society—all things being equal." It was illogical, Brown argued, to assume that white and black could not live in harmony and that expatriation of the blacks was necessary for them to achieve equality. Every emigration scheme would uproot blacks from the soil and the civilization that they had helped to enrich and to the benefits of which they were fully entitled.

James C. Pennington put the case for the antiemigrationists concisely in his lectures to English and Scottish audiences: *"The colored population of the United States have no destiny separate from that of the nation of which they form an integral part."* Not even in Africa, he wrote in a letter to Douglass, could Negroes escape the white man. "The Saxon is there! The real, land-stealing, unscrupulous, over-reaching Saxon is even in Africa, and is pushing his way into the interior."

The emigrationists did not deny the equality of man, but they were opposed to assimilationist doctrines and were especially hostile to the idea of amalgamation. They regarded each race as having its own genius and set of aptitudes, and they believed that each race ought to be preserved as a distinct entity. They had abandoned as hopeless the idea of solving their people's problems through agitation in the white community for equality. Through emigration, they hoped to create a utopia for black people, either on the North American continent or in Africa, a civilization reflective of the Negro's real capacities. Delany argued that the colored race possessed "the highest traits of civilization" among all peoples. He referred to the legendary superiority of Negroes in the artistic and aesthetic areas of life, claiming for black people self-evident excellence in the areas of music and oratory. The Book of Psalms, he declared, foretold that "Ethiopia shall soon stretch her hand unto God," and the emigrationists were determined to carry out the divine decree in its application to African peoples everywhere.

The emigrationists were far from united. Each of the key emigrationist leaders championed a different utopia. Some looked north to Canada as the true land of freedom, others regarded Haiti as the promised haven for black Americans, and still others viewed Africa as the promised land.

9

Black Emigration, 1850–1861
II: Canada, Central America, and
Haiti

CANADIAN EMIGRANTS AND THEIR PROBLEMS

Although some blacks did migrate to the Caribbean Islands and to Africa, the number of emigrants to all other areas combined did not equal that of those who settled in Canada. For decades, slaves had fled from bondage to a new life "under the paws of the British lion," but it was the Fugitive Slave Act of 1850 that provided the greatest stimulus for the black American exodus to Canada. Only weeks after passage of the hated law, the governor-general reported to his home government that Canada was "likely to be flooded with blackies." It proved to be an accurate (if somewhat racist) prediction, as thousands of blacks sought to escape from slave catchers in the United States. They moved mainly to towns and cities, although some lived on farms or established all-black hamlets.

In October 1857 the *National Anti-Slavery Standard* published a report stating: "There is in Canada a remarkable want of accurate statistical information regarding the people of colour. Even their numbers cannot be arrived at with any degree of accuracy. The census of 1852 is in this respect notoriously unreliable, and its inaccuracy is acknowledged by the authorities themselves." It is not possible, therefore, to obtain an accurate picture of the growth of the black population in Canada in the decade after the Fugitive Slave Act of 1850. It appears, however, that in 1851 approximately eight thousand blacks resided in Canada West (the present Ontario Province) and that by 1860, observers estimated that there were sixty thousand Negroes in Canada West.

Some of this influx was stimulated by Henry Bibb and his wife, Mary, who settled in Windsor, where they published *Voice of the Fugitive*. In the journal, they urged black Americans to follow them. Canada, they emphasized, offered the refugees full civil rights. They could vote, join political parties, and serve both on juries and in the Canadian militia. In contrast to conditions south of the border, Canada was indeed utopia.

But many who followed the Bibbs' advice found, upon arriving in Canada, that "utopia" did not provide them with a livelihood. An appeal from fugitives who had "recently arrived in Upper Canada" to "the Friends of Freedom and Humanity in the Free States of the United States of America," dated January 1851, pointed out:

We found your land turned into hunting grounds for the slavecatchers. The man-stealer was on our track. He came not like a thief in the night, shrouded in darkness, with stealthy step, but in the broad glare of day, armed with the law, and assisted by the physical force of a mighty nation.

Therefore, we have fled from the free States of the North to the dominion of Her Britannic Majesty, among a people of our kindred and language; and we have found them hospitable and generous, according to their means. We are numerous, and many of us destitute, with our little families. Winter is here; we cannot obtain labor without wandering far into the interior; our means are exhausted.

We appeal to you for some little assistance in money, clothing or provisions, to assist us during an inclement winter, and to assist us to provide, in some measure, for the education of our children, and to build a few chapels, in suitable places, for the propagation of the religion of Jesus among our people.

This was but one of many such appeals during the next few years. In the fall of 1854, J. J. Rice wrote to the *Albany* (New York) *Argus* asking for financial aid for the "starving fugitive slaves in Canada." Abolitionists, he complained, too often preferred mass conventions, political actions, and Underground Railroad activities "to caring for the passengers after they reach their uncomfortable destination."

THE REFUGEE HOME SOCIETY

Henry and Mary Bibb, too, began to show concern for the economic conditions of the many black newcomers from the United States. To help meet this problem, friends of the fugitives organized the Refugee Home Society in 1851 as a black settlement in Canada. The society placed the management of the enterprise in the hands of the Bibbs and David Hotchkiss, a white who privately disliked blacks. The society purchased land near Windsor and authorized its agents to administer its distribution. Each refugee family was to have twenty-five acres. If the family occupied, cleared, and cultivated the land during the first three years, they received the first five acres free. The remaining twenty acres were to be purchased at $2 per acre—the original cost to the society—in nine annual installments. The only limitation to the contract was that all twenty-five acres must remain with the original refugee, or his legal heir, for fifteen years.

Forty lots were settled in Refugee Home, and a church and a school were constructed. The following year, Mrs. Laura S. Haviland became the first teacher. Unfortunately, controversy over the management of the Refugee Home developed just a year after it opened. Some observers believed that more blacks had not settled there because of the "degrading serfdom under the Refugees Home Society." Agents of the society solicited aid from friends who sent boxes of clothing, blankets, and other provisions to Bibb. It was charged that these goods were stored in Bibb's stable instead of being distributed to needy blacks. Then when Bibb refused to allow the manufacture and sale of alcoholic beverages in the community, some settlers rebelled. Refugee Home suffered from too much paternalism and too many arbitrary rules to attract a large number of settlers. Mary Bibb died in 1854, and even before the Civil War began, the Refugee Home settlement had nearly disintegrated.

THE BUXTON COLONY

To the east, in the region north of Lake Erie and south of Lake Huron, several black communities flourished briefly. One of the most successful was Elgin, located at Buxton and named in honor of the governor-general of Canada (1849–1854). Reverend William King, a Presbyterian minister and Louisiana slave owner, was a most unusual founder of a black community in Canada. King had been born in Ulster, North Ireland, studied for the Presbyterian ministry in Scotland, emigrated to America, and married into a slaveowning Louisiana family. His wife died, and King, having inherited her property, found himself a slaveowner. Since both he and his church were opposed to slavery, King secretly arranged to emancipate his fifteen slaves, and several years later he moved them to Canada in 1849. There, with the support of the Presbyterian church and Lord Elgin's government, King founded the Buxton Mission and Elgin Association colony.

King's petition for lands for a black colony aroused resentment among an organized, racist white minority in nearby Chatham. Indeed, when King came to Chatham in August 1849, threats were made on his life, and a group of armed black men organized a constant bodyguard to protect him. "The coloured people," King wrote later, "were determined to fight if I should be attacked." As a result of this black resistance, the Elgin Association's boundaries were laid out and its land divided into fifty-acre "concessions."

Starting with a nucleus of his own ex-slaves, King enlisted 130 black families who settled in the Elgin (or Buxton) colony within the first three years, many of them fugitive American slaves. A school, church, minister's home, store, hotel, pearl ash factory, and blacksmith's shop were among the colony's first buildings. Buxton soon became one of the most successful of the black Canadian settlements. When Frederick Douglass visited Buxton in August 1854, he cited it as "one of the most striking, convincing and gratifying" proofs that the black man "can live, and live well, without a master and can be industrious without the presence of the blood-letting lash to urge him on to toil." Douglass reminded his readers that "four years and a few months" earlier the forest had been the only "dwelling" in the Buxton area. "How different now," he observed. There were now "SEVEN HUNDRED SOULS" in the settlements, who had "built themselves snug cottages." There were fields of corn, grass, and grain, and the area presented "an appearance of advancement equal to parts of our Western States settled a dozen years ago." In one direction, one might see "the colored farmer behind his plough—in another leveling the forest—in another erecting his cottage—in another making brick—and in another threshing his grain. . . . The people have thrown off the bowed look of slaves, and menials. They bear themselves like free men and women."

Although King's organizational ability was important to Buxton's success, the day-to-day operation of the colony was largely in the hands of its black residents, and a black court of arbitration gradually emerged as the community's controlling body. After a visit in 1856, Benjamin Drew reported that King was working out his belief in "the natural powers, capacity and capabilities of the African race" by placing the refugees "in circumstances where they may learn self-reliance, and maintain a perfect independence of aid: Trusting, under God, in their own right arm."

The colony required all heads of families to read and write and furnished night classes in the settlement's fine school. By 1864, illiteracy had been wiped out.

When William C. Nell and William H. Day visited Buxton in 1858, the settlement covered eighteen square miles of woodlands spotted with clearings where "neat cabins and smiling garden patches" were observed. Some residents had contracted to build brick cottages. Most inhabitants farmed on the fourteen hundred acres of cleared and fenced land. A majority had arrived in Buxton without capital, purchasing their homesteads from the Elgin Association on ten-year mortgages, similar to those of the Refugee Home Society. (One who had done so was William Parker, the hero of the Christiana resistance to the Fugitive Slave Act of 1850.) Much of the land had been abandoned by whites who had declared it "unproductive," but Nell, observing corn, wheat, oats, potatoes, buckwheat, and other crops, believed that no settler could lose his land by an inability to pay off the indebtedness.

Elginites were proud of their school and the fact that white children from Buxton attended because of its superiority. This, however, had not always been the case. On the contrary, when William King announced in April 1850 that the school would begin enrolling pupils of all colors, Chatham whites threatened to prevent the opening by force if necessary. But when a group of armed blacks ringed the new log school in the forest, fourteen black children and two whites enrolled without incident.

The Buxton school soon became famous for its excellence. Although education in Canada was generally segregated and color prejudice was strong, white people began to transfer their children to the black colony's school. The regular district school was soon forced to close down for lack of pupils. As time went on, the fame of the Buxton school spread, and applicants for admission came from all over Canada West, and even the United States. Two of the Buxton graduates who went on to Trinity College won the highest honors in the history of their institution up to that time. Among the graduates of the Buxton school were James T. Rapier, later the first black congressman from Alabama, and Thomas W. Stringer, a black leader of the Mississippi Constitutional Convention of 1868.

THE DAWN SETTLEMENT

Education was also a major factor in the success of Dawn, a black settlement in Dresden, Ontario. Dawn Industrial Institute, a grammar school, was established in 1842, and a black community grew around it. By 1852, an estimated three thousand to four thousand blacks lived at Dawn. In the summer of 1853, William Whipper, Pennsylvania's wealthy black moral reformer who had helped many fugitives escape to Canada, visited Dresden and was so impressed by the prospects that he purchased land on the Sydenham River. A year later, he completed construction of a substantial warehouse and other buildings in the village of Dresden. A strong opponent of emigration earlier in his career, Whipper had decided to move permanently to Canada in 1861, but the outbreak of the Civil War—with its promise of freedom—caused him to abandon his plan.

Benjamin Drew, who had visited Buxton, also spent time at Dawn and reported that the blacks at Dresden were generally prosperous farmers and mechanics, such as shoemakers and blacksmiths. One-third of the adult settlers possessed land that was either wholly or partly paid for. By 1861, however, the Dawn community suffered decay because of inner disputes, neglect, and mismanagement.

THE BLACK EXPERIENCE IN CANADA

Most of the Canadian black cooperative communities proved to be short-lived. William H. Pease and Jane H. Pease, who have studied them in detail in *Black Utopia: Negro Communal Experiments in America,* attribute the eventual collapse of the communities to inadequate direction and financial support, the persistence of white hostility, the middle-class nature of the experiments, and the indifference of most abolitionists who, the authors insist, indulged in moralizing cant when they should have been helping the free blacks adjust to life in a white society. But in their writing, Pease and Pease tend to slight the persistent efforts of many white abolitionists to combat racism in the North and Canada as well as slavery in the South, and they themselves admit that the failure of the communitarians to win support of the white society in which they operated was due to the strength of white racism rather than to abolitionist indifference.

Although black communities in Canada prospered briefly, most emigrants moved to Canadian towns and cities predominantly populated by whites. By 1858, Chatham's large, active black population occupied several entire streets.

They worked in most of the mechanical trades and manual labor occupations. James Madison Bell gained local recognition as a master builder and contractor during the 1850s. By 1861, one-third of Chatham's six thousand residents were black, and many considered the town their capital in Canada. It was the site of the Colored National Emigration Convention in 1858. That same year, John Brown was in Chatham, formulating his initial plans for the attack on Harpers Ferry.

Other urban areas had large black communities. Toronto, in 1861, was home to over a thousand fugitives who worked as domestics, bricklayers, blacksmiths, carpenters, shoemakers, and painters. Six Toronto blacks ran grocery stores, and a black physician, A. T. Augusta, operated a medical clinic. There were four black churches in Toronto—two Methodist and two Baptist—and other blacks attended the Church of England, while a few were Congregationalists or Catholics. Essex, Amherstburg, Port Stanley, Port Burwell, St. Catherines, Hamilton, Kingston, and Montreal had sizable black populations, while on the Pacific Coast, the number of blacks in Victoria and other towns in British Columbia was growing.

The *Provincial Freeman,* established by Samuel Ringgold Ward and edited by the remarkable Mary Ann Shadd Cary, was published first in Toronto, and after June 30, 1855, in Chatham, Ontario. The paper promulgated both antislavery and emigrationist principles. In 1856, H. Ford Douglass, then living in Chicago, became one of its proprietors, since its principles were in keeping with his views as an antislavery emigrationist. Convinced that Canada was the best place from which black people could struggle to end slavery in the United States, Douglass moved from Chicago to Chatham, from which he sent reports to his former associates arguing that the success of slaves who had become lawyers, doctors, merchants, and mechanics in Canada would have a positive influence on weakening slavery in the United States.

Douglass was so taken with Canada as a place where blacks could really enjoy freedom that he recommended that black Canadians become as thoroughly British as possible. He condemned separate organizations as relics of the United States and unsuited for a country like Canada, where blacks enjoyed equality. To support segregation in Canada, he argued, would only foster a caste system similar to that which black people had left behind when they emigrated. He even went so far as to urge Canadian blacks to ignore reform parties that might have been acceptable in the United States but that he felt were not needed in Canada. Canadian blacks, he maintained, should place the honor and dignity of Britain, their protector, above every other consideration.

While he did not go as far as H. Ford Douglass, William Parker, who fled to Canada after the resistance at Christiana, was optimistic about the future prospects for blacks in the country. "When I first settled in Buxton," he wrote, "the white settlers in the vicinity were much opposed to colored people. Their prejudices were very strong; but the spread of intelligence and religion in the community has wrought a great change in them. Prejudice is fast being uprooted;

indeed, they do not appear like the same people that they were. In a short time, I hope that foul spirit will depart entirely.''

Instead just the opposite took place. Throughout the 1850s, antiblack sentiment mounted in intensity in British North America. "This hydra-headed prejudice," Miflin Wistar, who had been among the first to emigrate from San Francisco to Victoria, British Columbia, reported sadly, "has pursued us to this country; and attempts to assert its supremacy through every ramification of society."

Soon enough, Canadian cities had their "black halls," "Negro quarters," and "darky lanes," indicating racial segregation. Although blacks competed with few white Canadian workers, doing mostly the type of work in urban areas that whites avoided or working on the railroads or farms, they met with prejudice from white Canadians. "I think colorphobia can hardly be worse in the Northern States than it is in this province," George Sumter, Jr., wrote from Windsor to the *Liberator* in August 1856. Sumter complained that he seldom found anyone "with humanity enough to do colored people justice." He felt that were it not for fear, many fugitives would have returned to the United States. "Niggers must be kept down" was a sentiment Sumter often heard. "Poverty of intellect and debasement of morals," he explained, "drive the poor, hard-up wretches to fall back on their white skins . . . as a ground for giving themselves airs of superiority." When Sumter attempted to get a permit from the reeve (the village mayor) and council to speak on "colorphobia," it was denied because "the subject ought not to be agitated; the colored people had privileges now, and almost too many." Nevertheless, Sumter made the speech and announced he would deliver another the following week. Local officials tried to persuade him not to do so, warning that he would have to take the consequences if trouble developed. The second speech was interrupted, first by the civil authorities and then by a mob that threw Sumter headlong from the platform.

When blacks emigrated north, they often looked forward to the educational opportunities provided by Canadian law. They soon learned that a gap existed between law and practice. In January 1846, Isaac J. Rice, a white missionary, wrote to Egerton Ryerson, the superintendent of schools for Canada West, on behalf of the Negro rate payers of the community. The local school trustees, he noted, had declared that rather than send their children "to school with niggers they will cut their children's heads off and throw them into the road side ditch." Despite many entreaties, the blacks could not gain admittance to the schools.

The situation grew worse as anti-Negro prejudice mounted in the 1850s. In the two provinces in which blacks were most numerous—Nova Scotia and Ontario—they were progressively restricted from access to the public schools as both provinces introduced forms of segregated school systems. While some blacks supported separate schools, the majority paid taxes for common schools and wanted access to them for their children, and they reminded the government that they had left the United States to escape from just such segregated practices.

After a study of educational conditions in Canada West, Samuel Gridley Howe of the Freedman's Inquiry Commission reported: "Notwithstanding the growing prejudice against blacks, the authorities evidently mean to deal justly by them in regard to instruction; and even those who advocate separate schools, promise that they will be equal to white schools." But as in the United States, the Negro schools lacked competent teachers; many schools met for only three months in the year or were closed. Most had no library of any kind. In Windsor, one Negro petitioner pointed out, a coop, sixteen feet by twenty-four feet, was used for thirty-five black pupils, while the white school remained unfilled. In some districts, school taxes were collected from Negro residents to support the common school from which their children were barred, even though this practice was illegal.

Nor was prejudice confined to education. A Branton grand jury in 1858 recommended the "separation of blacks and whites in jail." Many whites at Colchester inaugurated measures to drive out black residents and discourage further emigration. An Anderson township grand jury asked in 1859 that something be done about the blacks because, in the jury's opinion, "nine-tenths of the crimes committed in the county of Essex . . . are so committed by the colored people," a charge that had a familiar ring to emigrants from the United States. In Victoria, Reverend William F. Clarke, a Canadian-born Congregationalist and an outspoken enemy of slavery and champion of integration, aroused the fury of whites in his congregation because he told them that he would have nothing to do with tolerating a "negro corner," that the blacks were "as much sons of God as the whites," and that they had a perfect right "to seek those equal religious privileges to which they are by natural right and gospel grant, entitled." As a result, his congregation became mostly black, and in 1859, he was driven from his pulpit by the prejudiced whites, aided by an assistant pastor.

Even Samuel Gridley Howe changed his opinion of the Canadian attitude toward blacks, In an analysis of the position of the Negro in Canada, Howe wrote:

The Canadians constantly boast that their laws know no difference of color; that they make blacks eligible to offices, and protect all their rights; and the refugees constantly admit that it is so. The very frequency of the assertion and of the admission, proves that it is not considered a matter of course that simple justice should be done. People do not boast that the law protects white men.

The truth of the matter seems to be that, as long as the colored people form a very small proportion of the population, and are dependent, they receive protection and favors; but when they increase, and compete with the labouring class for a living; and especially when they begin to aspire to social equality, they cease to be "interesting negroes," and become "niggers."

H. Ford Douglass lived in Canada for only two years, returning to Chicago in late 1858, but it was long enough for him to realize how naively he had viewed the status of black Canadians. In 1855, William H. Day, formerly the publisher of the *Aliened American,* emigrated from Ohio to Canada, and for three years, he struggled against prejudice. He learned quickly that despite Canada's more liberal political practices, British North America was no utopia for blacks, and that socially and economically, life in Canada could be just as burdensome as was life in Ohio. In 1858, Day returned to Ohio to resume the struggle against slavery and for equality.

Day was not the only black to return to Ohio from Canada. The *Congregationalist* of September 23, 1857, reported: "The *Cleveland Plaindealer* says that the steamer *Telegraph* brings back from Canada, on every trip, families of negroes, who have formerly fled to the Provinces from the States."

Despite the increasing restrictions imposed on them, many Canadian blacks still considered themselves well off in Canada as compared with the status of their brothers and sisters in the United States. When J. D. Harris visited Chatham in October 1859 to promote Jamaican emigration, he met strong opposition. A resolution declaring loyalty to the crown as British subjects read in part:

We indignantly repudiate and denounce the scheme of endeavoring to effect a dislodgement of our people here, as inhuman, impolite and deceptive in the extreme and that in view of the course pursued, we regard the labor of the white yanke [*sic*] Mr. Stanley, engaged in the trick, as an ally and a confederate of those who put a price on human blood and we thus regard Mr. J. D. Harris, who has proved himself a willing tool in the matter, as a deceptive Judas, ready to betray his brothers for 30 pieces of silver.

But black emigrationists in the United States no longer shared this enthusiasm for Canada as a haven for the oppressed Negro. To be sure, in 1856, the National Emigration Convention met again in Cleveland and adopted the *Provincial Freeman,* issued in Canada, as its official organ, indicating that the dominant view was that Canada was the best source for black emigration. But after 1856, the emigration movement no longer held Canada to be the best place for black people to settle. The movement then split into two camps: one headed by Delany, which favored Africa, and the other led by James T. Holly, which preferred Haiti.

BLAIR'S CENTRAL AMERICAN PROJECT

Haiti was not the only area outside of Canada in the Western Hemisphere to be given consideration. The British government, having been assured that the United States had no objection, promoted the emigration of black Americans to the British West Indies. Britain sent agents to recruit both planters with capital and experience, and black laborers. As an inducement, the British offered to pay transportation costs. Reverend Josiah Henson and Reverend John Scoble were reported to be British agents promoting this movement, and antiemigration abolitionists charged that some of the contracts Scoble got blacks to sign bound them into slavelike conditions. It turned out that contracts between laborers who lacked funds for transportation and the British colonial governments did include terms under which their working conditions were not too far removed from slavery.

But J. Wesley Harrison, a middle-aged black who emigrated to Jamaica in 1851, returned to the United States two years later to deny these charges and to assert that he had improved his condition by emigrating to the island. Harrison was authorized to sell land in Jamaica at one dollar per acre, and interested blacks were invited to contact him at Reverend J.W.C. Pennington's church in New York City. The fact that Pennington, who up to that time was both a foe of emigration and one of America's respected black leaders, was connected with Harrison's efforts to persuade blacks to emigrate to Jamaica should have been a powerful stimulus to success. Few blacks, however, seemed to have responded.

Meanwhile sentiment was growing for emigration to Central America, stimulated by Francis P. Blair of Missouri and his two sons, Frank and Montgomery. The Blairs proposed that the United States sponsor the settlement of colonies of blacks in Central America. This was to be achieved either by the acquisition of land in Central America, which would then be distributed to blacks from the United States, or through the cooperation of the local governments. It was hoped that under the protection of the government of the United States, the initial colony would prove so successful that new ones would quickly follow. As slaves were freed in the Southern states, they would be transported to the black colonies, and "eventually the vast bulk of the Negro population in the United States would be removed."

To the Blairs, colonization was an essential part of a larger plan to destroy slavery within the Southern states and, at the same time, solve the race problem in the entire country by removing the blacks and leaving only a white population in the United States. In addition, the Negroes who emigrated to Central America would be "the black agents of the America Empire, they would help establish the commercial and political hegemony of the United States in Central America." The Blairs assured businessmen that the establishment of Negro colonies in Central America would ensure U.S. dominance in the area over Great Britain.

On January 14, 1858, in a speech before Congress, Frank P. Blair, Jr., a congressman from Missouri, presented the Blair colonization plan for free blacks to emigrate to Central America, where they would form colonies dependent on the U.S. government, which would assist the settlers in exploiting the area's riches. As a result of this joint venture of the U.S. government and emigrating Negroes, Blair declared, free blacks would realize happy and comfortable lives, which they could not expect to achieve in the United States because of the fundamental incompatibility of blacks in a white society. Blair contended that African colonization had failed and slaveholders were reluctant to manumit their slaves because there was no place for them to settle since many of the Northern states would not admit them. He argued that the federal government's policy of purchasing Indian lands and removing the Indians to Western reservations was sufficient precedent for acquiring territory and colonizing manumitted slaves and free blacks in Central America. Thus, at one stroke, the plan would eliminate the slaveowner's fear of the presence of the free Negro, thereby stimulating manumission, and at the same time would make the free black the principal factor in civilizing Central America and developing its commerce with the United States. In short, the result would be to "propagate freedom in the American tropics by colonizing free Negroes there."

In a lecture before the Boston Mercantile Association, Blair suggested Honduras as the ideal place for settlement because it would also help the United States in its rivalry with Great Britain by establishing control over trade in Central America. White Americans could not settle in that region, Blair argued, because of its climate, but blacks would decidedly prosper. In a statement foreshadowing the white man's burden theory of imperialism, Blair declared: "It is the true mission of a superior and enlightened race to protect and establish with well-founded institutions the feeble races within reach of its influence." He assured his audience that black Americans would easily dominate Honduras' inhabitants because of the intelligence, industry, and progressive spirit that they had developed from their contact with white Americans.

After Blair had established the Central American Land Company to promote his scheme, a number of black emigrationists expressed interest in the project. James T. Holly, James M. Whitfield, J. D. Harris, and Alfred V. Thompson were all eager to support Blair if funds were forthcoming. Delany expressed some interest, although he was hesitant to accept money from whites, and H. Ford Douglass became an agent of the Central American Land Company. Douglass was clearly impressed by Blair's argument that the emigration of manumitted slaves to Central America would induce slaveowners to resume freeing individual bondspeople.

But nothing came of Blair's vision. The U.S. minister in Honduras heard of the Missouri congressman's scheme and conveyed the information to the government of Guatemala, which controlled the region embracing Honduras. The Guatemalan government immediately denounced Blair's plan and decreed its failure by simultaneously announcing that it would welcome only white immigrants.

HAITIAN EMIGRATION

This left Haiti, which clearly would not follow Guatemala's lead in prohibiting black immigrants. On the contrary, when Reverend James Theodore Holly, a former shoemaker who became a Connecticut clergyman, conversed with Haitian officials in the summer of 1855, he received assurance that prospective black emigrants would be welcomed. On his return to the United States that fall, Holly delivered a lecture to black audiences entitled, "The Negro Race, Self-Government and the Haitian Revolution." He spoke in a number of states, including

Ohio, Michigan, New York, and Illinois, as well as Canada. In 1857, the lecture was published by the Africa-American Printing Company of New Haven, Connecticut, an organization formed to publish Negro literature, especially writings and speeches favoring emigration. Holly's lecture dealt at some length with the history of Haiti as a vindication of the ability of the Negro people to establish self-government and achieve progress, and he closed with a fervent appeal for black Americans to leave the United States and move to Haiti rather than to Africa. In so doing, they would offer their skills to a less-developed people, but a people with whom they would find easy assimilation. Holly saw the emigration of black Americans necessary ''for the political enfranchisement of the colored people of the United States'' but also as the only logical source from which Haiti could draw in its effort to improve. He was confident, moreover, that the emergence of Haiti as a powerful Negro nation would stop the African slave trade and portend the end of slavery itself. From Haiti, it was hoped, ''a reflex influence will irradiate, not only to uproot American slavery, but also to overthrow African slavery and the slave-trade throughout the world.'' But this was only the beginning of what would be accomplished:

If one powerful and civilized Negro sovereignty can be developed to the summit of national grandeur in the West Indies, where the keys to the commerce of both hemispheres can be held, this fact will solve all questions respecting the Negro, whether they be those of slavery, prejudice or proscription, and wheresoever on the face of the globe such questions shall present themselves for a satisfactory solution.

A concentration and combination of the Negro race of the Western Hemisphere in Haiti, can produce just such a national development. The duty to do so is therefore incumbent on them. And the responsibility of leading off in this gigantic enterprise Providence seems to have made our peculiar task by the eligibility of our situation in this country as a point for gaining an easy access to the island. Then let us boldly enlist in this high pathway of duty, while the watchwords that shall cheer and inspire us in our noble and glorious undertaking shall be the soul-stirring anthem of God and Humanity.

The Haitian emigration movement received a strong impetus in 1858 when the government of Haiti renewed its official invitation to black Americans and also sent two commissioners to the United States to further black sentiment for emigration to the island republic. They lectured to black audiences on tbe inducements their country offered to blacks but made it clear that the Haitian government sought only ''farmers and agricultural laborers or men of established character who designed to become active in agriculture.'' Several hundred emigrants were recruited, and some wrote back later to their former associates in the United States praising their way of life in Haiti. R. Stephen Baker, a Cincinnati black who settled in Haiti, wrote: ''So long as you continue to occupy boot-black and waiters' positions, so long will all whites disrespect, decide and trample upon you.'' He concluded his letter: ''Among men there should be no choice between liberty and political rights and an imaginary liberty without the right of suffrage.'' Although Baker's letter was widely published, it is difficult to determine if it stimulated further emigration to Haiti.

In 1859 and 1860, James Redpath, a white, British-born antislavery radical, visited Haiti three times as a reporter for the *New York Tribune.* He came away from the island deeply impressed by its beauty, fertility, and climate. A revolution in 1859 had brought to power in Haiti a new president, Fabre Geffard. Eager to develop the country's natural and human resources, Geffard approached Redpath and sought to convey to him a vision of a powerful, prosperous Haiti that would exhibit the capacity and genius of the Negro race to a skeptical world.

Redpath returned to Boston with a commission as general agent of the Haytian Bureau of Emigration. With an initial grant of $20,000 from the Haitian government, he opened a central office in Boston in the fall of 1860 and began to recruit agents and establish branch offices in several Northern cities. He published *Guide to Hayti* (which went through three editions), which described in glowing terms the physical and political characteristics of the island and urged black Americans to emigrate there for a new and better life. Haiti, he assured them, was the only country in the Western Hemisphere ''where the Black and the man of color are the undisputed lords . . . where neither laws, nor prejudices, nor historical memories press cruelly on persons of African descent; where the people whom America degrades and drives from her are rulers, judges, and generals . . . authors, artists, and legislators.''

Redpath pointed to the racist environment in the United States as an overwhelming impediment to black development and argued that success in Haiti could have the twofold effect of ''demonstrating the capacity of the race for self-government'' and ''of surrounding the Southern States with a cordon of free labor, within which, like a scorpion girded by fire, Slavery must inevitably die.''

Redpath informed prospective emigrants that the Haitian government would pay $15 apiece toward their passenger expenses and sell them land at low prices and low-term credits when they arrived. They would be exempt from military service and eligible for citizenship after one year. Complete religious freedom for all immigrants was guaranteed.

Redpath recruited several prominent blacks as agents and organizers for his bureau: James T. Holly (who published a series of articles in the *Anglo-American Magazine* promoting Haitian emigration), Henry Highland Garnet, William Wells Brown, H. Ford Douglass, and J. B. Smith, among others. He established an emigrationist paper, the *Pine and Palm,* in May 1861, which was published in both Boston and New York. The New York editor was George Lawrence, a black publicist. Redpath's black allies, led by Holly, gave scores of speeches and published dozens of letters on behalf of the emigration movement, and the *Weekly Anglo-African* devoted frequent editorials to the subject. On April 13, 1861, the black journal declared:

We can make of Hayti the nucleus of a power that shall be to the black, what England has been to the white race, the hope of progress and the guarantee of a prominent place. Look at her position; she is the centre of a circle in whose plane lie Cuba, Central America, and the Southern Slave states. From that centre, let the fire of Freedom radiate until it shall enkindle, in the whole of that vast area, the sacred flame of Liberty upon the altar of every black man's heart, and you effect at once the abolition of slavery and the regeneration of our race.

It was the sacred duty of black Americans to join in this divine missionary work by emigrating to Haiti.

In March 1861, H. Ford Douglass became an agent for Redpath's Haitian Bureau and a contributor to the *Pine and Palm*. As agent for the northwestern states, Douglass' duties were to invite individuals of African and Indian ancestry to migrate to Haiti, to explain the country's attractions, to describe the facilities offered by the Haitian government, and to distribute Redpath's *Guide to Hayti*. H. Ford Douglass also used the lecture platform to promote Haitian emigration. Indeed, following a lecture tour in Illinois together with H. Ford Douglass, Frederick Douglass reported that Chicago blacks were "in a ferment" about going to Haiti and that this was largely due to the efforts of his namesake.

Frederick Douglass himself briefly flirted with the idea of promoting Haitian emigration. He declared at the end of 1860:

While we have never favored any plan of emigration, and have never been willing to concede that this is a doomed country, and that we are a doomed race in it, we can raise no objection to the present movement toward Hayti. . . . If we go anywhere, let us go to Hayti. Let us go where we are still within hearing distance of the wails of our brothers and sisters in bonds. Let us not go to Africa, where those who hate and enslave us want us to go; but let us go to Hayti, where our oppressors do not want us to go, and where our influence and example can still be of service to those whose tears will find their way to us by the waters of the Gulf washing our shores.

In January 1861, Douglass published a long editorial reviewing the Negro's interest in Haiti over the preceding thirty years. For Douglass, the combination of favorable conditions in Haiti, increasing proscription at home, and other political considerations were sufficient to lead him to support the Haitian venture, especially since he realized that the black American's livelihood would be even further curtailed by the increasing influx of European immigrants who were taking over the jobs that he had once monopolized. Douglass was convinced that the inducements offered his people in the United States were now "few, feeble, and uncertain."

Douglass elaborated his new position on emigration in an answer to three questions posed to him by a black correspondent from Pottsville, Pennsylvania, and published in *Douglass' Monthly* of March 1861. The writer asked if Douglass was "positively in favor of the emigration of our people to Hayti," if he was "fully satisfied with the truthfulness of the representations of the Haytian Government, etc., as set forth by Mr. James Redpath's 'Guide to Hayti,' " and if he expected "to emigrate there, at any time." In his reply, Douglass indicated he opposed emigration en masse but contended that people could emigrate to better their moral or physical condition. Those who were well established and satisfied in the United States should not give up their dreams for Haiti: "We are far from calling upon any part of our people to emigrate, for public reasons, such as inability to live among white people or for the charms of a 'Colored Nationality.' The things for which men should emigrate are food, clothing, property, education, material prosperity, and he who has these where he is, had better stay where he is, and exert the power which they give him to overcome whatever of social or political oppression which may surround him." He was fully satisfied with the truthfulness of Redpath's representations of the Haitian government and did not personally intend to leave: "We have personal and peculiar reasons for staying just where we are. The same work to which we have given the first years of our manhood, require our last, and shall have them." However, he would rejoice in the success of people who sought homes in Haiti, and if ever able to do so, he was "resolved to visit them and see how they get along in their new homes."

Douglass' support of Haitian emigration drew criticism from some of his former allies in the struggle against emigration. A Philadelphia Negro declared that it was time that Douglass understood that "the idea of a great nationality in Hayti is all humbug; let us build up a nationality for ourselves here." The Progressive Library Association, a black society in Chicago, voiced the opinion that even if Douglass supported it, its members would not favor Haitian emigration but would continue to oppose all forms of expatriation, whether emigration or colonization. On the other hand, the Haytian Emigration Society of Toledo, Ohio, praised Douglass for his changed position and adopted the following resolutions:

Whereas, It is common for man, wherever placed, on the habitable globe, when deprived of his God-given rights, to devise so means to better his condition. . . .

Resolved, That we view in Hayti the chief cornerstone of an Ethiopic empire, and that we see in her the elements of a future that are nowhere to be found adjacent to the American continent.

Resolved, That we appeal to the blacks and men of color to form this nucleus around the chief cornerstone in our political edifice of the Antilles, and ere long from that radiating point the sable arm of Africa will belt the tropical regions of the globe.

The *New York Weekly Anglo-African,* which printed this resolution, also carried an account by its Philadelphia correspondent of a debate at the Banneker Institute, the literary and educational establishment for black youths, on the question: "Should the colored people emigrate to Hayti?" Alfred M. Green, a militant young black Philadelphian, spoke out in favor of Haitian emigration, "first, because it is calculated to elevate the colored people of both countries; secondly, because Hayti offers advantages which no other country offers at the present time," and finally, because a strong government in Haiti would help check the southward spread of slavery from the Southern states of the United States. Green advised black Americans to assist in helping "to build up a strong government in Hayti." J. Wesley Simpson, another black Philadelphian, also favored emigration to Haiti, arguing: "We can never obtain full enfranchisement in this country, and if you would preserve your race intact, go to Hayti and escape being absorbed in the American element. It can be proven by statistics that we can arrive at benefits sooner in Hayti, than in this country. Our educated youths have no avenues in which to develop their geniuses. If they go to Hayti, the field is open to them."

The opponents of Haitian emigration insisted that to speak of a mass migration was to indulge in illusions. "No such numbers as ours ever left this country; we are fixtures here." It would be wrong to emigrate when prospects for change for the better were emerging. "Not many years hence all our disabilities will be removed," J. C. Bowers predicted, "and we will have no need of going to Hayti." A detailed argument against Haitian emigration came from William P. Powell, a black visitor from New York and director of the Colored Seamen's Home in that city. Powell "took the floor and spoke at length in opposition to emigration." He suggested that advocates of emigration should look around in Philadelphia "and see the improvements that have been made among the colored people." He had once lived briefly in Philadelphia himself, he responded, and at that time there were few blacks in the city who could read or write, while now there were Negroes who were even Latin and Greek scholars. Emigration meant the abandonment of "4,000,000 of your brethren in bonds." He had emigrated to England a few years before and had enjoyed greater freedom under the British government than he knew in the United States, but he had returned to continue the struggle to end slavery, "to spend the remainder of my days with my friends," and to continue his work on behalf of free black seamen in New York City. Such work, he insisted, had to be continued in the United States rather than abandoning it by emigration to Haiti. There was no vote at the end by the audience, but the report indicated that "the debate was received . . . with much approbation and each speaker was greeted with applause."

Early in April 1861, Frederick Douglass made plans to visit Haiti so that he could investigate conditions for himself and report back to his people in the United States. He had accepted an invitation from the Haitian government to visit at its expense, and he now recognized that emigration was one of the answers to the black American's dilemma. "We propose to act," he wrote, "in view of the settled fact that many of the blacks are already resolved to look for homes beyond the boundaries of the United States, and that most of their minds are turned towards Haiti."

Douglass' steamer, chartered by the Haitian Bureau of Emigration in Boston, was scheduled to sail on April 25. He notified his readers that his trip would take about ten weeks. But ten days before his departure, the distant rumble of Fort Sumter's cannon roused Frederick Douglass from his Caribbean reverie. With the Confederate firing on Fort Sumter, Douglass added a paragraph to his editorial indicating that he would stand by and see what happened rather than go immediately to Haiti. "We shall stay here and watch the current developments," he wrote. "This is no time to leave the country."

Thereafter Douglass refrained from active support of Haitian emigration, although from June 1861 to well past the middle of 1862, a full-page advertisement from the Haitian government for black American immigration appeared regularly in *Douglass' Monthly.*

Actual emigration to Haiti began in 1861 when James T. Holly led a band of fifty Philadelphians to the Caribbean island. How many others joined the initial group is uncertain, but the settlement did not thrive. Holly stayed on and eventually became the Episcopal bishop of Haiti, but most of his followers found the island extremely difficult in terms of both health and economic existence. Few of them were farmers, and Haiti had little employment for the skilled workers Holly had convinced to accompany him. Early in 1863, the disillusioned emigrants returned to Philadelphia.

10

Black Emigration, 1850–1861
III: Africa

AGAIN LIBERIA

When Indiana blacks met in 1851, they concluded that they could always emigrate to Canada, Jamaica, Mexico, Central America, or Haiti, but, they insisted, they would never go to Liberia. During the next few years, this attitude changed somewhat. In May 1855, a meeting of the National Council of Colored People was held in Reverend S. S. Jocelyn's church in Brooklyn's Eastern District, at Eleventh and South Third streets, to hear reports from a number of blacks who had recently returned from Liberia. The speakers noted that emigrants would have to cope with "extreme heat and sickness since the African fever is very prevalent, and the duration is from six to eighteen months." However, those emigrants from the United States who had survived "are doing well and are principally engaged in manufacturing sugar and molasses and raising cotton. The labor is principally done by the natives, who carry lumber, bricks, stone, sand, and other materials upon their heads, sometimes a distance of several miles." The speakers urged emigration to Liberia but cautioned the prospective emigrants "to have some means in order to support themselves after assistance from the Colonization Society ceases, which is at the expiration of six months."

The mention of the American Colonization Society did not throw the meeting into a frenzy of anger, and the gathering adjourned with the promise to give the question of emigration to Liberia careful consideration. The incoming correspondence of the American Colonization Society in the Library of Congress reveals an increasing interest among Southern free blacks in emigration to Liberia, where they could hope to become useful citizens. That a number left for Liberia is evidenced by developments in the South during the late 1850s. Disturbed by the number of Liberian emigrants leaving Savannah and by the effect the exodus was having on local blacks, a special committee of the city council recommended in 1856 an ordinance calling for a $200 tax on each black emigrant leaving the city. The tax was quickly passed by the council. Mayor James P. Screven then directed Edward G. Wilson, clerk of the council, to inform William McLain, a Colonization Society official, that the tax was "intended as prohibitory and to prevent any further shipment of Negroes from this Port to Liberia."

Another evidence of growing Southern opposition to Liberian emigration from the South is the publicity given to the article "An Arrival from Liberia," originally published in the *Atlanta Examiner* and widely reprinted in the Southern press. Jefferson Waters had returned to Georgia with reports of a life of horrors he had undergone in Liberia. In fact, conditions in Liberia were so bad "that ninety-nine out of every hundred . . . would . . . gladly return to servitude upon the plantation." Part of the trouble was that Liberia was run by "northern negroes." The article was used in the South to encourage Southern blacks to stay at home and be satisfied with their circumstances.

GROWING INTEREST IN THE NIGER VALLEY

Meanwhile, interest in the Niger Valley region of Africa began to increase among black Americans, stimulated by the lectures and publications of Reverend Thomas Jefferson Bowen. Bowen, a Baptist missionary to Africa, had been dispatched to the Niger Valley by the Southern Baptist Convention and had established a mission at Abeokuta, in modern Nigeria. He returned to the United States in 1856 and, although weakened by fever, began a lecture tour on the opportunities awaiting black Americans in Central Africa. In 1857, he published "African Opening to Civilization and Christianity" in the *African Repository* and the book *Central Africa* (as he called the Yoruba country), in which he dispelled notions of African barbarism, stressed the advanced civilization of the Yoruba towns, and described their agricultural methods and the local weaving, dyeing, and cloth-making industries. In reporting one of Bowen's lectures, the *New York Journal of Commerce* declared on March 20, 1857: "Mr. Bowen says, if colonized by civilized blacks from America, it would soon command the trade of Central Africa." One of Bowen's repeated themes was that settlements by black Americans among the Yoruba people would both reap great commercial benefit and bring the Christian message to the African continent.

Bowen's lectures were widely attended and his publications widely read by blacks, and they resulted in a heightened interest in Africa. So, too, did Scottish minister and African explorer David Livingstone's *Missionary Travels and Researches in South Africa*. Henry Highland Garnet and Martin R. Delany both responded enthusiastically to the books by Bowen and Livingstone. Delany recommended *Central Africa* and *Missionary Travels* to his friends. After reading them on Delany's recommendation, Mary H. Freeman, the principal of Avery College in Pennsylvania, wrote on April 24, 1858: "I am more and more convinced that Africa is the country to which all colored men who wish to attain the full status of manhood, and bring up their children to be men and not creeping things, should turn their steps. I feel more and more every day that I made a great mistake in not going there when I was untrammeled by family ties and had the opportunity.''

THE YEAR 1858

The year 1858 marked a turning point in the African phase of emigrationism. The African Civilization Society was founded in the summer of 1858, with Henry Highland Garnet as president. Its immediate aim was to explore the Niger River area for the establishment of settlements of black Americans in Africa. Also in August 1858, the third National Emigration Convention met in Chatham, Ontario, Canada, "to consider all the information received during the year, as to all portions of the world in which the colored people are especially interested and without recommending any place now especially for emigration" but to give encouragement to all who might be determined to emigrate from the United States. The convention's aim was to bring all emigrationist views under the roof of one organization without promoting any one area. In fact, emigration was not even positively favored, and two amendments to the constitution were adopted that changed the nature of the organization to include "all colored people interested, and all who really sympathized with them." This change in policy reflected the strong antiemigrationist feelings of blacks in Chatham, who believed that blacks in the United States should "use all honorable means to hasten the day of enfranchisement and freedom."

Yet despite all this, the third National Emigration Convention was significant in the development of the African emigration movement. Upon his insistence, Martin R. Delany was permitted to head an expedition of five "to make a topographical, geological and geographical examination of the valley of the River Niger." But his commission explicitly stipulated that the expedition was for "the purpose of science and for general information, and without any reference to and with the [General] Board [of Commissioners] being entirely opposed to any Emigration there as such." Delany was authorized to name his own colleagues and to raise the funds necessary for the expedition.

THE THREE C'S

Thus, Henry Highland Garnet and Martin R. Delany became rivals in an effort to explore within the Niger area of Africa. But before examining what each of these two black emigrationist leaders did in the African phase of emigrationism, we should note the fact that black American emigrationists were not the only ones in the United States interested in Africa. On December 30, 1842, while he was presenting the Webster-Ashburton Treaty to the U.S. Senate, Secretary of the Navy A. P. Upshur explained that the reason for stationing a naval squadron in West Africa was not so much to curb the inhuman slave trade but to protect the growing commerce of the United States with West Africa. He noted, too, that "our commerce with that country . . . holds out at this time greater inducements to commercial enterprise than any other part of the world."

Important as the West African trade was considered to be, the Americans found themselves being pushed out by traders from other nations, especially the British and the French. As Commodore Matthew Callbraith Perry pointed out in 1844, the British "have monopolized at least two-thirds of the whole business while the Americans, contrary to the results of their usual enterprise, enjoy but a share of what is left." Hence, the American naval squadron in West Africa from the 1840s on was instructed to promote American commercial interests. Indeed, the suppression of the slave trade was regarded as the other branch of the squadron's duties. At a time when the United States had neither consuls nor commercial agents on the West Coast of Africa, the commanders of the naval squadron played the roles of both. Commodore Perry was particularly active in promoting American commercial interests in West Africa, and his successors picked up where he had left off, signing commercial agreements with African chiefs.

About the same time that Henry Highland Garnet and Martin R. Delany were preparing to explore the Niger River region, the American Colonization Society sought to develop interest in a U.S. Navy expedition to open Africa to commercial enterprise, just as Commodore Perry's expedition had opened Japan. The most immediate need in this connection was in the field of exploration. The society won the support of Reverend Bowen, and through his influence, a bill for a Niger expedition was introduced by Senator Robert Toombs of Georgia and passed the Senate early in 1857. The House of Representatives voted down the proposed Niger expedition, however, leaving the field open for Garnet and Delany.

Black American emigration leaders in the 1850s were keenly interested in the expansion of African trade with the United States. The resources of the new colonies that they hoped to establish in Africa had to be harnessed for this trade. Crummell saw commerce "under the benevolent influence of Christianity" as "the handmaiden of religion." Its successful exploitation would not only open the way for the introduction of Christianity and civilization but also bring to Africa the manufactured goods of developed nations.

A number of emigrationist leaders were more concerned with developing alternative sources to American slave-grown cotton. Their vision was to facilitate, through the establishment of colonies of black Americans in West Africa, "the production of those staples, particularly cotton, which now are supplied to the world chiefly by Slave Labour." It was a vision that struck a responsive chord among both British philanthropists, who saw the development of free labor produce as an instrument of antislavery activity, and British commercial and industrial interests, who, since 1848, had begun the serious search for alternative sources to American cotton on which the whole Lancashire cotton industry heavily depended. The formation of the Cotton Supply Association in 1848 was the beginning of an attempt to break the American monopoly.

In the view of the emigrationists who favored Africa as the area for the exodus of black Americans, the economy of the colonies they would establish would, in most cases, depend on the production of cotton, which within a few years would rival the South in the markets of Europe and thus begin to undermine the foundations of the Southern slave system, leading to the final emancipation of the slaves.

British industrialists began experimenting with West African cotton, and in 1850, Liberian President John J. Roberts welcomed an English agent sent to the African coast by some textile firms for that purpose. Roberts discussed a plan for growing cotton in Africa with Benjamin Coates, a Philadelphia Quaker, businessman, and active supporter of the American Colonization Society, who had become very enthusiastic about the idea. In 1858, Coates published a pamphlet, *Suggestions on the Importance of the Cultivation of Cotton in Africa in Reference to the Abolition of Slavery in the United States.* In it, he argued that the profit motive created and sustained slavery so that an alternative cheaper source of free-grown cotton in Africa would ultimately lead to the demise of slavery in the South. This effort should be led and controlled by enterprising black men emigrating to Africa from the United States over a period of years.

Commerce was only one of what has been called the "three C's" of African emigrationism. The other two were Christianity and civilization. The first duty and objective of every emigrationist was to spread Christianity. Racial affinity, they argued, made them uniquely suitable for the task. Garnet saw it as a duty and a privilege "to give the Gospel and Christian Civilization to our Fatherland." He sought, among other things, "to secure . . . the triumph of the Gospel in Africa, and the consequent overthrow of idolatry and superstition." Not one emigrationist, with the later exception of Blyden, ever questioned the utility of Protestant Christianity for Africa. William Craft, the famed fugitive slave, who, while not an emigrationist, spent almost five years in Dahomey, was an exception. Although he was an advocate of the spread of Christianity in Africa, he argued that missionaries should recognize and respect the fact that African societies did possess a body of religious beliefs, which had evolved over centuries and had met the needs of its followers. Paganism would never be removed and Christianity accepted, he insisted, unless Africans were approached in a spirit "of peace and with a doctrine averse . . . to the homily of physical force." "We strangers," he noted shrewdly, "are prone to lose sight of this spiritual background or are unacquainted with it altogether. We deliver our judgment dogmatically. 'Their God,' we exclaim, 'is a cloud; and so is the mud, and so are the streams, the beasts and storms!' If we could master their language, we should pause before we branded their style of adoration as the style of Paganism. In ignorance of their mode of giving vent to their thoughts, we hastily infer that the black face is the incarnation of a stolid school of idolatry; in the deceptive strength of self-sufficiency we degrade them to the condition of one who deifies and worships a cork, a bottle, a few feathers." And he concluded: "With equal show of logic and equal manifestation of intolerance, we might stigmatize the Roman Catholics as heathens, and might declare that their saints and relics, and their amulets, are nothing less than their gods." But Craft was a remarkable exception, and his influence was minimal.

Every African emigrationist saw the hand of God directing him toward the task of African redemption. Robert Campbell, a leader with Delany of a black expedition to explore the Niger River valley, argued that the slaves captured from slave traders and returned to Africa "have doubtless been the means of inaugurating a mighty work, which, now that it has accomplished its utmost," should be continued by black American emigrants to "a higher form by the more civilized of the same race, who, for a thousand reasons, are best adapted to its successful prosecution." As emigrationists saw it, slavery and the slave trade had provided blacks with the skills and talents for the work of African redemption. Crummell maintained that God had trained blacks in the New World for "His own great work in Africa." With their command of the "Anglo-Saxon tongue," the language of the Magna Carta and the Bible, blacks from the New World were to be the agents for shedding light on "benighted Africa." This vanguard would produce natives trained "to the spirit, moral sentiments, and practical genius of the language," a new moral order based on the precepts of Christianity.

Emigrationist leaders thus saw the black emigrants as the harbingers of African redemption. They would create in their new home a moral order that, through a combination of Christianity, economic strength, and social balance, would lead African societies toward "perfection." This moral order was to be achieved through hard work, seriousness, respectability, and self-help or, as Alexander Crummell put it, "forecast, wakefulness, industry, thrift, probity and tireless, sweatful toil." Addressing newly arrived Barbadian immigrants to Liberia, Crummell said: "Our mission is evidently to organize the native labor all around us; to introduce regulating and controlling law among them, to gather their children into schools, in order to train their intellects, to make these people civilized and Christian people; and to incorporate them into our Republic as citizens, and into the Church of God as brethren." To Crummell, as to many other emigrationists, the all-powerful and regulating hand of God had placed the emigrant in Africa to be "the guardian, the protector, and the teachers of our heathen tribes." The untutored natives, like adolescent children, were wards of superior talent and wiser heads, until such time as they acquired all the necessary skills and sophistication. This maturation would be achieved only through careful guidance and the judicious use of authority. "All historic fact," Crummell argued, "shows that force, that is authority, must be used in the exercise of guardianship over heathen tribes." "Here," observes black scholar R.J.M. Blackett, "was Manifest Destiny with a conscience."

Black emigrationist leaders believed that the technological aspects of civilization were destined to develop colaterally with Protestant Christianity. No other form of the faith was conducive to the civilization of Africa, Crummell was convinced, and he attributed the shortcomings of the Haitian experience to the influence of Roman Catholicism. Similarly, Delany called Christianity "the most advanced civilization that man had ever attained to," but he quickly added that "slavery was the legitimate successor of Roman Catholicism," as if it were the sole cause of the African slave trade. Strangely enough, for a man with a brilliant understanding of history, Delany praised the Protestants as the foes of slavery.

With one or two exceptions, black American emigrationists tended to display a contempt for things African. Delany shed this attitude upon contact with Africans, and Garnet seems not to have shared the contempt of other black emigrationists for them. Richard K. MacMaster points out that

in his view of Africa, Garnet made a significant break with the prevailing attitudes of the Liberian colonists. There is no hint of the open contempt with which the settlers there regarded their African neighbors. Missionaries often complained that the American Liberians freely criticized efforts to educate tribal Liberians as tending to raise the indigenous population to the same level as the immigrants.

Garnet, MacMaster notes, believed that the idea that "Africa was a land of half-naked savages" militated against the advancement of black Americans. By helping the citizens of Yoruba to develop a Christian civilization and a healthy economy, black American emigrants would further the cause of equal rights in the United States by creating "a nation of which the colored Americans could be proud." Garnet was clearly unaware of the fact that in putting it this way, he was conceding the argument of racism that Africa was then a continent of which black Americans could not be proud. In this respect, then, Garnet and Crummell saw eye to eye. Crummell combined the three C's in the following comment:

The kings and trades men of Africa, having the demonstration of Negro capacity before them, would hail the presence of their black kinsmen from America and would be stimulated by a generous emigration. . . . To the farthest interior, leagues and combinations would be formed with men of commerce, and thus civilization, enlightenment and Christianity would be carried to every state and town, and village of interior Africa.

GARNET AND THE AFRICAN CIVILIZATION SOCIETY

Garnet went further than Crummell, for he combined the principles of the three C's into an organization. Drawing upon his long experience with the free produce movement, especially its British aspects, where free labor competition with slave labor was allied with the usual boycotting of slave-grown sugar and cotton, Garnet was convinced that a carefully nurtured economic development in Africa would effectively end the slave trade. Growing and selling free-labor cotton from Africa not only would make fortunes for young black entrepreneurs but would supply the European market so well that southerners would be forced by economic self-interest to end slavery. Garnet knew from his own experience that British textile interests would welcome an effort to develop cotton growing in West Africa. This, he believed, would undercut the American cotton planter, make slavery less profitable, and pave the way for its abolition. To this Garnet added the proposal of Reverend Thomas Jefferson Bowen for colonizing the Yoruba area of Africa with black Americans who would introduce both Christianity and the English language. "The final result," Bowen wrote, "would probably be that all these countries . . . would exchange their language and religion for those of the immigrants." Garnet incorporated these ideas of Bowen with his own on cotton production in West Africa in the fundamental principles of the African Civilization Society.

Although Garnet was the founder and the most active proponent of the African Civilization Society, the new organization was the outgrowth of a great deal of planning and support from Philadelphia whites, most notably Benjamin Coates, a leader of the American Colonization Society, and it was therefore suspect to most blacks. Whether Coates was the leading spirit behind the formation of the African Civilization Society is difficult to determine, but he claimed credit for its formation and saw his suggestion as a matter of expedience aimed at avoiding "the obnoxious term of Colonization" associated with the hated society. While not exclusively a black organization, the African Civilization Society differed from the American Colonization Society in that it was devoted to the universal abolition of slavery.

On August 9, 1858, at a meeting at New York City's Spring Hall before a black audience, Garnet announced the formation of the African Civilization Society and presented his views on emigration to Africa. He told the audience that while blacks hated slavery and intended to continue fighting it until it was abolished, this did not conflict with the black man's love of Africa, the land of his ancestors. As for himself, he gloried in Africa's ancient glory, its science and art, and was proud to trace his origins to Africa, the land of early civilizations and of powerful empires. Love of country, he continued, was an essential part of man's nature, and for the black man in the United States, a void would exist until that was fulfilled. He expressed the hope that he would be able to see a national flag of which he was proud.

Garnet then turned to Africa's economic potential, which he described in glowing terms. He cautioned Negroes not to allow the whites to get too far ahead of them in Central Africa. A few thousand intelligent and enterprising black Americans, he maintained, would be enough to plant a Christian nation that would be a center for moral and religious, as well as commercial and social, influence for Africa. White men could not do this work as well as blacks, and God called upon the Negro people to join in this project. "Let those who wish to stay, stay here," Garnet concluded, "and those who have enterprise and wish to go, go and found a nation of which the colored American could be proud."

The constitution of the African Civilization Society was then made public. It announced its objectives as "the civilization and Christianization of Africa, and of the descendants of African ancestors in any portion of the earth, wherever dispersed. Also the destruction of the African Slave trade, by the introduction of lawful commerce and trade with Africa." Selective African repatriation was dedicated to supporting "the principle of an African Nationality," the African race being the ruling element of the nation, controlling and directing their own affairs. Since blacks would prove their fitness for freedom by demonstrating their capacity for self-government, the society would also help to destroy slavery in this way. Moreover, by the cultivation of cotton in Africa, the strongest support of slavery would be removed.

In an open letter to the British, Garnet stated the society's goals as follows: "We feel it to be our duty, as well as privilege, to give the Gospel and Christian civilization to our Fatherland. . . . With the blessing of God, we hope to secure, as the result of our efforts, the triumph of the Gospel in Africa, and the consequent overthrow of idolatry and superstition, the destruction of the African slave trade and slavery; the diffusion of Christian principles of religion, law and order, in Central Africa, and the elevation of our race everywhere." In a series of articles in the black press, Garnet presented an enthusiastic vision of what would be accomplished through the African Civilization Society. A first objective was "the immediate and unconditional abolition of slavery in the United States and in Africa, and the destruction of the African slave trade both in this and that country." A second objective was "the destruction of prejudice against colored people in the United States, especially in the nominal free states of the North; and we propose to do this by urging upon the abolitionists and the friends of humanity of every grade the necessity of giving trades and employment to ourselves and to our children." Third, he proposed "to assist in giving the Gospel to Africa, and thus render obedience unto the unrepealed command of Jesus Christ, to go into all the world and preach the Gospel to every creature." Fourth, he proposed "the advancement of the civilization of Africa, by the introduction into that country of lawful trade and commerce, by the cultivation of cotton to supply the world and relieve it of dependence on the cotton raised in the Southern states by slave labor, and by this means to strike the death-blow to American slavery." Through the establishment "of Christian industrial settlements" in Yoruba, west of the Niger, and the promotion of the growth of cotton and other products, "the natives may become industrious producers as well as consumers of articles of commerce." Fifth, he proposed "to establish a grand center of Negro nationality, from which shall flow streams of commercial, intellectual, and political power which shall make colored people respected everywhere." Finally, all these objectives were to be achieved through the voluntary cooperation of the friends of universal freedom, regardless of color.

Garnet further clarified his plans for the African Civilization Society in an address at Cooper Institute early in March 1860. He emphasized the need for sending out a select group and the educational and commercial aspects of the venture:

We regard the enslavement of our race to be the highest crime against God and man, and we hope, by teaching the Kings and Chiefs of Africa better things, to induce them to exterminate the slave trade and engage in lawful commerce, and in this way aid in destroying slavery in this and all other lands. We believe it would be preferable to sit down by the side, and not only teach the people by precept those principles which we desire them to cherish, but also to teach them by power of example those that will elevate their manhood and exalt their nature; and to make them feel that we are a part of themselves—interested in everything which promises to promote their happiness and increase their prosperity.

THE DEBATE OVER THE AFRICAN CIVILIZATION SOCIETY

Although Garnet stressed that the primary aim of the African Civilization Society was "the Evangelization and Civilization of Africa, and the descendants of Africa wherever dispersed," it was the antislavery aspects of the society that gave it its strongest appeal to a number of black Americans. William Whipper expressed full approval of the society's plan to aid American blacks in raising cotton as a means of undermining slavery in the South. "So far from feeling humiliated at the mere mention of Africa, or anything African," he wrote, "I wo'd summon her to meet on the ramparts of nations, and inaugurate a new destiny." He would like to see Africa flourish and attract the admiration of the world. The Reverend J. Sella Martin of Boston associated himself with the African Civilization Society as soon as it was formed and said, in explaining his reasons:

First that it would pay the passage of colored men who wished to go to Africa to assist in the development of the cultivation of cotton; Secondly, that the cultivation of cotton in Africa would break up the slave trade; thirdly, that cotton would be made cheaper in the United States by its cultivation in Africa, and thus the strongest support for slavery would be taken away.

A year later, Martin told a Boston audience that he "believed the Civilization Society would tend to break the link which held England to this country, and makes her dependent on the Southern states for cotton."

But although Garnet took great pains to deny any connection between the American Colonization Society and the African Civilization Society, the dominant role played by Benjamin Coates, long associated with the Colonization Society, earned it the opinion among blacks that the new society "was only a mask for the hated older one." As Jane H. Pease and William H. Pease note: "Whatever it gained in support among clerics drawn by its missionary dimension, it quickly lost in the denunciations of those who feared another white conspiracy to drive independent freemen in exile.'' Thus John T. Goines said he discerned in the African Civilization Society "the same old colonization *coon.*'' Reverend J.W.C. Pennington, who was at first in favor of the society because he believed it was formed for the purpose of educating young men and assisting to pay off the indebtedness of black churches, but later, having discovered, as he put it, that its real purpose was "to *secure the expulsion of the free colored people from this country,*'' came out vehemently against it. George T. Downing, too, insisted that the Civilization Society was merely "an off-shot of the American Colonization Society—all aimed at ridding the country of the free black population.'' Downing condemned the *New York Tribune* for having printed several letters in praise of Coates' 1858 pamphlet and the African Civilization Society. The whole idea of producing cotton in Africa, Downing charged, was a device to blind people to the society's real objective: to rid the United States of free Negroes. Africans were already doing a good job producing cotton themselves; why was it then necessary to send five thousand black Americans overseas to cultivate the crop? In concluding his attack on the society, Downing reminded Garnet that it was time he decided to use his talents at home:

Our friend Garnet it must be remembered left his country for Europe, afterward left Europe with his family for the West Indies, which was to have been his future home; afterward returned to his native home and settled himself down; and now we find him engaged in what I call a wild goose chase in Africa.

Shortly after the African Civilization Society was organized, Frederick Douglass, a vigorous opponent of all forms of emigration until he supported (for a few months) Haitian emigration, made his opposition clear. He objected to the formation of still another organization favoring the emigration of black Americans because, among other reasons, "the agitation of the removal of the colored people from the United States keeps them constantly in a perturbed, unsettled, neither-go-nor-stay, state of mind.'' A people so "disturbed, apprehensive, restless, and anxious, cannot improve the opportunities immediately surrounding them.'' Addressing himself to Benjamin Coates of the African Civilization Society, Douglass asked bluntly: "What right have Colonizationists, what right have you, Mr. Coates, what right have any, to take advantage of a popular prejudice, which else might soon die out, and keep this struggling people perpetually in a state of uncertainty and even alarm. . . . We Negroes are kept under a constant strain, either in contemplating magnificent enterprises, for which we have but little qualifications, or looking for the shadow of the cruel arm which we are told must sooner or later smite us, if we do not get out of this land.'' Garnet thereupon asked Douglass to tell his readers what his objections were "to the civilization and christianization of Africa.'' And, he went on:

What objection have you to colored men in this country engaging in agriculture, lawful trade, and commerce in the land of my forefathers? What objection have you to an organization that shall endeavor to check and destroy the African slave-trade, and that desires to co-operate with anti-slavery men and women of every grade in our own land, and to toil with them for the overthrow of American slavery?—Tell us, I pray you, tell us in your clear and manly style. "Gird up thy loins, and answer thou me, if thou canst."

In reply, Douglass listed several reasons that prevented him from cooperating with the African Civilization Society. The society continued the program of the American Colonization Society in trying to persuade blacks that "Africa, not America" was their home. "It is that wolfish idea that elbows us off the sidewalk, and denies us the rights of citizenship." The society would take forces and funds away from the struggle against slavery and for equality at home. The society proposed "to plant its guns too far from the battlements of slavery for us." The best way to put down the slave trade, "and to build up civilization in Africa, is to stand our ground and labor for the abolition of slavery in the U.S." The slave trade could be abolished by activity in the United States, for Douglass had no confidence that the African kings and chiefs would reverse the century-old practice of enslaving captives. There were 4 million slaves in the United States. "They are stigmatized as an inferior race, fit only for slavery, incapable of improvement, and unable to take care of themselves." Here, then, was the place and the free black Americans were the people "to meet and put down these conclusions concerning our race." Douglass advanced another argument aimed at undercutting a chief justification for the Civilization Society:

If slavery depended for its existence upon the cultivation of cotton, and were shut up to that single production, it might even then be fairly questioned whether any amount of cotton culture in Africa would materially affect the price of that article in this country, since demand and supply would go on together. But the case is very different. Slave labor can be employed in raising anything which human labor and the earth can produce. If one does not pay, another will.

His final argument was that the black person's search for his destiny would be held back by Garnet's scheme. "When in slavery, we were liable to perpetual sales, transfers and removals; and now that we are free, we are doomed to be constantly harassed with schemes to get us out of the country. We are quite tired of all this, and wish no more of it."

The *New York Colonization Journal,* an organ of the Colonization Society, leaped to Garnet's defense and accused Douglass of a lack of interest in Africa. He did not understand, it charged, that by developing Africa, the black American would more quickly attain higher status in this country than by working at home. Garnet agreed and, replying to his critics, argued that except for menial jobs, blacks were denied economic opportunity in this country:

You anti-emigrationists seem to desire to see the hundreds of colored men and women who have good trades to stay here and be the drudges and menials of white men who will not employ or work with them. Go to our hotels and private mansions of the rich, and on board of our steamboats, and you will find many skilful carpenters, masons, engineers, wheelwrights, and blacksmiths, millers, as well as female mechanics, who are wasting their talents for a mere pittance. You will see many of them borne down with discourage-ment, and they will tell you that the reason they do not work at their trades is because they have been told over and over again when they have applied for work—"We don't employ niggers."

For these and other black Americans, Garnet insisted, there was indeed no future in the United States but only in Africa. But the antiemigrationists ridiculed Garnet's conclusion, and, as J. McCune Smith informed the head of the African Civilization Society: "Our people want to stay, and will stay at home: We are in for the fight, and will fight it out here. Shake yourself free from these migrating phantasms, and join us with your might and main."

The debate that was developing between the pro- and anti-Civilization Society blacks reached a climax at a meeting in New York City's Zion Church on April 12, 1860. The call for the meeting invited the "colored people of New York and Vicinity"

to pass judgment in the African Civilization Society . . . and to declare openly whether they approve or condemn that society. The undersigned believe that in its operations and influence it is of kin to the old colonization scheme—a supporter of prejudice—and hence a co-worker in the ranks of our enemies.

Among the signers of the call were Jeremiah Powers, Reverend J.W.C. Pen-nington, George T. Downing, Reverend Charles B. Ray, and Charles L. Reason, all veterans of the struggle against slavery and for equality.

On the eve of the meeting, circulars were distributed in New York's black community with the following message:

COLORED MEN READ!

It is said we should be slaves! It is said we should go to Africa! A new society has been formed to send us there. It is collecting money for the purpose. Come out. Will you be shipped off? Let nothing prevent you, come out, crowd old Zion! Admittance free.

At about the same time, the *New York Weekly Anglo-African* published Garnet's plan under which the African Civilization Society would build schools and churches, instruct the inhabitants of Yoruba, west of the Niger, in the arts and sciences, and develop the natural resources of the country. "Our plan," he added, "is not to subvert the government and overthrow the reigning princes of those countries. We believe it would be more profitable to sit down by their side, and not only teach the people by precept those principles which we desire them to cherish, but also to teach them by the power of example and make them feel that we are part of themselves, interested in everything which promises to promote their happiness and increase their prosperity." But if Garnet thought that such missionary enterprise would satisfy his critics and win over the audience at Zion Church, he was mistaken.

Twelve hundred New York blacks turned out for the meeting. George T. Downing, the bitter foe of the Civilization Society, was elected chairman, and he began the proceedings by reading a letter he had received from Harriet Martineau, the British author. Martineau revealed that agents of the Civilization Society were in England asking for financial support and maintaining that the group's objectives had received the approval of the free black population of the United States. With the exception of Garnet and J. Sella Martin, the Boston black leader, the speakers at the meeting denounced this claim as a gross misrepresentation. The audience, too, shouted its disapproval by hissing at any favorable reference to the society.

When order had been restored, Downing read another letter, this one from Elizabeth Smith Miller, the daughter of Gerrit Smith, who was unable to send a personal communication but conveyed his views through his daughter. She reported that her father believed that some merit existed in the program to assist blacks who desired to emigrate to Africa, Haiti, and Central America, but he feared that it might work "great evil by the exaggerated views of their importance and effects." Her father believed, she continued, that "nothing is more indispensable . . . to the well-being of these Americans than the abiding sense that their native land is their own land; and that they have as much right and as much reason as the whites to look upon it as their home." She concluded by remarking: "Let the black man account no white man as his friend, or indeed, as other than his enemy, who does not accord as fully to the black race as to the white, political, civil, ecclesiastical and social rights, as well on this soil as on any other."

Before the meeting went much further, the discussion gave way to fist fights, and church officials threatened to turn out the lights if the gathering did not adjourn. At this, a resolution was hastily adopted:

Resolved, That we wish it to be most firmly fixed in the minds of our fellow-countrymen, the American people, that we as a body, in any number, do not intend to leave this, our home—that we intend to stay here; to have our children enjoy victory over hate and wrong, the promise of which is every day indicating itself.

At a second meeting, which they fully controlled, Garnet and J. Sella Martin made sure that a resolution endorsing the African Civilization Society and its work was adopted. But such a resolution represented only the few supporters of the society, and shortly thereafter their number was even further reduced. The setback in New York City was followed by other defeats for the African Civilization Society, partly caused by Garnet's practice of arranging controlled meetings after the Zion Church gathering had been broken up by fist fights. These controls ensured that opposition forces received virtually no representation, but even many emigration advocates objected to this kind of "undemocratic method of stifling critical debate.'' J. Sella Martin, for one, withdrew his active support of Garnet, first, as a protest against the practice of controlled meetings, and second, because, as he explained, England's Manchester Cotton Supply Association was developing adequate African resources.

On top of these setbacks, the Civilization Society sustained a serious blow when Reverend Elymas P. Rogers, pastor of the Plane Street Presbyterian Church in Newark, New Jersey, died during his trip to Lagos where he planned to select a station for the American Missionary Association and to establish a colony on behalf of the African Civilization Society. The fact that Rogers, one of the earliest and most active members of the Civilization Society, had to pay his own expenses on the trip indicated that the organization was already strapped for funds. But before we witness the demise of the Civilization Society, let us first turn our attention to the visit of Martin R. Delany to Africa and the consequences of the historic exploration of the Niger Valley.

THE DELANY-CAMPBELL EXPEDITION TO THE NIGER VALLEY

In August 1858 the convention of emigrationists in Chatham, Canada, had authorized Delany to undertake at his own expense a scientific expedition to the Niger, ''without any reference to, and with the Board being entirely opposed to any Emigration there as such''—as Delany put it later—in order to ascertain whether the Niger River valley was suited to permanent settlement by black American emigrants. Instead of the large expedition originally planned, only two men actually went, and they went separately. The other man was Robert Campbell, suggested as a replacement for Dr. James H. Wilson of Philadelphia, who had had to decline the invitation to accompany Delany.

Campbell was born in Jamaica in 1829 of mulatto and Scottish parentage. After being apprenticed as a printer for five years, he entered a normal school for two years and then became a parish teacher in Kingston. In 1853, he arrived in New York after spending some time in Central America. Two years later, he was appointed science teacher at the Institute of Colored Youth in Philadelphia.

Delany wrote to several white antislavery leaders to raise money for his expedition. His purpose, he explained to Reverend Henry Ward Beecher, was to lay the basis, through the signing of treaties with local chiefs, for the establishment of a colony of selected and skilled individuals. This colony would be composed of agriculturists, mechanics, competent businessmen, teachers, qualified clergy, a photographer and artist, a surveyor and civil engineer, a geologist and chemist, and ''persons to fill every vocation necessary to an intelligent and progressive community.'' Such a colony would bring enlightenment and Christianity to an otherwise benighted area. Delany requested support from the fund of $150,000 left by the Pittsburgh philanthropist Charles Avery "for the enlightenment and civilization of the African race on the continent of Africa."

Delany never received any support from the fund, but while he was unsuccessfully trying to raise money for his expedition, Robert Campbell met with Garnet and the other leaders of the African Civilization Society and, through them, with Benjamin Coates. To assist the expedition, Coates secured a large grant from the American Colonization Society. On April 3, 1859, Campbell sailed alone for England on the first stage of his expedition to Yoruba. In England, Campbell accepted more money to take him to Africa. He sailed on June 1859 on a British steamer bound for Lagos, taking with him two cotton gins and ten bushels of cotton seed.

Although Delany himself had solicited white financial support for his expedition, he drew the line at accepting aid from the American Colonization Society and was offended by Campbell's willingness to use their funds to finance his trip to Africa. Relations between the two were strained when Delany, having raised sufficient funds, sailed in May 1859 from New York for Liberia. As he departed, the *New York Colonization Journal* suggested that Delany's Niger expedition, if successful, would develop and expand commerce with Africa, extend markets for the manufactured goods of America and Britain, and in this way, "the commerce of the world will be stimulated, while Christianity and Civilization will advance to peaceful conquest of the great continent."

In the *Official Report of the Niger Valley Exploring Party,* Delany reported receiving courteous treatment at the hands of the Liberians, even though his fame as an opponent of the American Colonization Society's offspring had preceded him. He found it possible to explain his position to their satisfaction, and he, in turn, changed his opinion of Liberia and the Liberians. The *Liberian Herald* announced that "the arrival of Martin R. Delany in Liberia is an era in the history of African Emigration, an event doubtless, that will long be remembered by hundreds and thousands of Africa's exiled children." It noted that the news of the presence in Liberia of "the foremost champion of the elevation of the colored man in the United States, and this great antagonist to the American Colonization Society" had spread rapidly, and "persons from all parts of the country came to Monrovia to see the great man."

On his return to London, Delany was unstinting in his praise of Liberia. "It is a glorious country," he wrote, "and I only regret that we of America so long remained unacquainted of this noble band of brothers, who have always loved us with a heart's warm zeal, and though coldly and indifferently treated by us, ever bore it with patience, anxiously awaiting and hoping that the day might come when we would look on them with favor, and approbate their struggling efforts for liberty in an African nationality. I pledge them the heart and hand of a brother to stand by them in one common cause." In Monrovia, Blyden had asked whether Delany is the "Moses to lead in the Exodus of his people from the house of bondage," and recommended that he be encouraged and supported in his efforts. Little wonder, then, that Delany came back from Africa with an entirely new opinion of Liberia or that he had nothing to say about the condescending attitude of the black American emigrants toward the mass of the native population or their undemocratic conduct in controlling the country.

While Delany was on his protracted visit to Liberia, Robert Campbell was in Lagos, where he met with great encouragement in his project from both the British consul and the Reverend Samuel Adjai Crowther. Temporarily debilitated by a bout with fever and suffering from poor health, Delany stopped feuding with Campbell and joined his party in September 1859. In December, Campbell wrote from Abeokuta to the African Civilization Society: "Should circumstances permit, we propose affecting this week, a formal contract with the Alake [king] and chiefs of this place, in which we shall have clearly stated the conditions in which we shall be permitted to enjoy the privileges of civilized life. They are, as I have informed you, very favorable to our enterprise."

On December 26, 1859, Delany and Campbell signed a treaty with the Alake and chiefs of Abeokuta providing for the settlement of emigrants from the United States in the area around Abeokuta. As Campbell reported to the American Colonization Society, the treaty gave the two black Americans "the right of locating in common with the natives in any part of the territory, not otherwise occupied" and "to govern ourselves according to our own customs." In a letter to Garnet, Campbell explained that the laws of the native authorities would bind natives, and in case of a dispute between an American settler and a native, an equal number of commissioners representing each group would have the power to decide the case.

With the signing of the treaty, Delany and Campbell set out to explore Yoruba. They left Abeokuta on January 16, 1860, visiting Ikayem Objo, Obbomisharo, and Elorin on their outward trip. On the return trip to Abeokuta, they separated at Oyo because of the war that had broken out in Yoruba. Campbell and Delany returned to Abeokuta by separate routes. In spite of the fact that the war had engulfed the whole of Yoruba, the two black Americans were determined to establish their colony in Abeokuta. They set out for the United States, first stopping in England.

DELANY IN ENGLAND

During his stay in England, Delany became involved in a highly publicized international incident. His exploration of Africa brought him an invitation to attend the International Statistical Congress in July 1860, a distinguished gathering of scientists from all over the world. The entire diplomatic corps of the United States, including the American ambassador, a former vice-president of the country, was present. After an opening address by Prince Albert, the royal consort, several special guests were introduced by Lord Brougham, the eminent British legal reformer and antislavery advocate. At the close of his introductions, Lord Brougham turned to the American ambassador and said: "I hope our friend

Mr. Dallas will forgive me reminding him that there is a negro present, a member of the Congress.'' Since the others who had been introduced had responded to introduction, Delany decided to say a few words. "I pray your Royal Highness," he declared, "will allow me to thank his lordship, who is always a most unflinching friend of the negro and I assure your Royal Highness and his lordship that I am a man." The *London Times,* in reporting these remarks, noted: "This novel and unexpected incident elicited a round of cheering very extraordinary for an assemblage of sedate statisticians."

Ambassador Dallas, a native of Philadelphia, was enraged, but as he wrote in his diary: "Query: 'Is not the British government answerable for this insult? Or must it be regarded as purely the personal indecency of Lord Brougham?' " While Dallas did not withdraw from the congress, the official American delegate, Judge Augustus Baldwin Longstreet, then president of South Carolina College, did, and he was followed by the entire American delegation, except for one delegate from Boston. Not only did Judge Longstreet withdraw in protest, but he reported to the U.S. secretary of the treasury that Brougham's action had constituted "an ill-timed assault upon our country, a wanton indignity offered to our minister and a pointed insult offered to me." Because Dallas, much as he had detested Delany's presence and his introduction to the Congress, had not walked out, he was subjected to bitter abuse in the proslavery press in the United States. The *New York Herald,* a leading pro-Southern paper in the North, declared his action to be "deserving of the severest reprobation at the hands of the American people and the American government."

Delany was undisturbed by the rage his presence at the congress had aroused in his native land. Nor did the British appear to be concerned. In fact, before leaving London, Delany read a paper on his researches in Africa before the Royal Geographical Society. He continued to lecture on Africa in England and Scotland for almost seven months, dispelling myths about Africa's being a land of savages without any semblance of civilization. Not all the time Delany spent in England was devoted to educating the British about Africa. He and Campbell were successful in persuading a number of industrialists and antislavery men to support and promote their emigration scheme. The African Aid Society was founded in July 1860 with the express purpose of promoting emigration to Yoruba. Lancashire and Scottish cotton manufacturers supported the plan on the ground that a successful colony could provide them with an alternative source of cotton and relieve their dependence on the South. At a time when talk of secession and Civil War was widespread, Richard Blackett points out, "Delany and Campbell's plan came as a god-send to the English cotton interest." To this there was added the argument of antislavery advocates that the successful production of free-grown cotton in Abeokuta would ultimately undermine the basis of the South's economy and lead to the emancipation of the slaves.

In his bid for British support for his colony, Delany told a Scottish audience that land in Africa was available and free, labor was plentiful, crops were easily rotated, and black Americans could provide the expertise and supervision for the successful cultivation of cotton. All that was needed was a judicious infusion of British capital. He left England with great hope for the success of his project, having already discussed plans for the first group of settlers with William King, the leader of the Canadian Elgin community. The Scottish Presbyterian minister and former slaveowner was in Britain at the time of Delany's visit, raising funds and generally assisting Elgin settlers who planned to emigrate to Africa. He already had the support of the African Aid Society and agreed that Delany would lead the Elgin group to Yoruba country.

FAILURE OF AFRICAN EMIGRATION

Delany landed in Canada in 1861, six weeks after the Civil War had broken out, and he immediately began a lecture tour of Canada and the Northern states in the hope of winning support for the colony. He met with little success. The black communities were even more divided over emigration in 1861 than when Delany had left for Africa. Moreover, black Americans were turning to the Civil War in the hope of winning their freedom and rights as citizens, and emigration was furthest from their thought. William King, who had worked closely with Delany on the Abeokuta project, summed up the situation:

In the spring of 1861 I had several young men prepared to go out as pioneers of the colonies. While I was corresponding with the [African Aid] Society in London about sending the young men out, the Southern States seceded and the war was declared. I then wrote to the Society in London that the sword had been drawn from the scabbard and would not be returned, until liberty was proclaimed to the captives. The market for slaves as far as the United States was concerned would come to an end with the war. The young men interested to go out to Africa to colonize the West Coast were prepared to go south to fight for liberty as soon as the opportunity would be given them to enter the Northern Army.

In November 1861, the leaders of theAfrican Civilization Society conferred with Delany about the future of what had now become a joint project. This union was not entirely unexpected. While Delany and Garnet had been rivals, they still had much in common. Both had originally opposed emigration to Africa but had come to believe in it as a legitimate way of progress. Both now looked to Africa as the land of commerce. Both shared the view of the importance of the three C's of commerce, Christianity, and civilization.

The American Civilization Society and Delany resolved to discourage any general exodus of black Americans to Yoruba since it was obvious that any attempt to settle immigrant cotton planters in the war-torn area, which had become even more strife ridden since Delany left Africa, would have been impossible; however, they agreed to "aid such persons as may be practically qualified" to function in Africa individually. But nothing came of even this limited project. The African Civilization Society moved on to other projects and increasingly focused on Haiti as the destination for emigration. Indeed Garnet was actively promoting emigration to Haiti as well as Africa and accepted a position in James Redpath's Emigration Bureau. Though not entirely abandoning African emigration, Garnet soon turned his main attention to promoting a black exodus to Haiti. But Haitian emigration also failed. Delany was to be commissioned to raise black troops for the Union army and later given the rank of major. With that, his interest in African emigration largely receded. Of the entire group of African emigrationists interested in the Niger Valley area, only Robert Campbell settled there. In the last paragraph of the preface to his *A Pilgrimmage to My Motherland: An Account of a Journey among the Egbas and Yorubas of Central Africa, in 1859–60* he wrote: "I have determined with my wife and children, to go to Africa to live." The *Anti-Slavery Reporter* of April 18, 1863, carried the information that Campbell was operating a new paper, the *Anglo-African Weekly,* in Lagos.

Hopes of a renewed effort to settle the Yoruba area at a later time were shattered by a bitter controversy that developed over the legality of the treaty Delany and Campbell had signed with the African chiefs. The treaty with the Alake was ratified on December 28, 1859, by the "executive council of chiefs and elders." The version published in both Delany's and Campbell's reports of their journeys states that the kings and chiefs had given black Americans the right and privilege to settle in common with the Egba people on land not otherwise occupied; that the settlers had legal jurisdiction over matters affecting them; that they should be skilled and on arrival introduce plans for the dissemination of their skills and knowledge among the local people; that the laws of the Egbas would be strictly respected by the settlers; and that in matters affecting both groups, a commission of an equal number of Americans and Abeokutans would be appointed to settle the matter.

But the British enemies of the proposed settlement, mainly the traders who feared the breaking of their near monopoly of commerce in Yoruba, charged that the "Alake and chiefs declared that this [treaty] is a downright fabrication and that they signed no Treaty." It was soon clear that these forces had brought pressure on the Alake to rescind the concession. In 1862, the United Egba Association and the chiefs of the Abeokuta, yielding to the pressure of British traders, repudiated the agreement made in 1860 with Delany and Campbell. According to Richard Blackett, who has studied all of the pertinent documents, it seems that "both Delany and Campbell misunderstood Egba land laws." As a result, a conflict inevitably arose over the existence of a settlement within the Yoruba area with its own authority and laws.

Thus it was that although the privilege of settling was obtained in treaties signed by West African chiefs (and later repudiated), no emigration resulted from the labors of Martin R. Delany, Robert Campbell, and Henry Highland Garnet.

CONCLUSION

Black emigrationism was viewed by men like Delany, Garnet, Crummell, and Holly as a politically viable tactic at a time when the hopes and aspirations of black Americans were thwarted by increasing oppression. The 1850s was such a period. But with the 1860s, new hope arose, and as it did, emigrationist sentiment receded and almost vanished, for the time being. Even during the difficult years of the 1850s, emigrationist sentiment failed to engender black unity or to win widespread support in the Northern black communities. The emigrationist leaders failed to win widespread support because, in the main, black Americans continued to see in emigration a white plot to exile free blacks and further entrench the slave power. In Boston, where blacks did win some victories in the battle for equality in the fields of transportation, education, and intermarriage and where black males did have the right to vote, emigrationist appeals fell almost completely on deaf ears.

After investigating the migrations of free blacks into the American West and Spanish borderlands, George R. Woofolk concluded that there was a large black emigration in the decade following passage of the Fugitive Slave Act of 1850, but to neither Africa nor Haiti. Rather, many free blacks did "escape" to the West for asylum. Whether this conclusion is valid, it is certainly true that the record of colonization and emigration in terms of numbers of blacks involved, apart from those who fled to Canada, was not very impressive. By December 1860, after forty years of activity, the American Colonization Society had found only twelve thousand free blacks who were willing and able to expatriate themselves to Liberia. Black emigrationists of the period from 1850 to 1861 were no more successful than the Colonization Society had been in winning the confidence and cooperation of the black community. However noble and elevated their mission, as they sincerely believed it to be, the emigrationists could not overcome the feelings of many Northern blacks that endorsement of colonization in whatever form would only tighten the chains of their kinspeople in bondage and worsen their own status.

To be sure, at the height of the emigration fever, only a minority of black leaders seriously planned for a mass exodus to a foreign utopia. Even most emigrationists had reservations about deserting their brothers and sisters entrapped by slavery in the South and envisaged only a migration of a small number who would make a contribution to the new society to be built in a foreign land. Large-scale emigration, Delany, Garnet, and Crummell argued, would place insurmountable burdens on the fledgling colony. To achieve any measure of success, it necessarily had to be selective. These carefully selected and skilled emigrants would be the instruments for the redemption of the race, and after they had achieved this, then the mass of black Americans could follow them to the redeemed haven.

But if emigration did not offer to solve immediately the fundamental problems of the mass of black Americans, how could it be considered by them a viable alternative to continuing the struggle for liberty and equality at home, difficult though that might be? The emigrationist view that the existence of a successful black community in Africa or Haiti would by itself strengthen the struggle for the full freedom and equality of blacks who remained in the United States actually convinced few black Americans. Even Thomas Hamilton of the *Anglo-African*, Garnet's close associate, denied it would aid the cause "to found an empire in Yoruba." "After we had founded such a state," he wrote, "our work in the United States would remain to be done by other hands." But, black critics of emigration asked, why abandon this all-important struggle to "other hands"? As James McCune Smith put it to the emigrationist leaders:

There is a manhood in the colored race in the United States, and you cannot see it. You want to go to Africa to see gorgeous temples and governorships. You are so blind that you cannot see the grand throbbings of humanity in the heart of every black man.

Even though she spoke mainly from her experience in Boston, Sarah Parker Remond did not greatly overstate her case to a British audience in 1859 when she declared: "There is nothing that the free colored people of the United States hate like colonization. They are attached to their homes and their country, for America, not Africa, is their country, and they have no more idea of leaving it than the oppressed people have of leaving Africa."

The battle over emigration did not end in 1861, for emigration was more than a black reaction to white racism: It was a fundamental and vital aspect of the continuing struggle of black Americans for self-determination, for a black nationality in either Africa, the Caribbean, or the United States, and for a true understanding of African culture and the place of Africa in world history. In this last respect alone, Garnet felt that his efforts had not been in vain. Thus, he declared in 1860 "that if not a single person went to Yoruba, at this time, a strong interest had been awakened in Africa." Benjamin Coates made the same point in a letter to Alexander Crummell in April 1862, noting that before the formation of the African Civilization Society and Delany's expedition to the Niger River valley, the word *African* carried only the connotation of contempt, even among black Americans. Since these two events, respect for African history and civilization had emerged strongly among the Negro people in the United States.

Nonetheless, to most black Americans the whole emigration excitement was not more than a distraction from their struggle at home for emancipation in the South and equal rights in the North. Regardless of whether this was true, the main center of free black attention and activity during the period 1850 to 1861 was precisely in these two areas.

11

Kansas-Nebraska, Cuban Annexation, and the Early Republican Party

Following passage of the Compromise of 1850, a euphoria swept sections of the United States as the feared disruption of the Union was averted. However, a Georgia newspaper was closer to the truth when it observed: "It is the calm of preparation, and not of peace; a cessation, not an end to the controversy. . . . There is a feud between North and South which may be smothered, but never overcome."

KANSAS-NEBRASKA ACT

The illusory calm produced by the Compromise of 1850 was shattered four years later. On December 14, 1853, Augustus C. Dodge of Iowa introduced a bill in the Senate to organize the territory of Nebraska embracing the then-unorganized territory of the United States lying between the parallels of 36° 30' and 43° 30' North latitude. The bill made no mention of slavery, and it was referred to the Committee of Territories, of which Stephen A. Douglas, the "Little Giant" of Illinois, was chairman.

Although born in Vermont, with generations of New England ancestors, Douglas built his phenomenal political career in the Democratic party of the West. At twenty-one, he was Illinois state's attorney, at twenty-seven a member of the Illinois Supreme Court (called the "baby judge"), at thirty a congressman, and at thirty-five a U.S. senator. As early as 1848, Douglas became a champion of the doctrine of popular sovereignty (first formulated by Lewis Cass of Michigan) in dealing with the question of slavery in the territories. Let the settlers themselves decide, he insisted. Douglas also became one of the most fervent advocates of manifest destiny and a firm believer in unlimited territorial expansion. He also took the lead in promoting government support for the railroads.

Both the issue of popular sovereignty and that of railroad promotion became entangled in the way Douglas dealt with the bill for organizing the Nebraska territory. The bill he originally reported out of the Committee of Territories merely provided that the inhabitants had full power over their domestic institutions. But when Southern senators moved to insert an outright repeal of the Missouri Compromise of 1820 by permitting slavery to exist north of the line 36° 30'—leaving the matter to be decided by the settlers themselves—Douglas promptly included that demand into the bill.

Historians have long disagreed on the motives for Douglas' acquiescence. It appears clear, however, that the desire for a northern route for a Pacific railroad did play a significant role in his action. Since the discovery of gold in California in 1849, railroad promoters had been scheming to extend railroads across the Mississippi, west to the Pacific Coast. Congress had sponsored surveys of possible routes, and two principal plans had emerged: a northern railway to terminate in either St. Louis or Chicago or a southern one to New Orleans. Douglas was the senatorial sponsor of the Northern alternative. That project required that Kansas and Nebraska be given territorial rank, a step that required removing the Indians from their reservations and consolidating settlement there. Douglas was not in the least concerned over the Indian question, for he always looked upon the Indians as savages and their reservations as "barriers of barbarism." He believed that manifest destiny required their removal in order to permit "Christianity, Civilization and Democracy" to advance. But he did need to win Southern votes for his railroad project, and the southerners in Congress favored a southern route to the Pacific. In order to garner Southern votes for the Northern railroad scheme, Douglas agreed to allow the status of slavery in the Kansas-Nebraska region to be settled by popular sovereignty, even though a vote to permit slavery would repeal the Missouri Compromise barring slavery from most of the Louisiana Purchase territory.

According to Roy F. Nichols, a group of Southern Democrats, annoyed because President Franklin K. Pierce, elected in 1852 on the Democratic ticket, had been attempting to win the favor of Northern free soil Democrats by offers of patronage, decided to make the new Nebraska measure a test of the free-soilers' loyalty to the party. They told Douglas that they would not support any bill for organizing Nebraska that barred slavery from the territory. Eager to get the territory organized in order to open the door for a Northern railroad to the Pacific, Douglas speedily yielded. His bill virtually repealing the Missouri Compromise stirred an extremely bitter debate in both houses of Congress.

Although the North was slow to become aroused, many northerners were convinced that the sole purpose of the bill was to ensure the continued expansion of slavery. The famous "Appeal of the Independent Democrats in Congress to the People of the United States," written by Salmon P. Chase and Joshua Giddings, was first published in the *New York Times* of January 24, 1854, and was widely disseminated. It had much to do with arousing Northern hostility to the bill. It condemned the proposed repeal of the Missouri Compromise as "a criminal betrayal of precious rights, and part and parcel of an atrocious plot'' to extend slavery into the West, creating there ''a dreary region of despotism, inhabited by master and slaves.'' It closed with a warning that ''the dearest interests of freedom and the Union are in imminent peril'' and called for religious and political organization to defeat the bill.

Black reaction was mixed. Frederick Douglass was critical of opponents of the bill who, like Chase and Giddings, glorified the Missouri Compromise and insisted that ''the *true issue* should be kept in view'':

We regard this Missouri Compromise as scarcely fit to be made an incident issue with the slave power. . . . Our cause is not helped, but hindered, by pleading such compromises. That cause must fight its battles on broader and sounder principles than can be found in the narrow and rotten compromise of 1820. . . . The real issue to be made with the slave power, and the one which should never be lost sight of is this: Slavery, like rape, robbery, piracy or murder, has no right to exist in any part of the world—that neither north nor south of 36 deg. 30 min. shall it have a moment's repose if we can help it.

Douglass soon realized, however, that, as even Stephen A. Douglas had conceded some years earlier, the Missouri Compromise had been ''canonized in the hearts of the American people'' and could be disturbed only at the greatest peril.

Still, when Philadelphia blacks met on March 20, 1854, at an ''Anti-Colonization and Anti-Nebraska meeting,'' they made it clear that their basic opposition was not solely to the repeal of the Missouri Compromise. The meeting first denounced the American Colonization Society, attacked all efforts for ''expatriation to Africa,'' and went on to condemn the homestead bill, which had just been passed by Congress, providing that every settler should receive 160 acres of public land free from the federal government—but denied that right to all blacks. The Philadelphia meeting reminded the sponsors of the bill ''that color was not thought of as a hindrance to their suffering in two wars to maintain the rights of the American people.'' The meeting then resolved:

That our opposition to the Nebraska Bill is not based simply on the fact that it violates the Missouri Compromise of 1820, but grows out of our conviction that slavery cannot be legalized, and that therefore no opportunity whatever ought to be given the people in any new territory to declare hereafter as property HUMAN RIGHTS, who can never be made property.

Resolved, That whatever differences of opinion may be entertained on the right of new territories to legislate for themselves, we understand too well the policy of the South not to know the Nebraska Bill contemplates the extension of slavery, and we therefore regard it as peculiarly affecting us, by our identification with the slaves of the South.

Resolved, That we are opposed to all compromises between freedom and slavery, believing that slavery has no rights, but is pregnant with wrongs, and therefore we stop not to consider whether the Nebraska Bill violates this or that compromise, but seeing in it a foe to freedom, we stamp it as a document meriting the execration of every friend of man.

Finally, the meeting voted the thanks of Philadelphia's black community to Senators Seward, Chase, Sumner, and Wade and Gerrit Smith and Giddings in the House "for the able manner they defended our rights in opposing the bill."

As the Philadelphia blacks correctly noted, the introduction of the principle of popular sovereignty to replace the Missouri Compromise, for all its democratic sound, was deceitful. It opened a hitherto free area to the danger of being taken over by the slaveowners and opened all territory to slave settlement, paving the way for the forcible invasion of the West by the slaveholders. The Philadelphians were also prophetic when they declared that "we understand too well the policy of the South not to know the Nebraska Bill contemplates the extension of slavery." Even when the settlers in Kansas voted overwhelmingly for freedom, the slave power still refused it admission into the Union. Kansas was barred from admission until 1861, when the imminence of the Civil War sent most of the proslavery members of Congress home to the Confederacy.

The meeting of Philadelphia blacks was part of the wave of revulsion that swept the North against the Kansas-Nebraska bill. So great was the indignation aroused by the measure that Douglas, its author, wrote that he could have traveled from Boston to Chicago by the light of his own burning effigies. The reaction was particularly strong in Chicago, for it was the senator from that city who had sponsored the bill. A February protest meeting brought together Democrats, Whigs, and Free Soilers to accuse southerners and the "sectional traitor" Douglas of plotting to nationalize slavery. When Douglas finally returned to Chicago to defend his bill, he was shouted off the platform.

Undeterred, Douglas obtained President Pierce's backing and managed to push the Kansas-Nebraska bill through both houses of Congress. Pierce signed the measure on May 30, 1854. In his message to Congress, the president justified the repeal of the Missouri Compromise in the Kansas-Nebraska Act, blamed the North for any difficulties arising out of the Kansas situation, and praised the South for having made many concessions to the North in the interest of the Union. Referring to the danger of disunion, he asked if the American people were so intent upon upholding the "interests of the relatively few Africans in the United States as to abandon and disregard the interests of 25,000,000 Americans." Evidently, according to President Pierce, blacks were not Americans.

After Pierce signed the measure into law, the *Cincinnati Gazette* voiced a growing view in the North when it stated that "it is impossible to satisfy the South" and that the time had come to take a firm stand. William Wilson, the black correspondent who signed himself "Ethiop," agreed and wrote in *Frederick Douglass' Paper:* "The whole land trembles with the iniquities of the accursed system of slavery usurpation . . . let the tocsin be sounded, and to arms every man whose skin is not whitened with the curse of God; and let our motto be, 'hands off or death.' " Douglass himself declared in a leading editorial:

Let the whole North awake, arise; let the people assemble in every free State of the Union; and let a great party of freedom be organized, on whose broad banner let it be inscribed,

"All compromises with slavery ended—The abolition of slavery essential to the preservation of liberty." Let the old parties go to destruction, whither they have nearly sunk the nation. Let their names be blotted out, and their memory rot; and henceforth let there be only a free party and a slave party.

THE "AFRICANIZATION OF CUBA" SCARE

While the precise party Douglass envisaged did not yet materialize, the struggle against the Kansas-Nebraska bill was the greatest single factor that fused all antislavery elements into a new party. Another factor was the increasing appetite of the slave power for expansion outside of the United States as revealed in the Ostend Manifesto of October 1854, which advocated annexing Cuba by force, if necessary. Not all who opposed Cuban annexation did so on antislavery grounds; some were opposed because the Cuban population was largely Catholic, while the American system of government, they insisted, could "only be maintained . . . on the principle of Protestant liberty." But black Americans had only one reason for opposing annexation of Cuba in 1854: that it would expand the territory and the strength of the slave power and, at the same time, crush the movement in Cuba launched by Spanish officials to end slavery on the island.

The two issues were closely related. Spain was under British pressure, which was partly motivated by the desire to prevent Cuban-slave-produced sugar from severely damaging the prosperity of sugar producers in the British West Indies, where slavery was abolished in 1833. Desirous of securing British support against filibustering expeditions to annex Cuba being prepared in the United States, with the aid of the Pierce administration, Spain decided on a new slave policy in the Pearl of the Antilles. On September 23, 1853, the Marquis Juan de la Pezuela was appointed captain general of Cuba and explicitly charged with suppressing the slave trade. Pezuela arrived in Cuba on December 3, 1853, preceded by rumors that he had instructions to end not only the slave trade but slavery itself—all as part of a secret agreement reached with the British.

On December 23, Pezuela issued the first of several decrees, freeing all Negroes "known by the name of *emancipados*" and providing that anyone caught importing Africans would be heavily fined and banished from the island for a period of two years; and decreeing the removal from office of any governors or lieutenant governors who failed to advise him of clandestine landings of slave ships from Africa in their respective provinces. Another edict provided for the gradual introduction and regulation of Spanish, Indian, Yucatecan, and Chinese immigration to replace slave labor from Africa.

But Pezuela soon found himself in opposition to a provision in the law of 1845 that prohibited intrusion in the plantations in pursuit of contrabands—slaves brought into Cuba from Africa—and as Pezuela pointed out, once the slave ship had landed its cargo in an obscure inlet, it was virtually impossible to pursue the trader further. Since a Negro bought in Africa for 40 *duros* was sold in Cuba for

700, since the long and broken coast line made preventing landings difficult, and since the authorities could not follow the slaves into the plantations, the slave traders simply ignored Pezuela's edicts.

Pezuela's complaints, endorsed by the British, brought the necessary authorization from Madrid. In March 1854, the inviolability of the plantations was nullified; thereafter, they were subject to search to investigate their labor force.

On May 3, 1854, Pezuela issued his most celebrated decree. It authorized officials to enter all plantations suspected of contraband practices; warned civil and military officers that they would be discharged if, on hearing of a disembarkation of slaves, they failed to notify the government within twenty-four hours; applied the same penalty to all lesser officials, "since it is not possible to effect any embarkation without the connivance of minor officials"; subjected all those convicted of slave smuggling to a two-year exile; and provided for an annual registration of slaves after the August harvest. "Now," said Pezuela, in concluding his decree, "the spectacle of an impotent authority and the impunity of a few capitalists must come to an end. Avaricious interests that place private gain above the national interest can no longer be tolerated."

These measures filled the Cuban slaveowners with the wildest fears, and justifiably so. They recognized that the suppression of the slave trade, coupled with annual registration of the slave population, meant gradual abolition. Under Pezuela's decree, all slaveholders were to come before the local authorities and make a full declaration of their slave property. A slave whose master could not show a registered title to him could be declared free on the spot. All slave arrivals in Cuba after 1820 (when Spain agreed in a treaty with England to abolish the slave trade to the island) were declared illegal entries and their owners deprived of any clear title to them. The registration of slaves, it was hoped, would bring these irregularities into the open, and the illegally held slaves could be declared free at any moment the government chose. The death rate among the slaves on the island was extremely high and the birthrate correspondingly low. If their supply was not replenished and those who had been smuggled in were declared free, the only slaves left would be those imported before 1820 and their offspring. It would not be long before scarcely a slave remained in the island.

To meet this threat, the Cuban slaveowners raised the cry of Africanization. They prophesied that the decrees already published were the forerunners of more drastic ones—that Spain would send hordes of Negroes to the island and free them after a short period of enforced contract labor. These "barbarous" Africans would, in time, submerge the whites. Spain would then decree complete emancipation, and the blacks would take over the island. "A general descent in the scale of morality would run throughout the entire population," and soon "civilization and Christianity" would perish in the island. It was all part of the "diabolical plot" of Africanization. Spain had signed a treaty with Great Britain pledging itself to carry out this atrocious plan to reduce Cuba to a "howling wilderness."

The Cuban slave merchants and planters demanded the immediate rescinding of all of Pezuela's decrees and his removal from office. When Pezuela and Spain refused to accede to these demands, they intensified the cry of Africanization and turned to the United States for help:

In this state of things we turn our eyes to Washington, and with grief we see that there they do not know the danger that our lives and property are in, there they do not perceive the risk this country is in of being Africanized.

In March 1854, Pierce's secretary of state, William H. Marcy, dispatched a secret agent, Charles W. Davis, to Cuba to investigate whether "the Africanization of Cuba is contemplated by Spain, and [whether] she is even engaged in making arrangements to carry the measure in effect." If he found evidence that this was indeed the case, the president would ask Congress for immediate action: "Our forbearance is ceasing to be a virtue."

After a three months' stay in Cuba, Marcy's emissary returned with a report charging Britain with seeking to emancipate all slaves introduced into Cuba after 1820, the "immediate result" of which would be

the destruction of the wealth of the island, a disastrous bloody war of the races, a step backwards in the civilization of America—and in a commercial view, an immediate loss to the United States, it being one of the best markets for their produce, and in a political view, its loss would be incalculable as it would be a never-ending source of embarrassments and danger to the whole Union.

Davis predicted that the slaves, upon emancipation, would "destroy at one blow the production of the Island" and, armed with "the lifted torch and knife," proceed to "attack the whites they hate, and whose superior civilization they fear, and would not rest until they destroyed them or forced them to leave the Island." At the end of his report, Davis wrote:

The conclusion is irresistible that the emancipation of the Island and consequent Africanization of the Island is the true object had in view, and to which the march is as rapid as circumstances will allow. . . .

The danger is the more dreaded from the neighborhood of a Black Empire Haiti whose example they the emancipated slaves of Cuba would feel proud to imitate and whose asylum they could fly to in case they were conquered. Should the United States remain passive spectators of the consummation of the plans of the British ministry, the time is not distant in which they will be obliged to rise and destroy such dangerous and pernicious neighbors.

The conclusion to be drawn from Davis' hysterical report was obvious: send the U.S. Army to Cuba before Spain carried through the British-inspired scheme to Africanize the island, followed by the annexation of Cuba.

The Southern expansionist press swelled the outcry against Africanization. An Africanized Cuba would be bad enough in itself, but with Jamaica and Haiti, it would fasten a belt of Negro republics around the coast of the United States. These black republics would kindle a conflagration throughout the South, endangering "the very existence of slavery" through widespread slave insurrections and by offering refuge to fugitive slaves. "This [Africanization of Cuba] is monstrous," cried the proannexationist *Democratic Review,* "and we will not allow it. This continent is for white people, and not only the continent but the islands adjacent, and the negro must be kept in slavery in Cuba, and Hayti under white republican masters."

A major objection voiced in the Southern states to Pezuela's program was that it would end in the complete abolition of slavery in Cuba, and thus, as the *New Orleans Daily Picayune* frankly admitted on October 23, 1853, would render Cuba "worthless to the American Union, by fostering elements which would make it inadmissable into the confederacy." A free Cuba would be worthless to the slavery expansionists. Freedom for the slaves of Cuba was something that the slaveowners could not tolerate. As C. Stanley Urban writes: "Conservative planters understood Africanization to mean the adoption of any system of labor which had for its ultimate aim the extinction of slavery, and they so interpreted the labor decree in the island in 1854." Everything else—"the Negro republic," "the burning of the sugar-properties by the torch," "the destruction and expulsion of the white race," "the disappearance of civilization and Christianity"— was merely propaganda designed to conceal the real issue. As Robert Russell, a British visitor to the United States, reported: "The planters of the South cannot tolerate the idea of Cuba being made free, and they all declare that the United States would be justified in making war against Spain were she to free her slaves."

To many slaveowners, moreover, the annexation of Cuba for slavery was far more important than the opening up of Kansas and Nebraska for settlement by the slaveholders. Alexander H. Stephens of Georgia expressed the view of the Southern leaders when he wrote in May 1854 that while the Southern victory in the Kansas-Nebraska Act was significant, he doubted that it would produce an "actual extension of slavery. . . . We are on the eve of much *greater issues* in my opinion. The Cuba question will soon be upon us." In an editorial entitled "Nebraska and Cuba," the *New Orleans Daily Picayune* of June 9, 1854, stated frankly that Kansas and Nebraska, by themselves, were not important to the South: "The measure upon which the Nebraska principle will be tested is that of the acquisition of Cuba." At a public dinner in New Orleans, the participants drank to the following toast:

> Cuba:
> We'll buy or fight, but to our shore we'll lash her;
> If Spain won't sell, we'll then turn in and *thrash* her.

The "thrash her" was also a play on words, for it applied too to John S. Thrasher, an ardent proslavery, proannexationist Louisianian who had been for several years a resident of Cuba. Thrasher gained a good deal of notoriety in 1856 when he published an English translation of Alexander von Humboldt's *Ensayo Politico sobre la Isla de Cuba* under the title, *The Island of Cuba,* but completely omitted chapter seven dealing with slavery. In this chapter the German naturalist wrote: "Without doubt, slavery is the greatest of all the evils which has afflicted mankind."

"MANIFESTO OF THE BRIGANDS"

Spain, it turned out, did refuse to sell Cuba to the United States when Pierre Soulé, minister to Spain and prophet of Southern expansionism, offered the Madrid government up to $130 million for Cuba, on behalf of the Pierce administration. Upon receiving this rejection of the American offer, Secretary of State Marcy directed the ministers of the United States in London, Paris, and Madrid to assemble at a place designated by Soulé to consult on a Cuba policy. The conference of James Buchanan, James Mason, and Pierre Soulé, U.S. ministers, respectively, to Great Britain, France, and Spain, was held in Ostend, Belgium. Concluding their discussions on October 18, 1854, the ministers communicated the results of their deliberations in a dispatch to the State Department, which came to be known as the Ostend Manifesto.

In this notorious document, stigmatized by antiannexationists as the "manifesto of the brigands," the three American ministers argued that the immediate annexation of Cuba was essential to the security and "repose" of the American Union. The changes recently organized in Cuba by Pezuela threatened an insurrection that might have "direful" consequences to the American people since the slaves of Cuba might emulate their brethren of Haiti. But if Cuba belonged to the United States, it would not permit "the flames to extend to our neighboring shores, seriously to endanger or actually to consume the fair fabric of our Union." As long as Cuba belonged to Spain, Cuba would be an "unceasing danger" and "a permanent cause of anxiety and alarm" to the United States.

The manifesto recommended that "the United States ought, if practicable, to purchase Cuba as soon as possible," and, if Spain should refuse to sell, then

by every law human and Divine, *we shall be justified in wresting it from Spain, if we possess the power,* and this, upon the very principle that would justify any individual in tearing down the burning house of his neighbor, if there were no other means of preventing the flames from destroying his own house.

Under such circumstances, we ought neither to count the cost nor regard the odds which Spain might enlist against us.

In a private letter accompanying the manifesto, Soulé urged Marcy to prepare for war. This was the moment, he wrote, "to be done with" the Cuban problem—now, "while the great powers of this continent are engaged in that stupendous struggle in the Crimea, which cannot but engage all their strength and tax all their energies, as long as it lasts, and may, before it ends, convulse them all."

The proslavery, proannexationist forces, which the Pierce administration served, no longer dominated the American political scene, however. On November 4, the day the Ostend Manifesto arrived in Washington, New York voted every Democrat in Congress from that state out of office. This was only one of a series of electoral disasters for the administration. By the time all the returns were in, the Democrats had lost control of Congress. This was the answer of an electorate angered over the Kansas-Nebraska Act, and it was a repudiation of the administration's belligerent Cuban annexationist policy.

The administration debated its reply to the three ministers. On November 13, Marcy sent the answer. It repudiated the Ostend Manifesto and rejected its recommendations, but it still left the door open for action to seize Cuba in case a "material change in the condition of the island" occurred that might involve "immediate peril to the existence" of the United States. In short, should the Pezuela policy in Cuba be carried to the point of emancipating the slaves, this would justify the seizure of the island, and it would be the United States alone that would determine that the Spanish policy constituted a "clear and present danger" to its (that is, the Southern slaveholders') security.

In the end, the administration had to abandon every effort to annex Cuba for the benefit of the slave power. The Kansas-Nebraska Act did not sate the appetite of the Southern slaveowners, but the bitterness it provoked in the North demonstrated to all but the most rabid expansionists that the annexation of Cuba might easily break up the Union. Before this danger, even the annexation-obsessed Pierce administration had to retreat.

While black Americans hailed the defeat of the Pierce administration's efforts to obtain possession of Cuba, they lamented an unhappy concomitant of the administration's policy, for the protests of the slaveowners, the threat in the Ostend Manifesto, and Marcy's promise to act if Pezuela's policies continued, coupled with the indignant cries of rage from the slave merchants and planters in Cuba, forced Spain to replace the antislavery captain general. The man who succeeded Pezuela, José de la Concha, immediately announced that the major decrees of his predecessor would be abrogated. Pressured by the U.S. government to guarantee that there would be no return to Pezuela's policies, the Spanish secretary of state informed the American minister to Spain that the United States need have no fear. "He said," the minister reported joyfully, "that Spain regarded slavery as an indispensable element for the prosperous development of the resources of Cuba."

Black leaders in the United States pointed bitterly to the fact that, due largely to pressure from the Pierce administration, accompanied by threats of war and of seizure of Cuba, Spain's first sincere effort to extinguish the slave trade in the island, liberate the *emancipados*, and pave the way for gradual abolition of slavery had been nullified.

"BLEEDING KANSAS"

At about the same time, the naked aggression exhibited in the Ostend Manifesto had its counterpart in the opening shots of the struggle for Kansas as slaveholders sent their armed emissaries into the Kansas territory from Missouri to stuff ballot boxes and to seize Kansas for slavery by all possible means. This was countered by an organization which promoted migration to Kansas of free settlers from the North who came to combat the efforts to steal the territory for slavery. As the contestants came to grips in "bleeding Kansas," Frederick Douglass published "Our Plan for Making Kansas a Free State." Since Stephen A. Douglas had "given his plan for getting slavery into Kansas," he could "not see why Frederick Douglass should not submit his plan for keeping slavery out of Kansas." Convinced that there was nothing "slaveholders more dread than the presence of a numerous population of industrious, enlightened, and orderly Colored Men," he proposed that just such an organized group be sent to Kansas. He conceded that although the "infamous Nebraska Bill" did not bar blacks from entering the territory, the homestead bill just passed by Congress excluded them from its benefits. But he was convinced that this "injustice is so utterly base and scandalous" that most of Kansas' white population "would render it inoperative and void"—a vastly overoptimistic viewpoint, to say the least. Meanwhile, "Colored Men, Colored Citizens for such they really are—native-born citizens to boot, can emigrate to Kansas and can safely occupy land thereon." And when the day finally arrived for voting on the status of slavery in Kansas, let the champions of popular sovereignty try to exclude blacks. This would indeed make a mockery of the doctrine. But even if they were excluded from the ballot box, the black settlers "would not be without influence, and there is no question in which side the influence would be wielded."

So to begin, Douglass urged, let an association of wealthy men be formed, a fund of about $40,000 be raised, and the recruiting of black families for Kansas get underway:

Let the press of the North take hold of this idea and press it upon the public mind, and Kansas need not be a Slave State, and your cities need not have an unequal share of the free colored people of the North. Meanwhile, let the white free working men flock into the territory by themselves. There is room and work for all. . . .

Friends of Freedom! What say you to meeting the enemy on this vantage ground? You can meet them and beat them in the way here indicated, and if you do not do it, the responsibility is yours.

Nothing came of Douglass' plan. The proslavery "border ruffians" in Missouri, armed emigrants from Missouri, would not have hesitated to murder any black family who dared to venture into Kansas. Many of the free soilers who emigrated from the North to keep the territory free from slavery probably would not have protected the blacks. As they demonstrated later when they barred Negroes in the provisional state constitution they drew up for Kansas, neither slaves nor free blacks were welcome in the territory.

NORTHERN LABOR AND SOUTHERN SLAVERY

The same year that saw the passage of the Kansas-Nebraska Act and the "manifesto of the brigands" also witnessed the birth of the Republican party. A grass-roots movement, it came into existence in many places. At a celebration of the party's thirtieth anniversary in Maine, a speaker remarked that while seven cities claimed to be the birthplace of Homer, seven states claimed to be the birthplace of the Republican party.

Probably the first move toward the new party was taken at a meeting held in the town of Ripon, Wisconsin, in February 1854, pursuant to a notice sent out under the signatures of a Whig, a Democrat, and a Free-Soiler. The meeting, held in the Congregational church, resolved that if the recently introduced Kansas-Nebraska bill became law, old party lines were to be considered dissolved, and a new political party was to be formed, to be called Republican.

A second gathering at Ripon a month later took definite steps to organize the party on a local scale. The initiator of the Ripon meetings was Alvin E. Bovay, formerly the secretary-treasurer of the National Industrial Congress, one of the earliest attempts to organize labor on a nationwide scale, and a leader in the 1840s of the workingmen's movement of New York.

Before we proceed further into the formation of the Republican party, we must answer the question: How did it come about that a leader of white Northern labor became the initiator of a local movement that led to the formation of a new party—a party that grew in six years from a handful of men in Ripon's Congregational church to the political organization that elected the chief executive of the nation?

The answer to this question lies in the changing attitude toward slavery of the great bulk of white workers in the North during the 1850s. To be sure, sections of the Northern working class had expressed sympathy for the antislavery cause as early as the 1820s and 1830s. Thomas Wentworth Higginson, the Massachusetts abolitionist, later recalled that in Worcester the antislavery cause was "far stronger for a time in the factories and shoe shops than in the pulpits or colleges." In New York City, the largest numbers of signers of abolitionist petitions in the 1830s were the city artisans.

In 1836, the Working Men's Association of England asked the white workers of the United States: "Why, when she [the United States] has afforded a home and an asylum, for the destitute and oppressed among all nations, should oppression in her own land be legalized and bondage tolerated?" In transmitting this message to American workers, Lewis Gunn, a Philadelphia labor leader, wrote: "Our voice should *thunder* from Maine to Georgia, and from the Atlantic to the Mississippi—a voice of a nation of *Republicans* and *Christians* demanding with all the authority of moral power, *demanding* the immediate liberation of the bondsmen."

A workers' mass meeting assembled in Boston in May 1848 to hail the democratic revolutions then convulsing Europe resolved: "That while we rejoice in the organization of free institutions in the Old World, we are not indifferent to their support at home, and that we regard the despotic attitude of the slave power at the South, and the domineering ascendancy of a Monied oligarchy in the North, as equally hostile to the interests of Labor, and incompatible with the preservation of popular rights."

Nevertheless, the attitude of many Northern working people toward slavery during the 1830s and 1840s was ambiguous. For one thing, relations between the young labor movement and white abolitionists were often difficult and strained. Many abolitionists, property-owning members of the middle class, accepted Northern labor relations as natural and just and opposed both trade union organization and strikes. The first issue of William Lloyd Garrison's *Liberator* in 1831 included an attack on Northern labor reformers. "We are the friends of reform," Garrison wrote, "but this is not reform, which in curing one evil, threatens to inflict a thousand others." In response, labor spokesperson William West insisted that labor and abolition should work together. Each, he declared, was trying to secure from a group of employers "the fruits of their toil."

Aileen Kraditor contends that the Garrisonians made sincere efforts to join hands with the labor movement but that the approaches on both sides broke down fundamentally over ideas about the nature of social change. Kraditor argues that labor and abolition had common grounds for joint struggle, and she claims that Garrison's hostility to labor was not as deep as alleged but that he believed that while wage workers had real problems, they paled by comparison with those of the slaves.

But many labor leaders of the North, echoing the proslavery idealogues in the South, such as George Fitzhugh, John C. Calhoun, and other proslavery thinkers, argued that the free laborer of the North was as much a slave to capital as the Negro was of the slaveowner. The Northern white worker, they maintained, was the victim of wage slavery. In language strikingly similar to that of southerners, labor leaders in the North drew a picture of white wage slavery as being worse than black chattel slavery. New England labor leader Seth Luther declared that Northern factory workers toiled longer each day than did slave plantation workers. A New Hampshire labor paper echoed: "A great cry is raised in the northern states against southern slavery. The sin of slavery may be abominable there, but is it not equally so here? If they have black slaves, have we not white ones?"

When striking journeymen tailors in New York City were convicted of conspiracy in 1836, they issued the famous Coffin handbill, declaring, "The freemen of the North are now on a level with slaves of the South."

Some labor and utopian socialist leaders argued that growing industrial capitalism, or wage slavery, and not the Southern slave system was the main enemy
of the wage workers and that Northern free labor should unite with Southern
slaveowners to combat the capitalists. On the other hand, a small group of
abolitionist leaders attempted to forge an alliance with Northern labor leaders.
Nathaniel Rogers, editor of the *Herald of Freedom*, published in Concord, New
Hampshire, proposed a grand alliance of the "producing classes"—Southern
slaves and Northern workers—against the exploiters of labor in both sections.
Living amid the expanding factory system of New England, Rogers insisted:
"We have got to look to the working people of the North, to sustain and carry on
the anti-slavery movement." Frederick Douglass, one of the first to endorse
Rogers' projected alliance, agreed with his conclusion. "It is not the rich that we
are to look to, but the poor," Douglass told an antislavery audience in Ohio, "to
the hardhanded workingmen of this country. These are the men who are to come
to the rescue of the slave."

At the same time, several labor leaders and political figures sympathetic to
labor sought to link the interests of labor and antislavery in a different way. The
labor movement had been devastated by the depression of 1837–1842, and when
it reemerged in the mid-1840s, one of its major concerns was land reform. Many
workers came to agree with George Henry Evans, the English labor reformer
who had been living in the United States since the late 1820s. Evans was
involved in publishing, among other things, the *Working Man's Advocate* and
Young America, in both of which he insisted that land monopoly was the root of
the problems of Northern labor, a position that was also advocated by Horace
Greeley, editor of the *New York Tribune*. Both Evans and Greeley offered as
their solution the homestead plan under which every person who so desired
would receive 160 acres of public land free of charge from the federal government. This would enable Eastern workers to escape wage slavery altogether by
establishing their economic independence on farms of the West. Those who
remained behind would benefit by the reduction in the number of laborers, which
would lead to wage increases. Land reform would thus solve the problem of
urban poverty and offer every workingman the opportunity to achieve
independence.

It was Evans' belief that without the distribution of public lands, the slaves,
once they were emancipated, would be no better off than the white wage slaves
of the North. Thus, Evans wrote to abolitionist Gerrit Smith:

I was formerly like yourself, sir, a warm advocate of the abolition of slavery. This was
before I saw that there was white slavery. Since I saw this, I have materially changed my
views as to the means of abolishing Negro slavery. I now see, clearly, I think, that to give
the landless black the privilege of changing masters now possessed by the landless *whites,*
would hardly be a benefit to him in exchange for his surety of support in sickness and old
age, although he is in a favorable climate. If the Southern form of slavery existed at the
North, I should say the black would be a great loser by the change.

Evans therefore advised Northern workingmen to ignore the issue of chattel slavery and leave the blacks in their "favorable climate," enjoying "surety of support in sickness and old age," and to concentrate instead on emancipating themselves from wage slavery through the distribution of the public lands. After this was achieved, they could turn their attention to abolishing chattel slavery, confident that when the chains of the blacks were broken, they, too, through the agency of land reform, would be spared being hurled into wage slavery.

What Evans did not understand was that slavery was not content to remain stationary in the South, awaiting the day that the emancipated wage slaves would turn their attention to abolishing the peculiar institution. It expanded into territories outside the slave states and threatened to continue doing so indefinitely, unless checked. Evans also did not see that the slaveholders, because they wanted to expand their system westward, were the chief opponents of the homestead idea, or "free soil," as it came to be called. Thus, despite the protestations of Evans and those who echoed his views, the homestead idea was implicitly antislavery because free homesteads could not coexist with large plantations worked by slaves. Nor could free labor compete with slave labor on the public lands when the bondspeople were used in other economic pursuits besides growing agricultural products. In order for the homestead idea to be put into effect, the workers had to reject Evans' advice to ignore the slavery issue until they had achieved their own emancipation. They had to act immediately to check the spread of slavery into the Western territories.

In 1848, a coalition of antislavery politicians and some labor leaders formed the Free Soil party, the first substantial third party committed to halting the extension of slavery and to providing free land to settlers. The Free Soilers, with Martin Van Buren as their candidate for president, polled 10 percent of the popular vote and won considerable support from labor organizations. They succeeded in placing slavery and free soil in the center of the political stage and began the process of eliminating the breach that existed between the abolitionists and Northern labor. As slavery became the dominant issue in the North in the 1850s, a new group in labor circles joined the struggle against the institution. This was made up of refugees from the German revolution of 1848. The German-American Marxists were among these refugees, and, led by Joseph C. Weydemeyer, the pioneer Marxist in the United States, they first set out to overcome the influence of a few in the ranks of German-American workers who failed to see that the system of slavery was the major obstacle in the path of the labor movement. Among these was Herman Kriege, who echoed George Henry Evans when he stated in 1846 in a New York German labor paper: "We could not improve the lot of our 'black brothers' by abolition under the conditions prevailing in modern society, but make infinitely worse the lot of our 'white brothers.' . . . We feel constrained, therefore, to oppose Abolition with all our might."

The German-American Marxists challenged this backward view and set out to convince the German working class, and as many other workers as they could influence, that free labor could not emancipate itself as long as chattel slavery existed, that the expansion of slavery "would immensely undermine the power of free labor," and that unless the slave power was smashed, slave labor would become the dominant labor system in the public lands of the West, eliminating free labor in the process. Communist clubs established in the 1850s, notes Hermann Schleuter, "contributed liberally toward spreading the light on this question [of slavery among Northern workers] and they were so downright in their opposition to the slaveholders as to call any of their members promptly to account who fell under the slightest suspicion of sympathizing with the South."

In the Deep South itself, Dr. Adolph Douai, a German-American socialist educator and refugee from the Revolution of 1848, established an antislavery paper, the *San Antonio Zeitung,* which he published weekly from July 1853 to March 1856. So fervent was Douai in his antislavery, pro-free labor views that he was driven out of the state by Texas slaveowners, narrowly escaping being lynched. In 1868, Douai, now a leading Marxist, received a newspaper from Texas with the following announcement: "This paper, edited and set by negroes, is being printed on the same press from which Dr. Douai for the first time advocated the emancipation of the negroes in Texas. Let this serve him as a token of gratitude of the colored race that they preserve the memory of his efforts."

Late in February 1854, five thousand mechanics and workers met at the Broadway Tabernacle in New York City "to utter a protest against the efforts now being made by corrupt politicians to throw down the barriers erected to prevent the extension of Slavery to territory north of 36 deg. 30 min." The main theme struck by the speakers was that the public lands must remain open for free labor and that the extension of slavery north of the line prohibited by the Missouri Compromise would bar the free workers, including both those seeking refuge from "the wars and oppressors of the Old World" and those seeking escape from wage slavery in the East, and place these public lands under the domination of the owners of slave labor. Hence they resolved unanimously: "That we the mechanics and workingmen of New York heartily concur in the stern protest against the threatened repeal of the Missouri Compromise."

A few days later, the German-American workingmen of New York City took a similar stand, and at a mass meeting of the *Arbeiterbund* (Workers' League) on March 1, 1854, a resolution introduced by Joseph Weydemeyer received the unanimous approval of several thousand German-American workers. It asserted that since the Nebraska bill favored "capitalist land speculation" at the expense of the people, authorized the "future extension of slavery," and withdrew vast tracts of land, making them unavailable for any future homestead bill, the German-American workers of New York, who "have, do now, and shall continue to protest most emphatically against both black and white slavery," had no choice but to "solemnly protest against this bill and brand as a traitor against the people and their welfare everyone who shall lend it his support."

Similar meetings were held by workers in New Jersey, Illinois, Pennsylvania, Ohio, Massachusetts, Michigan, Vermont, Connecticut, Indiana, and Wisconsin. Each meeting adopted resolutions castigating the slave power and opposing the Nebraska bill. The workers of Philadelphia resolved that "we are opposed to the introduction of the curse and infamy of Human Slavery into the Virgin Territory of the North." Shortly after the repeal of the Missouri Compromise, the National Industrial Congress met in convention and reversed its former stand that chattel slavery was of minor importance to the working class. It now said that chattel slavery was first on labor's agenda and called upon the workers of the North to demand "the immediate repeal of the Nebraska Bill, the Fugitive Slave Law, and the restoration of the Missouri Compromise." The congress voted that "in the future we will have no representative in our State or National Councils who has not plighted his sacred honor to resent the aggressions of the southern slave power, and to stand by the liberties of the citizens who elected him to power."

BIRTH AND IDEOLOGY OF THE REPUBLICAN PARTY

Let us now return to Ripon, Wisconsin, where the former secretary-treasurer of the National Industrial Congress, Alvin E. Bovay, was uniting liberals and reformers who were disgusted with the Whig and Democratic parties into a new political organization dedicated to fight the further extension of slavery and pledged to support a free land program. Bovay bestowed upon this new political organization a name that his former leader, George Henry Evans, had used as far back as 1846. At that time, Evans had predicted that within a decade there would be only two political parties in America, "the great Republican Party of Progress and the little Tory Party of Holdbacks."

Evans had used land reform as the dividing line between the two parties, but by the time Bovay gave the name "Republican party" to the organization that emerged in Ripon, the campaign for land reform and opposition to the extension of slavery had become inseparable. Slaveowners knew that a homestead bill would prevent the expansion of slavery and give political strength to the antislavery forces. The *North Carolina Standard* said that it opposed the homestead bill because it would bring new·states into the Senate "to vote us down upon every question affecting our vital interest, and finally to control the government absolutely." Congressman Branch of North Carolina said that it was dangerous to slaveholders because it was supported by the labor movement and was therefore "the first step . . . towards introducing communism and socialism."

The Republican movement spread rapidly throughout the Northwest and soon became an influence in the industrial centers of the East. A general realignment was taking place in American political life. Democrats who refused to stay in their party when it was dominated by slaveowners and Whigs who were fed up with their party's straddling of the slavery question were looking for a new political organization. The newly formed Republican party represented a coalition of different classes united by their opposition to the future encroachment of the slave power.

The nature of the early Republican party has been a matter of controversy for many years. For a long time, historians were preoccupied with Republican ties with Northern business, with the authenticity of the Republican moral crusade against slavery, and with the personal motives of Republican politicians. In the last few years, however, the debate has taken several dramatic new turns. Eugene Berwanger has argued that the Republican party was essentially a movement to protect the Western states and territories from incursions by blacks, free or slave. James A. Rawley also sees the determination to keep America a white man's country as the motivating influence in the formation and development of the Republican party and the party itself as dominated by the pervasive race prejudice of the antebellum years. Kenneth Stampp concedes that "many Republicans appeared to be at heart more anti-slaveholder, or anti-Slave Power, or anti-southern, or even anti-Negro than they were anti-slavery on moral grounds." Nevertheless, he contends that the Democrats were more racist than the Republicans, hardly a great tribute to the new third party. Michael Holt has scrutinized the political life of one city, Pittsburgh, to suggest that the Republican party was a response more to local problems, particularly immigration and nativism, than to national issues. At least in Pittsburgh, he concludes, opposition to slavery was less influential than ethnic and religious antagonisms.

Thus, in general, the recent historical trend has been to argue that the Republican party was dominated by racism, that many leading Republican politicians displayed anti-Negro prejudices, and that the party itself embodied less of the antislavery impulse than had once been thought. But in his recent study of the ideology of the Republican party before the Civil War, Eric Foner has challenged all of these concepts and has called attention to the Republican party's belief in the superiority of free labor, its "extensive criticism of Southern society," and its stress on "the existence of a conspiratorial 'Slave Power' which had seized control of the Federal government." Fundamentally, Republicans opposed slavery on the basis of a free labor ideology—"an affirmation of the superiority of the social system of the North—a dynamic, expanding capitalist society, whose achievements and destiny were almost wholly the result of the dignity and opportunities which it offered the average laboring man."

At the center of Republican ideology, Foner argues, lay a passionate belief in the virtues of free labor, and to Republicans, the free labor concept symbolized an ideal society that they saw threatened by slavery. Thus, according to Foner, the early Republican party was the political expression of the free labor ideology, which was a product of bustling Northern capitalism of the 1840s and 1850s. By that time, a system of values incorporating the dignity of labor, economic progress, social mobility, and equality of opportunity permeated Northern society, accompanied by a boundless faith in the ability of all to improve their condition through hard work. "Political antislavery . . . ," Foner writes, "was an affirmation of the superiority of the social system of the North—a dynamic, expanding capitalist society.'' Ultimately the forward-looking free-labor outlook of the North became incompatible with the static, proslavery philosophy of the South, and the war between the two sections was inevitable.

It was, then, not merely accidental or as a result of political manipulation that slavery in the territories became the principal political issue of the 1850s. Convinced that ''free land in the West provided an insurance of continuing social mobility in the North,'' Republicans could not tolerate the further spread of slavery since it represented a social system ''whose values, interests and future prospects were in sharp, and perhaps mortal conflict'' with those of the free states.

Recognizing that most Republicans, like most Americans at that time, were ''deeply flawed by an acceptance of many racial stereotypes,'' Foner argues that they ''did develop a policy which recognized the essential humanity of the Negro, and demanded protection for certain basic rights which the Democrats denied him.'' In short, while the new party was by no means free of prejudice, a substantial body of Republicans defied prevailing opinion and fought for many of the rights of the black man. Moreover, Foner finds that antislavery was the main focus of the Republican party, being almost the one issue that could unite it. Foner defends the radical antislavery men who joined and remained in the Republican party, against recent charges that their opposition to slavery stemmed largely from their racism. ''Principles . . . were what made the radicals adhere to the Republican Party,'' he maintains.

Where did the Negro fit into the free labor ideology of the Republican party? According to Foner, they did have a place. He notes, for example, than when an amendment barring blacks from participating in homestead benefits passed the House and Senate in 1854, twenty-four Whig and Democratic congressmen, who later served in the Congress as Republicans, voted against the provision and that no political figure who was associated later with the Republicans favored it. In general, he argues, the Republican party upheld the basic natural rights of the Negro, including his right to an economic livelihood, and it emphasized that ''the fundamental civil rights of the Negro, short of suffrage, deserved legal protection.''

BLACKS AND THE EARLY REPUBLICAN PARTY

There were three distinct views among blacks toward the early Republican party. The majority took a wait-and-see attitude. They had discovered, to their sorrow, that the free soil movement was heavily laced with racism, and most of them shared the view expressed by Frederick Douglass in 1849: ''The cry of Free Men was raised, not for the extension of liberty to the black man, but for the protection of the liberty of the white.'' While they were impressed by the fact that the men who became Republican party leaders had voted in Congress against the amendment barring blacks from participating in homestead benefits, they were not sure that these same men would not yield to political expediency and take a racist position the next time the issue arose. Moreover, they had little confidence in the Northern white workers, who formed a considerable element within the Republican party coalition. These workers had completely barred free blacks from their trade unions and even from the workshops where the Negro might find employment. Certainly these workers did not seem to share the Republican party's view that the Negro had a right to an economic livelihood. Hence most blacks decided to wait and see how the new party acted on issues of immediate concern to them. The Republican party, in short, had to prove the sincerity of its intentions before blacks would give it widespread support.

But while most blacks did not immediately flock to the Republican banner, small groups did begin holding a pro-Republican ticket "worthy [of] the support of every man of our race who has the vote." Charles B. Ray urged black voters in New York to vote Republican and thus show that they understood "the science of liberty and [were] up to the practical doctrine of sustaining freedom when brought to the issue of tyranny."

Another group of blacks, including Frederick Douglass, J. McCune Smith, J. B. Loguen, and Henry Highland Garnet, refused to desert the Liberty party and, along with some three hundred Liberty party members, remained outside of the new coalition organized in the Republican party. They contended that the "signs of the times forbid the dissolution" of their tiny organization. It was the only party, they argued, willing to fight the battle of freedom on the ground that "slavery cannot be legalized" anywhere on the earth, and the only party calling for "the utter annihilation of slavery." In September 1854, thirty Liberty party men, with several blacks among them, met in Syracuse and nominated William Goodell for governor on a platform calling upon the federal government to abolish slavery. Following the convention, Douglass took the stump for Goodell.

Even though the *New York Tribune*, the leading Republican organ, had proposed that Frederick Douglass be nominated for Congress by the Republican party, he refused to abandon the Liberty party and ally himself with the Republican movement. The Republican party, he contended, did not go far enough; it gave aid and comfort to the slaveholders by its willingness "to let Slavery where it is." Yet that was precisely where slavery should be attacked. There was, he maintained, a need for a party that called for "a clean sweep of slavery everywhere" and that "by its position and doctrines, and by its antecedents, is pledged to continue the struggle while a bondman in chains remains to weep." Such was the Liberty party, and on its platform "must the great battle of freedom be fought out." While it could not boast of mass support, the Liberty party could fulfill an important function by keeping alive the demand for the abolition of slavery throughout the nation until such a time as events themselves compelled other political parties with greater numerical support to incorporate this program into their platforms.

From June 26 to 28, 1855, the convention of the Liberty party (now renamed the Radical Political Abolitionists) met in Syracuse, New York. James McCune

Smith, the prominent black physician, was elected chairman, and Douglass was designated to serve on the Business Committee. (Smith's election was an unprecedented act, even among abolitionists.) The convention challenged the non-extension-of-slavery policy of the Republican party on the grounds that it was immoral to fight slavery in one part of the nation while permitting its existence elsewhere, and impractical to expect to suppress crime in one part of the country, while admitting its legality in other areas. The delegates then challenged Garrison's policy of "no-union with slaveholders" on the ground that it was immoral to secede from the South and leave the slaves in their present condition and impractical to take steps that were unconstitutional and might lead to civil war. Instead the delegates proposed the more viable alternative of national abolition as the most moral and practical means for ending slavery.

The question of using violent means to abolish slavery was the most divisive issue at the convention. The appearance of John Brown at the Syracuse gathering and his appeal for arms to "defend freedom" in Kansas led to a heated debate. Frederick Douglass spoke in favor of Brown, as did Gerrit Smith. But "peace men" like Lewis Tappan, the philanthropist and abolitionist, and William Goodell succeeded in passing a motion calling for peaceful means "at the ballot box" to end slavery.

The convention finally endorsed a program that urged the use of the political power of the nation "to overthrow every part and parcel of American Slavery" and pledged to nominate a candidate on that platform in the forthcoming presidential campaign of 1856. "We shall . . . contribute our mite toward effecting this desirable consummation," Frederick Douglass assured his readers.

THE KNOW-NOTHINGS

When the Whig party was destroyed, a political vacuum was left that had to be filled, and one of the organizations that filled the void initially in some states was the Native American or Know-Nothing party. Nativism had been intermittently influential in the politics of the Eastern states since the 1830s, but with the influx of Irish-Catholic immigrants in the mid-1840s and refugees from revolution in Europe in the early 1850s, it began to appear for a short time that nativism, rather than slavery, might be the dominant issue of the decade.

In the early 1850s, nativists organized a distinct political force. The Order of the Star-Spangled Banner was founded as a sacred nativist society in New York City in 1850, and lodges sprang up quickly in the rest of New York State and elsewhere in the nation. In 1853, its offshoot, the Know-Nothing party, adopted a platform calling for restricted naturalization, a free nonsectarian school system, Bible reading in public schools, and nonclerical control of church property.

The Know-Nothings developed a large following, particularly in the Northeastern states and especially in Massachusetts, where the presence of so many Irish fed the flames of nativism and anti-Catholicism. The Know-Nothings achieved their greatest successes in Massachusetts, where in 1854 they over-whelmingly elected the governor, the mayor of Boston, every state senator, and 351 of the lower house's 359 representatives.

But in the presidential election of 1856, the Know-Nothing party's national convention in Philadelphia split over the issue of opposition to the extension of slavery. The convention reversed the party's previous stand by denouncing the repeal of the Missouri Compromise, but it also indirectly demanded that Congress not interfere with slavery in the territories. At that, the antislavery element left the convention. The remnant, emphasizing that preservation of the Union had to be given first priority, chose as its standard-bearer Millard Fillmore, who, as president, had signed the Compromise of 1850.

ELECTION OF 1856

On February 22, 1856, Republican leaders met in Pittsburgh. They planned a national convention for June and drew up an "Address to the People of the United States." The document was a disappointment to blacks. In the entire address, there was only the demand for freedom for Kansas. "Nothing said of the Fugitive Slave Bill," Frederick Douglass complained, "nothing said of Slavery in the District of Columbia—nothing said of the slave trade between States—nothing said of giving dignity of the nation to Liberty—nothing said of securing the rights of citizens from the Northern States, or the constitutional right to enter and transact business in the slave states. There is not a single warm and living position, taken by the Republican Party, except freedom for Kansas."

In an effort to pressure the Republican party to take a more radical stand on slavery and the rights of free blacks, the Radical Political Abolitionists met in the national convention at Syracuse on May 28, two weeks before the Republican convention was scheduled to meet in Philadelphia. Garrison was beside himself with glee as he wrote in the *Liberator*:

I see that Lewis Tappan, Douglass, McCune Smith, Goodell and Gerrit Smith have called a convention for the purpose of nominating candidates for the Presidency and Vice Presidency of the United States!! Can anything more ludicrous than this be found inside or outside of the Utica Insane Asylum?

Indifferent to such caustic comments, Frederick Douglass addressed the convention on its first day. He admitted that he was tempted to join the Republican party but said he was dissuaded by the realization that "they do not give a full recognition to the humanity of the Negro" and sought to limit slavery only in Kansas and Nebraska: "Liberty must cut the throat of slavery or have its own cut by slavery."

The Radical Political Abolitionists nominated Gerrit Smith for president. The convention hoped that its action might force the Republican platform to include a pledge against the admission of any more slave states, to call for the repeal of the Fugitive Slave Act, and to promise to abolish slavery in the District of Columbia. Since the Republican party in Chicago had already taken a stand calling for the abolition of slavery in the District of Columbia, the repeal of the Fugitive Slave Act, and, in addition, the repeal of the Illinois black laws, it was not outside the realm of possibility that the Radical Abolitionist pressure might bring the desired result.

While the greater portion of the platform adopted by the Republicans concerned itself with Kansas, asking for its admission as a free state, it also took a firm stand against the further extension of slavery, urging Congress to prohibit slavery in the territories. On this platform, John C. Frémont and William L. Drayton were nominated for president and vice-president of the United States.

The first blacks to endorse the Republican ticket were those in Brooklyn, New York. On July 29, 1856, they met, pledged to vote for Frémont and Drayton, and adopted a resolution asserting that in the Republican platform

we behold the embodiment of Northern sentiment against Southern impudence and oppression and tender it [the Republican party] our hearty good will, pledging as far as we are permitted (by yet the behest of slavery in our state) to exercise the right of American citizens in the use of the ballot box, to remember him [Frémont] in the coming election.

Early in September, a large group of Boston's blacks held a political rally at Reverend Grimes' church and pledged their support to the Frémont-Drayton ticket. However, they criticized the Republican platform for having endorsed the Kansas free state constitution, which would not allow blacks to enter the territory. They were also critical of the tendency of the Republicans "to ignore the colored man's interest in the party," all of which indicated that "it is not an anti-slavery party." Thus, they would not commit themselves completely to the Republican cause, cautiously asserting: "While we are willing to unite with them to resist the aggressions of the Slave Power, we do not pledge ourselves to go further with the Republicans than the Republicans will go with us."

State conventions of blacks in Ohio and New York were less reserved in their endorsement of the Republican ticket. The New York convention met in Williamsburgh, Brooklyn, on September 23, 1856, and heard Henry Highland Garnet urge the six thousand black voters in New York State (about half of whom lived in New York City and Brooklyn) to vote Republican. Garnet criticized any tendency to stay at home on Election Day because the Republican platform did not go as far as blacks would want it to. He insisted that blacks should act with those who came nearest to supporting their positions, and he expressed the belief that the Republican party met this requirement. The delegates agreed with Garnet, and the convention passed a resolution asserting "that inasmuch as the Republican Party of this country presents a platform more consistent with the principles of liberty and justice than that of any other party, we therefore pledge ourselves to use our best endeavors to secure the success of the candidates nominated by that party.'' Following the convention, the delegates organized ''Colored Republican Clubs'' throughout New York State and helped rally blacks around the Republican ticket.

Meanwhile, the Radical Political Abolitionists were facing a dilemma. Although it was clear that the Republican party was not an abolitionist organization, it was also clearly antislavery, and many abolitionists and blacks were engaged in helping the party win the election. Interestingly enough, according to Ralph Harlow, Gerrit Smith's biographer, Smith, the Radical Abolitionist presidential candidate, contributed five hundred dollars to Frémont's campaign.

It was thus not entirely surprising that on August 15, Frederick Douglass informed his readers of his purpose ''to support, with whatever influence we possess, little or much, John C. Frémont and William L. Drayton, the candidates of the Republican Party for the presidency of the United States in the present political canvass.'' His support of the Republican candidates, he explained, did not signify that he had abandoned his antislavery principles. He would continue to contend for the extinction of slavery in every part of the republic, but he felt he could best do this in the ranks of the Republican party, using his voice and pen to teach and influence the vast numbers who were flocking to its banner. The fact that the Republican party did not go as far as he wished on the slavery issue was no reason for withholding support for its candidates:

A man was not justified in refusing to assist his fellowmen to accomplish a good thing, simply because his fellows refuse to accomplish some other good things which they deem impossible. Most assuredly, that theory cannot be a sound one which would prevent us from voting with men for the Abolition of Slavery in Maryland simply because our companions refuse to include Virginia. In such a case the path of duty is plainly this; go with your fellow-citizens for the Abolition of Slavery in Maryland when they are ready to go for that measure, and do all you can, meanwhile, to bring them to whatever work of righteousness may remain and which has become manifest to your clearer vision.

Douglass was not the only one to surprise the public by his support of the Republican ticket. While warning his followers to eschew the ballot, William Lloyd Garrison observed in late October that ''if there were no moral barrier to our voting, and we had a million ballots to bestow, we should cast them all for the Republican candidate.'' He judged it inconceivable ''that any voter, desirous of frustrating the Slave Power,'' would cast his vote for the Democratic James Buchanan or the Know-Nothing Millard Fillmore. Republicanism had arisen as ''the legitimate producer of moral agitation'' of Northern voters by Garrisonians, and radicals could best promote antislavery feeling in all its manifestations by continuing to agitate in the traditional way. But those who sincerely believed they could help the antislavery cause by voting should vote Republican.

Buchanan, the Democratic candidate, won the election with an electoral vote of 174 and a popular vote of 1,838,169. But Frémont piled up an electoral vote of 114 and a popular vote of 1,341,264, trailing Buchanan by only 497,000 votes. The electoral votes were nearly geographically polarized, with all of the South voting Democratic and most of the North (apart from California, Illinois, Indiana, and New Jersey) voting Republican. The 1856 election marked the end of the Know-Nothing party as an effective force. Know-Nothing presidential candidate Fillmore won only in Maryland, gaining just eight electoral votes and 874,534 popular votes. It was evident that the agenda of national politics was to be set by the opposition over slavery between Republicans and Democrats. The third party had become the second party of the nation.

In a speech in Chicago on October 30, 1854, on the Kansas-Nebraska bill, in the midst of the gloom over the repeal of the Missouri Compromise, Frederick Douglass had predicted this outcome, saying:

The signs of the times are propitious. Victories have been won by slavery, but they have never been won against the onward march of antislavery principles. The progress of these principles has been constant, steady, strong and certain. Every victory won by slavery has had the effect to fling our principles more widely and favorably among the people—the annexation of Texas—the Florida war (against the Seminoles)—the war with Mexico—The Compromise measures and the repeal of the Missouri Compromise . . . all have and will unite the antislavery forces of the nation.

As he surveyed the election results of 1856, Douglass made another prediction in a brief note to Gerrit Smith: ''We have turned Whigs and Democrats into Republicans and we can turn Republicans into Abolitionists.'' He was soon to see his prediction fulfilled.

12

The *Dred Scott* Case, Its Repercussions, and the Election of 1858

The *Dred Scott* case has been called "the most famous of all American judicial decisions." However, after Judge A. Leon Higgenbotham, Jr., surveyed twenty-two of the major constitutional law books published from 1895 through 1973, he found that the vast majority did not even cite the case. Yet as Don E. Fehren-bacher has amply demonstrated in his recent comprehensive study, *The Dred Scott Case: Its Significance in American Law and Politics*, the case is truly one of the most important in the entire history of American race relations.

WHO WAS DRED SCOTT?

Dred Scott was a slave who had traveled with his owner to Illinois and to territory in which slavery had been prohibited under the Missouri Compromise and, after returning to Missouri, had sued in court for his freedom. In the *Dictionary of American Biography,* Dred Scott is portrayed as "shiftless and unreliable, and therefore frequently unemployed and without means to support his family." In the *Mississippi Valley Historical Review,* Frank H. Hodder charged that the case began because Dred Scott was a shiftless Negro who was entirely dependent on the white man, Taylor Blow, who had instituted the suit for his freedom. And in *The Negro Vanguard,* Richard Bardolph describes the famous defendant as "at best an illiterate, good natured, shiftless slave whose successive removals about the country by his owners furnished the pretext for the fateful court battles he himself scarcely understood."

But the real Dred Scott was a slave in Missouri who, although in poor health, had once run away, hiding in the Lucas swamps near St. Louis, a haven for slave runaways. He had a wife who was sold away from him and two male children who died. In 1835, he married another slave named Harriet, and they had two

214

daughters. He tried to buy his family from Mrs. Emerson, his owner, but she refused the offer. Dred Scott then took $300 he had saved, hired a lawyer, and brought suit for the liberty of the Scott family. For ten years and ten months the case dragged on, and during this time, he received some help from the white Blow family, who had once owned him.

THE *DRED SCOTT* CASE IN MISSOURI COURTS

After Peter Blow's death, Dred Scott was sold to Dr. John Emerson, who took him into the free state of Illinois and into territory made free from slavery by the Missouri Compromise. Emerson then took him back to Missouri, and when Emerson died, Dred Scott and his family were left as part of the estate provided for Mrs. Emerson's daughter, Henrietta. Mrs. Emerson's brother, John Sanford, was named in the will as one of the executors. It was at this time that Dred Scott offered to buy his and his family's freedom, but Mrs. Emerson refused. Since other Negroes had won their freedom in Missouri because of residence in free territory, Dred Scott was informed of his legal rights by several whites, and he brought suit to obtain freedom from Mrs. Emerson.

In the first of two actions brought by Dred Scott in the Missouri state court, he sued for freedom because his late master, Dr. John Emerson, had taken him from Missouri to military posts in Illinois and to territory made free by the Missouri Compromise. The trial court instructed the jury that if the facts were as claimed, Scott was entitled to freedom. The jury declared the Scott family free. But Mrs. Emerson appealed the case to the Missouri Supreme Court, which reversed its own precedents and denied freedom to the Scott family. In a statement irrelevant to the issue but explaining the reason for the court's refusal to follow its own precedent and rule, it declared:

Times now are not as they were when the former decisions on this subject were made. Since then not only individuals but States have been possessed with a dark and fell spirit in relation to slavery, whose gratification is sought in the pursuit of measures whose inevitable consequence must be the overthrow and destruction of our government. Under such circumstances it does not behoove the State of Missouri to show the least countenance to any measure which might gratify this spirit. She is willing to assume her full responsibility for the existence of slavery within her limits, nor does she seek to share or divide it with others. . . . As to the consequence of slavery, they are much more hurtful to the master than the slave. There is no comparison between the slave in the United States and the cruel, uncivilized negro in Africa. When the condition of our slaves is contrasted with the state of their miserable race in Africa; when their civilization, intelligence, and instruction in religious truths are considered, and the means now employed to restore them to the country from which they have been torn, bearing with them the blessings of civilized life, we are almost persuaded, that, the introduction of slavery amongst us was, in the providences of God, who makes the evil passions of men subservient to his own glory; a means of placing that unhappy race within the pale of civilized nations.

It is the opinion of some legal authorities that had the case been appealed directly from the Missouri Supreme Court to the U.S. Supreme Court, a clear precedent existed in *Strader* v. *Graham* under which the federal court would simply have held the state's ruling final. But instead another method was used. The former Mrs. Emerson had moved to Massachusetts and there married an antislavery politician, Dr. Calvin C. Chafee. The marriage cost her the control of her first husband's estate, because under Missouri law, a married woman could not administer an estate for a minor, and the estate was in trust for Henrietta. Therefore John Sanford, as a surviving original executor of Dr. Emerson's will, became the administrator of Henrietta's estate, which included Dred Scott.

A new case was therefore begun in federal circuit court alleging that the plaintiff and defendant were citizens of different states—Dred Scott of Missouri and Sanford of New York. Sanford denied that the federal circuit court had jurisdiction on the grounds that Dred Scott was not a citizen and could not sue in federal court. His plea was based on the argument that Dred Scott could not be a citizen because he was "a negro of African descent, whose ancestors were of pure African blood, and who were brought into this country and sold as slaves."

Dred Scott's attorneys, Montgomery Blair and George Ticknor Curtis, admitted the facts of their client's ancestry but denied that this precluded the possibility that he was a citizen. The circuit judge ruled for Dred Scott and assumed jurisdiction in the case, but in the end, he ruled that Dred Scott was still a slave. Thereupon, with some financial assistance by Henry Taylor Blow, a Free Soil supporter, and with the legal assistance of Blair and Curtis, both Republicans, Scott appealed to the U.S. Supreme Court.

THE *DRED SCOTT* CASE BEFORE THE U.S. SUPREME COURT

In February 1856, the case of *Dred Scott* v. *Sanford* was first argued before the Supreme Court. Chief Justice Roger B. Taney was from Maryland; four of the associate justices were from free states—John McLean of Ohio, Samuel Nelson of New York, Robert C. Grier of Pennsylvania, and Benjamin R. Curtis of Massachusetts—and four associate justices were from slave states—James M. Wayne of Georgia, John Catron of Tennessee, Peter V. Daniel of Virginia, and John A. Campbell of Alabama. Opposing attorneys brought a wide variety of arguments on both the issue of the jurisdiction of the lower court (involving the question of Negro citizenship) and the merits of Dred Scott's claim to freedom (involving the constitutionality of the Missouri Compromise, which had excluded slavery from the territory into which Dred Scott had been taken). The opposition to Dred Scott, represented by Reverdy Johnson of Maryland, former U.S. attorney general, and Senator Henry S. Geyer of Missouri, argued that slavery could exist for all time and that its expansion was essential for the preservation of constitutional freedom in the United States.

Such statements angered both blacks and abolitionists and focused a great deal of attention upon the case as it was argued before the Supreme Court. Then, too, it was fully recognized that Chief Justice Taney had been trying increasingly to use the Supreme Court's power to advance the interests of the slaveowners. As William M. Wieced points out:

Taney's determination to put down abolitionist constitutional theory intensified in the 1850's. Within the space of two years, he first denied to Congress any power that might be exercised to inhibit the spread of slavery into the territories, and then arrogated to the federal court powers to override state judicial power to protect state citizens in slavery.

In April 1856, the Supreme Court began consultation, but in the end, the case was ordered reargued at the end of the year. Reargument took place in December 1856, and in February 1857, in answer to President-elect Buchanan's query, Associate Justice Catron assured him that the case would be decided on February 15 but would settle nothing about such congressional power in the territories as had been exercised in the Missouri Compromise. The purpose of Buchanan's inquiry was so that he could use the information in his forthcoming inaugural address.

On February 14, the case was discussed, and a majority agreed that the decision would have to be based on the merits of the case and could rest upon the precedent of *Strader* v. *Graham*, which made each state the final judge of the status of slaves who had sojourned in free territory and returned. The circuit court decision was to be upheld on the grounds that it had properly considered itself bound by the ruling in the Missouri Supreme Court on Dred Scott's status.

Associate Justice Nelson was assigned to write this opinion, avoiding both the issue of Negro citizenship and the constitutionality of the Missouri Compromise. However, this agreement was not sustained, and on February 19, Catron again wrote to Buchanan to inform him that two dissenters, McLean and Curtis, had forced the majority to take up the constitutionality of the Missouri Compromise. Catron then reported that Buchanan's fellow Pennsylvanian, Justice Grier, was convinced that the Compromise was unconstitutional but might not say so in his opinion. Catron suggested that Buchanan write to Grier, urging him to join the majority openly and lend as much weight to the decision as possible.

Buchanan did write to Grier, who showed the letter to both Justices Wayne of Georgia and Taney; he then replied to the president-elect that he would join the majority. In his inaugural address on March 4, 1857, Buchanan defended popular sovereignty against the settlement in the Missouri Compromise. Only one question remained, he said, and that was of the exact time when the people of a territory might accept or reject slavery by the exercise of their sovereignty. That question, Buchanan announced, was about to be answered by a Supreme Court decision. As for his own opinion, he added, the decision should not be made until a constitution preparatory to statehood was drafted. Two days after the inauguration, the Supreme Court handed down its decision in the *Dred Scott* case in which it held the Missouri Compromise unconstitutional, denied the power of Congress to prohibit slavery in a territory, thus protecting slavery in the territories until statehood, and delivered a devastating blow to the basic rights of all black Americans, free as well as slaves.

After the decision was handed down, William H. Seward charged in the Senate that the whole case was a conspiracy on the part of the slavocracy in which President Buchanan and Chief Justice Taney were personally implicated and that there had been collusion between Buchanan and the Court. In his *History of the United States from the Compromise of 1850,* published in 1892, James Ford Rhodes dismissed Seward's charge with these words:

That either would stoop from the etiquette of his high office is an idea that may not be entertained for a moment; and we may be sure that with Taney's lofty notions of what belonged to an independent judiciary, he would have no intercourse with the executive that would brook the light of day.

In 1911, the final volume of *The Works of James Buchanan* was published. It contained the letters of Justices Catron and Grier of February 19 and 23, 1857, to Buchanan revealing that the original decision had been to avoid the controversial questions but that a change had occurred, that Catron had asked Buchanan to try to influence Grier, and that the president-elect had done so successfully. The letters also informed Buchanan exactly what the decision would be. In 1926, Philip Auchempaugh published *James Buchanan, the Court and the Dred Scott Case,* and revealed that Buchanan had originated the correspondence with Justice Catron, and that Catron had written the president-elect two letters—on February 6 and 10, 1857—prior to the ones revealed in *The Works of James Buchanan.*

In a revised edition of his *History* in 1920, after publication of the letters in Buchanan's *Works,* James Ford Rhodes conceded that the president-elect had meddled with the proposed decision in a manner unbefitting to the dignity of the presidency and that Taney had also descended from the standards long associated with his high office.

The opinions of the U.S. Supreme Court in the case of *Dred Scott* v. *Sanford* were read on March 6 and 7, 1857. "Neither of the two litigants were present in the courtroom," writes Don E. Fehrenbacher in his introduction to *The Dred Scott Case.* "Scott remained at home in St. Louis, still a hired-out slave eleven years after he had taken the first legal step in his long battle for freedom. As for his alleged owner, John F. A. Sanford, languished in an insane asylum and within two months would be dead."

CHIEF JUSTICE TANEY'S MAJORITY OPINION

Nine separate opinions were read during the two days. In the majority opinion, Chief Justice Taney held that the circuit court did not have jurisdiction because a

Negro could not be a citizen of the United States competent to sue in federal court. Then, noting that some members of the Court doubted that the question of jurisdiction of the lower court on the Negro issue was properly before the Supreme Court for review, he argued that there was another reason for denying that the lower court had jurisdiction: Dred Scott was a Negro and hence not a citizen of either Missouri or the United States and had no right to sue. He then declared that even if Scott had been allowed to sue, his residence in a free territory had not made him a free man, since this would deprive his master of property in violation of the due process clause of the Fifth Amendment to the Constitution—"No person . . . shall be deprived of life, liberty, or property, without due process of law." Taney, in short, rejected Dred Scott's claim to freedom based upon residence in free territory and a free state. He rejected the claim of residence in a territory made free by the Missouri Compromise on the ground that Congress had no power to prohibit slavery in a territory, thereby rendering the Missouri Compromise unconstitutional. As to Dred Scott's residence in Illinois, Taney held that his return to Missouri established his status as being whatever the Missouri courts decreed. Therefore he had never been freed from slavery.

Taney's tortuous efforts to deny Negro citizenship attributed to the founding fathers a great fear of the Negro, and he argued that the slave states would never have ratified the Constitution if free Negroes had been included in the meaning of citizens. Said Taney:

For if they were . . . entitled to the privileges and immunities of citizens, it would exempt them from the operation of the special laws and from the police regulations which they considered to be necessary for their own safety. It would give to persons of the negro race . . . the right to enter every other State whenever they pleased . . . to go where they pleased at every hour of the day or night without molestation, . . . and it would give them the full liberty of speech in public and in private upon all subjects upon which its own citizens might speak; to hold public meetings upon political affairs, and to keep and carry arms wherever they went. And all of this would be done in the face of the subject race of the same color, both free and slave, and inevitably producing discontent and insubordination among them, and endangering the peace and safety of the State.

Then for the first time, Chief Justice Taney held on behalf of the Supreme Court of the United States that under the Constitution, a black man

had no rights which the white man was bound to respect; . . . the negro might justly and lawfully be reduced to slavery for his benefit. He was bought and sold and treated as an ordinary article of merchandise and traffic, whenever profit could be made by it.

Taney did grudgingly concede that the states could make citizens of whomever they pleased, but this was offset by his denial that blacks might thereby become citizens, entitled to the privileges and immunities specified in article IV, section 2 of the Constitution and by his insistence that, upon migration, these black free-state citizens would lose their status and acquire whatever status the state they removed to might confer on them.

OTHER COURT OPINIONS

None of his eight colleagues directly challenged Taney's explicit assertion that his was the official opinion of the court, and in popular usage on all sides, the term *Dred Scott* decision came to mean the opinion read by the chief justice.

Justice Wayne concurred fully with Taney, and Campbell, Catron, Daniel, and Grier agreed with Taney that Dred Scott was not free and that the Missouri Compromise was unconstitutional, but each wrote a separate opinion and disagreed on various points. Nelson read the opinion he had originally prepared as the majority opinion, declaring Dred Scott still a slave without touching upon either Negro citizenship or the Missouri Compromise. But McLean and Curtis dissented at length, considering Dred Scott free and declaring that Negroes could be citizens and that the Missouri Compromise was constitutional because Congress did have the power to ban slavery from the territories. In their forceful dissents, McLean and Curtis emphasized that a "slave is not a mere chattel. He bears the impress of his Maker, and is amenable to the laws of God and man; and he is destined to an endless existence." Nevertheless, the dissenting justices accepted the legality of slavery within the Southern states. In order to counter Taney's argument that the slaveholder had a right to take his slave property anywhere in the Union, McLean and Curtis made the assumption that slavery was a domestic institution supported by law, having no force outside the jurisdiction of the slave states. Congress therefore had a right to restrict slavery in the territories as it did in the Missouri Compromise.

Shortly after the Supreme Court struck down their bid for liberty, Dred Scott and his family had a new owner, for John Sanford had died. Control of the Scotts reverted to the former Mrs. Emerson and her husband, Dr. Chaffee, who transferred title to Taylor Blow (the son of Dred Scott's former owner) who immediately emancipated the Scotts. Scott continued to live in St. Louis, where he worked at Barnum's Hotel and also helped his wife with a laundry business.

EVALUATION OF TANEY'S OPINION

The Supreme Court decision in *Dred Scott* v. *Sanford* aroused indignation in the North. Horace Greeley wrote angrily: "The judgment of the five slaveholders who compose a majority of the court is entitled to just so much moral weight as would be the judgment of a majority of those congregated in any Washington barroom."

Most Republican party spokespersons maintained that when Taney declared that the circuit court had been in error in assuming jurisdiction, he should have stopped there, and that his further pronouncements on the unconstitutionality of the Missouri Compromise were *obiter dicta* (incidental opinions not material to the decision of the case and therefore not binding). But gradually Taney's reputation has been rehabilitated by several generations of revisionist historians, Confederate apologists, and judicial supremacists to whom Taney is a highly worthy figure, since he was the most activist justice between Marshall and Warren. In a 1911 essay, Edwin Corwin defended Taney's *Dred Scott* opinion as grounded in precedent. Charles Warren attacked Taney's Republican critics in his 1923 history of the Supreme Court. Charles Evans Hughes, chief justice of the U.S. Supreme Court, praised Taney in his 1931 essay before the American Bar Association. In 1937, Supreme Court Justice Felix Frankfurter ridiculed the idea that Taney was "the bigoted provincial protector of slavery" and called him "second only to Marshall in the constitutional history of our country." In general, an entire mythology has grown up around Taney that has emphasized that he was not privately opposed to slavery; that he was forced to render a sweeping decision in the *Dred Scott* case, because the two antislavery justices planned to issue dissenting opinions; and that his opinion in this celebrated case was carefully and logically constructed.

In the April 1974 issue of the *University of Pennsylvania Law Review*, Judge A. Leon Higgenbotham, Jr., stated bluntly: "The *Dred Scott* holding was unquestionably racist. Chief Justice Taney's opinion constitutionally doomed only blacks to the status of mere property, whether they were born in this country or not, whether they were 'free' or slave." But it was Don E. Fehrenbacher in his monumental study of the case, published in 1978, who most effectively challenged and destroyed the revisionist interpretations of Chief Justice Taney. Dismissing the usual defenses of Taney's opinion in the *Dred Scott* case point by point, he called it an "extraordinary combination of error, inconsistency and misrepresentation, dispensed with pontifical self-assurance." As Fehrenbacher puts it: "The true purpose of Taney's Dred Scott opinion was to launch a sweeping counterattack on the antislavery movement and to reinforce the bastions of slavery at every rampart and parapet." He points out that Taney's *obiter dictum* in the decision, the statement that a territorial government could not forbid slavery, was "a question that had never arisen in the Dred Scott case." Then, citing Taney's statement that every citizen was a member of "the political body who, according to our republican institutions, form the sovereignty, and who hold the power and conduct the Government through their representatives," Fehrenbacher calls this a "gross inaccuracy": "A large majority of American citizens—namely, women and children, were not members of the sovereign people in the sense of holding power and conducting the government through their representatives." Negroes may not have been citizens, he adds, but not for the reason that Taney here described.

Taney's assertion that in the times of the founding fathers, Negroes "had no rights which the white man was bound to respect" was a "gross perversion of the facts." Taney's statement, Fehrenbacher points out, confused free Negroes with slaves, and even then, "the statement was not absolutely true, for slaves had some rights before the law." Fehrenbacher notes, too, that there were some respects in which "a [free] black man's status was superior to that of a married white woman, and it was certainly far above that of a slave." The free black man "could marry, enter into contracts, purchase real estate, bequeath the property, and most pertinently, seek redress in courts."

As Fehrenbacher shows, Taney went to such lengths to exclude Negroes from the possibility of being naturalized citizens that his opinion made them *"the only people on the face of the earth who (saving a constitutional amendment) were forever ineligible for American citizenship."* And he points out:

Rightly or not, permanently or not, the Supreme Court had written two new and provocative rules into the fundamental law of the nation: first, that no Negro could be a United States citizen or even a state citizen "within the meaning of the Constitution . . . ," and second, that Congress had no power to exclude slavery from the federal territories, and that accordingly the Missouri Compromise, together with all other legislation embodying such exclusion, was unconstitutional.

Fehrenbacher also argues (incorrectly I believe) that the case was not (as many historians have thought it was) a major factor in causing the Civil War. "It had no immediate legal effect of any importance except on the status of free Negroes," he writes, without any awareness that this was an important exception. The psychological frustration of intangible victory played a role, he says, but "only belatedly and indirectly." What was vital, he argues, were "certain later developments."

IMPACT OF THE DECISION ON NORTHERN FREE LABOR

But this ignores the immediate understanding among people in the North that if Taney's due process thesis was valid for the territories, thus prohibiting the barring of slavery there, it was equally valid for the states. The Vermont legislature complained immediately that the privilege-and-immunities clause of the Fifth Amendment, if read in the light of the *Dred Scott* decision, "would convert every State into a slaveholding State, precisely as it now makes every Territory a slaveholding Territory."

Even before the *Dred Scott* decision, Northern white workingmen had begun to be troubled by this issue. While sections of the Northern working class had defended the slaveowners on the grounds that by keeping black workers enslaved, they prevented them from coming North in huge numbers to compete with white workingmen, others began to fear that slave labor might spread to the shops and factories of the North. Did not the slaveowners openly call for enslaving all workers, black and white? Why be troubled with a free working class, they counseled Northern employers. Keep labor on a level with beasts of burden, for as soon as "the mere laborer has the pride, the knowledge, and the aspirations of a free man, he is unfitted for his situation." Slavery was "right, natural and necessary" for all workers, regardless of their complexion. "Slavery is the natural and normal condition of the laboring man," the *Charleston Mercury* pontificated. "Master and slave is a relation in society as necessary as that of parent and child, and the Northern states will yet have to introduce it. The theory of free society is a delusion."

Free society, the slaveowners argued, was not only a delusion but a danger. In a free society "greasy mechanics" and "filthy operatives" organized trade unions and engaged in strikes and other subversive activities. Slavery, boasted one planter, protected the South "from the demands for Land Limitation . . . anti-rent troubles, strikes of workmen . . . diseased philanthropy, radical democracy and the progress of socialistic ideas in general." Northern capitalists should institute the system of slave labor in their shops and factories. It would relieve them of all anxieties caused by trade unions. Only an alliance between Northern capitalists and the slavocracy could arrest the forces of abolition whose hidden object was the overthrow of all forms of property and the establishment of communism. Eventually, the slaveowners argued, the Northern capitalists would learn that slavery was necessary for them.

Most Northern workers did not take this threat seriously before the *Dred Scott* decision, but when the logic of the decision indicated that slavery could not be barred from a state any more than from a territory, they became alarmed. "Slavery National" seemed to be the clear purpose of the slaveowners. Color was no longer to be the barrier between the Negro slave in the South and the free white worker in the North. As one prolabor paper put it: "The negro slaves are valuable because they *can* be carpenters, and blacksmiths, and masons, etc., and hence every white laboring man in the country is compelled to have a direct interest in the question of the chattelization of labor."

Late in 1860, the issue heated up when the *Lemmon* case was brought before the Supreme Court (*Lemmon* v. *New York*, 1860). The case originated when eight slaves brought from Virginia to New York for shipment to Texas sued for their freedom. The highest court in the state affirmed that upon being brought to free soil, a slave automatically became free, but labor leaders feared that the Supreme Court would overturn this decision and establish the right of transit of slaves through the free states. Once the right of transit had been won, they believed, Southerners would set up slave markets in the North. "We shall see men buying slaves for the New York market," predicted Horace Greeley's *New York Tribune*. "There will be no legal power to prevent it."

While others charged that the whole issue was nothing more than a Republican party fantasy conjured up to win labor support, workers on strike reported that their employers reminded them that slave labor was used in industry in the South and might easily, under the principles set down in *Dred Scott*, be introduced into Northern shops. Bernard Mandel points out in his study, *Labor: Free and Slave*:

Many [Northern workers] perceived in the Nebraska Act and the *Dred Scott* dictum a logical pattern which led inevitably to the introduction of slavery even into the free states. The Mechanics and Workingmen's Central Union of New York condemned the decision and saw in it evidence that the slaveholders had a "settled determination" to make their institution legal in all the states, thus depriving free labor of the ability to protect itself against the competition of slave labor. The "nationalization of slavery" was seen not only in the logic and events and arguments, but as a conspiracy that was already in the making.

WERE FREE NEGROES CITIZENS?

In the weeks following the *Dred Scott* decision, the discussion was dominated by those sections of the Court's opinion invalidating the Missouri Compromise, opening the territories to slavery, and raising the possibility of the spread of slavery to the free states. Still, Taney's opinion that Negroes could not be citizens of the United States or of any state and had "no rights which the white man was bound to respect" did not go unnoticed. On the contrary, several state conventions of the Republican party in 1857 affirmed free Negro citizenship. The Republican legislatures of New Hampshire, Vermont, New York, and Ohio passed resolutions stating that color did not disqualify a resident of the state from citizenship, and Indiana Republicans defeated a Democratic attempt to have the legislature endorse Taney's views.

The Supreme Court of Maine pointedly rejected Taney's doctrine in its reply to a request from the state's senate to rule on whether, in view of the Supreme Court's decision, "free colored male persons of African descent" who met all other qualifications were still to be considered "citizens of the United States" and entitled to vote in Maine elections. Specifically announcing their disagreement with Taney's opinion, the Maine Supreme Court justices declared:

From the adoption of the Constitution to the present day, it is believed there has been no instance in the State in which the right to vote has been denied to any person resident within the State, on account of his color.

In view of these facts and considerations, we are of the opinion that our Constitution does not discriminate between the different races of people which constitute the inhabitants of our State; but that the term "citizens of the United States," as used in that instrument, applies as well to free colored persons of African descent as to persons descended from white ancestors. Our answer, therefore, is, that

Free colored male persons of African descent, of the age of twenty-one years and upwards, having a residence established in some town or plantation in this State, three months next preceding any election, and who are not paupers, aliens, nor persons under guardianship, are authorized, under the provisions of the Constitution of this State, to be electors for Governor, Senators, and Representatives.

BLACK PROTESTS AGAINST THE *DRED SCOTT* DECISION

In *The Coming of the Civil War,* Avery Craven argues that the *Dred Scott* decision excited little public passion. Although this conclusion is erroneous in general, it is especially so as it applied to the black communities of the North. There, the impact of the decision was immediate and intense. On April 3, 1857, a packed protest meeting of indignant blacks was held in Philadelphia's Israel Church. Robert Purvis introduced resolutions describing "this atrocious decision" as the "final confirmation of the already well known fact that under the Constitution and Government of the United States, the colored people are nothing, and can be nothing but an alien, disfranchised and degraded class." Hence, for any black man to support or pledge allegiance to such a government would be "the height of folly and depth of pusillanimity." Rather, the only duty owed to a Constitution "under which he is declared to be an inferior and degraded being, having no rights which white men are bound to respect, is to denounce and repudiate it, and to do what he can by all proper means to bring it into contempt."

Speaking in support of the resolutions prior to their adoption, Purvis told the enraged crowd that there was "nothing new" in the Supreme Court decision; "it was in perfect keeping with the treatment of the colored people by the American Government from the beginning to this day." He was followed by Charles Lenox Remond of Salem, Massachusetts, who agreed with Purvis' last statement and advanced the idea that the principles proclaimed by Taney had "lurked all the time in the Constitution, only waiting to be developed; and that now when it suits the slave oligarchy to assert that power, we are made to feel its grinding weight." Then Remond declared: "We owe no allegiance to a country which grinds us under its iron heel and treats us like dogs. The time has gone by for colored people to talk of patriotism." Remond, however, saw one ray of hope on the gloomy horizon. By threatening to extend slavery into the North, the *Dred Scott* decision held out the real possibility that

when our white fellow slaves in these so called free States see that they are alike subject with us to the slave oligarchy, the difference in servitude being only in degree, they will make common cause with us, and that [in] throwing off the yoke and striking for impartial liberty, they will join with us in our efforts to recover the lost boon of freedom.

A month later, at the annual meeting of the American Anti-Slavery Society in New York, Frederick Douglass characterized the decision (which he called "the Taney settlement of the slavery question") as a "judicial incarnation of wolfishness," the product of "the slaveholding wing of the Supreme Court." Douglass, however, refused to abandon his belief in the antislavery character of the Constitution and charged Taney with a monstrous distortion of history in his use of the document to justify his argument that Negroes could not be citizens. He cried: "As a man, an American, a citizen, a colored man of both Anglo-Saxon and African descent, I denounce this representation as a most scandalous and devilish perversion of the Constitution, and a brazen mis-statement of the facts of history."

Like Remond, Douglass saw hope for the future, but he saw it in the fact that the history of antislavery had already demonstrated that all efforts to crush the movement "have only served to increase, intensify, and embolden the agitation." This was the case with the Fugitive Slave bill, the Kansas-Nebraska bill, "and it will be so with this last and most shocking of all pro-slavery devices, this Taney decision":

By all the laws of nature, civilization, and of progress, slavery is a doomed system. Not all the skill of politicians, North and South, not all the sophistries of judges, not all the fulminations of a corrupt press, not all the hypocritical prayers, or the hypocritical refusals to pray of a hollow-hearted priesthood, not all the devices of sin and Satan, can save the vile thing from extermination.

While blacks were staging protest meetings voicing their indignation over the *Dred Scott* decision, a number of them, convinced that the federal government had abandoned them to the slaveholders and slavecatchers, left the United States. "Your national ship is rotten and sinking, why not leave it?" counseled Mary Ann Shadd Cary from Chatham, Ontario, Canada. Black clergyman Benjamin S. Tanner announced that he was going to "remove to Canada in the name of God."

But most blacks were determined to stay in the country their labor had helped to build and intensify their fight. As the resolutions adopted at a mass meeting of New Bedford blacks put it, the *Dred Scott* decision was "a palpably vain, arrogant animation, unsustained by history, justice, reason or common sense, and merits the execration of the world as a consummate villainy." Yet even though they were convinced that the design of the Court was "now more than ever before . . . to make our grievances permanent, by greatly multiplying the disabilities under which we labor; . . . nevertheless, we are determined to remain in this country, our title and right being as valid and indisputable as that of any class of people."

An interesting role in the protests of black Americans against the *Dred Scott* decision was played by William C. Nell, veteran leader of the long and successful battle to desegregate the public schools of Boston. Nell's reaction to the decision came swiftly: "Though Judge Taney, at slavery's bidding, has declared colored Americans are not citizens, the fiat of no judge has yet been potent enough to veto their equality with white Americans." Nell mobilized blacks in the state to memorialize the Massachusetts legislature to declare the *Dred Scott* decision unconstitutional, and, in keeping with his Garrisonianism, the memorial added that if such action by the legislature did not suffice "to protect the rights of all her citizens in the Union," it should take steps "to protect them outside of the Union, with such of her sister States as may be disposed to unite with her in the formation of a free and independent republic."

Speaking on behalf of the memorial before the legislature's Committee on Foreign Relations, Nell declared:

From early childhoood I have loved to visit the Eastern wing of this Senate House, and read from the four stones taken from the Monument which once towered from Beacon Hill summit, these lines:—

"Americans, while from this eminence scenes of luxuriant fertility, of flourishing commerce, and the abodes of social happiness, meet your view, forget not those who, by their exertion, have secured these blessings."

In the spirit with which these words are revered by the white inhabitants of Massachusetts, so do we, the colored citizens of this State, ask you, gentlemen, and through you, the Legislature, to remember that we, too, have at least done our part to secure to our beloved Commonwealth these blessings.

Feeling assured, gentlemen of the committee, that you are ready to do all in your power to shape the legislation of Massachusetts for the more perfect security of her colored citizens, our appeal is submitted to you in full confidence that it will not be made in vain.

But by linking the secession of Massachusetts and other states from the Union with the denunciation of the *Dred Scott* decision, the memorialists guaranteed that it would be rejected.

Nell, however, had another way to answer the *Dred Scott* decision. On March 5, 1858, he staged the first Crispus Attucks celebration in the United States, in honor of the black man killed in the Boston Massacre of March 5, 1770—the first to die in the American Revolution. Nell believed that the celebration of the black martyr for American liberty would "serve notice to the world that the Negro was indeed a citizen of the United States, and thereby entitled to the same freedoms as any other Americans."

The first annual Crispus Attucks Day celebration began with a parade to Faneuil Hall, which was decorated for the occasion. As Benjamin Quarles notes:

In front of the speaker's rostrum was an exhibit of Revolutionary War relics, which included a small cup allegedly owned by Attucks, a picture of Washington crossing the Delaware in which black Prince Whipple was seen pulling the stroke oar, and a banner presented by Governor John Hancock to a Negro military company, the Bucks of America. The meeting was graced by original songs, one of them by Charlotte Forten, who journeyed from Salem to be on hand. A hymn by Frances Ellen Watkins, "Freedom's Battle," was delivered by the Attucks Glee Club. This youthful quintet included Edward M. Bannister and George L. Ruffin, both destined for fame, one as a painter and the other as a judge.

Nell, the presiding officer, observed that

in view of the alarming spread of despotism in these United States, the suppression of Free Speech in one half of the Union—the subjugation of white citizens, and the annihilation of the citizenship of Colored Americans by the Dred Scott decision, it now seems a timely and significant hour for an application of that sentiment in the Constitution of Massachusetts which declares that frequent recurrence to its fundamental principles is absolutely necessary to preserve the advantages of liberty, and to maintain a free government.

The speakers who followed included Wendell Phillips, William Lloyd Garrison, and Theodore Parker, but it was the black schoolteacher, dentist, physician, and lawyer, John S. Rock, who stirred the largely black audience most deeply with his militant speech. Referring to statements of some whites that blacks had not resisted enslavement to the extent that native American Indians had or white Americans would have, Rock explained that the enslavement of blacks had nothing to do with black submission but rather with the fact that the whites had military power while the Africans had been "with no weapons and without a possibility of success." He appealed to history to prove the courage of the African and the Haitian people, reminding his listeners that the Haitian people's "bloody struggles for freedom" in which "the blacks whipped the French and the English and gained their independence . . . will be a lasting refutation of the malicious aspersions of our enemies." Moreover, Rock suggested that the slaves in the South might soon strike for their freedom:

Our fathers fought nobly for freedom, but they were not victorious. They fought for liberty, but they got slavery. The white man was benefitted, but the black man was injured. . . . We have had much sad experience in this country, and it would be strange indeed if we do not profit by some of the lessons which we have so dearly paid for.

Rock then predicted:

Sooner or later, the clashing of arms will be heard in this country, and the black man's services will be needed: 150,000 freemen capable of bearing arms, and not all cowards and fools, and three quarters of a million slaves, wild with the enthusiasm caused by the dawn of the glorious opportunity of being able to strike a genuine blow for freedom, will be a power which white men will be "bound to respect."

The last, of course, was a paraphrase of the wording of Taney's opinion in the *Dred Scott* decision. Rock then upbraided the Supreme Court and "this wicked Federal Government" and vowed that black people would outlast both. He turned next to the "prejudice which some white men have, or affect to have, against my color" and assured the audience that this gave him "no pain":

When I contrast the fine tough, muscular system, the beautiful, rich color, the full broad features and the gracefully frizzled hair of the Negro with the delicate physical organization, wan color, sharp features and lank hair of the Caucasian, I am inclined to believe that when the white man was created, nature was pretty well exhausted. But, determined to keep up appearances, she pinched up his features and did the best she could under the circumstances.

Rock's comments brought the house to its feet with laughter and applause. He continued:

I would have you understand that I not only love my race, but am pleased with my color; and while many colored persons may feel degraded by being called Negroes and wished to be classed among other races more favored, I shall feel it my duty, my pleasure and my pride to concentrate my feeble efforts in elevating to a fair position a race to which I am especially identified by feelings and by blood.

Neither black nor white protests against his opinion in the *Dred Scott* decision made any impression on Chief Justice Taney. On the contrary, on the eve of the Civil War, he drafted a supplement to his opinion, declaring that its principles extended to all blacks, not just those descended from slave ancestors. The American Revolution, he wrote, "was not designed to subvert the established order of society and social relations nor to sweep away traditional usages and established opinions." Similarly, the Declaration of Independence was "intended as a conservative measure, and not as a revolutionary" document; hence all blacks of necessity had to be deemed to have been excluded from its terms.

When this was drafted, a man had already been elected president of the United States during whose administration Taney's opinion in the *Dred Scott* case was to be rendered null and void. He was Abraham Lincoln, and it was the *Dred Scott* case that played a major role in catapulting him into national prominence in the famous 1858 Lincoln-Douglas debates.

LINCOLN, SLAVERY, AND THE NEGRO

It has become the tendency among some historians to see Abraham Lincoln as a white supremacist and a racist. Indeed, a headline in the *New York Times* of January 25, 1968, read: "Lincoln Termed Opportune Racist. Ebony Editor Tells Negroes to Reassess History." What followed was a summary of *Ebony*'s article, "Was Lincoln a White Supremacist?" by black historian Lerone Bennett, Jr., which was referred to as having "Exploded the 'Lincoln Myth.'" The article opened up a controversy over whether Lincoln, as Herbert Mitgang, who sharply disagreed with Bennett, put it, "was . . . just a honkie."

In a number of ways this was not a new controversy. From the moment of his cruel and untimely assassination immediately after the victory of the Union forces in the Civil War, two points of view emerged concerning the martyred president. The dominant one was that it was Lincoln who alone was the savior of the Negro. No mention in the adulation of Lincoln as the "Great Emancipator" was made of his political pragmatism on the race issue, of his deliberation of a plan for Negro colonization in Africa or the West Indies, or of his opinions on Negro inferiority.

But when on April 14, 1876, the monument to Abraham Lincoln was unveiled in Washington, with President Ulysses S. Grant, members of Congress, the Supreme Court, and other high officials in attendance, Frederick Douglass considerably altered the image of Abraham Lincoln. In his address, Douglass dealt both with Lincoln's limitations and his growth, his vacillation and procrastination, and his great advance over the years in dealing with the issues of slavery and the Negro. As Douglass made clear, Lincoln was a man of many contradictions. He was a firm believer in the philosophy of the Declaration of Independence but maintained that the Negro was inferior to the white man and opposed to their right to be voters or officeholders or to have social equality. He was opposed to slavery on moral grounds, but when he introduced a bill in Congress proposing gradual emancipation in the District of Columbia, he added a strong fugitive slave clause for the return of slaves escaping into the district, and later said, "I confess I hate to see the poor creatures hunted down . . . but I bite my lips and keep quiet." He was a Whig regular during most of his political career and came late to the Republican party, but he stood firm on the Republican platform dealing with slavery, and before the Civil War, Douglass himself had called him a "radical Republican" who could be counted on not to retreat from the Republican opposition to the further extension of slavery.

One thing is definite: Abraham Lincoln was not a white supremacist and not a racist. Although he often tended to obscure somewhat his position on slavery for political reasons, he never hid the fact that he hated the institution. "I have always hated slavery, I think, as much as any Abolitionist," Lincoln said in a Chicago speech in 1858, and he is reported to have told a Wisconsin audience that the underlying principle of the Republican party was "hatred to the institution of slavery; hatred to it in all its aspects, moral, social and political." He vehemently opposed the extension of slavery as hindering the expansion of free labor into the territories, but he insisted that slavery was not simply a political-economic but also a moral question. "If the negro is a man," he said, "why then my ancient faith teaches me that; 'all men are created equal,' and that there can be no moral right in connection with one man's making a slave of another."

Lincoln stood for the basic principle that the founding fathers had decreed that all men are created equal "with certain inalienable rights among which are life, liberty, and the pursuit of happiness." He held that it was the "actual presence" of slavery that had promoted the inclusion of the words *all men* in the Declaration of Independence.

Slavery, Lincoln added, was robbery—one person labored and another enjoyed the fruits. "I want every man to have a chance—and I believe a black man is entitled to it—in which he can better his condition," he declared. Speaking of a black woman, he added, "In some respects she is certainly not my equal, but in her natural right to eat the bread she earns with her own hands, without asking the leave of anyone else, she is my equal, and the equal of all others."

In denouncing Senator Stephen Douglas' statement regarding the principle of popular sovereignty, that he cared not "whether slavery is voted up or voted down," Lincoln said in 1854:

This declared indifference, but, as I must think, covert real zeal for the spread of slavery, I cannot but hate. I hate it because of the monstrous injustice of slavery itself. I hate it because it deprives our republican example of its just influence in the world; enables the enemies of free institutions with plausibility to taunt us as hypocrites; causes the real friends of freedom to doubt our sincerity.

In that same year, Lincoln said he opposed only the further extension of slavery and was not prepared to interfere with slavery where it already existed in the South—a statement that has enabled many historians to taunt him with being a hypocrite. But as Eric Foner points out:

Like other moderates, he was unwilling to jeopardize the Union by interfering directly with slavery in the states, but he was convinced that once the spread of slavery had been halted, the long process of decline would begin.

According to this view, if slavery were deprived of new land and political power, it would gradually disappear. "Like most western Republicans," Foner adds, Lincoln opposed Negro suffrage and was an ardent colonizationist, "though he insisted that emigration be voluntary." But Lincoln "never pandered to racial prejudice . . . and he consistently affirmed the basic humanity of the Negro— and his right to an economic livelihood."

"I now only oppose slavery in the territories," Lincoln wrote in 1854. But with the Kansas-Nebraska Act and the *Dred Scott* decision, he began to fear that slavery could legally be carried first into all territories and then, under the Supreme Court's application of the due-process clause of the Fifth Amendment in behalf of slave property, could spread into the free states as well. In his famous "house divided" speech in Springfield, Illinois, on June 16, 1858, Lincoln spoke of a conspiracy by the slave power and the federal government and a course of degeneration in government. The events of the four preceding years evinced "a common *plan* or *draft*," he charged, "drawn up before the first lick was struck." The position of moral neutrality officially taken in the Kansas-Nebraska bill served, in this design, to create an attitude of indifference among freemen to the expansion of slavery, and thus to prepare them for further steps. Meanwhile, the very language of the bill invited a constitutional ruling from the Supreme Court, for the power it accorded a territorial legislature to pass on slavery matters was made "subject only to the Constitution."

But the *Dred Scott* case, which had been initiated in a lower court at the precise time the Kansas-Nebraska bill was passing through Congress, was not finally decided by the high tribunal until after a national election had presumably given a mandate to the conspirators. In this fashion, the inauguration of Buchanan brought in its wake the fateful ruling by the Court that the Constitution carried slavery into all national territories. Only one more decision was needed, Lincoln warned, to break down the barriers of freedom in the Northern states themselves and to make slavery national everywhere. A "nice little niche might be filled with another Supreme Court decision," abrogating the power of the free states to exclude slavery.

Lincoln's criticism of the *Dred Scott* decision, Don E. Fehrenbacher argues, was not like the mainstream of Republican criticism, which tried to dismiss the controversial parts as mere *obiter dicta*. Lincoln instead took the position that a Supreme Court decision, although it must ultimately become authoritative, did not necessarily reach that status unless it was grounded in sound historical facts, repeated by the Court in several decisions, represented the views of the bulk of the justices, and met numerous other conditions that were functions of time. Likewise, Lincoln's first response to the decision was to denounce the historical absurdity of Taney's assertion regarding the state of opinion of the founding fathers on the Negro and to document a decline in recent times from the libertarian sentiments of the framers of the Constitution. As Lincoln put it, the *Dred Scott* opinion made it seem that "all the powers of the earth" were combining against the Negro, and "now they have him, as it were, bolted in with a lock of hundreds of keys, which can never be unlocked without the concurrence of a hundred men, and then scattered to a hundred different and distant places."

In his *Prelude to Greatness,* a study of Lincoln in the 1850s, Don E. Fehrenbacher has demonstrated that many of the qualities revealed during his presidency were already evident in the slavery debates from 1854 to 1860. However, G. S. Boritt in *Lincoln and the Economics of the American Dream,* takes this one step further. Boritt argues that Lincoln, throughout his career, adhered to certain unchanging economic principles. "The key to this persuasion," he writes, "was an intense and continually developing commitment to the ideal that all men should receive a full, good, and ever increasing reward for their labors so that they might have the opportunity to rise in life. . . . And this, Lincoln's American Dream, became a central theme throughout his political life." Lincoln, Boritt also argues, developed principles that became the foundation for a process of modernization in which all classes (including blacks) would share in the benefits of economic growth. Slavery, in that sense, was wrong because it denied the fundamental right of each individual to the fruits of his labor. Lincoln did not assert the political or social equality of blacks, but he did insist that in his "right to eat the bread, without the leave of anybody else, which his own hand earns," the slave was "my equal and the equal of Judge Douglas and the equal of every living man." Like whites, blacks had the natural right to try and better their economic position. Moreover, the expansion of slavery, an institution which curtailed the economic rights of blacks, threatened to deny whites the possibility of economic and social advancement as well.

One must be careful, in all of this, not to claim too much for Lincoln. A recent psychobiography of Lincoln asserts, for example, that there were "few Republican principles" until "Lincoln defined them in the debates" with Stephen A. Douglas in 1858. But, as we have already seen, the Republicans advanced a clear ideology (especially that of "Free Soil, Free Labor, Free Men") from the time of their founding in 1854. "It gives too much importance to Lincoln," George M. Fredrickson observes, "to claim that he invented basic Republican principles. What he did was articulate them in an exceptionally eloquent and politically effective way."

Clear evidence of this occurred during the Lincoln-Douglas debates of 1858.

THE LINCOLN-DOUGLAS DEBATES

The *Dred Scott* decision inevitably became the major issue in the congressional elections of 1858. Of these electoral contests, none attracted more nationwide attention than the one for the Senate seat in Illinois. This pitted the incumbent, Democratic Senator Stephen A. Douglas, author of the Kansas-Nebraska Act and a leader of his party in the Senate, against the Republican challenger, Abraham Lincoln. At that time U.S. senators were chosen in each state by vote of the state legislature. Democratic candidates for the legislature ran pledged to vote for Douglas, Republicans for Lincoln, and the choice of senator was thus determined by whose supporters won the most seats in the election for legislature.

The state convention of the Illinois Republican party met in Springfield on June 16, 1858, and nominated Lincoln as its "first and only choice" for U.S. senator. It was in his acceptance speech of June 16 that Lincoln delivered what is now known as the "house divided" speech. He said:

"A house divided against itself cannot stand." I believe this government cannot endure permanently half slave and half free. I do not expect the Union to be dissolved—I do not expect the house to fall—but I do expect it will cease to be divided. It will become all one thing, or all the other. Either the opponents of slavery will arrest the further spread of it, and place it where the public mind shall rest in the belief that it is in the course of ultimate extinction; or its advocates will push it forward till it shall become alike lawful in all the States, old as well as new, North as well as South.

This was based on the argument that if the Taney theory was valid for the territories, it could threaten the free states. Lincoln, however, struck another theme in the speech that he was to repeat in the campaign. He equated the revival of the African slave trade, being urged at that time in a number of Southern states, with Douglas' doctrine of popular sovereignty, which would allow the people in the territories to vote slavery up or down. "For years," Lincoln insisted, "he [Douglas] has labored to prove it a *sacred right* of white men to take negro slaves into the new territories. Can he possibly show that is *less* a sacred right to buy them where they can be bought *cheaper in Africa* than in *Virginia*?"

Douglas launched his campaign with a speech in Chicago on July 9 stressing that "this government of ours is founded on the white basis. It was made by the white man, for the benefit of the white man, to be administered by white men, in such manner as they should determine." To be sure, a Negro or an Indian, "or any other man of an inferior race to a white man," should be permitted to enjoy rights "that he is capable of exercising consistent with the safety of society." Which rights these should be, however, should be left to each individual state to determine. Then Douglas commented:

I do not subscribe to the doctrine of my friend, Mr. Lincoln, that uniformity is either desirable or possible. I do not acknowledge that the states must all be free or must all be slave. I do not acknowledge that the negro must have civil and political rights everywhere or nowhere. . . . He [Lincoln] goes for uniformity in our domestic institutions, for a war of sections, until one or the other is subdued. I go for the great principle of the Kansas-Nebraska Bill, the right of the people to decide for themselves.

Thus began the famous Lincoln-Douglas debates. Before Election Day, November 2, the candidates traveled a combined total of ten thousand miles by road, canal, river, and rail, speaking to groups of all sizes and descriptions. Lincoln challenged Douglas to fifty debates; Douglas agreed to seven.

The initial debate was held in Ottawa on August 21. Douglas spoke first (the comments in parentheses are the outbursts in the audience):

We are told by Lincoln that he is utterly opposed to the Dred Scott decision, and will not submit to it, for the reason that he says it deprives the negro of the rights and privileges of citizenship. . . . I ask you, are you in favor of conferring upon the negro the rights and privileges of citizenship? (*"No, no."*) Do you desire to strike out of our state constitution that clause which keeps slaves and free negroes out of state, and allow the free negroes to flow in, (*"Never,"*) and cover your prairies with black settlements?. . . If you desire negro citizenship, if you desire to allow them to come into the state and settle with the white man, if you desire them to vote on an equality with yourselves, and to make them eligible to vote on an equality with yourselves, and to make them eligible to office, to serve on juries, and to judge your rights, then support Mr. Lincoln and the Black Republican party, who are in favor of the citizenship of the negro. (*"Never, never."*) . . .

I do not question Mr. Lincoln's conscientious belief that the negro was made his equal, and hence is his brother, (*Laughter,*) but for my own part, I do not regard the negro as my equal, and positively deny that he is my brother or any kin to me whatever.

In reply Lincoln said:

I have no purpose directly or indirectly to interfere with the institution of slavery in the states where it exists. I believe I have no lawful right to do so, and I have no inclination to do so. I have no purpose to introduce political and social equality between the white and the black races. There is a physical difference between the two, which in my judgment will probably forever forbid their living together upon the footing of perfect equality, and inasmuch as it becomes a necessity that there must be a difference, I, as well as Judge Douglas, am in favor of the race to which I belong, having the superior position. I have never said anything to the contrary, but I hold that notwithstanding all this, there is no reason in the world why the negro is not entitled to all the natural rights enumerated in the Declaration of Independence, the right to life, liberty and the pursuit of happiness. (*Loud cheers.*) I hold that he is as much entitled to these as the white man. I agree with Judge Douglas he is not my equal in many respects—certainly not in color, perhaps not in moral or intellectual endowment. But in the right to eat the bread, without leave of anybody else, which his own hand earns, *he is my equal and the equal of Judge Douglas, and the equal of every living man.* (*Great applause.*)

Lincoln elaborated his views on the status of the Negro in Charleston on September 18, adding that not only had he never been "in favor of bringing

about in any way the social and political equality of the white and black races''
but that he was

not now nor ever have been in favor of making voters or jurors of negroes . . . nor of
qualifying them to hold office, nor to intermarry with white people; and I will say in
addition to this that there is a physical difference between the white and black races which
I believe will forever forbid the two races living together on terms of social and political
equality. And inasmuch, as they cannot so live, while they do remain together there must
be the position of superior and inferior, and I as much as any other man am in favor of
having the superior position assigned to the white race.

In his article, ''Was Lincoln a White Supremacist?'' Lerone Bennett, Jr.,
quotes the above from the Charleston speech and argues that in this statement,
''Lincoln made his position crystal clear.'' But he omits entirely the following
by Lincoln, which continues after ''to the white race'':

I say upon this occasion I do not perceive that because the white race is to have the
superior position the negro should be denied everything. I do not understand that because I
do not want a negro woman for a slave I must necessarily want her for a wife. (*Cheers and
laughter.*) My understanding is that I can just let her alone. I am now in my fiftieth year,
and I certainly never have had a black woman for either a slave or a wife. So it seems to
me quite possible for us to get along without making either slaves or wives of negroes. I
will add to this that I have never seen to my knowledge a man, woman or child who was in
favor of producing a perfect equality, social and political, between negroes and white
men.

On several occasions Douglas charged Lincoln and the Republican party with
having ''a different set of principles for each of these localities'': ''His principles
in the north are jet black, (*laughter,*) in the centre they are in color a decent
mulatto, (*renewed laughter,*) and in lower Egypt they are almost white. (*Shouts
of laughter.*)'' There was much truth in this observation. Compare, for example,
Lincoln's comment in Charleston, in southern Illinois, with the following remark
in Chicago, in northern Illinois:

Let us discard all this quibbling about this man and the other man, this race and that race
and the other race being inferior, and therefore they must be placed in an inferior position.
Let us discard all these things, and unite as one people throughout this land, until we shall
once more stand up declaring that all men are created equal.

It would be incorrect to conclude that the central issue of the debates revolved
around the arguments over racial equality. Douglas, as author of the Kansas-
Nebraska Act, favored popular sovereignty, and yet the *Dred Scott* decision,
which he also supported, appeared to undermine his position by implying that
slavery could not be prohibited in a territory. This seemed to leave it that while
people in a territory could vote on the question of slavery, they could not vote

slavery down. Lincoln's repeated prodding on this contradiction produced, in Freeport, the answer from Douglas that even though in theory slavery could not be specifically prohibited in a territory, in fact, slaveholders would not take slaves into certain territories unless there were laws upholding slavery on the books.

To some, the Freeport doctrine seemed a quibble, and Don W. Fehrenbacher has argued that its significance has been greatly exaggerated. Nevertheless, it seems to have irritated southerners so much that it played a role in Douglas' loss of support from that section in his quest for the Democratic presidential nomination in 1860.

In the final debate, held in Alton on October 15, the candidates summarized their views. Lincoln claimed that Republicans looked upon slavery "as being a moral, social and political wrong" and insisted "that it should as far as may be, *be treated* as a wrong, and one of the methods of treating it as a wrong is to *make provision that it shall grow no larger.*" He ended with one of his most eloquent and meaningful statements:

That is the real issue. That is the issue that will continue in this country when these poor tongues of Judge Douglas and myself shall be silent. It is the eternal struggle between these two principles—right and wrong—throughout the world. They are the two princi-ples that have stood face to face from the beginning of time, and will ever continue to struggle. The one is the common right of humanity and the other the divine right of kings. It is the same principle in whatever shape it develops itself. It is the same spirit that says, "You work and toil and earn bread, and I'll eat it." (*Loud applause.*) No matter in what shape it comes, whether from the mouth of a king who seeks to bestride the people of his own nation and live by the fruit of their labor, or from one race of men as an apology for enslaving another race, it is the same tyrannical principle.

In conclusion, Douglas said that each state should be able to do as it pleased on the issue of slavery. While Lincoln looked forward "to a time when slavery shall be abolished everywhere," he, Douglas, looked forward to a time "when each state shall be allowed to do as it pleased. If it chooses to keep slavery forever, it is not my business, but its own."

In the course of the debates, Lincoln had stressed the moral basis of Re-publicanism and had pointed to divergent attitudes on the morality of slavery as the essential point of conflict between North and South. Moreover, he had made it clear that his long-range goal was not merely the nonextension of slavery, although he was inflexible in adhering to this objective, but its "ultimate extinc-tion." In his racial views, he had reflected a consciousness of speaking on the Negro in a Negrophobic state, but he had refused to abandon his fundamental belief that the black man and woman were entitled to their freedom and to the right to keep for themselves what their own labor produced—a right to which they were entitled under the Declaration of Independence as clearly and fully as any white man or woman.

In its appeal to voters on the eve of the election, the *Chicago Times,* the Democratic party's chief organ, urged:

White laborers should all vote for Douglas candidates, as his opponent, Mr. Lincoln, is in favor of bringing into the state the free negro population of Kentucky and Missouri—to compete with and crowd out from our workshops and our farm hands the Irish, German, and all other laborers of foreign birth. Vote against Lincoln and negro equality.

On November 2, the voters elected forty-six Democrats to the state legislature and forty-one Republicans, thus assuring Douglas' reelection to the Senate. But as Frederick Douglass wrote of the defeated candidate: ''In his debates with Douglas, he came fully up to the highest mark of Republicanism.''

ELECTION OF 1858 IN NEW YORK

Since blacks were disenfranchised in Illinois, they had played no political role in the Lincoln-Douglas contest. The situation was different in New York State, where the gubernatorial campaign of 1858 confronted blacks with a dilemma. Three candidates were in the field: Edwin D. Morgan for the Republicans, Amos J. Parker for the Democrats, and Gerrit Smith for the Radical Abolitionist party. The Radical Abolitionists entered the campaign with tremendous enthusiasm, convinced that events were moving voters in their direction. They argued that the Republican position on slavery was beginning to be modified in a conservative direction, as evidenced by the fact that all ninety-two Republicans in the House of Representatives had supported the Crittenden-Montgomery bill. This measure provided for a referendum on the admission of Kansas into the Union on the basis of the proslavery Lecompton Constitution and promised the admission of Kansas as a slave state if the document were approved.

The Republican surrender of principle in the Lecompton affair was seized upon by the Radical Abolitionists to bolster their charge that the Republicans were betraying even their limited policy of preventing the extension of slavery through the action of Congress, and they rallied strongly behind Gerrit Smith's candidacy to take advantage of the situation. Smith himself campaigned extensively throughout the state and financed a well-publicized drive to win votes. A special effort was made to attract to Smith's banner the 11,500 black voters in New York State. Blacks were told that the Republican party had betrayed its limited principles, that it was on the verge of disintegration, and that Radical Abolitionism was the wave of the future. Only with the Republican party out of the way, the Radical Republicans maintained, would the field be open for a party that would make the complete and total abolition of slavery the key issue in American politics. Finally, they argued that the Republican party had disappointed the Negro with regard to equal suffrage in New York and protection from the Fugitive Slave Act and that the Republicans actually prided themselves on being the white man's party. A Gerrit Smith administration in New York State would guarantee blacks equal suffrage and equal civil and political rights. In October 1858, the *Radical Abolitionist,* the party's official organ published monthly in New York City, appealed directly to black voters:

What part do you propose to take at the approaching State election? Hitherto, the greater part of you have voted with the Whig, Free Soil, Free Democratic, and Republican Parties. You have done so, because you have expected to obtain from them equal suffrage and protection against the *Fugitive Slave Bill.* Your expectations have been disappointed. The leaders of the Republican party have now ceased to repeat their former professions of regard for you, as they did when they were Free Soilers or Whigs. They declare their party to be distinctively *"The white man's party."*. . .

Can you refuse to neglect voting for GERRIT SMITH and elect the Democratic candidate. Unless Smith be elected, a pro-slavery Democrat will be. And the vote of the colored people may, perhaps, decide the election.

Yet even though blacks were deeply moved by appeals on behalf of Gerrit Smith, their long-time friend and benefactor, they were convinced that the Radical Abolitionists did not have a chance to win and that if too many black votes were given to Smith, the Republicans would go down to defeat and the proslavery Democrat would be elected. Moreover, much of the effect of the Radical Abolitionist argument that the Republicans were adopting a conservative antislavery policy was dissipated by William H. Seward's "irrepressible conflict" speech in Rochester on October 25. It was partly to prevent radical voters from casting their ballots for Smith that Seward delivered his famous speech a week before the election in which, after describing the divergent interests of the sections, he declared:

Shall I tell you what this collision means? Those who think that it is accidental, unnecessary, the work of interested or fanatical agitators, and therefore ephemeral, mistake the case altogether. It is an irrepressible conflict between opposing and enduring forces, and it means that the United States must and will, sooner or later, become either entirely a slaveholding nation, or entirely a free-labor nation.

The Rochester speech was calculated to counter Smith's arguments that the Republican party had betrayed its antislavery principles, and as far as black voters were concerned, it succeeded. The statewide convention of New York blacks at Troy urged blacks to rally around the Republican party. Stephen Myers, editor of the *Voice of Freedom*, a black newspaper published in Albany, summed up the convention's feelings when he said: "A house divided against itself must fall. And we, the 11,000 colored voters of the State, must stand just where we can be of some service in the struggle. If we ever gain any political rights we must look to the Republican party, for that is to be the dominant party."

William J. Watkins, who had been appointed by the convention to travel around the state drumming up Republican votes among blacks, praised Smith for his integrity and magnanimity but considered that his "nomination, under the present circumstances, must operate disastrously upon the hopes of the disfranchised colored citizens of the Empire State, and of the country at large; for the precedent now sought to be established, and the result of the present election will tell materially upon the next Presidential contest." Watkins viewed the Democratic party "of the State and nation as the black man's most determined and efficient enemy, a consolidated despotism which must be utterly overthrown before we can obtain the right of franchise upon the same basis with our white fellow citizens."

Morgan was triumphant. Smith received only 5,470 votes in contrast to Morgan's 247,953. In fact, except for Illinois, the elections of 1858 proved to be a great triumph for the Republican party, which won in every other Northern state. While the Republican triumphs did not please all blacks, the vast majority looked forward to the future with considerably more optimism as a result of these victories.

13

Blacks and John Brown

"The morning papers," wrote the Philadelphia diarist Sidney George Fisher on October 19, 1859, "contained an account of an attempted negro insurrection on the 17th & 18th at Harpers Ferry of a very curious character. It seems that a man by the name of Brown was the ring leader." Going on to explain how John Brown planned to seize an arsenal and call upon slaves to strike for their liberty with the arms he could then put into their hands, and how the plan failed, Fisher concluded: "A more absurd scheme could not be imagined and the man is no doubt a monomaniac."

Thus, even a respectable Philadelphian who loathed slavery dismissed John Brown in 1859 as insane because he sought the revolutionary overthrow of slavery. Since then, most respectable Americans have similarly tried to dismiss him as a madman. But Frederick Douglass reported that when the slaves mentioned John Brown's name, they "dropped their voices to a whisper," regarding him with awe. In truth, from the time of Harpers Ferry to the present, black Americans have always called John Brown the greatest of all fighters against slavery.

What manner of man was John Brown?

EARLY LIFE OF JOHN BROWN

Brown was born of Puritan stock in Torrington, Connecticut, in 1800, but when he was five years old, his family moved to northern Ohio, an area that became famous for the intensity of its religious abolitionist convictions. While there is some disagreement among Brown's biographers over the degree to which religion in general, and Calvinism in particular, influenced his antislavery views, it does appear that Brown's abolitionism was grounded in intense religious convictions and was greatly influenced by an orthodox Calvinist home, where he was brought up to revere the Bible and regard slavery as a sin.

John Brown married twice and fathered twenty children. As a businessman, he was unsuccessful; a series of small businesses he founded in Ohio, Pennsylvania, Massachusetts, and New York ended in bankruptcy. Through it all, however, he was identifying himself ever more closely with the antislavery cause. In the 1830s and 1840s, he befriended abolitionists and free blacks, donated land to fugitive slaves, gave money for black education, and financed the publication of two important manifestos by black revolutionaries: David Walker's *Appeal* and Henry Highland Garnet's *Address,* both of which called upon the slaves to rise in rebellion and overthrow slavery. He gave freely of his time and money to the antislavery cause, even though his family found it difficult to make ends meet on his earnings from successive jobs as a tanner, wool merchant, and farmer. Yet in 1834, Brown informed his brother in Ohio that "having fully consulted the feelings of my wife and my three boys, we have agreed to get at least one negro boy or youth, and bring him up as we do our own."

BROWN'S ORIGINAL PLAN TO END SLAVERY

John Brown had no patience with the commitment of many abolitionists to "moral suasion"—the belief that once the slaveholders were convinced of their sins, they would voluntarily abandon the institution. Late in 1847, while on a lecture tour in New England, Frederick Douglass met Brown, then a merchant in Springfield, Massachusetts. In his editorial correspondence to the *North Star,* Douglass wrote of having had a "private interview" with Brown, who, "though a white gentleman, is in sympathy a black man, and as deeply interested in our cause, as though his own soul had been pierced with the iron of slavery." Douglass did not reveal the nature of the interview, merely reporting Brown's joy at the appearance of men "possessing the energy of head and heart to demand freedom for their whole people," the result of which "must be the downfall of slavery." Years later, he filled in the details. After dinner at Brown's simple home, his host expounded his views on slavery. Brown not only condemned the institution but added that the slaveholders "had forfeited their right to live, that the slaves had the right to gain their liberty in any way they could." "Moral suasion," he maintained, could never liberate the slaves nor could political action abolish the system.

It was at Brown's home in Springfield in 1847 that Douglass first learned of his plan to aid the slaves, a project that embraced the setting up of an armed force that would function in the heart of the South. At that time, Brown pointed to a large map of the United States. He told Douglass that the Allegheny Mountains, stretching from the borders of New York State into the South, afforded an excellent "pathway for a grand stampede from the Slave States, a grand exodus into the Free States, and, through the latter, into Canada." The mountains were full of hiding places, and once the slaves were brought there and scattered among the glens, deep ravines, and rocks, it would be difficult to find them and even more difficult to overpower them if they were found. "I know these mountains well," said Brown, "and could take a body of men into them and keep them there in spite of all the efforts of Virginia to dislodge me, and drive me out. I would take at first about twenty-five picked men and begin on a small scale, supply them arms and ammunition, post them in squads of fives on a line of twenty-five miles, these squads to busy themselves for a time in gathering recruits from the surrounding farms, seeking and selecting the most restless and daring." Once he had gathered a force of a hundred hardy men and drilled them properly, they would help slaves escape in large numbers, keeping the braver ones in the mountains and sending the others north by the Underground Railroad. Gradually the operations would be enlarged to cover the entire South, and in due course, the movement would seriously weaken slavery in two ways: by destroying "the money value of slave property" by making it insecure and by keeping alive antislavery agitation and thereby compelling the adoption of measures to abolish the evil altogether.

From eight o'clock in the evening until three in the morning, Douglass and Brown discussed the plan. Douglass called attention to serious flaws in the project. For example, he pointed out, once the plan went into operation, the slaveowners would sell their slaves farther South or would use bloodhounds and armed forces to track down and overpower Brown and his band. Also it would be almost impossible to keep the group in the mountains provided with supplies. Brown brushed aside these objections. If the slaves were removed to the lower South he would follow them, and even driving them out of one county into another would represent a victory. Regardless of any difficulties, he would persevere in his attempt, for some launching event was necessary to prevent the agitation over the slavery question from dying out. And even if he should die in the effort, he would be giving his life for the cause closest to his heart.

Douglass became convinced that Brown's plan had "too much to commend it," but he still felt that "moral suasion" would succeed in converting the entire nation, including the slaveholders, to the antislavery position. Nonetheless, Brown's belief that slavery was actually a state of war profoundly impressed him. "My utterances," Douglass wrote later, "became more tinged by the color of this man's strong impressions," and he called his meeting with Brown a major turning point in altering his hopes that slavery could be ended by peaceful persuasion.

BROWN IN NORTH ELBA

In 1849, after breaking with his business partner in Ohio, John Brown visited Gerrit Smith in Peterboro, New York. He had read in the papers that the wealthy philanthropist and abolitionist had made much of his inherited land—120,000 acres—available to any blacks who would clear and farm it. Smith offered a minimum of 50 acres to each Negro family, and his offer attracted a large number of takers. A sizable all-black settlement—nicknamed Timbuctoo by the uneasy whites of the area—sprouted in the wilderness of North Elba, New York, in flatlands below Lake Placid, known as the Plains of Abraham. The whites need not have been uneasy; it turned out that the blacks, mostly from the Deep South, could not stand the bitterly cold winter, and many left after the first year. The few who remained needed some inspired expertise if they were to make a success of the independent agrarian life in the wilderness of North Elba.

Brown pointed out to Smith that the blacks were both inexperienced in this type of work and unused to the climate. "I propose therefore to take a farm there myself," he declared, "clear it and show the Negroes just how such work will be done. I will also employ some of them on my land, and will look after them in all ways, and will be a kind father to them."

Brown arrived at the Plains of Abraham in 1849 with his wife and several children. He bought a 240-acre farm from Smith for a dollar an acre, and he planned to use it as an example of productive agriculture for the Negro farmers of the area. A New York State Agricultural Society report of 1850 referred to a "number of very choice and beautiful Devons from the herds of Mr. John Brown, residing in our most remote and secluded towns."

At a time when belief in white supremacy was an axiom of American culture, Brown not only preached the brotherhood of all men but practiced it in his own life. Richard Henry Dana, the antislavery novelist, visited Brown's farm in North Elba and was impressed by the fact that the hired hands, including three blacks, ate with the family at the breakfast table: "I observed that he called the negroes by their surnames, with the prefixes of Mr. and Mrs. The man was 'Mr. Jefferson,' and the woman, 'Mrs. Wait.' He introduced us to them in due form. 'Mr. Dana, Mr. Jefferson, Mr. Metcalf, Mrs. Wait.' It was plain that they had never been so treated or spoken to often before, perhaps never until that day." Notwithstanding Brown's personal success, however, the experiment in North Elba failed.

In 1851, Brown was back in Springfield, Massachusetts, and became so enraged by the Fugitive Slave Act of 1850 that he exhorted blacks to kill any southerner or federal officer who tried to enforce the infamous law. He enlisted twenty-four black men and women into a mutual defense organization, the Branch of the U.S. League of Gileadites, based on the biblical command in the Book of Judges. In the league's program, which he drew up, Brown included a provision for the Gileadites to arm and shoot to kill.

BROWN IN KANSAS

In 1855, John Brown followed five of his sons to Kansas with the aim of keeping the territory free from slavery. "His first public appearance in the territory," wrote J. Ewing Glasgow, a black American living in Scotland, who published the first work on the Harpers Ferry insurrection, "was at Osawatomie at a public meeting, at which accommodating politicians were carefully pruning a set of resolutions to suit every shade of free state men. What called him out to the forum was a resolution in favour of excluding all negroes from Kansas. Scarcely controlling his indignation, he rose and boldly asserted the manhood of the negro race, and gave freest expression to his anti-slavery convictions, with force and vehemence, which drew the greatest consternation among all present." It was not powerful enough, however, to prevent the barring of blacks from Kansas.

This was Brown's last public speech in the territory. Instead he resorted to action. The need for action, he felt, was urgent. By 1856, Kansas was in a turmoil compounded of violence, murder, and outright war in which the advocates of a free state were the main sufferers. On May 16, 1856, the wife of Reverend Samuel Lyle Adair, John Brown's brother-in-law, who was then a resident at Osawatomie, wrote a letter to her sister, depicting the fear of death with which the free-state settlers in the area lived:

It is believed that Osawatomie is in danger any day or night. You ask in one of your letters if we have any fear of our lives. I think we are constantly exposed and we have almost no protection. . . . A few have their guns and revolvers, but as a people and place we are without even those and the place is known and called an *abolition nest*.

A Leavenworth, Kansas, dispatch dated May 20, 1856, published in the *New York Tribune* read: "No man's life is safe; no kind of property is secure. A guerrilla war exists in Kansas, and unless the people in the States come to our rescue and relief speedily, we shall all likewise perish." In short, an undeclared war was being carried on in Kansas by proslavery men, helped by large marauding bands from the South, and supported by sheriffs, judges, and the official legislature created by these bands through the combined use of terror and electoral fraud. On the other side were the free-state settlers, a number of whom had been killed and many beaten, with their homes and goods stolen by proslavery men. In one attack alone in the area of Osawatomie, five antislavery men were killed.

Then late in the afternoon of May 21, 1856, a group of men led by Douglas County Sheriff Samuel J. Jones bombarded the Free-State Hotel in Lawrence with a cannon and then gutted the building with gunpowder and flame; they wrecked the equipment of two newspapers, the *Herald of Freedom* and the *Kansas Free State*. These acts of looting and vandalism became known as the "sack of Lawrence."

This, in brief, was the background of an act of John Brown that is one of the most controversial of his controversial career and gained him notoriety all over the United States: the seemingly senseless murders he committed in Kansas. On May 24 at midnight, three days after the Lawrence attack, Brown led four of his sons and two other men in a raid on a small settlement on Pottawatomie Creek, murdering five proslavery men: James Doyle and his two sons, William and Drury, Allen Wilkinson, and William Sherman. He limited the killings at Pottawatomie to the number of free-states settlers who had just been killed in the area, although he could have killed at least nine men. Despite frequent charges, no women or children were killed in this action. Brown said that he deliberately killed the men to create "a restraining fear" and that he had acted as an instrument in the hand of God.

While Brown was roundly condemned in both the Northern and Southern press (and by most later historians), only three years later, in 1859, one of the settlers in the Osawatomie area observed: "The old settlers, almost unanimously, justify this tragic act, and they feel as if a debt of thanks was due to John Brown and his confederates in checking the hand of the border ruffians in that section of the country." A year later, J. Ewing Glasgow voiced the opinion of all black Americans when he wrote:

The ballot-box had already been desecrated; the ruffians of Missouri had overwhelmed the few men of the north, and had done every violence on them. He endeavored to revive the wasted energies of this north, give her a new spirit, and teach the southerners that men were not thus to be tampered with.

To him, principally is owning that Kansas is now a free state.

And later, in a still unpublished speech, Frederick Douglass, discussing the Pottawatomie killings for the first time, insisted that they must be placed in their historical context: "On both sides deeds were done at which humanity shudders and which no man in a normal condition of society can defend. It was war, terrible war, barbarous and bloody war. All that redeems it is that liberty and civilization triumphed over slavery and barbarism!"

In January 1857, Brown arrived in Boston seeking support for his efforts to preserve Kansas as a free territory. He hoped "to raise $30,000 to arm and equip a company." He spent part of the time with Lewis Hayden and his family. Brown and the Boston black leader each considered the other as possessing integrity of purpose, and above all, both considered themselves "men of action." On April 18, 1857, Brown wrote to his first cousin, the Reverend Herman Humphrey, retired president of Amherst College, indicating that he had not visited him because he had had "to hide myself a little" to keep clear of "one of 'Uncle Sam's Hounds'" who was on his "track." He added:

I have been trying to secure the means of thoroughly arming & equiping, One Hundred, Regular, Minute men: who should be carefully *selected;* intelligent, *industrious, moral, temperate,* and *earnest;* ready to serve *without wages;* & willing to *sacrifice* in the great cause of *god* & of *humanity*. The men are now diffused amongst the people of the Territory; & what I want is simply the means of *supplying them properly*. It requires to equip, & mount; *furnish shelter;* Baggage, Wagons, Harness, Saddles & Bridles, & a

small amount to feed men, & beasts; at least Three Hundred Dollars to the man; & I have
secured about one half the amount. . . .

By the time Brown left for Ohio in May, he had acquired $13,000 worth of
supplies and about $2,360 in cash. It is clear from the list of contributors that
Brown's efforts in behalf of the antislavery settlers in Kansas who had been
attacked by the proslavery groups, especially by the "border ruffians" from
Missouri, were supported by a number of distinguished northerners, including
clergymen. Nor is this surprising. During the 1850s, more and more abolitionists
came to accept John Brown's view of the necessity for violence in overthrowing
slavery. These were years that witnessed armed rescues of fugitive slaves from
Northern communities, fistfights between Northern and Southern congressmen,
and civil warfare in Kansas, in which Brown and several of his sons participated.
The accelerating tempo of violence of these years explains why important abolitionists were willing to give Brown financial and moral support.

Brown read many works on guerrilla warfare, from accounts of the resistance
of Spanish tribes to Roman occupation in ancient times, to those of the exploits
of the Haitian slave rebel, Touissaint L'Ouverture, and the activities of Brown's
contemporary, Garibaldi, in Italy. Richard Realf, a British radical abolitionist
who had worked closely with John Brown (but did not participate in the Harpers
Ferry attack), testified before the Select Committee of the U.S. Senate on January 21, 1860:

John Brown stated he had read all the books on insurrectionary warfare which he could lay
his hands upon . . . the Roman warfare; the successful opposition of the Spanish Chief-
tains during the period when Spain was a Roman province; how with ten thousand men
divided and subdivided into small companies, acting simultaneously, yet separately, they
withstood the whole consolidated power of the Roman Empire through a number of years.
In addition to this, he said he had become very familiar with the successful warfare waged
by Schamyl, the Circassian chief, against the Russians; he had posted himself in relation
to the wars of Touissaint L'Ouverture; he had become thoroughly acquainted with the
wars in Hayti . . . etc.

Early in 1858, Brown led a band of men into Missouri and rescued a number
of slaves, bringing them into Kansas. Years later, the event was recalled by John
Swinton, a former editor of the *New York Sun* who left that paper in the 1880s to
found *John Swinton's Paper,* the outstanding labor paper of the decade. In a
lecture on February 17, 1883, before the Bethel Literary and Historical Association, the famous society established by blacks in the nation's capital, Swinton
told the entranced audience of black Washingtonians:

We had rough times twenty-seven years ago in Kansas, which was then, as it were, an
outpost at which we had the skirmishing preliminary to the great anti-slavery war that
ended victoriously in Virginia in 1865. . . . One night in the winter of 1858 we got news
that a band of eleven fugitives, of both sexes, from Missouri, were in full flight toward

Lawrence, and that old John Brown, who was at the head of them, desired the support of a few of his Lawrence friends. I stayed in a small stone house with a couple of these young friends, who, heavily clad against the frosty weather and heavily armed against the pursuer, kept watch till long after midnight for the summons to join the defenders of the fugitives. Morning came, not the summons; for it turned out that John Brown, almost overtaken by thirty slave hunters, had merely skirted the town, continuing without stoppage his northward march over the plains of Iowa, on the way to Canada. We soon got wind of an event that threw some fun over the flight. In John Brown's band there were but seven fighting men besides himself—four whites and three colored—and as the thirty horsemen of the enemy were closing in upon him, he determined to halt and give battle. He seized two log houses in the woods, and the enemy sent for reinforcements, which brought their strength up to forty-two. They were about to attack, when John Brown and his seven men suddenly sallied from the woods with their rifles. But the red-shirted forces of the enemy, where were they? So terrified were they at the aspect of Brown and his men, that they took to their heels, or rather put spurs to their horses, and galloped off in panic over the prairie. "Not a shot was fired, not a drum was heard," says the chronicler of the event; but four of the foe were made prisoners in what was humorously called the Battle of the Spurs, these being the only weapons brought into play on that occasion.

It was at this time that an incident occurred illustrative of John Brown's pious humor. When he took their horses, the four prisoners indulged in profanity, which brought them a warning that he would tolerate no blasphemy in his camp. They were guilty again. "Kneel!" sternly cried the old man as he drew his pistol, before which they knelt. He ordered them to pray, and during the five days that he held them he compelled them to pray night and morning; but they never swore again in the presence of Old Osawattomie.

I need not tell that the eleven fugitive slaves, under John Brown's guidance, at last reached a place of safety on the soil of freedom.

BROWN'S NEW PLAN

Having learned the ways of guerrilla warfare by 1858, John Brown was ready to move. In February of that year, he stayed at Frederick Douglass' home in Rochester, where once again, as he had on several previous occasions, he outlined his project of a chain of hideouts in the Maryland and Virginia mountains from which men could go down to the plantations and encourage the slaves to escape. What Brown did not tell Douglass, however, was that while in Kansas, he had added a significant detail to his original plan. He now believed that, given a few sound men, it would be possible to establish a base in the mountains to which slaves and free Negroes would come and where, after beating off all attacking forces, whether state or federal, a free state would be set up.

Brown remained at Douglass' home for several weeks, spending most of the time in his own room, writing to friends for financial assistance for his venture, the nature of which he did not reveal. At other times, Brown talked at length of his plan for mountain strongholds, even explaining them to Douglass' children and illustrating "each detail with a set of blocks." Before he left Rochester, he had secured a recruit, Shields Green, a runaway slave who was staying at

Douglass' home. Brown had also drawn up a constitution for his projected free state. Consisting of a preamble and forty-eight articles, the document provided a framework of government, under a military commander-in-chief, which would be put into operation after his forces had gained power.

On March 15, 1858, Brown met again with Douglass in Philadelphia at the home of Stephen Smith, the lumber dealer. Also present were Henry Highland Garnet and William Still, the leading Underground Railroad operator. His funds exhausted, Brown appealed to them for men and money, but without divulging the broad scope of his new plans. Nor did Brown add to Douglass' knowledge when he and his son spent the night in the Negro leader's home early in April. All Douglass knew was that Brown was still proceeding with his original plan of setting up hideouts in the mountains.

That same month, Brown went to Chatham, Ontario, in Canada, the center for blacks who had moved from the United States. He had a double purpose in mind: to enlist men in his guerrilla army and to have a representative group of black men consider and ratify the constitution for the free state that he had drawn up in Douglass' home. Because of the need for secrecy, such a meeting could not be held in the United States.

Brown left for Canada accompanied by Jeremiah W. Loguen, one of his closest black friends (who accompanied him on the first leg of his Canadian trip), Richard Richardson, a runaway slave from Lexington, Mississippi, Richard Realf, the British abolitionist, and several of his companions from the Kansas struggles. During Realf's testimony before the Select Committee of the Senate, the following exchange took place:

Question: Was Brown's intercourse with the negro of a character to show that he treated him as an equal and an associate?
Answer: It certainly was. . . . We went into one of the hotels [in Chicago, enroute to Canada] in order to breakfast. We took the colored man, Richardson, to table with us. The keeper of the hotel explained that it could not be allowed. We did not eat our breakfast. We went to another hotel, where we could take a colored man with us and sit down to breakfast.
Question: Where you could enjoy your rights, I suppose.
Answer: Yes, sir.

In an interview with Brown during this same period, William A. Phillips wrote that Brown launched on his usual discussion of Spartacus and other slave revolutionaries. "I reminded him," said Phillips, "that Spartacus and the Roman slaves were warlike people . . . [while] the negroes were a peaceful, domestic, inoffensive race. In all their suffering they seemed to be incapable of resentment or reprisal. 'You have not studied them right,' he said, 'and you have not studied them long enough. Human nature is the same everywhere.' "

Brown's Canadian trip proved to be even more successful than he had hoped. At St. Catharines, he met Harriet Tubman, the legendary "Moses" of Underground Railroad lore, whose trips to Maryland and Virginia had given her an intimate knowledge of the Allegheny Mountains. Tubman agreed to solicit her Canadian friends for money and recruits, and she herself volunteered to join Brown's guerrilla force. Dr. Martin R. Delany, who had moved to Canada two years earlier, helped Brown to call a convention to organize the provisional government preliminary to overthrowing the slave power. At it, thirty-four black men and the members of Brown's group, all white except for Richard Richardson, formally considered a Declaration of Liberty and a Provisional Constitution and Ordinance for the proscribed and oppressed people of the United States. The latter provided for a one-house legislature, a president, a vice-president, a supreme court, and a commander-in-chief to be elected by the mature members of the organization. The supreme court was to have no judicial power but was a war council in charge of military matters and all correspondence with allies. The government's financial assets were to be common property. Articles 28 through 45 established rules governing the social, economic, and moral behavior of citizens. Brown believed the constitution was necessary to prevent anarchy once the revolution began. Moreover, article 46 insisted that nothing in the constitution was to be construed "so as to in any way encourage the overthrow of the United States . . . it looks to no dissolution of the Union, but simply to amendment and repeal." In short, Brown planned to transfer power within the existing system. Specifically, it would be transferred (at least symbolically) to Frederick Douglass. This notion, however, proved abortive because Douglass would not agree to it. After some debate, the delegates unanimously approved the constitution. William H. Day, the former Ohio editor who was temporarily residing in Chatham, set the type and secretly printed the charter.

John Brown was elected commander-in-chief of the provisional government by acclamation; John Henri Kagi, his most trusted white lieutenant, was chosen secretary of war; and Richard Realf, the young Englishman, secretary of state. Two blacks—Alfred M. Ellsworth and Osborn Anderson—were elected as members of congress. The office of president went unfilled after several blacks had rejected the post. Owen Brown, John Brown's son, and George B. Gill, another white associate of Brown, became treasurer and secretary of the treasury. Shortly before adjournment, John Brown introduced a resolution calling for the appointment of a committee to fill, by election, all offices named in the provisional constitution that might become vacant after the convention. The resolution was passed unanimously. The committee was made up of fifteen men, three of them blacks: Richard Richardson, the fugitive slave, Alfred M. Ellsworth of Windsor, Canada, and Osborne Anderson of Pennsylvania.

The project for which Brown had been enlisting support since late in 1857 had taken shape at the Chatham convention. His plan was to establish a stronghold in the Blue Ridge Mountains in which slaves and free blacks could take refuge and that would serve as a base of operations for fomenting slave insurrections. The key to the abolition of slavery, he believed, was guerrilla warfare. Through small forces of volunteer soldiers making surprise raids against slave-operating plantations, he hoped to weaken the market value of the slave and eventually force the collapse of the slave system. Through small-scale surprise operations, he hoped to keep bloodshed to a minimum. During his testimony before the Select Committee of the Senate, Richard Realf was asked who Brown expected "to be his soldiers." Realf answered:

The negroes were to constitute the soldiers. . . . John Brown expected that all the free negroes in the United States would immediately flock to his standard. . . . All the slaves in the Southern States would do the same . . . as many of the free Negroes in Canada as could accompany him, would do so.

A YEAR'S DELAY

The first problem to be solved after Chatham was financial. As Brown wrote to Douglass (who knew nothing of the plan): "I expect to need all the help I can get by the first of May." Evidently this problem was largely solved, for on August 16, 1858, Delany wrote to Kagi, Brown's lieutenant, that "all are in good spirits here, hoping and waiting for the 'good time coming.'" As Brown's and Delany's letters indicate, Brown had intended to strike in 1858 instead of 1859.

The year's delay was made necessary by the treachery of Hugh Forbes, an Englishman who had fought with Garibaldi and who had joined Brown after they had met in Kansas. Forbes had agreed to drill Brown's men and to recruit army officers; his main interest in the project was financial. After getting as much money as he could from Brown, he began on his leader's friends. When that source of income dried up, he threatened to expose the conspiracy if further funds were not forthcoming.

Frederick Douglass had reluctantly assisted Forbes in November 1857 with "a little money" and with letters of introduction to friends. But he had reacted unfavorably to the adventurer; he was unimpressed by his tale of family woes and so was not surprised when he learned that Forbes was threatening to disclose Brown's plans. He relayed this information to Brown. Meanwhile, Forbes did betray Brown's plan to antislavery congressmen in Washington. Alarmed, Brown's white backers (five of the "Secret Six")—Samuel Gridley Howe, Gerrit Smith, Theodore Parker, George L. Stearns, and Thomas Wentworth Higginson—met at the Revere House in Boston and insisted on a delay. They counseled Brown to postpone his operations and leave for Kansas. Assured that he would receive additional funds in the spring, Brown eventually returned to Kansas and hid out under an assumed name.

The postponement had a serious effect on Brown's ambitious plan. The year's delay scattered his forces. Martin Delany went to Africa, William Day went to England, and Harriet Tubman was ill. Henry Highland Garnet turned Brown down flatly, not because he objected to an invasion to stir revolt but because "the time had not yet come for the success of such a movement," since slaves in the South were unprepared for it. They were "not sufficiently apprised of their rights and of the sympathy that existed on the part of the North for them." And blacks in the North, "in consequence of the prejudice that shuts them out from both the means and the intelligence necessary," were equally unready for the venture.

The Reverend John W. Gloucester, usually more conservative than Garnet, apparently collected funds for Brown but did nothing more. In an effort to obtain recruits, Brown and Kagi visited Cleveland in March 1859 at a time when Simeon Bushnell and Charles H. Langston were awaiting trial in connection with the Oberlin-Wellington rescue. At the jail, Brown expressed his personal support for all of the Oberlin-Wellington rescuers. The rest of his time in Cleveland was spent talking to blacks who might be interested in joining his band and raising funds by speaking and auctioning off two "abolitionist" horses and a mule. On March 25, Brown left for the East, but Kagi remained in the city to continue efforts to round up support; he spent time with Charles H. Langston, John M. Langston, Lewis Sheridan Leary, John A. Copeland, Jr., and James H. Harris, hoping to recruit these blacks into Brown's small army. The precise reason for such a force was still the secret of a chosen few.

On April 15, 1859, *Frederick Douglass' Paper* carried the piece, "Old Brown in Rochester," indicating that Brown was again visiting Douglass. The black editor was critical of the local Republicans for failing to honor the "hero among us":

He was received at the City Hall on Saturday evening by an audience exceedingly and discreditably small, considering the Republican professions of our citizens, and the character and history of the brave old man, to whose courage and skill, more than to those of any other man in Kansas, the freedom of that Territory is now indebted. It is hard to account for the indifference of the Republicans to the claims of John Brown, on any grounds which do not imply an impeachment of their sincerity and honesty. Have they been sincere in what they have said of their love of freedom? Have they really desired to head off, hem in, and dam up the desolating tide of slavery? If so, does it not seem that one who has suffered, and perilled everything in accomplishing these very ends, has some claims upon their grateful respect and esteem? Where were they on Saturday night?. . .

It is possible that Mr. Brown is a trifle too thorough in his devotion to the cause of freedom to suit the professed friends of the cause. His recent demonstration against slavery in Missouri, in which he released a dozen slaves from bondage by force, may have produced the conviction that he is not altogether so politic and discreet as a leader should be. Indeed, that act of his has raised a question both of his honesty and sanity in some quarters, and made him an object of suspicion in some others. For the benefit of all such, we would say that Mr. Brown is neither insane nor inconsistent. He says that slavery is only one form of robbery, and he acts just as he talks. . . . He takes this to be sound morality, and sound Christianity, and we think him not far from the right.

The reception Brown received in Rochester was part of a general discouragement he was encountering. Enthusiasm among blacks for his plan had cooled off.

Some who had agreed to go with Brown had married, had children, and bought farms. Others had reconsidered the venture and were no longer willing to take part. Although Lewis Hayden was sympathetic to Brown's plan, he was not convinced that the insurrection against slavery could succeed. Ohio blacks celebrated Brown's "bravery . . . strength, and manhood," but few were ready to join. Charles H. Langston, according to John Brown, Jr., would do all he could to help, but "his health" was "bad." James H. Harris, "a Cleveland friend," in Kagi's words, did not join either. John Mercer Langston was of the opinion that the project envisaged by Brown "would . . . drive . . . the enslaved away rather than draw them in needed numbers to it." In his view, the raid would never succeed.

"Inquire after your four Cleveland friends," Brown wrote Kagi in July 1859, "and have them come on to Chambersburg." Actually, there were only two: John A. Copeland, Jr., and his uncle, Lewis S. Leary. Copeland, a former student in the preparatory department at Oberlin College, had just been released from jail with the other Oberlin-Wellington rescuers, and he volunteered to help Brown with the same zeal that had led him to help Price a year earlier. His aim was "to assist in giving that freedom to at least a few of my poor and enslaved brothers who have been most foully and unjustly deprived of their liberty." Leary, a free-born black from Fayetteville, North Carolina, living in Oberlin with his wife and daughter, shared his nephew's feelings and left with him to join Brown's army.

DOUGLASS AND BROWN IN CHAMBERSBURG

In the early summer of 1859, Brown fixed upon Harpers Ferry as the base of his operations in Virginia. He rented the Kennedy farm in Maryland, a few miles from the Ferry, as a place to collect his arms and his band of followers. He had failed to win over a single Negro leader to join his expedition, but he still hoped that he could recruit Frederick Douglass.

On August 19, 1859, Douglass and Shields Green went to Chambersburg, Pennsylvania, at Brown's request. Douglass brought a letter from Mrs. J. N. Gloucester, a Brooklyn woman of means, with $25 enclosed. There, twenty miles from Harpers Ferry, at a secret meeting in an old stone quarry, the "old man" told Douglass that he intended to attack the arsenal. Douglass was shocked because he saw no hope for success. He was sympathetic to some action in the South, but he rejected Brown's plan to attack the federal arsenal rather than wage guerrilla activity in the southern Appalachians, as he had originally planned. He was prepared to join him in carrying out the plan of running slaves through the Alleghenies, but he considered the raid on Harpers Ferry an attack on the national government and doomed to failure. No amount of argument could dissuade Brown. The seizure, he argued, would dramatize the evils of slavery, capture the attention of the nation, and arouse the people to action.

Brown's eloquence and his burning enthusiasm for the cause moved Douglass tremendously, but the latter remained adamant to all entreaties to participate. After the abortive raid, he wrote that he would have been willing to "write, speak, organize, combine, and even to conspire against Slavery," but Brown's fantasy was too foolhardy to win his support. "I told him . . . ," Douglass later recalled, "that all his arguments and all his descriptions of the place convinced me that he was going into a perfect steel trap and that once in he would never get out alive."

As Douglass was preparing to leave, Brown made a final appeal: "Come with me, Douglass! I will defend you with my life, I want you for a special purpose. When I strike, the bees will begin to swarm and I shall want you to help me hive them." Douglass shook his head sadly, and turning to Shields Green, he asked him if he had made up his mind. The former slave indicated his decision with the now-famous reply that he would go with the "old man."

THE RAID AT HARPERS FERRY

At Harpers Ferry, the Potomac River breaks through the Blue Ridge Mountains and meets the Shenandoah River in a wide, sweeping curve, between tree-covered hills. Leaving the farm he had rented on the other side of the Potomac shortly after sundown, Sunday, October 16, 1859, John Brown crossed the river with twenty-two followers, five of them blacks: Shields Green, John A. Copeland, Jr., Lewis Leary, Dangerfield Newby, and Osborne Anderson. Their objective was the capture of the federal arsenal at Harpers Ferry, from which they planned to distribute arms to slaves in the surrounding region. Brown's final instruction to his men before attacking Harpers Ferry was to avoid killing except when absolutely necessary in self-defense.

Brown and his men marched through the night in a heavy rain, which kept their passage unobserved. They reached Harpers Ferry at 4 A.M. and severed the telegraph wires to the east and west. The main body moved through the town's darkened streets and captured three main targets: the armory, the arsenal, and Hall's Rifle Works. Copeland and Kagi held the latter position, and early Monday morning, they were joined by Leary.

Colonel Lewis W. Washington, a planter and great-grandnephew of the first president, and John Allstadt, another planter, were captured and taken prisoner. In the light of blazing torches held by his men, Brown spoke to the two prisoners, explaining his aim: "I came here from Kansas, and this is a slave state; I want to free all the Negroes in this state; I seek possession of the U.S. Armory, and if the citizens interfere with me I must only burn the town and have blood."

So far, things had not gone badly. But when the Wheeling to Baltimore night express rolled into the Harpers Ferry station and the conductor learned of the attack on the arsenal, the situation soon changed. When daylight came, the train pulled out for Baltimore. At Monocacy, a way station, the conductor wired officials in the head office that an armed insurrection had occurred at Harpers Ferry. Immediately President James Buchanan, Virginia Governor Henry A. Wise, and a number of military leaders were alerted.

By the next morning, wildly exaggerated rumors were being spread. The first dispatch to the world announced an "insurrection" of 250 white abolitionists aided by a "gang of negroes"—"all armed"—with reinforcements on the way, wires cut, and all streets in the town "in possession of the mob" and "barricaded and guarded." President Buchanan tried to suppress the "terrible news," fearing that the insurrection would spread, but he could not. He sent Colonel Robert E. Lee with one hundred marines to Harpers Ferry.

While Lee was in transit, a disorganized, fearful, drunken militia at Harpers Ferry had forced Brown into the locomotive roundhouse, where he kept them at bay. But the militia was hacking away at Brown's forces, picking off his men one by one. The reinforcements Brown hoped for from the plantation slaves did not materialize. When Lee arrived with the marines, he attacked the arsenal and killed or captured Brown's remaining men with relative ease. By the morning of October 18, less than thirty-six hours after the action had begun, it was over.

Ten of Brown's band, including his two sons, had been killed. Seven were captured, and five escaped. Of the five blacks with Brown, Green and Copeland were captured. Leary and Newby were killed in the fighting. Osborne Anderson managed to escape and made his way back to Canada. Newby, a former slave, was the first to die. A letter from his wife was found on his body; it read:

Dear Husband: I want you to buy me as soon as possible, for if you do not get me somebody else will. Dear Husband, the last two years have been like a troubled dream to me. It is said Master is in want of money. If so, I know not what time he may sell me, and then all my bright hopes of the future are blasted. There has been one bright hope to cheer me in all my troubles, that is to be with you. If I thought I should never see you, this earth would have no charms for me.

The children are all well. The baby cannot walk yet. It can step around everything by holding on. It is very much like Agnes. Write soon and say when you think you can come.

FIRST REACTIONS

Immediately after the attack on Harpers Ferry became known, the entire South was so convulsed with the fear that similar insurrections were imminent that an immediate search was made in every state to discover any antislavery sympathizers, and action was promptly taken to expel any person suspected of being one. In the American Anti-Slavery Society's publication, *The New "Reign of Terror" in the Southern States,* scores of violations of civil liberties and expulsions of northerners were reported, with the sources clearly indicated.

In the North, too, the news from Harpers Ferry produced an initial irrational reaction. After the legislature of Massachusetts had finally passed a bill removing the word *white* from the militia so that blacks would be allowed to serve, the news came of John Brown's ill-fated raid at Harpers Ferry. Immediately Republican governor Nathaniel P. Banks vetoed the bill on the ground that the climate had changed and white Massachusetts citizens would not tolerate the removal of the "white" provision from the militia requirements.

In this atmosphere, it is not surprising that those blacks who had been on intimate terms with John Brown were immediately placed in danger. This was particularly true for Frederick Douglass, for while he was not one of the famous "secret six" who had joined the Brown conspiracy, he probably knew more about John Brown than any of them.

Douglass received the news of Brown's capture while lecturing in National Hall at Philadelphia. He was informed that letters had been found in Brown's possession implicating him, among others, of knowledge of the plot. He knew at once that with the mounting hysteria, his life was in extreme danger. On the advice of his friends, he left Philadelphia and hastened to New York City. Later Douglass learned how fortunate he had been in following this advice. John W. Hurn, a telegraph operator and an admirer of Douglass, surpressed for three hours the delivery of a message to the sheriff of Philadelphia ordering him to arrest Frederick Douglass.

Douglass' alarm increased as he read the New York papers. The *New York Herald* headlined a report of Brown's alleged confession to Governor Wise of Virginia: "Gerrit Smith, Joshua Giddings, Fred Douglass and Other Abolitionists and Republicans Implicated." Enough it seems had been ascertained to justify a requisition from Governor Wise of Virginia, upon Governor Morgan of New York, "for the delivery over to the hands of justice of Gerrit Smith and Fred. Douglass, as parties implicated in the crime of murder and as accessories before the fact." From Richmond came an announcement that one hundred southerners were offering rewards for "traitors," among whom Douglass' name was prominently featured.

Upon Douglass' arrival in Rochester, several friends warned him that the New York governor would probably surrender him to the Virginia authorities upon request, and he was advised to cross over the border to Canada. Aware that President Buchanan would employ the full power of the federal government to bring about his arrest, Douglass took the advice of his friends and fled to Canada, and from there to England.

Douglass barely evaded his pursuers. He had already been charged in Virginia with "murder, robbery and inciting to servile insurrection in Virginia." Moreover, Governor Wise had asked President Buchanan and the postmaster general of the United States to grant two agents from Virginia authority to serve as detectives for the postal department for the purpose of delivering Douglass to the Virginia courts. Had Douglass been arrested by federal authorities at the time, the chances are that in the prevailing tense atmosphere, he would have suffered the same fate of those at Harpers Ferry who survived the attacks by the militia and marines. No evidence would have been required to sentence a black abolitionist to death in Virginia during the weeks following the attack on Harpers Ferry.

TRIAL, EXECUTION, AND FUNERAL

From Harpers Ferry, John Brown and his captured followers were taken to Charlestown, where they were imprisoned and indicted by a grand jury on charges of murder, conspiring with slaves to rebel, and treason against the state of Virginia.

Green and Copeland were tried on November 1, and the state attorney general, Hunter, became especially irritated by Green's "boldly careless bearing." George Bennett of Boston defended the two blacks and tried to save their lives. He argued that since the *Dred Scott* decision had denied blacks citizenship, the two men could not be guilty of treason. Hunter agreed but pressed for conviction on the murder and insurrection charges. In desperation, Bennett suggested that Green and Copeland had been justified in resisting slavery. But both men were found guilty and sentenced to die by hanging.

Two of the letters Copeland wrote shortly before he died have become available. One, to his brother, was dated December 10; the other, to his entire family, was penned a few hours prior to his execution. To his brother he wrote:

Dear brother, could I die in a more noble cause? Could I, brother, die in a manner and for a cause which would induce true and honest men more to honor me, and the angels more readily to receive me to their happy home of everlasting joy above? I imagine that I hear you, and all of you, mother, father, sisters and brothers, say . . . "No, there is not a cause for which we, with less sorrow, could see you die."

The *Baltimore Sun* reported that on his way to the gallows, Copeland called out: "If I am dying for freedom, I could not die for a better cause—I had rather die than be a slave."

Osborne Anderson, who left the only eyewitness account of the attack on Harpers Ferry (written with the help of Mary Ann Shadd Cary, editor of Chatham's black newspaper, the *Provincial Freeman*), described the "mockery of a trial and execution" of Green and Copeland, and asked: ". . . are they not part of the dark deeds of this era, which will assign their perpetrators to infamy, and cause after generations to blush at their remembrance"?

And what of the "old man"? Reporters swamped John Brown with questions as he lay wounded, exhausted but unrepentant, on the grass outside the building in which he had been captured. Senators and governors arrived in Charlestown, along with a new batch of reporters, to be on hand at the trial of the leader of the attack. Under a heading, "Curiosity of the Negroes," the *New York Tribune* correspondent wrote from Charlestown:

People may say what they please of the indifference of the negroes to the passing events, but it is not true. They burn with anxiety to learn every particular, but they fear to show it. A hotel servant busied himself the whole morning a day or two ago to extract from me something concerning the prospects of Brown, without appearing to ask a direct question. At last I told him that he better say what he wanted, "Well, sir," he said very timidly, "what do you think they'll do after all, with Mr. Brown?" I told him they would surely hang him. "Well, now," he said argumentatively, "Don't you see it would be a pity to do anything so 'brupt?'"

The *Tribune* reporter's prediction proved true. Over Brown's objections, the court assigned two southerners to defend him. When it was learned that he was too badly wounded to rise from his bed, he was brought in to the courtroom on a cot. The court ignored Brown's call for a postponement on the grounds of the state of his health: "I have a severe wound in the back, or rather in the kidney, which enfeebles me very much; but I am doing well, and I only ask for a short delay of my trial. . . . A short delay would be all I would ask." The court denied the request. Over Brown's objection, his court-appointed lawyer produced a number of affidavits from his friends and relatives in Ohio claiming that there was insanity in Brown's family—evidence seized upon by later historians to prove their contention that John Brown was a madman.

Quickly found guilty, Brown was asked on November 2, 1859, if he had anything to say before sentence was imposed. Though unprepared, he rose and addressed the court unhesitatingly, saying in part:

In the first place, I deny everything but what I have all along admitted—the design on my part to free the slaves. . . . That was all I intended. I never did intend murder, or treason, or the destruction of property, or to excite or incite slaves to rebellion, or make insurrection.

I have another objection: and that is, it is unjust that I should suffer such a penalty. Had I interfered in the manner which I admit, and which I admit has been fairly proved. . . . Had I so interfered in behalf of the rich, the powerful, the intelligent, the so-called great, or on behalf of any of their friends, either father, mother, brother, sister, wife or children, or any of that class, and suffered and sacrificed what I have in this interference, it would have been all right, and every man in this Court would have deemed it an act worthy of reward rather than punishment. . . .

I believe to have interfered as I have done, as I have always freely admitted I have done, in behalf of His despised poor, was not wrong, but right. Now, if it be deemed necessary that I should forfeit my life for the furtherance of the ends of justice, and mingle my blood further with the blood of my children, and with the blood of millions in this slave country whose rights are disregarded by wicked, cruel, and unjust enactments, I submit: so let it be done.

Having borne himself defiantly with fortitude and serenity from the moment he was captured, Brown continued to do so after he was sentenced to death by hanging on December 2, 1859. His words during these five weeks became world famous. In a statement published in the *New York Herald,* Brown said: "You had better—all of you people of the South—prepare yourselves for a settlement sooner than you are prepared for it, and the sooner you commence that preparation, the better for you. You may dispose of me very easily—I am nearly disposed of now; but this question is still to be settled—this Negro question, I mean. The end of that is not yet.'' In what was (with the exception of a hurriedly written note to his wife on the morning of his execution) his last farewell to his family, he wrote:

As I now begin what is probably the last letter I shall ever write to any of you . . . I am waiting the hour of my public *murder* with great composure of mind, & cheerfulness: feeling the strongest assurance that in no other possible way could I be used to so much advance the cause of God; & of humanity: & that nothing that either I or all my family have sacrificed or suffered: *will be lost.* . . . I have now no doubt but that our seeming *disaster* will ultimately result in the most *glorious success.* So my dear *shattered;* and *broken* family; be of good cheer; & believe & trust in God. . . . Do not feel ashamed on my account; nor *for one moment* despair of the cause; or grow *weary of well doing.* . . . John Brown writes to his children to abhor with *undying hatred . . .* that ''sum of all vilainies,'' Slavery.

As Brown was led to his execution, a slave woman said, ''God bless you, old man; If I could help you, I would.'' And as he mounted the wagon that led him to the gallows, Brown handed this memorandum to a guard: ''I, John Brown, am now quite certain that the crimes of this *guilty* land will never be purged away but with blood. I had, as I now think vainly, flattered myself that without very much bloodshed it might be done.''

The return home of the hanged corpse of America's most illustrious pre-Civil War martyr was a moment of sincere sorrow for many citizens. As the train bearing his body moved east and then north, solemn church bells rang out. But not all mourned. When Brown's remains were brought to the City of Brotherly Love, James Miller McKim, the Philadelphia abolitionist, planned to secure the services of an undertaker and allow Mrs. Brown, who was accompanying the coffin, a day's rest before proceeding to North Elba, where the burial was to take place. The mayor of Philadelphia met them at the railroad station and insisted that Brown's remains be sent out of the city aboard the next train because he feared that otherwise he would be unable to maintain order in the face of the rising tide of anti-Negro feeling in the city. He threatened to use the police and even the military, if necessary, to remove the remains of the great champion of black people from the city. Brown's body had to be taken to New York City, where no objection was raised to its being turned over to an undertaker for two days.

Then the coffin was brought by train to Westport in Essex County, New York, and a somber cortege accompanied it to Elizabethtown, where it lay in state in the county courthouse. Six men stood vigil over it all night long, one of them riding off at dawn to inform Brown's children that the ''old man'' was coming home. Then the procession trudged through the cold mountains to North Elba, situated high in the Adirondack Mountains, and his final resting place, where to this day, "John Brown's body lies a-moldering in the grave." As the families of the six men from the village who had lost their lives during the raid on Harpers Ferry, including two sons of John and Mary Brown, stood around the open grave of John Brown, Wendell Phillips, orator and abolitionist, said, in prophetic words:

He has abolished slavery in Virginia. . . . History will date Virginia Emancipation from Harpers Ferry. True, the slave is still there. So, when the tempest uproots a pine on your hills, it looks green for months,—a year or two. Still, it is timber, not a tree. John Brown has loosened the roots of the slave system; it only breathes,—it does not live,—hereafter.

Most northerners were profoundly shocked by Brown's action, but as the weeks passed and largely as a result of Brown's dignified conduct, calm defense, and the heroic manner in which he accepted the sentence of death, as well as his reiteration of his antislavery beliefs in his famous last utterances, support for the "old man" grew and Northern opposition to slavery increased. "I find the hatred of slavery greatly intensified by the fate of Brown," wrote an abolitionist on the day after Brown's execution, and he added, "Men are ready to march to Virginia, and dispose of her despotism at once."

In his address before the citizens of Concord, Massachusetts, on October 30, 1859, during the days that John Brown's trial was taking place in Charlestown, Virginia, Henry Thoreau said:

He did not recognize unjust human laws, but resisted them as he was bid. . . . No man in America has ever stood up so persistently and effectively for the dignity of human nature, knowing himself for a man, and the equal of any and all governments. . . .

It was his peculiar doctrine that a man has a perfect right to interfere by force with the slaveholder, in order to rescue the slave. I agree with him.

In pleading from France for Brown's life, Victor Hugo wrote to Governor Wise of Virginia that "if insurrection be ever a sacred duty, it is so against slavery." He warned that "the murder of Brown" would "penetrate the Union with a secret fissure, which would in the end tear it asunder." It "might consolidate Slavery in Virginia, but it is certain that it would convulse the entire American Democracy." He urged Americans to ponder well the effects of Brown's execution: "For—yes . . . there is something more terrible than Cain slaying Abel—it is Washington slaying Spartacus."

While Brown remained in jail, meetings in his honor were held in town halls, sermons were delivered from Sunday pulpits by the most influential ministers of the day, and innumerable prayer and sympathy gatherings were held throughout the North.

BLACK AMERICA MOURNS

But as Benjamin Quarles has pointed out, no meetings "were more fervent than those called by Negroes." In New York City, the Reverend James W. Pennington wrote a guest editorial for the *Weekly Anglo-African* entitled, "Prayer for John Brown." The black women of Brooklyn not only prayed for Brown, but they sent the following letter to him:

We . . . would fain offer our sincere and heartfelt sympathies in the cause you have so nobly espoused, and that you so firmly adhere to. We truly appreciate your most noble and humane effort, and recognize in you a Savior commissioned to redeem us, the American people, from the great National Sin of Slavery; and though you have apparently failed in the object of your desires, yet the influence that we believe it will eventually exert, will accomplish all your intentions.

We consider you a model of true patriotism, and one whom our common country will yet regard as the greatest it has produced, because you have sacrificed all for its sake. . . . We have always entertained a love for the country which gave us birth, despite the wrongs inflicted upon us, and have always been hopeful that the future would augur better things. We feel now that your glorious act for the cause of humanity has afforded us an unexpected realization of some of our seemingly vain hopes.

Ralph Waldo Emerson said that the slavocracy, in hanging Brown, was making the gallows as glorious as the cross. The reaction of the black community provided eloquent testimony to the truth of this assertion. On December 2, 1859, the day of Brown's execution, a solemn service of sympathy was held in New York's Shiloh Church at which the Reverend Henry Highland Garnet presided. The prayer was offered by the Reverend Charles B. Ray, who asked that the sacrifice of "this dear old friend of freedom may mark the downfall of this sinful system of bondage." In closing the meeting, Garnet declared that "henceforth the Second of December will be called 'Martyr Day.'"

That same day, all black businesses in Boston were closed, and the Negro people, wearing armbands of black crepe, held three prayer meetings—morning, afternoon, and night—in all of the city's colored churches, each packed to overflowing, with hundreds turned away. In Cincinnati, blacks honored the man who had led the most direct attack on slavery, and "labored selflessly in our behalf." Philadelphia blacks, like those in Boston, observed the day by closing down their businesses and held prayer meetings in the leading black churches. In Detroit, they gathered at the Second Baptist Church and passed a resolution vowing to venerate Brown's character, regarding him as "our temporal leader whose name will never die."

Frederick Douglass, having fled to Canada and from there to England, was unable to participate in any of the scores of meetings held by blacks throughout the North. But before he left for England, Douglass wrote an editorial, which was read at a number of meetings:

Posterity will owe everlasting thanks to John Brown for lifting up more to the gaze of a nation grown fat and flabby on the garbage of lust and oppression, a true standard of heroic philanthropy, and each coming generation will pay its installment of the debt. . . .

Capt. Brown has initiated a new mode of carrying on the crusade of freedom, and his blow has sent dread and terror throughout the entire ranks of the piratical army of slavery. . . . Like Samson, he has laid his hands upon the pillars of this great national temple of cruelty and blood, and when he falls, that temple will speedily crumble to its final doom, burying its denizens in its ruins.

John Brown was honored by blacks in other countries, as well as in the United States, and in none more so than in Haiti. There, in his memory, flagstaffs in the harbor were hung in black, and prayer meetings were held in the churches. The leading church in Port-au-Prince was draped in mourning, and the altar was covered with white drapery, on which were depicted a pen, a sword, and a Bible, with the inscription: "A John Brown. Martyr De La Cause Des Noirs." The *Feuille de Commerce,* the leading paper in the city, carried the following editorial on its front page:

The cause of the abolition of slavery has just counted another martyr. This fact, however indifferent it may be to others, cannot be so to us, descendants as we are of the persecuted race of Africa. The event must weigh upon our hearts as a public calamity. John Brown, with his noble co-workers, has been sent to an ignominious death on the gallows! And this in a country where liberty appears to have its grandest inspiration, and where nothing is said or done but in the name of liberty; it is in this country, it is in the United States, in fact, that this man, who demanded liberty for an unjustly oppressed and enslaved race, is shamefully dragged to the scaffold! John Brown and his friends, perhaps, too quickly abandoned themselves to despair, but shall we therefore say that the hour of emancipation for our unhappy brethren is not yet come? However it may be, the blood of John Brown guarantees that it is at hand. Reassure yourselves, ye slaves, nothing is lost; liberty is immortal. Brown and his companions have sown this slave land with their glorious blood, and doubt not that therefrom avengers will arise.

In the rush of sympathy and admiration for John Brown, the black men who had accompanied him to the gallows were not forgotten. The deaths of Shields Green and John A. Copeland, Jr., on December 16, 1859, were commemorated by a public meeting of blacks in Cleveland. In Philadelphia, however, the efforts to honor the two martyrs produced a split in the black community. When a committee of Philadelphia blacks sent a petition to Governor Wise of Virginia requesting the bodies of Green and Copeland and referred to the governor's conduct in the Harpers Ferry affair as being "noble," "generous," and "magnanimous," and that the men hanged at Charlestown had been "miserably misguided," the black community exploded in anger. A call was instantly issued for a public meeting at the Philadelphia Institute "for the purpose of reviewing said petition." It was signed by, among others, John C. White, William Still, Ebenezer D. Bassett, Charles H. Bustill, and William P. Price. The meeting unanimously adopted resolutions denouncing the petition to Governor Wise "as cringing, servile and hypocritical, and a libel against our good sense of manhood," and went on to declare:

That no honest man can believe that the disfranchised American supposes than any act in his [Gov. Wise's] conduct in the Harpers Ferry affair, was either "noble," "generous," or "magnanimous," or that the brave men whose lives were sacrificed on Virginia's scaffold were "poor" or "miserably misguided."

That it is unmanly and ungrateful in sentiment, false and contemptible in its elaborations and conclusions, and is a slander upon the character of the noble men it refers to, and also a blot upon their dear and cherished memory.

That the petition exhibits a total want of dignity, frankness and independence, and violates the sentiment and feelings of every true man, by bowing and virtually kissing the heel that would crush its authors.

HISTORICAL SIGNIFICANCE OF JOHN BROWN

John Brown's character, activities, and motivations have been the subject of historiographical debate. Many historians have accepted at face value the affidavits presented at his trial that there was insanity in the Brown family. Allan Nevins described Brown's ailment as "reasoning insanity," and David Donald rarely refers to him as anything but "crazy John Brown." Although David Potter never unequivocally declares Brown insane, his analysis points in this direction, and he maintains that no one could call him "a well adjusted man." In his *The South and the Sectional Conflict,* Potter raises the slander that Brown had no meaningful relationship with the black people he sought to save. Other anti-Brown historians, like James Malin, have portrayed him as a horse thief who had little real interest in the antislavery cause.

On the other hand, W.E.B. Du Bois, in his 1909 biography, and Oswald Garrison Villard, in his life of Brown published a year later, have treated John Brown as a man of the highest moral and ethical values, a sincerely devoted abolitionist, and a true believer in racial equality. Villard, however, called the killings in Kansas ordered by Brown "murders" and titled his chapter, "Murder at the Pottawatomie," while Du Bois pointed to the threats and physical attacks upon the free-state settlers, and the marauding Southern bands that had burned and killed in the territory as the background required to understand Brown's actions. Moreover, Du Bois was convinced that it was Brown's violence in Kansas that made the state free.

The greatness of Brown, Du Bois made clear, lies in his wholehearted commitment to the cause of black liberation, his recognition, at a time when most other antislavery advocates relied on moral and political action, that southerners would never abandon their peculiar institution without a struggle, and the fact that he was a complete egalitarian at a time when many other antislavery men harbored racist attitudes. Brown's deeds proved that he did not simply work for the black men but did so on an exact level with them, knowing their faults as well as their virtues, and feeling as deeply as they did "the bitter tragedy of their lot." To Du Bois, John Brown proved that the black man can trust some white men, that black man and white man can fight side by side, as they did at Harpers Ferry, and that their destiny is indivisible.

Stephen B. Oates, author of *To Purge This Land with Blood: A Biography of John Brown,* believes that previous biographers have been prisoners of the Brown legend. Setting out either to vindicate or to demolish this legend, they have lost sight of the man himself. His own book, Oates says, is "neither an indictment nor an eulogy of Brown," but instead an objective account of the man's life. The portrait that emerges is not wholly flattering. Brown, we are told, was stubborn and self-righteous, convinced of his own special mission to root out slavery, and intolerant of weaknesses in others. At the same time, Oates does not ignore the genuinely heroic aspects of Brown's life. He finds his fortitude in the face of severe hardships indisputable and asserts that his courageous conduct in the days between his trial and execution not only deeply strengthened his reputation in the North but impressed many southerners as well. Moreover, in his chapters on Brown's years in Kansas, Oates effectively disposes of the scurrilous interpretation of Brown's conduct put forth by James Malin and others. He also argues convincingly that there is no real evidence that Brown was insane, pointing out that not only were the affidavits presented at his trial designed to save Brown from the gallows, but they were dictated by men with no medical experience.

Why did Brown change his plan from the one he originally presented to Frederick Douglass to the idea of attacking and seizing Harpers Ferry? Oates believes, on the one hand, that Brown considered the slaves ready for revolt and expected such a massive outpouring of black rebels that he would be able to stand and fight at Harpers Ferry. But he also believes that Brown "probably knew" that the raid would fail and that he may have intentionally sacrificed himself in a dramatic and courageous action that he was politically astute enough to know would turn Northern public opinion against slavery and hasten the day of emancipation.

But then, having adopted the Harpers Ferry plan, why did he deviate from his planned operation? Had Brown made the quick foray into Harpers Ferry he had originally planned, he might have succeeded. Most authorities agree that at any time between 4 A.M. and 11 A.M., after he had seized the arsenal, he could have gathered all the arms and munitions his men could carry and established a stronghold in the mountains to which slaves could flee. Not only did he not do this, but even before the raid began, Brown made a series of errors that sealed his doom. For one thing, he never really explored the surrounding countryside in detail, nor did he reconnoiter the roads leading out of Harpers Ferry. He made no advance contact with the slaves he expected to join him, he did not establish a base of provisions and arms in the mountains, and he left his own arms three miles from the town. And he let the night express train pass through Harpers Ferry and spread the alarm in Baltimore and Washington.

How can we explain these mistakes by a man who was a student of guerrilla warfare and had been planning the attack for over a decade? Possibly Brown believed that he could best serve the antislavery cause by sacrificing himself as a martyr. There is no question that he had a streak of fatalism in his character. Intense religious feeling lay at the core of his antislavery commitment, and he often compared himself with religious martyrs of the past. One of his black associates later wrote that his conversations with Brown ''led me to think that he intended to sacrifice himself and a few of his followers for the purpose of arousing the people of the North from the stupor they were in'' concerning slavery.

On the other hand, it is Truman Nelson's thesis in his 1973 publication, *The Old Man: John Brown at Harpers Ferry,* that Brown planned a classic coup at the Ferry, as distinguished from both insurrection and revolution, and that it finally worked. Its success, however, took a different shape and required a longer time and a great deal more blood than he had imagined. In the long run, says Nelson (who is critical of Oates' biography), the strategy succeeded; even though Brown failed to carry out his entire tactical plan, he did galvanize the nation and the Republican party. Contrary to the usual view of Brown, Nelson believes that his tragic flaw lay precisely in his hope that by the tactics of actual but chiefly symbolic assault, by displaying his humanity to his hostages, by restraint, by shedding blood only in self-defense, he could succeed in his revolutionary aim. He failed not as a general planning his strategy but as a captain at the operational level. And he knew it. His last written words were these: ''I, John Brown am now quite *certain* that the crimes of *this guilty land* will never be purged *away* but with blood. I had *as I now think vainly* flattered myself that without *very much* bloodshed it might be done.''

It is unfortunate that Richard O. Boyer, author of the fine study, *The Legend of John Brown*, died before he could bring the story to Harpers Ferry, having only completed the account to the eve of his departure for Kansas. Boyer might have thrown genuine light on this still puzzling aspect of Brown's final assault on slavery. Nevertheless, however one views the events at Harpers Ferry, it cannot be denied that John Brown's raid was the prologue to the Civil War. In the end, it was to take the full mobilization of Northern power and resources and the arming of hundreds of thousands of men—black and white—rather than an isolated and suicidal raid by twenty-two men, to overthrow the slave system. But when the black and white Union soldiers marched into Virginia in the last phase of the war to end slavery, they sang, ''John Brown's Body.'' Among these black soldiers was a group from New Bedford, Massachusetts, who were fulfilling a pledge they had made in a resolution adopted by the black community of the New England town on the day Brown was executed:

Resolved, That the memory of John Brown shall be indelibly written upon the tablets of our hearts, and when tyrants cease to oppress the enslaved, we will teach our children to revere his name, and transmit it to the latest posterity, as being the greatest man in the 19th century.

14

Blacks and the Election of 1860

Throughout the early part of 1860, the memory of John Brown and the other martyrs of Harpers Ferry remained foremost in the thoughts of black Americans. In Boston, William C. Nell worked to raise money for a monument for Brown and the four blacks who had died with him. He was assisted in this activity by Thomas Wentworth Higginson, one of the "secret six" who had encouraged Brown in his fatal move. The sum required, however, proved too difficult to raise.

THE JOHN BROWN FUND

More successful was the campaign to secure contributions to aid the widows and children of John Brown and Lewis S. Leary. (Since the wife and children of Danger Newby were slaves and could not receive funds and neither John A. Copeland, Jr., nor Shields Green was married, the money raised went entirely to Mrs. Brown and Mary Leary.) Philadelphia blacks sent Mary Brown $150, the John Brown Relief Fund of New Haven raised $12.75 for her, and the John Brown Liberty League of Detroit contributed $25. Some blacks sent Mrs. Brown personal contributions, and all received gracious letters of acknowledgment. When the black women of Brooklyn and New York sent Mrs. Leary $140, she replied that although her loss had been great, she hoped that her husband and his associates had not died in vain in their "attack on that great evil, American Slavery."

Blacks also helped circulate Osborne P. Anderson's *A Voice from Harpers Ferry*, "both as a means of imparting the only authentic information of these memorable scenes, and of assisting the author, who, from a combination of causes, now happened to be in need." William C. Nell informed Boston's black community that Anderson's book "can be obtained at the anti-slavery office for $.15 each, or $10 a hundred."

When word of the plight of Leary's widow was conveyed to the Haitian government by James Redpath, its emigration agent in the United States, he received a letter in reply from W. W. Pleasance, secretary of state for foreign relations, finance and commerce, instructing him "to invite her, in the name of the government, to come to reside in our country, and to place at her disposal all the means necessary to enable her to effect the voyage. Preparations will be made to prepare a dwelling for her." The Haitian official enclosed a letter addressed to Mrs. Leary in French, which was translated by Albert de la Foret, professor of French at Oberlin College, and published in the *New York Weekly Anglo-African*. It read:

Madame: Our general agent of emigration, Mr. Redpath, has informed us of the misfortune that has afflicted you in the person of your husband, who died so heroically at Harpers Ferry, in the defense of a holy cause. Your misfortune, Madame, entitles you to the esteem and sympathy of the people of Haiti, and it is to give you a testimony of this sympathy that we now invite you to come and live in the midst of us. You will find in Haiti, Madame, we beg you to believe, aid and protection on the part of the government.

We have charged our agent, Mr. Redpath, to furnish you every facility in undertaking this voyage.

Although the Leary family did not depart for Haiti where, she was assured by the minister, she would "enjoy esteem and consideration to which the heroic death of her husband has given her an eternal right," she did receive evidence of that "esteem and consideration" in the form of the fund raised there for the survivors of the Harpers Ferry martyrs. The Haitian John Brown Fund continued to operate for several years. By the fall of 1862, the Port-au-Prince committee had raised over $3,000, which was distributed among the widows of the survivors, John Brown, Jr., Owen Brown, and Osborne P. Anderson, the last being referred to as the "only colored survivor of John Brown's men." In February 1864, the citizens of Aux Cayes sent $1,131.04 for distribution among "the sufferers of the memorable expedition on Harpers Ferry." James Redpath, one of the two men in the United States designated to supervise the distribution of the Haitian fund, wrote to Garrison (the other designee):

If the blessings of the heroic poor, and the sincere admiration of the friends of the colored race, in America, will be esteemed an equivalent for their bounty, the people of Hayti have been already abundantly repaid for their generous and unexampled liberality to John Brown's men and their survivors. Since their fathers expelled the French, they have done no act which has gained for them so much respect abroad.

A CHANGE IN THE ATMOSPHERE

Even as they were honoring Brown and his men and raising funds for the survivors of Harpers Ferry and families of those who gave their lives, blacks realized that John Brown's death had marked a critical turning point in the struggle against slavery. Up to that point, "moral suasion" had still exercised some influence in the black community. Brown's raid, coming on top of the years of resistance to the Fugitive Slave Act of 1850, subjected that approach to the sharpest challenge since the emergence of Garrisonianism. Frederick Douglass spoke for a growing number of people when he declared on the eve of his departure for England that "moral considerations have long since been exhausted upon slaveholders. It is vain to reason with them. . . . Slavery is a system of brute force. It shields itself behind *might* rather than right. It must be met with its own weapons."

Harriet Beecher Stowe now also agreed. When she wrote her second novel, *Dred,* she ended the story with the black insurrectionist dead, the Southern reformers in exile, and the proslavery mobs in full control. But by the end of 1859, she was able to see a different outcome—to see, in fact, a revolution set in motion by John Brown. As she explained from abroad to the readers of the *New York Independent:*

Thus do all the signs gather round this new year; and, when we hear from home, we find that in America the same demons of slavery are trembling and quailing before some advancing power. . . . John Brown is a witness slain in the great cause which is shaking Hungary, Austria, Italy, France, and his death will be mightier for that cause than even his success. The cross is the way to the throne.

As John Brown's body was being transported from Charlestown to North Elba, Congress convened. It was obsessed by Brown and Harpers Ferry. Southern congressmen and senators argued that as a result of the events of Harpers Ferry, the South had to move to contain antislavery, or, as Jefferson Davis said in the Senate, the Southern states had to become "foreign governments with police stations along each border and passports required, with such inquiry into the character of persons coming in as would secure immunity to peaceful women and children from the incendiary and the assassin." For the moment, however, Southern congressmen were content to await the report of the committee authorized by the Senate to investigate the "Harpers Ferry invasion." The committee was chaired by Senator James Mason of Virginia, already notorious for having drafted the fugitive slave law in 1850.

The committee's report, submitted on June 14, 1860, furnished clear evidence that the sentiment in the North around John Brown and those associated with him had changed, for the committee did not dare to submit a report that would have condemned the entire North for the action at Harpers Ferry. Rather, it submitted an innocuous document stating that although Brown had planned "to commence a servile insurrection" which he hoped to extend "throughout the entire South," he did not appear to have entrusted even his immediate followers with details of his plan. After much consideration, the committee announced that it was "not prepared to suggest any legislation."

This was the atmosphere when Frederick Douglass returned from England to resume his duties as editor of his paper in Rochester. Now it was possible for a black American who had been an intimate acquaintance of John Brown to proclaim the fact proudly. In a letter to a group of abolitionists assembling at North Elba on July 4, 1860, to honor the memory of John Brown, Douglass wrote:

To have been acquainted with John Brown, shared his counsels, enjoyed his confidence, and sympathized with the great objects of his life and death, I esteem as among the highest privileges of my life. We do but honor to ourselves in doing honor to him, for it implies the possession of qualities akin to his.

RETURN OF SUMNER

Frederick Douglass was not the only abolitionist to return to his post to resume the fight against slavery and for black equality. On June 4, 1860, after an absence of nearly fifty months, Charles A. Sumner returned to the Senate chamber. A long-time champion of black equality and a leading foe of slavery, Sumner had delivered a speech in the Senate on May 19, 1856, "The Crime against Kansas." In it Sumner aimed some of his sharpest epithets against Senator Andrew P. Butler of South Carolina, who was absent. Two days later, Congressman Preston S. Brooks of South Carolina accosted Sumner at his desk and denounced him for having uttered a libel on South Carolina, "and Mr. Butler, who is a relative of mine." Brooks then struck Sumner on the head with a heavy cane and continued to beat him until the Massachusetts senator fell bleeding and unconscious to the floor. The attack took place before fifteen to twenty people, but it was so sudden and so violent that Sumner was seriously injured before anyone could intervene.

Three and a half years passed before Sumner was sufficiently recovered to return to the Senate. Meanwhile he had been reelected by the almost unanimous vote of the Massachusetts legislature. The attack on Sumner aroused the greatest furor in the black communities of the North, and his return was hailed by special prayers of thanksgiving in all black churches. Sumner's first address after his return to the Senate was the monumental "barbarism of slavery" speech in which he detailed the many abuses of the slave system. The speech brought Sumner a deluge of praise from black Americans. Published in full in *Douglass' Monthly,* it drew plaudits from the editor, who wrote to Sumner: "The right word has been spoken. You spoke to the Senate and the nation, but you have a nobler and mightier audience. The civilized world will hear you, and rejoice at the tremendous exposure of meanness, brutality, blood-guiltiness, hell-black iniquity, and barbarism of American Slavery."

BLACKS AND REPUBLICAN CONSERVATISM

Sumner had a purpose in delivering his famous speech that went beyond the usual exposure of the peculiar institution. He was "motivated by concern over moderating tendencies within the [Republican] party, and he hoped to give the coming [presidential] campaign a moral tone.'' Blacks shared this concern. They watched with a feeling of anger and disgust as most Republican leaders after John Brown's raid frantically tried to disassociate their party from the venture. They were furious when Republican Governor Nathaniel P. Banks of Massachusetts again and again vetoed bills passed by the legislature ending black exclusion from the militia, vetoes that the legislature was unable to override. In New York, blacks were equally furious over the fact that Republican Governor Edwin D. Morgan, elected with overwhelming black support, refused to do anything for the black community. Frederick Douglass echoed the views of many black New Yorkers when he declared:

Governor Morgan, whose anti-slavery was so loudly proclaimed to the people before his election finds no occasion in his Annual Message, to utter an anti-slavery sentence. How frequently we were told, during the campaign, that we were doing a very wicked thing to advocate the election of *Gerrit Smith*, in opposition to the anti-slavery candidate of the Republican party. We feared then, what seems to us to be proved *now*, that the anti-slavery of Mr. Morgan was not the kind that would bear the test of office. We have looked in vain, through the entire Message, to find one word of advice to the assembled Legislature of New York, in favor of granting the Elective Franchise to all her sons, irrespective of color.

In March 1860, the House of Representatives prepared to vote on a bill, introduced by Republican Harrison Gray Otis Blake of Ohio, to repeal the Fugitive Slave Act of 1850. But before the vote could be counted, Blake offered an amendment to his own bill, which stated:

Whereas, The chatteling of mankind, and the holding of persons as property is contrary to natural justice and the fundamental principles of our political system, and is notoriously a reproach to our country throughout the civilized world, and a serious hindrance to the progress of republican liberty throughout the nations of the earth. Therefore,
   Resolved, That the Committee on the Judiciary be . . . instructed to inquire into the expediency of reporting a bill giving freedom to every human being, and interdicting Slavery, wherever Congress has the Constitutional power to legislate on that subject.

When the vote was taken on the amendment, it was rejected by 109 to 60. All of the 60 affirmative votes were cast by Republicans. But 12 Republicans voted in the negative, and what particularly angered blacks was the fact that 43 Republicans abstained from voting. Had the Republicans who abstained and those who voted against the resolution joined ''the faithful sixty,'' the amendment would have passed by a majority of 18. As New York blacks pointed out at a meeting called to criticize the Republicans who had failed to join the ''faithful sixty,'' the Republican party ought not to forget that ''a House divided against itself cannot stand.''

Several of the Republican leaders and important sections of the Republican press, eager to rid the party of the label of "black Republicans" which was increasingly being applied to it, went to great lengths to proclaim themselves white supremacists. The *Eastern Argus* of Portland, Maine, noted that "thanks to black republicanism . . . this idea of amalgamation, revolting, unnatural and destructive to the races as it is, is evidently growing in favor, as witness the six cases in Boston in one year of intermarriages between black men and white women." The Republican response was: "We, the Republican party, are the white man's party."

HELPER'S *IMPENDING CRISIS*

The complex situation confronting blacks in their relations with the Republican party in 1860 is well illustrated in their reaction to the Republican handling of Hinton Rowan Helper's *The Impending Crisis of the South: How to Meet It*. When he offered an outline of his work to a New York publisher, Helper stated: "The author is a Southerner, a member of a family whose home has been in North Carolina for more than a century. At the sacrifice of a considerable amount of time, labor, and money, he has endeavored to prepare the most thorough, truthful, convincing, and unanswerable Anti-slavery work ever issued from the American press."

In his book, Helper said that he had not intended to cast unmerited opprobrium upon slaveholders or to display any special sympathy for the blacks. He did, however, blame slavery for the impoverishment of free white labor in the South. His was the "voice of the non-slaveholding whites of the South," with whom he was identified by interest, feeling, and position. He stated that no kind of labor in the South was either free or respectable and that every workingman was treated like a "loathesome beast, and shunned with the utmost disdain." Any man who owned no slaves was a slave himself and "would be deemed intolerably presumptuous if he dared to open his mouth, even so wide as to give faint utterance to a three-lettered monosyllable, like yea or nay, in the presence of an august knight of the whip and the lash."

Helper warned the farmers, mechanics, and workingmen that the slaveholders who controlled the government had hoodwinked them and were using them as tools to maintain their power and their peculiar institution. By subterfuge and misrepresentation, by keeping the people in ignorance and inflaming their prejudices, they taught the people to hate the abolitionists and thus temporarily to avert the vengeance that was bound to overtake them. After urging the non-slaveholders to join the abolitionist movement and rescue the South from "the usurped and desolating control of these political vampires," Helper concluded that if the people of the South allowed the slavocrats to fasten slavery on Kansas, the entire nation would soon fall prey to their designs: "If you do not voluntarily oppose the usurpations and outrages of the slavocrats, they will force you into involuntary compliance with their infamous measures.''

The appearance of such a bitter attack on slavery by a white North Carolinian created a sensation almost equal to that of *Uncle Tom's Cabin. The Impending Crisis of the South* was received enthusiastically in the North, except among Irish Catholics and blacks. Helper attacked the Irish-American population as supporters of slavery and charged that ''the ignorant Catholic element of the Emerald Isle'' were allies of the slaveholders ''in their diabolical works in humanity and desolation.'' As for blacks, Helper made no bones about being a racist. ''There was no room in his South or in his United States for the black man,'' writes Joaquin Cardoso, who has made the most intensive study of Helper's ideas. ''The spectre of emancipated blacks living and associating equally in white American pursuit of the American dream frightened and angered him. Both publicly and privately he dedicated himself to proscription of the Negro from white society.'' For Helper, blacks were simply ''inert chattel to be freed and removed.'' With the destruction of slavery and the removal of the Negro, a ''truly democratic, white Southern society'' would be created.

Blacks were pleased by the wide distribution of any work that attacked slavery, and the fact that Helper's book was furiously denounced in the South (where few dared to admit having read the work) gave them additional cause for satisfaction that it was adding to the mounting criticism of the institution. Nevertheless, the fact that important sections of the Republican leadership endorsed the book and assisted in its wide distribution without disassociating either themselves or their party from Helper's racism infuriated many blacks. Moreover, it was becoming clearer than ever in 1860 that many Republicans appeared to share Helper's view that the solution of the ''Negro problem'' lay first in ending slavery and then in working ''to get rid of the negro.'' Indeed, some Republicans, like the Blairs of Missouri, were not even ready to wait for the end of slavery to ''get rid of the negro.'' The Blairs favored the immediate colonization of free blacks to Central America to achieve the elimination of at least that part of the black population from American society.

In general, many Republicans now argued that blacks, free or not, served only to intensify the social problems of whites. In view of this, it was best to end slavery, and as Benjamin Wade of Ohio, a radical Republican and ordinarily a supporter of black rights, put it, ''to get rid of the negro.''

BLACKS SPEAK OUT

As evidence mounted of increasing Republican conservatism and of growing racism in Republican ranks, blacks grew angrier and more frustrated. Nor did they hesitate to voice these feelings. In January 1860, a group of Philadelphia blacks publicly debated the question: ''Would the success of the Republican party in the present canvass be advantageous to our cause?'' The affirmative side pointed out that this party was the only major political organization that had taken any kind of stand against slavery and that a Republican victory would be a step in the right direction. The negative side emphasized that the Republican party officially was still opposed only to the extension of slavery into the territories and had not moved toward a position in favor of action against slavery where it already existed. Moreover, Republican speakers were often proclaiming their party to be a party of and for white men only, so blacks could hope for little from a Republican victory. The vote of the audience at the end of the debate overwhelmingly supported the negative position.

A month later, at a meeting of the Massachusetts Anti-Slavery Society, John S. Rock of Boston criticized the Republican party for its limited outlook:

The Republicans . . . have no idea of abolishing slavery. They go against slavery only so far as slavery goes against their interests; and if they keep on lowering their standard . . . they will soon say in New England, what they have said already in the Middle States, that the Republican Party is not only the white man's party, but that it aims to place white men and white labor *against* black men and black labor! Such Republicanism is no better than Democracy.

On May 8, 1860, Philadelphia's Robert Purvis told the American Anti-Slavery Society that since he was "disfranchised; have no vote . . . ; put out of the pale of political society," he could not be a member of either the "bogus democracy" or the Republican party. But he added:

I would not be a member of the Republican party if it were in my power. How could I, a colored man, join a party that styles itself emphatically the "white man's party"? How could I, an Abolitionist, belong to a party that is and must of necessity be a proslavery party? The Republicans may be, and doubtless are, opposed to the extension of slavery, but they are sworn to support, and they *will* support, slavery where it already exists. . . . No, sir, I am not a Republican. I can never join a party the leaders of which conspire to expel us from the country.

Purvis aimed his sharpest criticism at Horace Greeley, who, in answer to the Democratic charge that the Republicans, if they won the presidential election, would abolish slavery and extend civil rights to Negroes, had responded publicly that the Republican party sought no more than to restrict slavery to the existing states and did not wish to abolish slavery or to extend equal rights to free blacks. Purvis contrasted this with the viewpoint of "that noble martyr and saint, the innocent hero of Harpers Ferry," and noted that John Brown "believed that the black man was a man, and he laid down his life to secure for him the rights of man."

The *New York Weekly Anglo-African* of New York City, one of a few black papers published by and for blacks at this time, made its position clear by declaring in March 1860 that antislavery meant little more to the Republicans than "opposition to the black man." In fact, as between the Democratic and Republican parties, the latter, "though with larger professions of humanity," was by far the black man's "more dangerous enemy. Under the guise of humanity, they do and say many things—. . . . They oppose the progress of slavery in the territories, and would cry humanity to the world; but . . . their opposition to slavery means opposition to the black man—nothing else. Where it is clearly in their power to do anything for the oppressed colored man, why then they are too nice, too conservative, to do it." Hence, the *Anglo-African* concluded: "We have no hope from either of the political parties. We must rely on ourselves, the righteousness of our cause, and the advance of just sentiments among the great masses of the people."

Thus, as the crucial presidential campaign of 1860 was about to get under way, blacks were indicating that they had little faith in either the Democratic or the Republican party.

DEMOCRATIC AND REPUBLICAN CONVENTIONS

The Democrats were the first to hold their national convention, and the Southern wing demanded that the platform be adopted before candidates were chosen. The Southern Democrats adopted as their platform the *Dred Scott* decision and denied that even the territorial legislatures had a right to interfere with slavery. But when the convention adopted as its platform both the *Dred Scott* decision and the Freeport doctrine, under which the people of a territory might, through "unfriendly legislation," prevent the existence of slavery, the Southern Democrats bolted the convention. The remaining delegates then voted that two-thirds of the original number should be needed to nominate the candidates for president and vice-president. While Stephen A. Douglas consistently ran first, he still had not gained the required number after fifty-seven ballots. The convention then suspended to reconvene six weeks later, when it nominated Douglas by a vote of two-thirds of the members in attendance.

The Independent Southern Democrats nominated John C. Breckenridge of Kentucky, on the *Dred Scott* decision platform, and the Constitutional Union party nominated John Bell of Tennessee on a platform that sought to preserve the Constitution and the Union by ignoring the slavery issue. With the Democratic party hopelessly divided by the time the Republicans met in convention in Chicago on May 16, 1860, the prospects for a Republican victory were bright indeed.

The Republican platform denounced the "new dogma,—that the Constitution, of its own force, carries slavery into any or all of the territories of the United States—[as a] dangerous political heresy . . . ; revolutionary in its tendency and subversive of the peace and harmony of the country." It went on to assert "that the normal condition of all the territory of the United States is that of freedom, . . . and we deny the authority of Congress, of a territorial legislature, or of any individuals, to give legal existence to slavery in any territory of the United States, . . . and we deny the authority of Congress, of a territorial legislature, or of any individuals, to give legal existence to slavery in any territory of the United States.'' It called for the admission of a free Kansas and urged the enactment of protective tariffs for the encouragement of industry, a homestead act, and internal improvements, including a railroad to the Pacific. It opposed any change in the naturalization laws abridging the rights of noncitizens or making naturalization more difficult.

At first, the Republican platform omitted the words of the Declaration of Independence that all men are created equal, which had been incorporated in the 1856 platform. But this was reinserted after a dramatic protest on the convention floor by Joshua Giddings and was endorsed by the vociferous sympathy of the galleries. The 1860 platform thereupon called the ''maintenance of the principles promulgated in the Declaration of Independence and embodied in the federal Constitution'': namely, the principle that all men are created equal and endowed with the rights of life, liberty, and the pursuit of happiness, as ''essential to the preservation of our republican institutions.'' It went on to affirm the principle that ''the federal Constitution, the rights of the states, and the union of the states must and shall be preserved,'' and assured the South that ''the maintenance inviolate of the rights of the states, and especially the right of each state to order and control its own domestic institutions according to its own judgment exclusively,'' was ''essential to that balance of power on which the perfection and endurance of our political fabric depends.''

The leading contender for the Republican nomination for president was William H. Seward of New York, regarded as abolitionist in his leanings. Abraham Lincoln, a candidate from the West, received strong support from those who considered themselves to be moderates on the slavery issue. In addition, there were other candidates who were generally less adamant on the slavery question than either Seward or Lincoln. Nomination required 233 votes. Lincoln was so close on the third ballot that four delegates switched their vote, giving him the nomination.

Hannibal Hamlin of Bangor, Maine, the Republican vice-presidential candidate, was not black, as sometimes has been alleged, but he did fight in Congress for the abolition of slavery; he was credited with a major role in the passage of the Wilmot Proviso, prohibiting slavery in the territory gained from Mexico, and had resigned as governor of Maine to continue his fight against slavery on the national scene. ''Black or white,'' wrote a reporter recently for the *Bangor Daily News,* ''he certainly stands out in the forefront of those opposed to slavery.''

BLACK OPINION OF LINCOLN IN 1860

The readers of *Douglass' Monthly* of June 1860 were treated to a lengthy discussion of Lincoln's nomination. Frederick Douglass did not share the prevailing opinion among Eastern journalists that ''the Rail-Splitter candidate'' for president was a nonentity, whose nomination was the result of pure accident plus vote swapping, logrolling, and wire pulling. "Mr. Lincoln," he wrote, "is a man of unblemished character; a lawyer, standing near the front rank of the bar of his own State; has a cool well balanced head; great firmness of will; is persevering, industrious; and one of the most frank, honest men in political life. . . . His political life is thus far to his credit, but it is a political life of fair promise rather than one of rich heritage." Lincoln, he said, merited the support of the more radical elements among the Republicans. In his debates with Douglas, "he came fully up to the highest mark of Republicanism."

Douglass criticized the Republican party for its campaign slogan, "No More Slave States," instead of "Death to Slavery." He conceded, however, that the people were not yet ready for the more advanced slogan, and as a result, "we are compelled to work and wait for a higher day, when the masses shall be educated to a higher standard of human rights and political morality." But as between the Democratic and the Republican party, "incomplete as its platform of principles" was, he would not hesitate to choose the latter: "While we should be glad to cooperate with a party fully committed to the doctrine of 'All rights to all men,' in the absence of all hope of rearing up the standard of such a party for the coming campaign, we can but desire the success of the Republican candidates."

Two months later, Douglass went even further and wrote that the Republican party was "now the great embodiment of whatever political opposition to the pretensions and demands of slavery is now in the field. . . . A victory by it in the coming contest must and will be hailed as an antislavery triumph. In view of this fact, we have no sympathy with those who regard all the parties alike, and especially those who go so far as to prefer the defeat of the Republican party at the coming election to its triumph." Among those Douglass was criticizing was a black orator from Illinois who bore the same surname: H. Ford Douglass.

At a mass meeting sponsored by the Massachusetts Anti-Slavery Society on July 4, 1860, the Illinois Douglass not only cataloged the reasons why no friend of the slave could support Lincoln but went on to assert that no party deserved the votes of abolitionists "unless that party is willing to extend to the black man all the rights of a citizen." He said plainly:

I do not believe in the antislavery of Abraham Lincoln, because he is on the side of this Slave Power of which I am speaking, that has possession of the Federal Government. What does he propose to do? Simply to let the people and the Territories regulate their domestic institutions in their own way. . . .

I care nothing about the anti-slavery which wants to make the Territories free, while it is unwilling to extend to me, as a man, in the free States, all the rights of a man. (*Applause.*) In the State of Illinois . . . we have a code of black laws that would disgrace any Barbary State, or any uncivilized people in the far-off islands of the sea. Men of my complexion are not allowed to testify in a court of justice, where a white man is a party. If a white man happens to owe me anything, unless I can prove it by the testimony of a white man, I cannot collect the debt. Now, two years ago, I went through the State of Illinois for the purpose of getting signers to a petition, asking the Legislature to repeal the "Testimony Law," so as to permit colored men to testify against white men. I went to prominent

Republicans, and among others, to Abraham Lincoln and Lyman Trumbull [senator from Illinois], and neither of them dared to sign that petition, to give me the right to testify in a court of justice! (*"Hear, hear."*)

Douglass also accused Lincoln of being "in favor of carrying out that infamous Fugitive Slave Law" and of being dominated by "pro-slavery character and principles."

As the campaign progressed, the position of Frederick Douglass moved toward that of H. Ford Douglass. On August 29, he attended the convention of the Radical Abolitionists at Syracuse and participated in drawing up the resolutions presented to the gathering. These resolutions not only condemned the Democratic party but also indicted the Republican party for its "almost infinitessimal amount of anti-slavery professions," which were "inadequate . . . to 'quiet the agitation' upon the subject of the slave's right to liberty." Unwilling to go along with the Republicans, the convention nominated Gerrit Smith and Samuel McFarland on a strong antislavery platform. Douglass was chosen as one of two presidential electors-at-large, the first time a Negro was nominated for such a position.

In October, Douglass advised his readers that 10,000 votes for Gerrit Smith would accomplish more for the abolition of slavery than 2 million for Lincoln, "or any man who stands pledged before the world against the interference with slavery in the slave states and who is not opposed to making free states a hunting ground for men under the Fugitive Slave Law." He charged that the "sentiments of the Republican party, as expressed by its leaders, have become visibly *thin* and *insipid* as the canvass has progressed." Douglass concluded:

Let Abolitionists, regardless of outside pressure, regardless of smiles or frowns, mindful only of the true and right, vote in the coming election for the only men in the field who believe in the complete manhood of the negro, the unconstitutionality of slavery, and are pledged to the immediate and unconditional abolition of slavery.

By this time, however, hatred of Lincoln and his party had become intense throughout the South, which was terrified that Lincoln intended to use the power of the presidency to free the slaves and turn them on their former masters. In South Carolina especially, Lincoln was seen in a quite different light from that being described by both Frederick Douglass and H. Ford Douglass. To one South Carolinian, he was "a fanatic in his policy"; another insisted that of Seward and Lincoln, the latter was "the most dangerous of the two." Indeed a large section of the South Carolina press argued that it was Lincoln, not Seward, who was the author of the "hated 'irrepressible conflict' doctrine." They reminded their readers that months before Seward's address at Rochester, Lincoln had delivered his famous speech at Springfield, Illinois, accepting his party's nomination for the Senate, in which he had denied that the nation could permanently be "half slave and half free." Lawrence Massilon Kent, a South Carolinian, wrote on September 10, 1860, to James Hammond:

If Lincoln is elected—what then! I am in earnest—I'd cut loose through fire and blood if necessary—poison in the wells in Texas and fire for the Houses in Alabama—Our Negroes are being enlisted in politics—with poison and fire how can we stand it?

Instead of one John Brown and his black allies, he feared, there would be thousands.

Most blacks did not share the sentiments of either Douglass that there was no difference between the Democratic and Republican candidates. While Northern blacks were aware that in the 1858 debates, Lincoln, the pragmatic politician, had articulated at least two contradictory positions on racial equality, they also knew that in a speech at Columbus, Ohio, on September 16, Lincoln said: "Did you ever, five years ago, hear of anybody in the world saying that the negro had no share in the Declaration of National Independence; that it did not mean negroes at all, and when 'all men' were spoken of negroes were not included? I am satisfied that five years ago that proposition was not put upon paper by any living being anywhere." Lincoln had gone on to assert boldly and firmly that the Negro was included in the principles of the Declaration of Independence and that those who denied it were insulting the finest traditions of the American nation. Blacks were also aware of and impressed by a speech Lincoln made early in 1860 in New Haven, Connecticut, in reference to a shoe strike then in progress in New England, in which he had declared:

I am glad to see that a system of labor prevails in New England under which laborers can strike when they want to, where they are not obliged to labor whether you pay them or not. I like the system which lets a man quit when he wants to, and wish it might prevail everywhere. One of the reasons why I am opposed to slavery is just here. . . . If you give up your convictions and call slavery right . . . you let slavery in upon you. Instead of white laborers who can strike, you'll soon have black laborers who can't.

It was with good reason, then, that blacks in Northern cities formed Republican clubs. The Colored Republican Club in Brooklyn raised a "Lincoln Liberty Tree" in July 1860. The colored "West Boston Wide Awakes" marched in a massive Republican parade in Boston. Samuel Smothers, a black educator in Indiana, spoke for the majority of Northern Negroes when he wrote:

The colored people are looking hopefully, and some of them are laboring earnestly, for the general reform of the Republican party. Yes, we are looking forward with bright anticipation to the day when the Republican party in Indiana, Ohio, Illinois, and throughout the entire North, shall be educated up to the principles of their platform, and when we shall be recognized as men, not only in New England, but all over the nation. Another thing that cheers our hopes and revives our drooping spirits is this: The best anti-slavery men in the nation are rallying under the Republican banner. This causes us to look hopefully throughout the entire nation, and the elevation of our race to social and political equality.

Faced with the political realities of the election, even Frederick Douglass concluded that the friends of abolition should not waste their vote on the Radical Abolitionist candidate. Douglass recalled throwing himself into the campaign for Lincoln's election "with firmer faith and more ardent hope than ever before, and what I could do by pen or voice was done with a will." This was, however, an overstatement of Douglass' commitment to Lincoln in October 1860.

THE CAMPAIGN DRAWS TO A CLOSE

Most of Douglass' energy during the closing weeks of the campaign, like that of a number of other New York blacks, including Henry Highland Garnet, was directed toward securing the repeal of the New York state law requiring that Negro citizens own real estate valued at $250 as a condition for voting. Some idea of the hysteria whipped up in the press over the proposed measure, which would place Negro citizens on an equal footing with others in the exercise of the right of suffrage, can be gleaned from the following appeal in the *Brooklyn Daily Times:*

Give the negroes an unlimited suffrage, and the logical and inevitable result is a negro alderman, a negro representative on the county ticket, and so forth.

. . . If [the negro] alderman officiates in places of civil honor, with his badge and staff of office, can you deny him the entree to your semi-public assemblies—can you keep him from meeting even the ladies of your family, on many semi-public occasions, as a social equal?

. . . It needs no prophetic eye to foresee that ere long, the countless millions of Asiatic barbarians, Chinese and Japanese—will overflow the narrow limits in which these fecund hordes have been confined—and spread through the Pacific states, all over this continent. Gladly will the negro voters of this State welcome these allies. The unrestricted franchise which we are now asked to extend to negroes, may be a fearful weapon when turned against us.

In the face of such vicious outpourings, New York blacks conducted a vigorous campaign for an unrestricted franchise. Twenty-five thousand tracts, *Suffrage Question in Relation to Colored Voters,* were issued and distributed by the New York City and County Suffrage Committee of Colored Citizens. William C. Nell, the prominent Boston black abolitionist, issued a pamphlet setting forth reasons why all blacks should vote. After recounting the accomplishments of New York blacks in military service, business, and social organizations, he asked: "Are not these patriotic, industrious, prudent, exemplary citizens deserving equal rights at the ballot boxes?"

Blacks formed suffrage clubs to distribute these pamphlets, even circulating foreign-language literature among foreign-born Democrats explaining why simple justice demanded equal suffrage.

On the eve of Election Day, the Democrats raised the cry that a victory for "Black Republican Abolitionism" would soon bring thousands of slaves and free Negroes to the North to compete with white workers. General Leslie Coombs of Kentucky told a Democratic mass meeting in New York on October 24, 1860:

Let the four million slaves in the South be set at liberty, and left to their own free will and desires, and we should very soon have, not the great conflict so long predicted between free labor and slave labor, but a terrible conflict between white labor and black labor. (*Applause.*) The unemployed slaves will be found among you in sufficient numbers to compete with you at your wharves and your docks, and in every branch of labor in which white people alone are now employed.

Even free Negroes in Boston were warned to vote against Lincoln because the emancipation of the slaves following a Republican victory would endanger their jobs. On the day before the election, the *New York Herald* warned: "Hundreds of thousands will emigrate to their friends—the Republicans—North, and be placed by them side by side in competition with white men. Are you ready to divide your patrimony with the negro? Are you ready to work with him in competition—to work more than you do now for less pay? If you are, vote for the Republican candidate." And on election day itself, the pro-Southern *Herald* pleaded: "If Lincoln is elected to-day, you will have to compete with the labor of four million emancipated negroes. . . . The North will be flooded with free negroes, and the labor of the white man will be depreciated and degraded."

The anti-Lincoln "reign of terror" failed. While many Irish immigrants in the urban centers of the East and the factory towns of New England voted Democratic, most other labor groups, especially the skilled urban workers, voted for Lincoln. Where they could vote, blacks, dismissing the Radical Abolitionists as ineffectual, cast their ballots in overwhelming numbers for the Republican party, although some did so with misgivings.

BLACK REACTION TO LINCOLN'S ELECTION

The victorious Republicans obtained less than 40 percent of the total votes cast: 1,857,610 for Lincoln (who carried all the free states except New Jersey); 1,291,574 for Douglas (who carried only Missouri and New Jersey); 850,082 for Breckenridge (who carried eleven Southern states); and 646,124 for Bell (who carried Virginia, Kentucky, and Tennessee). The electoral vote, however, guaranteed Lincoln's election: 180 for Lincoln, 12 for Douglas, 72 for Breckenridge, and 39 for Bell.

Those New York blacks who could vote had voted almost unanimously for Lincoln and rejoiced in his victory, but they were saddened by the defeat of the equal suffrage amendment and were bitter at the Republicans for failing to take a strong stand in favor of repeal of the restrictive suffrage law. ''The black baby of negro suffrage was thought too ugly to exhibit on so grand an occasion,'' Douglass wrote angrily in his paper as he reported the vote of 337,984 against ratification of the equal suffrage amendment to 197,503 for. ''We were told by some of our Republican friends to keep still—make no noise—they would do the work. Now the fox is out of the well, and the goat is in it.'' What, asked Douglass, had the antislavery cause gained by Lincoln's election? He answered:

Not much, in itself considered, but very much when viewed in the light of its relations and bearings. For fifty years the country has taken the law from the lips of an exacting, haughty and imperious slave oligarchy. The masters of slaves have been masters of the Republic. Their authority was almost undisputed, and their power irresistible. They were the President makers of the Republic, and no aspirant dared to hope for success against their frown. Lincoln's election has vitiated their authority, and broken their power. It has taught the North its strength, and shown the South its weakness. More important still, it has demonstrated the possibility of electing, if not an Abolitionist, at least an *anti-slavery reputation* to the Presidency of the United States.

''Will the election of Abraham Lincoln be advantageous to the colored people?'' was the question debated by leading blacks before the Philadelphia Library Company shortly after the election. William P. Price opened the debate by asserting that ''much good would result from the election in the future. We can endorse many of their [Republican] principles without sacrificing any of our antislavery principles.'' Price emphatically disagreed with any blacks who declared that they ''did not care which party gained the ascendancy, for when great issues are involved, men who are staunch for their principles must always feel interested when they find those nearest their own about to prevail.'' John O. Bowers disagreed, arguing that the success of the Republican candidate was not as important as it appeared, ''for if they the Republicans have a disposition to benefit us they have not a majority in Congress.'' He was convinced that the Republicans would ''back down'' in the face of Southern hositility to Lincoln's election. This position, however, was challenged by Isaiah C. Wears who declared:

The election of Lincoln will certainly benefit us, for although they [Congress] may not be able to legislate for us, Lincoln can hold them in check. The legislation has ever been against us and that has been our trouble. The question was a political one, not a moral or religious question, and I, for one, am confident that Lincoln will act in a political way which will prove to be beneficial to us all.

But J. Wesley Simpson and Alfred M. Green differed sharply with Wears. Simpson said flatly that ''one of the reasons Lincoln was elected was because he said in his debate with Douglas that the negro can never attain to equality with the white man in this country. The policies of the Republicans and Democratic parties are identical.'' Green read an extract from the life of John Brown ''to show that the old hero had not much faith in the Republican party'' and added that it was an opinion he shared.

In the end, the debate closed without a final vote to determine which side had made a stronger case. Instead it was decided to await the response of the Republican party to the challenge from the South before concluding if Lincoln's election had been ''advantageous to the colored people.''

15

The Coming of the Civil War

THE SECESSION CRISIS

A few days after the election of Lincoln, a Southern paper declared: "All the powers of a government which has so long sheltered it [slavery] will be turned to its destruction. The only hope for its preservation, therefore, is out of the Union." On December 20, 1860, by unanimous vote of a specially elected convention of 169 members, overwhelmingly slaveowners, South Carolina left the Union. In the "Declaration of the Immediate Causes Which Induce and Justify the Secession of South Carolina from the Federal Union," the defenders of slavery declared that the policy of containment advocated by the victorious Republicans was so dangerous to their interests as to signify "that a war must be waged against slavery until it shall cease throughout the United States."

To Southern leaders, opposition to the spread of slavery was intolerable because it convinced them that the ultimate aim of the North was to abolish slavery in the South. Since many southerners regarded slavery as a positive good, they could not accept restrictions on the institution. The alternative was to secede from the Union. Several recent studies have also emphasized that secession was an effort on the part of the planters to preserve their domination in the face of declining support for the slave regime and a declining proportion of slaveholders. In any case, by January 26, 1861, all of the Gulf states from Florida to Louisiana had seceded. In February, at a convention in Montgomery, Alabama, delegates from South Carolina, Georgia, Florida, Alabama, Mississippi, and Louisiana formed a provisional Confederate government. As Georgia's former senator and vice-president of the Confederate States of America, Alexander H. Stephens, put it in characterizing the objective of the new government: "Its foundations are laid, its cornerstone rests upon the great truth that the negro is not the equal of the white man; that slavery, subordination to the superior race, is his natural and normal condition."

In his diary, Edmund Ruffin, one of the wealthiest slaveowners in Virginia and founder of the League of United Southerners, noted a significant fact about the Montgomery convention, which founded the Confederate States of America. Recording a conversation with a former governor of South Carolina, John P. Richardson, he wrote:

Heard (confidentially from ex-Governor Richardson, a member of the) [South Carolina Secessionist] convention, that it was certain, (as communicated privately to members of each delegation to the General Convention at Montgomery), that it was supposed by the delegates that the majority of the people of every State except S. Ca. was indisposed to the disruption of the Union—and that if the question of reconstruction of the former union was referred to the popular vote, that there was probably little chance of its being approved.

That is why at that convention in Alabama, the question of submitting secession to a vote prior to the states' seceding was rejected. But then, as ex-governor Richardson of South Carolina put it: "I do not believe that the common people understand it, in fact I know that they do not understand it; but whoever waited for the common people when a great move was to be made. We must make the move and force them to follow."

This is exactly what the advocates of secession did. In fact, given the censored press, the hysteria that was whipped up following Lincoln's election, the years of propaganda about the Black Republicans and the idea of a great slaveholding empire in the Caribbean, and the constant appeal to the basest racial prejudices, the surprising thing is that so many southerners resisted the secession movement. The only way the disunionists could be assured of success was by carrying out secession in the undemocratic manner in which the South had long been accustomed to governing itself. Texas, which joined the Confederacy on March 11, 1861 (even though Governor Sam Houston of that state opposed secession and was illegally deposed from his office for his loyalty), was the only state to submit its resolution to a popular vote. Elsewhere the decision was by newly chosen conventions dominated by slaveowners.

A month before Georgia's secession, Charles Colcock Jones, Jr., the young mayor of Savannah, soon to become a Confederate army officer, wrote to his father:

I have long since believed that in this country have arisen two races which, although claiming a common parentage, have been so entirely separated by climate, by morals, by religion, and by estimates so wholly opposite of all that constitutes honor, truth, and manliness, that they cannot longer coexist under the same government. Oil and water will not commingle. We are the land of the rulers; fanaticism has no home here. The sooner we separate the better.

Jones' view represented that of the dominant slaveholder class, which had not the shadow of a doubt about the justice of slavery; it also had few doubts about secession or about the Confederacy's ability to win, if war came. Edmund Ruffin, one of the foremost of the secession advocates, whose diary reveals that when secessionism mounted in the South, his bodily complaints disappeared and his health improved, even argued that free Negroes ought to be reenslaved so that they could benefit from the master's direction; he strongly opposed schemes to send Negroes back to Africa, favoring instead the reopening of the African slave trade. Since slavery was such a benevolent system, Ruffin urged, with serious-ness, that "the only means to greatly extend civilization and Christianity in the now savage Africa" would be through the "enslavement to white and Christian masters" of the whole African population. Ruffin excused any "suffering and unhappiness" among the enslaved blacks on the ground that hardships have occurred "in every great movement of portions of mankind, and even in the most beneficial of general and great changes." It was quite appropriate that this was the man whom the commander of the Palmetto Guard of Charleston invited to fire the first shot against Fort Sumter during the early hours of April 12, 1861.

The lame duck Buchanan administration did nothing either to encourage or impede secession, although pro-Confederate cabinet members sent shipments of arms to forts under Confederate control. In his State of the Union address on December 3, 1860, Buchanan announced that the federal government could not act in the crisis. Secession, Buchanan argued, was theoretically unconstitutional, yet neither the president nor Congress had the power to prevent it.

BLACK REACTION TO SECESSION

Two weeks after Lincoln's election, H. Ford Douglass reflected the views of Garrisonian abolitionists when he advised the South: "Stand not upon the order of your going, but go at once. . . . There is no union of ideas and interests in this country, and there can be no union between freedom and slavery." Although he was no Garrisonian, Frederick Douglass also favored disunion during this peri-od. The prospects for ending slavery looked so bleak that Douglass believed that the dissolution of the Union might be necessary for the cause of liberty. His own course, he told his readers in December, was clear: "We shall join in no cry, and unite in no demand less than the complete and universal *abolition* of the whole slave system. Slavery shall be destroyed."

If the Union could be preserved without achieving this, Douglass insisted, then let it be dissolved. Speaking at a meeting to honor John Brown at Boston's Tremont Temple on December 3, 1860, Douglass said:

I am for a dissolution of the Union—decidedly for the dissolution of the Union! Under an abolition President, who would wield the army and navy of the Government for the abolition of slavery, I should be for the union of these States. . . . My opinion is that if we only had an anti-slavery President, if we only had an abolition President to hold these men in the Union, and execute the declared provisions of the Constitution, execute that part of the Constitution which is in favor of liberty, . . . if we could have such a government, a government that would force the South to behave herself, under those circumstances I should be for the continuance of the Union. If, on the contrary—no *if* about it—we have what we have, I shall be glad of the news, come when it will, that the slave states are an independent government, and that you are no longer called up to shoulder your arms and guard with your swords those States—no longer called to go into them to put down John Brown, or anybody else who may strike for liberty there—*(Applause)*.

Douglass was cheered when he called for slave uprisings in the South and also when he predicted that after the South established an independent nation, "a Garibaldi would arise in the North who would march into those States with a thousand men, and summon to his standard sixty thousand, if necessary, to accomplish the freedom of the slave." This reference to Giuseppe Garibaldi, who led the victorious expedition to Sicily and Naples in 1860 and with his thousand "red shirts" overthrew the Bourbon monarchy and made possible the accession of these states to a united Italy, did not please the strict Garrisonians in the audience. But Douglass reminded them that it was not enough merely to appeal to the moral sense of a slaveholder, and he repeated, to laughter and applause, his familiar argument that "the only way to make the Fugitive Slave Law a dead letter is to make a few dead slave-catchers."

Douglass had barely completed his speech when he was forced to demonstrate his principles in action. A mob, made up mainly of Irishmen hired by merchants engaged in the Southern trade, invaded the hall, disrupted the proceedings, and singled out Douglass for attack. Fighting "like a trained pugilist," the black abolitionist was "thrown down the staircase to the floor of the hall."

The meeting was adjourned to the black church on Joy Street. As the audience poured into the street, Negroes were seized, knocked down, and trampled upon, and a number were seriously injured. "The mob was howling with rage," Douglass recalled years later. "Boston wanted a victim to appease the wrath of the south already bent upon the destruction of the Union."

The *Boston Pilot,* the city's Irish Catholic organ, expressed the view that the rioters had spoken for all white Bostonians except the small group of abolition-ists. The editor was glad to see that in Boston there was

no irrational desire to interfere with the property of the south. . . . It is particularly gratifying to find Boston speaking thus out, at the present time. The fact cannot but have a good effect on the enthusiastic people of the south, whose secession movement may be justly attributed to the abolitionists of the Northern cities. If our city had acted in this matter before, it is quite certain that the country would not be so agitated as it now unfortunately is. But better late than not at all; the present ebullition of true patriotic sentiment may be followed by a great many.

Frederick Douglass answered this defense of mob violence a few days later at Boston's Music Hall where he presented one of the most stirring pleas for free speech in American history. He described at length the attack on the meeting by both respectable gentlemen and rowdies and affirmed that the right of free speech was basic to all other rights. No other right "was deemed by the fathers of the Government more sacred than the right of speech." "Liberty is meaningless," cried Douglass, "where the right to utter one's thoughts and opinions has ceased to exist." Nor did the right of free speech belong to only the rich and powerful. In words that have never lost their meaning, Douglass concluded:

There can be no right of speech where any man, however lifted up, or however old, is overawed by force and compelled to suppress his honest sentiments. . . . When a man is allowed to speak because he is rich and powerful, it aggravates the crime of denying the right to the poor and humble. . . .

A man's right to speak does not depend upon where he was born or upon his color. The simple quality of manhood is the solid basis of the right—and there let it rest forever.

Douglass agreed with Republican leaders that secession was unconstitutional, and he called upon the incoming president to act on this principle. Lincoln, he wrote, was "elected to preside over the United States, and if any of them have been permitted, by the treachery and weakness of his predecessor, to break away from the Government, his business will be to bring them back, and see that the laws of the United States are duly extended over them and faithfully executed. . . . He is pledged to the maintenance of the Union; and if he has the will he will not lack the power to maintain it against all foes. . . . South Carolina must conquer the United States, or the United States must conquer South Carolina. But there must be more than windy resolutions, to oppose the rebellion. There must be swords, guns, powder, and men behind them to use them."

Above all Douglass opposed any compromise that would keep the South in the Union by giving additional guarantees to slavery:

If the Union can only be maintained by new concessions to the slaveholders, if it can only be stuck together and held together by a new drain on negro's blood; if the North is to forswear the exercise of all rights incompatible with the safety and perpetuity of slavery . . . then will every right-minded man and woman in the land say, let the Union perish, and perish forever. As against compromises and national demoralization, welcome ten thousand times over the hardships consequent upon a dissolution of the Union.

To all blacks, not merely to Douglass, the key to the situation lay in whether the Republican party would compromise and appease the South to save the Union. At a debate sponsored by the Philadelphia Library Company on how blacks should view the secession crisis, the majority opinion expressed was that there was no way by which "we black Americans would be benefitted by the dissolution of the Union." But all speakers on both sides of the question voiced concern that the Republicans would "back down" and "ask pardon of the Southerners whom the election of Lincoln has offended."

THE CRITTENDEN COMPROMISE

Although there were many compromise plans, moderate hopes centered on the program introduced into the Thirty-sixth Congress by John J. Crittenden, the Whig-Constitutional Union senator from Kentucky. His legislation, introduced two days prior to South Carolina's withdrawal, was designed to reassure southerners that despite Lincoln's election, slavery would be safe if their states remained in the Union. Crittenden had little hope of keeping South Carolina from seceding, but he believed that if his legislation passed, the rest of the South would feel secure enough to stay.

Crittenden's program consisted of a series of constitutional amendments and suggested congressional resolutions. The first amendment reinstated the old Missouri Compromise line of 1820 and extended it to the Pacific Ocean. Slavery could be prohibited north of that line and protected south of it, both in existing U.S. territory and in all territory "hereafter acquired." Other amendments prohibited congressional interference with the interstate slave trade, slavery in the Southern states, and slavery in the District of Columbia; provided that owners of fugitive slaves who could not be recovered because of "violence or intimidation" could be compensated by the U.S. government; and called for stricter enforcement of the fugitive slave law and more effective suppression of the African slave trade. Crittenden's last amendment gave further assurances to the South by forbidding any future amendment of the program or of the proslavery provisions of the original U.S. Constitution.

Crittenden's resolutions reaffirmed the legality of the fugitive slave law; they suggested that Congress write laws to punish individuals who helped runaway slaves and called upon the federal government to require any states that had personal liberty laws to repeal them. The plan also included provisions for the disfranchisement and colonization abroad of free Negroes, from both the North and South.

Although Republican congressmen voted against Crittenden's proposal, he and his followers refused to admit defeat. The Virginia legislature invited all the states to send representatives to a Peace Convention in Washington in February 1861. The invitation specifically stated that the Crittenden resolutions "constitute the basis of such an adjustment of the unhappy controversy which now divides the states of this Confederacy." Although none of the states that had seceded sent delegates, twenty-one states did join the conference.

On February 6, a petition signed by "J. Sella Martin and 125 other colored citizens of Boston" was presented to the Massachusetts legislature. The document stated that the petitioners, "as citizens of the Commonwealth of Massachusetts," had up to then felt "perfectly secure in the enjoyment of the rights pertaining to such citizenship." They urged the legislature, when sending commissioners to Washington to represent the state in the convention, "to keep in view the following facts":

That Virginia, who invited Massachusetts to join her in convention with the above view, disfranchises her colored citizens.

That this is coupled with certain propositions, one of which is as follows: That "the elective franchise and the right to hold office, whether Federal, State, Territorial or Municipal, shall not be exercised by persons who are in whole or in part of the African race."

That therefore your honorable body instruct the commissioners appointed in behalf of the State, to oppose and vote against every proposition which may have in view or which may be perverted to the disfranchisement of the colored citizens of this Commonwealth.

On February 14, Massachusetts' Negro citizens held a mass meeting in the Joy Street Baptist Church of Boston and heard a series of speeches by representatives of black communities throughout the state. Dr. J. B. Smith of New Bedford urged the meeting not to accept any further concessions to the slaveholding states that imposed restrictions on rights of free blacks. "They have nothing to live for if their liberties are further infringed," he cried, declaring that he would "submit to no more oppression on the part of this barbaric nation." Resolutions were offered to the audience for their acceptance that declared that no compromise would settle the question agitating the nation—"nothing but the abolition of Slavery itself"; that the "colored people will never be driven from the United States by any compulsion"; that the personal liberty law must be retained on the statute books; and ended with a pledge that the blacks of the commonwealth "will continue to demand from the Legislature of Massachusetts the most absolute equality in every respect before the laws."

Speaking in favor of the resolutions, J. Sella Martin denounced the provisions of the Crittenden compromise and charged that even though it was acknowledged that the votes of black men had not brought on the present difficulties, "the North wishes only to offer up as a sacrifice those few colored men who have received a portion of the common liberty." He warned that there was a real danger that the forthcoming convention in Washington would, in its secret sessions, adopt a provision disenfranchising free blacks "and force it upon us" and also call for the forced removal of free Negroes from the United States. According to the reporter present, Martin concluded his speech as follows:

He would not submit to any forced expatriation, but would stay until he was carried away, or stand and drive back the driver if need be. They had appealed to the humanity of the country as Christians and peaceable citizens, and if we must go, we will leave our blood behind. (*Applause.*) There never was a darker hour for the colored people in this country than now, and they should speak earnestly to their fellow-citizens, and let them know if they are struck down, it shall be with a protest upon their lips; and if they die, it shall be like martyrs. And the God who has punished other nations for their inhumanity may enforce the penalty of national sins with annihilation.

George T. Downing, the Negro restauranteur, abolitionist, and fighter for black equality, then introduced the following manifesto:

APPEAL TO THE WHITE CITIZENS OF THE STATE

We have not the strong arm of power; we have not wealth and its influence; we cannot DEMAND, save in the name of justice. In the name of justice, WE DO DEMAND at least a hearing.

The appeal warned that there were "men in power—influential men" who were "laboring to disfranchise us . . . not for any crime or improper acts of ours, but to satisfy a party that we have never wronged—a power outside of the State." Pointing to the convention about to meet in Washington, the manifesto noted that the seventh clause of the Crittenden compromise, which was to be considered at the gathering, "deprives us of the right of voting in Massachusetts," and the eighth "looks to our expatriation." The manifesto then warned that the real purpose of these proposals was not merely to strike "at so small a political power as ourselves, but at the white citizens of the States of New England," and to punish them "because of their fidelity to that portion of the Declaration of Independence which declares, 'That all governments derive their just powers from the consent of the governed,'" which in the New England States was understood to "include the colored citizen." The manifesto concluded:

The injustice against which we protest is so self-evident that we have not deemed it necessary to argue. We have confined ourselves to an appeal to you as men and as Christians—in the name of social justice—in the name of American patriotism—in the name and by the sacred memory of the entombed fathers—in the name of the great God, before whom we must all appear, *hear us*! Speak out, Massachusetts! You are acknowledged head of New England. The movers in this injustice will not disregard the voice of New England.

In the debate on the resolutions and the address, William Wells Brown argued that neither the Peace Convention nor Congress would ever adopt the Crittenden compromise, and even if it were adopted, it would have to be submitted to a popular referendum. Therefore, he declared, there was really nothing to worry about: "They had only to sit still, and the law of progress shall give the black man his freedom." In essence, he did not believe the address should be adopted "because there is now no occasion for it."

Brown was answered by Martin, Hilton, and Downing, all of whom emphasized that the North had "always obeyed the Slave Power," and all signs pointed to a continuation of this trend unless protests were mounted and were heard. This latter viewpoint prevailed, and both the resolutions and address were adopted and forwarded to the Massachusetts legislature with a plea for that body to respond.

The Massachusetts legislature did respond. It instructed its commissioners to the Peace Convention to oppose the Crittenden compromise. Despite this opposition and that by the Republicans in general, the convention, on February 26, passed a watered-down version of the Crittenden plan. The new version stated that the Missouri Compromise line should be extended to include only present U.S. territories and that new territories could be acquired only with the consent of dual majorities of both Northern and Southern senators. The two provisions especially obnoxious to blacks, relating to voting and colonization, were retained.

George T. Downing now had "no doubt that the North would sacrifice the whole race of colored people to save the Union." At least in this instance, he was proved wrong. Republican voters by the thousands cautioned their congressmen and leaders not to compromise with the South. Mainly they opposed Crittenden's territorial plan countenancing the extension of slavery. Especially important was the fact that Lincoln abhorred Crittenden's plan because it would allow slavery to expand indefinitely: "The Missouri line extended . . . would lose us everything we gained by the election. . . . There is in my judgment, but one compromise which would really settle the slavery question, and that would be a prohibition against acquiring any more territory."

The supreme importance that Lincoln attached to the territorial issue was indicated in his letter of February 1, 1861, to William H. Seward, soon to take office as his secretary of state, in which he made clear his adamant stand against any further extension of slavery by any means. He also made it clear that he was quite willing to accept other features of the Crittenden compromise:

As to fugitive slaves, District of Columbia, slave trade among slave states, and whatever springs of necessity from the fact that the institution is amongst us, I care but little, so that what is done be comely, and not altogether outrageous.

But, he went on, "I say now, . . . as I have all the while said, that on the territorial question—that is, the question of extending slavery under the national auspices,—I am inflexible. I am for no compromise which *assists* or *permits* the extension of the institution on soil owned by the nation."

Lincoln and the Republicans were prepared to support an ironclad guarantee that the Constitution would never be amended in such a way as to interfere with the institution of slavery within the slave states. Indeed, an unrepealable amendment to that effect passed the House on February 12, 1861, and the Senate on the night of March 3–4, 1861, by the necessary two-thirds vote. The incoming president announced that he had "no objection" to the pending amendment, and three states (two of them free) actually gave their ratification in 1861.

Meanwhile, the Peace Convention reported its plan to Congress on February 27, and the Senate rejected it in the early morning hours of the day of Lincoln's inauguration. Then the Senate voted on the original Crittenden plan and defeated it by a 20 to 19 vote. Not one Republican supported the plan. The House also voted on the original Crittenden compromise on February 27 and defeated it by a 113 to 80 vote. Republicans in the lower House, as in the Senate, voted unanimously against the measure.

The rejection marked the end of any efforts to resolve the secession problem through legislation. Free blacks in the North heaved a huge collective sigh of relief. While they had opposed the territorial settlement aspects of the Crittenden compromise, they had particularly fought the plan because of the danger of disfranchisement and forced expatriation, and they were happy over the narrow escape.

LINCOLN'S INAUGURAL ADDRESS AND BLACK GLOOM

Now blacks, along with other northerners and southerners, awaited Lincoln's inauguration. Douglass' admiration of Lincoln had increased in the weeks following the election. He observed with satisfaction the president-elect's determination not to capitulate to the demands for the compromise policy that would nullify the key plank of the Republican platform and "his refusal to have concessions extorted from him under the terror instituted by thievish conspirators and traitors."

Douglass and all of his black brothers and sisters looked forward to Lincoln's inaugural address. They were bitterly disappointed. The president reiterated a statement he had made earlier in his debates with Douglas: "I have no purpose, directly or indirectly, to interfere with the institution of slavery in the States where it exists. I believe I have no lawful right to do so, and I have no inclination to do so." But now he went as far as to state that he would not oppose a constitutional amendment permanently guaranteeing noninterference with the institution of slavery.

At the same time, Lincoln firmly proclaimed his duty to maintain the Union, but the tone of his speech was moderate and pacific. On the question of the federal forts and arsenals across the South that the Confederates had been seizing, Lincoln simply stated that "the power confided in me will be used to hold, occupy and possess the property and places belonging to the government." The address ended with an appeal to the South for peace: "You can have no conflict without being yourselves the aggressors."

Douglass saw little in this to gladden the hearts of the Negro people:

Some thought we had in Mr. Lincoln, the nerve and decision of an Oliver Cromwell, but the result shows that we merely have a continuation of the Pierces and Buchanans, and that the Republican President bends the knee to slavery as readily as any of his infamous predecessors.

Further analyzing the address, Douglass admitted that Lincoln's announcement "that the laws of the Union shall be faithfully executed in all of the United States" was a significant advance over Buchanan's "shuffling, do-nothing policy." But he doubted whether the president had the courage to carry out his program. "It remains to be seen," he concluded, "whether the Federal Government is really able to do more than hand over some John Brown to be hanged, suppress a slave insurrection, or catch a runaway slave—whether it is powerless for liberty and only powerful for slavery.''

Lincoln's willingness, indeed eagerness, to grant the slaveholders the constitutional right of owning their slaves enraged Douglass. This, he charged, amounted to conceding the whole argument. He found the president's heartless attitude toward those still in slavery obnoxious: "Mr. Lincoln has avowed himself ready to catch them if they run away, to shoot them down if they rise against their oppressors, and to prohibit the Federal Government *irrevocably* from interfering for their deliverance.''

Viewing the events following Lincoln's election, Douglass, for the first time since he had joined the antislavery movement, began to feel some doubt about the ultimate triumph of the cause. For years he had announced his conviction that the forces of history were on the side of the abolitionists and that while they might suffer setbacks, the final victory would be theirs. Antislavery men, he declared, must not allow temporary discouragements to cause them to forget that "the Principles which form the basis of the Abolition movement . . . must triumph.'' Precisely because he was convinced that the cause would triumph, he had used his pen and voice against all emigration schemes, believing that free blacks must remain in the land where they lived, where their brothers and sisters were held in slavery, and where they could contribute to the liberation of their people.

But events since the election of Lincoln—the repeal of the personal liberty laws by the Republican legislatures and the attacks upon black people by Northern mobs—caused Douglass to doubt whether his confidence had been justified, and he began to look with some favor on the emigration movement to Haiti.

Douglass' pessimism was shared by many other Northern blacks, The *Anglo-African* of New York City, for example, devoted more space during the months following Lincoln's election, and especially in the weeks following his inauguration, to news, articles, and letters about emigration to Africa and Haiti than it did to events connected with the growing secession movement. Reports of emigration meetings of Northern blacks were featured, while those dealing with issues related to secession or the Crittenden compromise either were ignored or received little attention.

By this time, many blacks had so completely lost faith in the American government that they were no longer interested in the events associated with its survival. Robert Purvis expressed the view of many blacks when he said: "I say your government—it is not mine. Thank God, I have no willing share in a government that deliberately, before the world, and without a blush, declares one part of its people, and that for no crime or pretext of crime, disfranchised and outlawed. For such a government, I, as a man, can have no feelings but of contempt, loathing, and unutterable abhorrence!'' An even more striking example of this attitude appeared in the *Anglo-African* of March 23, 1861, in an editorial, ''Arming the Slaves,'' which was published in response to one in the

New York Tribune of March 16. In it, Horace Greeley responded to reports from the South that the Confederate States of America were making ''plans for arming their slaves'' and that Jefferson Davis would soon let the Northern people ''smell Southern powder and taste Southern steel'' in the hands of these slaves. Greeley warned the Confederacy that if it did go ahead with the plan, it would be launching a war of races in which it would be destroyed, for the history of the War for Independence had demonstrated that ''free Northern colored men have been distinguished for fidelity and bravery,'' and while the North could rely fully upon its black population under arms, the South could not:

The North would arm her free blacks by thousands, and to such a standard they would rally with enthusiasm. It would be liberty to the whole race they were fighting for; abolition in the most practical form. Two such forces meeting face to face would be likely to fraternize on sight. Let Southern blacks be armed and Northern antagonism would speedily be developed in the way we indicate, so that the game is one which two can play at.

Thomas Hamilton, editor of the *Anglo-African,* replied:

In the first place no man in his senses believes the South would arm their slaves, and in the second, no man of our race believes the *Tribune* or its Republican conferees would, except in the last extremity, consent to put arms in the hands of the free colored men. Flattery is a good salve when skilfully applied, but it will neither heal nor hide the gaping wounds of injustice and oppression the North as well as the South have opened on us.

Before politicians prate of co-operation in the future, would it not be well to recognize our just claims upon the inheritance which our past efforts aided, (and by their own showing most efficiently,) to secure? Before we enter into any such compact as that indicated by the *Tribune,* we must have something better than flattery to convince us that after freely giving our blood to again build up the Union whose foot has bound us down for eighty-five years, that though free nominally, we shall not be as in the past, pariahs and outcasts. We remember how the blood of Crispus Attucks was paid for in the rendition of Sims and Burns; and that the first act in the drama of Republican triumph has been the rendition of woman Jane at Cleveland, the repeal of the Personal Liberty Law of Rhode Island, and the emasculation of those of Maine and Massachusetts. Knowing as the politicians do the long arrears of blood-bought rights this country owes us, as well as the dark record of crimes against our race of which it stands accused and condemned, how ought not their cheeks to tingle with shame, and their tongues to falter at the proposition to further use us as instruments to stir up this rotten sham, this hollow fraud, this charnel house of human rights,—the Federal Government.

This thing is even more contemptible, when we remember, that the suggestion . . . is thrown out as a menace wherewith to frighten the fearful slave-owner. Like the threat of the nurse in the fable, to throw the unruly child to the wolf, it is only held out *in terrorem*, to morally persuade the South to quit her capers. We are not so silly as to hang upon the hope of any such contingency.

Messrs. Republicans, before you hand us *bullets* give us *ballots*. Ere you talk to us about instruments of war, give us those civic rights, those social privileges, for those maintenance or defence only is war legitimate.

Since the *Anglo-African* did not expect any positive response to its conditions, it continued to support emigration as the best solution for the free black population of the North. Within a few weeks, however, a dramatic change would occur in the attitude of the *Anglo-African* and of all blacks in the country.

FORT SUMTER AND THE OUTBREAK OF CIVIL WAR

Early in January 1861, the merchant ship *Star of the West* sailed for Charleston with supplies and 200 troops aboard to reinforce the garrison at Fort Sumter. The fort was manned by 128 men, 9 officers, 68 noncommissioned officers and other ranks, 8 musicians, and 43 noncombatant laborers, all under the command of Major Robert Anderson. When the ship arrived off Charleston on January 9, it was fired on by South Carolina batteries and turned back without discharging its cargo. This halfhearted attempt by retiring President James Buchanan constituted his last effort to reinforce the beleaguered men at Fort Sumter. During the next two months, an uneasy and unofficial truce prevailed in Charleston and Washington. Buchanan refused to recognize the secession of the Southern states, and he did not surrender Fort Sumter; however, he would not go beyond that.

On April 6, 1861, Lincoln sent a message to the governor of South Carolina by a special courier, who reached Charleston two days later, in which he warned the governor that an attempt would be made to supply the Sumter garrison with provisions only. There would be no effort to add men or arms unless either the relief force or Fort Sumter itself was attacked. The Sumter expedition sailed on April 8–9 and was scheduled to assemble off the coast of Charleston on April 11–12. After consulting his cabinet, Confederate President Jefferson Davis ordered Pierre Beauregard, the Southern commander at Charleston, to demand the surrender of Sumter before allowing relief to reach it. On April 10, Major Anderson rejected this demand but admitted that his tiny force would be starved out in a few days. A last-minute attempt to settle the matter peacefully on this basis broke down.

At 4:30 A.M. on April 12, 1861, the first shot was fired. The bombardment lasted for over thirty hours until Anderson was persuaded to surrender.

The firing on Fort Sumter aroused the North and swept away most of its remaining doubts, divisions, and uncertainties. Lincoln called for 75,000 militia to deal with "combinations too powerful to be suppressed by the ordinary course of political proceedings." Virginia, North Carolina, Tennessee, and Arkansas rapidly seceded and joined the Confederacy.

The Civil War had begun.

The May 1861 issue of *Douglass' Monthly* carried a note from the editor reflecting how these developments had changed black opinion. The note was preceded by an editorial in which Douglass informed his readers that he would be visiting Haiti to investigate conditions for himself and report back to blacks in the

United States on the advisability of emigrating to the Caribbean island. Then followed this postscript:

Since this article upon Haiti was put into type, we find ourselves in circumstances which induce us to forgo our much desired trip to Haiti, for the present. The last ten days have made a tremendous revolution in all things pertaining to the possible future of the colored people in the United States. We shall stay here and watch the current of events, and serve the cause of freedom and humanity in any way that shall be open to us during the struggle now going on between the slave power and the government. When the Northern people have been made to experience a little more of the savage barbarism of slavery, they may be willing to make war upon it, and in that case we stand ready to lend in any way we can be of service. At any rate, this is no time for us to leave the country.

The events referred to were the firing on Fort Sumter by the Confederates, the call for volunteers by President Lincoln, and the outbreak of the Civil War.

16

Why the War Came

None of the works on the history of black Americans, in discussing the beginning of the Civil War on April 12, 1861, examine the highly controversial issue of what precipitated the war. They are usually content to note that a complex of events and emotions, differences in cultures and in the economic systems, and above all, slavery, contributed to the chain of crises that culminated in the firing on Fort Sumter. Before dealing with the Civil War itself as it affected and was affected by black Americans—North and South—we shall consider here what is perhaps the single most persistent question in American historiography: What caused the Civil War?

In 1954, Thomas J. Pressly wrote *Americans Interpret Their Civil War,* in which he outlined the changing interpretations of the cause of the war during the period of almost a century preceding its publication and analyzed the different theories advanced by historians, economists, and political scientists, as well as by political figures and businessmen turned historians. Six years later, on the eve of the Civil War centennial, David Donald, in "American Historians and the Causes of the Civil War," formally announced the demise of Civil War causation as a subject for serious historical analysis. Like that of Mark Twain's death, however, this report was much exaggerated, for barely had it appeared in print when the hundredth anniversary of the Civil War produced an inundation of books and articles reexamining the causes of the conflict, a flood that continued even after the centennial was over.

To cite only a few of the host of works relating to the subject that were published after 1961: Kenneth M. Stampp, ed., *The Causes of the Civil War* (Englewood Cliffs, N.J., 1970), and *The Imperiled Union: Essays in the Background of the Civil War* (New York, 1980); Hans L. Trefousse, ed., *The Causes of the Civil War* (New York, 1971); Barrington Moore, *Social Origins of Dictatorship and Democracy* (New York, 1971); Peter J. Parish, *The American Civil*

War, chapter 12, "Why the War Came" (New York, 1978); William Barney, *The Road to Secession* (New York, 1972); Eric Foner, "The Causes of the American Civil War: Recent Interpretations and New Directions," *Civil War History* 20 (1974): 197–210, and "Politics, Ideology, and the Origins of the American Civil War," in George M. Fredrikson, ed., *A Nation Divided: Essays on the Civil War and Reconstruction* (New York, 1974).

THE FIRST EXPLANATIONS

What was probably the first contribution to Civil War historiography appeared several months before Fort Sumter. This was Edmund Ruffin's *Anticipations of the Future,* which foresaw the outbreak of the war in 1867, a conflict that would be brought on, Ruffin predicted, by the steps taken in the Republican administrations of Presidents Abraham Lincoln and William H. Seward to accomplish "the ruin of the South" without a direct assault upon slavery, such as, for example, the total prevention of the institution's further expansion. Ruffin was convinced that in the war, which he considered irrepressible, the continued loyalty of the slaves would guarantee a glorious Southern military victory. New York City would be destroyed by a mob, and Washington would become the capital of a victorious new Southern republic.

But it was with the end of the Civil War that the historical presentation of the causes really got under way. Benjamin H. Hill pointed out that the one great resource left to his ravaged South was history—"impartial and unpassioned, un-office-seeking history." Just how "impartial and unpassioned" this history was soon became clear, as southerners presented the Southern interpretation of the causes of the Civil War. In 1866 and 1868, Edward A. Pollard, the unrepetant Richmond editor and historian, published *Southern History of the Great Civil War* and *The Lost Cause Regained,* in which he accused the North of aggression, of a fanatical desire to destroy Southern culture and society, and of encouraging the slaves to turn upon their masters and to take vengeance for their long years of servitude—all this out of a determination to reduce the Southern states to the position of colonial dependencies of the North and to stifle their voice in the federal government. In the face of such threats, Pollard declared, the South had no alternative but to leave the Union and to fight for its right to secede when its desire to do so was denied.

The year 1868 also witnessed the publication of Alexander H. Stephens' *A Constitutional View of the Late War between the States.* A Southern apologist, Stephens asserted that "this whole subject of Slavery so-called . . . was to the Seceding States, but a drop in the ocean compared . . . with other considerations." By "other considerations," he meant those of constitutional principles, for Stephens argued that the issue of states' rights, divorced from the social problem of slavery, was the major cause of the Civil War. Thus, in his view, the

Civil War was solely the culmination of a struggle for power between the federal government and the state governments.

The Northern counteroffensive was not long in coming. Henry Wilson, in his *History of the Rise and Fall of the Slave Power in America*, published between 1872 and 1877, and John A. Logan in his *Great Conspiracy*, published in 1886, both stressed that the primary cause of the Civil War was the threat of the expansion of slavery—first into Mexico, Cuba, and the Central American states and finally, on the basis that it was a positive good, into all the territories and free states. It was to prevent this that the North took up arms.

Thus, beginning with the war generation, official justifications for their conduct were presented by both sides, and these were characterized by the designations they gave to the conflict. The Union, placing the blame on the South for its long history of aggression, climaxed by secession, called it the War of the Rebellion, while the Confederacy's apologists, emphasizing Southern nationalism and Lincoln's attempt to keep them in the Union by force, preferred the War between the States. Already, however, a third group was beginning to emerge, which viewed the war as a needless one that could have been avoided if extremists on both sides had not resisted and ultimately prevented compromise.

THE NATIONALIST INTERPRETATION AND THE CHALLENGE TO IT

Starting with James Ford Rhodes, the next generation developed a nationalist interpretation of the war. No longer dominated by the emotional attachment of his predecessors and influenced by the businessmen's desire for conciliation between the sections, Rhodes, an Ohio capitalist, was less inclined to fix the blame for the war on individuals or sections, preferring to ascribe it to an impersonal and irrepressible conflict, which had its roots in the institution of slavery. In his seven-volume *History of the United States from the Compromise of 1850 to the Final Restoration of Home Rule in the South in 1877*, published between 1893 and 1906, Rhodes argued unequivocally that while slavery was the cause of the Civil War, it was the nation rather than the South that had been responsible for slavery.

"It may be safely asserted," Rhodes stated bluntly, "that there was a single cause—slavery." The first generation of trained historians, led by Frederick Jackson Turner, Woodrow Wilson, Edward Channing, and John Bach McMaster, played variations on this theme. Some added that the North fought the Civil War to abolish slavery.

The twentieth century produced several challenging interpretations to these nationalist views. Charles and Mary Beard, Louis Hacker, and other economic determinists introduced into Civil War historiography the thesis that the war was an inevitable clash between an agrarian South and an industrial North. In *The Rise of American Civilization*, published in 1927, the Beards argued that "the institution of slavery was not the fundamental issue.'' They then went on to assert that constitutional issues also ''were minor actors in the grand dispute.'' The economic conflict between the sections alone explained the war. At issue was not slavery but such matters as banks and tariffs, internal improvements, land grants to railroads, and free homesteads for settlers. In other words, the war had not been a contest over principles but a struggle for power—a clash of economic sections between the industrial and planter interests rather than between freedom and slavery.

Another group of historians—southerners like Ulrich B. Phillips, Charles Ramsdell, and Frank Owsley—offered a new vindication of the South, often defending slavery as a ''civilizing'' institution, which had provided a solution to the race problem, and generally placing war guilt on the abolitionists. The Civil War, they maintained, was solely the result of extremist agitation by fanatic and irresponsible antislavery men and women; slavery would have ended without the war, and thus the war was a needless waste of lives and treasure.

THE REVISIONIST HISTORIANS AND THEIR CRITICS

Beginning with Gerald W. Johnson's *The Secession of the Southern States*, published in 1933, and reaching its peak of influence around the time of the outbreak of World War II, there began to emerge the so-called revisionist interpretation of the causes of the Civil War. The revisionist historians, among them George Fort Milton, Avery O. Craven, and James G. Randall, minimized the importance of slavery or any other factor as a cause of the war, challenged the view that the Civil War was an ''irrepressible conflict,'' and attempted to explain the war as an unnecessary conflict brought on by an irrational exaggeration of the issues, and especially by the agitation of the abolitionists, which produced more problems than it solved. In short, the struggle was a ''needless war'' brought on by a ''blundering generation.''

Essentially, then, these historians believed the Civil War resulted from a breakdown in the political process. Thus the war itself was needless and preventable. The differences between the sections, they insisted, were not fundamental and the forces making for conflict were not irrepressible. Slavery could have been eliminated gradually and peacefully. All that was needed was astute political management. Instead, the revisionist historians argued, blundering politicians exaggerated sectional differences for electoral purposes, blew up the crisis artificially, and eventually undermined the political system's capacity for compromise.

In *The Civil War and Reconstruction*, published in 1937, James G. Randall argued that the ''larger phase of the slavery question . . . seemed to recede as the controversies of the fifties developed.'' The attention of the country was ''diverted from the fundamentals of slavery in its moral, economic, and social aspects'' and instead ''became concentrated upon the collateral problem as to what Congress should do with respect to slavery in the territories.'' Hence, it was this narrow phase of the slavery question that became, or seemed to become, central to the succession of political events that produced the Civil War. As Randall saw it, the struggle "centered upon a political issue which lent itself to slogan-making rather than a political analysis.''

In a later work, Randall described the issue of slavery in the territories, when debated by Lincoln and Douglas in 1858, as a "talking point rather than a matter for governmental action, a campaign appeal rather than a guide for legislation." Indeed, at the center of the revisionist argument is the charge that the question of slavery in the territories was an artificial issue, already made obsolete by economic and geographical facts.

"Needless war" historians accuse Lincoln of failing to give enough support to those who, like Crittenden, struggled to find some final ground for compromise and of throwing down the gauntlet to the South with the decision to reinforce Fort Sumter, for this made a resort to arms inevitable. These historians have concluded that unconditional opponents of the Crittenden compromise constituted a minority in most of the South from December 1860 to January 1861 and would have had trouble securing secession in their states without the help of the Republican rejection of the proposal. Kenneth M. Stampp, for example, argues that the "only slavery compromise that had an outside chance of satisfying Southerners was Crittenden's. . . . Unquestionably it would have been acceptable to most of the people in the slave states that had not seceded. It was at least conceivable that its passage would have started a reaction against secessionist leaders in the Deep South and thus prepared the way for eventual reunion.'' It is also conceivable that it would have done nothing of the sort.

More recently, David M. Potter has also suggested that compromise was possible in 1860, and he chastises Lincoln and the Republicans for underestimating both the gravity of the crisis and the extent of Union feeling that still existed in the South. Furthermore, he seems to suggest that Stephen A. Douglas' doctrine of popular sovereignty—giving each territory the right to decide on slavery—could have settled the sectional conflict.

In this respect, Stephen A. Douglas became the darling of the revisionists. He was viewed as the only statesman who had wrestled seriously with the problem of sectional antagonism and the only one to present a policy with regard to slavery that might have averted the Civil War.

In *The Emergence of Lincoln* and in *Ordeal of the Union,* Allan Nevins tried to combine the revisionist and nationalist viewpoints. Nevins saw the South as comparatively static culturally, while the North was driving forward into the modern world. Those in the North who were bitterly opposed to slavery were thus able to attack the South on the secondary issue of being backward, semi-civilized, and outside the mainstream of progress. Nevins, however, rejected the older idea that slavery as a moral issue lay at the heart of the controversy and offered in its stead the view that "the main root of the conflict (and there were minor roots), was the problem of slavery with *its complementary problem of race-adjustment."*

Nevins agreed with the revisionists that the "failure of American leadership" contributed to the breakdown of the Union, and he even enunciated the belief that "the War should have been avoidable," although he never declared that it could have been avoided. But Nevins rejected revisionism in devoting major attention to the harsh aspects of slavery and in his condemnation of Stephen A. Douglas, whom he called "a man of dim moral perceptions," who, by his own admission, did not care much whether slavery was voted up or down.

Perhaps Nevins' major contribution was to restore the contribution of slavery to the analysis of Civil War causation. Yet, he added, although this may have seemed to many to have been "the grand cause" of the war, it was "not primarily a war about slavery." In his view:

It was a war over slavery *and* the future position of the Negro race in America. Was the Negro to be allowed, as a result of the shift of power signalized by Lincoln's election, to take the first step toward an ultimate position of general economic, political and social equality with the white man. Or was he to be held immobile in a degraded, servile position, unchanging for the next hundred years as it had remained essentially unchanged for the hundred years past?

Although his article was entitled, "The American Civil War as Constitutional Crisis," and dealt primarily with this aspect of the conflict, Arthur Bestor agreed with Nevins on the importance of the slavery issue as a cause of the war: "Though other factors must be taken into account in explaining the configuration of events, these other factors, isolated from those connected with slavery, cannot explain why tensions mounted so high as to reach the breaking point of war."

In *A History of the Southern Confederacy,* Clement Eaton, like Nevins, attempted to combine the nationalist and revisionist interpretations. Like the revisionists, he believed that the war was neither inevitable nor necessary, but he noted that the South was swept along on a wave of emotional fanaticism whipped up by the extremists who either were ignorant of or exaggerated the real danger to their section. At the same time, he argued that there were genuine issues underlying the sectional conflict. There was, for example, the real danger that with the end of Southern control of the federal government, slavery and white supremacy would soon be abolished. In short, "The South could not accept the nineteenth century, and compromise was prevented by pride and an inflated notion of Southern rights." As for the immediate cause of the outbreak of the war, Eaton adopted a dual position. The South was the aggressor, but Lincoln unnecessarily forced the issue when he ordered Sumter reinforced. He could have evacuated Sumter and gained time for the ascendancy of Union sentiment in the South. Eaton argued that a majority of Southern whites opposed secession in November 1860 but that they had swung behind the rebellion in the next two months; however, he offers little evidence to bolster this belief.

While Nevins and Eaton both opposed and supported the revisionist historians, this school, with its thesis of the needless war, came under severe attack from Bernard De Voto, Arthur M. Schlesinger, Jr., Peter Geyl, Harry V. Jaffa, and others. These critics decried the belief that the Civil War could have been avoided had the problems of the day been confronted more rationally and had the moral emotionalism been dampened. On the contrary, they maintained, it was the moral issue of slavery that was paramount. Schlesinger asserted that "the emotion which moved the North finally to battlefield and bloodshed was moral disgust with slavery." He also argued that the focus of the slavery contest had fallen on the territories not because the emerging industrial capitalists were seeking power in new regions and were indifferent to the brutalization of slaves in the Southern states but because Americans found slavery an institution in conflict with their ideals and with their civic duty to obey the Constitution, even though it protected slavery. While the conflict over slavery in the territories may have seemed to obscure the moral aspects of the slavery issue, Schlesinger insisted that it actually did not do so and that slavery as a moral issue remained basic as the cause of the Civil War.

These historians also criticized the needless war idea. Schlesinger, for example, argued that war might be necessary at times to break such great moral logjams of history as slavery and that no historian could prove that slavery would have disappeared by itself. The critics of revisionism deplored the practice of equating abolitionists and the secessionists as fanatics. "There is surely a difference," wrote Oscar Handlin in 1950, "between being a fanatic for freedom and being a fanatic for slavery."

On one point, however, the revisionist historians and their critics, as well as Nevins and Eaton, all agreed: the Beardian thesis that the Civil War was purely the product of an economic conflict between the industrial capitalists and the slaveowners was fundamentally wrong. At the same time, however, they tended to equate Beardian economic determinism with the Marxist interpretation of Civil War causation, even after the publication in 1937 of a volume that should have revealed to them the incorrectness of this belief. The book was *The Civil War in the United States by Karl Marx and Frederick Engels*, edited by Richard Enmale. In this collection of newspaper articles (originally published in the *New York Daily Tribune* and the *Vienna Presse* in 1861 and 1862) and of letters written between 1860 and 1866, Marx interpreted the Civil War from the start as an inexorable revolutionary battle of the bourgeois industrialist, the small farmer, and the worker against the slave power. He wrote: "The present struggle between the South and the North is, therefore, nothing but a struggle between two social systems, between the system of free labor and of slave labor. The struggle has broken out because the two systems can no longer live peacefully side by side on the North American continent. It can only be ended by the victory of one system or the other." Marx insisted that the issue of states' rights was a pretext rather than a cause of the war. Furthermore, although he recognized the connection between the Morrill tariff of 1861 (which raised tariff rates to an average of 18.8 percent) and the vested interests of the industrial capitalists, he rejected completely the economic determinist argument that the issue was drawn "between protection and free-trade."

To Marx, the slave power symbolized not only the institution of slavery itself but also the economic structure that utilized slave labor; not only the oligarchic slavocrats who manipulated political programs, local and national, in their interests but also the ideologies through which they maintained power. Marx clearly set forth the dependency of the slave power upon territorial expansion:

The whole movement was and is based . . . on the *slave question*: Not in the sense of whether the slaves within the existing slave states would be emancipated or not, but whether the twenty million free men of the North should subordinate themselves any longer to an oligarchy of three hundred thousand slave holders; whether the vast territories of the republic should be planting-places for free states or for slavery; finally whether the national policy of the Union should take [the] armed propaganda of slavery in[to] Mexico, Central and South America as its device.

Marx also recognized the influence of the expanding Northwest in the struggle for power. In a letter to Engels, he wrote: "A closer study of the American business has shown me that the conflict between South and North . . . was finally . . . brought to a head by the weight thrown into the scales of the extraordinary development of the Northwestern states."

Marx emphasized that the setting up of the Confederacy was "not merely a question of seceding from the North, but of consolidating and intensifying the oligarchy . . . in the South." "The war of the Southern Confederacy," he wrote, "is not a war of defense, but a war of conquest, for the extension and perpetuation of slavery."

In general Marx argued that while stimulating up to a point capitalist development in the North, black slavery in the South increasingly acted as a brake on further capitalist development. The Northern industrialists depended to a great extent upon the South, which supplied cotton for the North's textile industry, and as a result, the capitalists of the North participated in the exploitation of black slaves alongside the Southern planters. Nevertheless, the contradictions between the slaveholding South and the capitalist North were becoming ever more irreconcilable. The industrialists of the North were vitally interested in creating a single national market and introducing high protective tariffs in order to protect the nation's young industry from European competition. For this reason the contradictions between the slaveholding South and the capitalist North were becoming ever more irreconcilable. In the struggle for power, hostility grew between the slaveholders and the Northern capitalists. As Marx wrote, the struggle for power between the North and South "was the general formula of the United States history since the beginning of this (19th) century."

Marx was not the only one to see this struggle for power at the root of the Civil War. Frederick Douglass, for example, wrote: "The masters of the slaves have been the masters of the republic. Their authority was almost undisputed, and their power irresistible." And since the Civil War more and more historians have come to agree with the significance of the issues emphasized by Marx and Engels. Indeed, writing in *New York History* for January 1938, Professor James Laughlin said of *The Civil War in the United States* by Marx and Engels: "As one reads, one frequently forgets that the opinions are those of a contemporary writer formed immediately after the fact, because they are, without exception, findings which were confirmed by political scientists of the following fifty years."

THE CENTENNIAL OF THE CIVIL WAR

The centennial of the Civil War was marked by a "Confederate tide" in the writing on the causes of the conflict. Secession, in the words of E. Merton Coulter, a historian of the Confederacy, was "a release from tyranny," "a counter-revolution against the excesses of Northern demagoguery, mob rule, and dangerous fanaticisms imported from Europe." Other Southern historians emphasized the economic and legal issues dividing the North and discounted the problem of slavery. They did not, of course, quote Lincoln's succinct statement in his letter to Alexander Stephens of December 22, 1860: "You think slavery is *right* and ought to be extended, while we think it is *wrong* and ought to be restricted. That I suppose is the rub, it certainly is the only substantial difference between us." Instead, they quoted Jefferson Davis, who insisted that slavery was "in no wise the cause of the conflict but only an incident."

It was the abolitionists who bore the brunt of the attacks by Southern writers during the centennial. In *The Legacy of the Civil War*, Southern novelist and poet Robert Penn Warren blamed them entirely for the war. They were men, he wrote, who repudiated society because they had lost personal control over it through the rise of cotton mill wealth in New England and the decline of government by the genteel. They were men, moreover, who opposed slavery because it produced the cotton that enriched and empowered their rivals, the manufacturers. Resurrecting the wage-slavery argument, Warren accused the abolitionists of ignoring the exploitation of white labor in Northern mills. They were, he charged, inflammatory, irresponsible, and determined to destroy the Union, and they succeeded in their objective. Warren ignored the wild rhetoric of Southern "fire eaters" and the fact that while Garrison may have condemned the Union, it was the South that shattered it. Rather, the political crimes of the secessionists are brought down upon the heads of the Northern reformers. No mention was made of the fact that the cotton states refused to allow the Crittenden compromise even to be discussed in the Senate and that on December 14, 1860, the Southern address in the Senate rejected any compromise. "The argument is exhausted. . . . All hope of relief in the Union is extinguished," the Southern senators said.

The great mentor of the Confederate version of Civil War causation during the Centennial was Avery Craven, who, in his *The Civil War in the Making,* insisted that "most of the incentives to honest and sustained effort to a contented, well-rounded life, might be found under slavery. . . . What owning and being owned added to the normal relationship of employer and employee is very hard to say." This may be true for a historian, but it can hardly be said about a slave.

Craven blamed the war entirely on the "abolitionist fanatics" and charged that Lincoln deliberately conspired to bring on the firing at Fort Sumter in order to make the Confederates appear to be the aggressors. Like Warren, Craven ignored the role of the Southern fanatics.

Reading such explanations for the Civil War, it is hardly to be wondered that Faith M. Brodie was moved to ask in the *New York Times Book Review* of August 25, 1962: "Who won the Civil War, anyway?"

Despite the effective rebuttals of the entire theory of revisionism during the late 1940s and the 1950s, it was revived during the centennial. In the centennial volume *Politics and the Crisis of 1860,* Norman A. Graebner, William E. Barringer, Don E. Fehrenbacher, and Avery Craven, argued that the sectional crisis called for "a wise and tolerable statesmanship," a quality that was exhibited, according to them, only by Stephen A. Douglas. But for the emergence of Lincoln, he might have united conservatives of North and South and have "blunted the secession movement and guided the nation past the danger of Civil War."

Norman A. Graebner had a simple explanation for the war. He argued that Lincoln and the Republicans could not "present to the nation any genuine alternative but civil war to the indefinite coexistence with slavery." Since the latter was politically impossible, the former became inevitable.

In *Patriotic Gore,* a centennial study of the literature of the antebellum era and the Civil War, Edmund Wilson advanced the by now familiar thesis that the moral issue of slavery had nothing to do with the war. Slavery, he maintained, was simply a useful theme in Northern propaganda in a war that was no more than an elemental struggle for power:

The institution of slavery, which the Northern states had by this time got rid of, thus supplied the militant Union North with the rabble-rousing moral issue which is necessary in every modern war to make the conflict appear as a melodrama.

The real issue of the struggle, as Wilson saw it, was expressed in the following zoological metaphor:

In a recent Walt Disney film showing life at the bottom of the sea, a primitive organism called a sea-slug is seen gobbling up smaller organisms through a large orifice at one end of its body; confronted with another sea-slug of an only slightly lesser size, it ingurgitates that, too. Now, the wars fought by human beings are stimulated as a rule primarily by the same instincts as the voracity of the sea-slug.

Yet while Wilson tries to remove "the whole subject from the plane of morality," the contents of the book often testify to the failure of his attempt. Thus, he quotes Abraham Lincoln, six years before the Civil War, as writing to a Kentucky friend:

In 1841, you and I had together a tedious low-water trip, on a Steam Boat from Louisville to St. Louis. You may remember, as I well do, that from Louisville to the mouth of the Ohio there were, on board, ten or a dozen slaves, shackled together with irons. That sight was a continual torment to me, and I see something like it every time I touch the Ohio, or any other slave-border. It is hardly fair for you to assume that I have no interest in a thing which has, and continually exercises, the power of making me miserable. You ought rather to appreciate how much the great body of the Northern people do crucify their feelings, in order to maintain their loyalty to the constitution and the Union.

Wilson does not comment on Lincoln's letter, which he quotes, but he does intercede when Ulysses S. Grant, in conversation with Bismarck, offers an explanation of the causes of the Civil War that Wilson has already rejected.

"Yes," said the prince, "you had to save the Union just as we had to save Germany." "Not only save the Union, but destroy slavery," answered the General. "I suppose, however, the Union was the real sentiment, the dominant sentiment," said the prince. "In the beginning, yes," said the General; "but as soon as slavery fired upon the flag it was felt, we all felt, even those who did not object to slaves, that slavery must be destroyed. We felt that it was a stain to the Union that men should be bought and sold like cattle."

At this point, Wilson comments: "Bismarck changes the subject. The General is quite unaware that, by putting the thing in this way, he has indicated that slavery, on the part of the Unionists, has at the last moment been recruited to justify their action in the struggle for power." But Grant meant nothing of the sort. It is true that the general exaggerated the degree of feeling in the North at the time of Fort Sumter "that slavery must be destroyed." But in the long run, Grant was correct, for "as soon as slavery fired upon the flag," it set into motion forces that made inevitable the emergence in the North of the view "that slavery must be destroyed." And while it is true that secession, not slavery, was the immediate cause of the war, it is also true that the cause of secession was the controversy over slavery: both the moral aspects of the issue and the economic and political aspects involved in the clash between the free labor ideology and that of the slaveowners, and the struggle over the South's attempt to extend slavery indefinitely.

Marxists and so-called Marxist scholars also presented their interpretations of the causes of the Civil War during the centennial. In the latter category was Eugene D. Genovese's argument that the internal contradictions in the South and the external conflict with the North placed the slaveholders hopelessly on the defensive, with little to look forward to except slow strangulation. Their only hope lay in a bold stroke to complete their political independence and to use it to provide an expansionist solution for their economic and social problems. The ideology and the social psychology of the proud planter class made surrender or resignation to gradual defeat unthinkable, for its entire civilization was at stake. Hence the war, which Genovese calls "the War between the States," was really a war for Southern independence.

But in "The American Civil War: A Centenary Article," Marxist historian Herbert Aptheker wrote:

In origin, the Civil War in the United States was an attempted counter-revolution carried out by a desperate slaveholding class. The aggressors were the dominant elements among the slaveowners, and the resort to violence was long planned, carefully prepared and ruthlessly launched. There was no unanimity among the slaveowners; some feared that the resort to violence would fail and that its result would be the destruction of the slave system. But those who so argued were overruled and the richest and most powerful among the planter-slaveholders carried the day for secession and war. . . . The Confederate assault upon Washington and the secession from the United States was a counter-revolutionary development. It was counter-revolutionary not only in its regressive motivations and its profoundly anti-democratic essence; it was counter-revolutionary, too, in that it was done secretly with malice aforethought, and *against the will of the vast majority of the Southern people.*

Aptheker saw "four great forces" that "drove the slaveholding class into the path of counter-revolutionary violence":

First: the momentous socio-economic transformation of the United States north of the Mason-Dixon line and extending from the Atlantic Ocean to the Mississippi River; second, the quantitative and qualitative growth of the Abolitionist movement; third: the intensification of mass unrest and class conflict within the South; fourth: the accumulating impact of certain organic contradictions within the plantation-slavery system.

SINCE THE CENTENNIAL

The years since the Civil War centennial have witnessed a decline of the influence of historians who deny that slavery was a moral issue and of those who blame the war on fanatics, dogmatists, cranks, ambitious or blundering politicians, and the propagandists who spread suspicion, paranoia, and irrational obsessions. There is still a historian like William Appleman Williams, who, during the bicentennial of American Independence in 1976, echoed the Southern writers on Civil War causation by bluntly asserting: "Put simply, the cause of the Civil War was the refusal of Lincoln and other Northerners to honor the revolutionary right of self-determination—the touchstone of the American Revolution." There were also the "new political historians," who, using the tools of quantitative history, portray an irrational electorate in the North responding to ethnic or nativist bigots and ignoring national issues while concentrating on the slavery issue. Then there are the political scientists who use the modernatization model to explain the causes of the Civil War by arguing that the North was determined to integrate the premodern South into a national political and economic system.

But the main result of the writings on Civil War causation since the centennial has been to move the issue of slavery back in the center of the picture, where it has remained. David M. Potter, in *The Impending Crisis, 1848–1861*, still preached the doctrine that compromise was possible in 1860 and blamed Lincoln and the Republicans for its failure. Yet he also insisted on the centrality of the slavery issue, declaring that as an ethical question, a vast economic interest, and the foundation of a distinct cultural life in the South, slavery lay at the root of the sectional conflict.

The conclusion of two studies of Civil War causation by British historians is similar. "The *prima facie* case for slavery as the fundamental cause of the Civil War is unanswerable," writes Peter J. Parish. Alan A. Conway notes:

Would there have been a Civil War without the existence of slavery in the Southern States? It seems unlikely that the war would have come over the tariff or state rights, although the belief in the right to secede from the Union cannot be dismissed lightly; but without slavery the desire of the Southern states to secede *en bloc* was unlikely to have arisen. . . . Slavery permeates—some might say, poisons every aspect of American life, North, South and West in the years before the Civil War and is the one factor common to all the subsidiary causes of the war.

Steven A. Channing's *Crisis of Fear: Secession in South Carolina*, published in 1970, was one more major contribution to the work of placing the slavery issue where it has always belonged: at the center of any discussion of the origins of the Civil War. "In South Carolina," Channing points out, "secession was a revolution of passion, and the passion was fear"—fear for the security of slavery and for the whole apparatus of social control that rested upon it. Fear of abolition and fear of servile insurrection lay at the core of the secessionist case and were not just its vehicle. "States' rights, economic grievances, social and cultural divergence from the North were all subordinate to the central issue."

Several recent studies, however, while agreeing that slavery was the central issue, emphasize that the secession of the South after the election of Lincoln was motivated not by paranoia or hysterical fear but by a realistic assessment that the unity of their society could not survive the open debate on the future of slavery that the Republican victory was destined to stimulate within the South.

All this does not mean that the "blundering generation" hypothesis of the revisionist school of the 1930s and 1940s, under the leadership of James G. Randall and Avery Craven, did not have new defenders. One was Michael F. Holt in his 1978 publication, *The Political Crisis of the 1850's*. Holt asks the question of why, if slavery-related sectional differences caused the Civil War, did the conflict not erupt during the 1830s and 1840s? His answer is that the political crisis of the 1850s, not slavery, generated the conflict. Once again, we are told that was all the result of blundering politicians. "Politicians," he writes, "who pursued very traditional party strategies were largely responsible for the ultimate breakdown of the political process." While Holt does not deny that sectional tensions may have had their roots in differences over slavery, these differences had existed since the Revolution, and they did not cause the Civil War. Rather it was the political crisis of the 1850s, a crisis precipitated not by slavery but by a temporary cleavage between the two parties, that started the conflicts that led to war. Of course, it is easy to eliminate slavery as playing a central role in Civil War causation by merely denying it, but once that is done, the rest of the analysis loses much of its meaning.

Even as late as 1981, James McGregor Burns reiterated the "revisionist" interpretation of the causes of the Civil War in the first volume of *The American Experiment,* subtitled, *The Vineyard of Liberty.* Despite all of the evidence demolishing the thesis, Burns continues to argue that proper leadership might have prevented the Civil War.

By way of contrast is Kenneth M. Stampp's *The Imperiled Union: Essays on the Background of the Civil War*, published in 1980. Stampp belongs to the school that believes the war was inevitable (although this does not mean he subscribes to the view that it was unavoidable), but he refuses to attribute the conflict to economic or cultural differences between the two sections. Rather, he attributes it to the clash of proslavery and antislavery forces. Stampp rejects the view that Lincoln was responsible for starting the war by relieving Fort Sumter. Moreover, he sees Fort Sumter as a triumph rather than a defeat for Lincoln, noting: "With consummate skill he had at once hamstrung the South, satisfied the great majority of Northerners that he contemplated no aggression, and yet conveyed his determination to defend the authority of the Federal government."

Few historians today would not agree that slavery was a crucial factor in bringing about the Civil War, but few also view the slavery issue solely as a moral question. In his study of the free labor ideology of the Republican party, Eric Foner notes that the Republicans created "an ideology which blended personal and sectional interest with morality so perfectly that it became the most potent political force in the nation. The free labor assault upon slavery and southern society, coupled with their idea of an aggressive Slave Power threatening the most fundamental values and interests of the free states, hammered the slavery issue home to the northern public more emphatically than an appeal to morality alone could ever have done." All of the elements that "were intertwined in the Republican world view"—"resentment of Southern political power, devotion to the Union, anti-slavery based upon the free labor argument, moral revulsion to the peculiar institution and racial prejudice, a commitment to the Northern social order and its development and expansion"—created a conviction that the "North and South represented two social systems, whose values, interests and prospects were in sharp, perhaps mortal, conflict with one another."

No single factor, whatever its nature, can account for the Civil War. Several forces converged, producing the conflagration. But in 1865, in his second inaugural address, Abraham Lincoln summed it up in a few words: "The Negro slaves in the Southern states," he said, "constituted a peculiar and powerful interest. All know that this interest is somehow the cause of the war."

In short, the Civil War was America's struggle over slavery.

17

The White Man's War

REASONS FOR SOUTHERN CONFIDENCE

When the Civil War started on April 12, 1861, the Confederacy believed it held several trump cards that would guarantee it victory. One was its confidence in the intervention on its behalf of Britain and France because of the all-powerful influence of cotton. As a Confederate song put it:

> Proud Independence is the cry
> Of Sugar, Rice and Cotton.
> King Cotton is a monarch
> Who'll conquer Abolition.

The British journal *Punch* paid its tribute to cotton with this jingle in its March 30, 1861, issue:

> Though with the North we sympathize
> It must not be forgotten
> That with the South we've stronger ties
> Which are composed of cotton.

William H. Russell, the *London Times* correspondent in the United States, reported the following remark made to him by a Confederate leader during his visit to the South on the eve of Fort Sumter: "Sir, we have only to shut off your supply of cotton for a few weeks and we can create a revolution in Great Britain. Four million of your people are dependent on us for their bread." These millions of workers, the argument continued, would join forces with the British upper class, who sympathized with the Southern aristocracy and hated and feared the Northern democracy, to demand Britain's intervention to break the inevitable Union naval blockade of Southern ports. France would follow Britain's lead, and with these two European countries ready to provide the Confederacy with money, arms, munitions, food, and drugs and ready to buy cotton, the Confederacy would be able to fight indefinitely. And should the Union government respond to such an intervention by a declaration of war—as it certainly would have to—it would be signing its own death warrant.

A second, and to many southerners the major, resource in Confederate hands was the fact that although seemingly hopelessly outnumbered—with 22 million people in the Union and 9 million in the Confederacy—the South would be able to put as many and possibly more soldiers into battle. (In fact, the South did possess a numerical superiority at the battles of First Bull Run, Pea Ridge, Gaines's Mill, Seven Days, Corinth, Chickamauga, Peach Tree Creek, and Atlanta.) The reason lay in slavery. At the outset of the war, the Southern press insisted that the 3,953,740 black slaves provided the Confederacy with a military advantage over the North that would practically guarantee it victory. The *Alabama Advertiser* pointed to the slaves as a "Military Element in the South," and noted:

The total white population of the eleven states now comprising the Confederacy is 5,000,000 and, therefore, to fill up the ranks of the proposed army, 600,000, about ten percent of the entire white population, will be required. In any other country than our own such a draft could not be met, but the Southern states can furnish that number of men, and still not leave the material interest of the country in a suffering condition.

The *Advertiser* continued:

Those who are incapacitated for bearing arms can oversee the plantations, and the negroes can go undisturbed on in their usual labors. In the North, the case is different; the men who join the army of subjection are the laborers, the producers and the factory operatives. Nearly every man from that section, especially those from the rural districts, leaves some branch of industry to suffer during his absence. The institution of slavery in the South alone enables her to place in the field a force much larger in proportion to her white population than the North. The institution is a tower of strength to the South, particularly at the present crisis, and our enemies will be likely to find that the "Moral Concern" about which their orators are so fond of prating, is really one of the most effective weapons employed against the Union by the South.

The *Savannah Republican* put the same idea more tersely: "Our cottonfields are tilled by slaves, and Georgia alone might send twenty thousand troops to the field, without diminishing the production of her crop to the amount of a hundred bales."

In short, the South believed that while its men went off to war, it could count on at least 4 million black slave laborers who would raise food and produce the sinews of war for it, work its plantations, and protect its families. An additional 261,918 free blacks would add to this element of black strength that would guarantee a Confederate victory.

But what if the slaves revolted or ran away, or the free blacks engaged in sabotage or other acts of interference with the Confederate war effort? On this, the Southern press at the opening of the war exuded only confidence. By that time, the slaveowners had so convinced themselves of the positive good of slavery and of the fact that the slaves of the Southern plantations were the happiest people on earth that the Confederate press could speak only of the "general fidelity and affectionate loyalty" of the slave population. Free blacks, too, would be "loyal and obedient," and a goodly number were even expected to take advantage of the recent legislation permitting free Negroes to select masters and voluntarily become slaves. The idea of "a general stampede of negroes" once the war really got under way was dismissed as an "absurdity."

"THE UPRISING OF A GREAT PEOPLE"—BUT NO
BLACKS WANTED

One prediction of the *Alabama Advertiser* was quickly proved correct. A majority of the men who joined the Union army in response to President Lincoln's call for 75,000 volunteers were the "laborers, the producers, and the factory operatives." So many members of trade unions volunteered that the labor movement, which had been slowly gaining in strength through the 1850s until the depression of 1857, almost ceased to exist. Trade unions organized fighting companies and enlisted as a body, posting notices on their union halls, reading: "Closed for the duration." German and Irish-American workers formed entire regiments. Exiled Poles, English Chartists, and Welsh miners joined the colors. The Garibaldi Guards, made up of Italian workingmen of New York City, was one of the first regiments to leave for Virginia. Many companies in the regiments of the Illinois Volunteers were composed of members of the Miners' Union, and the American Miners' Association, organized two months before the attack on Fort Sumter, sent large numbers of members into the ranks.

The socialist movement in America also contributed heavily to the armed forces. The Turner organization, made up largely of German-socialist workingmen, the *Arbeiterbund* (Workers' League), and the communist clubs sent more than half their members into the Union army. In New York, the Turners organized a regiment within a few days after Lincoln's call, and in many communities they sent one or more companies. There were three companies of Turners in the First Missouri Regiment, and the Seventeenth consisted almost entirely of Turners.

Where were the Northern blacks during this "uprising of a Great People"? When they sought to emulate the white workingmen who enlisted for service, they faced what seemed an insuperable obstacle. Despite the fact that Negro soldiers had fought for the United States in both the American Revolution and the War of 1812, there were neither any blacks in the U.S. Army nor the slightest preparation for their enlistment. Moreover, a federal law barred colored men from serving in state militias, and several states had their own exclusion in their constitutions, specifying white-only militias.

Despite these obstacles, during the first weeks after the fall of Fort Sumter, Northern blacks insisted on joining in the patriotic uprising and offered their services to the government to help suppress the rebellion. At a meeting of Philadelphia blacks on April 20, 1861, barely a week after Fort Sumter, Alfred M. Green, a schoolteacher, called upon Negroes to join the ranks of the Union army. It was time, he insisted, for blacks to say, "My country, right or wrong, I love thee still!" It was time, too, to forget past grievances:

It is true, the brave deeds of our fathers, sworn and subscribed to by the immortal Washington of the Revolution of 1776, and by Jackson and others in the War of 1812, have failed to bring us into recognition as citizens, enjoying those rights so dearly bought by those noble and patriotic sires.

It is true that our injuries in many respects are great; fugitive-slave laws, Dred Scott decisions, indictments for treason, and long dreary months of imprisonment. The result of the most unfair rules of judicial investigation has been the pay we have received for our solicitude, sympathy and aid in the dangers and difficulties of those "days that tried men's souls."

But, he continued, the duty of black Americans was "not to cavil over past grievances" but rather to "endeavor to hope for the future and improve the present auspicious moment for creating anew our claims upon the justice and honor of the Republic":

Let us, then, take up the sword, trusting in God, who will defend the right, remembering that these are other days than those of yore; that the world today is on the side of freedom and universal political equality; that the war cry of the howling leaders of Seccession and treason is: "Let us drive back the advance guard of civil and religious freedom; let us have more slave territory; let us build stronger the tyrant system of slavery in the great American Republic." Remember, too, that your very presence among the troops of the North would inspire your oppressed brethren of the South with zeal for the overthrow of the tyrant system, and confidence in the armies of the living God—the God of truth, justice and equality to all men.

The response to this appeal was felt all over the North. By the end of April, Boston blacks had petitioned the Massachusetts legislature to allow them to take an active role in "defending the Commonwealth against its enemies" by revising the militia law. They backed up their petition with a mass meeting at which resolutions were adopted urging the government "to modify your laws, that we may enlist—that full scope may be given to the patriotic feelings burning in the colored man's breast." Black women, too, were prepared to make their contribution, and the meeting urged that they be allowed to "go as nurses, seamstresses, and warriors, if need be, to crush the rebellion and uphold the Government." The meeting vowed to defend the American flag to the very end and announced that blacks were ready to raise an army of fifty thousand black men from all over the North if Massachusetts would only change its militia laws. Until that time, they decided to organize unofficial militia companies of their own for drilling purposes only to prepare them for service when the time came.

In support of these pleas for the right to serve in the armed forces, William C. Nell published a historical document citing numerous instances of Negro bravery and patriotism, "duly suggesting to the nation the propriety, if not indeed the necessity of the employment of colored soldiers in the Federal armies." John A. Andrew, Massachustts' new Republican governor, joined Nell in pleading for the federal government to permit blacks to join the armed forces. Andrews argued that if the Negro were to emerge from the war as an emancipated citizen, he had to make his own contribution to that goal and obtain immediately the right to bear arms.

But all of these pleas fell on deaf ears. In late April the following exchange of letters took place:

Washington, April 23d, 1861

Hon. Simon Cameron
Secretary of War

Sir: I desire to inform you that I know of some three hundred of reliable colored free citizens of this City, who desire to enter the service for the defence of the City.

I have been three times across the Rocky Mountains in the service of the Country with Fremont and others.

I can be found about the Senate Chambers, as I have been employed about the premises for some years.

Yours respectfully,
Jacob Dodson,
(Coloured)

War Department
Washington, April 29, 1861

Jacob Dodson (colored),
Washington City:

Sir: In reply to your letter . . . this Department has no intention at present to call into the service of the Government any colored soldiers.

With resp etc, &c.
Simon Cameron
Secretary of War

At about this same time, over one hundred black Wilberforce students formed a volunteer company and offered their services to the state and nation. "We were told," Richard H. Cain, one of the volunteers, recalled later when he was a member of Congress, "that this is a white man's war, and that the Negro has nothing to do with it." Undaunted, other Ohio blacks sought to enlist and serve their country. A public meeting of Cleveland blacks announced that "today, as in the time of '76, and the days of 1812, we are ready to go forth and do battle in the common cause of the country." But Ohio's militia commander informed the blacks that "the constitution will not permit me to issue the order." (His reference was to article IX, section 1 of the 1851 Ohio Constitution, which permitted only "white male citizens" to "be enrolled in the militia and perform military duty.") Unlike Governor Andrew, Ohio's Governor William Dennison supported the rebuff and announced that "the matter was in the hands of the white people" who "would take care of it."

In order to be prepared for the day when they might be needed to defend the city, Cincinnati blacks, at a public meeting, formed the "home guards" and established a recruiting station. But the authorities were so enraged by this that the police demanded the keys to the schoolhouse where they were scheduled to meet. The blacks were also forced to remove the national flag from the door of the recruiting station. Asked for an explanation, the police informed the press they wanted the "d——d niggers to keep out of this; this is a white man's war."

New York City blacks formed a military club and offered their services to the Union only a few days after the outbreak of hostilities, but the city's police department refused to permit further meetings on the ground that they "might lead to some unpleasantness in New York as well as exasperate the South." Nevertheless, on May 1, 1861, New York City blacks met to discuss the resolution "that we tender our services to the Governor of this State, to serve during the war, either as firemen . . . to act as a Home Guard, or to go South, if their services should be required." But several speakers opposed the resolution on the ground that earlier offers by blacks had been rejected and that they "did not think that we should offer ourselves to be kicked and insulted as others had been. . . . The whites knew that we were willing to fight, and therefore there was no need of laying ourselves liable to insult, simply for the privilege of saying so." The majority at the meeting agreed, and the resolution was defeated. However, several members of the minority began to drill in a privately hired hall until the chief of police warned that "he could not protect them from popular indigation and assault."

The *New York Weekly Anglo-African* heartily approved the decision to reject the proposed resolution. "Have We a War Policy?" the editor asked, and he answered that if there was one, it did not include blacks. While he insisted that blacks must assist their slave brothers and sisters, it was obvious that "no Governor would allow colored soldiers to muster into service and if he did, the General Government would reject such aid." Therefore the black weekly was "against the policy . . . [of] organiz[ing] volunteer companies." Instead, "let us . . . organize for military purposes . . . procure arms, and hold ourselves as Minute Men to *respond* when the *slave calls.*" What the *Anglo-African* envisaged was a private army of black liberators from the North moving into the South the moment news reached them of a slave uprising.

From his office in Rochester, New York, Frederick Douglass took up the battle for the full participation of blacks in the war. On the first page of the May 1861 issue of *Douglass' Monthly,* there appeared an American eagle and the flag, followed by the stirring slogan—''Freedom for all, or chains for all.'' The leading article carried the title, ''How to End the War.'' Douglass called upon the administration to proclaim freedom to the slaves, to call the slaves and free people of color into service, and organize them *''into a liberating army,* to march into the South and raise the banner of Emancipation among the slaves.'' The slaveholders, he reminded the government, did not hesitate to use Negroes in waging their war of aggression. Blacks (both the free and the slaves) were being impressed to serve the Confederacy in the mills, mines, and industries and were being employed as teamsters, cooks, hospital attendants, and stretcher bearers in the Confederate army. The important work of keeping roads, bridges, and railroads open for the movement of Confederate troops fell to Negro labor groups under the supervision of mounted troops. And the slaveholders openly boasted that the use of black labor in the fields and factories enabled them to send troops to the front without diminishing production behind the lines. Consequently, sound policy, no less than humanity, demanded that the government of the United States turn this powerful force to its own use by being ''as true to liberty as the rebels, who are attempting to batter it down, are true to slavery.'' One Negro regiment carrying the Stars and Stripes into the South would do more to educate the slaves ''as to the nature of the conflict . . . than . . . a thousand preachers.''

Thus, two themes were struck by Douglass from the moment the war started: free the slaves as a war measure and recruit Negroes into the Union army. He urged this policy without compromise. In editorials, speeches, letters, and interviews, he stressed again and again the idea that ''the negro is the key of the situation—the pivot upon which the whole rebellion turns.'' A proclamation of freedom to the slaves would ''smite rebellion in the very seat of its life,'' depriving it of the labor that kept the rebel army supplied with food, clothing, and the sinews of war. And one ''sable'' regiment would have the psychological impact of several white ones. Their color alone would have a more powerful influence than would ''powder and balls.''

Douglass called for petitions and delegations to convince the president that the people would support measures to bring the war to a victorious conclusion. He declared that if he could speak to Lincoln, he would tell him the story of the blacks of Rhode Island and Connecticut who had fought valiantly in the War for Independence and of blacks who had fought side by side with General Jackson in New Orleans. He would tell him that the North needed the same positive convictions that the South possessed and the same will to fight for freedom that southerners displayed in battling for slavery. He would urge him to ally with the pro-Union, antislavery popular forces in the border states rather than relying upon the slaveowners, who had never been friends of the Union and were now doing ''the work of enemies in the garb of friendship.'' He would tell him that the very life of the nation required revolutionary methods and that this was not time "to talk of constitutional power": "We should tell him that this is no time to fight with one hand, when both are needed; that this is no time to fight with your white hand, and allow your black to remain tied."

Influenced by Douglass' brilliant analysis, the *New York Weekly Anglo-African* altered its uncompromising hostility to blacks' offering to serve in the Union army. In the late summer of 1861, it advised its readers to seize arms and to prepare themselves for the government's call. Anticipating a certain amount of disappointment among some blacks over its new stand, the *Anglo-African* explained:

There are men among our people who look upon this as the "white man's war," and such men openly say, let them fight it out among themselves. It is their flag, and their constitution which have been dishonored and set at naught. . . .

This is a huge fallacy. In proof of which let us ask ourselves some questions. . . . What rights have we in the free States? We have the "right to life, liberty and the pursuit of happiness." We have the right to labor, and are secured in the fruits of our labor; we have the right to our wives and our little ones; we have to a large extent the right to educate our children. . . .

Are these rights worth the having? If they are then they are worth defending with all our might, and at any cost. It is illogical, unpatriotic, nay mean and unmanly in us to shrink from the defence of these great rights and privileges. . . . But some will say that these rights of *ours* are not assailed by the South. Are they not? What in short is the programme or platform on which the South would have consent to remain in the Union? It was to spread slavery over all the States and territories. . . .

Hence, talk as we may, we *are* concerned in this fight and our fate hangs upon its issues. The South must be subjugated, or we shall be enslaved. In aiding the Federal government in whatever way we can, we are aiding to secure our own liberty; for this war can only end in the subjugation of the North or of the South. We do not affirm that the North is fighting in behalf of the black man's rights, as such—if this was the single issue, we even doubt whether they would fight at all. But circumstances have been so arranged by the decrees of Providence, that in struggling for their own nationality they are forced to defend our rights. . . . Let us be awake, therefore, brethren; a generous emulation in a common patriotism, and a special call to defend our rights alike bid us to be on the alert to seize arms and drill as soon as the government shall be willing to accept our services.

REASONS FOR REJECTING BLACKS

"Why does the Government reject the negro?" asked Douglass. "Is he not a man? Can he not wield a sword, fire a gun, march and . . . obey orders like any other?" The official administration answer was that this was a war to preserve the Union, not to alter the nation's social conditions, that the enlisting of blacks would seriously alienate the border states and drive them into the Confederacy, and that the conflict would be of short duration and victory could be obtained without the use of black troops. Other arguments were that Negroes would not fight, that whites would refuse to fight with them, that enlistment would slacken, and that the enlistment of blacks would stiffen Southern resistance. Finally, to employ blacks as soldiers would imply their equality with white men.

The initial white response to the arming of blacks was consistent with the widespread racism in Northern society. In his study, "Billy Yank and the Black Folk," Bell Irwin Wiley points out that many Union soldiers "were deeply prejudiced before entering the service," that they enlisted solely to preserve the Union and had no interest in ending slavery, and that "the overwhelming majority of the rank and file appear to have been against the proposal" to enlist blacks. They opposed it because they thought it "unnecessary" and "a threat to white supremacy" and because they believed Negroes "deficient in soldiery qualities." When the blacks of Cleveland petitioned Governor David Todd and offered "two or more regiments of colored men" to replace the "well-drilled" white men guarding "rebel prisoners" so that their services "could be used for better purposes," the governor rejected the offer because of the hostility among Union soldiers to black enlistment. He reminded the petitioners: "Do you know that this is a white man's government; that the white men are able to defend and protect it, and that to enlist a Negro soldier would be to drive every white man out of the service?" In short, the United States was a white man's country, and the whites would fight this war.

FREE BLACKS ACCEPTED IN UNION NAVY

Yet when the Civil War began, a significant number of free black seamen volunteered for sea duty with the Union navy, and they were recruited on the same basis as whites. They were actively employed on federal ships from the start of the war and were utilized at nearly every job available to enlisted men. Moreover, they served aboard ship on an integrated basis.

This did not mean that the navy advocated a policy of racial equality, for the naval authorities and officers shared the prevailing view of Negro inferiority. But the navy's willingness to enlist blacks when the Union army was rejecting their services stemmed from its long history of using Negroes aboard naval vessels. While a newly recruited Union soldier was writing, "We don't want to fight side and side with the nigger. . . . We think we are a too superior race for that," sailors in the navy had a long experience of serving side and side with black shipmates and were willing to continue to do so now that the nation's life was at stake.

The same policy was followed in Washington's navy yard. Michael Shiner, a black navy yard worker, wrote in his diary:

On the first Day of June 1861 on Saturday Justice Clark was Sent Down to the Washington navy yard For to administer the oath of allegiance to the mechanics and the Labouring class of working men with out Distinction of Colour for them to Stand By the Stars and Stripes and defend for the union and captal Dalgreen Present and I believe at that time I Michael Shiner was the first coloured man that taken the oath in Washington D C and that oath Still Remains in my heart and when I taken that oath I taken it in the presence of God without prejudice or enmity to any man And I intend to Sustain that oath with the assistance of the Almighty God until I die for when a man Takes an oath for a Just cause it is more than taking a Drink of water or Sitting Down to his Breakfast

THE NEW FUGITIVE SLAVES

In addition to those Northern free blacks who volunteered for the Union army and actually joined the Union navy, another source of Negro manpower was becoming available to federal authorities. The legend that Southern slaves were indifferent to the course of events was riddled by their mass escapes when approaching Union armies gave them the opportunity. It is true that many families had several loyal slaves, especially the house servants, who did not take advantage of the opportunity to escape and who remained with their owners. Many white families took pride in the faithful servants who turned down opportunities to flee. But these loyal slaves constituted only a small percentage of the whole. Almost as soon as the guns of Fort Sumter quieted, a silent exodus of escaping slaves sought the protection of the Union lines, and the flood mounted with the passing months.

As the blacks deserted the plantations in large numbers, the South's early confidence in the loyalty of the slaves quickly diminished, and the Negroes began to appear in another light. Many letters from the summer of 1862 in *The Children of Pride: A True Story of Georgia and the Civil War* reveal the Confederacy's anxieties about slave loyalties:

The temptation of change, the promise of freedom and pay for labor, is more than most can stand; and no reliance can be placed *certainly* upon any. The safest plan is to put them beyond the reach of temptation . . . by leaving no boats in the water and by keeping guards along the rivers.

This was Reverend Charles Colcock Jones' opinion in July 1862. A few days later, he returned to the theme: "The temptation of cheap goods, freedom, and paid labor cannot be withstood," he told his son, Charles Colcock Jones, Jr., mayor of Savannah, then a Confederate general. In the same letter appeared an ominous note: "They are traitors who may pilot an enemy into your *bedchamber*. They know every road and swamp and creek and plantation in the country, and are the worst of spies. If the absconding is not stopped, the negro property of the county will be of little value."

From this time onward, the slaveowners knew no peace of mind. W.E.B. Du Bois put it well: "Every step the Northern armies took . . . meant fugitive slaves. . . . Wherever the army marched and in spite of all obstacles came the rising tide of slaves seeking freedom. . . . This was not merely the desire to stop work: It was a strike on a wide basis against the conditions of work. It was a general strike that involved directly in the end perhaps a half million people. They wanted to stop the economy of the plantation system, and to do that they left the plantations.'' Bell Irwin Wiley gives no specific figure as to how many slaves ran away to the Union forces during the war. ''But it can be said with safety,'' he adds, ''that the arrival of Union soldiers in any part of the South marked the beginning of a flow of black humanity toward the Federal camp; and that, in many cases, the flow was so great that it carried away the bulk of the male slave population.''

THE ''CONTRABANDS''

One of the first problems confronting military and government officials concerned the question of what to do with the flood of fugitive slaves. General George B. McClellan showed how much of a white man's war it was in the spring of 1861 by ordering his command to return fugitives within their jurisdiction to loyal masters. When McClellan entered western Virginia, he promised to protect slave property and crush any slave insurrection ''with an iron hand.'' At first many commanders, following McClellan's lead in the absence of a clear-cut executive policy to guide them, sent the fugitives back to their owners in accordance with the provisions of the fugitive slave law. Others forbade them to enter the Union lines or permitted masters or their agents to enter the lines to retrieve their property. Some Union navy officers also returned runaway slaves. Commander Thomas Craven, for example, returned twenty Negroes to Southern whites. Others even sold the fugitives back into slavery, pocketing the rewards they received from grateful slaveowners.

But in spite of slave patrols, the slaves continued to flock to the Union army encampments. Union officers sent most of the fugitives back to their masters. Slaveowners tried to scare the slaves by telling them that the Yankees ''kill all niggers.'' But still they came. The increasing number of fugitive slaves forced the Union army to make some use of them.

On May 24, 1861, a report sent to Union army headquarters read:

Three fugitives, the property of Colonel Mallory, commander of the Rebel forces near Hampton, were brought into Fortress Monroe by the picket guard. They represented that they were about to be sent South, and hence sought protection. Major Cary came in with a flag of truce, and claimed their rendition under the ''Fugitive Slave Law'' but was informed by General Butler that, under the peculiar circumstances, he considered the fugitives ''contrabands'' of war.

General Benjamin Butler refused to serve as a slave catcher and return fugitives ''to masters who were in actual war against the government.'' When he learned that the escaped slaves had been employed in building Confederate fortifications, he called them "contrabands of war." This was a technical term applied to military goods sold to an enemy nation by a neutral, but it acquired a new meaning in 1861, and thereafter for several years, all fugitive slaves were referred to as contrabands. They were not returned to their owners; instead, they were put to work in nonmilitary capacities, mostly in building fortifications for wages. By the end of July, over nine thousand such contrabands had sought the safety of the Union lines at Fortress Monroe alone.

The contrabands employed by General Butler were the first of thousands of fugitive slaves who served in labor battalions, which hauled supplies, dug trenches, and built fortifications. In addition, they frequently provided valuable intelligence on the location of Rebel troops and on the terrain in the area in which they had lived. In fact, they were so good as informers that the Confederates would often dress in Union army uniforms and go among the slaves to try to obtain information concerning Yankee troop movements.

A SLIGHT CHANGE IN POLICY

Since there was no national policy for contrabands, each military commander at posts other than Fortress Monroe pursued his own policy regarding the fugitive slaves. But this situation had to change. Northern newspapers carried more and more stories of the South's utilization of black labor for military purposes. While some of them were rumors, many were based on fact. Early in May 1861, the press reported that one hundred "negro soldiers" received blankets, shoes, and other provisions in Petersburg, Virginia, before their departure for Norfolk, where they were to be used in the "defense of Virginia soil and principles." Free blacks were reported to have offered their services to the Confederate cause in Nashville, Tennessee, and Amelia County, Virginia. Early in July, the press reported that on June 28, 1861, the Tennessee State General Assembly had passed the first act in the country to draft blacks for military service. The act had the following provisions: (1) All free black males between the ages of fifteen and fifty were eligible for the draft into military labor units; (2) each laborer was to receive eighteen dollars, clothing, and rations; and (3) sheriffs were to arrest those who refused to serve and charge these persons with a punishable misdemeanor.

In August, the press reported that batteries, rifle pits, and other military works, which had held back the advance of the Union army at Bull Run and elsewhere, "were constructed almost exclusively by Negroes." Although commentators insisted that the Confederacy did not have a single armed black company in the field (an accurate evaluation), rumors of armed blacks in Confederate uniforms persisted and grew. "We have had accounts of black regiments at Manassas, Memphis, New Orleans, in Mississippi, and in Alabama," cried the *Cleveland Morning Leader* in alarm on August 6, 1861, "and now the twentieth

New York regiment has been attacked by a body of seven hundred negro infantry in the vicinity of Fortress Monroe.''

Whatever the accuracy of these reports, the fact is that by the summer of 1861 the Confederate states were exploiting black labor to the full. Confederate officers used both their own slaves and captured blacks as teamsters and servants in the Confederate army. It is true that some generals did not trust blacks with their supplies and arms ''because blacks were known to be Union spies, and to run straight for the Yankee lines if they got half the chance.'' But the majority did use the blacks, and that use grew as the Confederates intensified their efforts to defend against approaching Yankee armies.

While it was still unwilling to accept blacks in the Union army, the administration was compelled by constant pressure to enact the First Confiscation Act of August 7, 1861. This measure, entitled ''An act of Congress to Confiscate Property used for insurrectionary purposes,'' provided that any slaves who had been employed by the Confederacy to help in the ''insurrection against the Government of the United States'' should be declared free once they fled to the protection of the U.S. forces. Thus a uniform policy in dealing with contrabands was finally emerging.

When General Butler outlined the policy he intended to follow to Secretary of War Edwin M. Stanton, he wrote: ''In a loyal State I should put down a servile insurrection, but in a state of rebellion I would confiscate that which was used to oppose my arms.'' General John C. Frémont, commander of the Western Department of St. Louis, did not make so fine a distinction. His military situation following the Union defeat at Wilson's Creek in the summer of 1861 was desperate. As a war measure, Frémont ordered martial law throughout Missouri on August 30, 1861, and proclaimed that ''the property, real and personal, of all persons in . . . Missouri who shall take up arms against the United States . . . is declared to be confiscated to public use, and their slaves . . . are hereby declared freemen.''

Even critics of Frémont admit that the people of the North hailed his action. ''The popular outburst endorsing this order was tremendous and spontaneous,'' writes T. Harry Williams, one of these critics. But Lincoln was not prepared to take the step to transform the war from one for preservation of the Union to a struggle for emancipation. The president informed Frémont that it was highly dangerous to confiscate property and liberate slaves of traitorous owners, for this would help turn friendly southerners against the Union. The general was instructed to modify his order to conform with the August 7 Confiscation Act. Shortly thereafter, Lincoln also voided the unauthorized military declaration by General David Hunter, which had given freedom to slaves in Georgia, South Carolina, and Florida.

Blacks were both depressed and enraged by Lincoln's orders. The *Weekly Anglo-African* denounced the president for having issued a decree ''which hurls back into the hell of slavery the thousands in Missouri rightfully set free by the proclamation of General Frémont, which deprives the cause of the Union of its chiefest hold upon the heart of the public, and which gives to the rebels 'aid and comfort' greater than they could have gained from any other earthly source.'' But this was mild compared to the denunciation voiced by Frederick Douglass. Many blunders had been committed by the administration since Fort Sumter, he cried, but this was the worst. The administration had been six months in office and what had it done? Had it set forth any principle? Any avowal of purpose? Not a line, not a word. The only step ''indicating an anti-slavery tendency on the part of the Government'' was the somewhat half-hearted approval of General Butler's ruling that slaves who had flocked into Union lines as contrabands of war should not be returned to their owners. On the other hand, when other Union officers returned all fugitive slaves and permitted owners of slaves to cross the Potomac and recover their property, the administration had assented silently. And it was only with the greatest reluctance that the president had signed the Confiscation Act of August 7, 1861, which granted freedom to slaves used by the rebels in prosecuting the war.

Now at last, Douglass declared, General Frémont had cleared the atmosphere with his bold proclamation. The president and his cabinet should have thanked him for furnishing ''an opportunity to convince the country and the world of their earnestness, that they have no terms for traitors . . . and that the rebels must be put down at all hazards, and in the most summary and exemplary way.'' Instead, the president had taken a stand that could ''only dishearten the friends of the Government and strengthen its enemies.'' Lincoln's letter to Frémont disapproving his act contained the key to ''all our misfortunes in connection with the rebellion.''

Douglass would not accept the argument of administration supporters that approval of Frémont's proclamation would have driven the slaveholders of the border states into the arms of the rebels, since the proclamation was directed only against slaveholding rebels. But even if it did, he would consider it a gain for the Union cause. He was weary of having the border state argument hurled at him every time he talked of emancipation. ''From the beginning,'' he declared, ''these Border Slave States have been the mill-stone about the neck of the Government, and their so-called loyalty has been the very best shield to the treason of the Cotton States.''

Reverend J. P. Campbell of Trenton, New Jersey, a prominent official of the African Methodist Episcopal church, explained Lincoln's action simply:

1st.   The President is not now, and never was, either an abolitionist, or an anti-slavery man.

2nd.   He has no quarrel whatever with the South, upon the slavery question.

3rd.   He, his cabinet, and all of his official organs most steadily proclaim that this is not a war against slavery, but a war for the Union, to save slavery in the Union.

Given this situation there was no reason to hope for any real change in the future. But even as attention was being focused on Lincoln's countermanding of Frémont's proclamation, events were occurring on the naval front that indicated important changes were taking place.

18

End of the White Man's War

SLAVES ACCEPTED IN UNION NAVY

At first, the navy also hesitated to enlist slaves. In addition to the continuing administration policy of not wishing to alienate the four border slave states still in the Union by openly recruiting slaves, there were the matters of white prejudice and the lack of naval skills on the part of many of the slaves. However, in July 1861, Commander James Glisson of the *Mount Vernon,* which was patrolling the waters of Virginia, informed his superior that contrabands were arriving daily and refusing to leave, that they brought valuable information with them, and that they were capable of performing useful work. He reported that he provided them with rations on his own responsibility, but his supplies would soon be exhausted. What should he do next?

On July 18, 1861, S. H. Stringham, flag officer of the Atlantic blockading squadron, sent these reports to Secretary of the Navy Gideon Welles and added his own opinion: "If negroes are to be used in this contest, I have no hesitation they should be used to preserve the government not to destroy it. These men are destitute, shall I ration them, they may be serviceable on board our store ships." Stringham's point was well taken for the Confederates were making extensive use of slaves in constructing fortifications and in running the Union blockade. At the same time, there was a growing need for men in the Union navy, and the contrabands could help solve the problem. Welles was forced to act. At first he replied that while it was not the "policy of the Government to invite or encourage this class of desertions . . . yet under the circumstances, no other course than that pursued by Commander Glisson could be adopted without violating every principle of humanity. To return them would be impolitic as well as cruel, and as you remark, they may be made serviceable on board our storeships; you will do well to employ them."

But as the floodtide continued and grew, this proved to be inadequate. In August came report after report similar to the following:

a small open boat [with five Negroes in it] came alongside mine demanding food and protection . . . discovered an open boat containing four negroes, with a white flag flying on the staff, and pulling for the ship. I took them on board, found them intelligent; they gave me useful information, and one of them informed me he had been a pilot to the steam brig. . . . We now have sixteen negroes on board this vessel; who are consuming our provisions and water faster than I think is desirable. . . . four fine-looking negroes, contraband, of war, have just arrived.

So it was that on September 25, 1861, the secretary of the navy officially authorized the employment of contrabands on board ships of war. As Welles informed his commanders:

The Department finds it necessary to adopt a regulation with respect to the large and increasing number of persons of color, common known as "contraband" now subsisted at the navy yards and on board of ships of war. They can neither be expelled from the service to which they have resorted nor can they be maintained unemployed; and it is not proper that they should be compelled to render necessary and regular service without a State compensation. You are therefore authorized, when their services can be useful, to enlist them for naval service under the same forms and regulations as apply to other enlistments. They will be allowed, however, no higher rating than boys, at a compensation of $10 per month and one ration a day.

The lower enlisted rank structure of the U.S. Navy in 1861 included third class boy, second class boy, first class boy, landsman, ordinary seaman, and seaman. Sailors progressed from rank to rank according to experience and age. In the "boy" ratings, age was the determining factor.

The contrabands were to be enlisted as boys at $8, $9, or $10 per month and one ration. "The enlistment of Contrabands was not a measure for racial equality, but a pragmatic move to gain more men and realize some return on the food and clothing given the blacks," concludes Lawrence Valuska in his study, "The Negro in the Union Navy, 1861–1865." However, Herbert Aptheker, in "Negroes in the Union Navy," points out that "these conditions would seem attractive to the Negro as compared to the offers of the army," and he notes that in October 1861, the Department of Virginia ordered that all contrabands employed as servants of officers or others were to receive their subsistence plus $8 per month ($4 for women) and that other Negroes under the protection of the troops, not employed as servants, were put to work and received, in the case of boys (from twelve to eighteen years) and infirm men, $5 per month, and ablebodied men $10 plus rations. (Even then, racist Union soldiers complained that contrabands were being pampered by the army.) Hence, it is not surprising,

Aptheker concludes, that a considerable number of contrabands found service in the Union navy desirable.

The squadron commanders quickly responded to Welles' order of September 25, 1861, and sent out notices to their junior officers to begin active recruiting. Since the Union army had not begun to recruit any blacks, the navy had the field to itself. By the middle of 1862 the demand for men was growing, and the navy was openly soliciting contraband recruits. On July 2, 1862, the secretary of the navy wrote to his squadron commanders informing them they would have to enlist contrabands since no more men could be sent; enlistments were not keeping pace with the needs of the service. (Among the reasons for this was the fact that enlistments in the navy, unlike those in the army, carried no bounty payments.) As the shortage of men became acute, the enlistment of contrabands became critical. By late 1862, all squadron commanders were eagerly employing contrabands.

Blacks who sought asylum aboard Union ships were not compelled to join the navy. They could either enlist or seek employment elsewhere. If the contrabands did not want to enlist in the navy, they were sent off the ships. Negroes not working for the navy would not be fed and clothed.

The contrabands also greatly aided the Union navy by providing military intelligence. The types of data received included reports on hidden weapons, supplies, and boats; Confederate plans of attack; and navigational data. In September 1862, six contrabands were picked up by Lieutenant Commander D. L. Braine. They told Braine that the Confederate gunboat *North Carolina* was to be launched within the week and that the gunboat was iron clad down to the water's edge. They further reported that the ship's guns were to be mounted on a covered deck, and its engines were to come out of the steamer *Uncle Ben*. Since the contrabands came from Wilmington City, North Carolina, they were able to discuss in detail the fortifications in and around that city. They pinpointed the forts on the Cape Fear River and pointed out where the Confederates had obstructed the river and how they could be bypassed. One of the contrabands told of an armory being developed in Fayetteville, North Carolina, and what type of weapons were being made. The contrabands also gave the officer information about several ships that had slipped through the Union blockade and how this had been accomplished. Union officers relied on this information extensively and as a result were able to conduct the blockade with greater efficiency.

The use of contrabands by the armed forces as laborers and intelligence agents increased in the spring of 1862. On March 30, 1862, President Lincoln approved a law passed by Congress entitled "An Act to Make an Additional Article of War." It prohibited all officers or persons in the military or naval services from using any of the forces under their commands "for the purpose of returning fugitives from service or labor who may have escaped from any persons for whom such service or labor is claimed to be due." Fugitive slaves escaping to the Union army or navy were not to be returned to their claimants.

SOME BLACK HEROES

The story of James Lawson is one of many about contrabands who made a major contribution to the war effort. Born a slave near Hampton, Virginia, Lawson left his wife and four children behind when he fled North shortly after the outbreak of hostilities. He worked briefly in the Union army. After the navy began to allow contrabands to enlist, Lawson shipped aboard the *Freeborn,* a gunboat in the Potomac flotilla under the command of Lieutenant Samuel Magraw. As soon as Lawson came aboard, Magraw sent him back ashore on a scouting expedition through Rebel fortifications in order to "test his reliability." Lawson passed the test.

A short while later, Magraw put Lawson ashore again below Mount Vernon in Virginia, and Lawson scouted inland for several miles but ran into Rebel sentries and was plucked off the shore by the captain's gig while in the midst of a hail of Rebel fire. By this time, Lawson had won Magraw's confidence and respect, and the naval officer agreed to land him in Virginia on a highly personal mission: the freeing of his family. Lawson slipped in, collected his wife and children, and led them to a rendezvous point where they were picked up by the gunboat.

Lawson was so good at his work behind enemy lines that high-ranking officers such as Generals Daniel E. Sickles and Joseph Hooker often picked him for difficult assignments. General Sickles sent Lawson on one mission to scout Rebel shore batteries near Fredericksburg and gave him his own pistol to carry for protection. Lawson took two other blacks with him. One was killed when they were discovered by Rebel sentries. Afterward Lawson hid in a hollow near a fence, crept through the woods to the shore, and was picked up by a boat after the sentries abandoned the pursuit.

Shortly after this, Lawson wound up on a new gunboat, the *Satellite,* which was ordered to Newborn, North Carolina. He and other blacks on the vessel proved as able at fighting as they were as scouts. The skipper of the *Satellite* reported that they manned his big guns "with more agility and skill in time of action than any white seaman he had ever seen."

The August 1861 issue of *Douglass' Monthly* carried a heading reading, "A Black Hero." The article told the story of William Tillman, a steward aboard the schooner *S. J. Waring,* which was captured by the Confederate privateer *Jeff Davis* near the waters of New York. The captain and the mate of the *Waring* were sent home, and a new crew was put on board. Three of the original crew, two seamen and William Tillman, the black steward, were retained. Tillman learned from conversations he overheard that the vessel was to be taken to Charleston, where he would be sold as a slave.

Tillman organized a plot to capture the vessel and return it to New York City, but only one of his fellow prisoners, a German named Hedding, agreed to take part in the dangerous plan. When the *Waring* was within fifty miles of Charleston and the crew was sleeping, Tillman seized a hatchet, killed the Rebel captain, mate, and second mate, and declared himself master of the ship. Although neither Tillman nor his companions knew anything about navigation, they managed to reach New York.

Tillman received a hero's welcome as well as $6,000 in prize money from the *Waring*'s owners. Horace Greeley wrote in his *New York Tribune* that the nation was indebted to the black steward "for the first vindication of its honor on the sea," and Douglass, in his *Monthly*, noted caustically that Tillman's great achievement occurred

while our Government still refuses to acknowledge the just demands of the negro and takes all possible pains to assure "our Southern brethren" that it does not intend to interfere in any with this kind of property; while the assistance of colored citizens in suppressing the slave-holder's rebellion is preremptorily and insultingly declined.

Tillman's bloody hatchet was placed on display at P. T. Barnum's American Museum. While visitors were viewing it, Jacob Garrick, a black cook aboard the schooner *Enchantress*, emulated Tillman's feat. Sailing from Boston to Cuba, the *Enchantress* was also overtaken by the *Jeff Davis*. Removing the crew except for Garrick, the Rebels took over. Hailed by a Union man-of-war, they passed themselves off as the original Union crew, but Garrick, risking death, gave away the scheme. He jumped overboard and cried out, "A captured vessel of the privateer *Jeff Davis*, and they are taking her into Charleston." The man-of-war's boat picked Garrick out of the water, the crew was seized, and the *Enchantress* was returned to Boston where the black cook received a hero's welcome.

The most famous of the black heroes in the early phase of the war was Robert Smalls, a twenty-three-year-old slave who, one night in May 1862, piloted the *Planter*, a former cotton boat converted into a Confederate armed vessel, past the fortifications in Charleston harbor to the Union naval force outside. In May 1864, at the AME General Conference in Philadelphia, Smalls told the fabulous story:

While at the wheel of the *Planter*, it occurred to me that I could not only secure my own freedom but that of numbers of my comrades. Moreover, I thought the *Planter* might be of some use to "Uncle Abe." I was not long in making my thoughts known to my wife. She desired to know the consequences in case I should be caught. I replied, "I shall be shot." "It is a risk, but you and I and our little ones must be free. I will go," said she, "for where you die I will die."

I reported plans to the crew (all colored) and secured their secrecy and cooperation. On May 13, 1862, we took on board several large guns at the Atlantic Dock. At evening of that day, the Captain went home, leaving the boat in my care.

At half past 3 o'clock in the morning of the 14th, I left the Atlantic Dock with the *Planter*, took on board my family and several other families, then proceeded down Charleston River slowly. On reaching Fort Sumter, I gave the signal which was answered from the fort, thereby giving permission to pass. I then made speed for the blockading fleet. When out of range of Sumter's guns, I hoisted a white flag and at 5 A.M. reached a

U. S. blockading vessel, commandered by Captain Nichols, to whom I turned over the *Planter.*

Smalls remained aboard the *Planter,* first as pilot and later as captain. In September 1862, the *Washington Republican* published a report that Smalls had applied to Senator Samuel Clarke Pomeroy of New Jersey for assistance in securing passage to Central America for himself and family. The black hero indignantly denied the report, writing to the *Republican:*

I wish it understood that I made no such application. . . . After waiting, apparently in vain, for many years for our deliverance, a party consisting of nine men, myself included, of the city of Charleston conferred freedom on our wives, five women and three children, and to the Government of the United States we gave the *Planter,* a gunboat which cost nearly thirty thousand dollars, together with six large guns, from a 21-pounder howitzer to a 100-pound Parrot rifle.

We are all now in the service in the navy, under the command of our true friend, Rear Admiral Dupont, where we wish to serve till the rebellion and slavery are alike crushed out forever.

CONTINUING DEBATE OVER RECRUITING BLACK SOLDIERS

The heroism of the black soldiers, cooks, and pilots played an important part in mobilizing public sentiment behind the recruitment of black soldiers. Black leaders, white abolitionists, and Radical Republicans continued to insist that the war could not be won and the Union restored without the abolition of slavery and without employing blacks to fight in the Union army. Thaddeus Stevens, the Radical Republican in Congress, kept arguing that slavery would have to be abolished in order to win the Civil War, that the army must enlist black troops, and that unless this was done soon, the Confederacy would triumph. Hailing Stevens' call, Frederick Douglass commented: "The side which first summons the negro to its aid will conquer."

"No measure could panic-smite the rebels like the use of black troops," the abolitionist *Oberlin Evangelist* insisted on July 16, 1862. "Let us have a new programme," it suggested, "and at the head of it, *colored regiments.*" This would deny the South nearly 4 million workers and would kill slavery, thereby taking supplies, food, and war materials away from the Rebels. "Black regiments," the *Evangelist* cried, "are the arm of the Almighty to decide the issues of this rebellion."

But others besides the abolitionists were now raising the same demand. On November 5, 1861, the *Cleveland Morning Leader* reminded its readers that in 1815 Andrew Jackson, a slaveowner, had asked for free blacks to aid in the defense of New Orleans. It asked what would be wrong if the North should follow his example and "use any club" that served "when there were heads that needed breaking." Five months later, the same newspaper was more explicit. "The rebels have deemed the blacks fit to bear arms against the Government," it editorialized, "and there is no reason why they are not equally fit to fight in its support."

The *Cincinnati Commercial* disagreed: "We have no squeamishness on the subject of arming negroes, provided it should appear indispensable—profitable." "Will it pay?" was the only question to be considered. "Our own judgment," it concluded, "is that it would not—certainly not outside of South Carolina." But this was mild compared to the open racism of other papers, particularly of the pro-Southern, or Copperhead, variety, which insisted that to employ blacks as soldiers would be a step toward racial equality, that it would be an insult to whites to have them wear the same uniform and receive the same pay as blacks, especially former slaves, and that their presence in the ranks would both cause white soldiers to desert and discourage others from enlisting.

But Parson Brownlow voiced the opinion of more and more Northern whites when he insisted late in October 1862 that although the North was not fighting for blacks, "let us . . . give them [the Confederates] their fill of the nigger and use him until they cry 'enough.' "

RECRUITING OF BLACK SOLDIERS

In July 1862, Lincoln's call for 300,000 volunteers met with a disheartening response; not enough white volunteers came forward. That same month, Congress passed an act revoking the provisions of the militia law excluding blacks and authorizing the president to use Negroes as laborers or in any other capacity he saw fit. But Lincoln, although willing to have blacks serve with the Union army as laborers, still refused to sanction their employment as combat soldiers. On August 4, Lincoln called for an additional 300,000 men to serve for a nine-month period. Only 87,588 men responded.

On August 5, 1862, the *New York Tribune* reported Lincoln's reply to the offer of Negro troops from Indiana. His reply was similar to his previous responses to offers of black regiments from Masachusetts and Rhode Island. The president told the deputation, which included two members of Congress, that "he was not prepared to go to the length of enlisting negroes as soldiers. He would employ all colored men offered as laborers, but would not promise to make soldiers of them." The report continued:

The deputation came away satisfied that it is the determination of the Government not to arm negroes unless some new and more pressing emergency arises. The President argued that the nation could not afford to lose Kentucky at this crisis, and gave it as his opinion that to arm the negroes would turn 50,000 bayonets from the loyal Border States that were for us against us.

But while Lincoln hesitated and while politicians, clergymen, and editors debated the issue of black participation in the Union army, the military commanders were acting, and several of them, operating on their own initiative, began to organize small units of blacks. In May 1862 in South Carolina, General David Hunter, without permission, undertook the recruitment of blacks for military service. Although not sanctioned officially, Hunter formed these men, mostly ex-slaves, into the First South Carolina Volunteer Regiment. The troops were used mainly in a support capacity for building bridges and digging trenches. Lack of War Department approval and support forced the disbanding of the organization in early August, with the exception of one company, which continued on active duty.

In August 1862, General James H. Lane, the colorful Kansas Jayhawker (a term applied to an antislavery guerrilla fighter in the Kansas-Missouri border disputes of the late 1850s), opened a Leavenworth recruiting office to enlist white, red, and black men. Lane informed Secretary of War Edwin M. Stanton of his action and asked if the administration objected. Although the president opposed Lane's recruiting of black men, enlistments continued.

General Benjamin Butler enlisted three regiments of black troops when his seizure of New Orleans was threatened by a Confederate attack in August 1862. Butler insisted that he would recruit only free blacks, but in practice, no one asked the recruits if they had been free or slave before the war. On September 1, Butler was able to write to Stanton that he expected within ten days to have a regiment of one thousand strong, "the darkest of whom is about the complexion of the late Mr. Webster." The War Department did not give Butler any specific approval for his action. Nevertheless, in rapid succession, he mustered in the First, Second, and Third Native Guards with their own officers.

Late in August 1862, a radical change occurred in War Department policy. This time, Secretary of War Stanton took the initiative by officially sanctioning the recruitment of blacks. On August 25, Stanton, in orders to General Rufus Saxton, military governor of Beauford, South Carolina, authorized him to arm and equip not more than five thousand blacks as part of the volunteer forces of the nation. Using Hunter's disbanded troops as a nucleus, Saxton organized an all-black regiment—the First South Carolina Volunteers—and appointed Thomas Wentworth Higginson, the Boston abolitionist and friend and associate of John Brown, as the commander.

THE BLACK BRIGADE OF CINCINNATI

As Confederate troops moved into Kentucky in August 1862, fear mounted in Cincinnati across the Ohio River. After a Union defeat in Richmond, Kentucky, Mayor George Hatich, in a proclamation issued on September 2, called "every man, of every age . . . citizen or alien" to assemble at their "usual place of voting" to organize for self-defense. Blacks were placed in a dilemma. Since they could not vote, they had no "usual place of voting." Were they, then, expected to respond?

Peter H. Clark recalled that a black delegation approached a policeman and asked: "Does the Mayor desire colored men to report for service in the city defense?'' The officer replied: ''You know d——d well he doesn't mean you. Niggers aren't citizens . . . all he wants is for you niggers to keep quiet.''

Local commander General Lew Wallace intended, however, to use black laborers in fortifications, but blacks were unaware of his desire. Rather than give them the opportunity to volunteer, the regular police force, composed mainly of Irishmen, went from house to house in the black community, searching closets, cellars, and garrets, arresting ''old and young, sick and well,'' and dragging them into the streets. The police marched their black captives like felons to a central location on Plum Street, where they were kept under guard.

Few of the victims knew why they were being repressed. By September 2, most of the city's black male population had been taken across the river into Kentucky, where General Wallace had decided to erect fortifications on the hills overlooking Newport and Covington. Cincinnatians, black and white, were ordered to help, but blacks were separated into small groups, and many of them feared they would be captured and enslaved. This harsh treatment continued until September 4, when General Wallace placed William M. Dickson in command of the Cincinnati blacks.

Dickson's Black Brigade recruited nearly a thousand blacks from Cincinnati and other parts of Ohio, and they operated as a civilian battalion working on the defenses. About three hundred were assigned to duties outside Dickson's jurisdiction. The official Black Brigade, under Dickson's command, included 706 blacks who were grouped into labor companies averaging forty-two men.

After the Black Brigade was organized on a quasi-military basis, Dickson marched the ''companies'' back to Cincinnati so that they could say farewell to their families before they departed for camp. But he had not anticipated the rage aroused among the Irish policemen by the sight of the Black Brigade. That evening, many blacks were arrested, beaten, and jailed. To get his men released, Dickson had to obtain a ''peremptory order'' from General Wallace ''prohibiting the arrest of any colored man, except for crime.''

The next morning over seven hundred black Cincinnatians reported for duty, this time with enthusiasm and under no coercion. The brigade was presented with a U.S. flag inscribed ''The Black Brigade of Cincinnati.''

From September 5 through 20, the brigade constructed ''miles of military roads, miles of rifle pits, cut down hundreds of acres of the largest and loftiest forest trees [and] built magazines and forts.'' One Union army commander reported that the blacks were ''the most efficient laborers on the fortifications.'' Some worked far in advance of the Union lines and came under Confederate sniper fire.

Most Black Brigadiers were eager to serve as combat troops, and the glory the brigade achieved through hard work on the fortifications, after the initial disgraceful conduct of the police and other city officials, helped them achieve their objective. ''Its service,'' wrote Edgar A. Toppin, ''proved to be an important step toward the use of black troops.'' That September, the *Cincinnati Daily Gazette* carried an editorial unstintingly praising the Black Brigade's accomplishments. Its service, the editorial concluded, "ends the idea of a white man's war."

FIRST MILITARY ACTION BY BLACK TROOPS

During the first week of October 1862, some of General James H. Lane's black troops participated in raiding missions into Missouri. Toward the end of the month, five companies of the First Kansas Colored Regiment met a Confederate guerrilla force near Butler, Missouri. The blacks fought well, and the *Chicago Tribune* correspondent expressed the belief that it was "useless to talk any more about negro courage." The news that black troops had demonstrated ability in battle received wide press coverage.

Both major attention was focused upon the First South Carolina Volunteers. These were not free blacks but former slaves from South Carolina, organized into a black regiment. Their officer, Thomas Wentworth Higginson, was a white abolitionist, and he wrote later:

There is no doubt that for many months the fate of the whole movement for colored soldiers rested on the behavior of this one regiment. A mutiny, an extensive desertion, an act of severe discipline, a Bull Run panic, a simple defeat, might have blasted the whole movement for arming the blacks.

One officer, an associate of Higginson, commented on his first encounter with the black volunteers: "The average plantation negro was a hard-working specimen, with about as much of the soldier to be seen in him as there was in the angel of Michaelangelo's block of marble before he applied his chisel." But, he went on, after drilling and teaching, "the plantation manners, the awkward bowing and scraping . . . with hat under arm and with averted look," were exchanged for "the upright form, the open face, the gentlemanly address and soldierly salute." In short, the First South Carolina Volunteers proved that the freed slaves were able to learn and master the complexities of warfare, and in so doing, they made a tremendous contribution in convincing the nation that the contrabands, together with free blacks, should be allowed to make their contribution to ensure a Union victory.

On March 30, 1864, General Lane reminded critics of President Lincoln that if the chief executive had ordered blacks into service earlier, white soldiers would have mutinied. "Not till thousands of them [whites] had been slain, and other thousands wounded and maimed," Lane pointed out, "did they give a reluctant assent to receive the aid of a black auxiliary." In most cases, personal prejudices had not altered, but simple pragmatism had won out over racism. It also transformed the war from one to simply preserve the Union to a war to preserve the Union by ending slavery.

19

Two Proclamations and a Day of Jubilee

CONSTITUTIONAL OR REVOLUTIONARY WAR?

At the beginning of the Civil War, the official policy of the Lincoln administration was that it was merely pledged to restore the Union to what it was before the opening of hostilities. Mention of slavery was to be avoided, and the Crittenden resolution, adopted in July 1861, declared that the war was not being fought for any "purpose of overthrowing or interfering with the rights or established institution of these States, but to defend and maintain the supremacy of the Constitution and to preserve the Union." Determined to mollify the border states and keep them in the Union, Lincoln turned a deaf ear to pleas that the war be turned into a war against slavery and that Negroes be recruited into the Union army.

Although it was often shaken, Frederick Douglass' faith that the war would result in an end to slavery remained intact. Even when Union soldiers seemed more concerned with hunting fugitives than shooting Rebels and when General George B. McClellan assured the slaveowners that his army would not interfere with their chattels and would "on the contrary, with an iron hand, crush any attempt at insurrection on their part," Douglass still believed that "the mission of the war was the liberation of the slave as well as the salvation of the Union."

This conviction did not stem from any single event or group of events. Rather it was the result of his fundamental understanding of what he called "the very core and vital element and philosophy of the strife." The American people and their government might refuse to recognize this for a time, but in the end the "inexorable logic of events" would compel the recognition of the truth that it was impossible to separate freedom for the slaves from victory for the Union. The end of slavery would be due "less to the virtue of the North than to the villainy of the South." The logic of the war itself would provide the necessary education. When the Union army had sustained defeat after defeat and after thousands of lives and millions of dollars had been sacrificed to the mistaken policy of expediency, the people and the government would be forced to recognize that the rebellion was "a war for and against slavery, and that it can never be effectually put down till one or the other of these vital forces is destroyed."

"Events themselves drive to the promulgation of the decisive slogan—*the emancipation of the slaves*," Karl Marx wrote in the Vienna *Presse* of November 7, 1861. The same dialectical approach to the basic issues of the Civil War that was revealed in Douglass' analysis led Marx to note in a letter to his colleague and coworker, Friedrich Engels, in which he chided him for his lack of faith in the final victory of the North as a result of its vacillating policies and its early defeats!

In my opinion all this will take another turn. In the end the North will make war seriously, adopt revolutionary methods and throw over the domination of the single border slave statesmen. A single Negro regiment would have a remarkable effect on Southern nerves. . . .

The long and short of the business seems to me to be that a war of this kind must be conducted on revolutionary lines, while the Yankees have so far been trying to conduct it constitutionally.

THE "SLOW COACH" PICKS UP SPEED

In 1864, in explaining the Emancipation Proclamation and his decision to recruit Negro soldiers into the Union army, Lincoln declared: "I claim not to have controlled events, but confess plainly that events have controlled me." Three years earlier, Frederick Douglass had written of Lincoln's administration: "It has been from the first, and must be to the last, borne along on the broad current of events. Its doctrines, its principles, and its measures are all subject to the modifying power of the great current." This was the basis of his faith, the foundation of his hopes. It was up to the people to bring the power of "this great current" to bear upon the government. And it was up to the abolitionists to educate the people on the home front and in the Union army to support a program that would bring freedom to the slaves and victory to the Union. Slowly—very slowly—but persistently, the "slow coach at Washington" moved in the direction of transforming the war into a war against slavery.

Two distinct aspects of the slave trade were destroyed by the Civil War. The domestic slave trade suffered a fatal blow early in the conflict. Slave trading in Alexandria, Virginia, for example, came to an abrupt end on May 24, 1861, as federal troops occupied the Confederate city without any opposition. George Kephart had remained active in the slave trade up to this very time, and he barely escaped from the city as federal troops occupied it. When they arrived at the slave headquarters in Duke Street, the pen was in disarray, and an old slave was still chained to the floor. He was promptly released and given his freedom. The slave pen continued in use, but not as a quarter for slaves in the domestic slave trade. It became a military prison housing captured Confederate soldiers.

At first it appeared that the war would open the way for an increase in the African slave trade. In August 1861, flag officer William Inman, commander of the U.S. Navy's African Squadron, received orders disbanding the squadron. Secretary of the Navy Gideon Welles needed Inman's cruisers to help blockade the Confederate ports. (Indeed, the secretary had also recalled the East India, Mediterranean, and Brazil squadrons.) Soon after receiving the orders, Inman began dispatching his warships to the United States, and by the end of the summer, only the sloop of war *Saratoga* remained on the station.

The effect on the slave trade of the demise of the African Squadron was immediately observed in the increase in the number of ships sailing from Africa with slaves on board. But if slave traders believed that the field was now open for them to operate freely, they soon learned they were mistaken. The Lincoln administration made clear its determination not to tolerate the trade. The president refused to mitigate Captain Nathaniel P. Gordon's sentence for commandeering an American slave ship. On February 2, 1862, Gordon was hanged—the first and only slave trader to suffer the death penalty under the 1819 law, which made piracy in slave trading punishable by death.

On June 7, 1862, the Lincoln administration took a step that really hit hard at the African slave trade. The United States and Great Britain concluded a treaty, kept secret at the time, that granted to each party the right to search the merchant vessels of either nation in African waters. This practice, which had been long repudiated by successive administrations in the United States, was finally to be permitted. Mixed courts, similar to those provided for in previous treaties concluded by Great Britain and several other European powers, were to be set up to try vessels captured by the cruisers of either Britain or the United States. The United States had finally done what it had vowed it would never do. Whether, as has been suggested, the motive was to woo Britain to support the Union, the important fact is that the Treaty of 1862 was a turning point in the effort to suppress the Atlantic slave trade.

On March 31, 1862, Lincoln signed a bill forbidding the Union army or navy to return fugitive slaves. Any officer violating the law would "be discharged from service and be forever ineligible to any appointment on the military or naval service of the United States." During an interview held that same month, Senator Charles Sumner of Massachusetts asked Lincoln the following question: "Do you know who is at this moment the largest slaveholder in the United States? It is Abraham Lincoln, for he holds all the 300,000 slaves of the District of Columbia." Congress was then debating a bill calling for the abolition of slavery in the district, with compensation to the slaveholders. The measure encountered bitter opposition from border state slaveholders, and their sympathizer, Senator Willard Saulsbury of Delaware, cried:

Senators, abandon now, at once and forever, your schemes of world philanthropy and universal emancipation, proclaim to the people of this whole country everywhere that you mean to preserve the Union as established by the fathers of the Republic, and the rights of the people as secured by the Constitution they helped to frame, and your Union can never be destroyed; but go on with your wild schemes of emancipation, throw doubt and suspicion in every man simply because he fails to look at your questions of wild philanthropy as you do, and the God of heaven only knows, after wading through scenes before which those of the French revolution "pale their ineffectual fires," what ultimately may be the result.

But popular pressure for the abolition of slavery in the nation's capital was too strong to be diverted by dire predictions of a reign of terror. On March 30, 1862, Senator Sumner, who, with Henry Wilson, the junior senator from Massachusetts, was most active in pushing the measure, delivered a notable address urging its speedy adoption. "It is the first installment," Sumner declared, "of the great debt which we all owe to an enslaved race, and will be recognized as one of the victories of humanity." The effect, he predicted, would soon be felt throughout the South. "What God and nature decree, rebellion cannot arrest," he concluded.

On April 3, 1862, the bill passed the Senate. Eight days later, it received final approval in the House. On April 16, the president signed the bill outlawing slavery in the District of Columbia and providing $300 in compensation to slaveholders for each slave emancipated under the act.

While some black and white abolitionists bitterly opposed the idea of compensating slaveowners, viewing it as a recognition of their right to hold human beings as property, Frederick Douglass called for hosannahs: "Let high swelling anthems (such as tuned the hearts and thrilled the hearts of ancient Israel, when they shouted to heaven the glad tidings of their deliverance from Egyptian bondage) now roll along the earth and sky." But less than a month later, the cheers died when the administration took a backward step. On May 9, 1862, General Davis Hunter, commanding the Department of the South, issued an order proclaiming that "slavery and martial law in a free country being altogether compatible, the slaves in Georgia, Florida, and South Carolina are therefore declared free." But on May 19, even before receiving official notice of Hunter's order but having learned of it through the newspapers, the president issued a message declaring the order unauthorized and null and void.

Then on June 19, 1862, Lincoln took another step forward. He approved a measure of Congress entitled "An Act to secure freedom to all persons within the territories of the United States." It provided that slavery should no longer exist in any territory "now existing, or which may at any time hereafter be formed or acquired by the United States." Thus, at one stroke, a major portion of the *Dred Scott* decision was rendered invalid, and the key plank in the Republican platform, on which Lincoln was elected in 1860, was fulfilled.

In June 1862, Lincoln recognized Liberia and Haiti, the two black republics that the United States had refused to consider worthy of recognition while the South had controlled the government.

On July 12, 1862, Lincoln proposed compensated emancipation to the border states, and on the same day, he summoned thirty congressmen from these four states to the White House where he urged them to recommend the plan to their constituents. "How much better for you and your people," he pleaded, "to take the step which at once shortens the war and secures substantial compensation for that which is sure to be wholly lost in any event. How much better to do it while we can, lest the war ere long render us pecuniarily unable to do it." His entreaties were in vain. The border states indignantly rejected the proposal.

BACKGROUND OF THE EMANCIPATION PROCLAMATION

On December 5, 1861, Lyman Trumbull of Illinois introduced a bill in Congress "to confiscate the property of Rebels and free their slaves." The first half of Trumbull's bill became law with the passage of the Second Confiscation Act of July 17, 1862. The second half, however, was delayed almost a full year until the promulgation by Lincoln of the Emancipation Proclamation.

The Second Confiscation Act was labeled by abolitionists "an emancipation bill with clogs on." It bestowed freedom on all slaves of persons "engaged in rebellion against the government of the United States" once they escaped into the Union armed forces. It was no longer necessary for them to prove that they were contrabands—that is, that they had been involved in the Confederacy's war effort. Much as he approved of the Second Confiscation Act, Frederick Douglass felt that it fell short of what was needed. The only choice left, he maintained, was the "abolition of slavery or destruction of the Union." "You must abolish slavery," he advised Lincoln, "or abandon the Union." He was certain that if only it had the will, the government would speedily abolish slavery. All that was needed was a proclamation by the president announcing the freedom of the slaves. His reply to the argument that a proclamation of emancipation would only be "a paper order" was simple and direct: "It would act on the rebel masters, and even more powerfully upon the slaves. It would lead the slaves to run away from the masters to Emancipation, and thus put an end to slavery."

Wendell Phillips, the eloquent Massachusetts abolitionist, shared Douglass' view. In a widely publicized prediction, he announced that the president would have to issue an emancipation proclamation: "Abraham Lincoln may not wish it; he cannot prevent it; the nation may not will it; but the nation can never prevent. I do not care what men want or wish; the negro is the pebble in the cog wheel, and the machine cannot go on until you get him out."

Unknown to Douglass and Phillips, Lincoln was being forced to the same conclusion. The forces that these two abolitionists, one black and the other white, had predicted would compel the government to pursue a revolutionary course of action were now in full operation. Lincoln was beginning to realize the impossibility of his own program. The slaveholders continued to use the labor of their slaves to wage their war, while the Union government continued to deprive itself of the valuable services of free blacks and slaves in the Union army, the very men who were the natural enemies of the slaveholders. Moreover, the failure of the Lincoln administration to make the war clearly one for the abolition of slavery was aiding the Confederate agents in Europe, especially in England, where they were sowing confusion among the working classes as to the real nature of the war. Only defining the war as an issue of slavery—for and against—would put an end to the danger of European recognition of the Confederacy and intervention against the Union. "It is my profound conviction," wrote Carl Schurz, U.S. ambassador to Spain, in a dispatch to Washington, "that as soon as the war becomes distinctly one for and against slavery, public opinion will be so strongly, so overwhelmingly in our favor, that in spite of commercial interests, or secret spies, no European government will dare to place itself by declaration or act, upon the side of a universally condemned institution."

During the trying weeks following General George B. McClellan's retreat after the Seven Days' Battle in June 1862, President Lincoln spent much time in the military telegraph office of the War Department. According to Major James Eckert, the officer in command, toward the middle of July the president told him that he was writing a proclamation to free the slaves in the South. In 1864, as he sat for a portrait depicting the signing of the Emancipation Proclamation, Lincoln recalled:

It had got to be . . . mid-summer, 1862. Things had gone from bad to worse, until I felt that we had reached the end of our rope in the plan of operation we had been pursuing; that we had about played our last card, and must change our tactics, or lose the game. I now determined upon the adoption of the emancipation policy; and without consultation with or knowledge of the Cabinet, I prepared the original draft of the proclamation.

On July 22, 1862, Lincoln surprised a cabinet meeting by laying before them a draft of the proclamation, which proposed to emancipate all slaves in areas still in insurrection against the central government on January 1, 1863. Included was a plan for compensating loyal slaveowners to encourage abolition by state action. Secretary of State William H. Seward supported the proposal but questioned its timing. Seward believed that the decision must be made from a position of strength and that a major Union victory must precede the announcement. Lincoln accepted his advice and set aside the draft until the Union's military fortunes should improve.

LINCOLN PROPOSES COLONIZATION FOR EMANCIPATED BLACKS

"What should be done with the freed slaves?" This question continued in Lincoln's mind as he waited for the right time to announce the emancipation message. Before the Civil War, Lincoln had concluded that racism was too powerful in the United States to enable blacks and whites to live together in domestic harmony. At that time, he had looked to voluntary colonization as the answer to the problem, and his views had not been altered by the presidency. Congress paved the way for funding such a project by passing an appropriation bill on July 16, 1862, to colonize the slaves of disloyal masters, and the House Committee on Emancipation and Colonization had recommended an appropriation of $20 million to relocate slaves outside the territory of the United States.

In August 1862, Lincoln summoned a five-man delegation of blacks to the White House, the first formal meeting between a president and a group of blacks. Describing the sharp physical differences between the two races and the consequent suffering for both blacks and whites, Lincoln insisted that "without the institution of Slavery and the colored race as a basis, the war could not have an existence." He asked for the support of such free Negroes as those before him—men "capable of thinking as white men"—for his colonization plans.

Frederick Douglass had only contempt for this speech of "our garrulous and joking President." In the September issue of *Douglass' Monthly,* he charged Lincoln with being "a genuine representative of American prejudice and negro hatred and far more concerned for the preservation of slavery, and the favor of the Border Slave States, than for any sentiment of magnanimity or principle of justice and humanity." By suggesting that the differences between the races were so great that separation was the only remedy, he declared, Lincoln had furnished "a weapon to all the ignorant and base, who need only the countenance of men in authority to commit all kinds of violence and outrage upon the colored people of the country." The logic that blamed blacks as the first cause of the war was the same as that which blamed the horse for the horse thief and the money in the traveler's pocket for the robbery:

No, Mr. President, it is not the innocent horse that makes the horse thief, nor the traveler's purse that makes the highway robber, and it is not the presence of the negro that causes this foul and unnatural war, but the cruel and brutal cupidity of those who wish to possess horses, money and negroes by means of theft, robbery and rebellion.

His answer to the president's plan was brief: "I repeat what I have said many times. We were born here, and here we choose to remain. We were coaxed and mobbed, and mobbed and coaxed; but we refuse to budge. This is our country as much as it is yours, and we will not leave it." If there were any to be colonized, let it be the slaveowners and not the emancipated slaves.

A few black spokespersons backed Lincoln's plan, including even Lewis Douglass, the son of Frederick Douglass, who was one of five hundred blacks who signed up to go to Central America. Henry Highland Garnet announced that he was one who did "sincerely approve" of the Central American plan of President Lincoln "*for the purpose of saving our emancipated brethren from being returned to slavery.*" "Where," Garnet asked, "are the freed people of the South to seek a refuge?" He went on:

Neither the North, the West, nor the East will receive them. Nay—even colored people do not want them here. They all say, white and black—"these Southern negroes if they come here *will reduce the price of labor and take the bread out of our mouths.*"

Let the government give them a territory and arm and defend them until they can fully defend themselves, and thus hundreds of thousands of men will be saved.

But it was Frederick Douglass, and not Henry Highland Garnet, who expressed the opinion of the overwhelming majority of Northern blacks. Robert Purvis, the Philadelphia black leader, assured the president and the nation that the blacks would not leave. A meeting of blacks in Queens County, New York, answered Lincoln tersely: "There is no country like our own. Why not declare slavery abolished, and favor our peaceful colonization in the rebel States, or some portion of them? We would cheerfully return there, and give our most willing aid to deliver our loyal colored brethren and other Unionists from the tyranny of rebels to our Government." Boston blacks met and adopted the following resolutions:

Resolved. That when we wish to leave the United States we can find and pay for that territory which shall suit us best.

Resolved. That when we are ready to leave, we shall be able to pay our own expenses of travel.

Resolved. That we don't want to go now.

Resolved. That if anybody else wants us to go, they must compel us.

Because of this patent hostility of those who were to be colonized, Lincoln's colonization scheme collapsed.

THE PRELIMINARY EMANCIPATION PROCLAMATION

On August 19, 1862, Horace Greeley addressed an editorial in his *New York Tribune* to President Lincoln, attacking his "seeming subserviency . . . to the slave-holding, slave-upholding interest." Greeley's editorial, entitled "The Prayer of Twenty Millions," insisted that most loyal citizens wanted Lincoln to enforce the Confiscation Acts, to use black troops, and to liberate the slaves of the Rebels:

On the face of this wide earth, Mr. President, there is not one disinterested, determined, intelligent champion of the Union cause who does not feel that all attempts to put down the Rebellion and at the same time uphold its inciting cause are preposterous and futile.

"What I do about slavery, and the colored race," Lincoln answered three days later, "I do because it helps to save the Union, and what I forbear, I forbear because I do not believe it would help save the Union." If he could save the

Union "without freeing any slaves," he would do it; if he could save the Union "by freeing all the slaves," he would do it; and if he "could do it by freeing some and leaving others alone, I would also do it."

Nothing in Lincoln's reply indicated that he was waiting for a military victory before acting against slavery. However, the chances for an early military victory suffered a setback on August 29 and 30 when General John Pope blundered at Manassas, in the second Battle of Bull Run, and the Union forces retreated toward Washington. Lincoln reluctantly asked General McClellan to assume command again of the Union armies in the East. The new commander had little time to reorganize. On September 5, Robert E. Lee invaded Maryland.

At this point, an accident of fate made it possible for the president to reveal his well-kept secret. Three cigars, sheathed in a copy of Robert E. Lee's orders giving the precise location of his segmented army, were lost in the field by a Confederate officer. A Union army private found the orders and passed them through the chain of command. At last General McClellan knew what Lee planned to do before the Confederate general did it. Lee's invasion was stopped in a major battle along Antietam Creek on September 17, 1862. Although Lee escaped total disaster by crossing the Potomac the following day, the Union's military fortunes had momentarily taken a turn for the better.

Disappointed that McClellan had allowed Lee to escape, Lincoln nevertheless took the opportunity to act. On September 22, 1862, the president issued the preliminary Emancipation Proclamation. He mentioned the possibility of compensated emancipation and said he would continue to encourage the voluntary colonization of Negroes "upon this continent or elsewhere." But, he declared, the time had come for direct action. The proclamation warned the Confederates to cease their rebellion within one hundred days. If not, he would proclaim

that on the first day of January, in the year of our Lord one thousand, eighteen hundred and sixty-three, all persons held as slaves within any State or any designated part of a state, the people whereof shall then be in rebellion against the United States, shall be then, thenceforward, and forever free.

Lincoln further ordered the military to recognize this freedom and to do nothing to interfere with those who would liberate themselves. Thus, in effect, the president was sanctioning slave insurrections in states that remained in rebellion after the first of the new year.

The reaction of Southern blacks was captured by "Cuffee's War Song, or, Hooray for Sixty-Three":

> Abram Linkon las' September
> Told de Souf 'less you surrender
> Afore de las' of next December,
> Away goes Cuffee!

Chorus:
For de cannon may boom when dey fight a big battle,
But de darkeys no more is de sheep and de cattle.
For freedom's watchman has sprung his rattle,
Hooray for sixty-three!

To prove that there were distinct limitations to the preliminary Emancipation Proclamation, a Washington newspaper, regularly read by Lincoln, reprinted an editorial from a French newspaper charging that the president, "far from striking at the root of the institution of slavery . . . reaffirms its constitutional legitimacy. He goes even further; he offers the protection of the Government as bounty and recompense to all slaveholders who will range themselves under his flag." The proclamation, it continued, did not cover all the slaveholding territory, and if the war should end and there were no states in rebellion on January 1, 1863, the Emancipation Proclamation would operate in no part of either the United States or the Confederate States. In short, the announcement was an empty gesture.

Frederick Douglass disagreed. Douglass could scarcely believe his eyes as he read the words *forever free* in the preliminary Emancipation Proclamation. He rushed into print to give vent to his happiness. "We shout for joy that we live to record this righteous decree," he wrote in his journal. His pen was jubilant:

Oh! long enslaved millions, whose cries have so vexed the air and sky, suffer on a few days in sorrow, the hour of your deliverance draws nigh.

Oh! ye millions of free and loyal men who have earnestly sought to free your bleeding country from the dreadful ravages of revolution and anarchy, lift up now your voices with joy and thanksgiving for with freedom to the slave will come peace and safety to your country.

Douglass insisted that this was the most important document ever signed by a president of the United States. When blacks in the South heard of it, they would flock by the thousands to the Union army. It was a "moral bombshell" to the Confederacy, more destructive than a hundred thousand cannon. The effect of the document on Europe, he predicted,

will be great and increasing. It changes the character of the war in European eyes and gives it an important principle as an object, instead of national pride and interest. It recognizes, and declares the real nature of the contest, and places the North on the side of justice and civilization, and the rebels on the side of robbery and barbarism. It will disarm all purpose on the part of European Government to intervene in favor of the rebels and thus cast off at a blow one source of rebel power.

The *National Anti-Slavery Standard* agreed wholeheartedly with Douglass. "We look forward . . . with bright anticipation to the First of January, 1863, as a day of jubilee for our country," it announced, "when if the chains do not actually fall from the limbs of the slaves, the government will be irretrievably committed to a course of action that will speedily bring about that glorious result.''

WOULD LINCOLN GO THROUGH WITH IT?

The real question, as many blacks now saw it, was not whether the proclamation would prove effective but whether Northern conservatives would be able to prevent its issuance in final form. Off-year elections were held in the fall of 1862, and in most state elections in the North, the administration candidates went down to defeat. Moreover, in the election for congressional representatives from these states, the administration's majority of forty-one was replaced by an opposition majority of ten. In fact, Lincoln had been informed that if he issued the proclamation on January 1, 1863, "the Legislature of Kentucky . . . will legislate the State out of the Union.''

Thus many in both North and South believed that Lincoln would never go through with the second Emancipation Proclamation on January 1, 1863. But Frederick Douglass was confident that the opposition to the proclamation would not prevail. "Abraham Lincoln may be slow,'' he argued, "Abraham Lincoln may desire peace even at the price of leaving our terrible national sore untouched, to fester on for generations, but Abraham Lincoln is not the man to reconsider, retract and contradict words and purposes solemnly proclaimed over his official signature.''

A mass campaign had to be mounted in support of the proclamation, Douglass maintained, in order to counteract the pressure being exerted on Lincoln by conservative elements in the North. Given this popular support, there would be no doubt where the president would stand on January 1, 1863:

Abraham Lincoln, will take no step backward. His word has gone out over the country and the world, giving joy and gladness to the friends of freedom and progress wherever these words are read, and he will stand by them and carry them out to the letter.

In a direct plea to the English public, entitled ''The Slave's Appeal to Great Britain,'' Douglass urged Englishmen to forget the past mistakes of the Lincoln administration and to be assured that the president's proclamation "will become operative on the first day of January 1863.'' He pleaded:

The hopes of millions, long trodden down, now rise with every advancing hour. Oh! I pray you, by all your highest and holiest memories, blast not the budding hopes of those millions by lending your countenance and extending your potent and honored hand to the blood-stained fingers of the impious slaveholding Confederate States of America.

Nevertheless, as the weeks passed, Douglass' anxiety increased, and he was worried lest perhaps emancipation would not be proclaimed. Perhaps the victories scored by the Democrats in the November elections, in which they carried seven important states, including New York, Pennsylvania, Ohio, and Illinois, would cause Lincoln to reconsider. Why had it been necessary for the president to wait three months before making his decree final? If only Lincoln had made his proclamation of freedom "absolute and immediate instead of conditional and prospective." A week before January 1, Douglass wrote: "The suspense is painful."

Douglass need not have worried. Congressman John Covode of Pennsylvania, upon visiting the White House, found the president pacing. He reported the following statement by Lincoln about issuing the Emancipation Proclamation: "I have studied the matter well, my mind is made up. . . . *It must be done. I am driven to it*. There is no other way out of our troubles."

Evidently the slaves in the South (who learned of it through the grapevine) had no doubt that the proclamation would be issued as promised. On December 11, 1862, Governor John Pettus of Mississippi received a letter from a Confederate officer at Camp Harris, which read: "The militia of the 5th Regiment at this place requests me to write to you asking your honor to disband us and give us the privilege of going home and remaining there fifteen to twenty days during Christmas time as we deem it highly necessary that we should be there for the defense of our families as the negroes are making their brags that by the first of January they will be free as we are and a general outbreak is expected by that time."

On December 30, members of the cabinet received copies of the final proclamation. On December 31, Lincoln called a meeting of the cabinet. Various members suggested changes. Secretary of the Treasury Salmon Chase contributed the penultimate paragraph. His further suggestion, that the proclamation be made applicable to entire states, was rejected by Lincoln on the grounds that the thirteen Louisiana parishes and the counties around Norfolk, Virginia, had held elections in conformity with the terms of the preliminary proclamation. Attorney General Edward Bates submitted an extensive legal opinion. Lincoln wrote out the final draft on the afternoon of December 31, and on January 1, 1863, one hundred days after issuing the preliminary proclamation, Lincoln signed the Emancipation Proclamation.

DAY OF JUBILEE

At about eight o'clock in the evening of December 31, Frederick Douglass entered the packed hall in Boston's Tremont Temple to join the audience of three thousand waiting for the word from the White House. He walked to the platform where a seat had been reserved for him and shook hands with William Wells Brown, the ex-fugitive slave who had become famous as an orator, novelist, and playwright; J. Sella Martin, the ex-slave who was a leading black preacher; and Anna M. Dickinson, the young advocate of women's rights and the abolition of slavery.

During the first hour of waiting, Reverend Martin and Anna Dickinson addressed the restless audience. By nine o'clock, a feeling of despondency descended upon the gathering. Douglass and Brown sought to revive the spirits of the audience with brief, hopeful speeches. But as ten o'clock passed without word from Washington, the gloom deepened. Suddenly a messenger burst into the hall shouting, "It is coming! It is on the wires." The cheers shook the hall. Soon the text of the proclamation was received and read. The words reverberated through the temple:

Whereas, on the twenty-second day of September, in the year of our Lord one thousand eight hundred and sixty-two, a proclamation was issued by the President of the United States, containing, among other things, the following to wit:

Then followed the text of the warning issued to the states in rebellion that "all persons held as slaves within any State or designated part of a State, the people whereof shall then be in rebellion against the United States, shall be then, thenceforward, and forever free." Since the warning had not been heeded,

Therefore, I, Abraham Lincoln, President of the United States, by virtue of the power in me vested as commander-in-chief of the army and navy of the United States, in time of actual armed rebellion, against the authority and government of the United States, and as a fit and necessary war measure for suppressing said rebellion, do, on this first day of January, in the year of our Lord one thousand eight hundred and sixty-three . . . order and declare that all persons held as slaves within said designated States and parts of States are, and henceforward, shall be free.

And the president further ordered "that such persons of suitable condition will be received into the armed service of the United States to garrison forts, positions, stations, and other places, and to man vessels of all sorts in said service."

The excited audience, unable to restrain its feelings, interrupted the reading of each paragraph with shouts of joy. Douglass led the audience in singing: "Blow ye the trumpet, blow!" A black preacher burst into the psalm:

> Sound the Loud Timbrel o'er Egypt's dark sea,
> Jehovah hath triumphed, his people are free.

At midnight, Tremont Temple had to be vacated, but the audience was in no mood to go home. A proposal was made that the meeting adjourn to the black Twelfth Baptist Church on Phillips Street. Within half an hour the church was filled. Reverend Leonard A. Grimes, the militant black pastor who had been imprisoned in Virginia for attempting to aid fugitive slaves, led in public prayer.

The demonstration of joy continued for several hours. The dawn was breaking when the meeting finally disbanded.

On the first day of the new year, three large meetings were held at Tremont Temple, conducted mainly by blacks. Douglass spoke at the afternoon session. A report of his address in the *Boston Journal* went in part:

Frederick Douglass thanked God that today he was living to see the end of slavery. He did not feel that emancipation would be successful in the immediate future, but in the end he had no doubt, for it was a struggle between the beautiful truth and the ugly wrong. Error cannot safely be tolerated unless truth is left free to combat it, and the only antidote to error is freedom, free speech and a free press. We have had a period of great darkness, but now we are having a period of illumination by the rosy dawning of the new truth of freedom, and we are here today to rejoice in it. (*Voices of "Amen," "Good," "Bless the Lord," etc.*)

. . . He was glad that the people of the country were finding out that the blacks were Americans, and that the color of a man's skin does not disqualify him from being a citizen of the United States. He concluded by rejoicing that he was here to share in the deliverance of his race from bondage.

The meetings in Boston were among many, as blacks gathered in churches and halls across the North to celebrate. Jonathan C. Gibbs, pastor of the Colored Presbyterian Church of Philadelphia, delivered a sermon on January 1 that opened:

The morning dawns! The long night of sorrow and gloom is past, rosy-fingered Aurora, early born of day, shows the first faint flush of her coming glory low down on the distant horizon of Freedom's joyful day. O day, thrice blessed, that brings liberty to four million native-born Americans. O Liberty! O sacred rights of every human soul! . . . The Proclamation has gone forth, and God is saying to the nation by its legitimate constitute head, Man must be free.

From Philadelphia, abolitionist B. Rush Plumbly wrote to President Lincoln:

I have been all day, from early morning until . . . [nearly midnight] in the crowded Churches of the colored people of this city. . . . Occasionally, they sang and shouted and wept and prayed. God knows I cried with them. . . .

As one of the speakers was explaining the effect of your Act, he was interrupted by a sudden outburst, from four or five hundred voices, singing "The Year of Jubilee. . . ."

The places of business, controlled by the colored people were, generally, closed. In the private houses of the better class, festivals and Love feasts were held. . . .

The black people do not believe that *you wish* to expropriate them, or to enforce upon them any disability, but that you *cannot* do *all* that you would. . . .

Some one intimated that you might be forced into some form of Colonization. "God won't let him," shouted an old woman. "God's in his *heart*," said another, and the response of the congregation was emphatic. . . .

Henry M. Turner, pastor of Israel Bethel Church in Washington, recalled the momentous day:

The first sheet run off with the proclamation was grabbed. . . . The third sheet I succeeded in procuring and off I went. Down Pennsylvania Avenue I ran as for my life. When the people saw me coming with the paper in my hand they raised a shouting cheer that was almost deafening. As many as could get around me lifted me to a great platform and I started to read. I had run the best of a mile. I was out of breath and could not read. Mr. Hinton to whom I handed the paper read it with great force and clearness.

While he was reading every kind of demonstration was going on. Men squealed, women fainted, dogs barked, white and colored people shook hands, songs were sung. . . . The jubilation that attended the proclamation of freedom I am sure has never been surpassed. Rumor said that the very thought of being set at liberty and having no more auction blocks, no more separation of parents and children, was so heart-gladdening that scores of colored people literally fell dead with joy. It was indeed a time of times and a half time. Nothing like it will ever be seen again in this life.

Turner's reference to "no more auction blocks" was also reflected in the Jubilee Song blacks sang in their joy:

> No more auction block for me,
>   No more, no more;
> No more auction block for me,
>   Many thousand gone.
>
> No more peck o'corn for me
>   No more, no more;
> No more peck o'corn for me,
>   Many thousand gone.
>
> No more driver's lash for me
>   No more, no more;
> No more driver's lash for me,
>   Many thousand gone.

At Port Royal on South Carolina's Sea Islands, where she was teaching ex-slaves and their children, Charlotte Forten described the January 1, 1863, celebration as "the most glorious day this nation has yet seen." Laura Towne, a white teacher, shared this feeling of excitement. She joyfully noted in her diary: "Not a legally held slave on the soil, Glory Hallelujah . . . to think that our country at last is free."

The day's festivities there took place under a grove of tall oak trees. After an opening prayer and a speech by General Rufus Saxton, Dr. William Brisbane read the president's proclamation. A spontaneous chorus of "My Country Tis of Thee" by the blacks in the audience brought tears of joy to the northerners. A visibly moved Colonel Thomas Wentworth Higginson then addressed the group.

After his remarks, Higginson presented Sergeants Prince Rivers and Robert Sutton, his two color bearers, with flags. A singing of "John Brown" concluded the program.

Before attending General Saxton's party at his headquarters, the guests viewed the First South Carolina Regiment's dress parade. Commenting on the precision and ease with which the men drilled, Charlotte Forten wrote: "To us it seemed strange as a miracle—this black regiment, the first mustered into the service of the United States, doing itself honor in the sight of the officers of other regiments, many of whom doubtless, 'came to scoff.'"

At Old Fort Grove in Beaufort, South Carolina, where the contrabands heard the news of the Emancipation Proclamation, a poem was read to the former slaves. It began:

> This day is the birth time of millions!
> The dawn of the year sixty-three
> Will be marked on the dial of ages,
> The hour when a RACE became free!

One of the contrabands, an old man "of the African persuasion," was called on to tell his experiences, which he did in the following statement:

Onst the time was, dat I cried all night. What's de matter? What's de matter? Matter enough. De next mornin my child was to be sold, an she was sold, an I never spec to see her no more till de day ob judgment! Now, no more dat! no more dat! no more dat! Wid my hands agin my breast I was gwine to my work, when de overseer used to whip me along. Now, no more dat! no more dat! When I tink what de Lord's done for us, an brot us thro' de trubbles, I feel dat I ought to go inter his service. We's free now, bress de Lord! (*Amens! were vociferated all over the building.*) Dey can't sell my wife an child any more, bress de Lord! (*Glory! glory! from the audience.*) No more dat! no more dat, now! (*Glory!*) Presufdund Lincum hav shot de gate! Dat's what de matter! (*And there was a prolonged response of Amens!*)

SIGNIFICANCE OF THE EMANCIPATION PROCLAMATION

There were grievous omissions in Lincoln's final proclamation. Missouri, Tennessee, Maryland, and Kentucky were left out of it, as were parts of Virginia and Louisiana. Cynics pointed out that Lincoln had excepted the only areas in the South occupied by the Union armies, and Secretary of State William H. Seward echoed this judgment when he said: "We show our sympathy with slavery by emancipating the slaves where we cannot reach them and holding them in bondage where we can set them free."

In this connection, it is worth noting that the Cherokee Act of Emancipation, issued February 21, 1863, freeing 2,504 Negro and other slaves of the Cherokee Nation, went beyond Lincoln's proclamation. For one thing the measure applied to all slaves within the Cherokee Nation and not merely, as in the case of the president's Emancipation Proclamation, to those who were under the control of Confederate armies. For another, the Cherokee laws defined freedom as permission to obtain unused Cherokee national land, "affording Cherokee Blacks," notes David R. Wrone, "an opportunity to earn a living. The term as used by the Federal government pertained to the person only and excluded property as part of its definition."

Although it fell short of granting actual freedom in the Confederate states and left untouched slave property in the loyal areas, almost all blacks saw in the Emancipation Proclamation the official death warrant of slavery. They rejoiced, moreover, that the final Emancipation Proclamation did not mention Lincoln's plans for either compensation or colonization. In the Sea Islands of South Carolina and Georgia, where she was teaching contrabands, Charlotte Forten noted in her journal under "New Year's Day—Emancipation Day—the greatest day in the nation's history": "Our hearts were filled with great gladness; for, although the Government had left much undone, we knew that Freedom was surely born in our land that day."

Historians have generally agreed that the Emancipation Proclamation marked the turning point of the Civil War. When news reached the South that President Lincoln had issued his preliminary proclamation, newspapers and Confederate leaders predicted that an edict freeing the slaves would serve to unify the South, bring extended foreign aid to the Confederacy, and turn the Union army into a mob of deserters as white soldiers threw down their arms and refused "to fight for the niggers."

These predictions proved totally inaccurate. The impact of the Emancipation Proclamation, both abroad and at home, was enormous. From England, Henry Adams, the son and secretary of Charles Francis Adams, the U.S. ambassador, wrote that "the Emancipation Proclamation has done more for us here than all our former victories and all our diplomacy." The British upper classes might be sympathetic to the Confederacy, he wrote, but the working classes, including those in Lancashire who suffered enormous privation because the lack of cotton had created widespread unemployment, were passionately on the side of the North after the news of the Emancipation Proclamation reached England. It was not merely that the North represented democracy, although this was an important consideration. It was mainly because Lincoln's decision to issue the Emancipation Proclamation had transformed the war for Union into a war for freedom as well. The South had always represented slavery, but the North now clearly represented freedom, and the British working classes (contrary to some recent interpretations challenging this view) would not tolerate any military or political support for the side of slavery.

The Emancipation Proclamation intensified internal dissension in the Confederacy by strengthening the antislavery and antiplanter sentiments of the small Southern farmers and other nonslaveholders. It is true that the Emancipation Proclamation did cause some soldiers in the Union army to turn against the war.

Most of those who volunteered in the Union army after the bombardment of Fort Sumter were not fighting for the abolition of slavery. They shared with Lincoln the belief that the only issue at stake in the war was "whether in a free government the minority have the right to break it up whenever they choose." To be sure, there were some in the Union army, the German socialists among others, who believed from the outset that the abolition of slavery was a major objective of the war. They were, however, opposed by powerful forces in the Union army. Copies of the *New York World,* the *New York Copperhead,* the *New York Herald,* the *New York Daily News,* and other pro-Southern papers were circulated in the ranks. Soldiers read they were giving their lives "for niggers and Mr. Lincoln."

General George McClellan not only did nothing to halt the circulation of these defeatist papers; rather, his officers, many of them Peace Democrats, gave every possible assistance to their reporters. Fitz John Porter, one of McClellan's closest advisers, wrote to Manton Marble, editor of the *New York World,* on April 26, 1862: "Your agents are here and I am with them. . . . This Army will cause a revulsion of opinion on its return home."

Nor was this all. Any effort to educate the soldiers to the fact that the war was a struggle for freedom and against slavery was quickly frustrated by McClellan and his subordinate soldiers. An interesting example involved the Hutchinson family, a troupe of singers who had used their talent before the war to advance the cause of abolition. Early in 1862, they were invited by Secretary of War Simon Cameron to sing to the soldiers of the Army of the Potomac. As was to be expected, the Hutchinsons got into difficulty with General McClellan and other officers who shared his belief that abolition of slavery was not the object of the war. Included in their program was a fervent abolition poem by John Greenleaf Whittier, set to the music of Luther's great hymn, "Eine feste Burg ist unser Gott." The words went in part:

> What gives the wheat fields blades of steel?
>   What points the rebel cannon?
> What sets the rabble's heel
>   On the star-spangled pennon?
> What breaks the oath
>   Of the men of the South?
> What whets the knife
>   For the Union's life?—
> Hark to the answer: Slavery!
>
> Then waste no blows on lesser foes
>   In strife unworthy freemen;
> God lifts to-day the veil and shows
>   The features of the demon!
> O North and South,
>   Its victims both,

Can ye not cry,
  "Let slavery die!"
And Union find in freedom.

It was too much to expect that this stirring battle cry for freedom would be
appreciated by McClellan and his subordinate officers who had assured the
slaveowners that the Union army did not intend to interfere in any way with their
chattels and who had forcibly returned to bondage slaves who came over to the
Union lines. General Kearny ordered the Hutchinsons to abandon their concert
and rebuked them furiously for their "incendiary" songs. "I think as much of a
Rebel as I do of an Abolitionist," he informed them. General McClellan revoked
the family's permit to sing in the camps.

But the Hutchinsons had faced stonings, beatings, and even worse during their
tours for the abolitionist cause, and they were not deterred by orders signed by
conservative army officers. Instead, they took their case to Secretary of the
Treasury Salmon P. Chase, who listened to their story and asked them to write
out the words of the song so that he could submit it to the cabinet. The next
morning Chase informed John Hutchinson:

I want to tell you that the poem was read at the cabinet meeting, and they were all in your
favor. Mr. Lincoln remarked that it was just the kind of songs he wanted the soldiers to
hear. He also said you should have the right to go among any of the soldiers where you
were invited to sing.

Readmitted by presidential order to the Union camps, the Hutchinson singers
advanced the cause of freedom through such songs as "The Slave Mother,"
"Emancipation Song," "The Slave's Appeal," "The Battle Cry of Freedom,"
and "Get Off the Track," the last one of the most famous of the abolitionist
songs.

But personal experience was proving even more effective than songs and
literature in convincing Union soldiers that slavery ought to be abolished. What
white soldiers saw with their own eyes of the horrors of slavery converted many
who had up to that time opposed abolitionists into antislavery fighting men. One
of these converts gave his reaction to the sight that greeted him when black
recruits were stripped for physical examination in Louisiana:

Some of them were scarred from head to foot where they had been whipped. One man's
back was nearly all one scar, as if the skin had been chopped up and left to heal in ridges.
Another had scars on the back of his neck, and from that all the way to his heels every
little ways; but that was not such a sight as the one with the great solid mass of ridges from
his shoulders to his hips. That beat all the antislavery sermons ever yet preached.

Another Union soldier wrote of an experience near New Orleans:

Visited during the day several plantations and saw enough of the horrors of slavery to make me an Abolitionist forever. On each plantation . . . may be seen the stocks, gnout, thumb screw, ball and chain, rings and chain, by which victims are fastened flat to the floor; and others by which they are bound to perpendicular posts; iron yokes of different patterns, handcuffs, whips and other instruments of torture, for the benefit of those who had been guilty of loving liberty more than life.

This soldier recorded in his diary having sawed heavy chains and weights from black refugees. A typical entry went: "Released another negro from his iron yoke, and ball and chain, with which he had traveled 18 miles. His ear had been cut off, to mark him, and he had been well branded with the hot iron. His flesh was badly lacerated with the whip and torn by dogs, but he escaped and I have just dressed his wounds with sweet oil. There is little hope that he will live."

Undoubtedly the Emancipation Proclamation did turn some white soldiers in the Union army against the war. A soldier in New Orleans under General Nathaniel P. Banks wrote home to Massachusetts on February 17, 1863: "As the aspect of the war has changed, it is now instead of being one to crush the rebellion, a war, the sole object being the freedom of the negroes. President Lincoln's Proclamation is outrageous. Had I my wish every nigger in the Union, would be sunk in the Atlantic Ocean or else remanded back to slavery. I hope no more niggers will be set free." But many more white Union soldiers in New Orleans, having developed a deep hatred of slavery from personal observations, welcomed the Emancipation Proclamation, and not only in New Orleans.

Not the least of the effects of the Emancipation Proclamation on the course of the Civil War was that under it, blacks were at last allowed to put on the Union army uniform. While the five hundred blacks, among them Lewis Douglass, were waiting for their chartered ship to depart for Central America, Lincoln issued the Emancipation Proclamation. Every one of them abandoned the plan to emigrate. A month later, the majority of them, including Lewis Douglass, joined the Union army.

20

Men of Color, To Arms!

A MONTH OF CELEBRATIONS

January 1863 was a month of jubilee celebrations for black Americans. In the slaveholding Confederacy, Negroes gathered secretly in their cabins to give thanks and to whisper: "We are free, we are free." In the North, the voices of jubilation rang loud and clear in a grand chorus of liberty as blacks met in a round of celebrations. Black churches and meeting halls were sites of thanksgiving gatherings. Frances Watkins Harper, the black abolitionist poet and lecturer, struck the dominant note of the meetings when she asked the audience at a Columbus celebration if they had "ever expected to see that day." Frederick Douglass traveled two thousand miles that month, making speeches "almost without intermission" at meetings from Boston to Chicago. He told a New York audience that "we can scarcely conceive of a more complete revolution in the position of a nation." At Cleveland's "grand celebration" on January 16 at National Hall, Douglass was the featured speaker, and John Mercer Langston, Peter H. Clark, David Jenkins, and other Ohio black leaders of the antislavery crusade were honored guests.

Everywhere he spoke, Douglass emphasized that it was time to stop fighting the Rebels with only the North's soft white hand and to unleash its iron black hand. He sharply criticized those who said Negroes could not fight:

In one breath the Copperheads tell you that the slaves won't fight, and in the next they tell you that the only effect of the Proclamation is to make the slaves cut their masters' throats [laughter] and stir up insurrections all over the South.—The same men tell you that the negroes are lazy and good for nothing, and in the next breath they tell you that they will come North and take the labor away from the laboring white men here. [Laughter and cheers.] In one breath they tell you that the negroe can never learn the military art, and in the next they tell you that there is danger that white men may be outranked by colored men.

356

THE MASSACHUSETTS FIFTY-FOURTH

While the administration had finally agreed to the conscription of blacks, including ex-slaves, into the Union army, it still refused to sanction the mixing of white and black enlisted men. Governor John Andrew of Massachusetts, who had been pressuring the War Department for official authorization to recruit Negro troops, was therefore authorized

to raise detached companies to volunteer heavy artillery, and such corps of infantry as he may deem expedient for three years, unless sooner discharged; and . . . to include in the corps . . . enlisted persons of African descent into separate corps.

Almost immediately, Governor Andrew dispatched a letter to Captain Robert Gould Shaw of Boston, who was at the time attached to the second regiment of Massachusetts Volunteer Infantry:

Captain, I am about to organize in Massachusetts a colored regiment as part of the volunteer quota of this state—the commissioned officers to be white men. . . . I offer you the commission of Colonel over it.

Within a week, Captain Shaw reached his father, Francis Shaw, a long-time supporter of abolitionist causes, and advised him to contact the governor and tell him that he would gladly accept. Immediately upon receipt of this information, Governor Andrew announced the formation of the Fifty-fourth Massachusetts Regiment, the first black regiment to be recruited in the North. But Massachusetts, with a comparatively small black population, could sign up only a hundred volunteers in the first six weeks. However, since other Northern states still excluded Negroes from their militias, recruiting the Fifty-fourth Regiment became a national rather than merely a state enterprise. Governor Andrew turned to his friend George L. Stearns, a leading New England Republican and formerly a close associate of John Brown, and persuaded him to take full charge of the recruiting. An able organizer, Stearns promptly collected $5,000, advertised widely for enlistments, and set up recruiting posts from Boston to St. Louis. To speed up the work, Stearns called on Negro leaders to act as recruiting agents. On February 23, 1863, Stearns left for Rochester to enroll Frederick Douglass as an agent. Douglass needed little prodding; he had been urging the recruiting of blacks into the Union army from the first month of the war. Within three days after Stearns' visit, Douglass issued his famous call, "Men of Color, to Arms!" Because their service had been rejected for nearly two years, during which time they had suffered both humiliation and harsh treatment, many blacks doubted that they would serve. But Douglass insisted that it was time for "Action! Action! not criticism." He condemned those blacks who opposed taking up arms as being "weak and cowardly," and he urged his people to "fly to arms, and smite with death the power that would bury the government and your liberty in the same hopeless grave.'' To be free, they must themselves strike the blow. Now they could prove their manhood and demonstrate their equality with the white man in fighting prowess and love of country. The gratitude of the country would be accorded to the Negroes and prejudice against them greatly diminished if they proved by force of arms that they deserved an improved status. ''Liberty won only by white men would lose half its lustre,'' he cried. He asked all to ''remember Shields Green and John Copeland, who followed noble John Brown, and fell as glorious martyrs for the cause of the slave,'' and he told them to remember Denmark Vesey and Nat Turner. ''This is our golden opportunity,'' Douglass asserted, to win ''the gratitude of the country and the best blessings of . . . posterity through all time.'' The call closed with the information that Douglass would forward all applications received within two weeks to Boston. This stirring message originally appeared in Douglass' journal and was republished by the leading papers of the North. Reprinted in pamphlet form, it was widely circulated and became the most important implement for recruiting black soldiers.

In addition to Douglass, Stearns employed other prominent blacks as recruiting agents: William Wells Brown, Charles Lenox Remond, Henry Highland Garnet, Martin R. Delany, William Cooper Nell, John Mercer Langston, and O.S.B. Wall. The expanded group of recruiters finally numbered one hundred and was named the Black Committee. These men produced results. From all over the Northeast, Negroes came to Boston. Recruitments opened on February 9, and by March 12, 1863, the regiment was full. Over three thousand blacks from Ohio alone reported to Fort Meigs, Massachusetts, for screening. The *Ohio State Journal* of Columbus reported that by May 22, 1863, nearly nine hundred volunteers had passed through Cleveland en route to Boston.

Some northerners spoke out against recruiting the black regiment. The *Boston Pilot,* an Irish-American Copperhead paper, sneered that ''one southern regiment of white men would put 20 regiments of them Negroes to flight in an hour. *20,000 negroes on the march would be smelled 10 miles distant.* No scouts need ever be sent out to discover such warriors.'' But the *Army and Navy Journal* reminded those who scoffed of the services of Negro soldiers in the War for Independence:

The record is clear that, from the beginning to the conclusion of the War of the Revolution, negroes served in the Continental armies with intelligence, courage, and steadfastness; and that important results in several instances are traceable to their good conduct.

The *Journal* was certain that when the history of the Civil War was written, it would record the fact that in this conflict, too, Negroes served ''with intelligence, courage, and steadfastness'' and contributed in many ways to the final victory of the Union.

The Fifty-fourth Massachusetts Regiment completed its training at Fort Meigs in mid-May. On May 18, 1863, Governor Andrew visited the training camp, and before over a thousand onlookers, presented the regimental colors to the commander, Colonel Robert Gould Shaw. The banner was a gift from black men and women of Boston, and as the governor held it out to Colonel Shaw, he spoke of the long struggle to create a regiment of blacks, how at last the dream had become a reality, and how on the battlefield all would see demonstrated "the manly zeal of the colored citizens of Massachusetts and of those other states which has cast their lot with ours."

Governor Andrew also presented Colonel Shaw with "the State colors of Massachusetts," which "have never been surrendered to any foe." The commander of the Fifty-fourth then took hold of the flag of his home state and said:

I know there is not one who will not be proud to fight and serve under our flag. May we have an opportunity to show that you have not made a mistake in entrusting the honor of the State to a colored regiment—the first State that has sent one to the war.

William Lloyd Garrison, who had discarded his pacifism and actively backed Governor Andrew's efforts to raise a black regiment, was one of the onlookers at this historic occasion. As he explained: "What would peace gain if men who will fight for other things will not fight for liberty? . . . When we get liberty, we shall have peace. . . . I am glad to see the men of the north who will not accept my peace views acting earnestly . . . in support of my liberty views."

On the morning of May 28, 1863, excitement prevailed in Boston. The *Boston Transcript* observed: "Since Massachusetts first began to send her brave sons in the field, no single regiment has attracted larger crowds into the street than the 54th." As the regiment of one thousand blacks, under the command of Colonel Robert Shaw, marched through the downtown streets on their way to the Common and then to board a ship for South Carolina, the crowd cheered. The soldiers made an excellent showing. One reporter noted the "general precision attending their evolution" and their "ease and uniformity in going through their manual."

After the dress parade on the Common, the regiment marched to Battery Wharf, passing over ground moistened by the blood of Crispus Attucks and along the route over which, less than ten years earlier, Anthony Burns had been led in chains back to slavery. As they marched off to war, the men of the Fifty-fourth Massachusetts sang a song that one of the volunteers had written:

McClellan went to Richmond with two hundred thousand brave,
He said, "keep back the niggers," and the Union he would save.
Little Mac he had his way still the Union is in tears—
    Now they call for the help of the colored Volunteers.

O, give us a flag, all free without a slave,
    We'll fight to defend it, as our Fathers did so brave.
The gallant comp'ny "A" will make the rebels dance,
    And we'll stand by the Union if we only have a chance.

So rally, boys, rally, let us never mind the past;
  We had a hard road to travel, but our day is coming fast,
For God is for the right, and we have no need to fear,
  The Union must be saved by the colored Volunteer.

Shortly before one o'clock, the black soldiers boarded the *DeMolay*. A few visitors were permitted on board, including Frederick Douglass, whose sons, Charles and Lewis, were leaving with the regiment, the latter in the uniform of a sergeant-major.

OTHER BLACK REGIMENTS

When the Fifty-fourth's roster was filled, the surplus black enlistees at Fort Meigs were organized into the Fifty-fifth Massachusetts Infantry Regiment. Composed mainly of Ohio blacks, the unit's colors came from the Buckeye State and were purchased for it by John Mercer Langston, the chief recruiter. En route to present the specially designed flags to the black regiment, Langston was summoned to the governor's mansion in Columbus where Governor James Tod asked him to recruit blacks for Ohio. But Langston informed the governor that he could not act without the authorization of George L. Stearns or Secretary of War Stanton. Still, when Governor Tod learned that the Massachusetts Fifty-fifth was made up almost entirely of Ohioans, he requested that the special colors be "exhibited from the eastern steps of the capitol." The colors were displayed and both the governor and Langston addressed an enthusiastic rally. The flags were then forwarded to Fort Meigs by express.

A breakdown of the trades and occupations of the Fifty-fifth Massachusetts Infantry revealed 596 farmers, 74 laborers, 34 barbers, 50 waiters, 27 cooks, 21 blacksmiths, 7 painters, 27 teamsters, 7 grooms, 9 hostlers, 3 coachmen, 5 coopers, 20 sailors, 8 butchers, 2 ironworkers, 9 shoemakers, 16 masons and plasterers, 3 brickmakers, 2 stonecutters, 6 boatmen, 5 clerks, 6 carpenters, 2 millers, 2 firemen, 1 coppersmith, 1 machinist, 1 rope maker, 1 fisherman, 1 tinker, 1 harness maker, 1 caulker, 1 grass grinder, 1 musician, 1 molder, 1 confectioner, 1 tobacco worker, 1 clergyman, 1 broom maker, 1 baker, 1 student, 2 whitewashers, 3 printers, 6 teachers, 5 porters, 2 wagon makers, and 3 engineers.

After the flags had been delivered to the Fifty-fifth Regiment, Governor Tod informed Langston that both Stearns and Secretary Stanton had instructed the black recruiter "to proceed at once to the recruitment of colored troops which would be credited to Ohio." The 127th Ohio Volunteer Infantry now came into existence. White officers were recruited after an examination of candidates by an appointed board. On November 1, 1863, the Ohio 127th boasted 1,094 men and officers ready for service. (To bypass the Ohio constitutional ban on black militia troops, the War Department activated the unit as the Fifth United States Colored

Troops.) A second Ohio black unit, the Twenty-seventh United States Colored Troops, was authorized by the War Department on January 11, 1864. More than 1,400 blacks served with the Twenty-seventh.

In June 1863, General Robert E. Lee's army moved northward toward an eventual showdown with the Union army at Gettysburg, Pennsylvania. Governor Andrew Curtin and Mayor Alexander Henry of Philadelphia issued proclamations calling for new recruits to bolster the state militia. The call to arms caused great excitement in the black community. Meetings were held in the city's black churches, and officers and drummers paraded in the streets. At the meeting in the basement of the Colored Bethel Church, held on June 29, 1863, George Trusty reported that he had spoken to both Mayor Henry and Major George L. Stearns and that they were both anxious that "a negro Brigade should be formed in the city." While most of the speakers called for immediate volunteers, Reverend J. P. Campbell cautioned against haste, for he did not "intend to be humbugged by the city government." Robert Purvis, however, criticized this stand, arguing that "this was not time to talk about being humbugged." An adjourned meeting held the following day adopted a resolution calling on Philadelphia blacks to respond to the call for soldiers and to help defend the state and city.

Headquarters were immediately opened at the Institute for Colored Youth for the purpose of recruiting a black company, and the students at the institute were the first company to respond. Led by Octavius V. Catto, the institute students volunteered en masse and left school to go off to fight Lee's army.

The newly organized company marched to the West Philadelphia train station, where a large number of blacks had gathered to say farewell. Upon reaching Harrisburg, they were fully mustered in and issued equipment, but Major Darius N. Couch of the Department of the Army of the Susquehanna area refused to allow them to be inducted. His excuse was that Congress had provided for the enlistment of blacks for not fewer than three years, and since this company was an emergency militia unit enlisted for limited service of a few months, they did not meet the qualification and could not serve. "Considering the dire state of the nation," Harry C. Silcox notes, "Couch's view indicates his prejudice." As soon as he learned of Couch's decision, Secretary of the Army Stanton telegraphed the major: "You are authorized to accept the service of any volunteer troops that may be offered, *without regard to color*." But the wire came too late. By then, the black company had returned to Philadelphia.

The entire black community and even sections of the white community of Philadelphia reacted indignantly to the treatment of the Negro volunteers. After Major Stearns had appealed to patriotic Philadelphians for help, a group of seventy-five organized themselves as the Supervisory Committee for Recruiting Colored Regiments. Cooperating with Stearns, this committee raised eleven regiments of U.S. troops for Pennsylvania and established the Free Military School at 1210 Chestnut Street for white officer candidates who were to become leaders of black regiments. Camp William Penn, located at Cheltenham Township in suburban Philadelphia, was the training ground for the black soldiers. No fewer than eleven regiments were formed at Camp William Penn before the end of the war: the 3d, 6th, 8th, 22d, 24th, 32d, 41st, 43d, 45th, and 127th Infantry. Of these the 6th and the 8th saw the most action. The 6th joined the Negro division under General Butler on the James River in May 1864 and later participated in the capture of Fort Fisher at Wilmington, North Carolina. The 8th, which suffered the heaviest casualties, fought first in the ill-fated Florida campaign and then joined the main Union army before Richmond. The 22d, which also served at Richmond, was detailed as part of the escort at Lincoln's funeral and was then sent to the Eastern Shore in pursuit of the conspirators in the plot to assassinate the president.

One of the men who joined the black regiments at Camp William Penn was Robert Forten, James Forten's second oldest son, who was fifty-one when he decided to enlist. Although his education and varied experience led him to believe he would be placed at the head of a black regiment, he soon learned that according to law, only white officers could command such units. Disappointed but undaunted, Forten accepted the rank of a private in Company A. But on April 8, 1865, Colonel H. Seymour Hall promoted Forten to sergeant major and transferred him to Maryland. In Baltimore, Forten recruited black soldiers. Suddenly, when it appeared that Forten was headed for a long and illustrious career in the service, tragedy struck. Overwork and unsanitary camp conditions made him seriously ill and forced him to receive sick leave. On April 25, he died of typhoid fever at the family's home on Lombard Street in Philadelphia.

In death, Robert Forten received the recognition due a loyal and patriotic soldier of his rank. His was the first military funeral given a black man in Philadelphia. On April 28, a huge crowd of soldiers and local residents gathered at Camp William Penn for the service. James Miller McKim and Lucretia Mott, abolitionist friends of the Forten family, offered brief remarks. Thomas Webster, chairman of the army's Supervisory Committee for black recruitment, spoke at the ceremony. Following the service, Forten's remains were escorted to St. Thomas Episcopal Church's cemetery. Soldiers fired three shots over the coffin before placing it in the family's vault.

In spite of his brief time in the military, Robert Forten's excellent record served a useful purpose. Supporters of a bill equalizing pay for black soldiers pointed to Forten's activities. William D. Kelly, a Philadelphia judge and congressman and a boyhood friend of Robert Forten, had been away from home during the sergeant major's funeral. Two days later in his speech before the House of Representatives, Kelly extolled the contributions of Robert Forten and other black soldiers from Pennsylvania, and he implored Congress to make the black soldier's treatment equal to that received by the whites.

The refusal of New York's Copperhead governor, Horatio Seymour, to raise black regiments left that state without any Negro units. Even the press began to complain that Seymour's unwillingness to cooperate was causing New York to lose too many black men to other states. On November 16, 1863, the Association for Promoting Colored Volunteers called a meeting to discuss Seymour's hostility to black recruitment. The circular calling upon New Yorkers to attend was signed by sixty-six people, including Peter Cooper, William Cullen Bryant, and P. T. Barnum. Reverend Henry Highland Garnet, one of the speakers, reminded New Yorkers that blacks were going to Rhode Island, Massachusetts, and Connecticut to enlist. Eventually, black units were authorized for New York, and the Twentieth, Twenty-sixth, and Thirty-first Regiments were established. Altogether, 4,125 black men enlisted in New York State, or about 2 percent of the total Negro enlistment during the Civil War.

On March 5, 1864, the Twentieth Regiment marched from Twenty-sixth Street to Union Square. At a mass rally, Charles King, president of Columbia College, told the regiment: "You are in arms, not for the freedom and law of the white race alone, but for universal law and freedom." "On! On! then, soldiers of the 20th . . ." King cried, "nowhere have they [colored troops] turned back from the bloodiest conflict or failed to follow their leader into the very jaws of death." President King climaxed the day by presenting the black regiment with a conquering eagle, a broken yoke, and the armed figure of liberty.

SOME BLACK RECRUITERS

By the summer of 1863, black soldiers were in great demand. A new conscription act required the states to draft men of military age if they could not fill their quotas with volunteers. Because every black who joined up made it possible for one white to stay out of the army, Connecticut, Rhode Island, Ohio, and Michigan sent agents across the country, to Canada, and to Union-held territory in the South to seek black volunteers. With the states competing against each other, blacks were offered substantial bounties for enlisting. Handbills similar to the following, which was handed out by Martin R. Delany on behalf of Connecticut, were distributed in black communities:

BLACK NATIONAL DEFENDERS!

The State of Connecticut is authorized to take Colored Troops; and any number of her quota of 5,000 may be colored men. 29th Regiment Connecticut Volunteers is now being formed at Camp Buckingham, composed entirely of Colored Men, located at the beautiful City of New Haven, the seat of Yale University.

STATE BOUNTY,
$200.00 CASH!
On being sworn in.

By an old law of the State, 30 dollars a year are allowed to each soldier for clothing, 10 dollars of which is paid down at the time of entering the service, the other 20 dollars being paid in four month payments each, making 10 dollars Bounty—cash, on joining the Regiment—and 20 dollars more during the year.

An important fact connected with this recruiting is, that the contract for raising the troops has been given to a Colored Man; and Connecticut is the first State, since the war commenced, which has been thus liberal and considerate.

This fact alone should be an inducement for COLORED MEN to rally to her standard.

Most of the state recruiters were men, but at least one was a woman—Mary Ann Shadd Cary, who left her home in Canada to work as a recruiter for the state of Indiana. The best woman recruiter was Harriet Tubman, but she did her recruiting in the South. Sent to South Carolina by Governor Andrew to work as a scout, she formed a corps of nine ex-slaves. They traveled through the countryside to collect information for army raids and to urge slaves to leave their masters. On March 6, 1863, General Saxton informed Secretary of War Stanton that "seven hundred and fifty blacks who were waiting for an opportunity to join the Union Army had been rescued from slavery under the leadership of Harriet Ross Tubman and the auxiliary command of Colonel James Montgomery." "This," Saxton added, "is the only military command in American history wherein a women, black or white, led the raid and under whose inspiration it was originated and conducted."

In a letter to Northern abolitionists requesting that they send her a pair of bloomers so she could move about the Southern countryside more easily, Harriet Tubman rejoiced:

We weakened the Rebels by bringing away 756 head of the most valuable livestock, known in your region as "contrabands," and this without the loss of a single life on our part, though we had good reason to believe that a number of Rebels bit the dust. . . . Of those 756 contrabands, nearly all the able-bodied men have joined the colored regiment here.

This and other successful raids made Harriet Tubman one of the best black recruiting agents.

Most blacks lived in the South, and that was where the largest number of black troops would have to be raised. On March 26, 1863, Secretary of War Stanton issued an order directing Adjutant General Lorenzo Thomas to raise black regiments in the Mississippi Valley. General Ulysses S. Grant gave Thomas active assistance in carrying out the new policy, issuing an order calling upon the officers to subordinate their prejudices. "It is expected," he said, "that all commanders will especially exert themselves in carrying out the policy of the administration, not only in organizing colored regiments and rendering them efficient, but also in removing prejudice against them." On October 3, 1863, the War Department, in general orders number 329, set up regulations for recruiting free blacks and slaves in Missouri, Tennessee, and Maryland. Under the order, the chief of the Bureau of Colored Troops received authority to establish recruiting offices in these slave states where free blacks and slaves, with their masters' consent, could be enlisted. Slaveowners could receive up to $300 if they permitted their slaves to enlist, but if within thirty days the enlistment of slaves had not been completed satisfactorily, the recruitment of slaves without the owner's consent was permissible. Fugitive slaves were usually signed up without the owner's permission, and free blacks joined readily.

By December 1863, fifty thousand blacks were in actual service, with the number swelling daily. Several factors, however, served to dampen the ardor of blacks to serve in the Union army.

DISCRIMINATION IN THE UNION ARMY

The lot of black soldiers in the Union army was made more difficult by the many forms of discrimination to which they were subjected by the government and by white, racist commanders. They were forced to serve in segregated units and were given inferior and insufficient equipment, food, clothing, lodging, and medical treatment, compared with that received by white soldiers. One newspaper characterized the barracks of the Michigan black volunteers as ''a disgrace to the community.'' ''There is not a barn or a pigsty in the whole city of Detroit,'' it observed, ''that is not more fit for habitation of a human than the quarters at Camp Ward.''

A Civil War song entitled, ''The Colored Brigade,'' a mixture of admiration and racism, contained the following lines:

> O when we meet de enemy I s'pec we make 'em stare,
> I tink he'll catch a tartar when he meets de wooly hair;
> We'll fight while we are able, and in greenbacks we'll be paid,
> And soon I'll be a colonel in de colored brigade.
> Chor.—A colonel, a colonel, in de darkey brigade,
> And soon I'll be a colonel in de colored brigade.

Very few blacks were commissioned as officers during the war. General Butler did commission more than seventy-five blacks in the regiments he raised in Louisiana in 1862; however, they were treated discourteously by white officers and were dismissed from the service by General Banks, who succeeded Butler. With Stanton's approval they were replaced by ''poorly qualified whites.''

Lousiana's black officers were not the only ones to experience discrimination. In 1864 James Monroe Trotter, who had risen to first sergeant and then to regimental sergeant major in the Fifty-fifth Massachusetts Regiment, was recommended for a commission as a second lieutenant, but several white army commanders were opposed to permitting a Negro to rise to officer status, and he was denied the commission. Probably as a result of William Lloyd Garrison's intervention, he did receive a commission on April 10, 1864, and served for the remainder of the war as a lieutenant. But for much of the time he, along with other black officers in the Fifty-fifth Massachusetts Infantry Regiment, performed their duties without actually being mustered into service by General William Foster who claimed, "There is no law *allowing* it, they being colored men." "I am sorry to have to tell you . . . that almost all the line officers give us the *cold shoulder*," Trotter wrote bitterly on August 2, 1864, to Francis Jackson Garrison (William Lloyd Garrison's son), and he added: "O how discouraging! How maddening, almost! A few, however, are sensible enough and kind hearted enough not to deny a poor oppressed people the means of *liberating themselves*." Trotter continued:

An officer told me that it was "too soon." That time should be granted white officers to get *rid of their prejudices* . . . yes . . . there is really more turning up the nose on account of the commissions *in our very midst* than elsewhere; *and no other reason is given except Color*. Several white officers have resigned because of it, and the disapproval of the muster papers alone prevented others from doing the same thing. This is a model way to promote military discipline and efficiency. They differ with Napoleon. He always secured the perfect good behavior of his soldiers by promoting the deserving. Every man knew that if he did well that he would be rewarded. But according to the *"Modern* Mode" no such rule is to be adopted because the soldiers are so *blamable as to have their skins dark*. Most awful crime! I wish if they hate us because we are black, that the colorphobia and "Negro Elevating" class would white wash us.

Reverend Henry M. Turner, the first black man commissioned as a chaplain to the Union army, had a different experience. Turner's entry in his journal for December 18, 1864, contained the following news: "I was amused this morning at a colored boy who came to wait on the tables. He was so much surprised at seeing me, a colored man, eating with white officers, that he did nothing but stand back and look at me. I suppose that he never saw such a sight before."

About one hundred blacks gained commissions during the war, which was a small percentage considering that 7,122 officers served with the black regiments. Twelve black chaplains and eight black surgeons were commissioned during the war.

A number of black soldiers had the opportunity of displaying extraordinary leadership on the battlefield even without being commissioned as officers. After all the white officers of the Ohio Fifth United States Colored Troops had been either wounded or killed during the battle at Chapins Farm, Virginia, on September 29, 1864, 4 black noncommissioned officers assumed command of companies. On April 6, 1865, they were awarded the Medal of Honor for gallantry in a battle in which 28 black soldiers lost their lives and 185 more were wounded.

Many Union commanders regarded trained black troops as fit only for fatigue duty, and they assigned all the unhealthy and unpleasant details to them. The weapons provided Negro troops were generally of an inferior quality. Suffering from poor arms and equipment, inferior training, and incompetent officers, black soldiers were often hurled into battle without adequate preparation. Under such circumstances, the slaughter of soldiers was fearful, and the expression *black cannon fodder* became fairly common.

The treatment of black soldiers who fell into the hands of the enemy was particularly cruel. In December 1862, Jefferson Davis announced that any Negro soldier who was taken prisoner would be turned over to state authorities and dealt with as an insurrectionist in accordance with the slave codes of the South. Since these codes stipulated death sentences for "subversive" activities, many free black soldiers died convicted of "conspiracy to murder or maim a white person." Under the regulation, no exchange of prisoners could be effected where Negroes were concerned. In most cases, blacks captured in battle were brutally murdered by the Confederates. Not even the wounded were spared.

The most serious problem for black troops was that of pay. In the beginning, it had been assumed that the black regiments would be used primarily in noncombat support and labor duties and that the whites would do the bulk of the fighting. Their pay, therefore, was set at the rates paid to laborers and not soldiers. White privates received thirteen dollars a month and a three-dollar clothing allowance, while black soldiers—both noncommissioned officers and privates—were paid at the rate of ten dollars a month.

Many blacks objected vigorously to this discrimination and refused to enlist because of the pay differential. The booming war economy and the availability of jobs had created an unusual prosperity for blacks in certain sections of the North, and the wages of Negro soldiers were hardly an inducement for them to leave the home front for the armed forces. As Reverend J. P. Campbell correctly pointed out at a Baltimore meeting of blacks to encourage enlistments:

It takes as much to clothe and feed the black man's wife as it does the white man's wife. It takes as much money to go to market for the black man's little boys and girls. We have yet to learn why it is that the black soldier should not receive the same compensation for labor in the service of his country that the white soldier receives. . . . Give us equal pay, and we will go to war—not pay on mercenary principles, but pay upon the principles of justice and equity.

The discriminatory pay scale also bred deep resentment among black troops. Rather than accede to this unequal treatment, large numbers of black soldiers refused, as a matter of principle, to accept any compensation at all when army paymasters sought to pay them less than a soldier's salary. In November 1863, the Massachusetts legislature provided for a special appropriation of state funds to make up the wage differential for the black soldiers of that state. However, these soldiers not only refused to accept this equalization offer because it violated their principle, but they continued to serve without compensation. James Henry Gooding, a black corporal in the Fifty-fourth Massachusetts, went beyond this. He wrote to President Lincoln:

Are we Soldiers, or are we Laborers? We are fully armed, and equipped, have done all the various duties pertaining to a Soldier's life, have conducted ourselves to the complete satisfaction of General Officers, who were, if anything, prejudiced against us, but who now accord us all the encouragement and honors due us. . . .

Now your Excellency, we have done a Soldier's duty. Why can't we have a Soldier's pay?

No reply from Lincoln has been preserved, but the Copperhead *New York World* answered: "To claim that the indolent, servile negro is the equal in courage, enterprise and fire of the foremost race in all the world is a libel upon the name of an American citizen. . . . It is unjust in every way to the white soldier to put him on a level with the black."

Writing to the *Christian Recorder* from Jacksonville, Florida, "A Soldier of the Eighth Regiment Colored Troops" drew a grim picture of what blacks faced in the Union Army:

Ever since I have been in the regiment, I have tried to discharge the duty that has been laid down for me to do, in the best way that I know how. I have always been ready for any duty that I have been called upon to perform; but things work so different with us from what they do with white soldiers, that I have got discouraged; and not only myself, but all of our company. Our treatment is quite different. Our rations are unequal. Our tents are nothing to be compared with those of the white soldiers. They have large tents, while we have small shelter-tents, that a good-sized man can hardly stand up in; and, if we want any comfort in them—if we want to have them so that we can get in to them, without getting down and crawling on our hands and feet—we must carry and beg boards and rails for nearly half a mile, and then, if they don't just put up to suit our commanding officers, they will have to be torn down or thrown down by them. . . .

It is really discouraging to think that men have to leave their families and friends, homes and fire-sides to go forth to the field of battle, go through the same drill as the white soldiers, do the same duty, march the same, and, if anything, harder than the white soldiers, fight just as well, and stand in contest just as long, and, if it comes to a hard struggle, they will stand longer, and with it all, they don't want to pay them the same wages that they pay the white soldiers. . . .

With all this, I would not think so hard of it, if they would treat us right in other respects. But we have, part of the time, only about half enough to eat. Our families at home are in a suffering condition, and send to their husbands for relief. Where is it to come from? . . . My wife and three little children at home are, in a manner, freezing and starving to death. She writes to me for aid, but I have nothing to send her; and if I wish to answer her letter, I must go to some of our officers to get paper and envelopes. . . . When we lie down to sleep, the pictures of our families are before us, asking for relief from their sufferings. How can men do their duty, with such agony in their minds?

Unlike the Union army, the navy, for the most part, adopted a policy that upheld equal treatment for all enlisted men. In contrast to the army, which maintained segregated units, identifying blacks by the designation USCT (U.S. Colored Troops), the navy integrated white and black sailors, and this, in turn, made it almost impossible for it to establish two administrative policies—one for whites and one for blacks. This did not mean, however, that white sailors treated blacks on board their ships as equals. Ridicule of blacks was common and found expression in stereotypes of Negroes presented in plays performed aboard naval vessels. Moreover, even though the men on board ships were not segregated, a form of segregation did take place. On some ships, Negroes were required to cook and eat their food in separate areas and were assigned the more menial tasks aboard ship. Although the Navy Department did not officially encourage such practices, it did nothing to prohibit them.

Like black army enlistees, Union naval Negroes suffered as a result of the Confederate attitude toward black prisoners of war. The black seamen captured by the Confederates were subject to the laws of the Southern states with regard to activities inciting slaves to rebel against their master.

While the status of the black seamen was not equal to that of their white counterparts, nevertheless, compared to the life that black soldiers endured in the Union army, they enjoyed relative equality.

DEALING WITH BLACK SOLDIERS' GRIEVANCES

At first, black recruiters tended to play down the importance of lack of equality for Negro enlistees. John Mercer Langston insisted that by enlisting, the volunteers would "aid in achieving the freedom of our slave brother: and win for themselves and their posterity equality before American laws." He brushed aside the pay difference with a call to duty: "Pay or no pay, let us volunteer." Frederick Douglass, too, insisted that nothing should interfere with the Negro's participation in the Union army. Discrimination against black soldiers must be consistently fought, he insisted, but it must not serve as a barrier against the full Negro's participation in the war. "Colored men going into the army and navy," Douglass wrote, "must expect annoyance. They will be severely criticized and even insulted—but let no man hold back on this account. We will be fighting a double battle, against slavery in the South and against prejudice and proscription in the North—and the case presents the best assurances of success."

Douglass admonished his people to join the Union army and fight regardless of the question of wages. If the government offered blacks a chance to enlist and to serve, even without salary, it would still be best to sign up. He saw in the black soldier the foundation for the black citizen:

Once let the black man get upon his person the brass letters U.S.; let him get an eagle on his button, and a musket on his shoulder, and bullets in his pocket, and there is no power on earth or under the earth which can deny that he has earned the right of citizenship in the United States.

But as reports detailing grievances and complaints of black soldiers mounted in both number and intensity, Douglass changed his stand. Infuriated, he published an open letter in which he lashed out at Lincoln for failing to redress the grievances of black soldiers. When white soldiers were threatened with assassination, he wrote, the president immediately informed the Confederacy that the federal government "will retaliate sternly and severely." But when black soldiers were murdered, "no word comes from the Capitol." Until Lincoln used his authority "to prevent these atrocious assassinations of Negro soldiers, the civilized world will hold him equally with Jefferson Davis responsible for them."

Douglass demanded that the black soldiers be adequately trained, that they be provided with competent officers, and that a halt be called to the practice of assigning Negro soldiers to demoralizing, unpleasant, and unhealthy garrison, fatigue, and labor details. Finally, he insisted that blacks be granted equal pay for equal work and the right to become commissioned officers. "Colored men," he wrote, "have a right not only to ask for equal pay for equal work, but that merit, not color, should be the criterion observed by government in the distribution of places."

Having set forth these demands, Douglass called a halt to his recruiting work until the government changed its policies toward black soldiers. His duty, he felt, was to provide decent conditions for blacks in the armed forces before asking any more to enlist. "I owe it to my long abused people," he informed Stearns in giving up his recruiting activities, "and especially of them already in the army, to expose their wrongs and plead their cause."

Stearns persuaded Douglass to travel to Washington and lay his grievances before Lincoln. The stairway to Lincoln's office was crowded with the usual throng of patronage seekers, and Douglass fully expected to have to wait "at least half a day" before he would be able to see the president. But two minutes after he had sent in his card, he was ushered through the crowd into Lincoln's office. Douglass later recalled, "I could hear, in the eager multitude outside, as they saw me pressing and elbowing my way through, the remark, 'Yes, damn it, I knew they would let the nigger through,' in a kind of despairing voice—'a Peace Democrat, I suppose.'"

The president arose and put his visitor at ease. When Senator Samuel Clarke Pomeroy of New Jersey, who had arranged the meeting, started to introduce Douglass, the president stopped him, saying: "Mr. Douglass, I know you; I have read about you, and Mr. Seward has told me about you." He referred to a speech Douglass had made in New York in which the black leader had listed "the tardy, hesitating, vacillating policy of the President of the United States" as "the most disheartening feature in our present political and military situation." Lincoln admitted that he had sometimes been slow, but denied the charge of vacillation. "I think it can not be shown," he told Douglass, "that when I have taken a position, I have ever retreated from it."

After these introductory remarks, Douglass came directly to the point. As a recruiting agent, he wished to present the case of the black soldier. If the War Department wished to recruit Negro men, it had to reverse its policies: it had to give the black soldiers the same pay white soldiers received; it had to compel the Confederacy to treat black soldiers, when taken prisoners, as prisoners of war; it had to promote Negro soldiers who distinguished themselves for bravery in the field just as white men were promoted for similar service and to retaliate in kind when any black soldiers were murdered.

Lincoln listened attentively and sympathetically to these proposals. The time was not yet ripe, he replied, to give black soldiers the same pay as white men, for opposition to recruiting Negroes in the Union army was still too strong. "I assure you, Mr. Douglass," he continued, "that in the end they shall have the same pay as white soldiers." He admitted the justice of Douglass' request for the promotion of blacks in the army and promised "to sign any commission to colored soldiers" that the secretary of war recommended. He agreed that black soldiers should be treated as prisoners of war when captured. But he balked at Douglass' suggestion for retaliation. "Once begun," he declared, "I do not know where such a measure would stop." Basically Lincoln's position was that black soldiers should be willing to serve under any conditions because they had stronger motives for fighting than did the white troops and that the prejudice against blacks could be overcome only gradually.

Douglass was not entirely satisfied with Lincoln's reactions to his request, but he "was so well satisfied with the man and with the educating tendency of the conflict" that he determined to continue recruiting black men for the Union cause. He was convinced that the government's treatment of black soldiers would soon radically change for the better.

Lincoln's prediction to Douglass that discrimination in pay would be abolished was to come true a year after his interview with the black leader. On July 14, 1864, Congress passed a bill granting black soldiers the same pay as white soldiers, retroactive to January 1, 1864. Arrears prior to that date would be paid only to those who had been free on that day. This led to the so-called Quaker oaths—many saying they had been free by God's law, if not man's. In September 1864, men of the Fifty-fourth Massachusetts received their full back pay since May 1863 at a rate equal to that of the white troops—constituting a sum of $170,000 for their "eighteen months of unsalaried service." Not until March 1865, however, was a fully retroactive equal pay law passed.

On April 18, 1864, Lincoln delivered a speech in which he told the audience: "A painful rumor—true, I fear—has reached us of the massacre by the rebel forces at Fort Pillow, in the west end of Tennessee, on the Mississippi River, of some three hundred colored soldiers and white officers, who had just been overpowered by their assailants." The rumor was soon confirmed. On April 11, 1864, General Nathaniel Forrest's Tennessee Confederate Cavalry took Fort Pillow by storming the place. Forrest's soldiers shot, stabbed, buried alive, and captured most of the fort's defenders. They then ordered those who surrendered to jump into the Tennessee River and shot those who refused. Because of the Confederate government's already announced no-quarter policy concerning black soldiers and because of the Confederate soldier's deep and ingrained hatred of blacks, the 262 black soldiers at Fort Pillow suffered an incredible 238 casualties. General Forrest, later a leader of the Ku Klux Klan, explained that this was "to demonstrate to the Northern people that negro soldiers cannot cope with Southerners."

In retaliation, Lincoln held a number of southerners as hostages, vowing not to return them to their former prisoner-of-war status until the Confederacy agreed to prevent such actions from happening in the future. Responding to the South's unwillingness to exchange captured black soldiers for white soldiers and to a Confederate resolution stating that white Union officers of Negro soldiers "shall, if captured, be put to death or be otherwise punished at the discretion of the court," Lincoln issued an order of retaliation:

It is the duty of every government to give protection to its citizens of whatever class, color or condition, and especially to those who are duly organized as soldiers in the public service. The law of nations, and the usages and customs of war, as carried on by civilized powers, permit no distinction as to color in the treatment of prisoners of war as public enemies. To sell or enslave any captured person on account of his color, and for no offense against the laws of war, is a relapse into barbarism and a crime against the civilization of the age.

The Confederacy was duly informed that the "government of the United States will give the same protection to all its soldiers" and that if the Rebels should sell or enslave any soldier because of his color, "the offence shall be punished by retaliation upon the enemy's prisoners in our possession." Then came this stern warning above the signature, "Abraham Lincoln":

It is therefore ordered that for every soldier of the United States killed in violation of the laws of war, a rebel soldier shall be executed; and for every one enslaved by the enemy or sold into slavery, a rebel soldier shall be placed at hard labor on the public works, and continued at such labor until the other shall be released and receive the treatment due to a prisoner of war.

With this proclamation by President Lincoln, the Confederacy's barbaric treatment of black soldiers captured as prisoners ceased.

Despite the extent and depth of their grievances, there were few disciplinary problems with the black troops. There was a near mutiny in the Fifty-fifth Massachusetts and a minor mutiny in the South Carolina regiment over the pay issue. The most serious event was the brief mutiny at Fort Jackson, Louisiana, but a study of the event concludes that the black troops were so brutally treated by a white racist and sadist officer and by other incompetent white officers that they were virtually "provoked to rebellion."

In the face of continuing discrimination, an enormous number of blacks did enlist and serve in the Union army. One black probably expressed the view of most Negroes when he reportedly prayed:

Great Doctor ob doctors, king ob kings and God ob battles help us to be well. Help us to be able to fight wid de union sojers the battles for de union. Help us to fight for de country—fight for our homes and our own free children and our children's children.

The "God ob battles" inspired almost 200,000 black men to enlist in the Union army. It is impossible to state definitely the exact number of Negro soldiers. The files in the adjutant general's office reveal a total of 186,017, but the number of those who actually enlisted is probably greater. One soldier who points out that when a black soldier died or was killed, another was substituted in his place under the same name, estimated the total number of black soldiers called into the ranks of the Union army at about 220,000. W.E.B. Du Bois, however, puts the figure at 300,000.

Herbert Aptheker estimates the number of blacks who enlisted in the Union navy at 29,511, or 25 percent of the total navy enlistments. However, Lawrence Valuska asserts that only 9,596 out of the total of 117,580 naval enlistees were blacks. Whatever the exact figures, it is clear that over 200,000 black men fought in the Union army and navy. Of this number over 160,000 were from the slave states and most of them were slaves or former slaves. In his poem "Battle-Pieces," Herman Melville wrote:

> All nature felt their coming,
> The birds like couriers flew,
> And the banners brightly blooming
> The slaves by thousands drew,
> And they marched beside the drumming.
> And they joined the armies blue.

The many thousands of black Americans who joined the Union's armed force despite various forms of discrimination participated in 449 military engagements during the last two years of the war, of which 39 were major battles. Several have special significance.

PORT HUDSON AND MILLIKEN'S BEND

The first major engagement in which black troops participated occurred at Port Hudson, Louisiana, in May 1863. Simultaneously with Grant's siege of Vicksburg, General Nathaniel P. Banks was given the task of taking Port Hudson, farther down the Mississippi River. On May 23, 1863, the assault was ordered, and the First and Third Louisiana regiments, composed of free blacks with Negro officers in command (the Native Guards of Louisiana had always had black officers), led the attack on the fort. The black regiments made six desperate charges into the teeth of the strongly entrenched enemy's artillery, in the course of which one out of five of the blacks fell. Here is how a white Union army officer described the assault on Port Hudson:

On their extreme right the two negro regiments advanced over the bayou toward the enemy's works. . . . A fire of musketry opened from the top of the bluff, and from the rifle-pits all the way down. The fire was supported by their batteries. . . . They stood up nobly, but it was impossible to cross the bayou. . . . Slowly they fell back, the enemy not daring to follow them. Hearing our heavy fire, another charge was made, and another, and a fourth with a like result. . . . A fifth charge was made. . . . They stood like veterans and were mown down, and finally a retreat was ordered which was made as if by old soldiers. . . . I find that many sneerers are very polite to Colonel Nelson of the Third Louisiana. . . . No regiment behaved better than they did. They never staggered under a fire from a superior force and batteries of the largest guns known to warfare. . . . They fought with desperation and carried all before them. They had to be restrained for fear they would get too far unsupported. They have shown that they can and will fight well. I hope the Copperheads will now stop their abuse.

As newspapers presented stirring accounts of the black troops, public sentiment in the North concerning the bravery of the Negro under fire underwent a remarkable change. The *New York Times* published a report that concluded: ''Nobly, indeed, they have acquitted themselves, and proudly may every colored man hereafter hold up his head, and point to the records of those who fell in that bloody field.'' In his official report of the battle, General Banks wrote:

Whatever doubt may have existed heretofore as to the efficiency of organizations of this character, the history of the day proves conclusively to those who were in a condition to observe the conduct of these regiments, that the Government will find in this class of troops effective supporters and defenders. The severe test to which they were subjected, and the determined measures in which they encountered the enemy, leaves upon my mind no doubt of their ultimate success.

Philadelphia's Union League issued a pamphlet honoring the black soldiers at Port Hudson. It began: ''There certainly does exist at this time a strong prejudice against employing negroes as soldiers, but the following extracts from authentic documents [describing the bravery of the Negro troops at Port Hudson] will show that this prejudice is unfounded.'' The account included a poem by George H. Boker, which concluded:

> Hundred on hundreds fell;
>   But they are resting well;
> Scourge and shackles strong
>   Never shall do them wrong.

Altogether 25,000 copies of three editions in English and one in German were distributed by the Union League.

Milliken's Bend, a Union outpost on the Mississippi River above Vicksburg, was the next scene of black military bravery. There, on June 7, 1863, two regiments of newly recruited freedmen beat back a Confederate attack, displaying great courage while forcing the rebels to retreat in a furious bayonet charge. Even the Rebel general commanding the assult on Milliken's Bend grudgingly conceded that the charge "was resisted by the negro portion of the enemy's force with considerable obstinacy, while the white or true Yankee portion ran like whipped curs almost as soon as the charge was ordered." Assistant Secretary of War Charles Dana visited Milliken's Bend a few days after the battle and later wrote that "the bravery of the blacks in the battle at Milliken's Bend completely revolutionized the sentiment of the army with regard to the employment of negro troops. I heard prominent officers who formerly in private had sneered at the idea of the negroes fighting express themselves after that as heartily in favor of it." General Lorenzo Thomas, the War Department's official recruiter of black troops in the Mississippi Valley, reported that when he undertook his task "the prejudice against colored troops was quite general, and it required in the first instance all my efforts to counteract it; but finally it was overcome, and the blacks themselves subsequently by their coolness and determination in battle fought themselves into their present high standing as soldiers." Port Hudson and Milliken's Bend were milestones in that fight.

FORT WAGNER

In mid-July 1863, units of the Fifty-fourth Massachusetts saw their first combat near Seceshville, South Carolina. During this encounter, Company K was completely cut off from the rest of the Union forces and surrounded by a Confederate regiment. The company, according to one participant, "only escaped by desparate [sic] fighting, with the loss of five killed, and six or eight wounded." A forced march of twenty miles brought the Fifty-fourth to Morris Island, where Fort Wagner, a major defensive position protecting Charleston, guarded the entrance to Charleston harbor. There, on July 18, 1863, in sight of Fort Sumter, the Fifty-fourth Regiment of the Massachusetts Volunteer Infantry waged its first real battle and exhibited a bravery that became legendary.

The Negro regiment was placed in the van. Colonel Robert Gould Shaw was among the first to scale the walls, his troops following closely. Shaw was shot and fell into the fort; his body was found with twenty of his men lying dead around him. Sergeant Major Lewis Douglass, the son of Frederick Douglass, jumped onto the parapet close behind Shaw and was the last man to leave it. A few units reached the top and planted the U.S. flag and the Massachusetts banner on the parapet. Sergeant Carney caught a flag as it was falling from the hands of its wounded bearer. In spite of his own severe injuries, he held it tightly until he reached the hospital, where he sank to the floor, saying, "The old flag never touched the ground, boys."

At Wagner, meanwhile, hand-to-hand combat pitted bayonet, clubbed rifle, and black men against rifle fire and grenades. New York and Connecticut units reached the salient but were ineffective because of darkness. Union forces held their positions for three hours, but as casualties mounted, the assault was abandoned. Fort Wagner remained in Confederate hands, but the *New York Tribune* said of the Fifty-fourth's performance at Wagner:

It is not too much to say that if this Massachusetts Fifty-fourth had faltered when its trial came, two hundred thousand colored troops for whom it was a pioneer would never have been put into the field, or would not have been put in for another year, which would have been equivalent to protracting the war into 1866. But it did not falter. It made Fort Wagner such a name to the colored race as Bunker Hill has been for ninety years to white Yankees.

Leaving aside the fact that blacks, too, fought at Bunker Hill, the praise lavished by the *Tribune* upon the black soldiers of the Fifty-fourth was both merited and shared by military men. On August 23, 1863, General Grant wrote in a private letter to Lincoln:

I have given the subject of arming the negro my hearty support. This, with the emancipation of the negro, is the heavyest [*sic*] blow yet given the Confederacy. . . . By arming the negro we have added a powerful ally. They will make good soldiers and taking them from the enemy weakens him in the same proportion they strengthen us. I am therefore most decidely in favor of pushing this policy to the enlistment of a force sufficient to hold all the South falling into our hands and to aid in capturing more.

And Lincoln himself wrote to Grant, not only urging the raising of Negro troops but adding: "I believe it is a resource which, if vigorously applied now, will soon close the contest." In short, Port Hudson, Milliken's Bend, and Fort Wagner had already demonstrated that the war could be speedily brought to an end with the use of black troops.

In the remaining months of 1863, black troops again and again proved their courage, determination, and desire to fight. Thomas Wentworth Higginson expressed a growing sentiment among Union generals when he wrote to Secretary of War Stanton:

Nobody knows anything about these men who has not seen them in battle. There is a fiery energy beyond anything of which I have read. . . . It would have been madness to attempt with the bravest white troops what I have accomplished with the black ones. . . . No officer in this regiment now doubts that the key to the successful prosecution of the war lies in the unlimited employment of black troops.

21

The Home Front—South

"Disloyalty of slaves to their masters has been a neglected phase of Confederate history," Bell I. Wiley wrote in 1938 explaining his reasons for publishing *Southern Negroes, 1861–1865*. Since the appearance of this book, historians have dispelled the "moonlight-and-magnolia" myth of loyal slaves who cheerfully supported the masters who fought to keep them enslaved.

There were, of course, household servants who hid the family treasure, took the livestock into the woods when the Yankees were near, and protected the mistress when the owner left for the Confederate army. Some house servants even took pride in the added responsibilities given them in the master's absence. There were Southern mistresses who depended on black drivers while their husbands were away at war. At the outset of the conflict, in fact, nearly all masters and mistresses had great faith and confidence in their slaves and black drivers.

If one reads the Southern press, that confidence appeared to be rewarded. "The general fidelity and affectionate loyalty of servants," wrote a Charleston editor, "is one of the more gratifying results and indications elicited by the war." Despite the Emancipation Proclamation, an Alabaman observed, "Our servants are still loyal and never rendered more cheerful obedience." As far as he was concerned, the war had wrought no substantial changes in the slaves' behavior.

The reality, however, was far different. So long as the Union army stood still, most of the slaves remained quiet. But the moment the federal troops moved into slave territory, the bondspeople joined them, and as federal patrols began inciting desertion, more and more did so. In 1862, a Confederate general estimated that slave desertion was costing North Carolina a million dollars every week. A year later, a report from a plantation in Snyder's Bluff, Mississippi, told of every

Negro having deserted. From Fort Gisbon, Mississippi, a planter wrote that "two men, three women, and eight children were all that remained with us, and they were much demoralized." In November 1863, a white resident of Warrentown, Alabama, predicted that in view of the high rate of desertion, the day was near when there "will not be a negro left in the country."

When asked to explain the flight of slaves to the Union army, Jefferson Davis replied: "The tempter came, like the serpent in Eden, and decoyed them with the magic word 'freedom.'" There were loyal slaves who resisted, but they were a small percentage. Examples of blacks who put the opportunity for freedom above every other consideration are the normal finding in the records of the period.

By the summer of 1862, many slaveowners were openly revealing bitterness at what they called the "fickleness" of the slaves. Their letters reveal real anxiety about slave loyalties. In July 1862, Reverend Charles Colcock Jones in Georgia wrote: "The temptation of change, the promise of freedom and pay for labor, is more than most can stand, and no reliance can be placed *certainly* upon any. The safest plan is to put them beyond reach of temptation . . . by leaving no boats in the water and by keeping guards along the rivers." A few days later, the Georgia slaveowner returned to the same theme: "The temptation of cheap goods, freedom and paid labor cannot be withstood," he wrote to his son, a Confederate lieutenant. In the same letter came the ominous note: "They are traitors who may pilot an enemy into your *bedchamber*! They know every road and swamp and creek and plantation in the country, and are the best of spies. If the absconding is not stopped, the negro property of the country will be of little value."

Even before this was written, the slaveowners knew no peace. A resident of Columbia, South Carolina, wrote on March 17, 1862: "Last night a house was set on fire; last week two houses. . . . Our troubles thicken indeed when treachery comes from that quarter." Incendiary activity among slaves was fairly common. "Indeed," writes Herbert Aptheker, "in January, 1864, Jefferson Davis's own domestic slaves, with the connivance and aid of at least one other slave, set fire to his official residence in Richmond, and this was discovered none too soon for the health of the President of the Confederate State."

The slaveowners were angered by the defections and other "disloyal" behavior of their most trusted slaves. They were shocked when they learned that their drivers had encouraged mass desertions to Union lines. John H. Ramsdell wrote bitterly to Governor Thomas O. Moore of Louisiana: "The drivers everywhere have proved the worst negroes." "This war has taught us the perfect impossibility of placing the least confidence in any negro," complained a Georgia planter bitterly. "In too numerous instances, those we esteemed the most have been the first to desert us."

INSUBORDINATION, STRIKES, INSURRECTIONS, AND GUERRILLA WARFARE

"Those that did not go on with the [federal] army," a Louisiana planter wrote, "remained at home to do much worse." For one thing, many displayed an attitude of "brazen insolence." The *Selma* (Alabama) *Reporter* of August 27, 1863, complained that "the negroes . . . are becoming so saucy and abusive that a police has become positively necessary as a check to this continued insolence." A law was passed in Georgia in November 1862 "to punish slaves and free persons of color for abusive and insulting language to white persons." In North Carolina, bills were introduced into the legislature enabling free blacks "to select masters and become slaves" and requiring that all free Negroes who had not "voluntarily sold their services for the term of ninety-nine years before January 1st, 1864, shall be removed from the State." By making all blacks slaves, the legislation would restrict the contacts between the free Negroes and the slaves and enable "the white people to control better the Negro population in the state."

A common complaint voiced by slaveowners was that blacks who did not run off to the Union lines refused to work. "We have had hard work to get along this season," a South Carolina planter wrote in August 1862, "the negroes are unwilling to do any work, no matter what it is." Some of these slaves were shot. Others were forced to work at gunpoint. Only such drastic measures had the desired results. J. C. Younger, a Louisiana planter who had killed the leader of slaves who refused to work, wrote to the governor of the state that all of the others had gone back to work "in low spirits."

"The refusal to work was sometimes a strike for wages," notes Bell I. Wiley. He cites the case of the slaves on Woodland Plantation in Louisiana who presented themselves before the overseer one morning in August 1862 and said that "they would not work any more unless they got pay for their work." After a discussion, they agreed to continue working without pay for another week. But inside of a few weeks, this owner and all the others on the surrounding plantations "had to go over to the wage basis." The presence of federal troops helped make the strikes a success: "A refusal to grant wages often resulted in a wholesale flight of the blacks to the Federal camp."

William Minor's work contract was typical:

I agreed with my negroes on the 28th of February 1863 that they should have one twentieth (1/20th) of the crop of sugar & molasses instead of wages by the month as soon as the Sugar is headed up & the molasses in barrels— . . . when their portion is sold the money will be brot. here & divided among the workers—according to the agreement— that is to say Mechanics thrice shares—full field hands two shares—women, half hands, & house servants one share—I agreed with the other hands that the mechanics should draw only two shares & I would make up to them the other share.

In many cases, a federal invasion of an area produced more than a strike. It was often followed by the "seizure and distribution of property, and a general celebration of the advent of freedom." When the federal troops passed on, many of the adult blacks followed them, taking as much of the master's property as they could. Those who remained were whipped and forced back to work. In the case of Louisiana's Rapid Parish, a Union army raid in 1862 produced a general upheaval among the slaves. On one plantation, they drove the overseer off and instantly "Rose and Destroyed everything, they could get hold of. Pictures, Portraits and Furniture were all smashed up with Crockery and everything in the House." On a nearby plantation, Wiley reports, "they erected a gallows in the quarter for the purpose of hanging their master. Some of them marched around through the neighborhood, with flags and drums, shouting 'Abe Lincoln and Freedom.'"

Wiley concludes that while "rumors of insurrections of slaves were numerous during the war, only a few plots were detected; actual outbreaks were fewer still, and these were immediately suppressed." Aptheker, however, cites at least twenty-five "distinct plots or harshly suppressed uprisings," which he traced in newspapers and records of the Confederate states. In his study, *Confederate Mississippi,* John Betterworth notes that "rumors of uprisings were occasioning considerable alarm" as early as May 1861. These rumors became reality by the summer of 1862 when A. K. Farrar, provost marshal of Adams County, Mississippi, wrote to Governor John Pettus:

According to instructions which you gave me by telegraph, I have detached militia men who are overseeing on plantations to do police and patrol duty upon the same. This is a matter of great importance to us here, as there is a great disposition among the negroes to be insubordinate, and to run away and go to the federals. Within the last 12 months we have had to hang some 40 for plotting an insurrection, and there has been about that number put in irons.

The governor was also informed that slaves were "enabled to harbor runaways who have fire arms, traverse the whole country, kill stock and steal generally." The situation had reached such a state that Farrar wrote despairingly: "Complaints are made to me to remedy the evil. I am however at a loss to know how to proceed. Something is necessary and I appeal to you for assistance."

Even where no revolt materialized, white southerners sensed that life had changed. "The fear of insurrection occasioned by the absence of the greater portion of the arms-bearing white population," declared the *Richmond Whig* anxiously on January 1, 1864, "has produced a leniency and indulgence among the farmers, which has encouraged the natural laziness of the slave, and resulted in a rapid and yearly increased diminution of the crops . . . and the danger is that famine will be superadded to insurrection."

Slave guerrilla activity was another aspect of black resistance in the Confederacy. In Virginia in 1862, a fugitive slave camp of one hundred blacks killed the whites who were hunting them and went on to raid the nearby plantations. Such activities continued in Virginia and North Carolina throughout the war. Referring to Camden and Currituck counties in North Carolina, the *Richmond Examiner* of January 14, 1864, declared:

It is difficult to find words of description . . . of the wild and terrible consequences of the negro raids in this obscure theater of the war. . . . In the two counties . . . there are said to be from five to six hundred negroes, who are not in the regular military organization of the Yankees, but who, outlawed and disowned by their masters, lead the lives of banditti, roving the country with fire and committing all sorts of horrible crimes upon the inhabitants.

What made the situation doubly dangerous, the Confederate newspaper added, was that "disloyal" whites were cooperating with the black "banditti."

Evidence of unity between blacks and poor whites in guerrilla bands was fairly widespread. Governor J. G. Shorter of Alabama requested reinforcements from the Confederate secretary of war to be sent to the southwestern counties of his state because "the county near the Coast is the common retreat of deserters from our armies, tories and runaway negroes." By "tories," he meant disaffected Southern white Unionists. In August 1864, Confederate General John K. Jackson reported from Lake City, Florida:

Many deserters . . . are collected in the swamps and fastnesses of Taylor, LaFayette, Levy and other counties, and have organized with running negroes, bands for the purpose of committing depredations upon the plantations and crops of loyal citizens and running off their slaves. These depredatory bands have even threatened the cities of Tallahassee, Madison and Marianna.

DISAFFECTION IN THE CONFEDERACY

In his widely heralded 1928 article, "The Central Theme of Southern History," Ulrich B. Phillips categorically declared: "When slavery was attacked, it was defended, not only as a vested interest, but with a vigor and vehemence as a guarantee of white supremacy and civilization. . . . Otherwise it would be impossible to account for the fervent secessionism of many non-slaveholders and the eager service of thousands in the Confederate army." But in spite of the argument of Phillips and most Southern white historians that secession and war were popular among white southerners who owned no slaves, they themselves have shown in discussions of labor strikes, antiwar activity, demonstrations (often by women), desertion, and anti-Confederate guerrilla warfare that the notion of popular support for the Confederacy is another myth. There is a mass of evidence proving this in the works of Roger W. Shugg, John W. Betterworth, E. Merton Coulter, Ella Lonn, Georgia Lee Tatum, G. C. Eggleston, Albert B. Moore, and others.

In its initial call for volunteers, the Confederacy received more state militia than it could arm and equip. Nevertheless, there soon emerged deep divisions among the people of the seceded states, divisions that contributed considerably to the ultimate defeat of the Confederacy. As the war dragged on, over 100,000

men deserted from the Confederate forces, and in 1865, officials wrote DE-
SERTER across the hundreds of discharges.

Much of this disaffection arose from military reverses or from the gradual
collapse of supplies. But at its root was a basic factor that existed from the outset
of the Civil War. In his *History of the Confederate War,* G. C. Eggleston cites
the economic factor as one of the main reasons for the disaffection of the poor
whites:

The often illiterate but shrewdly intelligent mountaineers . . . were very naturally jealous
of their better fed, better educated, and altogether more prosperous neighbors. It is hard
for a man who trudges afoot or astride an underfed mule for which his forage supply is
scant, to entertain kindly feelings toward the man who goes about in his carriage drawn by
sleek and negro-groomed horses. It is not easy for the man who houses his family in a
mud-daubed log hut and feeds his half-clad wife and children upon corn pone and an often
uncertain ration of salt pork or bacon, to avoid sentiments of discontent when he realizes
how much easier and more comfortable is the lot of those who wear purple and fare
sumptuously every day.

Although people in the uplands hoped to own slaves someday, they had
relatively few at the time the Civil War began. Many of them felt that slavery
was the cause of their poverty and their social inferiority, and they were not
going to do anything that might preserve such an institution. "These mountain
dwellers," Eggleston emphasized, ". . . saw no reason why they should fight
for a system which they resented, a system which somehow created the disparity
of fortune, social status, and personal comfort which existed between themselves
and their plantation owning neighbors."

As early as August 1861, Richmond newspapers were printing letters denouncing special military service exemptions for planters and the overseers and
other manifestations of preference for the "aristocracy." This hostility increased
with the enactment of conscription laws by the Confederate government and
subsequent attempts to enforce them. In mid-April 1862, the Confederate Congress passed its first Conscription Act, which called into service all white men
between the ages of eighteen and thirty-five. A week later, the Congress passed
an act establishing a system of class exemptions from military service. An
integral part of this system was the provision that men who were not liable for
service might be received for those who were. This allowed those who had
money to buy substitutes, leaving the poor to go to war. In the fall of 1862, the
Confederate Congress passed the second Conscription Act, which, among other
things, exempted the owners of twenty or more slaves. These two laws made it
clear that the war was basically a defense of slavery by men too poor to hire
substitutes or to own twenty slaves. As Georgia Lee Tatum points out, the
second exemption served "to convince both the poor and the non-slaveholders
that the planters were a favored class, that the only issue in the war was the
protection of slavery and the non-slaveholders were to be sacrificed for the

benefit of the slave owners.'' Indeed, so widespread was this feeling that the *Montgomery Weekly Advertiser* found it necessary to devote several editorials to the subject. In one entitled ''Slaveholders and Non-Slaveholders,'' the Alabama paper wrote:

We regret to discover a disposition to foster and strengthen a feeling of prejudice on the part of the non-slaveholding portion of the community towards those whom fortune or their own exertions have more highly favored by making them the owners of slave property. An insidious effort is being made to impress upon the minds of the poorer classes the conviction that it is the intention of the government of this country to promote the slave interest to the injury of those who are dependent on their own labor for support. . . .

But it is not true that the legislation of the country is intended to benefit the rich and not the poor. . . . The law in regard to exemptions may indeed appear to operate unequally in some instances, but such cases are in the nature of things unavoidable, and do not indicate that there is anything radically wrong in the system.

Having satisfied itself that nothing was wrong with the Conscription Act, the *Montgomery Weekly Advertiser* resorted to a technique long used in the South against all who opposed slavery and sought to abolish it:

The attempt to excite a feeling of enmity towards the slave-holders, as the part of those who are not, is due to a spirit of agrarianism which has found its way to the South from the hotbeds of French and Yankee fanaticism. It has its foundations in the belief that there is an irrepressible conflict between labor and capital, which must go on until all men occupy an equal footing in the world. It is the plea by which demagogues have ever sought to obtain control of the minds of the ignorant masses, and mold them to their wills. To give countenance to it in the South is to encourage the worst species of anti-slaveryism, as it places the institution of slavery on such a basis, that it is apparently the duty of every man, not owning slaves, to do everything in his power to remove that which is antagonizing with the white labor of the country. . . .

Until the pernicious ideas we have alluded to, are abandoned, and correct views are entertained on the subject, we can never be certain that we have escaped the dangers of revolution in the future.

Such warnings had little effect on the plain people of the South. Zebulon Baird Vance, war governor of North Carolina, acknowledged in 1886 that the discriminatory exemptions from military service ''did more than anything else to alienate the affections of the common people'' because they ''opened a wide door to demagogues to appeal to the non-slaveholding class, and make them believe that the only issue was the protection of slavery, in which they were sacrificing for the sole benefit of the masters.'' Since, Vance explained, ''seven-tenths of our people owned no slaves, and, to say the least of it felt no great and enduring enthusiasm for its preservation,'' it was not surprising that they also felt no enthusiasm for fighting for the Confederacy.

The poor whites were largely illiterate, but they knew instinctively that, as Ella Lonn, herself pro-Confederate, puts it, "this was a rich man's war and poor man's fight, since the wealthy seemed to bribe their way to freedom, or to comfortable posts as magistrates, overseers, or government officials." James Phelon, a leading Confederate of Mississippi, complained to Jefferson Davis on December 18, 1862: "It seems as if nine-tenths of the youngsters of the land, whose relatives are conspicuous in society, wealthy and influential, obtain some safe perch where they can doze with their heads under their wings."

The suffering that prevailed as a result of the war was an important factor fostering dissatisfaction. As usual, the poorest suffered the most. By 1863, many were firmly convinced that the situation had become one in which "the higher class was staying home and making money, and the lower class was thrust into the trenches." The blockade had deprived the people not only of luxuries but also of necessities. By 1863, food had become scarce, and in many sections medicine was lacking; prices had risen phenomenally due to the depreciation of currency, and it was commonly said that "one carried his money to market in a basket and brought his purchase home in his purse."

Rents in Richmond quadrupled in two years, and food prices climbed steadily. Four pounds of coffee, which cost $.50 in 1860, now brought $20. The price of bacon rose from $1.25 for ten pounds in 1860 to $10 in 1863. By late March 1863, the crisis in the Confederacy's capital city had reached unbearable proportions. Flour now commanded $30 to $35 per barrel, eggs $1.50 per dozen, and butter $2.70 to $3 per pound.

The necessities of fighting had led to the growth of industry, and additional thousands of workers poured into Richmond. In two years, the city's population doubled. Many of the new workers were employed at the Tredegar Iron Works, the Confederacy's largest plant. During the first year of the war, workers at Tredegar struck for higher wages, but we do not know the outcome of this struggle. By the spring of 1863, the workers were desperate because of the continuously rising prices. Their wives met to discuss their problems and decided to seek the help of Virginia Governor John Letcher.

The governor met the women, now joined by other complaining housewives, and told them that while he was sympathetic to their plight, there was nothing he could do. This, a Richmond woman of the upper class who was in the neighborhood reported, did not satisfy the women:

I sat on a bench near, and one of the number [of the women] left the rest and took a seat beside me. She was a pale, emaciated girl, not more than eighteen, with a sunbonnet on her head, and dressed in a clean calico gown. I was encouraged to ask: "What is it? Is there some celebration?"

"There is," said the girl solemnly: "We celebrate our right to live. We are starving. As soon as enough of us get together we are going to the bakeries and each of us will take a loaf of bread. That is little enough for the government to give us after it has taken all our men."

More than a thousand people followed Mary Jackson, a painter's wife, described as "a tall, daring Amazonian-looking woman." They included men, women, and boys. When the crowd reached the shops and wholesale houses on Main and Cary streets, the women shouted "Bread!" and took bread. General looting followed as the crowd seized hams, hats, and whatever else they could find. Troops were called in, and Confederate President Jefferson Davis warned the crowd that if they did not disperse in five minutes, he would give the order to fire. The crowd then dispersed, and the bread riot was over.

Meeting in emergency session, the Richmond City Council blamed the riot on "outsiders" and charged that it was "probably abetted by the machination of Yankee agents," but no proof of this charge was ever offered. A number of men and women who had been arrested received stiff prison sentences.

The Richmond press carried no report of any aspect of the bread riot. Assistant Adjutant General John Withers had dispatched a request to all Richmond newspapers:

> The unfortunate disturbance which occurred to-day in the city is so liable to misconstruction and misrepresentation abroad that I am desired by the Secretary of War to make a special appeal to the editors and reporters of the press at Richmond, and earnestly request them to avoid all references directly or indirectly to the affair.

Secretary of War James Sedden also requested the telegraph office to send "nothing of the unfortunate disturbance of today over the wires for any purpose." But if nothing was said about the bread riot, nothing was done either to halt the prices from continuing to skyrocket. On December 2, 1863, prices in Richmond were still high: apples, $65 a bushel; onions, $35 a bushel; potatoes, $6 a bushel; and wheat, $20 a bushel. Corn cost a Confederate soldier's full month's pay: $11 a bushel.

Efforts by workers to meet the mounting cost of living through strikes for higher wages proved futile. They were usually broken by the conscription of strikers into the army, and when conscription was not used, slaves were. "The impressment of slaves into the ordnance works, railroads (slaves were used in all positions, including those of brakemen and firemen), maritime, and some factory work," Herbert Aptheker points out, "could and did, vanquish war-time struggles of the free workers." Strikers were simply fired and replaced by slaves.

One right the plain white people of the South could exercise: they could refuse to fight and could desert if conscripted. By early January 1863, the second Conscription Act was unenforceable among the mountain folk who owned few slaves. Desertions from the Confederate army were so frequent by this time that Union generals were making rulings on the disposition of the deserters. At the insistence of President Lincoln, the deserters were given paid jobs constructing fortifications or doing other necessary work. Those who were unable to work were paroled and shipped home at federal expense. In some cases, the Union army sent out expeditions to rescue and bring into camp the families of the deserters left at home.

Robert E. Lee, the Confederate commander in chief, confessed that desertion was the main cause of his retiring from Maryland during the 1862 campaign—at a time when the Confederates, with the assistance of the Maryland slaveowners, hoped to wrest that state from the Union. By June 1863, the number of absentees in the Confederate army approached 30 percent. In a speech at Macon, Georgia, Jefferson Davis lamented that "if half the men, absent without leave and constituting one-third of the army, would return, the South would win."

But they did not return. Tens of thousands failed to report back from their furloughs, hiding out in the swamps and hills to harass the Confederacy. In the mountain areas, anti-Confederate partisans made frequent raids, destroying Confederate stores of ammunition and property. And on October 21, 1862, the *New York Times* reported that a Union meeting in Beaufort County, North Carolina, endorsed Lincoln's preliminary Emancipation Proclamation. This, it observed, was the result of the growth of a "free-labor feeling" and the widespread hatred of slavery among the small farmers who felt that slavery was the "prime cause of the rebellion."

The most spectacular expression of Union sentiment in the South was the breakaway of the western part of Virginia in 1861, its organization into another state, and its ultimate admission into the Union in 1863 as West Virginia. Mountainous east Tennessee also tried to constitute itself as a state, but in this case no federal troops came to its aid.

In many conscript regiments, Union sentiment was so strong that the Confederate soldiers even organized secret societies to take the South out of the war and thus leave the slaveowners without fighting men. Conscript soldiers in Clariton's Alabama Brigade formed a secret society with signs, grips, and passwords. Its members had planned to lay down their arms on Christmas Day 1864. Union soldiers in the opposing army had helped the white southerners organize the society before its existence was discovered by the Confederate military intelligence. Ella Lonn says of this society:

Its object was to deplete the ranks by desertion and to thwart the work of the Conscript Bureau. The password to escape from prison was "Washington"—repeated four times, which procured release in 24 hours. When approaching a Yankee guard post, after being halted and challenged, the member was to pronounce the word, "Jack," the sentinel would reply, "All right, Jack, pass on with your goose quills."

In the line of battle, the sign of membership was placing the gun against the right hip at an angle of about 45 degrees, holding it in this position long enough to be distinguished and then carrying it to the left shoulder in the position of shoulder arms.

Citizens of Taylor County, Florida, formed the Independent Union Rangers under the leadership of a deserter. This guerrilla band was governed by a constitution that pledged allegiance to the Union. Elsewhere in the Florida Everglades region, runaway white conscripts banded themselves together with runaway Negro slaves to liberate the remaining slaves and to confiscate the crop of the pro-Confederate planters. In Mobile, Alabama, twelve hundred Negroes impressed into Confederate labor battalions were persuaded by poor whites to desert, and they enlisted in the Union army. Lonn also describes the clever methods that the Southern Unionists used to escape detection:

Every road leading to a camp, where the men were living in groups, was so well picketed that not a man, woman, or child could come near them unheralded. All bands had spies and an elaborate system of signals to indicate the approach of danger. A quilt hung in the fence in varying positions, or quilts of different colors, conveyed a variety of messages to the deserter hiding within sight of his mountain cabin; hog-rolling was practiced through such a range of tones that it was exalted almost into an art; or songs, apparently caroled on the way to the spring, conveyed a warning. Horns and cowbells were also made to serve the same purpose.

Such precautions were necessary. It was, after all, "a rich man's war and a poor man's fight," and the poor of the South were determined not to fight. They did not, as in the past, blame the slaves for the difficulties that faced them. Rather, they now openly and clearly blamed the slaveowners. As a North Carolina small farmer put it concisely in a letter to Governor Vance, "the common people is drove of[f] in the war to fight for the big mans negro," while the slaveholders were allowed to remain at home, raising crops and setting prices because they had the power to do so. A leading spokesperson for the small farmers and poor whites said the same thing somewhat differently: "Men, for the protection of whose negroes the war is waged, get rich—those who have no negroes become poor."

A BLACK VOICE IN THE DEEP SOUTH

On April 26, 1862, one year after the Civil War began, New Orleans fell to federal troops. While the victorious fleet's guns were still trained on the city, a Confederate sympathizer tore the U.S. flag from its newly won position atop the Mint. The sheer recklessness of the act dumfounded most of the occupying troops. But the point struck home immediately to General Benjamin Butler, in command of the Union army, and he saw that his chief allies would have to come from the free people of color.

As a result, the status of the free people of color in New Orleans suddenly changed. They were not given political rights, but they were allowed freedom of press and the right to protest. In this new condition, the free Negroes took steps to launch an avenue of expression. In the summer of 1862, a group of educated and wealthy free Negroes, led by Dr. Louis Charles Roudanz, who held a medical degree from the University of Paris and was a highly successful physician in New Orleans, and Paul Trevigne, who had taught languages and had editorial experience, founded the newspaper *L'Union*. The first issue appeared on September 27, 1862. In it, editor Trevigne announced the start of a drive for Negro rights. "The hour has sounded," he wrote, "for the fight of great humanitarian principles against a vile and sordid interest which breeds pride, ambition and hypocrisy."

In its subsequent issues, *L'Union* spread the news of the Emancipation Proclamation and urged all former slaves in Louisiana to make the best of their new opportunities in freedom:

Brothers! The hour strikes for us; a new sun, similar to that of 1789, should surely appear on our horizon. May the cry which resounded through France at the seizure of the Bastille resonate today in our ears. . . .

Compatriots! The epoch in which we live exhorts us in a loud voice to unite all our efforts for the cause of liberty and justice. Let us all be imbued with those noble sentiments which characterize all civilized people. . . .

Enough of shame and submission; the break is complete! Down with the craven behavior of bondage! Stand up under the noble flag of the Union and declare yourself hardy champions of the right. . . . Fellow workers, plow in the vast field of the future the furrow of *Fraternité;* plant there firmly the tree of *Liberté,* whose fruits, collected by future generations, will be shared with the most perfect *Egalité* by the children of the same God.

In the spring of 1863 General Nathaniel P. Banks began to recruit a "Corps d'Afrique" from the Negro population of New Orleans. *L'Union* supported Bank's efforts editorially:

To Arms! It is our duty. The nation counts on the devotion and the courage of its sons. We will not remain deaf to its call; we will not remain indifferent spectators, like strangers who attach no value to the land. We are sons of Louisiana, and when Louisiana calls us we march.

To Arms! It is an honor understood by our fathers who fought on the plains of Chalnette. He who defends his fatherland is the real citizen, and this time we are fighting for the rights of our race. . . . We demand justice. And when an organized, numerous, and responsible body which has rendered many services to the nation demands justice— nothing more; but nothing less—the nation cannot refuse.

L'Union did demand the justice Negroes had earned through their armed contributions to the Union, but the paper's effectiveness was limited by the fact that while it did publish an English section, it was mainly perfunctory and was relegated to a remote section. Basically its major sections appeared only in French, and a French-language newspaper, even in Louisiana, could reach only a limited audience. This handicap led to *L'Union*'s dissolution in the summer of 1864, but the defunct journal's printing equipment was purchased by Dr. Louis Roudanz, and several days later, the *New Orleans Tribune* was launched, first as a triweekly paper, then as a daily in English and French. Thus, even before the Civil War was ended, the first daily black newspaper in American history had been launched, and in the Deep South.

Dr. Roudanz hired Jean-Charles Houzeau, a radical Belgian scientist and abolitionist who identified himself completely with New Orleans Negroes, to be co-editor with Paul Trevigne of the black daily. Houzeau, who wrote most of the editorials for the *New Orleans Tribune,* was born in Mons, Belgium, on October 7, 1820. He attended the College of Mons and later the University of Brussels, where he displayed brilliance in both science and the humanities; however, he withdrew from school before receiving his degree in order to devote himself to travel and scientific research. From 1840 to 1845, he toured Europe and studied in the great libraries of Switzerland, Germany, and France. After being influenced by the ideas of Louis Blanc and Pierre Proudhon, both utopian socialists, he returned to Brussels to engage in political reform movements while serving as assistant to the director of the Royal Observatory. He was removed because he attempted to foment an uprising against monarchy in Belgium following the Paris Revolt of 1848, but he was soon restored to his position and appointed director of a project for making a new national map based on astronomical triangulation. His scientific prowess was widely recognized, and he was nominated for membership in both the Belgium Royal Academy and the French Institute. His hatred of monarchy, however, remained intact, and after completing the map in 1857, Houzeau left Belgium to settle in the more democratic United States.

His destination was New Orleans. Arriving in 1857, he occupied himself with studying English but then left for Texas, where he hoped to establish a settlement for alienated Belgians like himself. Although nothing came of the plan, he remained in San Antonio for five years, continuing his scientific research and becoming involved in the antislavery movement. In addition to attacking slavery in letters to European newspapers, Houzeau was active in the underground movement that helped slaves escape to Mexico.

After the efforts of Texan slaveowners to silence him had failed, Houzeau was warned that he would be lynched if he remained in San Antonio. In Mexican disguise, he fled to Matamoras, Mexico, but after a brief sojourn in Mexico, he left for New Orleans. Arriving in the city in February 1863, he met Dr. Roudanz, who warned him that his antislavery reputation had stirred up hatred toward him among the city's proslavery elements. Houzeau adopted the pseudonym "Cham," which he used in articles he published in *L'Union.* For the sake of safety, however, he moved to Philadelphia, and from September 1863 to July 1864 he published articles in French in *L'Union,* under his pseudonym, dealing with politics, military events, President Lincoln, Copperheads, black soldiers, slavery, and abolition. In addition, Houzeau wrote a 220-page antislavery work, *Question de l'esclavage* [*The slavery question*], which has never been translated into English and was published in 1863 in Brussels.

After Roudanz had purchased *L'Union* and changed its name to the *New Orleans Tribune,* he persuaded Houzeau to accept the editorship. In November

1864, the Belgian scientist and abolitionist returned to New Orleans and began editing the first daily black paper published in the United States. "Dalloz," as Houzeau now called himself, threw himself wholeheartedly into the cause of New Orleans's black community. He was convinced that a major weakness of *L'Union* had been that its main articles and reports had appeared only in French. "It isolated these colored men from the general life of the country," he wrote later. "They could address themselves neither to the national government, to the Northern press, to public opinion, nor even to the slaves." He called the English section of *L'Union* a "scissor job," and he quickly altered the situation. As he wrote of the English section, "It had to be our great arm of attack and defense and it was the one which deserved most attention and care."

Houzeau then set out to build an alliance between the free blacks and the former slaves. This was not easy to achieve. *L'Union* had tended to write of the former slaves as crude and uncivilized and to argue that it was the duty of the free people of color to teach the newly free "that the word 'liberty' is not the sign of anarchy and laziness" and that liberty would be useful to them only if they were industrious and orderly. It called upon the free people of color "to inculcate in our freed brothers this principle that true liberty is achieved only by practice of all the religious and social virtues."

A number of the free people of color had owned slaves, and although they had usually done so out of philanthropic motives, cases of cruelty and exploitation were both frequent and well remembered by the former slaves. In general, the former slaves believed that the free people of color did not really have their interests at heart. On the contrary, they were convinced that many of the free people of color believed that they could more quickly secure their own rights if they abandoned the mass of the blacks. As Houzeau put it later in summing up the attitude of the former slaves and free people of color:

The free people of color, they said, were closer to the whites. And it did seem to the free pepole of color that it would be easier for them to obtain civil equality if the former slaves were excluded. Strange error in a society where prejudice struck alike everyone with African blood in his veins, no matter how small in proportion.

In every issue of the *New Orleans Tribune,* Houzeau hammered away the theme that if mulattoes, octoroons, and quadroons alone were given civil rights, they would find themselves "lost in the mass; an imperceptible minority in the legal state, a minority without possible influence, condemned to nothing but a resemblance of rights." But if the free people of color took their logical place as leaders of all blacks, they would constitute a political force. Above all else, he emphasized, history proved that in a social upheaval it was always best to base oneself on principle. It would be "easier to claim the emancipation of all, in virtue of natural rights, rather than asking for the elevation of a handful of men of varied colors as a simple expedient."

Under the ownership of men from the ranks of the free people of color and the editorship of Jean-Charles Houzeau, the *New Orleans Tribune* exercised an important influence in Louisiana and even affected events on behalf of black Americans on a national scale. As Houzeau wrote on the eve of his departure in 1868 from New Orleans for Jamaica:

The cause that we defended was after all but a chapter in the great universal cause of the oppressed of all colors and all nations—in the end the same denial of justice. I understood the situation of the New Orleans colored men, I identified with them, because if the people were different the situation was not strange. I found again on one side a dominating class, and the other, a dominated class that was crushed under foot and which had no influence in society. We set out to change this.

22

The Home Front—North

As the Lincoln administration moved cautiously toward emancipation in 1862, Democratic editors and Copperhead demagogues stirred white fears that freed blacks would migrate North, drive white workers from their jobs, swell the relief rolls, and endanger white women. "The Irish and German immigrants, to say nothing of native laborers of the white race, must feel enraptured," the pro-Southern *New York Herald* thundered, "at the prospect of hordes of darkeys overrunning the Northern states and working for half wages," and thus ousting them from employment.

The propaganda of fear and hate was doubly effective because during its early months, the Civil War disrupted normal commerce, severely hampered business, and caused real economic hardship. In 1861 alone, there were nearly six thousand reported business failures. The Northern economy remained depressed until late the following year, and to make matters worse, the short depression was accompanied by inflation. Jobs became scarce at the same time that prices were increasing. Black as well as white laborers suffered from the economic slump and inflation, but the Copperheads emphasized only the effect on the whites and left the impression that blacks were reaping benefits from white suffering.

The situation for dock workers was especially acute. Hard times, race prejudice, and competition for jobs created an explosive combination on the docks of Northern cities. The hostilities that had been brewing between blacks and Irish immigrants who competed for menial jobs, especially on the docks, came to a head.

TOLEDO AND CINCINNATI

During July 1862, Toledo stevedores, a large number of them Irishmen, struck for higher wages to compensate for higher prices. Company officials thereupon increased the number of black laborers. When the *New York,* a propeller-driven steamer, arrived at the Wabash docks, black stevedores began moving freight. Irish strikers bombarded the workers with stones and brickbats. Three blacks were injured before they all found shelter aboard the *New York.*

Whites then raided the black section along the canal, burned shanties, and, according to one account, damaged "every house inhabited by negroes." On July 8, city officials brought in a special police force to end the violence. On July 10 and 11, leaders of the riot were tried by municipal authorities; they were found guilty, fined $50, and sentenced to thirty days in jail. By July 18, most of the violence had subsided.

On the morning of the same day that the Toledo riot trials began, racial violence erupted in Cincinnati. The city had suffered a severe loss of trade when secession and war all but closed commerce on the river. Soon, however, government contracts began to stimulate heavy industry and the building trades, just as it did in other parts of the North. Skilled and semiskilled workers enjoyed increased wages. For unskilled laborers, however, jobs were still scarce. The river commerce did not recover. Irish, German, and black stevedores scrambled for work on the riverfront, many unsuccessfully. By the summer of 1862, the bitter hatred between white and black reached a breaking point.

On July 10, two blacks employed as stevedores to move freight on the steamboat *Aurora* were confronted by a group of whites who had gathered on the levee. Insults were hurled and an argument developed between the blacks and one white man. One of the stevedores allegedly hit the white with a board. Other whites came to the victim's aid, forcing the blacks to seek shelter aboard the steamer. Excitement spread along the wharves. Whites began attacking any black within sight. When a small band of blacks counterattacked, open warfare broke out. Both sides suffered injuries. The officers sent to the scene by the mayor arrested two white men on charges of inciting a riot and brought about order. But the whites threatened further riots and made clear their determination that "no d——d niggers should work on the levee."

On July 13, the city council ordered three-fourths of the 160-man Cincinnati police force to join military units moving South. John Hunt Morgan's Confederate cavalry had penetrated the Union lines, threatening Lexington, Kentucky. The council's decision left only forty policemen in Cincinnati to attempt to keep the peace.

That evening, rioting again broke out and initiated a week-long reign of terror for Cincinnati blacks. Mobs of whites assaulted blacks on the streets and stoned black houses. The following evening, after whites had attacked blacks near the levee, Negroes invaded an Irish neighborhood in the Thirteenth Ward, smashed windows, and broke into a house. A white mob then gathered on the edge of Bucktown, the black ghetto, and began to attack black houses and other buildings. The *Cincinnati Commercial* announced the following day:

There was a shameful and most deplorable riot in the Thirteenth Ward last night. The houses of negroes were stoned, a number of windows being broken, and doors battered.

The negro church on Sixth Street was stoned, and several shots were fired. We did not hear that any persons were seriously hurt, but the wonder is they were not. The city is indebted to the forbearance of the unoffending negroes, whose houses were assaulted, for the fact that the riot was not made a bloody one.

The *Commercial* concluded sternly:

It is imperatively necessary that this rioting should be stopped. If it continues any longer there is no telling how far it may go. The negroes are the victims thus far, but if the mob spirit is permitted to gather force, it will soon proceed to assault and destroy irrespective of color or condition.

Just as the editorial warning was being published, William Burke, a white man who was helping his Irish relative remove the contents of his grocery, was caught in a crossfire, severely wounded, and died two days later.

At this, the "better element" of the city's whites decided to act. Insisting that the rioting must be checked before it spread, they held two meetings and passed resolutions denouncing violence and pleading for law and order. "Their primary motive," Leonard Harding points out in his study of the Cincinnati riots, "was not compassion for the Negroes but fears that the property-damaging proclivities of the mob might get out of control and spill over into the rest of the downtown area."

Meanwhile white rowdies were chasing blacks through the streets and severely beating those who were caught. Most black residents of Bucktown and the levee departed with their families, and by July 17, the last day of rioting, most blacks had left the city. The police and volunteers, armed with Winfield rifles, maintained order. During the succeeding days, blacks returned to their homes and shops. Many suffered severe losses of property, but no white agency offered to assist them. Such aid as did come for victims of the white mobs came from the black community.

BROOKLYN AND DETROIT

The Toledo and Cincinnati riots were followed by attacks on blacks by white workers in Brooklyn, New York. Lorrillard and Watson's tobacco factory in Brooklyn employed twenty-five blacks, most of them women and children. In August 1862, a mob of Irish workers forced their way into the factory and set it afire, hoping to burn down the building with the black workers in it. Fortunately, the firemen arrived in time to extinguish the flames and rescue the workers. But the press reported that "the colored people dare not return to Mr. Lorrillard's factory." Frederick Douglass castigated Brooklyn, "the city of churches," for tolerating riots against blacks, and asked:

Will not all good citizens unite in stopping this wicked business? If suffered to go on, there may be a fearful reckoning ere long. . . . If men are to be killed like dogs because they are black, the same spirit will kill them because they are anything else that an unreasonable mob may not like. "They that sow the wind will reap the whirlwind."

This observation was voiced in September 1862 before the Emancipation Proclamation was issued. For with emancipation, notes Forrest G. Wood in *Black Scare,* "racist demagogues . . . launched a white supremacy crusade through pamphlets, newspapers, books, leaflets, songs, pictures, and speeches, and accused the government of leading the nation down the road to ruin."

Detroit was one of the first to feel the effects of this propaganda. When a rumor spread through the city that a black man had raped a white girl, mobs shouting, "Kill all the damn niggers," began a riot. "Yesterday was the bloodiest day that ever dawned upon Detroit," lamented the *Detroit Free Press* on March 7, 1863:

The mob first inaugurated the day by petty persecutions of any negroes who chanced to come in the vicinity of City Hall. Any of that unfortunate race who happened along were subjected to kicks, cuffs and blows, and were liable to be butchered upon the streets. Even women and children were not exempt, several of them being abused in a most shameful and outrageous manner.

From the city hall, the mob went on a rampage through the black ghetto. The account in the *Free Press* continued:

The first house where a negro family resided, one end of which was used as a copper shop, situated on Beaublen Street, was assaulted with bricks, paving stones and clubs. About a dozen negroes were at work in the shop, or stopping in the house at the time. The most of them were armed, and fired several shots into the crowd from the windows, taking effect in several instances, but not fatally injuring anyone, as far as could be ascertained.

As each shot from the negro hovel reverberated through the vicinity, the fiendishness of the mob became more manifest, and their desperation more dreadful. The firearms in possession of the negroes deterred them from entering, for it would have been almost certain death for any man to attempt it. Any missile that could be obtained was hurled at the rendezvous of the negroes, the windows and doors burst open, and everything destroyed which could be seen by those outside. Finally, finding that they could not be forced out of their hiding place in any other manner, the match of the incendiary was placed at one end of the building, and in a very short time the flames spread so as to envelop almost the entire building.

The scene at this time was one that utterly baffles description. With the building a perfect sheet of livid flame, and outside a crowd of blood-thirsty rioters, some of whom were standing at the door with revolvers in their hands, waiting for their victims to appear, it was a truly pitiable and sickening sight. The poor wretches inside were almost frantic with fright, undecided whether to remain and die by means of the devouring element, or suffer the almost terrible fate which awaited them at the hands of the merciless crowd. There was no more mercy extended to the suffering creatures than would have been shown to a rattlesnake. No tears could move, no supplications assuage the awful frenzy and demonical spirit of revenge which had taken possession of that mass of people.

One colored woman made her appearance at the door with a little child in her arms, and appealed to the mob for mercy. The monstrous fact must be told, her tearful appeals were met with a shower of bricks, stones and clubs, driving herself and the babe in her arms back into the burning building. At this juncture one man moved to mercy at this cowardly and inhuman act, rushed to her assistance, bravely and nobly protecting her person from the violence which threatened her. But the negroes found no such protection. They were driven gradually to the windows and doors, where they were mercilessly assailed with every species of weapons, including axes, spades and clubs, and everything which could be used as a means of attack. The frightened creatures were almost as insane with fright as their persecutors were with madness. As they came out, they were beaten and bruised in a terrible manner, their shrieks and groans only exciting the mob to further exertions in their brutal work. Several of them were knocked down with axes and left for dead, but who afterwards recovered only to be again set upon and cruelly beaten to insensibility.

Several men, including old men, some as much as eighty years of age, were killed, thirty-two houses destroyed, and more than two hundred made homeless. "The colored population of the city," frightened and distracted, hurried from the mob, scattering in every direction, a large number going over the river to Canada, while many fled to the woods with their wives and children. When it was all over, the rapist turned out to be white, and the girl, a prostitute.

COPPERHEAD PROPAGANDA AND THE DRAFT

By 1863, the serious inflation and the failure of wages to increase correspondingly had made the economic condition of many workers in the North desperate. By July 1863, a greenback dollar was worth only 35 cents in gold. When one considers that skilled workers were fighting for a daily wage of $2.50 and that women and children generally averaged that much money in a week, it is obvious that there was a fertile field for the Copperheads to cultivate. Their papers laid the plight of the workers at the door of the "New England Abolitionist oligarchy," which sought to flood the labor market with contrabands and emancipated slaves to keep wages down and limit employment opportunities for white workers. Under Lincoln, cried the *New York Daily News*, a leading Copperhead paper, the Union army was "employed in freeing the negro—striking the shackles from him . . . to be carried out even at the expense of transferring the chains to the limbs of the free laboring men."

Not only was the war without meaning or benefit to labor, Copperhead newspapers charged, but it was directly against the white workers' own best interest. The *New York Daily News* editorialized:

The war is of vast moment to shoddy contractors; shoulderstrap politicians and bounty jumpers, because they amass fortunes at the expense of the country. . . . It half starves the mechanics and laborers, it tears men from their families to toil, to bleed and to die in an unnatural and patricidal strife.

Peace will stay the slaughter—will put a stop to further demoralization—will put an end to starvation prices for labor, and will restore industry its regard. . . . No men have a greater stake than those whose labor constitutes the wealth of the nation. They are the most oppressed by the war.

According to the Copperhead press, the labor of white workers constituted "the wealth of the nation." "To white toil," declared the *Boston Pilot,* an Irish-Catholic racist journal, "the nation owes everything—to black, *nothing.*"

Anti-Negro feeling in the North, carefully nurtured by the Copperhead press, boiled over into several serious race riots in the summer of 1863. These riots were sparked by job competition between white and black laborers and by the white workingmen's fear that emancipation would loose a flood of Negroes upon the labor market and drive down wages. On top of this, there was the wartime draft, which discriminated in favor of the rich and against the poor. These factors became especially important when they were broadcast in Copperhead speeches, leaflets, and newspaper editorials.

In July 1862, Lincoln issued a call upon the states for an additional 300,000 men. The result of the call was a disaster, for it produced only 88,000 men. By this time, too, volunteers were so scarce that congressional legislation was adopted to provide men for the Union army. A comprehensive conscription law was enacted on March 3, 1863. Under it, a draftee was to be given ten days' notification, and, if he wished to escape military service, he could furnish a substitute or pay a $300 commutation fee. Draft resisters and those who obstructed the orderly prosecution of the law were subject to imprisonment and a fine.

Particularly galling was the $300 commutation fee, which the Copperheads seized upon and interpreted as an effort to make the conflict a rich man's war but a poor man's fight. While the wealthy could buy their way out of service, the impoverished worker or farmer would be "ruthlessly swept into the ranks to waste his blood and sacrifice his life." Thus, the Copperheads took full advantage of the class nature of the Conscription Act. Posing as friends of labor, they denounced the provision permitting all who "possess $300 in 'greenbacks' filched from the *people*" to escape military service. Handbills carrying the words of the "Song of the Conscripts" were circulated by the thousands in the summer of 1863. A typical excerpt went:

> We're coming, Father Abraham, three hundred thousand more,
> We leave our homes and firesides with bleeding hearts and sore;
> Since poverty has been our crime, we bow to thy decree;
> We are the poor who have no wealth to purchase liberty!

What would the workers fight for? the Copperheads asked. And they replied: "To enable 'abolition capitalists' to transport negroes into northern cities in order to replace Irish workers who were striking for higher wages." The *New York Copperhead* urged workingmen to obey only "laws which give the poor equal privileges with the rich," while the *Daily News* wrote: "The people are notified that one out of about two and a half of our citizens are to be brought off into Messrs. Lincoln and Company's charnel house. God forbid! We hope that instant measures will be taken to prevent this outrage."

They were.

NEW YORK CITY DRAFT RIOTS

The drawing of names for the draft began in New York City on Saturday, July 11, 1863. All went peaceably. But early on Monday morning, the usual large crowd of stevedores that milled around the piers for the shape-up was missing, an ominous sign. By 4:30 that afternoon, the city officials had their answer. Wild mobs began to riot, and for five days they stormed through the streets of New York City, unleashing their hatred against the Conscription Act and committing atrocities against the black community, murdering or maiming any Negro whom they came upon.

On Fifth Avenue, covering the entire block between Forty-third and Forty-fourth streets, was the Colored Orphan Asylum, which cared for some three hundred black children. The rioters surprised the asylum's staff. When they climbed the fences, surrounding the buildings, William K. Davis, the supervisor, demanded to know what the mob wanted. They told him in no uncertain terms: "We're here to clean out your nigger nest." Recognizing the insane mood of the mob, Davis moved to get the children off the grounds. As he marched the youngsters from the buildings, the mob charged across the lawn to get at the orphans. They were saved by the aid given by the firemen who came upon the scene at that moment, but they could not save the buildings. The Colored Orphan Asylum burned to the ground.

The Colored Seamen's Home was also attacked, "rifled of all its furniture, clothing and books," and the building partly damaged. William P. Powell, the home's owner and director, barely managed to save himself and his family from the mob. He published the following account:

My family, including my invalid daughter, took refuge on the roof of the next house. I remained till the mob broke in and then narrowly escaped the same way. This was about 8½ p.m. We remained on the roof for an hour. It began to rain, as if the very heavens were shedding tears over the dreadful calamity.

How to escape from the roof of a five-story building with four females—and one a cripple—without a ladder was beyond my *not* excited imagination. But God came to my relief in the person of a little deformed, despised Israelite who, Samaritan-like, took my poor helpless daughter under his protection in his house. He also supplied me with a long rope. Though pitch dark I took soundings with the rope to see if it would touch the next roof, after which I took a clove-hitch around the clothesline which led from one roof to the other over a space of about one hundred feet.

I managed to lower my family down to the next roof and from one roof to another, until I landed them in a neighbor's yard. We were secreted in our friend's cellar till 11 p.m. when we were taken by the police and locked up in the station house for safety. In this dismal place we found upward of seventy men, women and children—some with broken limbs—bruised and beaten from head to foot. All my personal property to the amount of $3000 has been scattered to the four winds.

Henry Highland Garnet escaped the mob only because his daughter had wrenched his nameplate from his door with an axe. But not all escaped. The tenement house at 147 East Twenty-seventh Street was inhabited by blacks, one of them Henry Nichols. He had not ventured out all day for fear of the mobs. His mother, Mrs. Mark Stoat, a seamstress, had spent the day with him, and the two had passed the time visiting with neighbors and talking about the riots. Some men in the building formed a defense group to guard the house.

A mob numbering several hundred had been driven by police from Jackson's Foundry. Enraged and frustrated, the rioters took out their feelings in acts of wanton terror. They set fire to a row of wooden shacks on Second Avenue at Twenty-eighth Street and then turned into East Twenty-seventh Street and attacked the Negro tenement building. The few blacks guarding it put up a fight but were soon overwhelmed. The rioters charged into the building and along the hallways, kicking in the doors of apartments. Irving Werstein describes what happened next:

In one dwelling, they came on a young woman lying in bed with her six-day-old baby. Her husband tried to stop them but was killed in cold blood. The blood-lust was raging in the rioters. Wildly glaring men grabbed the screaming woman and flung her through the window into the courtyard below. A man hurled the baby after the mother with the nonchalance he would show in tossing away a cigar butt.

This was only a brief incident in the horror to come. About ten Negroes, mostly women and children including Mrs. Stoat and her son, managed to reach the basement where they hid themselves in a wood bin and cowered there, listening to the stomping rioters smashing up the apartments on the upper floors.

The rioters were preparing to leave when the frightened group in the cellar was discovered. Instead of storming the basement the whites decided to have some fun. The main water pipe was cut and gallons of water cascaded into the basement. The water soon rose waist deep in the cellar. Women wept and shrieked and clutched their children. The rioters ringed the building and massed in the backyard which had an exit from the basement.

At last, the trapped Negroes could no longer remain where they were. They preferred the risks of a dash out into the darkness to drowning in the cellar. They made a concerted rush for the back door and stumbled out into the weed-choked yard, dripping wet and half mad with fear.

The yard was surrounded by a sagging, rotting picket fence. Several of the women managed to escape, for the few men fought with frenzied courage to give them time. The fight soon ended with the Negroes either killed or knocked unconscious. Rioters dashed after the fleeing women. Two men caught Mrs. Stoat and dragged her back into the yard. Nichols, bleeding from a dozen wounds, stumbled toward the men who held his screaming, struggling mother.

"Don't harm her. Kill me but don't harm my mother!" he cried. "Sure, nigger. Glad to oblige. Let the old cow go, boys. We got ourselves a volunteer!" a rioter called out, swinging a crowbar.

The men released Mrs. Stoat who slumped to the ground in a dead faint. Two rioters held Nichols by the arms while the one with the crowbar hefted it and cried, "Watch this, lads! I'll get this nigger with one stroke!"

He raised the bar high and brought it down on Nichols head with full force. There was a sound like a melon bursting open. Nichols was dead before he fell, his head caved in.

Hours later, Mrs. Stoat was found crouching by her son's body in the darkness and moaning unintelligibly, shocked into madness by her ordeal.

Small wonder that C. C. Chapin wrote in his "Personal Recollections of the Draft Riots": "Deeds were done and scenes occurred that one could not believe have occurred in a civilized country."

The attacks on blacks mounted with such intensity that Commissioner of Police Henry Acton sent a message to all police precincts: "Receive every colored person. Refuse no one."

The riots went unchecked until eleven Union regiments were released by the secretary of war to quell the rioters. By this time, the report of the Merchants' Committee on the Draft Riots pointed out,

blacks had been driven by the fear of death at the hands of the mob, who . . . had . . . brutally murdered by hanging on trees and lamp posts, several of their number, and cruelly beaten and robbed many others, burning and sacking their houses, and driving nearly all from the streets, alleys and docks upon which they had previously obtained an honest though humble living—those people had been forced to take refuge on Blackwell's Island, at police stations, on the outskirts of the city, in the swamps and woods back of Bergen, New Jersey, at Weeksville, and in the barns and out-houses of the farmers of Long Island and Morristown. At these places were scattered some 5,000 homeless men, women and children.

THE AFTERMATH

The New York City draft riots of July 1863 were the bloodiest race riots of American history. Police figures on deaths among the white rioters ranged from twelve hundred to fifteen hundred; thousands more died later of wounds. Losses of property through burning and pillaging came to many millions of dollars; at least one hundred buildings were completely destroyed, and more than twice that many were badly damaged or thoroughly looted. Whole blocks were burned to the ground. Much-needed troops were brought in to restore order.

Upwards of thirty blacks were lynched on the street corners or slaughtered in their homes. Some responsible estimates of blacks killed exceed one hundred, and contemporary guesses were even higher. "It is impossible to know how many bodies of Negro victims of the lynch mobs were borne away by the waters on either side of Manhattan Island," Albon P. Man, Jr., points out. "Significantly the Negro population of the metropolis dropped 20% between 1860 to 1865, declining from 12,472 to 9,945."

Few rioters were brought to trial; none were executed for murder. The riot, however, did mark a turning point in public feeling about black New Yorkers. To the surprise of the black community, New York's leading merchants came forward with offers of help. They raised almost $50,000 for the riot victims and helped rebuild the Colored Orphan Asylum. But in the main, they refused to offer blacks the jobs they had formerly held on the docks or in other menial occupations, fearing that Irish workers would destroy any establishments that continued to employ Negroes.

How should blacks meet the rioters? Reverend J.W.C. Pennington discussed this question in an address on August 14, 1863. His answer went: "First, we must study the use of arms for self-defense. There is no principle in civil or religious obligation that requires us to live on in hazard and leave our persons, property and our wives and children at the mercy of barbarians. Self-defense is the first law of nature."

In his account of his ordeal during the riots, William P. Powell concluded: "My oldest son is now serving my country as a surgeon in the United States army, and I myself had just received a commission in the naval service. . . . I am now an old man, stripped of everything which I once possessed, of all the comforts of life; but I thank God that He has preserved my life, which I am ready to yield in defence of my country."

Powell was not the only black to display his devotion to the Union cause despite the sufferings he had endured. When the Twentieth Regiment, U.S. Colored Troops, was organized in New York in December 1863, William Derickson, whose mother had been murdered by the rioters and who had narrowly escaped being burned alive himself, was one of the first to volunteer. When one considers that there were at that time only six thousand Negroes capable of bearing arms in the whole state and that fifteen hundred had already volunteered for regiments in other states, the fact that it was possible to raise three regiments so soon after the draft riots is ample proof that the black citizens of New York did not allow that shameful episode to blunt their loyalty.

On March 5, 1864, the first black regiment paraded through the streets of New York City as it prepared to leave for the front. At the clubhouse the wives of the city's most prominent citizens presented the regimental colors to the Twentieth. "In New York City," wrote Joseph T. Wilson, a black officer in the Fifty-fourth Massachusetts Volunteers, "where Negroes had been hung to lamp posts and where a colored orphan asylum had been sacked and burned, crowds gathered in

Broadway and cheered [Black] Phalanx regiments on their way to the front." So
impressed was Francis Lieber that he wrote the following day to Charles Sumner:

When I wrote to you yesterday . . . I omitted mentioning the historic fact—the, to me,
great symbolic fact—of the presentation of colors to the regiment of blacks in Union
Square by our club. There were drawn up in line over a thousand armed negroes, where
but yesterday they were literally hunted down like rats. . . . A few months ago the
question was put to us whether a Massachusetts colored regiment might march through
New York to embark. It was decided, and justly so, that it could not be done, without
being prepared for bloodshed; that was shortly before the riots; and now within a half a
year, a colored regiment is cheered, and handkerchiefs wave from every window. I was
deeply, deeply moved. It was for once a visible step forward.

ADVANCES ON THE CIVIL RIGHTS FRONT

Among many Northern blacks, the Emancipation Proclamation stirred a new
hope that white attitudes were really changing. Perhaps, they hoped, full equality
would soon be inaugurated throughout the North. This hope was partially realized. The Civil War did produce great changes in the status of Northern Negroes.
The State Department ignored Chief Justice Roger Taney's dictum in the *Dred
Scott* case that a Negro could not be an American citizen, and in August 1861 it
granted a passport to Henry Highland Garnet explicitly stating that Garnet was a
"citizen of the United States." In 1862, moreover, Attorney General Edward
Bates, in a lengthy opinion, denied the principles of the *Dred Scott* decision and
affirmed that every free person born in the United States was "at the moment of
birth, *prima facie* a citizen."

Under the leadership of Charles Sumner, Congress passed several anti-
discrimination measures during the war. In 1862, the Senate repealed an 1803
law barring blacks from carrying the mail. (The law was an aftermath of Gabriel
Prosser's slave conspiracy in Virginia.) Democrats and conservative Republicans
killed the bill in the House, but it finally passed both Houses and became law on
March 3, 1865. In 1862, Congress decreed that in all proceedings of the District
of Columbia courts, there must be no exclusion of witnesses because of race, and
in 1864 this legislation was broadened to cover every federal court in the nation.

Action against discrimination also occurred on the state level during the war.
In 1863, the California legislature, responding to the organized protests of black
Californians and their white abolitionist allies, repealed the law barring Negroes
from testifying against whites. Blacks could henceforth testify in any court case.

Illinois had perhaps the most repressive antiblack laws of all the free states.
Restrictions on free blacks prohibited their immigration into the state and denied
them access to the polls, courts, or schools. The state's repressive black laws and
the notorious antiblack sentiments of its white citizens had combined, by 1860,
to keep the black population under 0.5 percent. Despite the laws against immi-

gration and the denial of virtually all civil rights, Illinois' black population increased 268 percent between 1860 and 1865, reaching a little over 0.9 percent of the population. The majority of these illegal immigrants, most of them contrabands, settled in the southernmost counties of Illinois, along the Mississippi River, or in Chicago.

By the middle of the Civil War, Illinois had fallen under Democratic sway, but the 1864 elections returned the state to Union Republican control. Consequently, beginning with the new general assembly in 1865, there were significant advances in civil rights. These changes, however, were granted grudgingly, and only after pressure from the black community.

The repeal of the black laws did not go beyond allowing blacks to immigrate and testify in court. Blacks still could not sit on juries, vote, or hold office, nor could their children attend the free public schools. Indeed, Newton Bateman, Illinois superintendent of public instruction, admonished the general assembly to provide free public schools for the state's blacks, while assuring the more racist members of the legislature that "the question of co-attendance or separate schools, is an entirely separate and distinct one, and may safely be left to be determined by the respective districts and communities." At a state convention in Galesburg, Illinois, on October 16, 1866, black Illinois citizens declared that "it is necessary for us to take measures looking to the removal of such disabilities as now affect us by State laws, and without the repeal of which any favorable action on the part of Congress can be of but little avail." Among the rights they desired all blacks to enjoy (in addition to the right of suffrage) were admission to the state's public schools and colleges and the right to a fair trial by having the right to sit on juries.

By the spring of 1865, Indiana was the only Northern state that retained black laws against Negro immigration and testimony, and they were eliminated in the winter of 1865–1866 by court and legislative action.

BATTLE AGAINST SEGREGATION: THE PHILADELPHIA STORY

Although legal barriers fell in most parts of the North during and immediately after the war, other forms of discrimination proved more resistant. Even in Massachusetts, where Negroes enjoyed civil and political rights, black children attended integrated schools, and black men were admitted to the professions, Negroes were subjected to many kinds of discrimination. John S. Rock, a justice of the peace in Suffolk County, said bluntly in August 1862:

Massachusetts has a great name, and deserves much credit for what she has done; but the position of the colored people in Massachusetts is far from being an enviable one. While colored men have many rights, they have few privileges here. . . . The educated colored man meets, on the one hand, the embittered prejudices of the whites, and on the other the jealousies of his own race. . . . You can hardly imagine the humiliation and contempt a colored lad must feel by graduating the first in his class, and then being rejected everywhere else because of his color. . . .

We are colonized in Boston. It is five times as difficult to get a house in a good location in Boston as it is in Philadelphia, and it is ten times more difficult for a colored mechanic to get employment than in Charleston. Colored men in business in Massachusetts receive more respect and less patronage than in any place that I know of. In Boston we are proscribed in some of the eating-houses, many of the hotels, and all the theatres but one. . . .

The laboring men who could once be found all along the wharves of Boston, can now be found only about Central Wharf, with scarcely encouragement enough to keep soul and body together. You know that the colored man is proscribed in some of the churches, and that this proscription is carried even to the graveyards. This is Boston—by far the best, or at least the most liberal large city in the United States.

But compared to Philadelphia, Boston was almost a paradise for blacks. Following a visit to Philadelphia at the beginning of 1862, Frederick Douglass wrote indignantly:

There is not perhaps anywhere to be found a city in which prejudice against color is more rampant than in Philadelphia. Hence all the incidents of caste are to be seen there in perfection. It has its white schools and colored schools, its white churches and its colored churches, its white Christianity and its colored Christianity, its white concerts and its colored concerts, its white literary institutions and its colored literary institutions . . . and the line is everywhere tightly drawn between them. Colored persons, no matter how well dressed or how well behaved, ladies or gentlemen, rich or poor, are not even permitted to ride on any of the many railways through that Christian city. Halls are rented with the express understanding that no person of color shall be allowed to enter, either to attend a concert or listen to a lecture. The whole aspect of city usage at this point is mean, contemptible and barbarous.

Of Philadelphia's nineteen streetcar and suburban railroad companies, eleven refused to admit blacks to their cars. The other eight reluctantly allowed them to ride but forced them to stand in the front platform with the driver, even when the cars were half empty and even in rain or snow. In many parts of Philadelphia, blacks seeking transportation had to walk or hire an expensive carriage.

At the outbreak of the Civil War, a black passenger brought an action for damages against a conductor who ejected him from a car. He apparently believed that the fact that the nation was engaged in a struggle for survival might induce a change in policy. If he did, he was wrong. The court rejected the action and upheld the right of companies to exclude Negroes. Judge Richard Hare pointed to the fact that blacks were excluded "in our theatres, our schools, our lecture-rooms, our churches, and in fine, in all places where men congregate in public or private, for the transaction of business in common, or for enjoyment." It was too much to expect that a race "long civilized" would desire to travel in the company of those "emerging from the shades of barbarism." He concluded: "In the belief then, that the regulation excluding blacks now before us is a wise one or if not wise, will work its own cure best when least molested, we enter judgment for the defendant.'' The Philadelphia Female Anti-Slavery Society branded the decision ''an illustration of the hypocrisy of a people calling themselves democratic and Christian,'' but the companies, now reinforced by the court, continued their practice unchanged. Even black soldiers returning to their camps to fight for the Union were ejected from the horsecars. The Reverend Robert J. Parton of Chestnut Hill described the following incident:

A few minutes before six o'clock on Monday evening two non-commissioned officers of the United States army, belonging to a regiment now forming at Camp William Penn, stepped on the front platform of a Fifth-street car . . . on their way to the Berks-street depot of the North Pennsylvania Railroad. It was the last car by which they could reach the train to convey them out to their camp that night. When these well-dressed and well-behaved colored soldiers stepped on the platform there was none else on it except the driver. They were almost immediately seen by the conductor, who rushed through the car and ordered the men to ''get off.'' One of the soldiers replied, ''We want to reach the train to get out to camp tonight.'' ''I can't help that, you can't ride on this car,'' was the answer. As the men did not move at once, the conductor put them off. The men, without resistance, but with an indignation they could not express, *were forced from the platform.*

The men were then on the sidewalk, within a short distance from us, but the conductor would not listen to their being allowed to stand on the vacant platform. . . . We reached the Berks-street station just in time to take the train on the North Pennsylvania Railroad, and the two soldiers were left behind.

I have seen colored soldiers on the battlefield. I have seen them defending fortifications, which a few hours before, they had taken from the Southern rebels, at the point of a bayonet. I have seen them suffering from wounds received in our defence, but I never before saw them forcibly driven from the privilege of standing on the platform of a railway car.

Negro regiments were organized and trained at Camp William Penn, a few miles from the city. It was a common sight to see hundreds of Negro men and women walking on the road leading to the camp to visit their sons and husbands to say farewell before they left to fight for the Union. ''These are the people whom our City Railway Companies exclude from their cars,'' the Female Anti-Slavery Society declared bitterly. ''Our colored population promptly responded to the call for men to drive back the rebel invaders of Pennsylvania; they go willingly in the face of death, and worse than death, to bear their part in the fierce struggle for the Nation's life. Is it *thus* that Philadelphia should requite them?''

But Philadelphia was unmoved. Nor was it influenced by the fact that mothers and wives of wounded black soldiers found it impossible to visit their kinsmen in local hospitals, either because they could not ride in any of the cars in that direction or because they were compelled to stand on the front platform in the most miserable weather. One black woman wrote indignantly in 1864:

We have in this city three societies of ladies for the relief of the sick and wounded soldiers. . . . These ladies, whenever they desire to visit their brethren at the hospitals, either to minister to their wants or attending them when dying, are constrained to pay for carriage hire, at an expense of six or seven dollars, thus expending money that would be otherwise appropriated to the soldiers were they permitted to ride in the cars. . . . Now we do think this is a great outrage, not only upon us but upon the men who, regardless of the prejudice they have always encountered in this land of their birth, have at the call of their country rushed forth to aid in putting down the rebellion, and now they are wounded, many disabled for life, are deprived of seeing those dear to them, because the directors of the city passenger cars refuse to let colored people ride, which, to say the least, is a stigma upon the city of Philadelphia.

Here is what happened to the wives of two wounded soldiers when they attempted to visit them at the hospital. The description is by a white Philadelphian who witnessed the brutal incident:

On Thursday evening last, accompanied by a lady, I took a seat in a Spruce and Pine streetcar, going west. When the car arrived within a few feet of Eighth street it was hailed by two colored women. The car was stopped, and the women got in. All passed quietly for some time. The conductor received the fare from the women, and no objection was made to their presence until nearing Eleventh street, when the car was stopped and the women ordered to leave. This they declined doing in a mild and peaceable manner, pointing out that they were going to visit their wounded soldier husbands. Several minutes were spent in endeavoring to persuade the women to leave, but to no purpose. The car was then driven at a furious rate as far as Broad street, when it stopped to admit a passenger. The colored women attempted to get out, but were prevented, the conductor informing them that they would be taken to the depot and whitewashed. At Seventeenth street a lady wished to get out. The conductor would not stop for fear of losing his prisoners. At Nineteenth street I pulled the strap. The car stopped and I got out. The colored women rushed to the door to make their escape. One succeeded in reaching the platform, where she was seized by some ruffians. She cried frantically for help; and fear, I suppose, induced the outlaws to release her. The car had started when she sprang from the platform, she barely escaping injury. The other woman did not succeed in making her escape. During the trip the women were incessantly assailed with oaths, threats, and most disgusting language from the driver, conductor and the passengers, including a white woman, whose language was positively loathsome.

Robert Smalls, born a slave in Beaufort, South Carolina, in 1839, was catapulted to national fame in May 1862 when he led fifteen other slaves in delivering the *Planter,* a Confederate gunboat, to the Union navy outside Charleston harbor. He won commendation from Congress and President Lincoln and served throughout the war as a Union pilot. But while the *Planter* was at the navy yard in Philadelphia undergoing repairs, Smalls and a white sailor attempted to board a car to visit the famous vessel. The conductor would not allow the Negro to ride. The sailor pointed out who his companion was, but the conductor stuck to his statement: "Company regulations. We don't allow niggers to ride!" Smalls and his sailor friend had to walk several miles to the navy yard.

James M. McPherson has characterized the battle against streetcar segregation in Philadelphia as "a microcosm of the Negro's battle for equal rights and human dignity." The battle was waged throughout the Civil War by Philadelphia's blacks, aided by a few white abolitionists, by means of public appeals, action in the court, and lobbying in the state legislature. But while New York City and San Francisco both abolished segregation in their street railroads in 1864, Philadelphia refused to budge. Not even the fact that New York City, less than a year after the bloody draft riots during which wild mobs hanged, burned, and butchered Negroes, had ended streetcar segregation had the slightest effect. The only concession the presidents of the street railway companies made was to propose to a protesting committee of white and black Philadelphians that the issue be settled by a poll in the cars. They would let their passengers decide if blacks should be allowed to ride. Over the protests of the black community, the poll was held, and an overwhelming majority of the passengers voted "No" on the proposal: "Shall colored persons be allowed to ride in all the cars?"

That settled it as far as the streetcar companies were concerned. The Civil War ended with segregation on the streetcars of Philadelphia as firmly established as it had been when the war began. In a pamphlet entitled *Why Colored People in Philadelphia Are Excluded from the Street Cars?* a group of white Philadelphians, all of whom had been involved in the streetcar campaign, summarized the long and futile battle to end streetcar segregation and observed gloomily:

We are forced to the conclusion that this community, as a body, by long indulgence in the wicked habit of wronging and maltreating colored people, has become, like a moral lunatic, utterly powerless, by the exercise of its own will, to resist or control the propensity.

During the war abolitionists and black leaders pressed demands for black equality before the law in the North, and they made some progress against racial discrimination. The legislatures of Illinois, Iowa, and Ohio repealed state laws barring black immigration and denying the Negroes the right to testify in court. The Rhode Island lower house passed a school desegregation measure. In New York City and San Francisco, blacks and abolitionists forced the desegregation of transportation. Senator Charles Sumner persuaded Congress to take several antidiscrimination measures during the war. And, as George M. Fredrickson has noted, the effect of enrolling blacks in the Union army was "to dispel rather dramatically any lingering sentiment in favor of government-sponsored colonization." It was difficult to ask a man to fight for a nation without recognizing his right to live in it.

23

The Army and the Freed Slaves, 1863–1864

The rush of slaves into the Union army forced the high command to adopt a series of policy decisions that came to serve as guidelines for treatment of the Negro during and after the war. They established schools to educate black soldiers and freedmen and organized the refugees to work on the cotton fields of abandoned plantations under government auspices, usually employing the labor contract and wage payments as the instruments for carrying this into effect, and, in a few cases, selling or distributing sections of the abandoned plantations among the freedmen.

EDUCATION OF BLACKS DURING THE WAR

The Civil War witnessed the advent of an era of new educational opportunity for blacks, and the Union army played a major part in providing education for its black enlistees. In some cases they were taught by individual soldier-instructors who worked informally, sitting with one or more pupils under a tree, giving out words for spelling, putting words on slates for copying, and, in general, teaching the ABCs. Thousands of black enlistees learned to read and write in army schools conducted by Northern civilians, army officers and enlisted men, chaplains, and the wives of officers. So great was their desire for education that in a number of instances, the black soldiers built their own schoolhouses and pooled their money to hire teachers. One visitor to the hospital at Benton Barracks in Missouri reported that a "very large proportion of the blacks had books in their hands, or within reach of their beds," and the Negro convalescents were organized into a school. After their discharge, many of these men and other members of the Sixty-second U.S. Colored Infantry stationed at Benton contributed $5,000 and raised additional funds to help establish Lincoln University in Jefferson City, Missouri. The librarian of that university has written: "Lincoln . . . itself is a living memorial to the members of the 62nd and 85th Regiments who, having just emerged from slavery, gave of their meager savings so that a school could be established."

> So come bring your books and slates,
> And don't be a fool
> For Uncle Sam is rich enough
> To send us all to school.

This verse was sung "with a perfect gusto" at Uncle Sam's School at Arlington, Virginia. Not all freedmen and their children were sent to school during the Civil War, but a great many were. In Louisiana, under General Nathaniel P. Banks' general order number 23, provision was made for free education for Negro children. This, together with a supplementary order, number 38, established the Office of Education directed by three military men who were authorized to build schools, select teachers, and regulate instruction. By October 1864, more than half of the 15,340 black children in occupied Louisiana were attending the institutions, and within a few months, a large portion of the remainder were being educated.

Blacks of all ages came to these and other schools established in the Southern states occupied by the Union army. "Mother, child, and grandchild sometimes came hand in hand to the schoolroom," one historian has written. Of 160 pupils in a Newbern, North Carolina, school in 1863, 50 were between six and twelve years of age, 95 were between twelve and forty-five, and 15 were over forty-five. Young and old, they were all eager to learn. To the freed men and women, reading and schools were symbols of freedom and a guarantee against the return of slavery, especially if linked to the ownership of land. The following incident is typical:

Immediately after the occupation of Wilmington, North Carolina by the Federals, a teacher announced that he would meet the colored children at nine o'clock on a certain morning at the church to enroll them. Very early in the morning of the appointed day Negroes began to appear at the church ground. By seven o'clock, the yard was full and the street was blocked. Anxious parents would come pushing their way through the crowd with their dusky charges in train saying to the teacher that they wanted "dese yer four children's names tooken," or "Please, Sir, put down dese yer." Or, "I wants dis gal of mine to jine."

The adults usually attended school in the evening or in the afternoon after the day's work was done. They even took their spelling books and readers to the fields with them to study at intervals of rest, and "labor superintendents making their regular rounds of inspection were some times plied with questions by workers in the field as to the identification of letters of the alphabet and the pronunciations of words."

The *Report of the Board of Education for Freedmen, Department of the Gulf, for the Year 1864* observes that the black children were more determined to learn than any white children the teachers and supervisors had seen. The *Report* continued:

Another habitude of these colored children is their care of books and school furniture. There is an absence of that young American lawlessness so common on Caucasian playgrounds. The walls and fences about the colored schools are not defaced, either by violence or vulgar scratching. They do not whittle or ply the jack-knife at the expense of the desks and benches.

By war's end, army schools had educated about 200,000 black soldiers and freedmen. In the Department of the Gulf alone, 50,000 blacks were said to have learned to read and write. Many of the newly educated blacks were taught by Northerners who went South to teach. Coming particularly from earlier antislavery centers and sponsored by both the army and philanthropic organizations, they were dedicated to eradicating the impress of bondage. From the refugee centers along the Mississippi or the contraband camps around Fortress Monroe to Port Royal and other South Carolina Sea Islands, these northerners, many of them women, worked zealously and tirelessly at their task. They became teachers to the thousands of Negroes thrown up and dispossessed by the war. Many were prolific letter writers, and not only did they describe in detail their work and their daily lives but they commented at length about their pupils. From Baton Rouge, Louisiana, Frank H. Green wrote in July 1864:

The cause of the Freedman is prospering wherever schools have been established, the colored people are learning to read and write, with great success. If any one thinks that the negro is not capable of being educated, let him visit any one of the schools in this Department, and I think he will be convinced that the color of the skin does not affect the mental capacity. I have as intelligent children in my school as I ever saw any where in the North. I never saw children show greater eagerness for learning. It is a real pleasure to teach them. I am happy when surrounded with their dusky faces and glistening eyes.

THE PORT ROYAL EXPERIMENT

Port Royal is one of a complex of sea islands strung along the Atlantic Coast from Charleston to Savannah. In November 1861, a flotilla of Union ships sailed into Port Royal Sound, knocked out the tiny Confederate forts that put up a futile resistance, and steamed on to capture Beaufort, the principal town of the island. The masters and their families had fled to the mainland with what few slaves they could persuade or coerce into going with them. Most of the slave population, some ten thousand, had refused to move.

The island economy had been shattered by the war, by the flight of the planters, by looting and destruction by whites and blacks alike, including the burning of cotton gins, the loss of farm implements, and the waste of seed. Here was a chance for the Union government to try out experiments in education and training the freedmen and in the rehabilitation of the economy. Here, as Willie Lee Rose has put it in her definitive study of the Port Royal experiment, was an opportunity to rehearse for Reconstruction.

The collection and distribution of this abandoned property, both human and material, came under the Treasury Department's jurisdiction. Within a few months of the Sea Islands victory, Treasury Secretary Salmon P. Chase, an antislavery Republican from Ohio, seized the opportunity to launch the Port Royal experiment. The shipment of cotton to the North was the secretary's first consideration. In December 1861, Lieutenant Colonel William Reynolds arrived at Port Royal as Chase's agent to supervise this undertaking. Second, the secretary entrusted the gathering of information on the South Carolina blacks to Edward L. Pierce, a young Boston attorney. Having worked with General Butler supervising black workers at Fortress Monroe, Pierce brought substantial expertise to his new assignment. Writing for the September 1863 issue of *Atlantic Monthly,* Pierce recorded his impressions of the Virginia blacks. He observed that the contrabands were industrious and determined to be free, and he was convinced that the ex-slaves had the potential for citizenship. Pierce's article substantiated the antislavery argument that blacks would work without being coerced.

His visit to the Sea Islands confirmed Pierce in this belief, and on February 13, 1862, he returned enthusiastically to Washington. He presented his ideas to Chase, Frederick Olmstead of the Sanitary Commission, Robert Purvis, Wendell Phillips, and other abolitionists. He even met briefly with President Lincoln, who left any decision for implementing the project to Chase's discretion.

Pierce proposed that the government send teachers, ministers, and superintendents South to aid the blacks. Fearful that too much government involvement might lessen the antislavery thrust of the mission, Pierce suggested the northerners' salaries should be paid by private agencies.

As Pierce had hoped, Chase approved of the Port Royal project and many people simultaneously responded to the Sea Islands challenge. During February 1862, the New England Educational Commission and the Freedmen's Relief Association of New York came into existence. The following month, Philadelphians organized the Port Royal Relief Commission. All three groups pledged to provide financial support for the men and women chosen for the Southern work.

After considerable deliberation, the New England Education Commission chose thirty teachers, including four women, for the Port Royal assignment. On March 3, 1862, these appointees joined Edward Pierce and twenty-three others chosen by the Philadelphia and New York Commissions aboard the steamer *United States.* Embarking from New York harbor, they brought with them relief supplies, medicine, agricultural equipment, and books with which they were to begin a great effort to regenerate the South and prepare the blacks for freedom and citizenship. They called themselves Gideonites after Gideon and the five hundred Israelites who followed him and who, according to biblical history, armed only with trumpets and lamps put to flight an army of thousands.

As agents of the Treasury Department, the Gideonites would superintend the various abandoned plantations; as missionaries to the Sea Islands blacks, they would teach, minister, distribute supplies, and be paid a small salary by the three private associations that had financed and organized the venture.

Most Gideonites were young and well educated. According to Edward Pierce, Harvard, Yale, Brown, and the divinity schools like Cambridge and Andover provided many workers for Port Royal. All had strong antislavery backgrounds, which had been a prerequisite for their selection. Edward Philbrick's father, Samuel, for example, had served as the Massachusetts Anti-Slavery Society's treasurer. Her close friendship with both Salmon P. Chase and Charles Sumner influenced Susan Walker, a Bostonian, to become a Port Royal teacher. Laura Towne began a lifelong career as a teacher on St. Helena's island. A Philadelphian by birth, Towne had been raised in an antislavery family. Wendell Phillips' nephew, Samuel, became a Sea Islands teacher, as did twenty-five-year-old Charlotte Forten of the famous Philadelphia black abolitionist family.

Born in Philadelphia, the granddaughter of James Forten, Sr., and the daughter of his son, James, Jr., both wealthy blacks and militant abolitionists, Charlotte Forten became deeply involved in activities directed toward achieving equality for black Americans. By attending Lombard Street Primary School taught by her aunt, Margaretta Forten, young Charlotte avoided the city's segregated and often inferior facilities for black children. The necessity of securing a higher education for his daughter, however, caused Robert Forten to send Charlotte to Salem, Massachusetts. There the seventeen year old entered Higginson Grammar School, which afforded Charlotte Forten and other young women an excellent education. During the 1850s, Charlotte, the only nonwhite pupil among two hundred other girls, studied history, geography, drawing, and cartography. After she graduated, Charlotte secured a job in the city's school system, becoming the first Afro-American hired to teach integrated classes.

In 1862 when John Greenleaf Whittier first learned of the Sea Islands project, he thought Charlotte would make an excellent participant and suggested that with her teaching experience, she could make an important contribution to the project. After careful consideration, she decided to place an application with the New England Commission in Boston. But securing a teaching position proved to be more difficult than Charlotte had anticipated. Rumors circulated of the commission's reluctance to hire blacks. Although Edward Pierce denied the rumors, by mid-October when no word had arrived from the Boston group, Charlotte placed an application with the Philadelphia Port Royal Relief Commission, and within a few days, she received an assignment.

Whittier's prediction of Charlotte Forten's aptness for the Port Royal experiment had been accurate. Within one year of Charlotte's arrival in South Carolina, Laura Towne described her as "the pet and belle of the island." Besides her teaching assignment, Charlotte sewed for elderly women, nursed soldiers, and listended to the blacks' joys and sorrows. The local people found her musical talents delightful. They loved to hear her play the piano.

After enduring sea sickness and crowded quarters aboard ship, the early Gideonites reached their destination to discover fleas, mosquitos, and makeshift living accommodations. Unaccustomed to the tropical climate, many northerners fell victim to disease. During the winters of 1863 and 1864, Laura Towne, who had some medical training, attended her fellow teachers. Although the vast majority of northerners regained their strength with medical treatment and rest, others were not as fortunate. During August 1863, Sea Islands residents mourned the death of Samuel Phillips, a victim of tropical fever.

Because of the haste in which the Port Royal project had been organized, early arrivals lacked adequate living quarters. Further, the fear of a Confederate attack kept the Gideonites on the alert. During the spring of 1863, Charlotte Forten and Lizzie Hunn, who shared a bedroom at the Oaklands plantation, frequently slept with revolvers under their pillows. Packages from home supplied the Gideonites with many essentials and a few luxuries.

In time, adequate living quarters eased the northerners' initial discomforts. Charlotte Forten entered the work with enthusiasm and zeal even before this was accomplished. On October 20, 1862, after her first visit to a Sea Islands school, she remarked: "Dear Children! born in slavery, but free at last. May God preserve to you all the blessings of freedom, and may you be in every possible way fitted to enjoy them. My heart goes out to you. I shall be glad to do all I can to help you." On October 31, after her first day as a teacher, she described her students. "The children are well behaved and eager to learn," she wrote. "It will be a happiness to teach there."

Charlotte Forten's diary speaks of her growing understanding of and communication with the people of the island. She felt the depth of their religious beliefs as expressed in their songs, and she became a collector of the folksongs of her people. In her school classes she taught the children stories of black heroes, pointing up particularly the exploits of Touissaint L'Ouverture, the Haitian revolutionary. She recorded her objective in such lessons, writing, "I long to inspire them with courage and ambition of a noble sort, and high purpose." Upon Charlotte Forten's request, John Greenleaf Whittier wrote a hymn to celebrate her students' academic progress. The children quickly learned the song entitled, "O None in All the World Before," which had been composed in their honor. On Christmas day 1862, they sang the song before an audience of soldiers, teachers, and local blacks. The hymn's first stanza went:

> O None in all the world before
> Were ever glad as we!
> We're free on Carolina's shore,
> We're all at home and free.

In March 1863, Edward Pierce inspected two schools on St. Helena's, another on Ladies Island, and four in the town of Beaufort. While Pierce praised all the

Port Royal teachers, he took special notice of the two blacks. In the September 1863 issue of *Atlantic Monthly,* Pierce proudly described the diligent work of Ned Lloyd White, a former slave, who along with two white women taught a school in St. Helena's village. Pierce devoted a full page of his article to Charlotte Forten and her labors among the Sea Islands blacks. Besides mentioning the young Philadelphian's African ancestry, olive complexion, and cultural and educational attainment, Pierce described Forten's sincere dedication to the Port Royal project. He applauded her decision to remain in the United States instead of living in Europe. Pierce explained, "She would not desert herself from the fortunes of her people, and now, not with a superficial sentiment, but a profound purpose, she devotes herself to their elevation."

The elevation to which Pierce referred had come with surprising speed. Charlotte Forten's report to the Philadelphia Port Royal Relief Commission mentioned how easily the Sea Islands children learned their lessons. She wished only that the advocates of black inferiority could witness the children's rapid progress. Forten's experience in teaching white students in Salem, Massachusetts, afforded her the opportunity to compare the white and black children's educational ability. Mindful that whites had never experienced bondage, she remarked, "Yet I can say with truth, that these poor negro children, born to slavery and degradation, compare, in many respects, most favorably with those highly favored white children."

Like the children, Sea Islands adults also took advantage of this new educational opportunity. Northern teachers spent their evenings tutoring adult students. On November 13, 1862, Harry, an elderly man, arrived for his first tutoring session. Charlotte Forten, Harry's teacher, recorded how excited her new pupil had been at the prospect of acquiring an education. She hoped to tutor many other adults, but their daily work and the raising of families prevented many from attending classes. Realizing the importance of an education, however, parents endured numerous sacrifices so their children could learn. One such parent told Forten, "Do Miss let de chil'en learn eberything dey can. We nebber had no chance to learn nuttin' but we wants de chil'en to learn." Elizabeth Botume, another teacher, recorded a similar incident. After listening to her children recite their lessons, a proud black parent remarked, "Dem chillen knows a heap more'n me. When they come home they talk so smart, I ain't know what they say, but I is proud all the same."

One of the key figures at Port Royal was Edward Philbrick, a young Bostonian of abolitionist convictions and an efficient businessman who made a great success and a good deal of money out of plantation management. Philbrick's great idea was that free labor was intrinsically profitable and for that reason superior to slave labor. Liberating the slaves and giving them intelligent direction (which only whites could do) and paying wages would provide a new market for Northern manufacturing goods and enable blacks eventually to acquire the dignity of fully independent Americans.

But Philbrick's theory came into conflict with his desire for profits, and as an employer, this abolitionist proved to be a hard taskmaster. To his surprise, his black laborers did not take exploitation lightly and complained about the wages they were receiving. A group of women laborers came to Philbrick with a demand for a wage increase. When Philbrick remonstrated with them, one of the blacks said that they knew "very well" that Philbrick had been "jamming bills" into his safe for six months, "and there must be enough in it now to bust it." But Philbrick refused the demand for a wage increase, convinced that "after being idle for a few weeks to think about the matter and to hope for more, they would gradually go to work for the same wages which they had previously received." He proved to be correct, for the black laborers' choice was to yield or to starve.

The incident pointed up the most troublesome problem at Port Royal and elsewhere in the occupied South: the disposition of the abandoned or confiscated land. The issue had been discussed in the black community soon after the start of the war, and black leaders argued that education and political equality were not enough to enable the former slaves to get a new start in life. Unless they received land of their own, the ex-slaves would remain poorly paid laborers or sharecroppers on the land of their former masters. Hence, from the outset of the war, a number of black leaders and newspapers called for the breakup of large Southern plantations and their redistribution among the freedmen. Such action would accomplish two important objectives: it would foster democracy in the South by destroying the economic basis of the "landed aristocracy," and it would ensure the creation of a prosperous and independent black farming population. As early as November 1861, the *Anglo-African* replied to the question, "What Shall Be Done with the Slave?"

When the war is ended, there will be few, if any slaves, for the government to dispose of. There will be four million of free men, women and children, accustomed to toil, who have by their labor during sixty years past supported themselves, and in addition, an extravagant aristocracy. . . . Besides these laborers, lands will be confiscated to the government, and turned into public lands. . . . What course can be clearer, what course more politic, what course will so immediately restore the equilibrium of commerce, what course will be so just, so humane, so thoroughly conducive to the public weal and the national advancement, as that the government should immediately bestow these lands upon these freedmen who know best how to cultivate them, and will joyfully bring their brawny arms, their willing hearts, and skilled hands to the glorious labor of cultivating as their own, the lands which they have bought and paid for by their sweat and toil.

Frederick Douglass endorsed this policy in his own paper, declaring:

I call for distribution of land among the freedmen. They have watered the soil with their tears and enriched it with their blood, and tilled it with their hard hands during two centuries; they have leveled the forests, raked out the obstructions to the plow and hoe, reclaimed the swamps, and produced whatever has made it a goodly land to dwell in, and it would be a shame and a crime little inferior to the enormity of slavery itself if these natural owners of the Southern and Gulf States should be driven away from their country to make room for others.

Unfortunately, this was precisely what did happen.

The Confiscation Act of July 17, 1862, provided for the expropriation of all property belonging to traitors. But at Lincoln's insistence, Congress passed a joint resolution stating that nothing in the act should be construed to work a forfeiture of real estate beyond the life of the offender. As James M. McPherson points out, this meant that

when the original Confederate owner died, his confiscated property would revert to his heirs. No effectual land reform could be based on this legislation, and in fact only a relatively small amount of property was expropriated and sold to new owners under the act of July 1862. Later Congressional efforts to modify or amend the act to provide for permanent confiscation failed of passage.

On June 7, 1862, however, Congress authorized the president to appoint tax commissioners to determine the amount of taxes owed by occupied areas of the Confederacy in helping pay for the war effort and to offer the land of delinquent tax payers for sale at public auction. It was this policy that was carried out on a large scale on the South Carolina Sea Islands. In March 1863, 16,749 acres of abandoned lands were put up for general sale. Members of Gideon's Band—that is, those not infected by the speculative fever—worked and fought to preserve most of the land for the freedmen. They were supported by General Rufus Saxton whose plan was to put as many of the freedmen on their own land as he could. His ideal was the small freehold—as many as possible. Indeed, so zealous was Saxton in his effort to realize his plan that he circumvented government orders prior to the sale of the Sea Islands lands by encouraging freedmen to squat anywhere. Saxton reasoned—correctly it turned out—that if they were not allowed to do this while awaiting the sale, the extent of available land would be greatly reduced, and they would be frustrated in their hope of staying on what they felt was their homes.

Meanwhile, contrary to Southern propaganda and widespread Northern belief, the blacks had proved that they could work without being coerced. During 1862, 3,817 Sea Islands laborers planted modestly successful crops of corn, potatoes, and cotton. The vast majority of this harvest supplied local needs, while the remainder was shipped to the North. While credit for the Sea Islands' productivity must be also given to the Northern superintendents whose managerial and agricultural expertise assisted the black laborers, the ex-slaves provided most of such knowledge themselves, which they had acquired during their long experience in slavery.

On March 9, 1863, as the Gideonites celebrated their first anniversary on the Sea Islands, the Commissioner's Office conducted the first land sales. By combining their meager savings, blacks were able to purchase only 2,000 of the 16,479 acres placed on sale. A description of one such black purchaser read:

Harry, an ex-slave, with funds of his own and some borrowed money, bought, at a tax sale, a small farm of 300 acres for $350. Beside paid duty for services to an officer, he does the work of a full hand on his place. His wife and two teenaged daughters also work. He lives in the house of his former overseer and by April 10, 1863, one third of his crop was then in.

The bulk of the land, however, was bought by Northern investors and speculators. A company that Edward Philbrick helped to form bought up 8,000 acres at less than a dollar an acre.

The sale of nearly 90 percent of the auctioned property to rich capitalists and other outsiders caused considerable anger among the freedmen and most of the Gideonites. The government still held 60,000 acres of land on the islands for nonpayment of taxes, and on December 31, 1863, these teachers and missionaries, with the support of General Saxton, managed to obtain an order from Secretary of the Treasury Salmon P. Chase allowing Negro heads of families to preempt any of this land, up to forty acres apiece, for a nominal price of $1.25 per acre. But the tax commissioners denounced the order, and with the aid of wealthy Northern investors, they persuaded Chase to rescind it. At a second public auction held on February 18, 1864, freedmen were able to buy only 2,750 acres.

Some Negroes who had saved a little money but were unable to pay competitive prices for the land on which they had worked most of their lives were disappointed by the rescinding of the preemption order. Several expressed their feelings in letters to President Lincoln, usually dictating them to their teachers. One freedman's letter, put down by the teacher exactly as dictated and later published in the *Philadelphia Press* of May 31, 1864, went in part:

Do my missus, tell Linkum dat we wants land—dis bery land dat is rich wid de sweat ob de face and de blood ob we back. We born here; we parents' graves here; we don wants oder country, dis yere our home. De Nort folks hab home, antee? What a pity dat dey don't love der home like we love we home, for den dey would never come here for buy all way from we.

Do my missus, beg Linkum for lef us room for buy land and live here. We don't ask for it for notins. We too tankful. We too satisfy to pay jist what de rich buckra pay. But dey done buy too much a 'ready, and lef we no chance. We could a bin buy all we want, but dey make de lots too big, and cut we out.

Lincoln took no steps to satisfy these yearnings, but in subsequent years Sea Islands blacks did manage to buy several thousand acres from the original Northern wartime purchasers. Edward Philbrick, for example, had insisted that he would eventually resell most of the land he acquired to blacks at somewhere near cost. During the first year of operation, however, he made so great a profit that when he finally did sell the land in 1865, his scruples did not prevent him from taking four or five times the amount he had paid for it.

A revolutionary land reform did get under way for Sea Islands blacks early in 1865, during General William T. Sherman's march through Georgia, and, in one way or another, the Sea Islands freedmen came in to own more land per capita than Negroes in any other part of the South.

LOUISIANA

In neither of the two other major areas occupied by the Union army was any land distributed among the ex-slaves, nor were they even allowed, as in Port Royal, to purchase land. In Louisiana, General Butler assigned a supervisor to take care of the abandoned plantations and supplied the necessary labor from the refugee camps, stipulating a ten-hour day and wages at $10 a month for first-class hands.

Under the land system administered by General Nathaniel P. Banks, his successor, the plantations in Louisiana were either leased to loyal whites or retained by those owners who took an oath of allegiance. Banks issued order number 12 on January 29, 1863 (part of which dealt with the education of black children), which required the former slaves to select an employer and remain under contract for one year. It also set wages and standards of treatment, prohibited the freedmen from leaving the plantations without a pass, and authorized provost marshals to enforce discipline. The order assured employers that "all the conditions of continuous and faithful service, respectful deportment, correct discipline and perfect subordination" would be enforced by the officers of the government.

Banks' new labor regulations were issued after several private negotiations the general held with forty leading planters at the St. Charles Hotel in New Orleans in February 1863, where he acceded to virtually their basic demands. Banks pledged that "the officers of the Government will induce the slaves to return to the plantations where they belong" and will "require them . . . to work diligently and faithfully for one year . . . [in] perfect subordination." The planters, who had insisted that they retained property rights in black people despite the Emancipation Proclamation, were particularly gratified by Banks' reference to blacks as "slaves."

Banks' order aroused widespread indignation among blacks. Speaking in Boston, Frederick Douglass attacked the policy, calling it

our chief danger at the present time; that it practically enslaves the negro, and makes the Proclamation of 1863 a mockery and delusion. What is freedom? It is the right to choose one's own employment. Certainly, it means that, if it means anything; and when any individual or combination of individuals undertakes to decide for any man when he shall work, where he shall work, at what he shall work, and for what he shall work, he or they practically reduce him to slavery. He is a slave. That I understand Gen. Banks to do—to determine for the so-called freedman when, and where, and what, and for how much he shall work, when he shall be punished, and by whom punished. It is absolute slavery. It defeats the beneficent intentions of the government, if it has beneficent intentions, in regard to the freedom of our people.

The *New Orleans Tribune,* the black newspaper, was the sharpest critic of Banks' policy. After praising the general's order for providing education for black children, it expressed its rage over the manner in which Banks dealt with the freedmen's economic needs. It labeled the federal land policy in Louisiana "a travesty on justice and little better than slavery." As an alternative, the newspaper advocated "universal confiscation of rebel property." The plantations should be "divided into five acre lots, and portioned among the tillers of the soil," who "should hold [the land] directly from the United States, as owners or lessees, at a *nominal price.*" Such measures were justified as punishment for the slaveholders, who were "guilty of bloody treason and as just compensation to the freedmen for generations of unrequited toil."

Instead of land, however, the *Tribune* went on, the freedmen, under General Banks, received an ultimatum that forced them to work under one-year contracts at ridiculously low wages. Moreover, openly catering to the planters, Banks deprived the black laborers of the freedom to come and go, requiring them to secure a pass from their employers if they wanted even to visit a neighboring plantation. All of these measures, the *Tribune* concluded, established "de facto slavery":

If we except the lash . . . one is unable to perceive any material difference between the two sets of regulations. All the important prohibitions imposed upon the slave, are also enforced against the freedmen. The free laborer, as well as the slave, has to retire into his cabin at a fixed hour in the evening; he cannot leave on Sunday, even to visit friends or simply to take a walk in the neighborhood, unless he is provided with a written authorization. . . . It is true that the law calls him a freeman; but any white man, subjected to such restrictive and humiliating prohibitions, will certainly call himself a slave. . . . Our freedmen, on the plantations, at the present time, could more properly be called, mock-freedmen. . . . If we do not take care, slavery will never be practically abolished in Louisiana.

But this had no effect on either the national administration or the local army officers.

MISSISSIPPI VALLEY

In the Mississippi Valley, under General Lorenzo Thomas, the army leased abandoned plantations to any whites willing to work Negro refugees for set wages. The lessees would take over the army's responsibility for supervising the refugees in their daily labor. The idea was that the vast majority of the refugees would find work on the plantations as hired hands. The lessees pledged to hire Negroes, to furnish them with rations of food and clothing at cost to be deducted from wages due, and to pay the low scale of $7 a month for adult males, $5 for women, and $3.50 for all hands aged twelve to fifteen. In addition, the hired

Negroes would pay a tax based on wages earned for the support of sick and dependent refugees.

Bell Irwin Wiley correctly calls these wages "pitiably low; so low in fact as not to constitute real wages." Apart from everything else, the planter was required to pay the freedman only for the actual day's work at the rate of $7 for a month's work of twenty-six days, or 27 cents a day. If a laborer, either because he was ill or because the planter failed to provide something for him to do, worked only ten days during the month, he received only $2.70 for his month's labor. Since this amount was further reduced by deductions for clothing and for the support of dependents, the laborer usually ended the year in debt to the planter.

In his *A Report on the Condition of the Freedmen of the Mississippi*, based on a thorough investigation of the operation of Thomas' policy, James A. Yeatman summed up the gloomy state of the freedmen:

The poor negroes are everywhere greatly depressed at their condition. They all testify that if they were only paid their little wages as they earn them, so that they could purchase clothing, and were furnished with the provisions promised they could stand it; but to work and get poorly paid, poorly fed, and not doctored when sick, is more than they can endure. Among thousands whom I questioned none showed the least unwillingness to work. If they could only be paid fair wages they would be contented and happy. They do not realize that they are free men. They say that they are told they are, but then they are taken and hired out to men who treat them, so far as providing for them is concerned, far worse than their "secesh" masters did. . . .

The parties leasing plantations and employing these negroes do it from no motives either of loyalty or humanity. The desire of gain alone prompts them, and they care little whether they make it out of the blood of those they employ or from the soil. There are of course exceptions; but I am informed that the majority of the lessees were only adventurers, camp followers, "army sharks," as they are termed, who have turned aside from what they consider their legitimate prey, the poor soldier, to gather the riches of the land which his prowess has laid open to them. . . . Lessees are now allowed to lease as many plantations as their cupidity may lead them to grasp. . . . No one party should be permitted to lease over one. Lessees of more than one plantation are unable to give their personal supervision and so employ the old overseers whom the former masters had employed. Whether these men can ever be brought to regard as freemen those whom they had always known and treated as slaves is very doubtful.

The unscrupulous activities of Northern capitalists and others interested solely in speculation so demoralized the refugees that many blacks refused to return to the fields. These speculators paid Negroes in the cheapest supplies at inflated costs, skipped out in mid-season without settling wage bills, and in many cases made no attempt even to plant cotton. Instead they rented plantations as fronts for their illegal business of gathering up cotton abandoned in the countryside or else obtained them from agents who hoped in this way to evade paying federal taxes. As Ronald Davis points out in his study of the operations of the abandoned plantations in the Natchez, Mississippi, District:

Agents of the federal government . . . conspired with unscrupulous leaseholders in intricate plots for practicing fraud upon the Negro. . . . More than a few officers later faced courts-martial charged with taking bribes, supplying planters from military depots in return for payoffs, and forming partnerships in conspiracy against the interests of the government and freedmen alike.

On March 11, 1864, the Army and Treasury departments issued order number 9. Under it freedmen were to function as wage laborers, and the army's responsibility was to prepare the Negro "for the time when he can render so much labor for so much money, which is the great end to be attained." Under it, too, employers would be given enough control over labor to protect investments and organize the ways in which the freedmen could be trained to work "as disciplined field hands." The order forbade Negroes to leave the plantations unless authorized; contracts were made binding upon both the employer and laborer alike under military law; and vagrancy on the part of blacks was to be punished by putting the unemployed to work on public works, roads, and levees.

With the lash no longer usable to force blacks to labor—"flogging and other cruel or unusual punishment" was prohibited by military order—the military men were convinced that the only recourse left lay in the employers' control over the freedmen's livelihood. Hence order number 9 provided that disobedience, insolence, and time lost due to illness would be at the freedmen's expense and not at that of the employers and would be immediately followed by a forfeiture of wages. In the case of repeated refusal to do the employer's bidding, Negroes "would be turned over to the Provost Marshal of the police district for labor upon public works without pay."

Many freedmen believed that under order number 9, they would be returning to the working conditions they associated with slavery. Believing, too, that freedom meant at least the right to reject such working conditions, large numbers of them abandoned the plantations for army camps or for nearby towns. Still another reason for their exodus from the plantations was the growing belief among the freedmen that they would receive land of their own from the abandoned plantations. They were therefore unwilling to tie themselves to any contracts, and especially those under order number 9, which was designed to restore conditions they associated with slavery.

24

Blacks and Abraham Lincoln, 1863–1864

In September 1863, the Brooklyn correspondent of the *Christian Recorder* wrote:

I am of the opinion that it is the duty of every colored man to uphold the present administration, because it is doing more for his race than has ever been done since the organization of the government. Never has a President, or cabinet officer stood forth to vindicate the rights of black men before. Never before have black men been recognized as citizens by the Secretary of State, and the giving of passports to them when embarking for foreign ports. Then the recognition of the republics of Liberia and Haiti, the acceptance of ambassadors from these countries, all demonstrate that this administration is the friend of the black race, and desires its prosperity no less than the good of all the races of men.

Yet at the time that this opinion was being published, the man who was being so lavishly praised was still convinced that there was no place for blacks in the United States and was seeking to colonize them in some other land.

COLONIZATION, AGAIN

The 1862 law that emancipated slaves in the District of Columbia included a provision of $100,000 to ship blacks out of the country and colonize them in a foreign land. Lincoln was determined to make use of that appropriation to carry out his long-planned scheme of colonizing Negroes. As he told the deputation of black men who visited him at his request in the White House on August 14, 1862, the broad physical differences between the two races was disadvantageous to both. ''I think your race suffers very greatly, many of them living among us,'' he declared, ''while ours suffers from your presence. . . . If this is admitted, it

422

affords a reason at least why we should be separated." He reminded his audience that in the United States at least, freedom had not brought equality for the blacks, for "on this broad continent, not a single man of your race is the equal of a single man of ours." Nor, he insisted, would they ever be equal.

Despite the rejection of his proposal by the vast majority of blacks, Lincoln still clung to the colonization scheme. Indeed, in his message to Congress on December 1, 1862, he advanced a new argument in favor of colonization, the Negro labor competition argument: "Reduce the supply of black labor by colonizing the black laborers out of the country, and by precisely so much you increase the demand for, and the wages of white labor." He indicated, too, that he was still convinced that all Negroes would prefer to emigrate rather than remain in the United States as second-class citizens.

Hence it is not surprising that when Ambrose W. Thompson, an American capitalist who had, by questionable means, secured control of a land grant of 2 million acres in the northern part of present-day Panama, incorporated the Chiriqui Improvement Company to develop the coal mines and other resources on his land and offered to sell coal to the American government for its navy at half the prevailing price if the government would supply him with Negro colonists to work the mines, Lincoln immediately expressed interest in the offer. In the summer of 1862, the president appointed Senator Samuel C. Pomeroy as U.S. colonization agent to recruit colonists and arrange transportation. Pomeroy issued a pamphlet addressed to "the Free Colored People of the United States," praising the wonderful climate and opportunities for blacks in Chiriqui.

But most black leaders were not impressed. Robert Purvis urged Pomeroy to inform the president that he was making a mistake by reviving the worn-out, discredited idea of colonization:

Sir, we were born here and here we choose to remain. Don't advise me to leave, and don't add insult to injury by telling me it's for my own good. Of that I am to be the judge. It is in vain you talk to me about "two races" and their "mutual antagonism." In the matter of rights, there is but one race, and that is the *human race.* . . .

Sir, this is our country as much as it is yours, and we will not leave it.

To this Frederick Douglass added the following advice: "Instead of sending any of the loyal people out of the country . . . at this time our great nation should hail with joy every loyal man, who has an arm and a heart to fight as a kinsman and clansman, to be marshalled to the defence and protection of a common country."

In spite of this opposition to the Chiriqui scheme, Lincoln encouraged Senator Pomeroy to continue, and by October 1862, he had recruited five hundred black emigrants, purchased the necessary equipment, and chartered a ship. But members of Lincoln's cabinet had begun to question the validity of Ambrose Thompson's title to the Chiriqui lands; scientist Joseph Henry of the Smithsonian Institute reported that the coal deposits in Chiriqui were virtually worthless; and several Latin American nations protested against any North American effort to establish a colony in Central America. When Secretary of State Seward recommended that the whole Chiriqui project be abandoned, Lincoln reluctantly agreed, and Pomeroy's shipful of emigrants never sailed. Frederick Douglass pronounced a fitting epitaph to the Chiriqui scheme: "A wise ending to a singularly foolish beginning."

Lincoln was still not discouraged. In September 1862, Bernard Kock, another capitalist, offered to provide employment for colonized blacks in the Ile à Vache, a small island off the southern coast of Haiti, agreeing to supply the Haitian government with 35 percent of the timber he cut. Kock wanted black labor to cut down the trees and hoped to obtain it in Washington. He made a favorable impression on Lincoln, who signed a contract with him on December 31, 1862, to transport five hundred Negroes to Ile à Vache for fifty dollars apiece. But when investigation revealed that Kock was a shady character, the government canceled the contract.

Lincoln still did not give up. A few months later, the president authorized a similar contract with Paul S. Forbes and Charles K. Tuckerman, two New York businessmen, who promptly hired Kock as manager of the enterprise, and in May 1863, a group of 453 Negroes from Washington and Hampton, Virginia, arrived at Ile à Vache.

The Ile à Vache emigration experiment was a dismal failure. Kock confiscated the colonists' American money and failed to provide them with adequate housing. Smallpox, mutiny, and starvation stalked the colony. Nearly a hundred blacks died. Lincoln gave up the experiment, and in February 1864 he ordered a ship to bring the surviving colonists back to the United States. Five months later a disgusted Congress repealed all provisions of the 1862 legislation appropriating funds for colonization purposes.

Long after the event, Benjamin F. Butler, the Massachusetts Republican leader and former Union officer, maintained that in April 1865, Lincoln had asked him to work out the logistics of shipping Negroes to "some fertile country with a good climate, which they could have for themselves." But all indications point to the fact that after the Ile à Vache fiasco, Lincoln simply gave up on colonization. John Hay, Lincoln's secretary, reports that the president had finally "sloughed off that idea of colonization." Once he had done so, the president had to confront the fact that the Negro people were here to stay, and inevitably he had to deal with them in his plan for Reconstruction of the South.

LINCOLN'S RECONSTRUCTION PLAN AND BLACK REACTION TO IT

The issue of Reconstruction arose in December 1863 with Lincoln's Proclamation of Amnesty and Reconstruction, granting pardon, with certain exceptions, to participants in the rebellion who would take a prescribed oath of allegiance to the Union, to the Constitution, and to the Northern Civil War enactments regarding slavery. It provided that where one-tenth of the voters qualified to vote in 1860 took the oath of allegiance and reestablished a state government, it would be recognized by the federal government. The new state governments were to be permitted to maintain the codes of law and constitutions—except for the provisions regarding slavery—that had existed before the war.

Black Americans immediately condemned the president's plan, partly because it placed the freedmen at the mercy of a small group of people but mainly because it denied the vote to the Negro while granting it to those who had been guilty of rebellion. (No Negroes voted in the South in the election of 1860.) "The Negro is deemed good enough to fight for the Government," Frederick Douglass wrote bitterly, "but not good enough to enjoy the right to vote for the Government. We invest with the elective franchise those who with bloody blades and bloody hands have sought the life of the nation, but sternly refuse to invest those who have done what they could to save the nation's life." "All I ask," Douglass declared, "is that whatever rule you adopt, whether of intelligence or wealth, as the condition of voting, you should apply it equally to the black man." He lashed out against the racist contentions that voting Negroes would introduce "baseness, brutality, coarseness, ignorance, and bestiality" into the electorate and lampooned the lack of these traits in the existing body politic. Douglass argued that black soldiers should be allowed to vote and made a special case for enfranchisement of Southern Negroes. He held that with the cessation of hostilities, black voters would support the reestablishment of republican institutions in the South and declared that the former slaves would need the vote to protect themselves from the vengeance of the defeated rebels.

General Benjamin F. Butler, first commander of the Union army of occupation in New Orleans, agreed with Douglass, and he hoped to unite white unionists (particularly those among the white workers in the city) with blacks. It is significant that the first black suffrage proposal in Louisiana was presented at a meeting of the Workingmen's National Union League in New Orleans, and the large white working-class audience greeted it with "immense applause."

Unfortunately, the alliance envisaged by Butler was never realized. Louisiana began the process of Reconstruction outlined by Lincoln in December 1863, and as the state, under the direction of military authorities, prepared for a convention of pardoned white citizens who would draw up a new state constitution and apply for readmission to the Union, the free black population raised the demand to participate. Before the war New Orleans included eleven thousand black free men, and as a result of the war, the number had greatly increased. The black elite of the city owned property of considerable value, played a vital role in the urban economy, and were frequently well educated. Their sophisticated leadership and strong organization made it possible for them to play a central role in local Reconstruction politics. Peyton McCrary, in his study, *Abraham Lincoln and Reconstruction: The Louisiana Experiment*, notes that in 1864 and 1865 the black community was "seething with creative activity," and he mentions their organization of a farmers' cooperative movement, and the campaign to boycott segregated streetcars, as well as their demands for equal citizenship and voting rights.

But the black community of New Orleans was not a unified one. The black elite felt that by reason of their wealth and education, they were entitled to the suffrage, but they had no intention of including the black masses, especially the newly freed slaves, in the demand for the ballot.

In November 1863, a group of the elite black leaders in New Orleans presented a petition to General George F. Shipley, military governor of Louisiana, asking for the right of the free Negro population to vote. In support of their request, they listed their services to the nation and the state, as well their record of payment of substantial taxes. Shipley referred the matter to General Banks, who rejected the petition, stating that he thought it "unfeasible to draw the line between freemen of color and the recently emancipated Negroes." He did not, however, suggest that the petitioners draw up a new document including the "recently emancipated Negroes" in their demand. Thus, only whites were allowed to vote in the election of February 1864.

When Banks ordered a convention to meet in March 1864 to amend the Louisiana constitution of 1852, the elite black leaders in New Orleans decided that a request should be made directly to President Lincoln for the right of qualified free black men to vote. For this purpose, they prepared a petition with over one thousand signatures, and on March 10, 1864, they sent a copy of it to Congress, as well as to Lincoln. After detailing the wealth, patriotism, and military history of the signers—twenty-seven were veterans of the Battle of New Orleans in 1815—they concluded by asking that all citizens of "Louisiana of African descent, born free before the rebellion, may be, by proper orders, directed to be inscribed on the registers, and admitted to the rights and privileges of electors."

Two of the signers—Jean-Baptiste Roudanez, an engineer and the brother of Dr. Louis Charles Roudanez, and Arnold Bertonneau, a wine merchant who was a captain in the first Negro regiment raised by General Butler—were selected to present the petition to the president. When they arrived in Washington with it, they were persuaded by Radical Republicans that the phrase *born free before the rebellion* created a distinction between free and freed blacks, so they added a final paragraph to the petition:

Your memorialists pray that the right of suffrage may be extended not only to natives of Louisiana born free, but also to all others, whether born slave or free, especially to those who have indicated their right to vote by bearing arms, subject only to such qualifications as shall equally affect the white and colored citizens.

On March 2, the two delegates presented the revised petition to Lincoln. (Three days later, Senator Sumner presented it to the Senate.) Lincoln received the delegates with courtesy but said: "I regret, gentlemen, that you are not able to secure all your rights, and that circumstances will not permit the government to confer them on you." Greatly disappointed, the two Negroes departed. Before they returned to New Orleans, however, they were invited by Republican leaders in Massachusetts to a dinner in their honor in Boston. After an introduction by Governor John A. Andrew, Bertonneau delivered a speech in which he detailed the contributions of the free Negroes of Louisiana to the nation during the War of 1812 and the Civil War. He expressed regret over the fact that their contributions had been ignored in the plans for the reorganization of civil government in Louisiana. Still, the Negro citizens of Louisiana were not content to remain silent:

> To influence the action and to obtain the elective franchise for our people, we, as delegates of the free colored population of Louisiana, visited Washington to lay the matter before President Lincoln and the Congress of our country. We ask that, in the reconstruction of the state government there, the right to vote shall not depend on the color of the citizen; that the colored citizen shall have and enjoy every civil, political and religious right that white citizens enjoy; in a word, that every man shall stand equal before the law. To secure these rights, which belong to every free citizen, we ask the aid and influence of every true loyal man all over the country.

As they departed for New Orleans, the two delegates did not know that on the day after their visit, Lincoln had sent a private letter to Governor Michael Hahn in which he had written: "I barely suggest, for your private consideration, whether some of the colored people might not be let in, for instance, the very intelligent, and especially those who have fought gallantly in our ranks. They would probably help in some trying time in the future."

James G. Blaine, the Republican senator from Maine, considered this letter "of deep and almost prophetic significance. It was perhaps the earliest proposition from an authentic source to endow the Negro with the right of suffrage." But Blaine overlooked the fact that it was a private letter, and Hahn had no intention of taking Lincoln's advice. The constitutional convention met on April 6, 1864, without a Negro delegate.

The constitution produced by the delegates did, however, include several concessions to Negroes, largely at Banks' insistence. It abolished slavery, rejected a proposal to ban perpetually the extension of suffrage to blacks, and recommended that in the future, the legislature should grant the vote to Negroes who had such qualifications as past military service, taxable property, or manifest intelligence. (Whites did not have to possess such qualifications.) It also arranged for public education for blacks as well as whites, and initiated a progressive income taxation, as well as a nine-hour day and minimum wage for laborers on public works. But when the newly elected legislature met, it rejected Negro suffrage.

When Louisiana's representatives were then sent to Congress, however, they were denied their seats. Although the state had fulfilled the reconstruction requirements established by Lincoln, it had not met those set by Congress. These, as specified in the Wade-Davis bill, which was passed over Lincoln's veto, demanded as a precondition for reentry to the Union that one-half the number of the state's qualified voters in 1860 take the amnesty oath.

BLACKS AND THE ELECTION OF 1864

Lincoln's response to the New Orleans petition and his failure to act in favor of Negro suffrage when Hahn rejected his advice was disappointing to not only New Orleans blacks. His refusal to intervene decisively in their favor stoked a growing disillusionment with the president among some blacks that was to make itself felt in the presidential campaign of 1864, when Lincoln ran for reelection.

Most Negroes appeared to support Lincoln without any hesitation. Even though they could not vote in the presidential election, a mass meeting of San Francisco blacks on New Year's Day, 1864, marking the first anniversary of the Emancipation Proclamation, unanimously adopted a resolution endorsing Lincoln's reelection to the presidency. In an editorial supporting the resolution, the *Pacific Appeal,* San Francisco's black weekly, stated:

The nomination of Mr. Lincoln by acclamation, at the celebration held on January 1st . . . in commemoration of the Emancipation Proclamation . . . was a tribute of respect and the high appreciation felt by the colored citizens of San Francisco for him. They were made happy in this opportunity to bestow a humble mark of their approbation. He is the man who, of all others who have occupied the Presidential chair, since the formation of the Government or the adoption of the Constitution, has stood up in defiance of the slave-power, and dared officially to maintain the doctrine, by his official actions, that we are citizens, though of African descent—that the army and navy shall protect and defend such citizens in common with all others—that provision ought to be made for the education of freedmen. . . . For these, and other more weighty reasons, we have duly considered him to be the right man in the right place in the present crisis, and also the man to fill the Presidential chair in 1864.

But other blacks reacted to what they called the president's "indecisiveness," and they were indignant at his retention of conservative Republicans in key positions, his seeming approval of the system of labor introduced by General Banks in Louisiana, and his unwillingness to do anything to remove the disabilities against Negro soldiers. Frederick Douglass voiced the sentiments of the black critics of Lincoln when he wrote to an English correspondent:

The treatment of our poor black soldiers—the refusal to pay them equal compensation, though it was promised them when they enlisted; the refusal to insist upon the exchange of colored prisoners, when colored prisoners have been slaughtered in cold blood, although the President has repeatedly promised thus to protect the lives of his colored soldiers—have worn my patience threadbare.

The major cause of the conflict, however, lay in the difference over Reconstruction. The majority of blacks, like most Radical Republicans and white abolitionists, viewed Lincoln's reconstruction plan as opening the door for ex-Confederates, especially the slaveowners, to gain control of the Southern states as they came under Union control. Their view of Lincoln's plan was expressed in the resolution offered by Wendell Phillips, probably Lincoln's severest critic, at the annual meeting of the Massachusetts Anti-Slavery Society on January 28, 1864, which affirmed that "the Government, in its haste, is ready to sacrifice the interest and honor of the North to secure a sham peace, thereby risking the introduction into Congress of a strong confederate minority to embarrass legislation, and leaving the freedmen and the Southern States under the control of the late slaveholders."

During the early months of 1864, a group of Radical Republicans and abolitionists, dissatisfied with Lincoln's policies, began a movement to prevent his renomination. A campaign got under way to gain support for Salmon P. Chase, encouraged by the secretary of treasury himself, but the Chase bubble collapsed in March. Meanwhile, John C. Frémont's star was rising. The Republican presidential candidate in 1856 had the support of many of the radicals, and especially of the large German element, particularly in the West, where he had served as a general. The Radical Republicans and abolitionist opponents of Lincoln issued a call for a convention under the name of Radical Democracy, to meet in Cleveland, Ohio, on May 31, 1864, "for consultation and concert of action in respect to the approaching election." Frederick Douglass, believing that the proposed assembly was in the best interest of the Negro people, publicly supported the convention call:

I mean the complete abolition of every vestige, form and modification of Slavery in every part of the United States, perfect equality for the black man in every State before the law, in jury box, at the ballot-box and on the battlefield; ample and salutary retaliation for every instance of enslavement or slaughter of prisoners of color. I mean that in the distribution of offices and honors under this Government no discrimination shall be made in favor of or against any class of citizens, whether black or white, of native or foreign birth. And supposing the convention which is to meet at Cleveland means the same thing. I cheerfully give my name as one of the signers of the call.

On May 31, 1864, four hundred delegates, including some outstanding abolitionists (but not including William Lloyd Garrison, who was committed to supporting Lincoln), met in Cosmopolitan Hall in Cleveland and nominated John C. Frémont and John Cochrane, nephew of Gerrit Smith, for president and vice-president, respectively. The platform they adopted called for the uncompromising prosecution of the war, the constitutional prohibition of slavery, free speech and free press, a one-term presidency, reconstruction to be administered exclusively by Congress, and the confiscation of rebel lands to be divided among soldiers and actual settlers.

The week following Frémont's nomination, the Union party, a coalition of Republicans and War Democrats, gathered in Baltimore. Among the state delegations seeking to influence the convention's proceedings was a contingent from the Sea Islands. The group of sixteen included four blacks, of whom Robert Small, the hero of the *Planter*, was the most prominent. These delegates received seats on the convention floor but gained no official recognition from the chairman. "The Republicans were simply not prepared to treat Negroes as political equals," observes Larry E. Nelson in describing the incident.

The Union Convention adopted a platform calling for preservation of the Union, a constitutional amendment ending slavery, and retaliation for Southern atrocities against black soldiers. On this platform, Lincoln was unanimously named to stand for reelection, and Andrew Johnson of Tennessee was nominated for vice-president in order to win the support of the War Democrats.

Despite Frémont's strong antislavery record, his candidacy did not rouse enthusiasm among many blacks. James W. C. Pennington came out for Lincoln as soon as he was nominated. "The wisest, the safest, and the soundest policy of colored Americans," Pennington declared, "is to exert all our influence to keep our present Chief Magistrate where he is for four years from next March." But other black leaders could not bring themselves to support Lincoln. Like many Republicans, they believed that Lincoln could not win. The failure of the Union armies to move decisively to end the war while the staggering toll in lives and treasure continued to mount; the open clamor of the Copperheads and even Republicans like Horace Greeley for peace at any price; the dissension in the president's cabinet; the conflict between Congress and the chief executive—all weakened the support of the administration and the chances for Lincoln's reelection. "Mr. Lincoln is already beaten," cried Greeley. "He cannot be elected." Senator John Sherman predicted that if the Democrats should select a candidate who had "any particle of patriotism or sense," they would "sweep the Republicans out of office like an avalanche."

Similar gloomy views were expressed at a meeting of black Bostonians. William Wells Brown told the gathering: "I am most discouraged. We have an imbecile administration, and the most imbecile management that it is possible to conceive of. If Mr. White's God is managing the affairs of this nation, he is making thereby a miserable failure." Lincoln, he declared, did not deserve to be reelected. Drawing upon a biblical analogy, John S. Rock told the dispirited audience: "I fear the Republicans, and I confess that it looks to me now as though we shall be like Jacob serving Laben for Rachel, and wake up some morning only to find we have got Leah."

Frederick Douglass not only joined Wendell Phillips in denouncing the president's policies, but he called upon his friends in England to expose "*the swindle* by which our Government claims the respect of mankind for abolishing slavery."

Early in August, Douglass met Reverend John Eaton in Toledo, Ohio. During his discussions with the young army chaplain who had been appointed by General Grant a superintendent of freedmen in the Department of Tennessee, Douglass criticized Lincoln's failure to redress the grievances of Negro soldiers and his readiness to reconstruct the Southern states without Negro suffrage. Eaton conveyed Douglass' misgivings to Lincoln when he met the president. Lincoln questioned Eaton further, admitted that he was concerned about Douglass' attitude, and declared "that considering the condition from which he had arisen and the obstacles that he had overcome, and the position to which he had attained that he regarded him as one of the most meritorious men, if not the most meritorious man in the United States." He expressed a desire to see Douglass. Eaton promptly arranged the interview.

Around August 25, Douglass met Lincoln for the second time. He found the president in an "alarmed condition," frightened by the repercussions of his "To Whom It May Concern" letter in which he had guaranteed a careful hearing and safe conduct to anyone who brought an authoritative proposition "which embraces the restoration of peace, the integrity of the whole Union, and the abandonment of slavery." The letter had been written on July 18, 1864, at the request of Horace Greeley, the editor of the *New York Tribune,* who was about to hold an interview with two Rebel emissaries in Niagara Falls. Greeley had asked Lincoln to grant a safe conduct to these emissaries in order that they might come to Washington and discuss terms of peace. In reply, the president sent the "To Whom It May Concern" letter by a special messenger, John Hay, one of his private secretaries.

Although nothing came of the peace negotiations, since it was soon apparent that the Rebel emissaries had no authority to deal for peace, the publication of the letter produced a cry of dismay from Copperheads and moderate Republicans alike. Lincoln was denounced for having said in so many words that even if the war were ended and the Union saved by a negotiated peace, the conflict would go on until slavery was abolished. Pressure was being exerted upon him by Republicans to modify his conditions for peace.

Lincoln had framed a letter to answer the charges. When Douglass entered, the president read the contents to him and asked him if he should release it. Lincoln's letter denied the accusation that he stood in the way of peace, first, because no person authorized to speak for the Confederate government had ever submitted a proposition for peace to him, and second, even if he wanted to commit himself and the country to an abolition war rather than a war for the Union, he would not have been able to do so since the country would not support such a war. In response to the president's query as to whether the letter should be released, Douglass replied:

Certainly not. It would be given a broader meaning than you intend to convey; it would be taken as a complete surrender of your anti-slavery policy, and do you considerable damage. In answer to your Copperhead accusers, your friends can make the argument of your want of power, but you cannot wisely say a word on that point.

Whether Douglass' advice was considered, the fact remains that Lincoln did not release the letter. Undoubtedly Douglass felt highly honored that the president should have sought his advice on so vital a matter of national policy. He was equally impressed by the fact that at no time during the discussion did Lincoln assert, as he had in the past, that his aim was to save the Union with or without slavery. "What he said on this day," Douglass wrote later, "showed a deeper moral conviction against slavery than I have ever seen before in any thing spoken or written by him."

Lincoln told Douglass that the acute feeling of despondency to the North, the growing clamor for peace, and the efforts by Greeley and others to discuss peace terms with the Confederacy might force him to conclude the war by a negotiated peace. He himself was convinced that no real and lasting peace could be had "short of absolute submission on the part of the rebels," but he feared that he might have to yield to the pressure for a speedy end to the conflict. In that event, all Negroes who had not come into the Union lines would continue in slavery after the war was over. He therefore wished to set in motion a plan to bring as many slaves as possible within the Union territory. He asked Douglass to organize a band of scouts, composed of black men, to move into the rebel states, beyond the lines of the Union army, to spread the news of the Emancipation Proclamation, and to conduct squads of runaways into the Union lines. What a far cry this plan was, Douglass must have thought, from the days when the administration had permitted Union officers to return fugitive slaves to their owners and had even allowed the slaveowners to cross the Potomac and recover the property.

Lincoln's proposal reminded Douglass of John Brown's original plan to send trained men onto the plantations to lead slaves into mountain hideouts and conduct them to the North and Canada. He was somewhat concerned over the fact that the president believed that his proclamation of freedom would cease to operate once the war was over. But he eagerly undertook the task assigned him, believing that even if the war did not end quickly, the more slaves brought into the Union lines, the better. As he informed Lincoln from Rochester on August 29 after consulting "several Trustworthy and Patriotic colored men" about the president's plan:

All with whom I have thus far spoken on the subject, concur in the wisdom and benevolence of the Idea, and some of them think it practicable. That every Slave who Escapes from the Rebel States is a loss to the Rebellion and a gain to the Loyal cause. I need not stop to argue the proposition is self-evident. The Negro is the stomach of the rebellion.

Douglass submitted a detailed outline to Lincoln. It called for the appointment of a general agent who would employ twenty-five assistants "having the cause at heart," who, operating at various points in the Union army, would send sub-agents into Rebel territory to conduct squads of slaves into the Union lines. But the plan never was put into operation. The fall of Atlanta on September 2 and Farragut's victory in Mobile Bay soon after knocked the bottom out of the peace-at-any-price maneuver.

On August 29, the same day that Douglass sent his outline to Lincoln, the Democratic party met in Chicago. With no difficulty, General George B.

McClellan was nominated for president. The convention's attitude toward the war was summed up by Congressman Clement L. Vallindigham of Ohio, the leading Copperhead in the North and the dominant figure at the convention:

The war for the Union . . . is a most bloody and costly failure. War for the Union was abandoned, war for the negro openly begun. With what success? Let the dead at Fredericksburg make answer. Ought this war to continue? I answer, "No, no, no!" Stop fighting. Make an armistice.

The Democratic platform was drawn up by the Copperhead group in the party and included a plan, written by Vallindigham, that asserted:

That this Convention does explicitly declare, as the sense of the American people, that after four years of failure to restore the Union by the experiment of War . . . justice, humanity, liberty, and the public welfare demand that immediate efforts be made for a cessation of hostilities, with a view to an ultimate convention of the States or other peaceable means, to the end that at the earliest possible moment peace may be restored on the basis of the Federal Union of the States.

The Democratic campaign cry was racism personified:

> For the Sovereign People's President
> For the white man free;
> 'Tis for Pen and Little Mac,
> And a glorious victory.
> And with thirty million voices clear,
> We'll shout the white man free. . . .
>
> We've got our armor on,
> And ready for the fight
> For the White Man Free:
> 'Tis Ten and Little Mac,
> And a Glorious victory.
> Trot out your Nigger!
> And with two hundred million voices clear
> We'll shout the White Man Free.

The results of the Democratic convention compelled blacks who had thrown their support to Frémont or refrained from endorsing Lincoln to reevaluate their position. Douglass did not hesitate; as soon as he learned of the proceedings at Chicago, he decided to support Lincoln. "All dates changed with the nomination of McClellan," he declared. The election of McClellan and the victory of the policy avowed in the Chicago platform would be "the heaviest calamity of these years of war and blood, since it would upon the instant sacrifice and wantonly cast away everything valuable purchased so dearly by the precious blood of our brave sons and brothers on the battlefield for the perfect liberty and permanent peace of a common country." He urged that "every man who wishes well to the slave and to the country should at once rally with all the warmth and earnestness of his nature to the support of Abraham Lincoln."

Nearly every prominent Negro leader and black newspaper joined Douglass in switching to Lincoln from Frémont. The outstanding exception was the *New Orleans Tribune*, which refused to endorse Lincoln and the Republican party. Throughout the campaign, the *Tribune* opposed the election of either Lincoln or McClellan. In a front-page editorial, the newspaper characterized both candidates as "third or even fourth-rate men, and utterly unworthy to be head of a great nation like ours, at the present emergency." As for Lincoln, his goal was "TO MAINTAIN, IF HE CAN, UNION AND SLAVERY." If the Negro people wanted justice, they would have to find another president.

But by now, the *Tribune* was a solitary voice in the black community. Although they could not vote, Baltimore Negroes expressed their support for Lincoln in September by presenting him with an elegantly bound Bible as a gift from the entire black community. The cover of the Bible carried a design showing Lincoln in a cotton field striking the shackles from the wrists of a slave.

Black leaders now not only endorsed Lincoln but tried to campaign for his reelection, but Republican committees were cool to the idea. When Frederick Douglass offered to take the stump for Lincoln, he was turned down. A campaign pamphlet issued by the Democrats, entitled *Miscegenation Indorsed by the Republican Party,* quoted from Douglass' speech at the meeting of the American Anti-Slavery Society in December 1863, describing his first visit with Lincoln. The Democrats pointed gleefully to Douglass' statement that "the President of the United States received a black man at the White House just as one gentleman received another." Republican politicians, frightened by the label attached to their candidate, felt that Douglass' campaign speeches would only provide further ammunition for the Democrats. As Douglass put it: "I am not doing much in this Presidential canvass for the reason that Republican committees do not wish to expose themselves to the charge of being the 'Nigger' party. The negro is the deformed child, which is put out of the room when company comes."

Meanwhile developments on Southern battlefields dramatically revived the Northern war spirit. The triumphant armies of General William T. Sherman and General Philip Sheridan, with their victories in Georgia and the Shenandoah Valley, spurred the revival of war sentiment, and the Republicans put pressure on Frémont to withdraw. On September 22, Frémont withdrew his candidacy, making clear that he was acting not because he approved of Lincoln's policies but because General McClellan had come out for restoration of the Union with slavery and the Democrats must therefore be defeated at all costs.

There were now only two candidates in the field: Lincoln and McClellan. Although barred from direct participation in Republican political activity, black leaders made a concerted effort to bring their views before the electorate. Ten days after Frémont's withdrawal, the National Convention of Colored Men, which had not met for almost a decade, gathered in Syracuse, New York. One hundred and forty-four delegates from eighteen states, including seven slave states, were present. The *Syracuse Joural* commented: "Almost every one of the representative colored men of the United States is attending the convention."

The Reverend Henry Highland Garnet, at whose initiative the convention was called, opened the sessions; John Mercer Langston was elected temporary chairman, and Frederick Douglass was chosen to preside over the assembly. Accepting the position, Douglass announced the purposes of the meeting: "We are here to promote the freedom, progress, elevation, and perfect enfranchisement of the entire colored people of the United States." He noted with delight the presence on the platform of young men who "had come up in this time of whirlwind and storm." Douglass sounded a defiant note: "In what is to be done we shall give offense to none but the mean and sordid haters of our race."

After several speakers, including a black woman from Syracuse, had addressed the convention, the delegates organized the National Equal Rights League, to promote self-help in the black community and to obtain "recognition of the rights of colored people of the nation as American citizens." In the declaration announcing the league's formation, the delegates expressed confidence that the "nation will ultimately concede our just claims, accord us rights, and grant us our full measure of citizenship." They then demanded that Congress remove "insidious distinctions, based upon color, as to pay, labor and promotion" among black soldiers and called upon the legislative body to grant the vote to Negro citizens of the District of Columbia. The delegates labeled any effort to restore the Union with slavery a flagrant breach of faith and called upon "the whole power of the civilized world" to resist such an eventuality. They praised the "unquestioned patriotism and loyalty" of black troops who ignored past injustice and answered the call to the colors. Their dedication and courage, the delegates declared, "vindicate our manhood, command our respect, and claim the attention and admiration of the civilized world." The delegates also passed resolutions expressing sympathy and support for Southern freedmen, urging Negroes to settle as much as possible on the public domain, and endorsing the efforts of Negro schools, associations, and newspapers. They thanked the president and Congress for abolishing slavery in the District of Columbia, for the recognition of the black republics of Liberia and Haiti, and for the retaliatory military order invoked as a result of "barbarous treatment of colored soldiers of the Union army by the rebels." A special resolution expressed the gratitude of the delegates to Senator Sumner and General Butler for their activities on behalf of the Negro people.

The convention also endorsed a "Declaration of Wrongs and Rights," written by Dr. P. B. Randolph of New York, which eloquently described the grievances suffered by blacks and summarized the rights they claimed. Vehemently denouncing white racism, slavery, and colonization, it demanded the abolition of slavery, "the immunities and privileges of all other citizens and defenders of the nation's honor," and an "equitable share of the public domain, whether acquired by purchase, treaty, confiscation, or military conquest."

The ''Address of the Colored National Convention to the People of the United States,'' written by Frederick Douglass and unanimously adopted, was the outstanding document of the convention. It made clear in bold and unmistakable language where the Negro people stood in the election of 1864, as well as what they expected in the future. Every point raised by Douglass in the address was, in the words of Carl Sandburg, ''a living issue that had taken on new intensity with every month of the war.''

Douglass realistically approached the problems confronting his people. Vast advances had been achieved in a relatively short time, he declared, but powerful forces were at work to ''reverse the entire order and tendency of the events of the last three years'' and prevent further progress. The Negro people not only had to contend with the bitter opposition of proslavery forces, but they were also confronted by the timidity and confusion in the ranks of antislavery men. With the *National Anti-Slavery Standard* denying that the American Anti-Slavery Society advocated the ballot for Negro people and with Garrison's *Liberator* apologizing ''for excluding colored men of Louisiana from the ballot box,'' black Americans realized that they had to suffer with the ''injudicious concessions and weaknesses'' of their friends, as well as the strength of their enemies. Such astonishing remarks by abolitionist journals ''injure us more vitally than all the ribald jests of the whole proslavery press.''

The address analyzed the policies of the contending political parties in the campaign. Despite the fact that the Republican party was composed of ''the best men in the country'' and had been responsible for the enactment of progressive measures, it was ''largely under the influence of the prevailing contempt for the character and rights of the colored race.'' The Republican party still was not prepared to make the abolition of slavery a precondition for the reestablishment of the Union. ''However antislavery in sentiment the President may be, and however disposed he may be to continue the war till slavery is abolished, it is plain that in this he would not be sustained by his party.'' A single reverse on the battlefield would arouse strong opposition in the party to the president. Moreover, Secretary Seward, the leading administration spokesperson next to the president, had said in a recent speech that when the insurgents ''laid down their arms, the war will instantly cease; and all the war measures then existing, including those which affect slavery, will cease also.'' Freedom for the Negro people thus hung upon the slender thread of Rebel power, pride, and persistence.

Yet with all its weaknesses and prejudices, Douglass went on, the Republican party was the only party the Negro could support. Compared to its rival, it officially proclaimed abolition as its goal. ''In the ranks of the Democratic party, all the worst elements of American society fraternize.'' From that quarter Negroes ''need not expect a single voice for justice, mercy, or even decency.'' A victory at the polls for the Democratic party would ''comprise the sum of all social woes'' for black Americans.

The main body of the address dealt with the need for the complete abolition of slavery and the granting of the ballot to the Negro. In discussing the first point,

Douglass issued a warning whose validity was all too soon to be proved. "Be not deceived," he told those who argued that slavery had "already received its death-blow":

Slavery is still the vital and animating breath of Southern society. The men who have fought for it on the battle-field will not love it less for having shed their blood in its defence. . . . Let Jefferson Davis and his Confederate associates, either in person or by their representatives, return once more to their seats in the halls of Congress—and you will then see your dead slavery the most living and powerful thing in the country.

Douglass went into great detail in presenting the claims of the Negro to the ballot. The right to vote was "the keystone of the arch of human liberty." Why did the Negro want to vote? "Because we don't want to be mobbed from our work, or insulted with impunity at every corner. We are men, and want to be as free in our native country as other men":

We are asked, even by some abolitionists, why we cannot be satisfied, for the present at least, with personal freedom; the right to testify in courts of law; the right to own, buy, and sell real estate; the right to sue and be sued. We answer, Because in a republican country, where general suffrage is the rule, personal liberty and the other foregoing rights become mere privileges, held at the option of others. What gives to the newly arrived emigrants, fresh from lands governed by kingcraft and priestcraft, special consequences in the eyes of the American people? Not their virtue, for they are often depraved; not their knowledge, for they are often ignorant; not their wealth, for they are often very poor; why, then, are they courted by the leaders of all parties? The answer is, that our institutions clothe them with the elective franchise, and they have a voice in making the laws of the country.

But Douglass did not press the demand for Negro suffrage only from the standpoint of the benefits to be derived by his people. With prophetic insight, he pointed out that once the rebellion in the South was suppressed, "a sullen hatred toward the National Government" would be "transmuted from father to son as sacred animosity." Treason, crushed by the federal armies, would go underground and strive in various ways "to disturb the peaceful operation of the hated Government." The ballot and, "if need be, arms," in the hands of 4 million Negroes in the South would be the most effective counterpoise against Southern treason and hostility: "You are sure of the enmity of the masters,—make sure of the friendship of the slaves; for, depend upon it, your Government cannot afford the enmity of both."

During the convention's final session, the emigration issue surfaced in a heated debate swirling around Henry Highland Garnet and the African Civilization Society. Garnet wanted an endorsement of the society, which was then mainly engaged in providing aid for the freedmen. The delegates, however, were wary of endorsing emigration and made clear their opposition to any plan to leave the country. In an effort to end on a note of unity, however, they endorsed the society before adjourning at noon on October 7, 1864. With the close of the Syracuse convention, the position of black Americans in the presidential election was made clear. Abraham Lincoln was their unquestionable choice.

The election returns gave Lincoln a majority of 484,567 out of a total vote of 4,166,537. In the country at large, Lincoln received the electoral votes of twenty-two out of twenty-five states. Of the 150,635 soldiers who voted, 116,887 cast their ballots for Lincoln. The new Thirty-ninth Congress had 145 Unionists to 40 Democrats. "Let the tidings go forth," cried Charles Sumner at an impromptu victory rally on Election Day: " 'To whom it may concern,'—to all the People of the United States, at length now made wholly free,—to foreign countries . . . that this Republic shall live, for Slavery is dead." Even the *New Orleans Tribune* rejoiced, declaring: "We are beginning a new era; the sovereign people . . . [have] reaffirmed their devotion to freedom. . . . Mr. Lincoln has just been elected on a platform which authorizes him to follow a more radical policy than he has hitherto shown."

25

Union Victory

It was the last year of the war—from the Red River campaign in Louisiana in April 1864 to Appomattox in Virginia in April 1865. The year 1864 had opened very badly for the Confederacy. Its manpower was exhausted, its armies in retreat before the powerful offensives of Grant and Sherman, its forts blockaded by the Union fleet, and half its territory invaded. It seemed that with the forces arrayed against it, defeat for the Confederacy was inevitable.

But the Union generals were not prepared to let the inevitable happen by itself. They were determined to provide the Confederacy with the necessary persuasion to surrender. "All that has gone before is mere skirmishing," General William T. Sherman wrote to his wife.

In March 1864, General Grant was appointed commander in chief of the Union forces and transferred from the western front to Virginia, where the last and decisive battles of the Civil War were impending. Grant did not take a single white regiment with him. All he had were 20,000 blacks, the same 20,000 who had fought so well under his command in the West. Soon after, he supplemented them with white soldiers.

SHERMAN'S MARCH TO THE SEA

Grant, Sherman, and Farragut had reconquered the West and freed the Mississippi River. Then Sherman moved on Atlanta, the most important remaining source of supplies for the South. Sherman ordered those sections of the city that the Confederacy had used, and might use again, for military purposes (especially arsenals, depots, and railroad machine shops) burned to the ground. Whatever further destruction occurred in Atlanta was the work of civilian marauders who moved in on the city after Sherman departed.

Now Sherman decided to put into operation the bold plan he had been nurturing—a plan entirely new to military science. He would break all railroad and telegraph connections with his rear and start a march of three hundred miles to Savannah on the coast, destroying the Confederacy's last line of communications and supplies and cutting the Rebel territory in two. From Savannah, Sherman would swing north to join the Army of the Potomac and end the resistance of Lee at Richmond.

The plan astounded military experts. The reaction of the British *Army and Navy Gazette* was typically of that of many other military organs when it wrote: "If Sherman has really left his army in the air and started without a base to march from Georgia to South Carolina, he has done either one of the most brilliant or one of the most foolish things ever performed by a military leader."

That Sherman was well aware of the political significance of the march is shown by a letter he wrote to Grant on November 6, 1864, describing his plan as the military counterpart of Lincoln's reelection. The march and the election, he wrote, would form "a complete, logical whole."

The army that Sherman led to the sea was composed of veterans of many battles and marches, all in perfect physical condition. Included among the marchers were men from sixteen states comprising 218 regiments or fragments of regiments. A company of white Alabama Unionists rode in the cavalry, and there was the First Georgia Regiment, made up of men who had been drafted into Confederate service and who had deserted at the first opportunity to join the Union. The strength of Sherman's force was 55,329 infantry, 5,063 cavalry, and 1,812 artillery—in all, 62,042 officers and men.

This army was to divide into two main sections. One column would move on Macon, the other on Augusta, and in seven days they would join forces at the state capitol, Milledgeville. This division of forces was intended to confuse the Confederacy and prevent it from concentrating its men.

In his *Memoirs,* Sherman recorded the following:

About 7 A.M. of November 16, we rode out of Atlanta by the Decatur road, filled by the marching troops and wagons . . . and reaching the hill we naturally passed to look back upon the scenes of our past battles. Below us lay Atlanta, smoldering in ruins, the black smoke rising high in the air, and hanging like a pall over the ruined city. Away off in the distance was the rear of Howard's column, the gun-barrels glistening in the sun, the white-topped wagons stretching away to the South. Some band, by accident, struck up the anthem of "John Brown's soul goes marching on," and the men caught up the strain, and never before have I heard the chorus of "Glory, glory, hallelujah" done with more spirit, or in better harmony of time and place.

The song they sang first appeared in the *Kansas Herald* and was sung by the black soldiers of the Kansas Colored Volunteers. It was reprinted in the *Christian Recorder,* official organ of the African Methodist Episcopal church, in its issue of April 23, 1864, and went in part:

Old John Brown's body lies mouldering in the grave,
While the bondsmen are all weeping, whom he came to save;
But though he lost his life a-fighting for the slave,
His soul is marching on.

He captured Harpers Ferry with his nineteen men so few,
And frightened old Virginia till they trembled through and through;
They hung him as a traitor—themselves a traitor crew,
But his soul is marching on.

The battle that John Brown begun he looks from heaven to view,
On the Army of the Union, with its flag—red, white and blue;
And the angels shall sing praises o'er the deeds we mean to do,
As we go marching on. . . .

Glory, glory, hallelujah!
Glory, glory, hallelujah!
  Glory, glory, hallelujah!
    His soul is marching on.

Systematically, day by day, Sherman's men tore up the rails of the Confederacy's last important road. At night they heated the rails in the flames of bonfires and twisted them, still glowing hotly, around trees and telegraph poles. Two hundred miles of road and every bridge along the way suffered destruction.

The food for this immense army, which started with only twenty days' supply of rations and five days' supply of forage, came from the fields of Georgia. Soldiers especially selected for the task—they became known as "bummers"—gathered the crops and drove in the livestock. In view of the long-standing slander of Sherman's foragers, the general's exact orders, contained in special field order 119, are of special interest:

Soldiers must not enter the dwellings of the inhabitants, or commit any trespass. . . . In districts and neighborhoods where the army is unmolested no destruction of . . . property should be permitted; but should guerrillas or bushwackers molest our march . . . then army commanders should order and enforce a devastation more or less relentlessly according to the measure of such hostility. As for horses, mules, wagons, etc., belonging to the inhabitants, the cavalry and artillery may appropriate freely and without limit, discriminating however between the rich, who are usually hostile, and the poor and industrious, usually neutral to friendly.

Soldiers caught disobeying these orders were severely punished.

The two columns of Sherman's army, sometimes as many as fifty or sixty miles apart, moved forward with such exactness of calculation that on November 23 they reached Milledgeville together. There they found that the state government had fled, taking with it furniture, carpets, and food but leaving behind the public archives, muskets, and ammunition. Sherman ordered that the arsenal and other buildings that could be used for war be destroyed and that the rest of the city be spared.

At Fort McCallister, on the coast near Savannah, Sherman met his first serious resistance. A fast march and a determined assault captured the fort, and Sherman opened communications with the blockading Union Fleet. The sole remaining task was to take Savannah, a city with 15,000 men and heavy cannons. Unexpectedly, while the Union army was planning to attack, the city was evacuated. On December 20, 1864, Sherman entered Savannah and at once sent a telegram to Lincoln in Washington: "I beg to present to you as a Christmas gift, the city of Savannah with one hundred and fifty heavy guns and plenty of ammunition, also about twenty-five thousand bales of cotton."

All along the route of Sherman's march to the sea, the Negro people gave the Union army a memorable welcome. Sherman wrote in his *Memoirs* that he found them "simply frantic with joy." About four miles east of Covington, the army made camp. Sherman wrote:

Here we made our bivouac, and I walked to a plantation-house close by, where were assembled many negroes, among them an old gray-haired man. I asked him if he understood about the war and its progress. He said he did; that he had been looking for the "Angel of the Lord" ever since he was knee-high and, though we professed to be fighting for the Union, he supposed slavery was the cause, that our success was to be his freedom. I asked him if all the negro slaves comprehended this fact, and he said they surely did.

Black women as well as men understood the meaning of the march. Sherman watched a young Negro woman, formerly a slave, embrace a regimental flag. An old black woman who walked along with the cattle at the rear, upon being questioned, answered simply: "I's going where you go." Fearing restoration of the slaveowners after Sherman's army had passed and dreading slavery for their children more than separation, black mothers begged the army to take the children along. An officer wrote to his wife: "It was very touching to see the vast number of colored women following after us with babies in their arms. . . . One poor creature, while nobody was looking, put two boys, five years old, in a wagon, intending, I suppose, that they should see the land of freedom if she couldn't."

From first to last, resistance to Sherman's army was slight, and the Union casualties were amazingly small: 103 killed and 428 wounded. The ease and safety with which the Union army reached its objectives may be credited to three factors: Sherman's superb tactics, especially his division of the enemy forces; the unwillingness of the poor white people of Georgia, themselves opposed to the Confederacy's "rich man's war and poor man's fight," to harass the Union army in any way; and the help given by the blacks. About 25,000 blacks joined the march, and on Sherman's order, the ablebodied men were organized into pioneer battalions.

THE FIFTY-FOURTH AND FIFTY-FIFTH IN SOUTH CAROLINA

Having delivered his knock-out blow to Georgia, Sherman turned to South Carolina. On November 30, 1864, while the Union army had been awaiting Sherman's move into the area, there had been a battle at Honey Hill, South Carolina. As the pickets of the Confederate force defending Honey Hill came into firing range of the Union troops, the rebel forces could hear the men in the Union brigade singing:

> Oh, boys, chains are breaking
> Bondsmen fast awaking
> Tyrant hearts are quaking
> Southward we are making.

The singers were members of the Colored Brigade, composed of the Fifty-fourth and Fifty-fifth Massachusetts Regiments, commanded by Colonel Alfred S. Hartwell. Serving with them were the Thirty-second and Thirty-fifty Colored Regiments. These black combat troops, together with some white regiments, made up a striking force of about five thousand men under the command of Major General John A. Foster.

The battle that day ended in the defeat of the Union force, but the conduct of the black troops was exemplary. Unfortunately, the Negro soldiers were badly misused by their white commanders and were not able to reap the fruits of their courage. Nor was this the first time. The Fifty-fourth Massachusetts, heroes of the Fort Wagner battle, had fought bravely at Olustee, Florida, in February 1864 and there, too, they had been led poorly by white commanders. The black regiment had gone into battle at Olustee crying, "Three cheers for Massachusetts and seven dollars a month." The reference in this bitter cry was to the fact that regular pay for privates was thirteen dollars a month but seven dollars for the black soldiers. Despite their anger and frustration, the Fifty-fourth had fought bravely, only to find themselves poorly led. Now again at Honey Hill, they were subjected to the heaviest fire, and the men held firmly to their places. Soon their companion regiment, the Fifty-fifth, moved up to their support. In the wild fighting that ensued, Colonel Hartwell sustained severe wounds but refused to leave the scene where his gallant men were again proving the worth of Negro soldiers. The black regiments were finally compelled to retreat, but they left the field in good order, never relaxing their discipline. The men of the two regiments fully justified their pledge before the battle that

> No more for trader's gold
> Shall those we love be sold

Nor crushed be manhood bold
In slavery's fold.

Recovering from the defeat, the black regiments joined Sherman's army in the attack on South Carolina. On February 21, 1865, the soldiers of the Fifty-fourth and Fifty-fifth had the satisfaction of entering the citadel of slavery—Charleston, South Carolina. There the exuberant black soldiers broke open the slave pens and inscribed on their walls mottoes from Isaiah, Garrison, and John Brown. The auction block, from which countless thousands of unfortunate blacks had been sold, was borne away by the regiment and sent to Boston, where Garrison mounted it to deliver an abolitionist oration.

"When black troops entered Charleston singing the John Brown song," writes Leon F. Litwack, "they found themselves immediately surrounded by the black residents. Upon seeing the soldiers, one elderly slave woman threw down her crutch and shouted the year of the Jubilee had finally arrived. Some of the soldiers and their officers, after what they had witnessed, confessed that 'the glory and triumph of this hour' simply defied description. 'It was one of those occasions which happen but once in a lifetime.' " When Major Martin R. Delany arrived in Charleston, the newly commissioned black officer could barely restrain himself at the thought of entering the city "which, from earliest childhood and through life, I had learned to contemplate with feelings of the utmost abhorrence."

A CELEBRATION IN CHARLESTON

March 21, 1865, was a joyous day in Charleston. The occasion was a grand celebration by the freed blacks in honor of their release from bondage. On the Sunday preceding the day of the celebration, the organizing committee, headed by Major General Rufus Saxton, announced to a large black congregation, assembled at Zion Church, that arrangements were in progress to give the former slaves an opportunity to express their "delight at the new freedom they were enjoying." This announcement was greeted with cheers, and the black community immediately undertook the task of making the necessary preparations.

The designated place for assembling was Citadel Square, and at noon on March 21, 1865, not only the space within the enclosure but the streets on either side were crowded with men, women, and children, all waiting to form a procession. At two o'clock, the number of people assembled reached four thousand, and shortly after that hour, the black marshals took their positions in the line.

Two black marshals on horseback led the procession, each wearing badges and rosettes of red, white, and blue. They were followed by a society of about fifty black butchers, who carried their knives at their sides and in front of whom was displayed a huge pig. Next in order came the Twenty-first Regiment, Lieutenant Colonel Bennett commanding, preceded by a band. A company of school boys, the leading boy carrying a banner with the inscription, "We know no masters but ourselves," followed the military, and after them came a car of liberty drawn by black horses and decorated with flags, streamers, and banners. Within the car were seated thirteen young black girls, costumed in white, with colored trimmings, and each wearing a white headdress.

The preachers, elders, Sunday school teachers, and Bible societies of the various denominations in Charleston followed. Then came eighteen hundred black school children, boys and girls, with their white teachers walking beside them, displaying mottoes such as "We know no caste of color." The tailors, carrying shears as the emblem of their trade, and the coopers, with hoops in their hands, turned out in large force. After them came the firemen—no fewer than ten organizations marching—dressed in red shirts, with belts around their waists. The various trade associations, including painters, blacksmiths, carpenters, wheelwrights, and barbers, all came in regular order. They were followed by a cart drawn by a mule and containing an auctioneer, who was standing over two women seated on a block, with their children standing over them. A small black boy stood near them ringing a bell. The cart bore the announcement, "A number of negroes for sale," and as it moved along, the auctioneer appealed to the crowd for a bid. The bystanders were informed that one of the slaves to be auctioned was an excellent cook, or an expert seamstress, or a valuable field hand. Attached to the cart was a long rope, tied to which were a number of men and women.

Next came a hearse, bearing a coffin, and the inscriptions, "Slavery is dead"; "Who Owns him? No one"; "Sumter dug his grave on the 13th of April, 1861." The hearse was followed by mourners dressed in deep black.

Fifty sailors with their officers, a company of wood sawyers, a band of newspaper carriers, and several clubs and associations brought up the rear of the great procession.

The procession moved through the principal streets of Charleston below the Citadel; its length was estimated to have been about three miles. Stands had been erected at the Citadel Square for the speakers, but a sudden downpour of rain forced a postponement. Hence a little after dark, the celebration ended, and the participants returned to their homes. It was a day Charlestonians would long remember.

GRANT'S VIRGINIA CAMPAIGN

While Sherman's troops, including the black regiments, had been conquering Georgia and South Carolina, General Grant had opened his Virginia campaign. Grant's relentless determination to defeat the Confederates, regardless of the cost in lives, became legendary. Within one month after it had crossed the Rapidan River, the Army of the Potomac under Grant had lost no fewer than half as many men as it had lost in the previous three years of bloody fighting in Virginia. "For thirty days it has been one funeral procession past me," protested one of Grant's generals, "and it has been too much." Yet it was only the beginning. By the time he had crossed the James and besieged Petersburg, Grant's losses came to nearly 75,000 men—more than Lee and Beauregard had had in both their armies at the start of the campaign a month and a half before. In one charge before Petersburg, a Maine regiment of 850 lost 632 men, more than 74 percent, in less than half an hour.

Casualties among the Confederates were much smaller in number but larger in proportion to their available manpower, and therefore costlier in military terms. Knowing this, Grant never abandoned his meat-grinder tactics, pouring black and white soldiers into the grinder.

As one Confederate support after another fell to the Union armies, Fort Fisher, the strongest fortification yet built in North America, still guarded the approach to Wilmington, North Carolina, the last haven for blockade-running supply ships and Lee's major supply depot for his army in Virginia. As the noose closed around Lee's army, Grant decided to launch the largest amphibious attack of the Civil War against the fort.

Among the nearly eight thousand federal troops sent to sea were several regiments of black soldiers. The First Regiment, U.S. Colored Troops, recruited in Washington early in 1863, formed part of the amphibious army that would attack and conquer Fort Fisher. It had on its roster of its otherwise all-white officers the first black man commissioned as a chaplain to the Union army: Henry M. Turner, pastor of the Israel African Methodist Church on Capitol Hill, black civil rights advocate, and an outstanding journalist. Turner's account of the assault on Fort Fisher, published in the *Christian Recorder,* is a vivid report of the battle, of the tremendous contributions of the black soldiers to the Union victory, and of the enormous losses sustained by the combatants.

THE CONFEDERACY AND BLACK SOLDIERS

In a desperate effort to stave off defeat, the Confederacy grudgingly decided to use black troops. At least six Southern states had already impressed into service and utilized free blacks as well as slaves. The mayor of Richmond advised the free blacks that "it was no less their duty than that of the whites to do something for the good of the country; since they could not fight they could work." From the beginning, impressed slave labor had been used by the Confederacy to build fortifications, in the transportation of supplies, as laborers, in armories, mines, and factories, and in a variety of other activities.

Early in the war, the American correspondent of the Russian publication *Severnaya Pechela* [Northern star] wrote from Washington: "Many are saying that the slave owners could arm the slaves, but the question is whether they will be able to disarm them easily." Even arms in the hands of free blacks were feared in the Confederacy. About one thousand free blacks in New Orleans had been permitted to serve in a militia unit in 1861, but they performed only parade, drill, and guard duty during their period of service. Yet as the Russian correspondent noted, there were some in the Confederacy who felt the need for the use of slaves in the Confederate army. Patrick Cleburne, a Confederate major general, was one of the first to suggest this. In 1863 he recognized the need for more troops and pointed to slaves as the only potential source of fresh recruits. In a proposal to Jefferson Davis in December 1863, Cleburne traced the South's desperate situation to the lack of white manpower resources. Valueing victory for the Confederacy far more than slavery, he advocated the immediate training of a large reserve of slaves, guaranteeing freedom to any slave "who shall remain true to the Confederacy in this war."

Although several of his fellow officers approved of Cleburne's proposal a council of the Army of Tennessee rejected it, and General Albert Sidney Johnston refused to refer it through channels to President Davis. The views of the plan's opponents were summarized by General Clement H. Stevens:

I do not want independence if it is to be won by the help of the negro. . . . I contend that slavery was the initiating cause of the war . . . and the cry of Union and rebellion are only a subterfuge to enlist the masses in a crusade against slavery. . . . The justification of slavery is the inferiority of the negro. If we make him a soldier, we concede the whole question.

General Howell Cobb vigorously supported the position that slaves must not be permitted to fight. "Use all the negroes you can get for all the purposes for which you need them, but don't arm them," he pleaded. "The day you make soldiers of them is the beginning of the end of the revolution. If slaves will make good soldiers our whole theory of slavery is wrong—but they won't make good soldiers."

But blacks, the majority of them former slaves, had made and were making good soldiers for the Union army. The Russian magazine *Russkoye Slavo* [Russian World], describing the heroism of the black soldiers, commented:

No one now doubts the courage of Negro soldiers in the battlefield. Nor do their former masters have any reason to doubt that, having exchanged bayonet charges with them. . . . For they have seen for themselves what an army of Negroes can do; equipped with axes and knives it attacked plantations. Now that this fierce mob has the benefit of military organization, it is winning victory after victory in a calm and confident way and laying siege to towns.

In November 1864, President Davis stated bluntly that "should the alternatives ever be presented of subjugation or the employment of the slaves as a soldier, there seems no reason to doubt what should be our decision." But even though it was now impossible to keep the Confederate armies filled with white soldiers, the Confederate Congress refused to act. In *The Gray and the Black:*

The Confederate Debate on Emancipation (a collection that gathers together selections from newspaper editorials, letters, and speeches to provide an overview of the public debate in the last months of the war on whether to arm and emancipate the Confederate blacks), Robert F. Durden concedes that the debate on Davis' proposal showed that "most articulate Southerners, despite certain fascinating exceptions, made it tragically clear that they yet lacked, even in the ultimate crisis, the intelligence, moral courage, and imagination to begin voluntarily to abandon the peculiar institution."

In 1865 Robert E. Lee released a letter in which he said:

I think we must decide whether slavery shall be extinguished by our enemies, and the slaves used against us, or use them ourselves at the risk of the effects which may be produced upon our social institutions. My own opinion is that we should employ them without delay.

Lee predicted that the slaves' habit of obedience would make them good soldiers.

Finally, in March 1865, the Confederate Congress authorized the enlistment of 300,000 slaves. These "slave soldiers" were not to be emancipated without the consent of the owners and of the states in which they resided. Nevertheless, everyone seemed to take it for granted that freedom was to be the reward for service. "Freedom would be given to the negro soldier," the *Richmond Enquirer* editorialized, not because we believe slavery is wrong, but because we must offer to the negro inducements to fidelity which he regards as equal to if not greater than those offered by the enemy."

But this measure came so late that even though some companies were raised, and a week before the fall of Richmond, black Confederate soldiers drilled in the Capitol Square, none of them actually participated in any military campaign. The only slave to die in military combat wearing a Confederate uniform was James Jones, who lies buried in a tiny cemetery at Great Bridge in Chesapeake, Virginia. His marker says simply: "James Jones, Co. C 1 Va. Inf. C.S.A." The records in the National Archives tell us that Jones joined the Confederate Army for one year at Manassas, Virginia, on May 1, 1861; that his name appears on the company muster roll for July and August 1861, and that he was last paid on June 30, 1861.

While speaking to the men of the 140th Indiana Regiment a few weeks before the war's end, President Lincoln made some comments regarding the question of the Confederate use of Negro troops:

The great question with [the South] was whether the negro, put in the army, would fight for them. I do not know, and therefore cannot decide. (*Laughter.*) They ought to know better than we. I have in my lifetime heard many arguments why the negroes ought to be slaves, but if they fight on the side of those who would keep them in slavery it will be a better argument than any I have yet heard. (*Laughter and applause.*) . . .

He who will fight for that ought to be a slave. . . . While I have often said that all men ought to be free, yet I would allow those colored persons to be slaves who want to be; and next to them those white persons who argue in favor of making other people slaves. (*Applause*.) I am in favor of giving an opportunity to such white men to try it on themselves. (*Applause*.)

Bell I. Wiley takes the position that he does know whether "the negro being put into the [Confederate] army would fight for them." He wrote in *Southern Negroes, 1861–1865*:

It hardly seems likely that slaves who greeted the "Yankees" and grasped freedom with such alacrity . . . would by the mere donning of Confederate uniforms have been transformed into loyal and enthusiastic fighters for . . . the perpetuation of the institution of slavery.

END OF THE CIVIL WAR AND ASSASSINATION OF LINCOLN

"I am glad to see the end so near at hand," Lincoln declared in concluding his talk to the men of the 140th Indiana Regiment. He was correct. One main hope remained for the Confederate cause. The Army of Tennessee, under the command of General John Bell Hood, had massed its forces to take the city of Nashville and to conquer Tennessee and Kentucky, with the intention of marching on the North via Cincinnati to take the pressure off Lee's army bottled up in Virginia. If such a plan had worked, the Union might have been forced to accept a peace on terms favorable to the South. But the effort failed. With the black troops playing a prominent role, the Confederate army of General Hood was at first contained and then destroyed in the battle of Nashville.

When Richmond, the last hope of the insurgents, fell in April 1865, it was the black regiments who first entered the city singing "John Brown's Body." During the battle of Richmond, the Twenty-ninth Connecticut black regiment distinguished itself. In the period from February to April 1864, the regiment had captured as many as 500 artillery pieces and 6,000 muskets and taken prisoner a large number of enemy troops. Other black regiments took part in the assault on and capture of the capital city of the Confederacy. Lee now had no choice but to surrender. The inevitable occurred on April 9, 1865, at Appomattox, Virginia. The Civil War was at an end.

The joy of black Americans, North and South, at the end of the bloody war was temporarily dashed by the sorrowful news three days after Appomattox of the assassination of Abraham Lincoln. Their sadness turned to anger when they learned that the New York City Common Council had voted to exclude Negroes from the funeral procession when Lincoln's body passed through the city. Black New Yorkers met at Cooper Institute to protest the decision, and Frederick Douglass, the featured speaker, denounced the council's action as "the most disgraceful and scandalous proceeding ever exhibited by people calling themselves civilized.'' In a letter of protest to the *New York Evening Post,* black minister J. Sella Martin wrote:

The last public words of Mr. Lincoln leave no doubt that had he been consulted he would have urged, as a dying request, that the representatives of the race which had come to the nation's rescue in the hour of peril, and which he had lifted by the most solemn official acts to the dignity of citizens and defenders of the Union, should be allowed the honor of following his remains to the grave.

Martin's reference to Lincoln's ''last public words'' could have been to the fact that before he was assassinated, the president approved the congressional bills providing for the abolition of discrimination on horse-drawn streetcars in Washington, for the acceptance of Negro witnesses in federal courts, and for the equalizing of penalties for the same crime. But most likely it referred to Lincoln's last public address on April 11, 1865, in which he indicated his belief that as the Southern states drew up new constitutions for readmission into the Union, the right of suffrage should be conferred on ''the very intelligent [blacks] and those who serve our cause as soldiers.''

It appears from recent research that Lincoln's stand for limited black suffrage was not entirely a new development. Peyton McCrary in his 1978 study, *Abraham Lincoln and Reconstruction: The Louisiana Experiment,* presents convincing evidence to demonstrate that Lincoln would have supported this policy when the state constitution was being drawn up in 1864 but for the fact that he was furnished with ''misinformation'' by General Banks to the effect that such a position would delay the operation indefinitely. This, McCrary conclusively demonstrates, was ''a deliberate distortion of the facts.'' When it became clear to Lincoln that by themselves white unionists could not challenge planter political domination, he endorsed limited enfranchisement of blacks in his last speech.

In *Lincoln and Black Freedom: A Study in Presidential Leadership,* LaWanda Cox advances the thesis that Lincoln's opposition to slavery and his wartime commitment to emancipation were motivated by moral principle, not by mere expedience, and that his wartime policies moved beyond a limited conception of emancipation as the abolition of chattel bondage toward a broader conception of equal citizenship. To this she adds that despite Lincoln's statements in favor of white supremacy during the 1850s, which have often been quoted to prove his racism, his racial views remained flexible and underwent progressive liberalization during the war. It would thus appear that, as one scholar has put it, ''The aspiring Illinois politico of the 1850's who had pandered to the racial prejudices of his audience had, by the end of the Civil War, arrived at a remarkable sensitivity to the plight of blacks in American society.'' In any event, neither Lincoln's last public words nor black protests had any effect on the New York City Common Council. Only a telegram from Assistant Secretary of War Charles A. Dana to General Dix, in command of the arrangements, reversed this decision. On April 25, 1865, about two thousand blacks made up the end of the long line behind the Emancipator's coffin.

Seven men and one woman went on trial in 1865 as accomplices of John Wilkes Booth, Lincoln's assassin, who was killed during his flight. They were indicted for conspiracy in the murder of Lincoln and in the attempted murder of Secretary of State Seward and with conspiring to murder Vice-President Johnson and Lieutenant General Grant. The government charged that the conspirators had combined with Jefferson Davis, president of the Confederacy, and with his agents in Canada. After a trial by a military commission, four of the accused, including Mary Surratt, were hanged; the other four went to prison.

"The rebellion," said the U.S. counsel at the trial, "was itself a criminal conspiracy and gigantic assassination." But it was the attorney for the defense of Seward's attacker who most clearly pointed to the link between slavery and assassination:

It was a custom for masters to whip slaves, to sell them, kill them. Under slavery murder of a companion with a bowie-knife, or in a duel was an index of spirit; torture of negroes evidence of a commanding nature. Now let me ask whether in the world there is another school in which the prisoner could so well have been trained for assassination? [He had] the cheap regard for life which comes from trading in and killing slaves. We now know that this is the spirit of slavery, stripped of its disguise. . . . We see again . . . in assassination the social bowie-knive and pistol; and in this prisoner the legitimate moral offspring of slavery.

26

Why the North Won

FIVE HISTORIANS EXPLAIN THE NORTHERN VICTORY

In *Why the North Won the Civil War*, a volume of essays edited by David Donald and published in 1960, five leading American historians seek to explain the fact of the Northern victory. Richard Current, in assessing the relative economic strength of North and South, comes down unequivocally in support of the inevitability of Northern victory. Economic factors, he writes, must have been the prime cause of the outcome of the war. The South was never a match for the massive potential of the North; the only Southern hope might have been immediate victory—before the North had time to organize its material and human forces—or large-scale foreign intervention at some critical early points of the war. Once these dangers to the North had been averted, the South was slated for defeat. Materially, the North was so much stronger that it could, Current concludes, "almost lick the South with one hand tied behind her back."

In contrast to Current, the other authors regard the outcome of the war as much less predetermined by material factors. The South, they feel, might have won in spite of its agrarian economy and lack of industrial potential, had it been equal in other ways to its adversary. A case in point, according to Norman Graebner, was diplomatic policy; the South might have emerged victorious had it been able to secure European intervention and important British or French assistance to its war effort.

In their essays, T. Harry Williams, David Donald, and David Potter attribute Southern defeat to human factors—the deficiencies of both the leaders and the led—that blunted the Southern drive for victory. Williams discusses the problem of military leadership, the individual talents, and strategic and tactical preconceptions of Northern and Southern commanders. Both groups, he argues, were students of traditional military concepts, trained in the strategic theories of the eighteenth century. But while the southerners were "brilliant practitioners" of conservative principles of the massed offensive—the concentration on single important sectors of enemy territory—Lincoln and Grant led the Northern forces to victory with the radical formula of massive attack all along the enemy lines and of seizing the Southern armies rather than Southern territory.

David Donald offers the theory that the South "died of democracy" and that Southern institutions and traditions precluded a cooperative and coordinated mobilization of resources. In the Southern army, Donald insists, stubbornly individualistic habits of thought and behavior made the most elementary organization and maintenance of discipline almost impossible. In the final essay, David Potter details the case against Jefferson Davis in an indictment that found the Confederate president, in contrast to Abraham Lincoln, wanting in common sense, cautious and unimaginative in the conduct of government and army, and a petty bureaucrat concerned with insignificant details and with a "conspicuous lack of an instinct for victory."

THE SIGNIFICANCE OF SLAVERY

Twenty years after the publication of *Why the North Won the Civil War,* Kenneth M. Stampp published an essay, "The Southern Road to Appomattox," which offered a suggestion of "one of the conditions, among several, that may help explain why the South lost the Civil War." Stampp advances the hypothesis that many southerners—"enough to affect the outcome of the war—who outwardly appeared to support the Confederate cause, had inward doubt about its validity, and that, in all probability, some, perhaps unconsciously, welcomed its defeat." He believes that there was no "genuine southern nationalism" and that, except for slavery, Southern whites had little in the way of distinctive culture, either in the bulk of their population or in their political and religious belief. They were driven to secession not out of nationalism but by fear and anger, as a last painful resort. Some of them, he suggests, seemed to have regarded secession as a means of eventually negotiating a better position in the old Union than could be obtained from negotiating from within.

Guilt and shame over slavery, Stampp adds, were largely responsible for the South's defeat, for slavery could never serve as an effective rallying cry. It is significant, he points out, that there was an almost total lack of partisan resistance and sabotage in many Union-occupied zones of the South during the Civil War.

Whether guilt and shame over slavery were as prevalent in the Confederacy as Stampp suggests is open to question. From the records of slaveowners' journals, diaries, and letters, we can discover hardly a flicker of doubt over the basic issue of slavery. Even when everything was crumbling around them, the slaveowners still resolutely regarded the slaves as their rightful property. When emancipation came, most had no difficulty in viewing it as an act of brazen robbery. But at least Stampp, unlike the historians in *Why the North Won the Civil War*, emphasizes slavery as a basic reason for the South's defeat.

Other historians stress the fact that the need to maintain slave control forced the Confederacy to exempt slaveowners and their sons from military service and place the burden of fighting in a war to protect slavery on the backs of the nonslaveholding, poorer whites. This in turn caused internal cleavages, desertions, and eventually what Charles H. Wesley aptly calls *The Collapse of the Confederacy*. Armstead L. Robinson put it well when he wrote: "Slavery caused the American Civil War and active slave resistance helped bring the Confederacy to its knees." And he adds:

The slaves' expectations and actions precipitated deep conflicts among Southern whites, conflicts which preceded emancipation and which devastated the Southern war effort. The evidence suggests that the fear of slave revolt acted as a cancer within the body of the Southern Republic, a cancer first sapping Confederate morale and then ultimately consuming the South's will to fight for national independence. Fears of wartime slave revolts were based on hard facts, not mere fantasy. . . . The slaves wanted to be free and the South knew it. In turn, it was the Confederate reaction to these facts which set in motion the conflicts among Southern whites which lay at the heart of the Confederate's inability to win the Civil War.

In short, Robinson concludes, the relationship between "slave actions and the collapse of the Confederacy demonstrates how blacks' involvement in wartime society led to their own emancipation."

THE SIGNIFICANCE OF BLACK SOLDIERS

While Kenneth M. Stampp has stressed the role of slavery in the Confederacy's defeat, like most other white historians, he, too, neglected the role played by blacks, especially the slaves, in the Northern victory.

Before the Civil War ended, more than 230,000 black men had fought in the Union army and navy. More than 186,000 (134,111 of them recruited or conscripted in the slave states) had fought in the Union army, making up nearly 10 percent of the total enrollment. Almost as many blacks, men and women, mostly freedmen, were employed as teamsters, carpenters, cooks, nurses, laundresses, stevedores, blacksmiths, coopers, bridge builders, laborers, servants, spies, scouts, and guides.

Once the Lincoln administration decided to use Negro troops, the Union army's heavy utilization of blacks gave it an overwhelming advantage over the rebel forces, an advantage the Confederacy could never overcome.

It was Abraham Lincoln, commander in chief of the Union army, who testified to the fact that the blacks won the Civil War. In 1864, Lincoln told a delegation seeking to halt the recruiting of black soldiers and the disbandment of Negro regiments already in service:

There are now in the service of the United States near two hundred thousand able-bodied colored men, most of them under arms, defending and securing Union territory. . . . Abandon all the posts now garrisoned by black men; take two hundred thousand men from our side and put them in the battlefield or cornfield against us, and we would be compelled to abandon the war in three weeks.

After Appomattox, Lincoln was even more positive. "Without the military help of black freedmen, the war against the South could not have been won," he declared in a victory speech. Lincoln also urged his listeners never to forget that in the war to save the Republic, 38,000 black soldiers were killed in action—a mortality rate that was 35 to 40 percent greater than among other troops, notwithstanding their late entrance into the armed forces. In this connection the *New York Tribune* observed: "The Negro gave one in three of his number to the cause of freedom. Did we with our valor do half as well?"

HISTORIANS AND BLACK CONTRIBUTIONS TO NORTHERN VICTORY

Two years after the war, William Wells Brown, one of the earliest and most prolific of black historians, published *The Negro in the American Rebellion, His Heroism and His Fidelity*. In his preface, Brown wrote modestly that he had hoped one more qualified than he would record the services of Negro soldiers in the war, but, none appearing, he had undertaken the task. The book, based on firsthand narratives of battles and experiences obtained from men who had been involved personally, ended with the sentence: "From the commencement of the enlistment of colored troops, to the close of the war, there were engaged in active service one hundred and sixty-one thousand six hundred and twenty-four colored men." In 1888, black historian George Washington Williams, himself a veteran of service with the Massachusetts Fifty-fourth Regiment, published *A History of the Negro Troops in the War of Rebellion,* which added further details on the significant military contributions of black soldiers.

Yet when James Ford Rhodes published, between 1893 and 1906, his seven-volume *History of the United States from the Compromise of 1850 to the Restoration of Home Rule in the South in 1877*, his only comment on the military contribution of black soldiers was to call it insignificant. He concluded that throughout the war, the slaves were "patiently submissive and faithful to their owners." But worse was still to come. In an 1928 biography of General Ulysses S. Grant, a man who had expressed to President Lincoln his opinion that "by arming the negro we have added a powerful ally," W. E. Woodward had the effrontery to write:

The American negroes are the only people in the world, so far as I know, that ever became free without any effort of their own. . . . The Civil War was not their business. They had not started the war, nor ended it. They twanged banjoes around the railroad station, sang melodious spirituals, and believed that some Yankee would soon come along and give them forty acres of land and a mule.

The view that the slave was a passive, docile, uncomprehending recipient of freedom in 1865 and that 4.5 million black Americans in the United States played no important or effective role in the Civil War continued. (Even as late as 1972, Robert F. Durden could assert in a book published by the prestigious Louisiana State University Press that black freedom was purely the "gift of the Federal armies, Lincoln and the Thirteenth Amendment." Not a word about black Union soldiers and sailors who were attacking the Confederate slave nation from without, or of countless acts of escape, espionage, work slowdowns, and sabotage by the slaves who attacked it from within.) But there have been exceptions. In spite of serious failings—such as the use of terms like *darky* and *buck,* the failure to mention the amazing exploit of Robert Smalls, the absence of any discussion of the armed Negroes in runaway camps who carried on a guerrilla warfare in Louisiana, South Carolina, Mississippi, Alabama, Virginia, and especially North Carolina and Florida, the ignoring of the treatment of captured black soldiers by the Confederates, and the disparaging of the labor performed by the freedmen under federal direction and of the education of blacks under federal auspices—Bell Irwin Wiley's *Southern Negroes, 1861–1865,* published in 1938, made it difficult for anyone again to say, with Rhodes, that the slaves had been "patiently submissive and faithful to their owners." Wiley's work proved, despite its shortcomings, that the Negro in the United States earned his freedom by fighting for it.

Wiley may have made it difficult to ignore this fact, but not impossible. E. Merton Coulter, in his 1951 book, *The Confederate States of America*, devoted 14 of the 644 pages to the 4 million blacks in the South. In these pages, he found "happiness" and "loyalty" their characteristics and dismissed the black Union troops as a nuisance who "cluttered up operations." Ignoring the fact that blacks constituted over a third of the Southern population, Clement Eaton, in his 1954 *History of the Southern Confederacy*, devoted four pages to their life and activity during the war, an equal number to the tribulation of plantation mistresses, and four more to the literary work of three minor writers.

Little wonder, then, that Benjamin Quarles still found it necessary in 1953 to publish *The Negro in the Civil War* in order "to set the record straight, to restore the Negro to his rightful active place in the war that set him free." Or that three years later, Dudley Taylor Cornish felt compelled, for the same reason, to publish *The Sable Arm: Negro Troops in the Union Army, 1861–1877.* Quarles and Cornish succeeded admirably in their efforts, but this did not prevent David Potter, on the occasion of the hundredth anniversary of the outbreak of the Civil War, to refer to their works as part of the "fantastic interest in tangential and peripheral subjects" that had accomplished the boom in books about the Civil

War. Indeed, as late as 1978, Raimondo Luraghi, who superficially pretends to a Marxist analysis, wrote in his *The Rise and Fall of the Plantation South* that black loyalty to the Confederacy was a sign of "the political maturity of southerners of African origin."

As the United States prepared to celebrate the centennial of the Civil War, it began to appear as if the conflict were a colorful contest that had nothing to do with such ugly matters as slavery, in which blacks played no role whatsoever, and which somehow both sides had gloriously won. To honor the anniversary of the Confederate firing on Fort Sumter on April 12, the National Civil War Centennial Commission met in Charleston under the guidance of Major General Ulysses S. Grant III, a grandson of the Union commander. One of the chief speakers was Robert E. Lee IV, a great-grandson of the Confederate commander. One of the officials attending was Madeline A. Williams, a member of the New Jersey State Commission, but she was present only because of the intervention of President John F. Kennedy. For Ms. Williams being black, the New Jersey delegation was advised that the Charleston hotel where the rites were to be held would be unable to accommodate her. Her colleagues appealed to General Grant to take action, but the descendant of the man who wrote that "by arming the negro we have added a powerful ally" showed no interest in having Ms. Williams as an "ally." The New Jersey group withdrew from the affair, followed by those from Illinois, New York, and California. Even Kennedy's first attempt to impress Grant with the impropriety of his arrangements failed, the commission replying that it had "no authority or jurisdiction to dictate" to hotelkeepers. It was only when the president said flatly, "We cannot leave the situation as it is," that action followed. Ceremonies took place in Charleston, but the dining and business of the commission were carried on at the U.S. naval base, which, being federal property, was free of local custom. But neither in Charleston nor at the U.S. naval base was there any reference to the role played by some quarter of a million black Americans in the Union army and navy.

Noting later that year the tendency and determination during the centennial of the Civil War to forget the contribution of the black American, W.E.B. Du Bois wrote: "There is little that I can say to stem the tide. But perhaps some will listen to the conservative voice of Booker T. Washington." And he quoted Washington's observation:

The services which the Negro troops performed in the Civil War in fighting for the freedom of their race not only convinced the officers who commanded them and the white soldiers who fought by their side that the Negro race deserved to be free, but it served to convince the great mass of the people in the North that the Negroes were fit for freedom. It did, perhaps, more than any other thing to gain for them, as a result of the war, the passage of those amendments to the Constitution which secured to the Negro race the same rights in the United States that are granted to white men.

The amendments referred to were the Thirteenth, Fourteenth, and Fifteenth. The last two lie outside the scope of the present volume and will be discussed in volume 4. But let us turn our attention to the first of the three.

27

Free at Last!

Away in the days of bondage they thought to see in one divine event the end of all doubt and disappointment; few men ever worshipped Freedom with half such unquestioning faith as did the American Negro for two centuries. To him, so far as he thought and dreamed, slavery was indeed the sum of all villainies, the cause of all sorrow, the root of all prejudice; Emancipation was the key to a promised land of sweeter beauty than even stretched before the eyes of wearied Israelites. In song and exhortation swelled one refrain—Liberty. . . . At last it came,—suddenly, fearfully like a dream.

So W.E.B. Du Bois wrote lyrically in *The Souls of Black Folks*. It came to all black Americans in the words of the Thirteenth Amendment:

1. Neither slavery nor involuntary servitude, except as a punishment for crime, whereof the party shall have been convicted, shall exist within the United States, or any place subject to their jurisdiction.
2. Congress shall have power to enforce this article by appropriate legislation.

ORIGIN OF THE THIRTEENTH AMENDMENT

In his second inaugural address on March 4, 1865, Abraham Lincoln pointed to the fact that when the Civil War began, "One-eighth of the whole population were colored slaves, not distributed generally over the Union, but localized in the southern part of it. These slaves constituted a peculiar and powerful interest." "All knew," Lincoln continued, "that this interest was somehow the cause of the war. To strengthen, perpetuate and extend this interest was the object for which the insurgents would rend the Union, even by war, while the Government claimed no right to do more than to restrict the territorial enlargement of it."

At the beginning of the war, President Lincoln had disavowed emancipation as a war aim. He stood on the Republican platform of 1860, which supported "the right of each state to control its own domestic institutions," and he also stood behind the Crittenden resolution of July 1861, which said that the war's only immediate objective should be to preserve the Union.

But the war itself had changed everything. As Lincoln also said in his second inaugural address: "Neither party expected for the war, the magnitude or the duration, which it has already attained. Neither anticipated that the *cause* of the conflict [slavery] might cease with, or even before the conflict itself should cease."

Slavery did cease in parts of the South as the war progressed. To be sure, the Emancipation Proclamation applied only to those areas yet unconquered as of January 1, 1863, but slavery was abolished in the months that followed in several of the states not included in the proclamation. It came to an end in Louisiana in January 1864 by military order, and the following summer, a state constitutional convention formally outlawed slavery. In Maryland, slavery was abolished by the ratification of the state constitution of 1864. Actually the popular vote was against the constitution by 29,536 to 27,541, but the soldier vote being overwhelmingly for the constitution by a majority of ten to one, the majority for the constitution was 263 out of a total of 59,973 votes recorded. There was no compensation for the owners in 1864, but three years later, with the Democrats in control of the constitutional convention, they proposed in the new constitution that while slavery would not be restored, compensation was due from the federal government to the former owners. No compensation was forthcoming, however.

Meanwhile the pressure for complete and permanent emancipation grew. The successes of the Union army early in 1864, coupled with the Republican successes at the polls in November 1863, seemed to indicate that both military and popular strength had been found to bring about an early victory for the North. Believing the end of the war was in sight, abolitionists and most Unionists began urging a constitutional amendment that would incorporate emancipation into the fundamental law. As a policy it existed only because Lincoln had proclaimed it, and upon his death or failure of reelection, a stroke of the pen could reverse the policy and destroy the fruits of three years of war. "The President's Proclamation has nobly paved the way," declared Robert Dale Owen, "but AN ACT OF EMANCIPATION is needed to endorse that Proclamation and enlarge its operation; a sanction of that great measure by the National Legislature under the solemn form of law."

The largest signature drive up to that time was mounted to urge Congress to adopt a constitutional amendment freeing the slave. Early in 1864, the Women's Loyal National League presented Congress with petitions bearing 400,000 signatures. With Lincoln's approval, Charles Sumner introduced a resolution in the Senate proposing an amendment abolishing slavery, and it was reported out of committee by Senator Lyman Trumbull. Overjoyed, Francis Lieber wrote to Sumner:

I cannot bring to my mind any change of opinion, conviction, and feeling . . . equal to the change that has been wrought in the American mind concerning slavery within the last one year. . . . I, for one, would never have dared to believe it possible that but yesterday that Taney could give his opinion boldly and an Abolitionist was treated like a leprous thing, and that today a Winter Davis can declare in Congress that the Constitution of the United States never acknowledged man as property. I rub my eyes, and say, "Where are we?"

But though the people may have been ready for the amendment, the Democrats in Congress were not. From the time it was introduced into the Senate, until it was finally passed on April 8, 1864, they used parliamentary measures to prevent its passage. Similar tactics met its appearance in the House, and it was not until June 25 that it was voted on. The vote clearly reflected the cleavage between the two parties, each voting en bloc—the Republicans for the measure, the Democrats against it. A two-thirds vote was necessary for its passage, and it failed, ninety-five to sixty-six.

In the presidential campaign of 1864, the Frémont platform announced that "the rebellion has destroyed slavery" and called for a constitutional amendment to prevent its revival. At Lincoln's insistence, the National Union (regular Republican) platform said that slavery should be extirpated by supplementing previous executive and legislative acts with an amendment to the Constitution. The Democrats came out for states' rights, the Union under the Constitution, the cessation of hostilities, and a convention of states to restore the Union. They said nothing about slavery, but in speeches at the convention and during the campaign, the Democrats insisted that the abolition of slavery had nothing to do with ending the war and attacked those Republicans who, like Lincoln, were willing to fight on until slavery was overthrown.

In supporting a constitutional amendment to end slavery, Lincoln called the measure "a very fitting if not indispensable adjunct to the winding up of the great difficulty." Although his popularity was at a low point, many people were demanding an early end of the slaughter, and influential voices were raised for overtures to the Confederacy to return to the Union with slavery, Lincoln refused to retreat from the position advanced in the Republican platform calling, at his own insistence, for complete emancipation. It will be recalled that in the "To Whom It May Concern" letter of July 18, 1864, to Horace Greeley, Lincoln set down the following terms for ending the war: "Any proposition which embraces the restoration of peace, the integrity of the whole Union, and the abandonment of slavery." To be sure, Lincoln did draft a letter on August 17 in which he stated that the fact that he had insisted upon peace upon the basis of renunciation and emancipation did not mean "that nothing else or *less* would be considered, if offered." But Lincoln neither made this new position public nor sent the letter to the Confederates. Moreover, when, on August 22, Henry J. Raymond, chairman of the Republican National Executive Committee and editor of the *New York Times,* warned Lincoln of the damage being done to his candidacy by the belief that abolition was being made a precondition of peace, and urged him to offer the

Confederates peace on the sole basis of "acknowledging the supremacy of the Constitution," Lincoln convinced Raymond and other Republicans who agreed with him "that to do so would be to surrender the election in advance."

Secretary of State Seward did insist during the campaign that there was no truth to the Democratic charge that Lincoln was making abolition a prerequisite for peace and that when the war ceased, the measures already taken against slavery would also cease. But Lincoln did not publicly endorse Seward's position, for while he regarded the Emancipation Proclamation as a war measure that would cease to operate when the war ended, it was precisely because of this that Lincoln supported a constitutional amendment abolishing slavery.

CONGRESS ADOPTS THE THIRTEENTH AMENDMENT

With the reelection of Lincoln and the overwhelming victory of the Republicans at the polls in 1864, guaranteeing them a majority in both houses of Congress, the movement for the Thirteenth Amendment picked up tremendous steam. In his annual message to Congress on December 6, 1864, Lincoln urged passage and submission to the states of the amendment. Directly after this was read to Congress, the amendment was once again introduced into the Senate. The language proposed was borrowed almost word for word from the Northwest Ordinance of 1787. ("There shall be neither slavery nor involuntary servitude in the said territory, otherwise than in the punishment of crimes, whereof the party shall have been duly convicted.") However, Senator Sumner at one point in the Senate debate suggested a broader formulation: "All persons are equal before the law, so that no person can hold another as a slave; and the Congress may make all laws necessary and proper to carry this article into effect everywhere within the United States and the jurisdiction thereof." But Senator Lyman Trumbull objected to this formulation, and he had the support of many Republican senators. Senator Charles Howard, for one, was disturbed by the fact that Sumner's language was drawn from the constitution of the French Revolution, which abolished slavery. French governments, he argued, were notably unstable, and he preferred "the good old Anglo-Saxon language employed by our fathers in the ordinance of 1787, an expression which has been adjudicated upon repeatedly, which is perfectly well understood both by the public and judicial tribunals." In the face of this opposition, Sumner withdrew his formulation. The language of the Ordinance of 1787 was accepted.

On February 1, 1865, the Thirteenth Amendment was approved by Congress. On that same day, reported the *New York Tribune,*

at three minutes before 11 o'clock in the morning, Charles Sumner entered the court-room (of the Supreme Court) followed by the Negro applicant for admission, and sat down within the bar. At eleven the procession of gowned Judges entered the room with Chief-Justice Chase at their head. . . . The Associate-Justices seated themselves nearly at once. . . . The Chief-Justice standing to the last, bowed with affable dignity to the Bar, and to his central seat with great pleasure. Immediately the Senator from Massachusetts arose, and in composed manner and quiet tone said "May it please the Court, I have the honor to present John S. Rock, Esq., a counsellor of the Supreme Court of Massachusetts, and ask that he be admitted to practice in the Supreme Court of the United States."

The chief justice bowed and replied: "Let Mr. Rock advance to the clerk's desk and take the oath." The oath was duly administered, and Rock "was at once accepted by Chief Justice Chase, and sworn in without objection."

A correspondent of the *Boston Journal* who witnessed the oath taking of the first black lawyer admitted to the bar of the U.S. Supreme Court wrote joyfully: "The slave power, which received its constitutional death-blow yesterday in Congress (via the passage of the Thirteenth Amendment), writhes this morning on account of the admission of a colored lawyer, John S. Rock of Boston, as a member of the bar of the Supreme Court of the United States." The *New York Tribune* commented that "the Dred Scott Decision [was] Buried in the Supreme Court." At this "funeral," "Senator Charles Sumner and the Negro lawyer John S. Rock, [were] the pall-bearers—the room and the Supreme Court of the United States the Potter's Field—the corpse the Dred Scott Decision."

"LET THE MONSTER PERISH"

On the second Sunday of February 1865, the Reverend Henry Highland Garnet, minister of New York's Fifteenth Street Presbyterian Church, was invited to deliver the sermon at the exercises in the House of Representatives celebrating that action. Garnet's speech was published as a pamphlet with the interesting title: *The First Sermon Delivered in the Hall of the House of Representatives, Washington, D.C., by an American Citizen of African Descent.*

In his sermon, delivered on February 12, 1865, Garnet not only praised the action of Congress but included an eloquent appeal for equal rights. The speech of the first black American to speak in the halls of Congress concluded, "Let the Monster Perish":

Let slavery die. It has had a long and fair trial. God himself has pleaded against it. The enlightened nations of the earth have condemned it. Its death warrant is signed by God and man. Do not commute the sentence. Give it no respite, but let it be ignominiously executed. . . .

The nation has begun its exodus from worse than Egyptian bondage, and I beseech you that you say to the people that they go forward. With the assurance of God's favor in all things done in obedience to his righteous will, and guided by day and by night by the pillars of cloud and fire, let us not pause until we have reached the other and safe side of the stormy and crimson sea. Let freemen and patriots mete out complete and equal justice to all men and thus prove to mankind the superiority of our democratic, republican government.

Favored men, and honored of God as his instruments, speedily finish the work which he has given you to do. Emancipate, enfranchise, educate and give the blessings of the gospel to every American citizen.

The largest audience ever to assemble in Boston's Music Hall gathered on February 5, 1865, "To Rejoice over the Amendment prohibiting Human Slavery in the United States forever." The main speech was delivered by William Lloyd Garrison, and practically every sentence he spoke was greeted with enthusiastic applause. The audience reached the heights of enthusiasm when the veteran abolitionist declared that while the joyful news from Washington that Congress had passed the Thirteenth Amendment

causes within me no feeling of personal pride or exultation—God forbid! . . . I am unspeakably happy to believe, not only that this vast assembly, but that the great mass of my countrymen are now heartily disposed to admit that, in disinterestedly seeking, by all righteous Instrumentalities, for more than thirty years, the utter abolition of slavery, I have not acted the part of a madman, fanatic, incendiary, or traitor (*immense applause,*) but have at all times been of sound mind, (*laughter and cheers,*) a true friend of liberty and humanity, animated by the highest patriotism, and devoted to the welfare, peace, unity and ever increasing prosperity and glory of my native land! (*cheers.*) And the same verdict you will render in vindication of the clear-sighted, untiring, intrepid, unselfish, uncompromising Anti-Slavery phalanx, who, through years of conflict and persecution— misrepresented, misunderstood, ridiculed and anathemized from one end of the country to the other—have labored—"in season and out of season"—to bring about the glorious result. (*Renewed applause.*) You will, I venture to think and say, agree with me, that only RADICAL ABOLITIONISM, is at this trial hour, LOYALTY, JUSTICE, IMPARTIAL FREEDOM, NATIONAL SALVATION—the Golden Rule blended with the Declaration of Independence! (*Great applause.*)

The greatest outburst of enthusiasm that historic evening came when, in listing those who should be credited with having contributed to the passage of the amendment by Congress, Garrison paused and said:

And to whom is the country more immediately indebted for this vital and saving amendment of the Constitution perhaps, than to any other man! I believe I may confidently answer—to the humble rail-splitter of Illinois—to the Presidential chain-breaker for millions of the oppressed—to ABRAHAM LINCOLN! (*Immense and long continued applause, ending with three cheers for the President.*) I understand that it was by his wish and influence, that that plank was made part of the Baltimore Platform (of the Union Party in 1864); and taking his position unflinchingly upon that Platform, THE PEOPLE have overwhelmingly sustained both him and it, ushering in THE YEAR OF JUBILEE. (*Renewed cheering.*)

Be assured, Abraham Lincoln can be trusted to the end. You may rely upon his honesty and integrity, in whatever he has said or done for the overthrow of slavery. In spite of all the wiles of all the so-called Peace Commissioners, he will be true to his word (*cheers*); he will never consent, under any circumstances, to the reenslavement of any one of the millions whose yokes he has broken. (*Loud applause.*)

The Year of Jubilee ended in December 1865 with the ratification of the Thirteenth Amendment by the states, thereby abolishing slavery in the United States forever—and with no compensation to the former slaveowners.

How truly revolutionary this development was is clearly seen if one recalls that on the eve of the Civil War, Lincoln and the Republicans were prepared to support an ironclad guarantee that the Constitution would never be amended in such a way as to interfere with the institution of slavery within the slave states. Indeed, an unrepealable Thirteenth Amendment to that effect passed the House on February 12, 1861, and the Senate on the night of March 30, 1861, by the necessary two-thirds vote. The incoming president, Abraham Lincoln, announced that he had "no objection" to the pending amendment, and three states (two of them free) actually gave their ratification in 1861. But the amendment that was finally ratified four and a half years later abolished slavery in the United States forever.

MEANING OF THE THIRTEENTH AMENDMENT

In the congressional debate on the proposed amendment, a number of congressmen emphasized that they expected the abolition of slavery would result in the enjoyment by "the oppressed slave [of] his natural and God-given rights," and in "the political and social elevation of negroes to all the rights of white men." In his study of the congressional debate on the Thirteenth Amendment, Professor tenBroek concluded that the framers intended to work a revolution in federalism, authorizing federal protection of "natural rights." Viewing the amendment as "the constitutional consummation of organized abolitionists . . . repeated and re-enacted by the 14th Amendment," tenBroek suggests that the framers used the term *natural rights* very broadly and intended to attack even the disabilities of Northern Negroes. He sees the framers as having not taken merely the "first step" toward the full protection of Negroes' civil rights but as intending to cover most of the ground specified later in the Fourteenth Amendment.

Other scholars, however, point out that only a minority of the members of the Thirty-eighth and Thirty-ninth Congresses, which debated and finally passed the Thirteenth Amendment, were Radicals, sharing the abolitionist sympathy for the Northern Negro, that their attention was focused south of the Mason-Dixon line, and that they were concerned only with the "incidents of slavery," such as the destruction of the slaves' capacity to acquire and hold property and the denial of the right to testify in court. As these scholars see it, the framers' conception of emancipation was limited to these formal rights.

Regardless of the exact purpose of the framers—and this is almost impossible to determine—it is certainly true that the opposite of slavery is freedom, and there can be no doubt that the framers' purpose was to free the slaves. But what is freedom? If slavery means the ownership of one person by another, is freedom then no more than the absence of such ownership? It is significant, for example, that in upholding the constitutionality of the 1866 Civil Rights Act, Justice Swayne in *United States* v. *Rhodes* held that the Thirteenth Amendment supported the protection of the Negro's rights to testify in court. The abolition of slavery, he said, inevitably created "hostility of the dominant class" endangering the freedmen. Congress was empowered under section 2 to attack manifestations of that hostility which might make "the gift of freedom . . . a curse instead of a blessing." Five years later, Justices Swayne and Bradley delivered a dissenting opinion, again involving the right to testify, arguing that the Thirteenth Amendment authorized Congress to eliminate the "disabilities" that had been "incidental to slavery, and the effects flowing from them." Furthermore, Congress could act to "institute the freedmen in the full enjoyment of that civil liberty and equality which the abolition of slavery meant."

But it was in 1968, in the case of *Jones* v. *Alfred H. Mayer Co.,* that the Supreme Court took the position that the Thirteenth Amendment supported a broad protection of civil rights. The petitioners in *Jones* had been denied housing in a private development because Jones was a Negro. The Court held this denial to be in violation of a provision of the 1866 Civil Rights Act, granting to all citizens of the United States "the same right . . . as is enjoyed by white citizens . . . to inherit, purchase, lease, sell, hold, and convey real and personal property." The Court then held that the enabling clause of the amendment grants Congress the power not only to outlaw forced labor but also to identify "badges of slavery" and pass legislation "necessary and proper" to eliminate them. It was not irrational, the Court argued, for Congress to find that discrimination against Negroes in the sale of private property constituted such a "badge." The Thirteenth Amendment, the Court continued, contains a "promise of freedom" that might become a "mere paper guarantee" if Congress could not act to secure at least the "freedom to buy whatever a white man can buy, the right to live wherever a white man can live. If Congress cannot say that being a free man means at least this much, then the 13th Amendment made a promise that the Nation cannot keep."

One can add to this judgment that in a very real sense, the Thirteenth Amendment did make a promise that the nation did not keep. As the amendment was making its way through the states to eventual ratification, a racist song mocked the freedom proclaimed in the new constitutional guarantee. Entitled "Who Will Care for Niggers Now?" the song parodied the popular "Who Will Care for Mother Now?" and went in part:

> Listen to me, plantation niggers,
> As I in die mud-hole lie;

> Though I feel starvation's rigors,
>   Let me say a word, and die.
> Niggers, does dis look like Freedom?
>   I can't see it anyhow,
> Blacks are fools, and white folks lead em:
>   But who cares for niggers now?
>
> *Chorus:*   Look heah! niggers, I am dying.
>   See the death-sweat on my brow.
>   Dis am Freedom, no use crying:
>   Who will care for niggers now?
>
> White folks say dey gib us Freedom;
>   What dey gib is all my eye:
> Free to suffer, free to languish;
>   Free to starve, and free to die.
> No potato, corn-cake, bacon,
>   We must to starvation bow;
> If dis Freedom, I's mistaken—
>   But who cares for niggers now?

The racist mockery of the freedom embodied in the Thirteenth Amendment failed to mention that the freedmen did not look yearningly for someone to care for them, as the former slaveowners, on whose behalf the song had been composed and distributed, had supposedly so magnanimously done. The former slaves wanted and were determined to take care of themselves, provided that the nation, whose existence they had done so much to preserve, offered them the opportunity to do so. And they made this clear to the Lincoln administration.

On January 11, 1865, several weeks after Sherman occupied Savannah, the revenue cutter *Spaulding* put in at the city with a distinguished cargo, including Secretary of War Edwin M. Stanton, Quartermaster General Montgomery C. Meigs, and other federal representatives. Secretary Stanton went immediately into conference with General Sherman. At this conference, Stanton proposed that Sherman arrange a meeting with the leaders of the local Negro community for the purpose of putting the question: "What do you want for your own people?" Accordingly, a meeting was arranged for the following evening, January 12, at 8 P.M. in General Sherman's headquarters in the spacious and palatial home of Charles Green, a British subject and wealthy Savannah cotton broker.

On February 12, 1865, a month later, a verbatim report of this meeting was read to the Sunday evening congregation of Brooklyn, New York's, Plymouth Church by its famed minister, Henry Ward Beecher. A copy of the minutes of the meeting had been turned over to Beecher by Secretary Stanton himself. The following day it was published in the *New York Tribune*.

As reported by the *Tribune,* there were twenty blacks present: five were born free; the others were former slaves. Three had been freed by the wills of their owners, two had purchased their freedom, and the others were freed by the

Union army. The majority were ministers or preachers. Garrison Frazier, one of the blacks who had purchased his freedom, was chosen by the group to express their common sentiments upon the matters of inquiry. Here are the key questions and answers:

1. State what your understanding is in regard to the acts of Congress and President Lincoln's proclamation touching on the condition of the colored people in the Rebel States.

Reply: So far as I understand President Lincoln's proclamation to the Rebellious States, it is, that if they would lay down their arms and submit to the laws of the United States before the first of January, 1863, all would be well, but if they did not, then all the slaves of the Rebel States would be free henceforth and forever. That is what I understand.

2. State what you understand by slavery and the freedom that was to be given by the President's proclamation.

Reply: Slavery is, receiving by *irresistible power* the work of another man, and not by his *consent.* The freedom as I understand it, promised by the proclamation, is taking us from under the yoke of bondage, and placing us where we would reap the fruit of our own labor, take care of ourselves, and assist the Government in maintaining our freedom.

3. State in what manner you think you can take care of yourselves, and how can you best assist the Government in maintaining your freedom.

Reply: The way we can best take care of ourselves is to have land, and to turn it and till it by our own labor—that is, by the labor of the women and children and old men; and we can soon maintain ourselves and have something to spare. And to assist the Government, the young men should enlist in the service of the government, and to serve in such manner as they may be wanted. (The Rebels told us that they piled them up and made batteries of them, and sold them to Cuba; but we don't believe that.) We want to be placed on land until we are able to buy it, and make it our own. . . .

7. State whether the sentiments you now express are those only of the colored people in the city, or do they extend to the colored population throughout the country, and what are your means of knowing the sentiments of those living in the country?

Reply: I think the sentiments are the same among the colored people of the State. My opinion is formed by personal communication in the course of my ministry, and also from the thousands that follow the Union Army, leaving their homes and undergoing much suffering. I did not think there would be so many; the number surpassed my expectation.

In conveying the verbatim report of the Savannah meeting to Henry Ward Beecher, Secretary Stanton expressed the opinion that for the first time in the history of the nation, the representatives of the government had gone to these "poor debased people to ask them what they wanted for themselves." He could have added that for the first time, too, the government had quickly responded to their most cherished demand.

The reply to the question as to how the freedmen "can best take care of themselves" came as no surprise to Sherman, and the general knew that the speaker spoke for the freedmen in the countryside, as well as those in Savannah. The blacks on plantations visited by Sherman during the march to the sea repeatedly expressed their belief that the land abandoned by the slaveowners "would be apportioned out to them." General Slocum, who commanded a wing of Sherman's army during the march through Georgia and South Carolina, declared before a New York audience: "You seldom hear of the numerous cases where the freedmen have laid claims to the lands of their former masters and have quietly informed them that they held title under the United States Government."

Shortly after the meeting in Savannah with the delegation representing the black community, steps were taken to provide an orderly way in which the process referred to by General Slocum could be carried out, and, at the same time, give effective meaning to the promise embodied in the Thirteenth Amendment. On January 16, 1865, Sherman, with the full concurrence of the secretary of war, issued his special field order number 15 authorizing the freedmen to take possession of the land on the Sea Islands off the coast between Charleston, South Carolina, and Augusta, Georgia, and abandoned rice plantations for thirty miles inland. Each freedman was granted possessory title over forty acres of land for the duration of the war, with the understanding that the land would be given them permanently by Congress. General Rufus Saxton, who was made inspector of the settlements and plantations in this region, testified that in urging the blacks to cross to the Sea Islands, "the faith of the government was solemnly pledged to maintain them in possession." Saxton was the military governor of the Sea Islands region, and he had unusual opportunities to become acquainted with the desires of the freedmen. "The object which the freedmen have most at heart is the purchase of land," he reported. "They all desire to get small homesteads and locate themselves upon them, and there is scarcely any sacrifice too great for them to accomplish this object."

On February 2, 1865, the freedmen of Savannah and vicinity held a meeting at the Second Baptist Church, at which General Saxton explained the details of his order and urged all to enter at once upon the business of locating where they could support themselves and families in comfort and peace by their own industry, "calling no man master, and with none to deprive them of the fruits of their toil." In a short time, 40,000 freedmen settled on the land and proceeded to work it as their own. On some of the islands the freedmen established civil government, with constitutions and laws for the regulation of their internal affairs, with all the different departments for schools, churches, building roads, and other improvements. On one of the islands, the black farmers within a few months had carried through improvements amounting to a sum "large enough to have purchased the whole island three years ago, with all the improvements of two hundred years under the rule and culture of its white inhabitants."

General Sherman's order, as carried out by General Saxton, gave concrete meaning to the freedom envisaged in the Thirteenth Amendment. It turned the Sea Islands into the most advanced outpost of the black freedom struggle. Even here, however, as we shall see in volume 4, the blacks were to retain their land only after a long and bitter struggle. But the first clear-cut, unequivocal action of the government in response to the freedmen's own answer as to how they could best take care of themselves in freedom aroused and heartened the black masses and gave a special significance to the constitutional guarantee of freedom.

THE HALF ABOLITION OF SLAVERY

Tragically, however, the government refused to take Sherman's order as its springboard. A more or less uniform land policy was established in the bill of March 1865 creating the Bureau of Refugees, Freedmen and Abandoned Lands (the Freedmen's Bureau) under the supervision of the War Department and the administration of General O. O. Howard. The main purpose of the bureau, which was set up in each Southern state under the direction of a commissioner, was to manage the abandoned lands, supervise the labor relations of the freedmen with their employers, and extend temporary relief to refugees and former slaves. The bill made it clear that redistribution of the land in the form of free grants to freedmen was not contemplated. Instead, the commissioners of the bureau were authorized to assign to each freedman and "loyal white refugee" not more than forty acres of land from the abandoned and confiscated plantations. The land was to be leased for a term of three years at an annual rent of 6 percent of its value. At the end of the rental period, the lessee would be permitted to purchase it.

At the most, then, the plan was to permit blacks to rent land on the confiscated plantations that had not yet been leased to large contractors. No further measures were contemplated, and the land that the bureau took over, amounting to about 800,000 acres, could hardly supply 4 million landless blacks with enough land to build cabins upon. Only further confiscation of all the large estates could supply the necessary land. Instead, the bureau sold most of its best land to large operators and to speculators. Ironically, during its first year the bureau collected enough rent, paid mostly by blacks, to meet its expenses.

Had the Sherman-Saxton policy been put into effect, settling hundreds of thousands of freedmen and their families on their own land, the purpose of the Thirteenth Amendment would have been fully realized. But, as we shall see in volume 4, the Sherman-Saxton policy was swept away by President Andrew Johnson's pardoning policy restoring land to the former slaveowners. The more radical of the Freedmen's Bureau commissioners, including General Saxton, who had been in charge of the bureau for the state of South Carolina, were forced out and replaced by men more favorable to the interests of the large plantation owners and land speculators.

Historians commonly agree that in its consequences, the Civil War witnessed, if not a second American Revolution, at least a major reconstructing of national life. The Homestead Act, passed in May 1862, made it possible for any citizen of the United States, upon payment of a registration fee of $10, to receive 160 acres of the public lands, and after five years of work upon the land, to obtain ownership. Although the implementation of the Homestead Act was often marred by abuses and speculation in public land, it nevertheless represented the realization of a dream long held by small farmers and workers in the North.

The war gave a tremendous boost to industrial expansion in the North. With the Homestead Act, the free lands in the West were occupied not by slaveholders but by millions of free people who furnished a growing market for the industries of the North. The war laid the foundations for an expanding American capitalism in other ways as well. Protective tariffs, long sought by American industrialists in their competition with British industry but opposed by importing slaveholders, were adopted during the war, and a new national banking system was instituted to serve the needs of expanding capitalism. The war also laid the foundation for a revitalized labor movement, proud of its part in the overthrow of slavery yet insisting that workers share in the fruits of the new industrial society. Among the resolutions adopted at a mass meeting of Boston workers held at Faneuil Hall on November 2, 1865, was the following:

We rejoice that the rebel aristocracy of the South has been crushed, that . . . beneath the glorious shadow of our victorious flag men of every clime, lineage and color are recognized as free. But while we will bear with patient endurance the burden of public debt, we yet want it to be known that the workingmen of America will demand in the future a more equal share of the wealth their industry creates . . . and a more equal participation in the privileges and blessings of those free institutions, defended by their manhood on many a bloody field of battle.

For Northern blacks, the war also brought advances in the field of civil rights: the repeal of black laws, the desegregation of public schools in several communities, and the integration of public transportation in several cities. In 1865, Massachusetts enacted the first comprehensive public accommodations law in American history, forbidding the exclusion of any person because of race or color from restaurants, inns, theaters, and places of amusement. On February 1, 1865, John S. Rock, the Massachusetts black laywer, was sworn in by Chief Justice Salmon P. Chase as the first Negro to be accredited to argue cases before the Supreme Court.

It is true that race prejudice still continued to exercise influence in the North, and discrimination continued to prevail in many walks of life. Blacks in 1865 were able to vote on equal terms with whites in only five Northern states. But there had been more progress in the field of civil rights in four years of war than in the decades preceding the conflict.

It is true that equality in law did not translate into equality in fact, but it would be wrong to view the Civil War as an unrelieved tragedy for black Americans. It may have been for many blacks a "flawed victory" (the title of a book published in 1975, which claimed to offer "A New Perspective on the Civil War"), but it was not marked by only "hollow achievements," as John Rosenberg maintains, as he projects the idea that more would have been accomplished through peaceable secession.

It was in the South that the greatest changes had occurred. Before the war, 4 million blacks in the South had been property, subject to the will and the whim of their owners. The Northern victory lifted the burdens of slavery, and now the basic personal freedom and the integrity of the families of these millions of black Americans were guaranteed by a constitutional amendment.

A controversy has recently developed among historians concerning the degree of freedom that blacks experienced under the Thirteenth Amendment. Some have argued that blacks enjoyed a high degree of freedom and made marked economic progress after slavery in the postbellum South. Hyman Belz, author of the prize-winning *Reconstructing the Union* and of *Emancipation and Equal Rights: Politics and Constitutionalism in the Civil War Era,* argues that the "fundamental" task of Reconstruction was not to resolve what he calls "the freedmen's problems" but rather to organize new state governments in the South and restore them to the Union. In that sense, he calls Reconstruction a "success." But he goes on to argue further that Reconstruction was a success also for blacks and not only because they also won the "freedom" of sharecropping and the "decided gain" of racial segregation. He argues that sharecropping "made sense economically" and was "efficient."

Belz argues still further that many historians have been "unhistorical" in maintaining that confiscation and distribution of plantation land to freedmen would have provided an economic basis for their new political rights. Such an analysis, Belz believes, is not "realistic"; it errs in analyzing Reconstruction policies "in relation to present day concerns, rather than in the context of their own time."

In his 1977 book, *A Right to the Land: Essays on the Freedmen's Community,* Edward Magdol effectively demolishes Belz's entire thesis. He highlights the demand of ex-slaves across the South for land as well as for the vote and education. At the end of the Civil War, Magdoll finds a common thread among the strivings of black people in the South, and the desire for economic independence by obtaining land was widespread. He quotes Robert Wyatt, a freed slave in Virginia, as voicing this common feeling: "We has a right to the land where we are located. For why? I tell you. Our wives, our children, our husbands, has been sold over and over again to purchase the lands we are now located upon, for that reason we have a divine right to the land."

Considerable contrary evidence challenging the thesis of Hyman Belz, Stephen J. De Canio, and Robert Higgs, who argue that blacks made economic progress after slavery, has been put forward by Roger Ransom and Richard Sutch, Harold D. Woodman, Gavin Wright, and Jay Mandle, among others, who have demonstrated that blacks experienced a very limited freedom and were entrapped in an economic system that left most of them impoverished. We can address this controversy here only in a limited way. But we must note that the overwhelming evidence proves that black freedom was fragile in large part because the former slaves did not have a secure economic foundation in the ownership of small farms. As George Washington Julian, congressman from Indiana, had pointed out: "Of what avail would be an act of Congress totally abolishing slavery, or an amendment of the constitution forever prohibiting it, if the old agricultural basis of aristocratic control shall remain." But remain it did, and as a consequence, for the former slaves, freedom was extremely limited. Emancipation brought with it a new era of hope for 4 million blacks now added to the American free labor force. But it also brought burdens that were especially onerous for a people set free to face enormous obstacles, for they had been set free with neither education nor wealth and property, and they were despised and feared by their former masters whose power, it soon became clear, persisted in the postbellum South. Although blacks had performed most of the work in Southern agriculture for centuries, they came to freedom with no capital, possessing neither cash nor land. They had only the ability to work. But without land, most of them would have to return to the same plantations they had labored on before the war and to work under circumstances not much different from those of slavery.

Blacks viewed such labor as unacceptable and held out hope that the government would confiscate the property of Southern rebels and redistribute it among the loyal people of the South. As we have seen, activities of several Union generals who had in fact confiscated land and distributed it among blacks during the war had given grounds for hope. But in the end the government acceded to Southern white demands and refused to redistribute land in the South. This action placed blacks at the mercy of their former owners and locked them into a system of perpetual poverty.

In short, it had been only "half an abolition." This was how Joaquin Nabuco, the nineteenth-century Brazilian abolitionist, characterized the process of freeing the Negro without freeing the land and turning it over to its "natural owners," the former slaves, whose labor for over two hundred years had made it valuable. The tragedy that accompanied the joy felt by millions of black Americans at being free at last—a tragedy that would seal the failure of Reconstruction—-was expressed most poignantly by Frederick Douglass:

When the Hebrews were emancipated, they were told to take spoil from the Egyptians. When the serfs of Russia were emancipated, they were given three acres of ground upon which they could live and make a living. But not so when our slaves were emancipated. They were sent away empty-handed, without money, without friends and without a foot of land to stand upon. Old and young, sick and well, they were turned loose to the open sky, naked to their enemies.

Bibliography and Sources

1. THE COMPROMISE AND THE FUGITIVE SLAVE ACT OF 1850

Background of the Compromise
For the letter of John C. Calhoun, see *Annual Report of the American Historical Association for 1929*, p. 440; for the *Charleston Mercury*, see Ray Ginger, *People on the Move: A United States History to 1877* (Boston, 1975), pp. 367–68; for the views of Philip Hone, see Philip S. Foner, *Business and Slavery: The New York Merchants and the Irrepressible Conflict* (Chapel Hill, N.C., 1940), pp. 21, 23; Allan Nevins, ed., *The Diary of Philip Hone* (New York, 1936), pp. 112–16. For the secession movement in the South, see Arthur C. Cole, "The South and the Right of Secession in the Early Fifties," *Mississippi Valley Historical Review* 1 (December 1914): 376–99.

Background for the New Fugitive Slave Law
For the laws passed by Pennsylvania, see William R. Leslie, "The Pennsylvania Fugitive Slave Act of 1826," *Journal of Southern History* 18 (November 1952): 429–45. For the relation of black opposition to seizure of fugitives to the 1834 anti-Negro riot in Philadelphia, see *Register of Pennsylvania*, December 10, 1834. For the *Prigg* case, see Joseph L. Nogee, "The Prigg Case and Fugitive Slavery, 1842–1850," *Journal of Negro History* 39 (July 1954): 185–205; *Prigg* v. *Pennsylvania* 16 Peters 539–42. For the personal liberty laws passed after *Prigg*, see Thomas D. Morris, *Free Men All: The Personal Liberty Laws of the North, 1780–1861* (Urbana, Ill., 1971), pp. 118–29. The account in the *Carlisle* (Pennsylvania) *Herald* of June 3, 1847, is reprinted in Jonathan Katz, *Resistance at Christiana: The Fugitive Slave Rebellion, Christiana, September 11, 1851: A Documentary Account* (New York, 1974), pp. 50-51. For the Crosswhite story, see John E. Yzenbaard, "The Crosswhite Case," *Michigan History* 53 (Summer 1969): 131–43.

Fugitive Slave Bill of 1850 and Nature of Bill
For Senator Underwood, see *Congressional Globe*, 30th Cong., 1st sess., p. 51; for Senator Butler, see ibid., p. 222; for Senator Mason, see 31st Cong., 1st sess., ibid.,

appendix, p. 79; for Senator Clay, see ibid., pp. 115, 123. For the role of the commissioners, see George M. Dowell Stroud, *A Sketch of the Laws Pertaining to Slavery in the Several States of the United States of America* (Philadelphia, 1856), pp. 272–74; for Judge Robert Kane's statement, see Pennsylvania Anti-Slavery Society, *Fourteenth Annual Report* (Philadelphia, 1851), p. 20. For the actual terms of the Fugitive Slave Act of 1850, see *United States Statutes at Large,* September 18, 1850, pp. 462–65. For the opinion of Attorney General Crittenden, see Benjamin F. Hall, ed., *Official Opinions of the Attorneys General of the United States, 1791–1948* (Washington, D.C., 1852–1949), 5:258.

Reaction to Fugitive Slave Bill

For William H. Seward's "higher law" speech, see *Congressional Globe,* 31st Cong., 1st sess., pt. I, pp. 263–69; William M. Stzasz, "Antebellum Appeals to the 'Higher Law,' 1830–1860," *Essex Institute Historical Collections* 100 (January 1974): 46.

For Horace Mann's speech, see Horace Mann, *Slavery: Letters and Speeches* (Boston, 1853), pp. 390–472. For Webster's March 7 speech, see H. D. Porter, "Webster's Seventh of March Speech," *American Historical Review* 27 (January 1922): 254–62, and Claude Fuess, *Daniel Webster* (Boston, 1930), 2:200–32. For the proceedings of the anti-Webster meeting in Boston, see *Liberator,* April 5, 1850; see also Philip S. Foner, ed., *The Voice of Black America: Major Speeches by Blacks in the United States, 1797–1973* (New York, 1975), 1:115–18.

Compromise of 1850 Becomes Law

For the enactment of the Compromise, see David Potter, *The Impending Crisis, 1848–1861,* completed and edited by Don E. Fehrenbacher (New York, 1976), pp. 118–38. For Hone's comment, see Foner, *Business and Slavery,* p. 34. For the views that there are evil features of the Fugitive Slave Act but still it should be supported and efforts made to revise it, see *Cleveland Daily Herald,* September 30, 1850; *Cincinnati Daily Gazette,* September 19, 1850; *Columbus Daily Ohio Statesman,* October 17, 1850; *Dayton Daily Journal,* October 19, 1850, reprinted in Richard Folk, "Black Man's Burden in Ohio, 1849–1863" (Ph.D. diss., University of Toledo, 1972), p. 319.

For Walt Whitman's poem, see Thomas L. Brasher, ed., *Walt Whitman: The Early Poems and the Fiction* (New York, 1963), pp. 36–37, 47–48. For the manifesto of the congressmen and the defeat of proposals to modify the Fugitive Slave Act, see *Journal of the Senate,* 31st Cong., 2d sess., pp. 88–90; Carl Schurz, *Henry Clay* (Boston, 1887), 2:378.

2. BLACK REACTION TO THE FUGITIVE SLAVE LAW OF 1850: TERROR IN THE BLACK COMMUNITY

For the effort to kidnap Henry "Box" Brown, see *Liberator,* September 6, 1850; for the case of Adam Gibson, see *Pennsylvania Freeman,* December 20, 26, 1850; American and Foreign Anti-Slavery Society, *Eleventh Annual Report* (New York, 1851), p. 75. For Elizabeth Williams, see *Voice of the Fugitive,* August 13, 1851. For the letter to the counterfeiters, see Kempes Y. Schell, "Court Cases Involving Slavery: A Study of the Application of Anti-Slavery Thought to Judicial Argument" (Ph.D. diss., University of

Michigan, 1955), p. 230; the report in the *New York Tribune* is reprinted in American and Foreign Anti-Slavery Society, *Ninth Annual Report* (New York, 1850), p. 30. For Gerrit Smith's comment, see Gerrit Smith, *Abstract of the Argument of the Fugitive Slave Law. Made by Gerrit Smith of Syracuse, June, 1852, on the Trial of Henry W. Allen, U.S. Deputy Marshall for Kidnapping* (Syracuse, N.Y., 1852), pp. 16–17. For the comment of the Massachusetts Anti-Slavery Society, see *Nineteenth Annual Report* (Boston, 1851), p. 36.

Flight to Canada

For the discussion in this section, see William Breyfogle, *Make Free* (Philadelphia, 1958), p. 209; Benjamin Quarles, *Black Abolitionists* (New York, 1969), pp. 200–201; James Oliver Horton and Lois E. Horton, *Black Bostonians: Family Life and the Community Struggle in the Antebellum North* (New York and London, 1979), p. 103; A. E. Dorn, "A History of the Anti-Slavery Movement in Rochester and Vicinity" (masters's thesis, University of Buffalo, 1932), p. 77; American and Foreign Anti-Slavery Society, *Twelfth Annual Report* (New York, 1852), pp. 31, 36; Gordon Casey, "Significance of the Fugitive Slave Law of 1850" (master's thesis, Columbia University, 1924), p. 37; George Walker, "Black Resistance to the Fugitive Slave Law of 1850, 1850–1856" (master's thesis, Columbia University, 1970), pp. 26–27, 45; *Pennsylvania Freeman,* September 26, October 3, 1850; John Weiss, *The Life and Correspondence of Theodore Parker* (New York, 1864), 2:94; Wilbur H. Siebert, "The Underground Railroad in Massachusetts," *New England Quarterly* 9 (March 1936): 457; *Cleveland True Democrat,* April 7, 1851.

Garrisonian Advice

For the view of Horace Mann, see Ernest Cassara, "Reformer as Politician: Horace Mann and the Anti-Slavery Struggle in Congress, 1848–1853," *Journal of American Studies* (Cambridge, England) (December 1971), 5:253. For Garrison's characterization of the Fugitive Slave Act, see *Liberator,* September 26, 1851. For his views on how to react to the Fugitive Slave Act, see ibid., April 5, October 4, 11, 1850. For Boston as a refuge for fugitive slaves, see Harold Swartz, "Fugitive Slave Days in Boston," *New England Quarterly* 27 (June 1954): 191; Wilbur H. Siebert, *The Underground Railroad* (New York, 1928), p. 246. For the statement of the board of managers of the Massachusetts Anti-Slavery Society, see *Liberator,* September 27, 1850, and for Wendell Phillips, see ibid., October 18, 1850.

Advice of Black Leaders

For the letter of the Negro to the *Liberator,* see issue of November 1, 1850. For the black Baptist, *see* American and Foreign Anti-Slavery Society, *Twelfth Annual Report,* p. 31. For Reverend Loguen's statement, see Herbert Aptheker, *Essays in the History of the American Negro* (New York, 1945), p. 130. For Delany, see William Loren Katz, *Eyewitness: The Negro in American History* (New York, 1967), p. 189. For the views of Samuel Ringgold Ward, see *Impartial Citizen,* reprinted in *Liberator,* September 20, October 11, 1850. For Loguen's speech to the Syracuse meeting, see Philip S. Foner, ed., *The Voice of Black America: Major Speeches by Blacks in the United States, 1797–1973* (New York, 1975), 1:119–21; Samuel J. May, *Some Recollections of our Anti-Slavery Conflict* (Boston, 1869), p. 357; Walker, op. cit., pp. 41–42. For Douglass' observation on his refusal to leave the country, see *Frederick Douglass' Paper,* November 27, 1851.

For Douglass' views on physical resistance to the Fugitive Slave Act of 1850, see Leslie F. Goldstein, "Violence as an Instrument for Social Change: The Views of Frederick Douglass, 1819–1895," *Journal of Negro History* 41 (January 1976): 68–69; *National Anti-Slavery Standard*, November 28, 1850; *North Star*, October 24, 1850, January 16, August 21, September 24, 1851; *Frederick Douglass' Paper*, August 29, 1852; Philip S. Foner, *Life and Writings of Frederick Douglass* (New York, 1950), 2:206–8, 284–89, 462, 487–88, 537; *Liberator*, October 18, 1850; Massachusetts Anti-Slavery Society, *Nineteenth Annual Report*, p. 43.

Black Protest Meetings

For copy of an early handbill, see *Frederick Douglass' Paper*, October 23, 1851. For the meetings in Boston, see Massachusetts Anti-Slavery Society, *Nineteenth Annual Report*, p. 41; Horton and Horton, op. cit., p. 103; William C. Nell, *The Colored Patriots of the American Revolution* (Boston, 1855), pp. 392–93; Donald M. Jacobs, "A History of the Boston Negro from Revolution to Civil War" (Ph.D. diss., Boston University, 1968), pp. 271–73; *Liberator*, October 4, 11, 1850; "Declaration of Sentiments of the Colored Citizens of Boston, on the Fugitive Slave Bill!!!!" handbill containing proceedings of the Belknap Street Church meeting of October 5, 1850, and "Address to the Clergy of Massachusetts," copy in Library of Congress, Rare Book Room, and reproduced in Horton and Horton, op. cit., following p. 80. For the "Abolition Riot," see Leonard W. Levy, "The Abolition Riot: Boston's First Slave Rescue," *New England Quarterly* 25 (1952): 85–92.

For the New York meeting, see Philip S. Foner, *Essays in Afro-American History* (Philadelphia, 1978), pp. 95–96; *National Anti-Slavery Standard*, October 10, 1850; *North Star*, October 24, 1850; *Liberator*, October 4, 1850; American and Foreign Anti-Slavery Society, *Twelfth Annual Report* (New York, 1852), p. 30. For the Cleveland meeting, see E. D. Preston, "The Fugitive Slave Acts in Ohio," *Journal of Negro History* 18 (October 1943): 471–72; for the Philadelphia events, see *Pennsylvania Freeman*, October 14, 31, 1850; *Philadelphia Evening Bulletin*, November 5, 7, 1850. For the Anti-Fugitive Slave Convention in Syracuse, see *North Star*, January 23, 1851, and *Voice of the Fugitive*, February 26, 1851; for the Ohio State Convention, see Philip S. Foner and George Walker, eds., *Proceedings of the Black State Conventions, 1840–1865* (Philadelphia, 1979), 1:259–60, 267; for the New York State convention, see ibid., pp. 54, 72–73.

Arming for Self-Defense

For the *Anti-Slavery Bugle* statement, see issue of October 12, 1850. On the dispatches from Springfield and western Massachusetts, see *Liberator*, October 4, 11, 1850. For Pittsburgh, see Irene E. Williams, "The Operation of the Fugitive Slave Law in Western Pennsylvania from 1850–1860," *Western Pennsylvania Historical Magazine* 4 (July 1921): 157. For Pillsbury, see Parker Pillsbury to Oliver Johnson, October 6, 1850, *Anti-Slavery Bugle*, October 12, 1850.

On the Gap Gang, see Franklin Ellis and Samuel Evans, *History of Lancaster County, Pennsylvania* (Philadelphia, 1883), p. 71; Hugh R. Filton, "Lancaster County in the War for Union," in John Klein, ed., *Lancaster County, Pennsylvania: A History* (New York, 1924), p. 602. On Parker's recollections, see William Parker, "The Freedman's Story," *Atlantic Monthly* 17 (February 1866): 157–62; Jonathan Katz, *Resistance at Christiana: The Fugitive Slave Rebellion, Christiana, Pennsylvania: A Documentary Account* (New

York, 1974), pp. 22–34. For the 1833 Detroit resistance, see David M. Katzman, *Black Detroit in the Nineteenth Century* (Urbana, Ill., 1973), pp. 8–12. For the case of John Read, see Philip S. Foner, *History of Black Americans: From Africa to the Emergence of the Cotton Kingdom* (Westport, Conn., 1975), pp. 505–7; Philip S. Foner, "The Two Trials of John Read: A Fugitive Slave Who Resisted Reenslavement," in *Essays in Afro-American History* (Philadelphia, 1978), pp. 6–18. For the view that blacks would return to passivity despite meetings and resolutions, see *United States Magazine and Democratic Review* 28 (April 1851): 352–59.

For the views of Ralph Waldo Emerson, Samuel P. Chase, and Joshua R. Giddings, see *National Era,* December 26, 1850; Eric Foner, *Free Soil, Free Labor, Free Men: The Ideology of the Republican Party before the Civil War* (New York, 1970), p. 134. For Casey's comment, see Casey, op. cit., p. 4.

3. BLACK RESISTANCE TO THE FUGITIVE SLAVE ACT OF 1850: EARLY PHASE

Purchase of James Hamlet

For the incident in Philadelphia, see *Anti-Slavery Bugle,* November 2, 1850; *Philadelphia Evening Bulletin,* October 29, 1850; George Walker, "The Afro-American in New York City, 1827–1860" (Ph.D. diss., Columbia University, 1972), pp. 52–53. The discussion of the case of James Hamlet is based on the following sources: Henry Wilson, *History of the Rise and Fall of the Slave Power in America* (Boston, 1874), 2:304–5; William Harned, *The Fugitive Slave Bill . . . with an Account of the Seizure and Enslavement of James Hamlet and His Subsequent Restoration to Liberty* (New York, 1850); "The Fugitive Slave Law and Its Victims," *Anti-Slavery Tracts,* no. 18, p. 7; *Liberator,* October 11, 18, 1850; *North Star,* October 3, 1850; *National Anti-Slavery Standard,* October 17, 1850; American and Foreign Anti-Slavery Society, *Eleventh Annual Report* (New York, 1851), pp. 23–24; Philip S. Foner, *Business and Slavery* (Chapel Hill, N.C., 1940), pp. 35–36; Benjamin Quarles, *Black Abolitionists* (New York, 1969), p. 198; *New York Journal of Commerce,* October 1, 6, 8, 9, 1850; Walker, op. cit., pp. 48–52; Philip S. Foner, *Essays in Afro-American History* (Philadelphia, 1978), pp. 94–97.

Return of Henry Long to Slavery

The discussion in this section is based on the following sources: Foner, *Business and Slavery,* pp. 60–61; letter of W. W. Parker to *Richmond Enquirer* reprinted in *New York Journal of Commerce,* January 16, 1851; Philip S. Foner, *Life and Writings of Frederick Douglass* (New York, 1975), 5:170–71; *North Star,* January 16, 1851.

Defense of William and Ellen Craft

The discussion in this section is based on the following sources: William Craft, *Running a Thousand Miles to Freedom . . .* (London, 1860), pp. 319–20; Archibald H. Grimké, "Anti-Slavery Boston," *New England Magazine,* n.s., 3 (December 1980): 458; *Liberator,* December 6, 1850; Henry Steele Commager, *Theodore Parker* (Boston, 1954), pp. 214–16; William Still, *The Underground Railroad* (Philadelphia, 1872), pp. 368–77; James Oliver Horton and Lois Horton, *Black Bostonians* (New York, 1979), pp. 103–4; Donald M. Jacobs, "A History of the Boston Negro from Revolution to Civil

War'' (Ph.D. diss., Boston University, 1968), pp. 273–74; Larry Gara, ''The Real Story of the Underground Railroad,'' *Civil War Times* 3 (August 1964): 44; Stanley J. Robboy and Anita W. Robboy, ''Lewis Hayden: From Fugitive Slave to Statesman,'' *New England Quarterly* 46 (December 1973): 600–601.

Rescue of Shadrach

The discussion in this section is based on the following sources: *Liberator,* February 11, May 30, 1851; *Boston Courier,* February 17, 1851; *Report of the Case of the United States vs. Charles G. Davis* (Boston, 1850); *National Era,* February 20, 1851; Horton and Horton, op. cit., pp. 104–5; Jacobs, op. cit., pp. 274–79; Walker, op. cit., pp. 54–57; Massachusetts Anti-Slavery Society, *Twentieth Annual Report* (Boston, 1852), p. 11, *National Intelligencer,* March 1, 4, 29, April 24, May 29, June 7, 21, November 13, 1851, June 12, 1852; James D. Richardson, ed., *A Compilation of the Messages and Papers of the Presidents, 1789–1897* (Washington, D.C., 1899), 5:101; Wilson, op. cit., 2:330.

Failure of the Sims Rescue

The discussion in this section is based on the following sources: *Trial of Thomas Sims, an Issue of Personal Liberty, on the Claim of James Potter of Georgia, against Him, as an Alleged Fugitive from Service, Arguments of Robert Rantoul, Jr., and Charles G. Loring, with a Decision of George T. Curtis* (Boston, 1851), pp. 31–32; Leonard W. Levy, ''Sims Case: The Fugitive Slave Law in Boston in 1851,'' *Journal of Negro History* 35 (January 1950): 40–45; *Liberator,* April 18, 1851; Massachusetts Anti-Slavery Society, *Twentieth Annual Report,* p. 22; Anonymous, ''Boston and the Fugitive Slave Law,'' *Business Historical Society Bulletin* 4 (May 1930): 4–5; Wilson, op. cit., 2:334–35; *North Star,* April 14, 1851; *National Anti-Slavery Standard,* April 17, May 15, 1851; *National Era,* April 10, 1851; Walker, op. cit., pp. 57–61; *Boston Commonwealth,* April 25, 26, 28, 1851; *Boston Courier* reprinted in *Liberator,* April 11, 1851; *Boston Courier,* April 12, 1851; Jacobs, op. cit., pp. 281–85; *Liberator,* May 15, 1863; Ethel Kime Ware, ''Lydia Maria Child and Anti-Slavery,'' *Boston Public Library Quarterly* 4 (January 1952): 39–40; Horton and Horton, op. cit., pp. 105–7, 114; Lawrence Lader, *The Bold Brahmins* (New York, 1961), pp. 178–80. For Parker's comment, see Theodore Parker, *The Slave Power* (Boston, 1917), p. 382.

The Jerry Rescue

The discussion in this section is based on the following sources: *Liberator,* October 10, 1851; Horace McQuire, ''Two Episodes of Anti-Slavery Days,'' *Publications of the Rochester Historical Society* 4 (1925): 213–22; Earl Evelyn Sperry, *The Jerry Rescue October 1, 1851 . . . Delivered before the Onondaga Historical Association, October, 1921 . . . Additional Jerry Rescue Documents and Rescue of Harriet Powell in Syracuse, 1839,* comp. and ed. Franklin H. Chase (Syracuse, N.Y., 1924), pp. 20–34; Ralph Volney Harlow, *Gerrit Smith, Philanthropist and Reformer* (New York, 1939), pp. 296–99; *National Anti-Slavery Standard,* October 29, 1853; *Frederick Douglass' Paper,* January 29, February 5, April 8, 1852, June 17, 1853; George Walker, ''The Afro-American in New York City, 1827–1860'' (Ph.D. diss., Columbia University, 1972), pp. 75–78; Carleton Mabee, *Black Freedom: The Nonviolent Abolitionists from 1830 through the Civil War* (New York, 1970), pp. 307–8. For Samuel J. May's views on the Fugitive Slave Act of 1850 and his regret at not being among those indicted in the rescue trial, see

Samuel J. May to William Lloyd Garrison, November 23, 1851, Garrison Papers, Boston Public Library, Rare Book Room; Samuel J. May to William H. Seward, September 7, 1853, William H. Seward Papers, University of Rochester Library; *Liberator,* October 25, 1850; Jane H. Pease and William H. Pease, "Confrontation and Abolition in the 1850's," *Journal of American History* 58 (March 1972): 927–29.

4. BLACK RESISTANCE TO THE FUGITIVE SLAVE ACT OF 1850: "FREEDOM'S BATTLE" AT CHRISTIANA, PENNSYLVANIA

The discussion in this chapter is based on the following sources: David R. Forbes, *A True Story of the Christiana Riot* (Quarryville, Pa., 1898); W. U. Hensel, *The Christiana Riot and the Treason Trials of 1851: An Historical Sketch,* 2d and rev. ed. (Lancaster, Pa., 1911); Jonathan Katz, *Resistance at Christiana: The Fugitive Slave Rebellion, Christiana, Pennsylvania, September 11, 1851: A Documentary Account* (New York, 1974); Albert W. Hostetter, "The Newspapers and the Christiana Riot," *Lancaster County Historical Society Papers,* December 1, 1911, pp. 296–308; [W. A. Jackson], *History of the Trial of Castner Hanway and Others for Treason* (Philadelphia, 1852); Roderick W. Nash, "The Christiana Riot: An Evaluation of Its National Significance," *Journal of the Lancaster County Historical Society* 6 (Spring 1961): 65–91; Roderick W. Nash, "The House Divided: A Study of Contemporary Editorial Reaction to the Christiana Riot of 1851" (honor's thesis, Harvard College, 1960); Roderick W. Nash, "William Parker and the Christiana Riot," *Journal of Negro History* 46 (January 1961): 23–35; William Parker, "The Freedman's Story," *Atlantic Monthly* 17 (February–March 1866): 152–66, 276–95; James R. Robbins, *Report of the Trial of Castner Hanway for Treason* (Philadelphia, 1852); Wilbur H. Siebert, *The Underground Railroad from Slavery to Freedom* (New York, 1899); Robert C. Smedley, *History of the Underground Railroad in Chester and the Neighboring Counties of Pennsylvania* (Lancaster, Pa., 1883); Thomas Whitson, "The Hero of the Christiana Riot," *Lancaster County Historical Society Papers* 1 (1896): 122–38; Richard Gray, "The Christiana Riot of 1851: A Reappraisal," *Journal of the Lancaster County Historical Society* 6 (1944): 172–85.

Background

The discussion in this section is based on the following sources: M. D. Maclean, "The First Bloodshed in the Civil War," *Crisis* (October 1911): 247–49; Katz, op. cit., pp. 6–40; *Lancaster Examiner and Express,* October 27, 1811, clipping in West Chester Historical Society, West Chester, Pennsylvania; Pennsylvania Anti-Slavery Society, *Fourteenth Annual Report* (Philadelphia, 1851), p. 33; *Pennsylvania Freeman,* March 27, June 18, 1851; James Miller McKim to William Lloyd Garrison, April 1851, Garrison-McKim Collection, New York Public Library, Manuscripts Division; George Walker, "The Afro-American in New York City, 1827–1860" (Ph.D. diss., Columbia University, 1972), pp. 61–63; Forbes, op. cit., pp. 7–9; Robbins, op. cit., pp. 114–18, 147, 162; *Lancaster Examiner and Herald,* September 17, 1851; Forbes, op. cit., pp. 7–9, 24; Parker, op. cit., pp. 283–86; Smedley, op. cit., pp. 102, 107, 147.

"Freedom's Battle"

The discussion in this section is based on the following sources: Still, op. cit., p. 350; Robbins, op. cit., pp. 41, 56, 58, 59, 74, 81, 83, 84, 96–99, 100, 102, 103, 120; Parker, op. cit., pp. 284–85; Forbes, op. cit., p. 25; Katz, op. cit., pp. 81–103; Joseph S. Gorsuch, "The History of the Christiana Riot," *Baltimore Daily Sun*, September 18, 1851, original ms. in Lancaster County Historical Society, Lancaster, Pa.

Flight to Canada

The discussion in this section is based on the following sources: Benjamin Quarles, *Black Abolitionists* (New York, 1969), pp. 61–62; Katz, op. cit., pp. 247–66; *Voice of the Fugitive*, April 3, 1852; Philip S. Foner, *Frederick Douglass* (New York, 1964), pp. 132–33, 398; Amy Hamner Croughton, "Anti-Slavery Days in Rochester," *Publications of the Rochester Historical Society* 15 (1936): 133–34; Parker, op. cit., pp. 290–91.

Reaction

The discussion in this section is based on the following sources: Nash, "The House Divided," pp. 12–16, 23–30; Nash, "The Christiana Riot," pp. 66–72; Hostetter, op. cit., pp. 296–99; Katz, op. cit., pp. 136–55; *Philadelphia Public Ledger*, September 13, 22, 1851; *Liberator*, September 26, 29, 1851, February 13, 1852; *New York Tribune*, September 13, 1851; *Philadelphia North American*, September 13, 1851; *Philadelphia Evening Bulletin*, September 14, 1851; *Philadelphia Pennsylvanian*, September 16, 1851; *Frederick Douglass' Paper*, September 25, October 16, November 13, 1851, January 8, 29, 1852; Phillip S. Foner, *The Life and Writings of Frederick Douglass* (New York, 1975), 5:204–8; *National Anti-Slavery Standard*, September 25, 1851, February 12, 1852; *Lancaster Sunday Evening Express*, September 29, 1851; Charles L. Remond in *Liberator*, February 4, March 12, 1851; Theodore Parker in ibid., November 1, 1851; "The Fugitive Slave Law and Its Victims," *Anti-Slavery Tracts*, no. 11, p. 21; *Voice of the Fugitive*, December 3, 1851, January 15, February 12, 1852; William and Ellen Craft to *Liberator*, reprinted in Carter G. Woodson, ed., *The Mind of the Negro as Reflected in Letters Written during the Crisis* (Washington, D.C., 1926), p. 263.

Treason

The discussion in this section is based on the following sources: Katz, op. cit., pp. 156–76; *Voice of the Fugitive*, January 15, 1852; Hensel, op. cit., pp. 39–40; Still, op. cit., pp. 357, 362; Robbins, op. cit., pp. 268–72; *Frederick Douglass' Paper*, September 25, 1851; Gray, op. cit., pp. 172–73.

The Trial

The discussion in this section is based on the following sources: Thomas Frederick Woodley, *Thaddeus Stevens* (Harrisburg, Pa., 1934), pp. 140–42; Katz, op. cit., pp. 177–243; Robbins, op. cit., pp. 18, 24–49, 109–11; *Philadelphia Evening Bulletin*, September 12–15, November 24, 1851; *Frederick Douglass' Paper*, September 25, October 2, 1851; *National Anti-Slavery Standard*, December 4, 11, 18, 25, 1851; William Still in *Voice of the Fugitive*, January 1, 1852; John William Wallace, Jr., *Cases in the Circuit Court of the United States for the Third Circuit* (Philadelphia, 1854), 2:134–40; Robert James Brent, *Report to His Excellency Governor E. L. Louis Lowe in Relation to the Christiana Trials* (Annapolis, Md., 1852); Helen T. Catterall, ed., *Judicial Cases Concerning American Slavery and the Negro* (Washington, D.C., 1936), 4: 310; *United States* v. *Williams*, 28 Fed. Cases 631 (1852).

Aftermath

The discussion in this section is based on the following sources: William Still in *Voice of the Fugitive*, January 1, 1852; Katz, op. cit., p. 144; Quarles, op. cit., pp. 211–12; Allan Nevins, *Ordeal of the Union* (New York, 1957), 1:349–50; *Papers Read before the Lancaster County Historical Society*, June 30, 1911, special supplementary number 15 (1911): 206.

5.   BLACK RESISTANCE TO THE FUGITIVE SLAVE ACT
OF 1850: THE MIDDLE PHASE

Conflicting Advice

The discussion in this section is based on the following sources: *Frederick Douglass' Paper*, April 13, 20, 27, 1852; Samuel Ringgold Ward, *Autobiography of a Fugitive Negro* (Toronto, 1855), pp. 16–17.

New Rescues

For the rescue in Sandusky, Ohio, see *Cleveland Daily Herald*, October 22–24, 1852; Stanley V. Campbell, *The Slave Catchers: Enforcement of the Fugitive Slave Law, 1850–1860* (New York, 1968), pp. 137–38; *Liberator*, November 5, 1852; Keith David Churchman, "The Social and Economic Status of the Negro in Ohio in 1860" (master's thesis, Miami University, 1929), pp. 110–11; Richard Albert Folk, "Black Man's Burden in Ohio, 1849–1863" (Ph.D. diss., University of Toledo, 1972), pp. 317–18. For the self-rescue of Lewis, see Folk, op. cit., pp. 319–22; *Cincinnati Daily Gazette,* October 11–13, 1853. For the self-rescue of William Thomas, see *New York Tribune*, September 24, 1853; *Liberator*, September 28, 1853; *National Anti-Slavery Standard*, October 22, 1853.

Rendition of Anthony Burns

The only recent book devoted to the Anthony Burns case is Jane H. Pease and William H. Pease, *The Fugitive Slave Law and Anthony Burns: A Problem in Law Enforcement* (New York, 1975), which has a detailed discussion and pertinent documents but is weak on the role of blacks in the whole struggle to prevent Burns' rendition. The discussion in this section is also based on the following sources: Anthony Burns Case Collection, compiled by Thomas Wentworth Higginson, Boston Public Library, Rare Book Division; Tilden G. Edelstein, *Strange Enthusiasm: A Life of Thomas Wentworth Higginson* (New York, 1970), pp. 155–61; "The Fugitive Slave Law, and Its Victims," *Anti-Slavery Tract*, no. 18, pp. 25–27; *National Anti-Slavery Standard*, June 3, 1854; "Trial of Anthony Burns," *Massachusetts Historical Society Papers* 44 (January 1911): 322–25; *Liberator*, August 29, 1854; Samuel Shapiro, "The Rendition of Anthony Burns," *Journal of Negro History* 44 (January 1959): 34–50; George Walker, "The Afro-American in New York City, 1827–1860" (Ph.D. diss., Columbia University, 1972), pp. 81–82; Jane H. Pease and William H. Pease, "Confrontation and Abolition in the 1850's," *Journal of American History* 58 (March 1972): 927–29; Herbert Aptheker, ed., *Documentary History of the Negro People in the United States* (New York, 1951), p. 368; *The Boston Slave Riot and Trial of Anthony Burns* (Boston, 1854); *Liberator*, October 23, 1850, February 23, March 9, May 24, 1855, June 26, October 30, 1857, March 26,

August 13, 1858, October 7, 1859; Reverend Hiram Wilson to Reverend Leonard A. Grimes, July 28, 1862, in *Liberator,* August 22, 1862; Donald M. Jacobs, "A History of the Boston Negro from Revolution to Civil War" (Ph.D. diss., Boston University, 1968), pp. 286–91; Larry Gara, "The Fugitive Slave Law: A Double Paradox," *Civil War History* 10 (September 1954): 240–41; David R. Maggines, "The Case of the Court House Rioters in the Rendition of the Fugitive Slave Anthony Burns, 1854," *Journal of Negro History* 56 (January 1970): 31–42; Stanley J. Robboy and Anita W. Robboy, "Lewis Hayden: From Fugitive Slave to Statesman," *New England Quarterly* 46 (December 1973): 605–7; Charles E. Stevens, *Anthony Burns: A History* (Boston, 1876), pp. 56, 72–75, 270–71; Charles F. Adams, Jr., *Richard Henry Dana* (Cambridge, Mass., 1890), 1:271–73, 301; Harold Schwartz, "Fugitive Slave Days in Boston," *New England Quarterly* 27 (June 1954): 191–212; Lawrence Leder, *The Bold Brahmins: New England's War against Slavery, 1831–1863* (New York, 1961), chap. 5; *Boston Journal,* May 27, 1854; *Boston Globe,* June 1, 1854; Thomas W. Higginson, *Cheerful Yesterdays* (Cambridge, Mass., 1898), chap. 2; *Boston Slave Riot and Trial of Anthony Burns* (Boston, 1854), pp. 10–13; Ann Phillips to Anne and Deborah Wilson, May 22, 1854, Weston Family Papers, Anti-Slavery Collection, Boston Public Library; Pease and Pease, "Confrontation and Abolition," op. cit., p. 927.

Repercussions

Herbert Aptheker, *The Negro in the Abolitionist Movement* (New York, 1941), p. 22; *Liberator,* August 13, 1858; *Frederick Douglass' Paper,* June 2, 9, 1854; Donald M. Jacobs, "A History of the Boston Negro from Revolution to Civil War" (Ph.D. diss., Boston University, 1968), pp. 290–94; *Boston Evening Globe,* evening edition, April 8, 11, 1889; William C. Nell, *Colored Patriots of the American Revolution* (Boston, 1855), pp. 372–73.

Other Rescues and a Court Decision

See *Anti-Slavery Tract,* no. 19, pp. 23–24; John C. Hurd, *The Law of Freedom and Bondage in the United States* (Boston, 1858), 2:773; *Acts and Resolves Passed by the General Court of Massachusetts, in the Year 1855* (Boston, 1855), p. 924; "The Removal of Judge Loring," *Monthly Law Reporter* 7 (new series, 1856): 8–10; *Milwaukee Free Democrat* in *New York Tribune,* February 22, 1855; Alex Johnson, "The Constitutionality of the Fugitive Slave Acts," *Yale Law Journal* 31 (December 1921): 161–82; *Abelman* v. *Booth* 21 Howard 506 (1859); Julius Yanuck, "The Fugitive Slave Law and the Constitution" (Ph.D. diss., Columbia University, 1953), pp. 86–89; Vroman Mason, "The Fugitive Slave Law in Wisconsin, with Reference to Nullification Sentiment," *Proceedings of the State Historical Society of Wisconsin* 43 (1895): 122–40; Richard Albert Folk, "Black Man's Burden in Ohio, 1849–1863" (Ph.D. diss., University of Toledo, 1972), pp. 282–86.

The Philadelphia Rescue

The discussion in this section is based on the following sources: *Christian Recorder,* August 1, 1854; *Frederick Douglass' Paper,* June 23, 1854, September 7, 1855; *Anti-Slavery Bugle,* September 15, 1852; Ralph Lowell Eckert, "Anti-Slavery Martyrdom: The Ordeal of Passmore Williamson," *Pennsylvania Magazine of History and Biography* 90 (October 1976): 522–38; *Narrative of the Facts in the Trial of Passmore Williamson* (Philadelphia, 1855); *Case of Passmore Williamson, Report on the Proceedings on the*

Writ of Habeas Corpus (Philadelphia, 1856); William Still, *The Underground Railroad* (Philadelphia, 1872), pp. 90–96, 610–12.

A Partial Rescue

The discussion in this section is based on the following sources: *Ex Parte Robinson,* 20 Federal Cases 969 (1855); "The Fugitive Slave Law, and Its Victims," *Anti-Slavery Tract,* no. 18, p. 32; Folk, op. cit., pp. 326–29; Levi Coffin, *Reminiscences of Levi Coffin* (Cincinnati, 1876), pp. 554–55; Campbell, op. cit., pp. 141–42; *Cleveland Daily Herald,* March 26, 30, 31, 1855; *Cincinnati Daily Gazette,* March 31, 1855; *Liberator,* April 27, 1855.

6. BLACK RESISTANCE TO THE FUGITIVE SLAVE ACT OF 1850: THE LAST PHASE

The Tragedy of Margaret Garner

The discussion in this section is based on the following sources: *Liberator,* February 8, 22, 29, March 7, 1856; Levi Coffin, *Reminiscences* . . . (Cincinnati, 1876), pp. 557–60; Stanley V. Campbell, *The Slave Catchers* (New York, 1968), pp. 144–47; *National Anti-Slavery Standard,* March 15, April 26, 1856; "Fugitive Slave Law and Its Victims," *Anti-Slavery Tract,* no. 18, pp. 41–45; Richard Folk, "Black Man's Burden in Ohio, 1849–1863" (Ph.D. diss., University of Toledo, 1972), pp. 329–30; Julius Yanick, "The Garner Fugitive Slave Case," *Mississippi Valley Historical Review* 40 (January 1953): 47–66; Marion Gleason McDougall, *Fugitive Slaves, 1819–1865* (Boston, 1891), pp. 47–49; *American Anti-Slavery Society, Twenty-third Annual Report* (New York, 1856), pp. 45–47; *New York Times,* February 2, 4, 7, 8, 16, 1856; J. Winston Coleman, Jr., *Slavery Times in Kentucky* (Chapel Hill, N.C., 1940), p. 208; *Cincinnati Daily Gazette,* January 29–February 2, 18, 28, March 12–19, 1856.

The Archy Lee Rescue

The discussion in this section is based on the following sources: Rudolph M. Lapp, "Negro Rights Activities in Gold Rush California," *California Historical Society Quarterly* 45 (March 1966): 8–13; Crawford Killian, *Go Do Some Great Thing: The Black Pioneers of British Columbia* (Vancouver, 1978), pp. 19–24, 34, 36, 40, 46, 48, 81, 137; *San Francisco Evening Bulletin,* January 10–February 14, April 20–May 5, 1858; *Ex parte Archy,* 9 1858, Cal. 147; Lucille Eaves, *A History California Labor Legislation* (Berkeley, Calif., 1936), pp. 99–103.

The Oberlin-Wellington Rescue

The discussion in this section is based on the following sources: John Mercer Langston, "The Oberlin-Wellington Rescue," *Anglo-African,* July 23, 1859, pp. 209–16; Linda Rose McCabe, "The Oberlin-Wellington Rescue: An Anti-Slavery Crisis Which Almost Precipitated the Civil War in 1857 Through the Secession of the North," *Godey's Magazine* (October 1896): 361–65; Wilbur H. Siebert, *The Underground Railroad from Slavery to Freedom* (New York, 1899), pp. 335–37; William C. Cochran, "The Western Reserve and the Fugitive Slave Law: A Prelude to Civil War," *Western Reserve Historical Society Publications* 10 (January 1920): 118–204; "The Oberlin-Wellington Rescue,

1856," *Midwest Journal* 7 (Spring 1955): 80–93; *Liberator,* December 17, 1858, April 29, May 6, 1859; *Oberlin Evangelist,* September 29, 1858, May 25, 1859; Campbell, op. cit., pp. 164–69; *Cleveland Daily Herald,* April 5–25, May 2–12, December 7, 17, 1859; Folk, op. cit., pp. 334–41; John M. Langston, *From the Virginia Plantation to the National Capital* (Hartford, Conn., 1894), pp. 185–86; Karl F. Geiser, "The Western Reserve in the Anti-Slavery Movement, 1840–1860," Mississippi Valley Association, *Proceedings* 5 (1911–1912): 96–97; *Douglass' Monthly* (May, June, August 1859); *Should Colored Men Be Subject to the Pains and Penalties of the Fugitive Slave Law? Speech of C. H. Langston before the District Court for the Northern District of Ohio, May 12, 1859* (Cleveland, 1859); Philip S. Foner, *The Voice of Black America: Major Speeches of Blacks in the United States, 1797–1973* (New York, 1975), 1:230–37.

The Last Crisis

The discussion in this section is based on the following sources: Richard Albert Folk, op. cit., pp. 351–55; *Liberator,* March 8, 1861; *Cleveland Daily Herald,* January 19, 1861; Alan Peskin, ed., *North into Freedom: The Autobiography of John Malvin, free Negro, 1795–1880* (Cleveland, 1966), pp. 22–25, 79–82.

The Fruits of Resistance

The discussion in this section is based on the following sources: Campbell, op. cit., pp. 49, 81, 88–89, 111–16, 168; *Liberator,* March 19, 1852, November 18, 1853; *Frederick Douglass' Paper,* April 29, 1852; David Potter, *The Impending Crisis, 1848–1861,* completed and edited by Don E. Fehrenbacher (New York, 1976), p. 138; Joel Parker, *Personal Liberty Laws and Slavery in the Territories* (Boston, 1861), pp. 28–29; *New York Tribune,* September 17, 1851; Amy Hammer Croughton, "Anti-Slavery Days in Rochester," *Publications of the Rochester Historical Society* 15 (1936): 133; Samuel J. May, *Some Recollections of Our Antislavery Conflict* (Boston, 1869), pp. 353; James Oliver Horton and Lois E. Horton, *Black Bostonians* (New York, 1979), pp. 112–22; George Walker, "The Afro-American in New York City, 1827–1860" (Ph.D. diss., Columbia University, 1972), pp. 85–91; Philip S. Foner, *Life and Writings of Frederick Douglass* (New York, 1950), 2:232–34; Jane H. Pease and William H. Pease, "Confrontation and Abolition in the 1850's," *Journal of American History* 58 (March 1972): 930–34; Thomas D. Morris, *Free Men All: The Personal Liberty Laws of the North, 1780–1861* (Baltimore and London, 1972), pp. 153–79.

7.   BLACKS AND *UNCLE TOM'S CABIN*

The Writing of Uncle Tom's Cabin

The discussion in this section is based on the following sources: Annie Fields, *Life and Letters of Harriet Beecher Stowe* (Boston and New York, 1898); Charles Edward Stowe, *Life of Harriet Beecher Stowe, Compiled from Her Letters and Journals* (Boston and New York, 1889); Edward Wagenknecht, *Harriet Beecher Stowe: The Known and the Unknown* (New York, 1965); Forrest Wilson, *Crusader in Crinoline: The Life of Harriet Beecher Stowe* (Philadelphia, 1941); Charles Dudley Warner, "The Story of *Uncle Tom's Cabin,*" *Atlantic Monthly* 78 (September 1896): 311–18; Samuel Sillen, "Mrs. Stowe's Best-Seller," *Masses and Mainstream* (February 1952): 20–29; Ellen Moers, *The Great*

Writers (New York, 1976), pp. 3–4; Alice C. Crozier, *The Novels of Harriet Beecher Stowe* (New York, 1969).

The Miracle of Uncle Tom's Cabin

In addition to the sources just cited, this section is based on: Donald E. Liedel, "The Antislavery Publishing Revolution in the 1850's," *Library Journal* 2 (1972): 67–80.

Reaction to Uncle Tom's Cabin

In addition to the sources cited above, this section is based on: Theodore Tilton, "Out of Jail: The Black Man Who Was Imprisoned for Reading *Uncle Tom's Cabin*," *Liberator*, July 4, 1862. All quotations from Mrs. Stowe's work in this and the following sections are from *Uncle Tom's Cabin, or, Life Among the Lowly*, 2 vols. (Boston, 1852); *Dred, A Tale of the Great Dismal Swamp* (Boston and New York, 1856); *A Key to Uncle Tom's Cabin* (Boston, 1853).

Harriet Beecher Stowe and Frederick Douglass

For Harriet Beecher Stowe and Frederick Douglass see Philip S. Foner, *Frederick Douglass* (New York, 1964), pp. 90, 120–25, 150–52, 180–82. For the view, a mistaken one in my judgment, that by invoking Stowe's financial assistance for the black college project, Douglass followed a course later developed to its full extent by Booker T. Washington, see Vincent Harding, *There Is a River: The Black Struggle for Freedom in America* (New York, 1981).

Harriet Beecher Stowe and Slavery and "Uncle Tom"

In addition to the sources cited above, the discussion in this section is based on the following sources: Donald K. Pickens, "Uncle Tom Becomes Nat Turner: A Commentary on Two American Heroes," *Negro American Literature Forum* 3 (Spring 1969): 46–47; Severn Duvall, *"Uncle Tom's Cabin:* The Sinister Side of the Patriarchy," *New England Quarterly* 36 (March 1963): 3–22; Theodore R. Hovet, "Christian Revolution: Harriet Beecher Stowe's Responses to Slavery and the Civil War," *New England Quarterly* 47 (December 1974): 530–48; Elizabeth Ammons, "Heroines in *Uncle Tom's Cabin*," *American Literature* 49 (May 1977): 161–79; Ellen Moers, "Mrs. Stowe's Vengeance," *New York Review of Books*, September 3, 1970, pp. 5–6; Thomas P. Ruggio, "Uncle Tom Reconstructed: A Neglected Chapter in the History of a Book," *American Quarterly* 28 (Spring 1976): 64–79.

George Harris and The Colonization Controversy

In addition to sources cited above, this section is based on the following sources: Randall M. Miller, "Mrs. Stowe's Negro: George Harris' Negritude in *Uncle Tom's Cabin*," *Colby Library Quarterly* (December 1974): 521–26; George T. Downing to Frederick Douglass, December 6, 1854, in *Frederick Douglass' Paper*, December 22, 1854; American and Foreign Anti-Slavery Society, *Thirteenth Annual Report* (New York, 1853), pp. 192–93; Lyman B. Stowe, *Saints, Sinners and Beechers* (New York, 1934), pp. 188–90; Thomas Graham, "Harriet Beecher Stowe and the Question of Race," *New England Quarterly* 46 (December 1973): 614–22.

Recent Estimates of Uncle Tom's Cabin

The discussion in this section is based on the following sources: James Baldwin, "Everybody's Protest Novel," *Partisan Review* 16 (June 1949): 580–88; J. C. Furnas,

Goodbye to Uncle Tom (New York, 1956); Wagenknecht, op. cit.; Alex Haley, "In 'Uncle Tom' Are Our Guilt and Hope," *New York Times Sunday Magazine*, March 1, 1964, pp. 23–24; Ernest Kaiser, "J. C. Furnas, Mrs. Stowe and American Racism," *Freedomways* (Spring 1961): 33–34; Edmund Wilson, *Patriotic Gore: Studies in the Literature of the American Civil War* (New York, 1962), pp. 3–58; Sterling Brown, *The Negro in American Fiction* (Washington, D.C., 1938), p. 122.

Few historians doubt the influence of *Uncle Tom's Cabin*, but one who does is Lee Benson. See his "Causation and the American Civil War," *History and Theory* 1 (1967): 174.

8.   BLACK EMIGRATION, 1850–1861 I: ISSUES AND PERSONALITIES

Liberia and Its Meaning

For the view of colonization as a scheme of the American Colonization Society, see Howard H. Bell, preface to Martin R. Delany and Robert Campbell, *Search for a Place: Black Separatism and Africa, 1860* (Ann Arbor, Mich., 1969), pp. 4–5. The quotations from the *African Repository* are from volumes 4:110–19, 5:276, 328. For the letter of N. D. Artist, see Carter G. Woodson, ed., *The Mind of the Negro As Seen in His Letters* (Washington, D.C., 1922), p. 103. For Douglass' comments, see *Life and Times of Frederick Douglass* (Hartford, Conn., 1881), pp. 325, 335; *Liberator,* September 3, 1850. For Lewis Woodson, see *Colored American*, May 3, September 28, 1838; Floyd J. Miller, "The Father of Black Nationalism," *Civil War History* 17 (December 1971): 310–19. For black praise of Liberia, see *African Repository* 25 (January 1849): 22, ibid. 28 (February 1852): 49.

Henry Highland Garnet: Champion of Liberian Emigration

For Garnet's opposition to emigration before 1849, see Henry Highland Garnet, *The Past and Present Condition and the Destiny of the Colored Race* (Troy, N.Y., 1848), p. 8; Richard K. McMaster, "Henry Highland Garnet and the African Civilization Society," *Journal of Presbyterian History* 48 (Summer 1970): 99. For Garnet's support of Liberia, see *North Star*, March 2, 1849; Earl Ofari, *Let Your Motto Be Resistance: The Life and Thought of Henry Highland Garnet* (Boston, 1972), p. 179. For the conflict between Douglass and Garner, see *North Star,* January 26, 1849, reprinted in Philip S. Foner, *The Life and Writings of Frederick Douglas* (New York, 1950), 1:35–52, and Garnet's letters and circulars in the Weston Papers, Boston Public Library, Rare Book Room. For the anticolonization meeting in New York City, see *National Anti-Slavery Standard*, May 3, 1849 reprinted in Foner, op. cit., 5:113.

Fugitive Slave Act of 1850, Blyden and Crummell

For Blyden's career, see Hollis R. Lynch, *Edward Wilmot Blyden, Pan-Negro Patriot, 1832–1912* (New York, 1969). The characterization of Blyden is from a review of Lynch's biography by John Henrik Clarke in *Freedomways* (2d quarter 1969): 168. For Blyden's articles favoring Liberian emigration, see *Anglo-African Magazine* (June 1859). There is as yet no real biography of Alexander Crummell, but see William B. Ferris, *Alexander Crummell: An Apostle of Negro Culture*, Occasional Papers, no. 20, American

Negro Academy (Washington, D. C., 1920), and Rosita Kornofe, "Alexander Crummell: Nineteenth Century Afro-American" (unpublished study, Swarthmore College, 1964). For Crummell's experience in Canaan, New Hampshire, see Alexander Crummell, *Africa and America* (Springfield, Mass., 1880), pp. 277–79. Crummell's other experiences before he left for England are set forth in his sermon, "The Shades and Lights of a Fifty Years Ministry," and the introduction to the Crummell letters and sermons in *Calendar of Manuscripts in the Schomburg Collection* (New York, 1948). For Crummell's views on Liberia and Liberian emigration, see Alexander Crummell, *The Future of Africa* (New York, 1862).

Emigrationism and Nationalism

For the views of von Herder and Schleiermacher, see Louis L. Snyder, ed., *The Dynamics of Nationalism: Readings in Its Meaning and Development* (Princeton, N.J., 1964), pp. 137–38. For Blyden's statement, see Edward Wilmot Blyden, *The African Problem and the Method of Its Solution* (Washington, D.C., 1890), and Lynch, op. cit., p. 27. For Crummell's comments, see Crummell, op. cit., p. 46, and for the Caribbean aspect, see Howard H. Bell, ed., *Black Separation and the Caribbean, 1860* (Ann Arbor, Mich., 1970), pp. 64–65. For Delany's comment, see Martin R. Delany, *The Condition, Elevation, Emigration and Destiny of the Colored People in the United States* (Philadelphia, 1852), p. 203.

New York Blacks Reject Colonization

The story of Putnam's program, Governor Hunt's message, and the victory of New York blacks is based on the following sources: *Federick Douglass' Paper,* November 13, 1851, January 15, February 26, 1852; *New York Tribune,* January 7, 27, 1851; *Liberator,* March 5, May 14, 1852; *National Anti-Slavery Standard*, January 22, 29, March 4, 1852; George Walker, "The Afro-American in New York City, 1827–1860" (Ph.D. diss., Columbia University, 1972), pp. 222–24; Jane H. Pease and William H. Pease, *They Who Would Be Free: Blacks' Search for Freedom, 1830–1861* (New York, 1974), p. 258.

Martin R. Delany, Emigrationist

For biographies and studies of Delany, see Floyd J. Miller, "The Search for a Black Nationality: Martin R. Delany and the Emigrationist Alternative" (Ph.D. diss., University of Minnesota, 1970); Victor Ullman, *Martin R. Delany: The Beginnings of Black Nationalism* (Boston, 1971); Dorothy Sterling, *The Making of an Afro-American: Martin Robison Delany* (New York, 1971); Frank A. Rollins, *Life and Public Services of Martin R. Delany* (Boston, 1883; reprint ed., New York, 1969). For the statements by Delany in this section, see *Liberator,* May 21, 1852; Delany, op. cit., pp. 48–49, 160, 171, 179, 193, 203. The National Negro Convention at Rochester, New York, 1853, is discussed in Philip S. Foner, *History of Black Americans,* Vol. 2: *From the Emergence of the Cotton Kingdom to the Eve of the Compromise of 1850* (Westport, Conn., 1983). But see Philip S. Foner, *Frederick Douglass* (New York, 1964), pp. 119–22.

The National Emigration Convention of 1854: The Call and the Controversy

For the Ohio convention of 1852, see *Proceedings of the Convention of Colored Freemen of Ohio, Held in Cincinnati, January 14–19, 1852* (Cincinnati, Ohio), pp. 5–9, and Philip S. Foner and George Walker, eds., *Proceedings of the State Black Conventions, 1840–1865* (Philadelphia, 1979), 2:222–25. For the text of the call for a National Emigration Convention, see "Call for a National Congregation of Colored Men" in Howard H. Bell, ed., *Search for a Place: Black Separatism and Africa* (Ann Arbor, Mich., 1969), pp. 27–29. For the controversy over the call, see *Frederick Douglass' Paper*, August 26, September 30, October 28, 1853, March 19, July 6, 21, 1854; Foner, *Life and Writings of Frederick Douglass*, 5:290–302; Pease and Pease, op. cit., p. 263.

The National Emigration Convention of 1854: Proceedings and Reaction

For the discussions at the convention, see *Proceedings of the National Emigration Convention of Colored People; Held at Cleveland, Ohio, August 24–26, 1854* (Pittsburgh, Pa., 1854); *Speech of H. Ford Douglass, in Reply to Mr. J. M. Langston before the Emigration Convention at Cleveland, Ohio. Delivered on the Evening of the 27th of August, 1854* (Chicago, 1854), extracts from which appear in Herbert Aptheker, ed., *Documentary History of the Negro People in the United States* (New York, 1951), pp. 366–68; "Political Destiny of the Colored Race, on the American Continent," in *Proceedings of the National Emigration Convention*, pp. 33–43; Richard Blackett, "Martin R. Delany and Robert Campbell: Black Americans in Search of an African Colony," *Journal of Negro History* 62 (January 1977): 2–3; Robert L. Harris, Jr., "H. Ford Douglass: Afro-American Antislavery Emigrationist," *Journal of Negro History* 62 (July 1977): 216–17; Floyd J. Miller, *The Search for a Black Nationality: Black Colonization and Emigration, 1787–1863* (Urbana, Ill., 1975), pp. 67–82.

Emigrationists and Antiemigrationists

The discussion in this section is based on the following sources: *Frederick Douglass' Paper*, January 27, 1854, February 16, March 8, 1855; Frederick Douglass to Benjamin Coates, April 17, 1856, in Foner, *Life and Writings of Frederick Douglass*, 2:388; William Wells Brown, *The Black Man: His Antecedents, His Genius and His Achievements* (New York, 1863), pp. 35, 47; William Edward Farrison, *William Wells Brown, Author and Reformer* (Chicago, 1969), 385–87; Benjamin Quarles, *Black Abolitionists* (New York, 1969), pp. 214–22; *Frederick Douglass' Paper*, April 22, 1852; Pease and Pease, op. cit., p. 260; Sterling Stuckey, ed., *The Ideological Origins of Black Nationalism* (Boston, 1972), p. 203; Delany, op. cit., pp. 40–43.

9.   BLACK EMIGRATION, 1850–1861 II: CANADA, CENTRAL AMERICA, AND HAITI

Canadian Emigrants and Their Problems

For the comment of the Canadian governor-general, see James Bruce, Eighth Earl of Elgin, to Henry George, Third Earl Grey, October 6, 1850, in Sir Arthur Doughty, ed., *The Elgin Grey Papers, 1846–1852* (Ottawa, 1937), p. 720, and Jane H. Pease and William H. Pease, *They Who Would Be Free: Blacks' Search for Freedom, 1830–1861* (New York, 1974), pp. 255–56. For the role of the *Voice of the Fugitive* in stimulating Canadian emigration, see issues of January 1, August 13, 1851. For the appeal of the fugitives, see *Liberator*, January 10, 1851, and for the letter of J. J. Rice, see *Albany Argus* reprinted in *Liberator*, September 8, 1854.

The Refugee Home Society

The story of the Refugee Home Society is set forth in Fred Landon, "Henry Bibb, A Colonizer," *Journal of Negro History* 5 (1920): 437–47; William H. Pease and Jane H. Pease, *Black Utopia: Negro Communal Experiments in America* (Madison, Wis., 1963), pp. 116–21; Robin W. Winks, *The Blacks in Canada, A History* (Montreal, New Haven, and London, 1971), pp. 233–40; Wilbur H. Siebert, *The Underground Railroad from Slavery to Freedom* (New York, 1898), pp. 220–22.

The Buxton Colony

The story of the Buxton Colony is set forth in Victor Ullman, *Look at the North Star: A Life of William King* (Boston, 1969), pp. 110–265; Pease and Pease, *Black Utopia: Negro Communal Experiments in America,* pp. 132–54; Winks, op. cit., pp. 314–20; *Frederick Douglass' Paper,* August 15, 1854; Benjamin Drew, *Northside View of Slavery* (Boston, 1856), pp. 297–98; *Liberator,* December 24, 1858; Jonathan Katz, *Resistance at Christiana: The Fugitive Slave Rebellion, Christiana, Pennsylvania, September 11, 1851, A Documentary Account* (New York, 1972), pp. 270–76.

The Dawn Settlement

The story of the Dawn settlement is set forth in Winks, op. cit., pp. 178–204; *Liberator,* December 24, 1858; Siebert, op. cit., pp. 206–7; John K. A. Farrell, "The History of the Negro Community in Chatham, Ontario, 1707–1865" (Ph.D. diss., University of Ottawa, 1955), pp. 124–30, 183–84; Richard P. McCormick, "William Whipper; Moral Reformer," *Pennsylvania History* 43 (January 1976): 40–41.

The Black Experience in Canada

The discussion in this section is based on the following sources: *Liberator,* September 5, 1856, December 24, 1858; Winks, op. cit., pp. 247–79; *Provincial Freeman,* March 8, May 31, November 25, 1856, March 21, 28, April 11, 1857, copies in University of Pennsylvania Library; Robert L. Harris, "H. Ford Douglass, Afro-American Antislavery Emigrationist," *Journal of Negro History* 62 (July 1977): 221–23; Crawford Kilian, *Go Do Some Great Thing: The Black Pioneers of British Columbia* (Vancouver, B.C., 1978), pp. 56–59, 68; Robin W. Winks, *Canada and the United States: The Civil War Years* (Baltimore, Md., 1960), pp. 9–10; *African Repository* 34 (December 1958): 380; Robin W. Winks, "Negro School Segregation in Ontario and Nova Scotia," *Canadian Historical Review* 50 (June 1969): 164–91; Samuel Gridley Howe, *The Refuge from Slavery in Canada West, Report to the Freemen's Inquiry Commission* (Boston, 1864), p. 11; Robin W. Winks, "The Canadian Negro: A Historical Assessment," *Journal of Negro History* 53 (October 1968): 293–95; *Congregationalist,* reprinted in *National Anti-Slavery Standard,* November 21, 1857; *Chatham Tri-Weekly Planet,* October 8, 1859 reprinted in Richard Blackett, "Martin R. Delany and Robert Campbell: Black Americans in Search of an American Colony," *Journal of Negro History* 62 (January 1977): 7.

Blair's Central American Project

For the emigration activities to Jamaica, see *Liberator,* November 7, 1851. The discussion of the Blair project is based on the following sources: Eric Foner, *Free Soil, Free Labor, Free Men* (New York, 1970), pp. 267–74; Hon. Francis P. Blair, Jr., *Speech on the Acquisition of Central America, Delivered in the House of Representatives, January*

14, 1858 (Washington, D.C., 1858); Frank P. Blair, Jr., *The Destiny of the Races of This Continent: An Address Delivered before the Mercantile Library Assn. of Boston, Massachusetts, January 26, 1859* (Washington, D.C., 1859); Beverly L. Clarke, U.S. Minister to Guatemala and Honduras, to Hon. Lewis Cass, June 22, July 22, 1859, National Archives, Washington, D.C., Microcopy N. 219, Dispatches from United States Ministers to Central America, 1824–1906, Roll 6, Guatemala, vol. 3, May 10, 1850–March 25, 1860, and cited in Harris, p. 224.

Haitian Emigration

The discussion of this section is based on *Cleveland Daily Herald*, October 8, November 26, 1861; *Cleveland Morning Leader*, September 16, 1858; James A. Redpath, *A Guide to Hayti* (Boston, 1866), pp. 9–11; James M. McPherson, *The Negro's Civil War* (New York, 1965), pp. 79–80; James Theodore Holly, *A Vindication of the Capacity of the Negro Race, for Self-Government as Demonstrated by Historical Events of the Haitian Revolution; and Subsequent Acts of That People, Since Their National Independence,* in Howard H. Bell, ed., *Black Separatism and the Caribbean, 1860, by James Theodore Holly and J. Dennis Harris* (Ann Arbor, Mich., 1970), pp. 24–25, 64–66; Philip S. Foner, *The Voice of Black America: Major Speeches by Blacks in the United States, 1797–1973* (New York, 1975), 1:191–218; *Anglo-African Magazine* 1 (September 1859): 300, (October 1859): 327–29; Pease and Pease, *They Who Would Be Free,* pp. 274–76; *Weekly Anglo-African,* February 16, March 26, April 27, 1861; *Pine and Palm* (Boston and New York), July 13, August 17, 1861; James Redpath to H. Ford Douglass, February 7, 21, 23, March 8, April 10, 24, May 6, 12, 1861, in James Redpath Letterbook, William R. Perkins Library, Manuscript Department, Duke University; Willis D. Boyd, "James Redpath and American Negro Colonization in Haiti, 1860–1862," *Americas* 12 (October 1955): 120–38; James Redpath Correspondence, December 1861–May 1862, Schomburg Collection, New York City Public Library; James Redpath, Letters and Reports of James Redpath, General Agent of Emigration to Hayti, to M. Pleasance, Secretary of State of Exterior Relations of the Republic of Hayti and Others, March 31–December 27, 1861, Library of Congress, Manuscripts Division; Harris, op. cit., p. 228; *Douglass' Monthly* (December 1860, January–May 1861); Philip S. Foner, *Frederick Douglass* (New York, 1964), pp. 188–89; William F. Farrison, *William Wells Brown, Author and Reformer* (Chicago, 1967), pp. 334–36.

10. BLACK EMIGRATION, 1850–1861 III: AFRICA

Again Liberia

The discussion in this section is based on the following sources: *Voice of the Fugitive,* August 27, 1851; *Frederick Douglass' Paper,* October 2, 1851; *New York Tribune,* May 10, 1855; Edward G. Wilson to William McLain, July 27, 1856, Letters Received, Ser. 1, vol. 144; Withington to McLain, August 18, 1856, ibid.; American Colonization Society Papers, Library of Congress, Manuscripts Division; James M. Gifford, "Black Hope and Despair in Antebellum Georgia: The William Norn Correspondence," *Prologue* 8 (Fall 1976): 159–61.

Growing Interest in the Niger Valley

The discussion in this section is based on the following sources: T. J. Bowen, "Africa Opening to Civilization and Christianity," *African Repository* 33 (April 1857): 97–114;

Howard H. Bell, ed., *Search for a Place: Black Separatism and Africa* (Ann Arbor, Mich., 1969), p. 41.

The Year 1858

The discussion in this section is based on the following sources: Richard Blackett, "Martin R. Delany and Robert Campbell: Black Americans in Search of an African Colony," *Journal of Negro History* 62 (January 1977): 6–8; *Chatham Weekly Planet*, August 26, 1858; M. R. Delany, *Official Report of the Niger Valley Exploring Party* (New York, 1861), pp. 11–12.

The Three C's

The discussion in this section is based on the following sources: Senate Executive Document, U.S. Congress, 27 Cong., 3d sess., vol. 2, no. 20; Commodore Matthew Perry to Secretary of the Navy, African Squadron Letters: 1844–45, no. 32, National Archives; Adewunme Fajang, "Africa in the Western Acculturation of West Africa 1820–1860" (master's thesis, Atlanta University, 1960), pp. 61–63; Blackett, op. cit., pp. 11–12; K. O. Dike, *Trade and Politics on the Niger Delta, 1830–1885* (Oxford, England, 1956), pp. 66–75; Robert S. Wetherall, "The African Squadron, 1843–1861" (master's thesis, University of Delaware, 1968), pp. 122–34; Omniyi Aderwaye, "The United States' Naval Squadron and the Suppression of Slave Trade in West Africa 1820–1861" (master's thesis, Howard University, 1970), pp. 114–26; Richard K. Mac-Master, "The United States Navy and African Exploration 1851–1860," *Mid-America* 46 (1964): 187–203; Benjamin Coates, *Suggestions on the Importance of the Cultivation of Cotton in Africa in Reference to the Abolition of Slavery in the United States through the Organization of an African Civilization Society* (Philadelphia, 1858); Alexander Crummell, *Hope for Africa: A Sermon in Behalf of the Ladies' Negro Education Society* (London, 1853), p. 42; Alexander Crummell, *The Future of Africa* (New York, 1862), pp. 47–48; Robert Campbell, *A Pilgrimage to My Motherland: An Account of a Journey among the Egbas and Yorubas of Central Africa in 1859–60*, in Bell, op. cit., p. 201; Alexander Crummell, *Africa and America: Addresses and Discourses* (New York, 1969), pp. 34–38; Blackett, op. cit., p. 8; Wilson J. Moses, "Civilizing Missionary: A Study of Alexander Crummell," *Journal of Negro History* 60 (April 1975): 46–50; Martin R. Delany in Bell, op. cit., pp. 103–4.

Garnet and the African Civilization Society

The discussion in this section is based on the following sources: *African Repository* 33 (1957): 280–81; Richard K. MacMaster, "Henry Highland Garnet and the American Civilization Society," *Journal of Presbyterian History* 48 (January 1970): 101–3; Joel Schor, *Henry Highland Garnet: A Voice of Black Radicalism in the Nineteenth Century* (Westport, Conn., 1977), p. 156; *New York Tribune*, August 11, December 18, 1858; Benjamin Coates to Alexander Crummell, Philadelphia, April 14, 1862, Benjamin Coates Papers, Historical Society of Pennsylvania; Blackett, op. cit., p. 8; *Weekly Anglo-African*, September 10, 1859, March 17, 1860; Schor, op. cit., pp. 161, 166; *Douglass' Monthly* (October 1859); MacMaster, "Garnet and American Civilization Society," p. 104.

The Debate over the African Civilization Society

The discussion in this section is based on the following sources: *Douglass' Monthly* (March 1859); Howard H. Bell, "Negro Nationalism: A Factor in Emigration Projects,"

Journal of Negro History 47 (January 1967): 47; Richard P. McCormick, "William Whipper, Moral Reformer," *Pennsylvania History* 43 (January 1976): 42; *Weekly Anglo-African,* August 5, 1850, April 21, May 5, 1860, January 5, 12, 26, 1861; James McPherson, *The Negro's Civil War* (New York, 1965), pp. 83–84; MacMaster, "Garnet and the Civilization Society," p. 105; *New York Tribune,* November 19, December 8, 10, 1858; Floyd J. Miller, "The Search for a Black Nationality: Martin R. Delany and the Emigrationist Alternative" (Ph.D. diss., University of Minnesota, 1970), pp. 217–19; Schor, op. cit., pp. 158–60; Jane H. Pease and William H. Pease, *They Who Would Be Free: Blacks' Search for Freedom, 1830–1860* (New York, 1974), pp. 271–72; *Liberator,* September 24, 1858, May 4, 1860; James Oliver Horton and Lois E. Horton, *Black Bostonians: Family Life and Community Struggle in the Antebellum North* (New York, 1979), p. 122; Philip S. Foner, *Life and Writings of Frederick Douglass,* 2:387–88, 441–47, 5:411–18.

The Delany-Campbell Expedition to the Niger Valley

The discussion in this section is based on the following sources: Delany, op. cit., pp. 11–12, 40–52; MacMaster, "Garnet and American Civilization Society," op. cit., 108, 109; *African Repository,* October, November 1859; *New York Colonization Journal,* November 1859, June 1860; Blackett, op. cit., pp. 7, 15; E. A. Ayandele, *The Missionary Impact on Modern Nigeria 1842–1914: A Political and Social Analysis* (London, 1966), p. 8.

Delany in England

The discussion in this section is based on the following sources: *Times* (London) reprinted in *New York Evening Post,* July 31, 1860; *Diary of George Mifflin Dallas* (Philadelphia, 1892), pp. 407–8; John Donald Wade, *Augustus Baldwin Longstreet* (New York, 1924), pp. 325–27; Frank A. Rollin, *Life and Public Services of Martin R. Delany* (Boston, 1868), pp. 106–8, 121; *New York Herald,* August 2, 1860; Theodore Draper, *The Rediscovery of Black Nationalism* (New York, 1970), p. 131; Blackett, op. cit., p. 12; Pease and Pease, op. cit., pp. 273–74.

Failure of African Emigration

The discussion in this section is based on the following sources: Blackett, op. cit., pp. 16–24; J.F.A. Ayaji, *Christian Missions to Nigeria, 1851–1891: The Making of a New Elite* (London, 1965), pp. 110–23; Delany, op. cit., pp. 12–15; Bell, op. cit., pp. 47–52, 77–78, 157–67, 248–59; *Douglass' Monthly* (August 1862); MacMaster, "Garnet and Civilization Society," pp. 110–11; *Anti-Slavery Reporter* (London) 10 (1862): 213; Jean H. Kopytoff, *A Preface to Modern Nigeria* (Madison, Wis., 1965), p. 435.

Conclusion

The discussion in this section is based on the following sources: George R. Woofolk, "Turner's Safety Valve and Free Negro Westward Migration," *Pacific Quarterly* 13 (July 1965): 125–30; Richard B. Morris, ed., *Encyclopedia of American History* (New York, 1960), p. 543; Cyril E. Griffity, *The African Dream: Martin R. Delany and the Emergence of Pan African Thought* (University Park, Pa., 1975), pp. 13–14; Benjamin Coates to Alexander Crummell, April 14, 1862, Benjamin Coates Papers, Historical Society of Pennsylvania; *Anglo-African Magazine* 1 (1859): 3–4; MacMaster, "Garnet and American Civilization Society," p. 111; *Anti-Slavery Advocate* (London), November

1, 1859; *Frederick Douglass' Paper,* May 27, 1852; Pease and Pease, op. cit., p. 259; Blackett, op. cit., p. 9.

11.   KANSAS–NEBRASKA, CUBAN ANNEXATION, AND THE EARLY REPUBLICAN PARTY

Kansas–Nebraska Act

The discussion in this section is based on the following sources: *Congressional Globe,* 35th Cong., 1st sess., pp. 221–22; David Potter, *The Impending Crisis, 1848–1861,* completed and edited by Don E. Fehrenbacher (New York, 1976), pp. 110–26; Roy F. Nichols, "The Kansas–Nebraska Act: A Century of Historiography," *Mississippi Valley Historical Review* 43 (September 1956): 201–11; Theodore Clark Smith, *Parties and Slavery, 1850–1859* (New York, 1904), pp. 95–97, 211; Robert W. Johannsen, *Stephen A. Douglas* (New York, 1973), pp. 188–202; Robert R. Russell, "The Issues in the Congressional Struggle over the Kansas–Nebraska Bill, 1854," *Journal of Southern History* 19 (May 1963): 191–96; *Chicago Tribune,* February 2, 9, 12, March 14, June 1, September 12, 1854; George Fort Milton, *The Eve of Conflict: Stephen A. Douglas and the Needless War* (Boston, 1934), pp. 171–77; *Frederick Douglass' Paper,* February 24, April 7, May 26, June 9, 1854; Philip S. Foner, *The Life and Writings of Frederick Douglass* (New York, 1950), 2:282–84; Jane H. Pease and William H. Pease, *They Who Would Be Free: Blacks' Search for Freedom, 1830–1860* (New York, 1974), p. 243; *Cincinnati Gazette,* June 13, 1854, quoted in Eric Foner, *Free Soil, Free Labor, Free Men: The Ideology of the Republican Party before the Civil War* (New York, 1970), pp. 95–96.

The "Africanization of Cuba" Scare

The discussion in this section is based on the following sources: Philip S. Foner, *History of Cuba and Its Relations with the United States* (New York, 1963), 2:75–85; Arthur E. Smith, "Spain and the Problem of Slavery in Cuba, 1817–1873" (Ph.D. diss., University of Chicago, 1958), pp. 117–23, 133–36, 178; C. Stanley Urban, "The Africanization of Cuba Scare, 1853–1855," *Hispanic American Historical Review* 37 (February 1957): 29–33; Robert Russell, *North America, Its Agriculture and Climate* (Edinburgh, 1857), pp. 240–42; William H. Marcy to Charles W. Davis, March 15, 1854, Davis to Marcy, May 22, 1854, State Department, Special Mission, III, Consular Despatches, Havana, XXIX, National Archives, Washington, D.C. In *Odious Commerce: Britain, Spain, and the Abolition of the Cuban Slave Trade* (New York, 1980), p. 239, David Murray points out that the departure of Pezuela from Cuba was "a sad blow to British hopes of ending the Cuban slave trade." But he does not see that it also seriously retarded the possibility of ending slavery in the island. For Alexander von Humboldt's criticism of John S. Thrasher for omitting chapter 7 from the translation of the work on Cuba, see his letter in the *New York Times* of August 5, 1856.

"Manifesto of the Brigands"

The discussion in this section is based on the following sources: Foner, *History of Cuba,* pp. 95–96; Robert Benson Leard, "Bonds of Destiny: The United States and

Cuba, 1848–1861'' (Ph.D. diss., University of California, Berkeley, 1953), pp. 176–78; Robert Leslie Stephens, "The Diplomacy of William L. Marcy, Secretary of State, 1853–1857'' (Ph.D. diss., University of Virginia, 1949), pp. 160–63; Sidney Webster, "Mr. Marcy, the Cuban Question, and the Ostend Manifesto," *Political Science Quarterly* 8 (March 1893): 23–25; Marcy to Soulé, July 13, 1853, April 3, 1854, Buchanan, Mason, and Soulé to Marcy, October 17, 1854, Soulé to Marcy, October 20, 1854, State Department, Diplomatic Despatches, Great Britain, LXVI, Spain, XXXIX, National Archives; Dodge to Marcy, August 26, 1855, State Department Despatches, Spain, XL, National Archives.

"Bleeding Kansas"

The discussion in this section is based on Potter, op. cit., pp. 178–83; Foner, *Life and Writings of Frederick Douglass,* 2:311–15; *Frederick Douglass' Paper,* September 15, 1854.

Northern Labor and Southern Slavery

The discussion in this section is based on the following sources: Philip S. Foner, *History of the Labor Movement in the United States* (New York, 1947), 1:266–96; Herman Schleuter, *Lincoln, Labor and Slavery* (New York, 1913), pp. 12–49; *National Laborer,* September 13, 1836; *Working Man's Advocate,* March 16, April 20, 1844; *Young America,* January 3, 1846; John R. Commons, "Horace Greeley and the Working Class Origins of the Republican Party," *Political Science Quarterly* 24 (September 1909): 488–92; Eric Foner, "Ante-bellum Labor and the Slave System," *In These Times,* August 22–September 2, 1980, pp. 10–11; *Herald of Freedom,* July 8, 1844; *Anti-Slavery Bugle,* January 1, 1853; Philip S. Foner, *American Socialism and Black Americans: From the Age of Jackson to the Eve of World War II* (Westport, Conn., 1978), pp. 23–60; Morris Hilquit, *History of Socialism in the United States* (New York, 1903), p. 191; *New Yorker Volkszeitung,* no. 4, 1888; Aileen Kraditor, *Means and Ends in American Abolitionism: Garrison and His Critics on Strategy and Tactics, 1834–1850* (New York, 1969), pp. 110–11.

Birth and Ideology of the Republican Party

The discussion in this section is based on the following sources: Eugene Berwanger, *The Frontier against Slavery* (Urbana, Ill., 1967); James A. Rawley, *Race and Politics: "Bleeding Kansas" and the Coming of the Civil War* (Philadelphia, 1969); Kenneth M. Stampp, *The Imperiled Union: Essays on the Background of the Civil War* (New York, 1980); Michael Holt, *Forging a Majority* (New Haven, 1969); Eric Foner, *Free Soil, Free Labor, Free Men* (New York, 1970). For the view that the significance of the free labor ideology in shaping the Republican party has been exaggerated and that it is "highly questionable" if it "divided Republicans from northern Democrats," see William Eugene Gienapp, "The Origins of the Republican Party, 1852–1856" (Ph.D. diss., University of California, Berkeley, 1980), pp. 1056–58.

Blacks and the Early Republican Party

The discussion in this section is based on the following sources: *North Star,* January 12, 1849; Foner, *Life and Writings of Frederick Douglass,* 2:81; Benjamin Quarles, *Black Abolitionists* (New York, 1969), p. 188; Philip S. Foner, *Frederick Douglass* (New York, 1964), pp. 167–69; George Walker, "The Afro-American in New York City,

1827–1860'' (Ph.D. diss., Columbia University, 1972), pp. 203–4; *Proceedings of the Convention of Radical Political Abolitionists, Held at Syracuse, N.Y., June 26, 27, 28, 1855* (New York, 1855); M. Leon Perkal, ''American Abolition Society: A Viable Alternative to the Republican Party?'' *Journal of Negro History* 65 (Winter 1980): 58–60; Frederick Douglass to Gerrit Smith, March 27, August 14, 1855, Gerrit Smith Papers, Syracuse University Library; *Radical Abolitionist* (April 1856).

The Know-Nothings

The discussion in this section is based on the following sources: Joel H. Silbey, *The Transformation of American Politics, 1840–1860* (Englewood Cliffs, N.J., 1967), pp. 14–25; Thomas J. Curran, ''Know-Nothings of New York State'' (Ph.D. diss., Columbia University, 1963), pp. 49–53; Louis Dow Sisco, *Political Nativism in New York State* (New York, 1907), pp. 85–87.

Election of 1856

The discussion in this section is based on the following sources: *New York Tribune,* July 30, 1856; *Frederick Douglass' Paper,* November 24, 1854; *National Anti-Slavery Standard,* September 27, 1856; Walker, op. cit., pp. 204–6; Foner, *Life and Writings of Frederick Douglass,* 2:72, 81–85, 332, 389, 404, 5:35; Foner, *Frederick Douglass,* pp. 170–72; *Liberator,* September 5, 1856; James Oliver Horton and Lois Horton, *Black Bostonians* (New York, 1979), p. 88; *Chicago Tribune,* September 16, 19, 26, 1854; Ralph Harlow, *Gerrit Smith, Philanthropist and Reformer* (New York, 1966), p. 364; Perkal, op. cit., p. 60.

12.   THE *DRED SCOTT* CASE, ITS REPERCUSSIONS, AND THE ELECTION OF 1858

Who Was Dred Scott?

The discussion in this section is based on the following sources: William Loren Katz, ''Historians and Racism,'' *Freedomways* (first quarter 1970): 371–72; Frank H. Hodder, ''Some Phases of the Dred Scott Case,'' *Mississippi Valley Historical Review* 16 (1929–1930): 3–4; Walter Ehrlich, ''History of the Dred Scott Case Through the Decision of 1857'' (Ph.D. diss., Washington University, St. Louis, 1950), pp. 20–35; A. Leon Higgenbotham, Jr., ''Race, Racism and American Law,'' *University of Pennsylvania Law Review* 122 (April 1974): 1052–53; Will D. Gilliam, Jr., ''Some Textbooks on the Dred Scott Case,'' *Negro History Bulletin* 14 (February 1951): 122; Walter Ehrlich, *They Have No Rights: Dred Scott's Struggle for Freedom* (Westport, Conn., 1978), pp. 65–85; Richard Bardolph, *The Negro Vanguard* (New York, 1959), p. 122.

The Dred Scott Case in Missouri Courts

The discussion in this section is based on the following sources: Don E. Fehrenbacher, *The Dred Scott Case: Its Significance in American Law and Politics* (New York, 1978), pp. 72–100; Ehrlich, ''History of the Dred Scott Case,'' pp. 76–94; *Scott* v. *Emerson* 15 Mo. 576, 582 (1852); Walter Ehrlich, ''The Origins of the Dred Scott Decision,'' *Journal of Negro History* 59 (April 1974): 132–42; Walter Ehrlich, ''Was the Dred Scott Case Valid?'' *Journal of American History* 55 (September 1968): 256–58.

The Dred Scott Case before the U.S. Supreme Court and Chief Justice
Taney's Majority Opinion

The discussion in this section is based on the following sources: Thomas B. Alexander, "Historical Treatments of the Dred Scott Case," *Proceedings of the South Carolina Historical Association, 1953* (Columbia, S.C., 1954), pp. 37–59; Vincent C. Hopkins, *Dred Scott's Case* (New York, 1951), pp. 172–75; *Dred Scott* v. *Sandford* 19 How. 393 (1857); William M. Wieced, "Slavery and Abolition before the United States Supreme Court, 1820–1860," *Journal of American History* 55 (January 1968): 120–35; Philips Archempaugh, "James Buchanan, the Court and the Dred Scott Case," *Tennessee Historical Magazine* 9 (1925–1926): 231–40; James Ford Rhodes, *History of the United States from the Compromise of 1850 to the End of the Roosevelt Administration* (New York, 1892), 2:249–71; Hopkins, op. cit., 167–95; Fehrenbacher, op. cit., pp. 280–327.

Other Court Opinions

For the discussion in this section, see Fehrenbacher, op. cit., pp. 330–56; 60 U.S. (19 How.) 529; (McLean, J. dissension), 564; (Curtis, J. dissension), 550.

Evaluation of Taney's Opinion

The discussion in this section is based on the following sources: Edwin S. Corwin, "The Dred Scott Decision in the Light of Contemporary Legal Doctrines," *American Historical Review* 17 (October 1911): 52–69; Charles Warren, *The Supreme Court in United States History* (Boston, 1923), 3:1–51; Charles Evans Hughes, "Roger Brooke Taney," *American Bar Association Journal* 17 (December 1931): 785–90; Felix Frankfurter, *The Commerce Clause under Marshall, Taney, and Waite* (Chapel Hill, N.C., 1947), p. 48; Higgenbotham, op. cit., pp. 1050–51; Fehrenbacher, op. cit., pp. iv–v, 285–87, 320–21, 382; *New York Tribune*, March 5, 7, 1857.

Impact of the Decision on Northern Free Labor

The discussion in this section is based on the following sources: Philip S. Foner, *History of the Labor Movement in the United States* (New York, 1947), 1:280–88; Bernard Mandel, *Labor: Free and Slave* (New York, 1955), p. 127; *Charleston Mercury*, July 5, 1858; *DeBow's Review* (August 1960): 199; Wilfred Carsel, "The Slaveholders' Indictment of Northern Wage Slavery," *Journal of Southern History* 6 (November 1940): 514–20; *Milwaukee Free Democrat*, August 21, 1857; Eric Foner, *Free Labor, Free Soil, Free Men* (New York, 1970), pp. 97–98; *New York Tribune*, April 21, 1860; *Liberator*, April 24, 1857; *National Era*, August 27, 1857; "Opinions of the Justices . . . 1857," 44 Maine 505 (1857). For the *Lemmon* case, see Helen C. Catterall, ed., *Judicial Cases Concerning American Slavery and the Negro* (Washington, D.C., 1936), 5:246–52.

Black Protests against the Dred Scott Decision

The discussion in this section is based on the following sources: Avery Craven, *The Coming of the Civil War* (New York, 1937), pp. 381–82; Robert P. Smith, "William Cooper Nell, Crusading Black Abolitionist," *Journal of Negro History* 55 (July 1970): 192; *Liberator*, May 8, July 10, 1857, March 2, August 3, 1858, January 28, April 8, 1859; James Oliver Horton and Lois Horton, *Black Bostonians* (New York, 1979), pp. 188–200; Herbert Aptheker, *Documentary History of the Negro People in the United States* (New York, 1951), pp. 394–96; Philip S. Foner, *The Voice of Black America:*

Major Speeches of Blacks in the United States, 1797–1973 (New York, 1975), 1:226–30; Philip S. Foner, *The Life and Writings of Frederick Douglass* (New York, 1950), 2:407–24; Benjamin Quarles, *Black Abolitionists* (New York, 1969), pp. 233–34.

Lincoln, Slavery, and the Negro

The discussion in this section is based on the following sources: Lerone Bennett, Jr., "Was Lincoln a White Supremacist?" *Ebony* 10 (January 1968): 23–35; *New York Times*, January 26, 28, 1968; Herbert Mitgang, "Was Lincoln Just a Honkie?" *New York Times Sunday Magazine*, February 11, 1968, pp. 99–107; Eric Foner, op. cit., pp. 215–16, 294; Roy F. Basler et al., eds., *The Collected Works of Abraham Lincoln* (New Brunswick, N.J., 1953–1955), 2:255, 316, 320, 461–69, 492, 3:379, 387–88, 390–91, 482; John G. Nicolay and John Hay, eds., *Abraham Lincoln, Complete Works* (New York, 1920), 1:186, 195, 508–9, 534; Philip S. Foner, *Abraham Lincoln: Selections from His Writings* (New York, 1944), pp. 22–26; Carl Sandburg, *Abraham Lincoln: The Prairie Years* (New York, 1926), 2:408; Don E. Fehrenbacher, *Prelude to Greatness: Lincoln in the 1850's* (Stanford, Calif., 1962), pp. 33–47, 59–65; Benjamin P. Thomas, *Abraham Lincoln, A Biography* (New York, 1952), pp. 170–78; Marvin R. Cain, "Lincoln's Views on Slavery and the Negro: A Suggestion," *Historian* 19 (August 1964): 502–20; G. S. Boritt, *Lincoln and the Economics of the American Dream* (Memphis, 1978), pp. xiii–xiv, 130–39. The psychobiography of Lincoln is Dwight G. Anderson, *Abraham Lincoln: The Quest for Immortality* (New York, 1982). George M. Fredrickson's comment appeared in *New York Review of Books*, July 15, 1982, p. 16. For other psychobiographical studies of Lincoln, which advance positions hardly rooted in sound analysis, see George B. Forgie, *Patricide in the House Divided* (New York, 1979) and Charles B. Strozier, *Lincoln's Quest for Union: Public and Private Meanings* (New York, 1982).

The Lincoln–Douglas Debates

The discussion in this section is based on the following: Harry V. Jaffa, *Crisis of the House Divided: An Interpretation of the Issues in the Lincoln–Douglas Debates* (Garden City, N.Y., 1959), pp. 252–93; Ronald N. Satz, "The African Slave Trade and Lincoln's Campaign of 1858," *Journal of the Illinois Historical Society* 32 (June 1972): 269–79; Richard Allen Heckman, *Lincoln vs. Douglas: The Great Debates Campaign* (Washington, D.C., 1967): 25–51; Nicolay and Hay, eds., op. cit., 3:2, 110–12, 117, 265, 393–400; Basler, op. cit., 2:461, 498, 3:225–26, 312, 349–50; *Chicago Times*, October 30, 1858; Philip S. Foner, *Life and Writings of Frederick Douglass*, 2:484.

Election of 1858 in New York

The discussion in this section is based on the following sources: *Congressional Globe*, 35 Cong., 1st sess., pp. 774, 1437, 1957; *Radical Abolitionist* (September, October, November 1858); *National Anti-Slavery Standard*, October 9, November 20, 1858; Perkal, op. cit., pp. 63–64; *New York Tribune*, October 5, 26, 1858; George Walker, "The Afro-American in New York City, 1827–1860" (Ph.D. diss., Columbia University, 1972), pp. 205–7.

13. BLACKS AND JOHN BROWN

Early Life of John Brown

The discussion in this section is based on the following sources: Oswald Garrison Villard, *John Brown, 1800–1859: A Biography Fifty Years After* (New York, 1943), pp.

23–74; Stephen B. Oates, *To Purge This Land with Blood: A Biography of John Brown* (New York, 1970), pp. 14–65; Louis Ruchames, ed., *John Brown: The Making of a Revolutionary* (New York, 1969), pp. 12–46. (This is a shortened version of his *John Brown Reader*, published in 1959.) Thelma D. Perry, "Race Conscious Aspects of the John Brown Affair," *Negro History Bulletin* 34 (April 1974): 312; Barrie Stavis, *Harpers Ferry: A Play about John Brown* (South Brunswick, N.J., 1967), pp. 9–11; Richard J. Hinton, *John Brown and His Men* (New York, 1899), pp. 12–36; F. B. Sanborn, *The Life and Letters of John Brown* (Boston, 1885), pp. 15–38.

Brown's Original Plan to End Slavery

The discussion in this section is based on the following sources: Philip S. Foner, *Frederick Douglass* (New York, 1964), pp. 174–76; *Life and Times of Frederick Douglass* (Hartford, Conn., 1882), pp. 225, 339–41; *John Brown—An Address by Frederick Douglass at the Fourteenth Anniversary of Storer College, Harpers Ferry, West Virginia, May 30, 1881.*

Brown in North Elba

The discussion in this section is based on the following sources: Oates, op. cit., pp. 78–92; Villard, op. cit., pp. 74–76; Ralph Volney Harlow, *Gerrit Smith* (New York, 1939), pp. 320–29; Benjamin Quarles, *Black Abolitionists* (New York, 1969), pp. 236–37; Sanborn, op. cit., pp. 125–26; Stavis, op. cit., p. 12.

Brown in Kansas

The discussion in this section is based on the following sources: James C. Malin, "Judge Lecompete and the Sack of Lawrence, May 21, 1856," *Kansas Historical Quarterly* 20 (August, November 1953): 465–94, 553–97; Ruchames, op. cit., pp. 31–36; R. Haven, "John Brown and Herman Humphrey: An Unpublished Letter," *Journal of Negro History* 52 (July 1967): 220–24; Sanborn, op. cit., pp. 350–67; Villard, op. cit., pp. 283–88; J. Ewing Glasgow, *The Harpers Ferry Insurrection* (Edinburgh, 1860), p. 10; *John Brown—An Address by Frederick Douglass; New York Globe*, February 24, 1883; Perry, op. cit., p. 313; Stanley J. Robboy and Anita W. Robboy, "Lewis Hayden: From Fugitive Slave to Statesman," *New England Quarterly* 46 (December 1973): 607–8.

Brown's New Plan

The discussion in this section is based on the following sources: *Life and Times of Frederick Douglass*, p. 387; Foner, *Frederick Douglass*, p. 176; Sanborn, op. cit., p. 434; Hinton, op. cit., pp. 165–66; Oates, op. cit., pp. 241–51; Perry, op. cit., pp. 313–14; Ruchames, op. cit., pp. 294–95; Quarles, op. cit., pp. 337–38; *Weekly Anglo-African*, November 12, 1859; Fred Landon, "Canadian Negroes and the John Brown Raid," *Journal of Negro History* 6 (April 1921): 174–75; Fred Landon, "From Chatham to Harpers Ferry," *Canadian Magazine* 53 (October 1919): 447–48; Jane H. Pease and William H. Pease, *They Who Would Be Free: Blacks' Search for Freedom, 1830–1860* (New York 1974), pp. 246–48; Frank A. Rollin, *Life and Public Services of Martin R. Delany* (New York, 1969), pp. 87–89; William E. Burghardt Du Bois, *John Brown* (Philadelphia, 1909), pp. 259–66; Robin W. Winks, *The Blacks in Canada: A History* (Montreal, New Haven, and London, 1971), pp. 267–69; Richard Albert Folk, "Black

Man's Burden in Ohio, 1849–1863'' (Ph.D. diss., University of Toledo, 1972), pp. 345–46.

A Year's Delay
The discussion in this section is based on the following sources: *Liberator*, December 9, 1859; Du Bois, op. cit., pp. 248–59; Foner, *Frederick Douglass*, pp. 176–77; Philip S. Foner, *The Life and Writings of Frederick Douglass* (New York, 1950), 5:428–30; Harlow, op. cit., p. 339; Dorothy Sterling, *Speak Out in Thunder Tones: Letters and Other Writings of Black Northerners, 1787–1865* (New York, 1973), pp. 273–77.

Douglass and Brown at Chambersburg
The discussion in this section is based on the following sources: Foner, *Frederick Douglass*, pp. 177–78; *Life and Times of Frederick Douglass*, pp. 387–90; Sanborn, op. cit., pp. 538–41; Hinton, op. cit., p. 507; Oates, op. cit., pp. 282–83; Foner, *Life and Writings of Frederick Douglass*, 2:314, 331–32, 458–60, 464, 484, 487, 517–18, 533–35, 5:459, 467–71; Leslie J. Goldstein, "Violence as an Instrument for Social Change: The Views of Frederick Douglass, 1819–1895," *Journal of Negro History* 41 (January 1976): 71; Herbert Aptheker, "The Drama of Frederick Douglass and John Brown," in Herbert Aptheker, *Toward Negro Freedom* (New York, 1956), pp. 60–72.

The Raid at Harpers Ferry
The discussion in this section is based on the following sources: Oates, op. cit., pp. 289–310; Allan Keller, "John Brown's Raid," *American History Illustrated* 11 (August 1976): 35–44; Osborn Anderson, *A Voice from Harpers Ferry* (Boston, 1861), pp. 32–69; Herbert Aptheker, *Documentary History of the Negro People* (New York, 1951), 1:435–38; Sterling, op. cit., pp. 280–84.

First Reactions
The discussion in this section is based on the following sources: *The New "Reign of Terror" in the Slaveholding States for 1859–60, Anti-Slavery Tracts*, n.s. no. 4 (New York, 1860); *Liberator*, December 23, 1859, January 20, 1860; Foner, *Frederick Douglass*, pp. 178–80; *Life and Times of Frederick Douglass*, p. 379; *New York Herald*, October 22, 28, 1859; Richard Scheindinhelm, ed., *The Response to John Brown* (Belmont, Calif., 1972).

Trial, Execution, and Funeral
The discussion in this section is based on the following sources: Stavis, op. cit., p. 18; "Trial of John Brown," *American Heritage* (August 1967): 26–30; Aptheker, *Documentary History*, 1:443–46; Oates, op. cit., pp. 325–29; *Testimonies of Capt. John Brown, at Harpers Ferry, with His Address to the Court, Antislavery Tracts*, n.s. 8 (New York, 1860); Sterling, op cit., pp. 285–88; *Baltimore Sun*, December 3, 1859; *Liberator*, January 13, 1860; Jean Libby, *Black Voices from Harpers Ferry* (Palo Alto, Calif., 1979); Benjamin Quarles, *Allies for Freedom, Blacks and John Brown* (New York, 1974).

Black America Mourns
The discussion of this section is based on the following sources: Quarles, op. cit., pp. 240–43; *Weekly Anglo-African*, November 5, 1859; George Walker, "The Afro-Ameri-

can in New York City, 1827–1860'' (Ph.D. diss., Columbia University, 1972), pp. 253–54; Aptheker, *Documentary History,* 1:441–44; *National Anti-Slavery Standard,* February 18, March 3, 23, 31, 1860; *Le Progres* reprinted in ibid., February 18, 1860; *Cleveland Morning Leader,* December 19, 22, 1859; *Frederick Douglass' Paper,* February 17, 1860; *Douglass' Monthly* (November–December 1859); Foner, *Frederick Douglass,* pp. 181–82.

Historical Significance of John Brown

The discussion in this section is based on the following sources: Stephen B. Oates, " 'In Thine Own Image': Modern Radicals and John Brown,'' *South Atlantic Quarterly* 73 (Autumn 1974): 417–27; Herbert Aptheker, "Du Bois as Historian,'' *Negro History Bulletin* 32 (April 1969): 6–7; the heated dispute in the *New York Review of Books* aroused by Willie Rose Lee's review headed "Killing for Freedom,'' December 3, 1970, pp. 12–19, and the replies by Louis Ruchames and Philip S. Foner, ibid., February 11, 1971, and the letter of Stephen B. Oates, April 22, 1971; the rather weak effort of Thelma D. Perry, op. cit., p. 314, to prove by the composition of the Provisional Government that Brown, whose "conduct with Blacks was exemplary,'' illustrated a flaw in his approach to the Negro. For Malin, see James C. Malin, *John Brown and the Legend of the Fifty-Six* (Philadelphia, 1942); for Potter, see David M. Potter, *The South and the Sectional Conflict* (Baton Rouge, La., 1968); for Nevins, see Allan Nevins, *The Emergence of Lincoln* (New York, 1950); for David Donald, see *The Irrepressible Conflict, 1850–1860* (New York, 1972). For Truman Nelson's interpretation of Harpers Ferry, see his *The Old Man: John Brown at Harpers Ferry* (New York, 1973), for his review of the Oates biography, see *Nation,* March 29, 1971, pp. 405–7, and for Oates' reply see ibid., May 3, 1971, p. 546. For Oates' biography, see Oates, *To Purge This Land with Blood: A Biography of John Brown* (New York, 1970). For Du Bois, see W.E.B. Du Bois, *John Brown* (New York, 1909). For another strained interpretation of what Brown may have had in mind at Harpers Ferry, see Albert Fried, *John Brown's Journey: Notes and Recollections on His America and Mine* (New York, 1978). For Richard O. Boyer, see his *The Legend of John Brown: A Biography and a History* (New York, 1973).

14.   BLACKS AND THE ELECTION OF 1860

The John Brown Fund

The discussion in this section is based on the following sources: *Liberator,* December 16, 1859, January 20, 1860, January 11, 1861, February 19, 1864; William C. Nell to Thomas Wentworth Higginson, February 6, 1860, Anti-Slavery Letters, Boston Public Library, Rare Book Room; Benjamin Quarles, *Black Abolitionists* (New York, 1969), pp. 243–44; *Weekly Anglo-African,* January 5, February 11, March 10, April 14, June 23, 1860; *National Anti-Slavery Standard,* October 4, 1862.

A Change in the Atmosphere

The discussion in this section is based on the following sources: Philip S. Foner, *Frederick Douglass* (New York, 1964), pp. 181–82; *Douglass' Monthly* (December 1859); Henry Wilson, *History of the Rise and Fall of the Slave Power in America* (Boston and New York, 1877), 2:606; Douglass to James Redpath, June 29, 1860, in *Liberator,*

July 27, 1860; Truman Nelson, *The Old Man: John Brown at Harpers Ferry* (New York, 1973), p. 328; Richard Scheindinhelm, ed., *The Response to John Brown* (Belmont, Calif., 1972), pp. 25–32; Forrest Wilson, *Crusader in Crinoline: The Life of Harriet Beecher Stowe* (Philadelphia, 1941), p. 449.

Return of Sumner

The discussion in this section is based on the following sources: *Douglass' Monthly* (July 1860); *Works of Charles Sumner* (Boston, 1880), 5:170–72; Quarles, op. cit., pp. 246–47.

Blacks and Republican Conservatism

The discussion in this section is based on the following sources: Eric Foner, *Free Soil, Free Labor, Free Men: The Ideology of the Republican Party before the Civil War* (New York, 1970), p. 112; *Liberator*, December 16, 1859; *Douglass' Monthly* (February 1859); *Eastern Argus*, January 8, 1858; *Principia*, January 14, 1860.

Helper's Impending Crisis

The discussion in this section is based on the following sources: Hinton Rowan Helper, *The Impending Crisis of the South: How to Meet It* (New York, 1857), pp. 120–25; J. J. Cardoso, "Hinton Rowan Helper, as a Racist in the Abolitionist Camp," *Journal of Negro History* 55 (October 1970): 324–25, 326; Eric Foner, op. cit., pp. 276–77; Hans L. Trefousse, "Ben Wade and the Negro," *Ohio Historical Quarterly* 48 (October 1959): 161–76; *New York Tribune*, December 18, 1860.

Blacks Speak Out

The discussion in this section is based on the following sources: *Liberator*, February 3, 1860; James M. McPherson, ed., *The Negro's Civil War: How American Negroes Felt and Acted during the War for the Union* (New York, 1965), p. 5; Philip S. Foner, ed., *The Voice of Black America: Major Speeches by Blacks in the United States, 1797–1973* (New York, 1975), 1:252–53; *New York Anglo-African*, March 1860.

Democratic and Republican Conventions

The discussion in this section is based on the following sources: Eric Foner, op. cit., p. 133; Jim Byrnes, "Was Hannibal Hamlin a Black Man or White?" *Bangor Daily News*, May 2, 1971; Kirk H. Porter, *National Party Platforms* (New York, 1924), pp. 50–58.

Black Opinion of Lincoln in 1860

The discussion in this section is based on the following sources: Foner, *Frederick Douglass*, pp. 184–85; *Douglass' Monthly* (June, July, August, September, October 1860); *Liberator*, July 13, October 19, 1860; McPherson, op. cit., pp. 6–7, 10; Foner, *Voice of Black America*, 1:254–65; Allan Nevins, *Emergence of Lincoln* (New York, 1950), 2:221–22; Steven A. Channing, *Crisis of Fear: Secession in South Carolina* (New York, 1970), pp. 78–82, 88, 93, 161, 231, 235–39; John G. Nicolay and John Hay, eds., *Complete Works of Abraham Lincoln* (New York, 1905), pp. 186–87, 189; *Life and Times of Frederick Douglass*, p. 327; *Principia*, September 8, 1860.

The Campaign Draws to a Close

The discussion in this section is based on the following sources: Don E. Fehrenbacher, *Prelude to Greatness: Lincoln in the 1850's* (Stanford, Calif., 1962), pp. 155–59; Philip S. Foner, *History of the Labor Movement in the United States* (New York, 1947), 1:293–96; *New York Herald*, October 20, 30, November 2, 1860; William C. Nell, *Property Qualification or No Property Qualification* (New York, 1860), pp. 20–22; George Walker, "The Afro-American in New York City, 1827–1860" (Ph.D. diss., Columbia University, 1972), p. 186; Phyllis F. Field, *The Politics of Race in New York: The Struggle for Black Suffrage in the Civil War Era* (Ithaca and London, 1982), p. 125.

Black Reaction to Lincoln's Election

The discussion in this section is based on the following sources: Foner, *Frederick Douglass*, pp. 186–87; *Douglass' Monthly* (December 1860); *Principia*, February 16, 1861; *Anglo-African*, December 22, 1860.

15.   THE COMING OF THE CIVIL WAR

The Secession Crisis

The discussion in this section is based on the following sources: *Journal of the Convention of the People of South Carolina, Held in 1860, 1861, and 1862* (Columbia, S.C., 1862), p. 465; Ronald T. Takaki, *A Pro-Slavery Crusade: The Agitation to Reopen the African Slave Trade* (New York, 1971), p. 470; Robert E. May, *The Southern Dream of a Caribbean Empire, 1854–1861* (Baton Rouge, La., 1973), p. 233; William K. Scarborough, ed., *The Diary of Edmund Ruffin*, Vol. 1: *Toward Independence, 1856–1861* (Baton Rouge, La., 1972), pp. 238, 241–42, 516; Herbert Aptheker, "Toward Counter-Revolution: The Slaveowners and Secession," *Political Affairs* (April 1973); 30, 55–57; Robert Manson Myers, ed., *The Children of Pride: A True Story of Georgia and the Civil War* (New Haven and London, 1973), pp. 342–43; Michael P. Johnson, *Toward a Patriarchal Republic: The Secession of Georgia* (Baton Rouge, La., 1977), pp. 108–23.

Black Reaction to Secession

The discussion in this section is based on the following sources: James McPherson, *The Negro's Civil War* (New York, 1965), pp. 11–13; *Douglass' Monthly* (December 1860, January 1861); *Liberator*, December 7, 1860; Philip S. Foner, *Frederick Douglass* (New York, 1964), pp. 187–88; Philip S. Foner, *The Life and Writings of Frederick Douglass* (New York, 1950), 2:526–30, 536–37, 3:59, 61; *Anglo-African*, December 22, 1860; *Boston Pilot* in *Liberator*, December 21, 1960.

The Crittenden Compromise

The discussion in this section is based on the following sources: Don E. Fehrenbacher, *Prelude to Greatness: Lincoln in the 1850's* (Stanford, Calif., 1962), pp. 90–96; *Congressional Globe*, 36th Cong., 2d sess., pp. 112–14, 237, 1093–94, 1259, 1264, 1368, 1403, 1405; David Potter, *Lincoln and His Party in the Secession Crisis* (New Haven, 1942), pp. 71–75; Kenneth M. Stampp, *And the War Came: The North and the Secession Crisis, 1860–1861* (Baton Rouge, La., 1950), pp. 131, 138–65; *Liberator*, February 22, 1861; McPherson, op. cit., pp. 14–16, publishes the petition and the manifesto but not the resolutions or the discussions at the mass meeting in the Joy Street Baptist Church of Boston; *Anglo-African,* December 22, 1860; Roy P. Basler et al., eds., *The Collected Works of Abraham Lincoln* (New Brunswick, N.J., 1953–1955), 3:18, 4:150, 154–55, 172, 183, 268–69.

Lincoln's Inaugural Address and Black Gloom

The discussion in this section is based on the following sources: Basler, op. cit., 4:262–71, 5:263; John G. Nicolay and John Hay, eds., *Complete Works of Abraham Lincoln* (New York, 1905), 6:169–71, 173, 175, 180, 183; *Anglo-African,* February 2, 16, March 9, 23, 1861; Foner, *Life and Writings of Frederick Douglass,* 3:71–80; *Douglass' Monthly* (April 1861); McPherson, op. cit., p. 12; *Anglo-African,* March 23, 1861.

Fort Sumter and the Outbreak of Civil War

The discussion in this section is based on the following sources: P. J. Parish, "Lincoln and Fort Sumter," *History Today* (April 1961): 262–70; Foner, *Frederick Douglass,* pp. 189–90; Foner, *Life and Writings of Frederick Douglass,* 3:579; *Douglass' Monthly* (April, May 1861).

16.   WHY THE WAR CAME

The discussion in this section is based on the following sources: Thomas J. Pressly, *Americans Interpret Their Civil War* (Princeton, N.J., 1954); David Donald, "American Historians and the Causes of the Civil War," *South Atlantic Quarterly* 59 (Summer 1960): 351–55.

The First Explanations

The discussion in this section is based on the following sources: [Edmund Ruffin], *Anticipations of the Future* (Richmond, Va., 1860), pp. viii–ix; Edward A. Pollard, *Southern History of the Great Civil War* (Philadelphia, 1866); Edward A. Pollard, *The Lost Cause Regained* (Philadelphia, 1868); Alexander H. Stephens, *A Constitutional View of the Late War between the States* (Philadelphia, 1868–1870), 1:542–45; Henry A. Wilson, *History of the Rise and Fall of the Slave Power in America* (Boston, 1872–1877); John A. Logan, *Great Conspiracy* (New York, 1886).

The Nationalist Interpretation and the Challenge to It

The discussion in this section is based on James Ford Rhodes, *History of the United States from the Compromise of 1850 to the Final Restoration of Home Rule in the South in 1877* (New York, 1893), 1:18–45; Charles A. and Mary R. Beard, *The Rise of American Civilization* (New York, 1927), 2:40–42; Arthur M. Schlesinger, *New Viewpoints in American History* (New York, 1922); Louis M. Hacker, *The Triumph of American Capitalism* (New York, 1933). For evidence that Northern business interests and plantation owners were tied together economically, see Philip S. Foner, *Business and Slavery: The New York Merchants and the Irrepressible Conflict* (Chapel Hill, N.C., 1940), and Thomas H. O'Connor, *Lords of the Loom: The Cotton Whigs and the Coming of the Civil War* (New York, 1968). For Phillips, see among others, Ulrich B. Phillips, *The Course of the South to Secession: An Interpretation,* ed. Merton Coulter (New York, 1939). For Ramsdell, see Charles W. Ramsdell, *Confederate States of America* (Durham, N.C., 1941). For Frank Owsley, see among others, *The South, Old and New Frontiers: Selected Essays of Frank Lawrence Owsley* (Athens, Ga., 1969).

The Revisionist Historians and Their Critics

The discussion in this section is based on the following sources: Gerald W. Johnson, *The Secession Crisis of the Southern States* (New York, 1933); James G. Randall, *The Civil War and Reconstruction* (Boston, 1937); James G. Randall, *Lincoln the President* (New York, 1945–1955), 1:125; James G. Randall, "The Civil War Restudied," *Mississippi Valley Historical Review* 27 (June 1940): 3–28; James G. Randall, "When the War Came in 1861," *Journal of Southern History* 6 (November 1940): 430–57; Arthur M. Schlesinger, Jr., "The Causes of the Civil War: A Note on Historical Sentimentalism," *Partisan Review* 16 (October 1949): 469–81; Harry V. Jaffa, *Crisis of the House Divided: An Interpretation of the Issues in the Lincoln-Douglas Debates* (New York, 1959); Kenneth M. Stampp, *And the War Came* (Baton Rouge, La., 1950), p. 166; Bernard De Voto, "The Easy Chair," *Harper's* 192 (February 1946): 123–26; Peter Geyl, "The American Civil War and the Problem of Inevitability," *New England Quarterly* 24 (June 1951): 147–68, reprinted in Peter Geyl, *Debates with Historians* (Gröningen, 1955), pp. 216–35; *The Civil War in the United States by Karl Marx and Frederick Engels,* ed., Richard Enmale (New York, 1937); Herbert Aptheker, "Marx and Engels on the Civil War," *New Masses,* July 30, 1946, reprinted in *Toward Negro Freedom* (New York, 1956), p. 81; Allan Nevins, *The Emergence of Lincoln* (New York, 1950), 2:122–24; Allan Nevins, *Ordeal of the Union* (New York, 1947), 1:118; Clement Eaton, *A History of the Southern Confederacy* (New York, 1954); Arthur Bestor, "The American Civil War as a Constitutional Crisis," *American Historical Review* 69 (January 1960): 330.

The Centennial of the Civil War

The discussion in this section is based on the following sources: E. Merton Coulter, ed., introduction to Ulrich B. Phillips, *The Course of the South to Secession* (New York, 1939, reprinted 1961); Robert Penn Warren, *The Legacy of the Civil War* (New York, 1961); Avery Craven, *The Civil War in the Making* (New York, 1961); William E. Barringer et al., *Politics and the Crisis of 1860,* ed. Norman A. Graebner (Urbana, Ill., 1961); Faith M. Brodie, "Who Won the Civil War Anyway?" *New York Times Book Review,* August 25, 1962, pp. 1, 22–23; Eugene D. Genovese, "The Slave South: An Interpretation," *Science and Society* 30 (December 1961): 295–96, reprinted in Allan Weinstein and Frank O. Gattel, eds., *American Negro Slavery: A Modern Reader* (New York, 1968), pp. 295–96; Herbert Aptheker, "The American Civil War: A Centenary Article," *Mainstream* (April 1961): 11, and *The American Civil War* (New York, 1961), pp. 6, 15; Edmund Wilson, *Patriotic Gore* (New York, 1961).

Since the Centennial

The discussion in this section is based on the following sources: William Appleman Williams, *America Confronts a Revolutionary World, 1776–1976* (New York, 1976), p. 113; John H. Sibley, "The Civil War Synthesis in American Political History," *Civil War History* 10 (June 1964): 130–40; Raimondo Luraghi, "The Civil War and the Modernization of Society: Social Structure and Industrial Revolution in the Old South before and during the War,'' *Civil War History* 18 (September 1972): 242–68; Steven A. Channing, *Crisis of Fear: Secession in South Carolina* (New York, 1970), pp. 181–82; William Birney, *The Road to Secession* (New York, 1972), pp. 130–40; Michael P. Johnson, ''Secession and Conservatism in the Lower South: The Social and Ideological Bases of Secession in Georgia, 1860–1861'' (Ph.D. diss., Stanford University, 1933); Eric Foner, ''The Causes of the Civil War: Recent Interpretations and New Directions,'' *Civil War History* 20 (Summer 1974): 208–9; David M. Potter, *The Impending Crisis, 1848–1861*, completed and edited by Don E. Fehrenbacher (New York, 1976), pp. 128–32; Peter J. Parish, *The American Civil War* (New York, 1975), p. 88; Alan A. Conway, *The Causes of the American Civil War: An Historical Perspective* (London, 1961, 1966), pp. 10–11; Michael F. Holt, *The Political Crisis of the 1850's* (New York, 1978), pp. vi–viii, 132–35; James McGregor Burns, *The American Experiment*, Vol. 1: *The Vineyard of Liberty* (New York, 1981), pp. 88–89, 92; Kenneth M. Stampp, *The Imperiled Union: Essays on the Background of the Civil War* (New York, 1980), pp. 88–89, 92–94; Eric Foner, *Free Soil, Free Labor, Free Men: The Ideology of the Republican Party Before the Civil War* (New York, 1970), pp. 222–25; Roy P. Basler et al., eds., *The Collected Works of Abraham Lincoln* (New Brunswick, N.J., 1953–1955), 8:332.

17.   THE WHITE MAN'S WAR

Reasons for Southern Confidence

The discussion in this section is based on the following sources: Irwin Silber, comp. and ed., *Songs of the Civil War* (New York, 1960), p. 173; *Bunch*, March 30, 1861, reprinted in Belle Becker Sideman and Lillian Friedman, eds., *Europe Looks at the Civil War* (New York, 1960), pp. 36–37; William H. Russell, *My Diary North and South* (London, 1861), pp. 66–67; W.E.B. Du Bois, ''The Negro in the Civil War,'' *Science and Society* 25 (December 1961): 348; *New Orleans Crescent*, April 16, 1861; *Savannah Republican*, March 12, 1861.

''The Uprising of a Great People''—But No Blacks Wanted

The discussion in this section is based on the following sources: Alfred Green, *Letters and Discussions on the Formation of Colored Regiments* (Philadelphia, 1862), pp. 3–4; Philip S. Foner, *The Voice of Black America: Major Speeches of Blacks in the United States, 1797–1973* (New York, 1975), 1:271–72; *Boston Bee*, April 19, 1861; *Liberator*, May 3, 10, 17, 31, September 6, 1861; Robert P. Smith, ''William Cooper Nell: Crusading Black Abolitionist,'' *Journal of Negro History* 55 (July 1970): 194; Herbert Aptheker, *Documentary History of the Negro People* (New York, 1951), pp. 463–65; Henry G. Pearson, *The Life of John A. Andrew, Governor of Massachusetts, 1861–1865* (Boston, 1904) 2:70; Philip S. Foner, *History of the Labor Movement in the United States* (New York, 1947), 1:300–310; U.S. Congress, House, 56th Cong., 1st sess., *The War of the Rebellion* (Washington, D.C., 1899), ser. III, 1:107, 133; Charles H. Wesley, *Ohio Negroes in the Civil War* (Washington, D.C., 1955), p. 15; Peter H. Clark, *Black Brigade of Cincinnati* (Cincinnati, Ohio, 1872), pp. 4–5; James McPherson, *The Negro's Civil War* (New York, 1965), pp. 30–32; *New York Weekly Anglo-African*, April 27, May 11, 1861; William Seraile, ''The Struggle to Raise Black Regiments in New York State,

1861–1864," *New-York Historical Society Quarterly* 58 (July 1974): 215–16; Philip S. Foner, *Frederick Douglass* (New York, 1964), pp. 190–93; *Douglass' Monthly* (May, September 1861): 62; Philip S. Foner, *The Life and Writings of Frederick Douglass* (New York, 1950), 3:94–98.

Reasons for Rejecting Blacks

The discussion in this section is based on the following sources: McPherson, op. cit., pp. 31–32; Bell Irwin Wiley, "Billy Yank and the Black Folk," *Journal of Negro History* 36 (January 1951): 35–36; Jack D. Foner, *Blacks and the Military in American History* (New York, 1974), p. 32.

Free Blacks Accepted in Union Navy

The discussion in this section is based on the following sources: Herbert Aptheker, "Negro in the Union Navy," *Journal of Negro History* 32 (April 1947): 169–74; Harold D. Langly, "The Negro in the Navy and the Merchant Service, 1789–1860," *Journal of Negro History* 52 (October 1976): 274–75; Lawrence Valuska, "The Negro in the Union Navy: 1861–1865" (Ph.D. diss., Lehigh University, 1973), pp. 5–21; Benjamin Quarles, *The Negro in the Civil War* (Boston, 1953), pp. 65–66; Philip S. Foner, *History of Black Americans* (Westport, Conn., 1975), 1:481–82, 486–87, 491–92; Michael Shiner Diary, Library of Congress, Manuscripts Division.

The New Fugitive Slaves

The discussion in this section is based on the following sources: George Washington Williams, *A History of the Negro Troops in the War of the Rebellion, 1861–1865* (New York, 1887), pp. 83–85; Bobby C. Lovett, "The Negro's Civil War in Tennessee, 1861–1865," *Journal of Negro History* 41 (January 1976): 36–37; Robert Manson Myers, ed., *The Children of Pride: A True Story of Georgia and the Civil War* (New Haven and London, 1972), pp. 453–56, 459–62; W.E.B. Du Bois, *Black Reconstruction in America* (New York, 1935), pp. 62, 65, 67; Bell Irwin Wiley, *Southern Negroes, 1861–1865* (New Haven, 1938), p. 8.

The Contrabands

The discussion in this section is based on the following sources: Elizabeth H. Botume, *First Days amongst the Contrabands* (Boston, 1892), p. 10; Edward L. Pierce, "The Contrabands at Fortress Monroe," *Atlantic Monthly* 8 (November 1861): 627–30; James M. McPherson, *The Struggle for Equality* (Princeton, N.J., 1964), pp. 70–71; Valuska, op. cit., pp. 49–50; Herbert Aptheker, *The Negro in the Civil War* (New York, 1938), p. 23.

A Slight Change in Policy

The discussion in this section is based on the following sources: Henry Wilson, *History of the Antislavery Measures of the Thirty-seventh and Thirty-eighth Congresses, 1861–1865* (Boston, 1865), pp. 235–59; John G. Nicolay and John Hay, eds., *The Complete Works of Abraham Lincoln* (New York, 1905), 6:368–69; *Douglass' Monthly* (September, October, November, December 1861, February 1862); Foner, *Frederick Douglass*, pp. 197–99; Foner, *Life and Writings of Frederick Douglass*, 3:145–69; McPherson, op. cit., pp. 42–43; *Christian Recorder*, October 12, 1861. T. Harry Williams, *Lincoln and the Radicals* (Madison, Wis., 1941), p. 32.

18.   END OF THE WHITE MAN'S WAR

Slaves Accepted in Union Navy

The discussion in this section is based on the following sources: Lawrence Valuska, "The Negro in the Union Navy, 1861–1865" (Ph.D. diss., Lehigh University, 1973), pp. 25–50; Herbert Aptheker, "Negro in the Union Navy," *Journal of Negro History* 32 (April 1947): 170–76; Henry Wilson, *History of the Antislavery Measures of the Thirty-seventh and Thirty-eighth Congresses, 1861–1865* (Boston, 1865), p. 22.

Some Black Heroes

The discussion in this section is based on the following sources: *Bangor Daily News,* February 20, 1971; *Douglass' Monthly* (August 1861); *New York Tribune,* July 12–14, 1861; Dorothy Sterling, *Speak Out in Thunder Tones: Letters and Other Writings of Black Northerners, 1787–1865* (New York, 1973), pp. 308–12; William Smith, *The Jeff Davis Piracy Cases* (Philadelphia, 1861); W.E.B. Du Bois, *Black Reconstruction in America* (New York, 1935), pp. 206–7; *AME Review* (January–March 1865); *Washington Republican* reprinted in *Liberator,* September 12, 1862.

Continuing Debate over Recruiting Black Soldiers

The discussion in this section is based on the following sources: *Oberlin Evangelist,* July 16, 1862; Richard Folk, "Black Man's Burden in Ohio, 1849–1863" (Ph.D. diss., University of Toledo, 1972), pp. 363–64; *Douglass' Monthly* (July–August 1862); *Cleveland Morning Leader,* November 5, 1861, April 29, October 31, 1862; *Cincinnati Commercial,* July 12, 1862.

Recruiting of Black Soldiers

The discussion in this section is based on the following sources: Jack D. Foner, *Blacks and the Military in American History* (New York, 1974), pp. 32–35; James McPherson, *The Negro's Civil War* (New York, 1965), pp. 164–65; Roy P. Basler et al., eds., *The Collected Works of Abraham Lincoln* (New Brunswick, N.J., 1953–1955), 5:356–57; David Taylor Cornish, *The Sable Arm: Negro Troops in the Union Army, 1861–1865* (New York, 1966), pp. 70–78; Benjamin Quarles, *The Negro in the Civil War* (Boston, 1953), pp. 113–14; *Chicago Tribune,* November 10, 1862.

The Black Brigade of Cincinnati

The discussion in this section is based on the following sources: Peter H. Clark, *Black Brigade of Cincinnati* (Cincinnati, Ohio, 1872), pp. 5–25; Edgar A. Toppin, "Humbly They Served: The Black Brigade in the Defense of Cincinnati," *Journal of Negro History* 48 (April 1963): 77–90; *National Anti-Slavery Standard,* September 17, October 18, 1862; Folk, op. cit., pp. 367–70; *Cincinnati Daily Gazette,* September 3–5, 1862; *Cincinnati Daily Commercial,* September 3–6, 1862.

First Military Action by Black Troops

The discussion in this section is based on the following sources: Thomas Wentworth Higginson, *Army Life in a Black Regiment* (New York, 1962), pp. 38–39; *New York Tribune,* March 31, 1864.

19. TWO PROCLAMATIONS AND A DAY OF JUBILEE

Constitutional or Revolutionary War?

The discussion in this section is based on the following sources: T. Harry Williams, *Lincoln and the Radicals* (Madison, Wis., 1941), p. 251; *Douglass' Monthly* (May, June 1861, February 1862); Philip S. Foner, *Frederick Douglass* (New York, 1946), pp. 194–95; Karl Marx and Friedrich Engels, *The Civil War in the United States* (New York, 1937), p. 253.

The "Slow Coach" Picks Up Speed

The discussion in this section is based on the following sources: WPA, *The Negro in Virginia* (New York, 1940), pp. 166–72; John G. Nicolay and John Hay, eds., *Complete Works of Abraham Lincoln* (New York, 1905), 7:270–73, 10:68–69; *Douglass' Monthly* (August 1861, May 1862); Foner, *Frederick Douglass*, p. 195; Henry Wilson, *History of the Rise and Fall of the Slave Power in America* (Boston and New York, 1877), 3:274–76, 291–95, 383; Carl Sandburg, *Abraham Lincoln: The War Years* (New York, 1939), 1:384–86, 577.

Background of the Emancipation Proclamation

The discussion in this section is based on the following sources: James M. McPherson, *The Struggle for Equality* (Princeton, N.J., 1964), pp. 98–101; John G. Nicolay and John Hay, *Abraham Lincoln: A History* (New York, 1890), 6:128–30; James G. Randall, *Lincoln the President* (New York, 1952), 2:154–57; Philip S. Foner, *History of the Labor Movement in the United States* (New York, 1947), 1:312–17; Carl Schurz, *The Reminiscences of Carl Schurz* (New York, 1909), 2:285–86.

Lincoln Proposes Colonization for Emancipated Blacks

The discussion in this section is based on the following sources: Herbert Aptheker, ed., *Documentary History of the Negro People in the United States* (New York, 1951), pp. 471–73; Dorothy Sterling, *Speak Out in Thunder Tones: Letters and Other Writings of Black Northerners, 1787–1865* (New York, 1973), pp. 297–98; Foner, *Frederick Douglass*, pp. 203–5; Foner, *Life and Writings of Frederick Douglass* (New York, 1951), 3:266–70; Benjamin Quarles, *The Negro in the Civil War* (Boston, 1953), pp. 146–48; Philip Van Doren Stern, ed., *The Life and Writings of Abraham Lincoln* (New York, 1940), pp. 715–23.

The Preliminary Emancipation Proclamation

The discussion in this section is based on the following sources: John Hope Franklin, *The Emancipation Proclamation* (Garden City, N.Y., 1963), pp. 148–62; *New York Tribune*, August 19, 1862; Lincoln to Horace Greeley, August 22, 1862 in Roy P. Basler et al., eds., *Collected Works of Abraham Lincoln* (New Brunswick, N.J., 1953–1955), 5:388–89; Foner, *Frederick Douglass*, pp. 204–5; *National Anti-Slavery Standard*, September 17, 1862; *Douglass' Monthly* (October 1862); Willard A. Heaps and Porter W. Heaps, *The Singing Sixties: The Spirit of Civil War Songs from the Music of the Times* (Norman, Okla., 1960), p. 281; Herbert Mitgang, *Lincoln as They Saw Him* (New York, 1961), pp. 319–20.

Would Lincoln Go Through with It?

The discussion in this section is based on the following sources: Foner, *Frederick Douglass*, pp. 206–7; Nicolay and Hay, op. cit., 8:161–64; Sandburg, op. cit., 2:14–18; Basler, op. cit., 6:42; Horace Greeley, *The American Conflict: A History of the Great Rebellion in the United States of America, 1860–1865* (Hartford, Conn., 1866), 2:254–55.

Day of Jubilee

The discussion in this section is based on the following sources: Foner, *Frederick Douglass*, pp. 208–9; Philip S. Foner, *The Voice of Black America: Major Speeches of Blacks in the United States, 1797–1973* (New York, 1975), 1:284–85; B. Rush Plumly to Abraham Lincoln, Philadelphia, January 1, 1863, Abraham Lincoln Papers, Library of Congress; *Liberator*, January 26, 1863; Henry M. Turner, *The Negro in Slavery, War and Peace* (Philadelphia, 1913), pp. 112–15; Sterling, op. cit., pp. 316–17; Elizabeth Hyde Botume, *First Days among the Contrabands* (Boston, 1892), pp. 75–77; Charlotte Forten, "Life in the Sea Islands," *Atlantic Monthly* 13 (June 1864): 668–70.

Significance of the Emancipation Proclamation

The discussion in this section is based on the following sources: David R. Wrone, "The Cherokee Act of Emancipation," *Journal of Ethnic Studies* 1 (Fall 1973): 87–90; James Truslow Adams, ed., *A Cycle of Adams Letters* (New York, 1949), 1:243; Mary Ellison, *Support for Secession: Lancaster and the American Civil War* (Chicago, 1972); Philip S. Foner, *British Labor and the American Civil War* (New York, 1981); Philip S. Foner, *Morale Education in the American Army* (New York, 1944), pp. 30–32; John J. Lynch Papers, Chicago Historical Society; Bell Irwin Wiley, "Billy Yank and the Black Folk," *Journal of Negro History* 36 (January 1951): 41–42; Franklin, op. cit., pp. 157–59; James G. Randall, *Constitutional Problems under Lincoln* (Urbana, Ill., 1951), pp. 343–85; Harold D. Moses, "Reaction in North Carolina to the Emancipation Proclamation," *North Carolina Historical Review* 52 (June 1970): 320–23; Sterling, op. cit., p. 298.

20. MEN OF COLOR, TO ARMS!

A Month of Celebrations

The discussion in this section is based on the following sources: *Cleveland Morning Leader,* January 14, 1863; Benjamin Quarles, *The Negro in the Civil War* (Boston, 1953), p. 174; Philip S. Foner, *The Life and Writings of Frederick Douglass* (New York, 1951), 3:321–27; *Cincinnati-Daily Gazette,* January 18, 1863; Richard Albert Folk, "Black Man's Burden in Ohio, 1849–1863" (Ph.D. diss., University of Toledo, 1972), pp. 381–82.

The Massachusetts Fifty-fourth

The discussion in this section is based on the following sources: Benjamin P. Thomas and Harold M. Hyman, *Stanton, The Life and Times of Lincoln's Secretary of War* (New York, 1962), p. 63; *War of the Rebellion: A Compilation of the Official Records of the Union and Confederate Armies* (Washington, D.C., 1880–1901), p. 215; Dorothy Sterling, *Speak Out in Thunder Tones: Letters and Other Writings of Black Northerners, 1787–1865* (New York, 1973), pp. 323–25; *Boston Journal,* January 27, May 19, 1863; *Liberator,* January 30, May 23, 28, June 5, 1863; Peter Burchard, *One Gallant Rush: Robert Gould Shaw and His Brave Black Regiment* (New York, 1965), pp. 71–74; Louis F. Emilio, *History of the Fifty-fourth Regiment of the Massachusetts Voluntary Infantry, 1863–1865* (Boston, 1894), pp. 11–16; Philip S. Foner, *Frederick Douglass* (New York, 1964), pp. 210–13; *Douglass' Monthly* (March 1863); *National Anti-Slavery Standard,* March 14, 1863; James M. McPherson, *The Negro's Civil War* (New York, 1965), pp. 173, 177–78; Folk, op. cit., pp. 385–86; *Boston Pilot* in *Liberator,* May 15, 1863; *Army and Navy Journal,* September 26, 1863; Philip S. Foner, *Morale Education in the American Army* (New York, 1944), p. 44; *Boston Transcript,* May 28, 1863; William Wells Brown, *The Negro in the American Rebellion* (Boston, 1867), p. 128.

Other Black Regiments

The discussion in this section is based on the following sources: *Official Roster of the Soldiers of the State of Ohio in the War of the Rebellion* (Akron, Ohio, 1893), 1:625–58; Folk, op. cit., pp. 388–93; Whitelaw Reid, *Ohio in the War: Her Generals and Soldiers* (Cincinnati, 1868), 2:905–7; John M. Langston, *Plantation to Capital,* pp. 209–17; *Record of the Service of the Fifty-fifth Regiment of Massachusetts Volunteers* (Cambridge, Mass., 1868), p. 112; *The War of the Rebellion,* series 1, 27, pt. 3, p. 203; Frederick M. Binder, "Pennsylvania Negro Regiments in the Civil War," *Journal of Negro History* 37 (October 1952): 383–417; Harry C. Silcox, "Nineteenth Century Philadelphia Black Militant: Octavius Catto, 1839–1871," *Pennsylvania History* 44 (January 1977): 59–60; *Philadelphia Press and U.S. Gazette,* June 20–25, 1863; George W. Williams, *A History of the Negro Troops in the War of the Rebellion* (New York, 1888), pp. 119–21; *New York Tribune,* March 7, 1864; William Seraile, "The Struggle to Raise Negro Regiments in New York State, 1861–1864," *New-York Historical Society Quarterly* 58 (July 1974): 218–23; Jeffrey D. Wert, "Camp William Penn and the Black Soldier," *Pennsylvania History* 46 (1979): 335–46.

Some Black Recruiters

The discussion in this section is based on the following sources: Jack D. Foner, *Blacks and the Military in American History* (New York, 1974), pp. 45–46; "The Colored Brigade," issued by Johnson, Song Publisher, 7 North Tenth Street, Philadelphia, Copy in Library Company of Philadelphia; Jack Abramowitz, "A Civil War Letter: James M. Trotter to Francis J. Jackson Garrison," *Midwest Journal* 4 (Summer 1952): 113–22; Edwin S. Redkey, " 'Rocked in the Cradle of Consternation,' " by the Reverend Henry M. Turner, *American Heritage* 31 (October–November 1980): 79–84; Lawrence Valuska, "The Negro in the Union Navy, 1861–1865" (Ph.D. diss., Lehigh University, 1973), pp. 119–35; Rowland Stafford True, "Life Aboard a Gunboat," *Civil War Times Illustrated* 9 (February 1971): 36–43; Sterling, op. cit., pp. 327–29; *Liberator,* October 7, 1864; *Boston Commonwealth,* July 17, 1863; Earl Conrad, *Harriet Tubman* (New York, 1943), pp. 168–69; *New York Tribune,* January 5, 1864.

Discrimination in the Union Army

The discussion in this section is based on the following sources: Sterling, op. cit., pp. 345–46; *Christian Recorder,* March 19, April 23, 1864; *New York World,* December 13, 1863; *Baltimore Sun,* March 1, 1864; *Douglass' Monthly* (February 1863); Herbert Aptheker, *To Be Free: Studies in American Negro History* (New York, 1948), pp. 83–92, 94–98; Brainerd Dyer, "The Treatment of Colored Union Troops by the Confederates," *Journal of Negro History* 20 (July 1935): 173–86; Corporal James Henry Gooding to President Abraham Lincoln, National Archives, Washington, D.C., War Records Office; Herbert Aptheker, ed., *A Documentary History of the Negro People in the United States* (New York, 1951), pp. 482–84.

Dealing with Black Soldiers' Grievances
    The discussion in this section is based on the following sources: *Cincinnati Daily Gazette*, July 9, 1863; Folk, op. cit., p. 391; Foner, *Frederick Douglass*, pp. 213–15; *Douglass' Monthly* (August 1863); *Liberator*, January 29, 1864; *Proceedings of the Thirteenth Anniversary Meeting of the American Anti-Slavery Society, 1864* (New York, 1864), pp. 116–18; *Address of Frederick Douglass at National Hall, Philadelphia, July 15, 1863* (Philadelphia, 1863); John W. Blassingame, "The Organization and Use of Negro Troops in the Union Army, 1863–1865" (master's thesis, Howard University, 1961), pp. 113–14; David Taylor Cornish, *The Sable Arm: Negro Troops in the Union Army, 1851–1861* (New York, 1966), pp. 264–67; *Baltimore Daily Gazette*, October 23, 1863, reprinted in John W. Blassingame, "The Recruitment of Negro Troops in Maryland," *Maryland Historical Magazine* 58 (July 1963): 28–29; John Sprague, "The Fort Jackson Mutiny," *Journal of Negro History* 27 (October 1942): 420–26; Joyce Sparer Adler, "Melville and the Civil War," *New Letters* 40 (Winter 1973): 109; W.E.B. Du Bois in *Science and Society* 25 (December 1961): 351; Herbert Aptheker, "Negro in the Union Navy," *Journal of Negro History* 32 (April 1947): 169–70; Valuska, op. cit., pp. 125–26; John G. Nicolay and John Hay, eds., *The Complete Works of Abraham Lincoln* (New York, 1905), 8:48–49, 239; George W. Williams, *A History of the Negro Troops in the War of Rebellion* (New York, 1888), p. 251; "The Fort Pillow Massacre," *Congressional Report No. 65* (Washington, D.C., 1865); Albert Castel, "Fort Pillow: Victory or Massacre?" *American History Illustrated* 10 (April 1974): 4–10, 46–48.

Port Hudson and Milliken's Bend
    The discussion in this section is based on the following sources: McPherson, op. cit., pp. 183–88; *New York Times*, June 11, 1863; [Matthew H. Meschert], *Washington and Jackson on Negro Soldiers: General Banks on the Bravery of Negro Troops. Poem—The Second Louisiana*, by George H. Boker, Philadelphia (1863), copy in Library Company of Philadelphia.

Fort Wagner
    The discussion in this section is based on the following sources: Cornish, op. cit., pp. 152–56; McPherson, op. cit., pp. 189–92; Emilio, op. cit., pp. 67–104; Roy P. Basler et al., eds., *Collected Works of Abraham Lincoln* (New Brunswick, N.J., 1953–1955), 6:409–10; Thomas Wentworth Higginson, *Army Life in a Black Regiment* (Boston, 1882), pp. 243–44.

21.   THE HOME FRONT—SOUTH

Were Slaves Loyal?
    The discussion in this section is based on the following sources: Bell I. Wiley, *Southern Negroes, 1861–1865* (New Haven, 1938), pp. 50–51, 72; Benjamin Quarles, *The Negro*

in the Civil War (Boston, 1953), pp. 50, 262; George Rawick, ed., The American Slave: A Composite Autobiography (Westport, Conn., 1971–1979), South Carolina Narratives, part IV, 3:45–46; Charleston Daily Courier, March 5, 1864; Robert D. Read, "The Negro in Alabama during the Civil War," Journal of Negro History 35 (July 1950): 273–74; Robert Munson Myers, ed., The Children of Pride: A True Story of Georgia and the Civil War (New Haven and London, 1972), pp. 322–27; G. P. Whittington, "Concerning the Loyalty of Slaves in North Louisiana in 1862," Louisiana Historical Quarterly 14 (October 1931): 491–93; Herbert Aptheker, Essays in the History of the American Negro (New York, 1945), pp. 178–79; Howard Swiggett, ed., A Rebel War Clerk's Diary at the Confederate States' Capital, by J. B. Jones (New York, 1955), 2:133; Kenneth M. Stampp, The Era of Reconstruction, 1865–1877 (New York, 1965), p. 121.

Insubordination, Strikes, Insurrections, and Guerrilla Warfare

The discussion in this section is based on the following sources: Whittington, op. cit., p. 492; Wiley, op. cit., pp. 73–78; John Hope Franklin, "The Enslavement of Free Negroes in North Carolina," Journal of Negro History 29 (October 1944): 413–15; B. H. Nelson, "Some Aspects of Negro Life in North Carolina during the Civil War," North Carolina Historical Review 21 (April 1948): 150–51; Harold D. Moser, "Reaction in North Carolina to the Emancipation Proclamation," North Carolina Historical Review 48 (April 1973): 413–18; W.E.B. Du Bois in Science and Society 25 (December 1961): 349; Harvey Wish, "Slave Disloyalty under the Confederacy," Journal of Negro History 23 (October 1938): 435–50; Herbert Aptheker, American Negro Slave Revolts (New York, 1952), pp. 356–67; A. K. Farrar to Governor Pettus, July 17, 1862, quoted in Herbert Aptheker, "Notes on Slave Conspiracies in Confederate Mississippi," Journal of Negro History 29 (January 1944): 76; Joel Gray Taylor, "Slavery in Louisiana during the Civil War," Louisiana History 8 (Winter 1967): 27–33; Aptheker, Essays in American Negro History, pp. 184–86; John Betterworth, Confederate Mississippi (New York, 1942), pp. 122–23; William J. Minor, Plantation Diary, 1863–1868, Louisiana State University Library, Baton Rouge, Louisiana.

Disaffection in the Confederacy

The discussion in this section is based on the following sources: Ulrich B. Phillips, "The Central Theme of Southern History," American Historical Review 24 (April 1928): 122; Ella Lonn, Desertion during the Civil War (New York, 1928), pp. 7, 11, 12, 14, 17, 19, 222, 245; G. C. Eggleston, History of the Confederate War (New York, 1910), pp. 4, 196; Georgia Lee Tatum, "Disloyalty and Disloyal Organizations in the Confederacy" (Ph.D. diss., Vanderbilt University, 1932), pp. 141–42; Albert Burton Moore, Conscription and Conflict in the Confederacy (New York, 1924), pp. 49, 143, 187–88, 279–80, 283, 284; Wilfred B. Yearns, "The Peace Movement in the Confederate Congress," Georgia Historical Quarterly 41 (March 1957), p. 1; E. Merton Coulter, The Confederate States of America (Baton Rouge, La., 1951), Volume 7 of A History of the South, ed Wendell H. Stephenson and E. Merton Coulter, pp. 134, 148–52; Georgia L. Tatum, Disloyalty in the Confederacy (Chapel Hill, N.C., 1934), pp. 114–15; Bell I. Wiley, The Plain People of the Confederacy (Baton Rouge, La., 1943), pp. 116–17; Thomas L. Livermore, Numbers and Losses in the Civil War in America: 1861–1865 (Bloomington, Ind., 1957), pp. 125–30; Charles W. Ramsdell, Behind the Lines in the Southern Confederacy (Baton Rouge, La., 1944), p. 47; Clement Dowd, Life of Zebulon B. Vance (Charlotte, N.C., 1897), pp. 447–48; Dominick R. Crup, "A Brief Survey of Disaffection, Disunity, and Disloyalty in the Confederacy,'' *Journal of Social Studies* 3 (Spring 1951): 52–61; "Proceedings of the First Confederate Congress," *Southern Historical Society Papers* 46 (January 1928): 244–45; Wilfred Buck Yearns, *The Confederate Congress* (Athens, Ga., 1960), pp. 65–67; *Carolina Watchman*, December 8, 1862; *Montgomery Daily Advertiser*, October 21, 1863; *Richmond Dispatch* and *Richmond Whig*, August 12, 16, 24, 1861, April 3, December 3, 4, 1863; Emory M. Thomas, "The Richmond Bread Riot of 1863," *Virginia Cavalcade* (Summer 1968): 44–47; Herbert Aptheker, *The Labor Movement in the South during Slavery* (New York, n.d.), pp. 19–21; *The War of the Rebellion: A Compilation of the Official Records of the Union and Confederate Armies* (Washington, D.C., 1880–1901), ser. IV, 3:813–14, 975.

A Black Voice in the Deep South

The discussion in this section is based on the following sources: *L'Union*, September 27, December 30, 1862, partly reprinted in James M. McPherson, *The Negro's Civil War* (New York, 1965), pp. 61–62; Jean-Charles Houzeau, "Le Journal Noir, Aux Etats-Unis de 1863 a 1870," *Revue de Belgique* 7 (June 1872): 120–21; Amistead Scott Pride, "A Register and History of Negro Newspapers in the United States, 1827–1850" (Ph.D. diss., Northwestern University, 1950), p. 19; Charles Reuleus and General Liagre, "Jean-Charles Houzeau," *Société Royal Belge de Geographie Bulletin* 4 (Fall 1888): 367–68; Jean-Charles Houzeau, *Etudes sur les Faculties Mentales des Animaux comparés a celles de l'Homme, par un voyageur Naturaliste* (Mons, 1872); Jean-Charles Houzeau, *Question de L'Esclavage* (Brussels, 1863); Rodolphe L. Desdunes, *Nos Hommes et Notre Histoire: Notices Biographiqués Accompagnées de Reflexions et de Souvenirs Personnels: Hommage a la Population Créole en Souvenir des Grands Hommes qu'elle Accomplies* (Montreal, 1911), pp. 160–76; John Blassingame, *Black New Orleans* (Chicago, 1973), pp. 130–31; David C. Rankin, "The Origins of Black Leadership in New Orleans during Reconstruction," *Journal of Southern History* 40 (August 1970): 433, 440.

22. THE HOME FRONT—NORTH

The discussion in this section is based on the following sources: Frank L. Kleement, *The Copperheads in the Middle West* (Chicago, 1943), pp. 12–17, 23, 45; Wood Gray, *The Hidden Civil War: The Story of the Copperheads* (New York, 1942), pp. 23, 29, 30; *New York Herald,* October 20, 1862; Ralph Andreano, ed., *The Economic Impact of the American Civil War* (New York, 1962), pp. 12–16.

Toledo and Cincinnati

The discussion in this section is based on the following sources: Ralph C. Dawnes, *Lake Port* (Toledo, 1911), pp. 374–90; Richard Albert Folk, "Black Man's Burden in Ohio, 1849–1863" (Ph.D. diss., University of Toledo, 1972), pp. 371–76; Edgar A. Toppin, "Humbly They Served: The Black Brigade in the Defense of Cincinnati," *Journal of Negro History* 48 (April 1963): 75–79; Leonard Harding, "The Cincinnati Riots of 1862," Cincinnati Historical Society, *Bulletin* 30 (October 1967): 229–38; Willston H. Lofton, "Northern Labor and the Negro during the Civil War," *Journal of Negro History* 34 (July 1949): 251–73; Charles R. Wilson, "Cincinnati during the Civil

War," *Journal of Southern History* 2 (November 1936): 468–79; *Cincinnati Commercial,* July 14, 17–18, 1862.

Brooklyn and Detroit

The discussion in this section is based on the following sources: *Brooklyn Daily Eagle,* August 1–4, 1862; *Douglass' Monthly* (September 1862); Forrest G. Wood, *Black Scare: The Racist Response to Emancipation and Reconstruction* (Berkeley and Los Angeles, 1968), pp. vii, viii; *A Thrilling Narrative from the Lips of the Sufferers of the Late Detroit Riot, March 6, 1863* (Detroit, 1863); Dorothy Sterling, *Speak Out in Thunder Tones: Letters and Other Writings of Black Americans, 1787–1865* (New York, 1973), pp. 334–35; *Detroit Free Press,* March 7–9, 1863.

Copperhead Propaganda and the Draft

The discussion in this section is based on the following sources: *New York Copperhead,* May 16, 30, July 18, 1863; *New York Daily News,* April 14, 22, 23, 1864; James G. Randall and David Donald, *The Civil War and Reconstruction* (Boston, 1961), pp. 480–86; Fred Shannon, *The Organization and Administration of the Union Army* (Cleveland, 1928), 1:305–7; Eugene Converse Murdock, *Patriotism Unlimited, 1862–1865: The Civil War Draft and the Bounty System* (Kent, Ohio, 1967), pp. 18–22, 88–95; Arnold Shankman, "Draft Resistance in Civil War Pennsylvania," *Pennsylvania Magazine of History and Biography* 101 (April 1977): 193; Philip S. Foner, *History of the Labor Movement in the United States* (New York, 1947), 1:320–22.

New York City Draft Riots

The discussion in this section is based on the following sources: J. T. Headley, *The Great Riots in New York* (New York, 1873), pp. 261–68; *New York Times,* July 14–19, 1863; *New York Tribune,* July 14–19, 1863; *New York Daily News,* July 12, 15, 1863; Augustine Costello, *History of the New York Police* (New York, 1885), pp. 161–68; Philip S. Foner and Ronald Lewis, eds., *The Black Worker: A Documentary History* (Philadelphia, 1978), 1:286–301; C. C. Chapin, "Personal Recollections of the Draft Riots, New York City, 1863," Manuscript, New-York Historical Society; Philip S. Foner, "William Powell: Militant Champion of Black Seamen," in *Essays in Afro-American History* (Philadelphia, 1978), pp. 104–5; *Liberator,* July 24, 1863, and reprinted in part in James McPherson, *The Negro's Civil War* (New York, 1965), pp. 73–74 and Sterling, op. cit., pp. 337–38; Irving Werstein, *July, 1863: The Incredible Story of the New York City Draft Riots* (New York, 1957), pp. 214–15; Albon P. Mann, Jr., "Labor Competition and the New York Draft Riots of 1863," *Journal of Negro History* 36 (October 1951): 375–76; James McCague, *The Second Rebellion: The Story of the New York City Draft Riots of 1863* (New York, 1968), pp. 128–35.

The Aftermath

The discussion in this section is based on the following sources: Philip S. Foner, ed., *The Voice of Black Americans: Major Speeches by Blacks in the United States, 1797–1973* (New York, 1975), 1:298–99; Mann, op. cit., pp. 375–76; McCague, op. cit., pp. 245–50; Joseph T. Wilson, *The Black Phalanx* (Hartford, Conn., 1899), p. 377; T. C. Perry, ed., *Life and Letters of Francis Lieber* (Boston, 1886), p. 342; Powell, in Philip S. Foner, *Essays in Afro-American History* (Philadelphia, 1978), p. 105.

Advances on the Civil Rights Front

The discussion in this section is based on the following sources: McPherson, op. cit., pp. 249–54; *Douglass' Monthly* (November 1861); Edward McPherson, *The Political History of the United States of America, during the Great Rebellion* (Washington, D.C., 1865), pp. 239–40, 242–43, 378–84, 593; *Pacific Appeal*, July 5, August 2, September 6, 1862; Arthur Charles Cole, *The Era of the Civil War, 1848–1870, Centennial History of Illinois* (Springfield, Ill., 1919), 3:225–26, 333–37, 417–18; Charles Noye Zucker, "The Free Negro Question: Race Relations in Ante-Bellum Illinois, 1801–1860" (Ph.D. diss., Northwestern University, 1972), pp. 169–76; Dennis Frank Ricke, "Illinois Blacks through the Civil War: A Struggle for Equality" (master's thesis, Southern Illinois University, 1970), pp. 122–35; Charles A. Gliozzo, *John Jones and the Repeal of the Illinois Black Laws* (Duluth, Minn., 1975), pp. 32–56; Arna Bontemps and Jack Conroy, *Anyplace But Here* (New York, 1966), pp. 43–52; John Jones, *The Black Laws and a Few Reasons Why They Should Be Repealed* (Chicago, 1864), pp. 3–7; Emma Lou Thornbrough, *The Negro in Indiana* (Indianapolis, 1957), pp. 203, 233.

Battle against Segregation: The Philadelphia Story

The discussion in this section is based on the following sources: *Liberator,* August 15, 1862; McPherson, *Negro's Civil War,* pp. 255–56; Philip S. Foner, "The Battle to End Discrimination against Negroes on Philadelphia Streetcars" (Part I): "Background and Beginning of the Battle" (Part II): "The Victory," *Pennsylvania History* 40 (July 1973): 261–90, (October 1973): 355–79, and reprinted in Philip S. Foner, *Essays in Afro-American History* (Philadelphia, 1978), pp. 19–76; *A Brief Narrative of the Struggle for the Rights of the Colored People of Philadelphia on the City Railway* (Philadelphia, 1867); *Report of the Committee Appointed for the Purpose of Securing to Colored People of Philadelphia the Right to Use of the Streetcars* (Philadelphia, 1869); George M. Fredrickson, *The Black Image in the White Mind: The Debate on the Afro-American Character and Destiny, 1817–1914* (New York, 1971), pp. 184–85.

23. THE ARMY AND THE FREED SLAVES, 1863–1864

Education of Blacks during the War

The discussion in this section is based on the following sources: Bell I. Wiley, *Southern Negroes, 1861–1865* (New Haven, 1938), pp. 279–81; Jack D. Foner, *Blacks and the Military in American History* (New York, 1974), pp. 40–41; Henry L. Swint, ed., *Dear Ones at Home: Letters from Contraband Camps* (Nashville, Tenn., 1966); letter of Frank Green, Baton Rouge, La., July 1864, Amistad Collection, Dillard University, New Orleans.

The Port Royal Experiment

The discussion in this section is based on the following sources: Willie Lee Rose, *Rehearsal for Reconstruction: The Port Royal Experiment* (New York, 1964); Ray Allen Billington, ed., *The Journal of Charlotte Forten* (New York, 1961); Charlotte Forten, "Life on the Sea Islands," *Atlantic Monthly* 13 (May 1864): 591; Elizabeth Ware Pearson, ed., *Letters from Port Royal* (Boston, 1906); extracts from *Letters of Teachers and Superintendents, New England Commission* (Boston, 1864); *Philadelphia Press,* May 31,

1864; Friends' Association of Philadelphia, *Statistics of the Operations of the Executive Board of Friends' Association of Philadelphia, and Its Vicinity, for the Relief of Colored Freedmen* (Philadelphia, 1864); Edward L. Pierce, "The Freedman at Port Royal," *Atlantic Monthly* 12 (September 1863): 22–36; Edward L. Pierce, *Report on the Negroes at Port Royal to Salmon P. Chase* (Boston, 1862); *Anglo-African* (November 1861); *Douglass' Monthly* (November 1862); James M. McPherson, *The Struggle for Equality* (Princeton, N.J., 1964), pp. 248, 256; James M. McPherson, *The Negro's Civil War* (New York, 1965), pp. 293–96.

Louisiana

The discussion in this section is based on the following sources: *Liberator,* February 10, 1865; *New Orleans Tribune,* August 13, September 10, 15, 22, 24, December 8, 1864; Peter C. Riley, *Slaves and Freedmen in Civil War Louisiana* (Baton Rouge, La., 1976), pp. 56–62; Peyton McCrary, *Abraham Lincoln and Reconstruction: The Louisiana Experiment* (Princeton, N.J., 1978), pp. 116–18.

Mississippi Valley

The discussion in this section is based on the following sources: Ronald L. C. Davis, "The U.S. Army and the Origins of Sharecropping in the Natchez District—A Case Study," *Journal of Negro History* 42 (January 1977): 60–80; *New York Times,* August 10, 1863; Thomas W. Knox, *Camp-Fire and Cotton-Field* (New York, 1865), pp. 305–440; John Eaton, *Grant, Lincoln, and the Freedmen* (New York, 1901), pp. 1–29, 46–61, 142–66; Wiley, *Southern Negroes,* pp. 184–90; Martha Mitchell Bigelow, "Freedmen of the Mississippi Valley 1862–1865," *Civil War History* 8 (March 1962): 38–47; Ulysses S. Grant, *Personal Memoirs of U.S. Grant* (New York, 1888), 1:424–26; James A. Yeatman, *A Report on the Condition of the Freedmen of the Mississippi* (St. Louis, Mo., 1864), pp. 7–9; William L. Harris, *Presidential Reconstruction in Mississippi* (Baton Rouge, La., 1967), p. 93; Special Order of Gen. Lorenzo Thomas, number 9, March 11, 1864, in *The War of the Rebellion: A Compilation of the Official Records of the Union and Confederate Armies* (Washington, D.C., 1880–1900), ser. III, 4:166–70.

24. BLACKS AND ABRAHAM LINCOLN, 1863–1864

Colonization, Again

The discussion in this section is based on the following sources: Tyler Dennett, ed., *Lincoln and the Civil War in the Diary and Letters of John Hay* (New York, 1939), p. 203; Philip S. Foner, *The Life and Writings of Frederick Douglass* (New York, 1950), 3:290; Paul J. Scheils, "Lincoln and the Chiriqui Colonization Project," *Journal of Negro History* 37 (July 1950): 419–30; James M. McPherson, *The Negro's Civil War* (New York, 1965), pp. 95–97; Warren A. Beck, "Lincoln and Negro Colonization in Central America," *Abraham Lincoln Quarterly Magazine* 6 (September 1950): 162–83; Benjamin F. Butler, *Autobiography and Personal Reminiscences of Major-General Benj. F. Butler* (Boston, 1892), p. 903; Roy P. Basler et al., eds., *The Collected Works of Abraham Lincoln* (New Brunswick, N.J., 1953–1955), 2:132, 3:15, 4:561, 5:48, 318, 370–75, 434, 520–21, 530–31, 534–35.

Lincoln's Reconstruction Plan and Black Reaction to It

The discussion in this section is based on the following sources: Basler et al., op. cit., 5:462–63, 504–5; 6:364–66, 7:1–2, 6, 66–67, 89–91, 123–25, 161–63, 185, 243, 248, 486–87, 8:106–7, 131, 164–65, 206–7, 404–14; Fred H. Harrington, *Fighting Politician: Major General N. P. Banks* (Philadelphia, 1948), pp. 164–65; Willie M. Caskey, *Secession and Restoration of Louisiana* (University, La., 1938), pp. 101–7; Benjamin Quarles, *Lincoln and the Negro* (New York, 1962), pp. 226–28; Annie Lee West Stahl, "The Free Negro in Ante-Bellum Louisiana," *Louisiana Historical Quarterly* 25 (Spring 1942): 301–16; Foner, op. cit., 3:378–86; James G. Blaine, *Twenty Years of Congress: From Lincoln to Garfield* (Norwich, Conn., 1884), p. 40; W.E.B. Du Bois, *Black Reconstruction in America* (New York, 1935), p. 157; *Liberator,* April 1, 1864; McPherson, op. cit., pp. 278–79; *L'Union,* May 24, 1864; *New Orleans Tribune,* July 21, August 11, 1864; John Blassingame, *Black New Orleans* (Chicago, 1973), pp. 9–22; D. E. Everett, "Free Persons of Color in New Orleans, 1803–1865" (Ph.D. diss., Tulane University, 1952), pp. 320–26; William E. Highsmith, "Louisiana during Reconstruction" (Ph.D. diss., Louisiana State University, 1953), pp. 159–65; Louis Ruchames, "William Lloyd Garrison and the Negro Franchise," *Journal of Negro History* 50 (January 1965): 37–49; Peyton McCrary, *Abraham Lincoln and Reconstruction: The Louisiana Experiment* (Princeton, N.J., 1978), pp. 148–75.

Blacks and the Election of 1864

The discussion in this section is based on the following sources: Foner, op. cit., 3:42–51, 386–87, 393–94, 403, 408, 424; Larry E. Nelson, "Black Leaders and the Presidential Election of 1864," *Journal of Negro History* 63 (January 1978): 42–58; Christopher Breiseth, "Lincoln and Frederick Douglass," *Journal of the Illinois State Historical Society* 68 (February 1975): 22–25; *Anglo-African,* January 9, 21, May 21, August 13, October 29, 1864; *New Orleans Tribune,* August 6, 9, 16, September 15, 22, 24, October 26, November 23, 1864; Jane H. Pease and William H. Pease, *Bound with Them in Chains* (Westport, Conn., 1972), pp. 162–90; William Wells Brown, *The Black Man* (New York, 1863), pp. 149–51; Martin Dann, ed., *The Black Press, 1827–1890* (New York, 1971), p. 23; I. Garland Penn, *The African-American Press and Its Editors* (Springfield, Mass., 1891), pp. 23–33; Frederick Douglass, "Address to American Anti-Slavery Society December 4, 1863," in *Proceedings of the American Anti-Slavery Society at Its Third Decade* (New York, 1864), pp. 111–15; Blassingame, op. cit., pp. 20–29; *Liberator,* February 5, March 11, April 1, 15, July 22, September 16, 23, 1864; *New York Times,* May 27, 1864; Edward McPherson, ed., *The Political History of the United States of America during the Great Rebellion* (New York, 1864), p. 413; Kirk H. Porter and Donald B. Johnson, eds., *National Party Platforms, 1840–1968* (Urbana, Ill., 1970), pp. 34–36; Ruhly J. Bartlett, *John C. Frémont and the Republican Party* (Columbus, Ohio, 1930), pp. 104–5; *Proceedings of the National Convention of Colored Men Held in Syracuse, New York, October 4–7, 1864* (New York, 1864), pp. 4–62; *Syracuse Journal,* October 7, 1864, reprinted in *National Anti-Slavery Standard,* October 15, 1864; Sidney Kaplan, "The Miscegenation Issue in the Election of 1864," *Journal of Negro History* 35 (July 1949): 274–343; Leonard Newman, "Opposition to Lincoln in the Election of 1864," *Science and Society* 32 (Fall 1944): 305–27; Lee Norton, *War Elections, 1862–1864* (New York, n.d.), pp. 44–46; J. W. Shively, *An Extra of the Sovereign People's Magna Charta* (n.p., 1864).

25.   UNION VICTORY

Sherman's March to the Sea

The discussion in this section is based on the following sources: Shelby Foote, *The Civil War: A Narrative: Red River to Appomattox* (New York, 1975), pp. 110–225; W. T. Sherman, *Memoirs of W. T. Sherman* (New York, 1888), pp. 162–65, 186–90, 212–15; *Christian Recorder,* April 23, 1864.

The Fifty-fourth and Fifty-fifth in South Carolina

The discussion in this section is based on the following sources: Jack Abramowitz, ed., "A Civil War Letter: James Trotter to Francis J. Garrison," *Midwest Journal* 4 (Summer 1952): 117–22; George W. Williams, *A History of the Negro Troops in the War of the Rebellion* (New York, 1888), pp. 209–11; Frank Moore, ed., *The Rebellion Record* (New York, 1871), pp. 118–20, 405–17; Leon F. Litwack, "Black Liberators," in Thomas R. Frazier, ed., *The Underside of American History* (New York, 1982), 2:24; Frank A. Rollin, *Life and Public Service of Martin R. Delany* (Boston, 1883), pp. 197–98.

A Celebration in Charleston

The discussion in this section is based on the *New York Times,* April 4, 1865; *New York Tribune,* April 4, 1865.

Grant's Virginia Campaign

The discussion in this section is based on the following sources: Foote, op. cit., pp. 240–445; Edwin S. Redkey, " 'Rocked in the Cradle of Consternation,' " *American Heritage* 31 (October–November 1980): 70–79, which reprints Turner's article in the *Christian Recorder.*

The Confederacy and Black Soldiers

The discussion in this section is based on the following sources: Charles H. Wesley, "The Employment of Negroes as Soldiers in the Confederate Army," *Journal of Negro History* 4 (July 1919): 239–53; W.E.B. Du Bois, *Black Reconstruction in America* (New York, 1935), pp. 117–18; Jack D. Foner, *Blacks and the Military in American History* (New York, 1974), pp. 48–50; Roy P. Basler et al., eds., *The Collected Works of Abraham Lincoln* (New Brunswick, N.J., 1953–1955), 8:361–62; Barbara C. Ruby, "General Pattick Cleburne's Proposal to Arm Southern Slaves," *Arkansas Historical Quarterly* 30 (Autumn 1971): 125–40; James H. Brewer, *The Confederate Negro* (Durham, N.C., 1969), pp. 213–43; Bell I. Wiley, *Southern Negroes, 1861–1865* (New Haven, 1938), p. 322; Carl Cahill, "Note on Two Va. Negro Civil War Soldiers: One Union, One Confederate," *Negro History Bulletin* 29 (November 1965): 39–40; *Severnaya Pchela* and *Russkoye Slavo* quoted in R. Ivanov, *American History and the Black Question* (Moscow, 1976), pp. 92–93, 109; Robert F. Durden, *The Gray and the Black: The Confederate Debate on Emancipation* (Baton Rouge, La., 1972), pp. vii–viii.

End of the Civil War and Assassination of Lincoln

The discussion in this section is based on the following sources: Bobby L. Lovett, "The Negro's Civil War in Tennessee, 1861–1865," *Journal of Negro History* 41 (January 1976): 46–47; *Liberator,* May 5, 1865; Herbert Aptheker, *Documentary History of the Negro People in the United States* (New York, 1951), pp. 499, 507; *The Assassination of Abraham Lincoln and the Trial of the Conspirators. The Courtroom Testimony as Originally Compiled by Benn Putnam,* introduction by Philip Van Doren Stern (New York, 1954), pp. 87–88, 172–73; Ludwell H. Johnson, "Lincoln and Equal Rights. The Authenticity of the Wadsworth Letter," *Journal of Southern History* 32 (1966): 83–87; Harold M. Hyman, "Lincoln and Equal Rights for Negroes: The Irrelevancy of the 'Wadsworth Letter,'" *Civil War History* 12 (1966): 258–66; Ludwell H. Johnson, "Lincoln and Equal Rights: A Reply," *Civil War History* 13 (March 1967): 66–73; Peyton McCrary, *Abraham Lincoln and Reconstruction: The Louisiana Experiment* (Princeton, N.J., 1978), pp. 202–3; LaWanda Cox, *Lincoln and Black Freedom: A Study in Presidential Leadership* (Columbia, S.C., 1981).

26. WHY THE NORTH WON

Five Historians Explain the Northern Victory

The discussion in this section is based on David Donald, ed., *Why the North Won the Civil War* (Baton Rouge, La., 1960).

The Significance of Slavery

The discussion in this section is based on Kenneth M. Stampp, "The Southern Road to Appomattox," in *The Imperiled Union: Essays in the Background of the Civil War* (New York, 1980); Charles H. Wesley, *The Collapse of the Confederacy* (Washington, D.C., 1922); Bell Irwin Wiley, *Plain People of the Confederacy* (Baton Rouge, La., 1943); Lawrence H. Gibson, "The Collapse of the Confederacy," *Mississippi Valley Historical Review* 4 (1918): 444–57; Charles Ramsdell, *Behind the Lines of the Southern Confederacy* (Baton Rouge, La., 1943); Armstead L. Robinson, "In the Shadow of Old John Brown: Insurrection Anxiety and Confederate Mobilization, 1861–1863," *Journal of Negro History* 65 (Fall 1980): 281–97.

The Significance of Black Soldiers

The discussion in this section is based on the following sources: John G. Nicolay and John Hay, eds., *Complete Works of Abraham Lincoln* (New York, 1905), 2:542; *New York Tribune,* December 26, 1865; Herbert Aptheker, "Negro Casualties in the Civil War," *Journal of Negro History* 32 (January 1947), reprinted in *To Be Free: Studies in American Negro History* (New York, 1942), pp. 75–112; W.E.B. Du Bois, *Black Reconstruction in America* (New York, 1965), p. 716.

Historians and Black Contributions to Northern Victory

The discussion in this section is based on the following sources: William Wells Brown, *The Negro in the American Rebellion* (Boston, 1867); George Washington Williams, *A History of the Negro Troops in the War of the Rebellion 1861–1865* (New York, 1888); James Ford Rhodes, *History of the United States from the Compromise of 1850 to the Restoration of Home Rule in the South in 1877* (New York, 1901), 3:322; W. E. Woodward, *Meet General Grant* (New York, 1928), p. 112; Robert F. Durden, *The Gray and the Black: The Confederate Debate on Emancipation* (Baton Rouge, La., 1972), p. viii; Bell Irwin Wiley, *Southern Negroes, 1861–1865* (New Haven, 1938); E. Merton Coulter, *The Confederate States of America* (Baton Rouge, La., 1951), pp. 256–63; Clement Eaton, *A History of the Southern Confederacy* (New York, 1954); Benjamin Quarles, *The Negro in the Civil War* (New York, 1953); Dudley Taylor Cornish, *The Sable Arm: Negro Troops in the Union Army, 1861–1867* (New York, 1956); David M. Potter, *The Causes of the Civil War* (Washington, D.C., 1961), p. 32; *New York Herald Tribune,* March 29, 1961; *New York Times,* April 2, 10, 12, 13, 1861; W.E.B. Du Bois in *Science and Society* 25 (December 1961), p. 352; Raimondo Luraghi, *The Rise and Fall of the Plantation South* (New York and London, 1978), p. 141.

27.   FREE AT LAST!

Origin of the Thirteenth Amendment

The discussion in this section is based on the following sources: W.E.B. Du Bois, *The Souls of Black Folk* (New York, 1903), pp. 5–6; Charles Lewis Waganalt, *The Mighty Revolution: Negro Emancipation in Maryland, 1862–1864* (Baltimore, 1964), pp. 232–35; Jeffrey R. Brackett, *The Negro in Maryland* (Baltimore, 1889), p. 262; J. R. Randall and David Donald, *The Civil War and Reconstruction* (New York, 1961), p. 370; James M. McPherson, *The Struggle for Equality* (Princeton, N.J., 1964), pp. 99–127; T. L. Perry, ed., *Life and Letters of Francis Lieber* (Boston, 1882), p. 341; Robert Dale Owen, *Emancipation Is Peace,* Loyal Publication Society No. 12 (New York, 1863); Thomas Hudson McKee, *The National Conventions and Platforms of All Political Parties, 1789–1905* (Baltimore, 1906), pp. 121–22; Ludwell H. Johnson, "Lincoln's Solution to the Problems of Peace Terms, 1864–1865," *Journal of Southern History* 34 (November 1968): 576–86; Roy P. Basler et al., eds., *The Collected Works of Abraham Lincoln* (New Brunswick, N.J., 1953–1955), 5:388–89, 7:435, 451, 8:151–52, 332–33, 411, 9:214, 215; John C. Nicolay and John Hay, *Abraham Lincoln: A History* (New York, 1890), 9:199, 215, 217–22; Ernest Francis Brown, *Raymond of the Times* (New York, 1951), pp. 259–61; George E. Baker, ed., *The Works of William H. Seward* (Boston, 1884), 5:502–4, 508.

Congress Adopts the Thirteenth Amendment

The discussion in this section is based on the following sources: *Congressional Record,* 38th Cong., 1st sess., pp. 1481, 1483, 1487, 1488, 1489, 2987, 2990; George A. Levesque, "Boston's Black Brahmin: Dr. John S. Rock," *Civil War History* 26 (1980): 335–36; *New York Tribune,* February 11, 1865; *Boston Journal,* February 1, 1865.

"Let the Monster Perish"

The discussion in this section is based on the following sources: Philip S. Foner, *The Voice of Black America: Major Speeches of Blacks in the United States, 1797–1973* (New York, 1975), 1:335–44; *A Memorial Discourse by Rev. Henry Highland Garnet, Delivered in the Hall of the House of Representatives, Washington, D.C., on Sabbath, February 12, 1865,* with an introduction by James McCune Smith, M.D. (Philadelphia, 1865); *Liberator,* February 10, 1865.

Meaning of the Thirteenth Amendment

The discussion in this section is based on the following sources: Jacob tenBroek, "Thirteenth Amendment to the Constitution of the United States," *California Law Re-*

view 39 (1951): 171–79; James Hamilton, "The Legislative and Judicial History of the Thirteenth Amendment," *National Bar Journal* 9 (1951): 26–28; "*Jones* v. *Mayer:* The Thirteenth Amendment and the Federal Anti-Discrimination Laws," *Columbia Law Review* 69 (June 1969): 1019–56; "The 'New' Thirteenth Amendment: A Preliminary Analysis," *Harvard Law Review* 82 (1969): 1294–1321; Arthur Kinoy, "The Constitutional Right of Negro Freedom Revisited: Some First Thoughts on Jones v. Alfred H. Mayer Company," *Rutgers Law Review* 22 (1968): 537; Arthur Kinoy, "The Constitutional Right of Negro Freedom," *Rutgers Law Review* 21 (1967): 387; *United States* v. *Rhodes* 27 F.Cas. 785 (No. 16, 151) (C.C.Ky. 1866); *Blyen* v. *United States,* 80 U.S. 581, 601 (1871); *Jones* v. *Alfred H. Mayer Co.* 392 U.S. 409 (1968); "Who Will Care for niggers now?" copy in Library Company of Philadelphia; Josef C. James, "Sherman at Savannah," *Journal of Negro History* 13 (January 1928): 127–37; *New York Tribune,* February 13, 1865; *Memoirs of General W. T. Sherman,* 2:247–49; *Savannah Herald,* February 3, 1865.

The Half Abolition of Slavery

The discussion in this section is based on the following sources: George R. Bently, *A History of the Freedmen's Bureau* (reprint ed., New York, 1970), pp. 49–102; William S. McFeely, *Yankee Stepfather: A Study of General O. O. Howard and the Freedmen's Bureau* (New Haven, 1968), pp. 64–83; James E. Sefton, *The United States Army and Reconstruction, 1865–1877* (Baton Rouge, La., 1967), pp. 46–49; Ronald C. F. Davis, "Good and Faithful Labor: A Study on the Origins, Development and Economics of Southern Sharecropping, 1860–1880" (Ph.D. diss., University of Missouri, 1974), pp. 22–26; *National Freedman* (June 1865); J. H. Wilson, *Under the Old Flag* (New York, 1907), p. 564; Manuel Gottlieb, "The Land Question during Reconstruction in Georgia," *Science and Society* 3 (Summer 1939): 383–85; James S. Allen, "The Struggle for Land during the Reconstruction Period," *Science and Society* 1 (Fall 1937): 378–416, reprinted in chapter 2 of his *Reconstruction: The Battle for Democracy* (New York, 1937); *Liberator,* February 24, 1865; Special Field Order Number 15, Official Records, I, *War of the Rebellion,* 47, Part II: 60–62. For "Flawed Victory," see William L. Barney, *Flawed Victory: A New Perspective of the Civil War* (New York, 1975); John Rosenberg's comment is in his article, "Toward a New Civil War Revisionism," in Barney, op. cit., p. 128.

For the controversy that has recently developed among historians over the degree of freedom among blacks in the postbellum South, see Hyman Belz, *Emancipation and Equal Rights: Politics and Constitutionalism in the Civil War Era* (New York, 1978); Edward Magdol, *A Right to the Land: Essays on the Freedmen's Community* (Westport, Conn., 1977), and p. 172 for the Wyatt quote; Stephen De Canio, *Agriculture in the Postbellum South: The Economics of Production and Supply* (Cambridge, Mass., 1974); Robert Higgs, *Competition and Coercion: Blacks in the American Economy, 1865–1914* (New York, 1977); Richard Sutch and Roger Ransom, "The Ex-Slave in the Post-Bellum South: A Study of the Economic Impact of Racism and Market Economy," *Journal of Economic History* 33 (March 1973): 131–48; Roger C. Ransom and Richard Sutch, *One Kind of Freedom: The Economic Controversies of Emancipation* (New York, 1977). For additional recent works on the social and economic system prevailing in the postbellum South and the position of blacks within the system, see James C. Roark, *Masters without Slaves: Southern Planters in the Civil War and Reconstruction* (New York, 1977); Daniel A. Novak, *The Wheel of Servitude: Black Forced Labor after Slavery* (Lexington, Ky.,

1978); Jay R. Mandle, *The Roots of Black Poverty: The Southern Plantation Economy after the Civil War* (Durham, N.C., 1978); Jonathan M. Wiener, *Social Origins of the New South: Alabama, 1860–1885* (Baton Rouge, La., 1978); Dwight B. Billings, Jr., *Planters and the Making of a "New South": Class, Politics, and Development in North Carolina, 1865–1900* (Chapel Hill, N.C., 1979); Pete Daniel, "The Metamorphosis of Slavery, 1865–1900," *Journal of American History* 66 (June 1979): 88–99; Jonathan M. Wiener, "Class Structure and Economic Development in the American South, 1865–1955," *American Historical Review* 84 (October 1979): 970–1006; Joseph Reid, "Sharecropping as an Understandable Market Response," *Journal of Economic History* 33 (March 1973): 106–30; N. Gorden Carper, "Slavery Revisited: Peonage in the South," *Phylon* 38 (March 1976): 85–105; William F. Cohen, "Negro Involuntary Servitude, 1865–1940," *Journal of Southern History* 42 (February 1976): 40–62; Harold D. Woodman, "Sequel to Slavery: The New History of the Postbellum South," *Journal of Southern History* 43 (November 1977): 540–62; Leon F. Litwack, *Been in the Storm So Long: The Aftermath of Slavery* (New York, 1979).

For the statement by Frederick Douglass, see Philip S. Foner, *Frederick Douglass* (New York, 1962), p. 222. For George W. Julian's statement, see W.E.B. Du Bois, *Black Reconstruction in America* (New York, 1935), p. 128.

Index

About the Author

PHILIP S. FONER is Professor Emeritus of History at Lincoln University in Pennsylvania. His books include the first two volumes of *History of Black Americans* (Greenwood Press, 1975 and 1983), and *American Socialism and Black Americans* (Greenwood Press, 1977), among many others.

Recent titles in Contributions in American History

Series Editor: Jon L. Wakelyn

John Eliot's Indian Dialogues: A Study in Cultural Interaction
Henry W. Bowden and James P. Ronda

The XYZ Affair
William Stinchcombe

American Foreign Relations: A Historiographical Review
Gerald K. Haines and J. Samuel Walker

Communism, Anticommunism, and the CIO
Harvey A. Levenstein

Fellow Workers and Friends: I.W.W. Free-Speech Fights as Told by Participants
Philip S. Foner

From the Old South to the New: Essays on the Transitional South
Walter J. Fraser, Jr., and Winfred B. Moore, Jr.

American Political Trials
Michael R. Belknap

The Evolution of American Electoral Systems
Paul Kleppner, Walter Dean Burnham, Ronald P. Formisano,
Samuel P. Hays, Richard Jensen, and William G. Shade

Class, Conflict, and Consensus: Antebellum Southern Community Studies
Orville Vernon Burton and Robert C. McMath, Jr.

Toward A New South? Studies in Post-Civil War Southern Communities
Orville Vernon Burton and Robert C. McMath, Jr.

To Free A People: American Jewish Leaders and The Jewish Problem in Eastern
Europe, 1890–1914
Gary Dean Best

Voting in Revolutionary America: A Study of Elections in the Original Thirteen
States, 1776–1789
Robert J. Dinkin

Good and Faithful Labor: From Slavery to Sharecropping in the Natchez District,
1860–1890
Ronald L. F. Davis

Reform and Reformers in the Progressive Era
David R. Colburn and George E. Pozzetta, editors

History of Black Americans: From the Emergence of the Cotton Kingdom to the Eve
of the Compromise of 1850
Philip S. Foner